WORLD POLITICS

Trend and Transformation

THIRD EDITION

Charles W. Kegley, Jr.
University of South Carolina

Eugene R. Wittkopf
Louisiana State University

ST. MARTIN'S PRESS ❑ NEW YORK

Editor: *Larry Swanson*
Project Editor: *Beverly Hinton*
Production Supervisor: *Julie Toth*
Text Design: *Leon Bolognese & Associates*
Cover Design: *Darby Downey*
Graphics: *G&H Soho Ltd.*

327

Library of Congress Catalog Card Number: 88-60540

Manufactured in the United States of America.

32109
fedcb

For information, write:
St. Martin's Press, Inc.
175 Fifth Avenue
New York, NY 10010

ISBN: 0-312-00499-0

200 28130

ACKNOWLEDGMENT

Selections from Hans Singer and Javed Ansari, *Rich and Poor Countries*, Fourth
edition, 1988. Published by Unwin Hyman Limited. Reprinted by permission.

To Suzanne, Debra, and Jonathan

Preface

In what fundamental ways has the world changed since 1945? How have previous patterns of relations among international actors been affected by the pace of change in today's world? To what extent do emergent trends presage the advent of a transformed global arena, and, conversely, to what extent has the transformation of world politics been inhibited by the force of persistent continuities? These questions provide the focus and theme of the third edition of *World Politics: Trend and Transformation*.

Although attention to what is new and what is enduring is not unique, the analysis presented here departs from others in a number of important ways. We have sought to provide a balanced treatment of the traditional topics in international politics, commonly referred to as matters of *high politics*, and the newer issues, often referred to as matters of *low politics*, that have come to compete for the attention of political leaders during the past two decades. Both are integral elements of the contemporary global agenda. Although among both international relations scholars and practitioners interest in and concern about the high politics of peace and security increased markedly during the 1980s, concern for the transnational economic and welfare issues that comprise low politics remains unabated. Many of the issues making up the agenda of low politics grow out of the increasingly complex web of international economic interdependence among many nations of the world, which became a primary concern of international relations students during the 1970s.

Part II serves as a prelude to the treatment of issues of low and high politics by examining the principal actors on the world political stage. Nation-states necessarily command particular attention, and we probe the nature of their decision-making processes, world views, national capabilities, and position in the international hierarchy that propel the major conflicts in contemporary world politics, namely, the East–West and North–South disputes. We also examine the role of nonstate actors in world politics by inquiring into their capacity not simply to be shaped by but to shape the trends and transformations unfolding in contemporary world politics.

Understanding the nature of the international political economy and the problems confronting it is a focal point of our analysis of transnational welfare issues; but we also examine others related to population, resources, and the environment. The transnational issues comprising low politics are examined in the four chapters comprising Part III; the questions relating to war, peace, and security—those comprising high politics—are analyzed in the four chapters making up Part IV.

Throughout, *World Politics: Trend and Transformation* takes a macro, or holistic, view of world politics. The historical roots that animate contemporary trends and controversies are put into perspective, and emphasis is placed on the major issues that transcend national boundaries in such a way as to affect many world political actors. Also, the topical organization of the book continually encourages readers to consider how change within one policy area influences the probability of change in others. To facilitate this, as early as Chapter Two we focus explicitly on contending analytic perspectives that scholars and policymakers have developed in order to comprehend the kaleidoscopic trends and transformations occurring in world politics. In subsequent chapters, we draw on these perspectives and related concepts in order to enhance readers' understanding of contemporary world politics. In this way we seek to broaden awareness of different, often competing, visions of global political "reality"; the emphasis reflects our conviction that it is important to draw on a broad spectrum of theory, as no single research perspective is likely to provide an understanding of the manifest changes unfolding in world politics or of their interrelationships.

No observer of the contemporary world scene can view it without a sense of urgency and even alarm. Because the world's problems have become so complex and intertwined, the challenges and dangers they pose are unprecedented. The available choices for resolving these problems are often unattractive; but the need to make a choice is unavoidable. By attempting to capture the nature of both change and continuity in world politics, *World Politics: Trend and Transformation* seeks to heighten awareness of both the dangers and opportunities posed; in the concluding chapters of Part V, concepts and controversies are introduced for the purpose of stimulating a more sophisticated understanding of the destiny shared by all.

Readers familiar with the earlier editions of *World Politics: Trend and Transformation* will immediately note the addition of a new chapter in Part II that examines how nations make foreign policy choices. They will also find that the structure and organization of the book remain the same, but that the treatment of the substantive elements of every chapter has been thoroughly revised and updated. In some cases—notably the chapters concerned with the population-food equation and the global energy situation—this required fundamental reanalysis and reinterpretation to account for dramatic new developments since the second edition was published in 1985. In other cases—such as the North–South dialogue and the Third World debt crisis—the emphasis has been altered to cast the issues and interpretations in a broader historical context. In many chapters, particularly in Part IV, the order of presentation has been altered to increase its clarity; and throughout, some concepts and issues—such as international regimes, long-cycle theory, and low-intensity conflict—have been highlighted or given expanded treatment. New empirical data related to the enduring issues covered in *World Politics: Trend and Transformation*, such as international crises and war, terrorism, the strategic balance, and trade and monetary issues, have also been incorporated. The result is a work thoroughly, substantively, and conceptually updated.

No book is possible without the help of many people. In addition to those who contributed their ideas and time to the earlier editions, we wish to acknowledge and thank those who contributed to the third: Virginia Anselman, Peter Auyeung, Mary Joyce Burns, William A. Clark, Gary Cornwell, Lawrence Eagleburger, James B. Holderman, Martha Houle, Scott Lawson, Gregory A. Raymond, Neil R. Richardson, Jo Scurria, Herbert K. Tillema, Jonathan Wilkenfeld, Kurt D. Will, Peter R. Zwick, and the staff of the Text Processing Center of the College of Arts and Sciences at Louisiana State University, particularly Joyce Grant and Diane LeNoir. The suggestions of a number of reviewers—Patrick M. Morgan, Washington State University; Nicholas G. Onuf, The American University; Philip A. Schrodt, Northwestern University; and Birol Yeshilada, University of Missouri–Columbia—and the aid and support of Larry Swanson, our editor at St. Martin's Press, Beverly Hinton, our project editor, and others on the St. Martin's staff are also gratefully acknowledged.

As we continue to look to the future with hope, we dedicate this, the most recent of our collaborative efforts sustained by bonds of mutual respect, to Suzanne, Debra, and Jonathan.

Charles W. Kegley, Jr.
Eugene R. Wittkopf

Contents

Part IV: High Politics: National Security, Arms, and War   349

PART I

Change and Transformation in World Politics

ONE

World Politics in Transition: A Thematic Introduction

I say we had best look at our times and lands searchingly in the face, like a physician diagnosing some deep disease.

WALT WHITMAN, 1888

In the aftermath of the Second World War, there began a massive reorganization of the world. . . . We are living through an era of the most extensive and intensive political change in human history. . . . Our generation is living through a genuine global political awakening.

ZBIGNIEW BRZEZINSKI, 1979

The spinning sphere we call earth is a planet in space approximately 8,000 miles in diameter and 25,000 miles in circumference. It is believed to be at least 4.5 billion years old. In the course of its evolution, it has undergone constant change. Only in the last 3 billion years of its existence, for instance, has it been meaningful to speak of the earth as possessing a biosphere—a system of life and living organisms. And a sociosphere—a system of human beings in interaction—is, in the history of the planet, a relatively recent development. A cosmic calendar would tell us that the drama of human history commenced only in the last 340,000 years (Childe, 1962). Humankind has been a component of the earth's biosphere for merely 1/1,000th of its existence, and only for the past 5,000 years or so can we speak of a record of human history.

Since Homo sapiens first began to roam the some 200 million square miles of the earth's surface, the earth's terrestrial habitat has been transformed by the ways in which humans have behaved. In the earth's ecosphere, the natural environment in which humans live, the quality of life has been influenced by the ways that humans have organized themselves politically for making decisions and managing disputes, how they have extracted from the earth's resources to sustain and enhance life, and how they have exchanged and transferred those resources. These basic processes have conditioned human existence. Although the modes of human behavior defined by these processes have been varied, they have not been random. Since antiquity, patterns of political, economic, and social behaviors have been discernible, and these make it meaningful to talk about characteristic ways in which people have acted toward one another politically. To understand contemporary world politics, therefore, we must trace continuities in human interaction and look for commonalities in past patterns.

But if we are to comprehend adequately the present condition of world politics, we must also appreciate changes in the way that humans interact with one another politically. The global system is dynamic, not static; it is marked by movement as well as constancy. The contemporary world political system is a product of processes that are themselves susceptible to long-term evolutionary modification. Hence we must heed both change and changelessness if we are to comprehend today's global politics.

In what ways has the international political system changed or remained constant, especially since World War II, which marks the beginning of contemporary world politics as we use that term in this book? What do recurrent historical practices and deviations from them tell us about contemporary world politics? What are the implications of emergent global trends for the future of world politics? These are principal among the questions addressed in *World Politics: Trend and Transformation*.

Perhaps at no other time in history has a consideration of the changes taking place in world politics been more urgent than now. This is not because the present age is unique; every age has been one of transition. Rather, what makes attention to global trends so timely is the unprecedented rapidity with which so many facets of global politics appear to be undergoing change. The dramatic rate of change for humanity as a whole perhaps explains why those willing to think about change and its implications often experience "future shock" (Toffler, 1970), a kind of disorientation and disillusionment and even despair encountered under frenzied conditions that disrupt traditions and circumstances assumed to be stable. Confusion, uncertainty, and a sense of chaos are produced by perceived discontinuities from the past. The fear and anxiety symptomatic of our times are therefore to be expected because they are often provoked by the uncertainty of a world in transition.

How can we best understand the worldwide political transformations that seem to engulf us daily, and how can we best understand their significance for the future? To begin, we must heed philosopher George Santayana's warning that those who ignore history are doomed to relive it. As Winston Churchill once remarked, "The further back you look, the further forward you can see."

Implicit in these admonitions is the necessity of observing world politics over an extended period. A long-term perspective helps differentiate a short-term fluctuation, which is of little ultimate significance, from a long-term trend, one that will affect the very fabric of world politics well into the future. Such a perspective also allows us to identify more accurately the transformations in international history that mark the turning points at which one pattern of characteristic behavior is replaced by another.

World Politics: Trend and Transformation incorporates historical perspectives into the analysis of contemporary world politics by focusing on *mac-*

ropolitical processes—those dynamics that influence the entire fabric of relations among global political actors as they have evolved through, and have been influenced by, historical circumstances as well as contemporary challenges.

The decades following World War II will command particular attention, because the war itself set in motion, and came to be symbolic of, a fundamental transformation of world politics. Power came to be concentrated in two states destined to become superpowers; Europe ceased to be the center of the international political system; self-determination came into its own as the European colonial empires began to dismantle, giving rise to the emergence of a "Third World" of newly independent states that had failed to advance economically in the same way as their colonizers had; and the atomic bomb revolutionized warfare by radically altering the role that the actual and threatened use of force would henceforth play in the game of nations. Together these and other changes set in motion by World War II clearly distinguish contemporary world politics from that of previous eras. Against this background, a question implicit in *World Politics: Trend and Transformation* is whether the world political system that came into being during and after World War II may not now be undergoing another equally profound transformation.

The macroscopic orientation of *World Politics: Trend and Transformation* implies not only that we be sensitive to the impact of the past on the present but also that we focus attention on some aspects of world politics and ignore others. We ask our readers to picture the world not as it might appear from the vantage point of where they now find themselves but as it might appear if they viewed it from space. Such a macroscopic approach sacrifices detail. It means that we cannot dwell on particular events, particular nations' foreign policies, particular individuals, or other transitory phenomena whose long-term significance is likely to diminish. But a macropolitical approach is warranted if our purpose is to depict behaviors that cohere into general global patterns that portend trends and transformations that will measurably affect the human political habitat as we move toward the twenty-first century.

The macropolitical orientation of *World Politics: Trend and Transformation* is not meant to denigrate the importance of examining political processes peculiar to individual nations and their impact on the larger context of world politics. On the contrary, because of their importance, we shall examine in Chapter 3 characteristics of the processes whereby national policymakers make choices necessary for protecting and advancing what they perceive to be the interests of their nations.[1] But a concern for the larger picture necessarily implies a greater focus on the general than on the particular, on the recurrent rather than the ephemeral.

---

1. Our previous work on American foreign policy and policy–making processes (Kegley and Wittkopf, 1987) demonstrates our commitment to understanding international politics from the viewpoint of individual actors as well as from the macropolitical perspective that underlies this book.

Any inventory of the basic changes in global politics must have established empirical bases. Because we wish to know what is new about political behavior at the global level and what is recurrent, we must have some basis on which to determine whether change has occurred or continuity has persisted. Fortunately, social scientists, governments, and international institutions have endeavored over the past several decades to collect empirical evidence about the characteristics and changing attributes of the global environment. Though sometimes limited, these data provide insight into what is occurring internationally and offer documentary evidence about change and continuity in world politics. Accordingly, *World Politics: Trend and Transformation* will draw on this information, as appropriate, to buttress our understanding about the nature of contemporary world politics.

Implicit in the preference for documentary evidence to support the arguments in *World Politics: Trend and Transformation* is our belief that the world is too complex to be understood by single-factor explanations. Instead, we must think in multicausal terms. No change stands alone; all interact simultaneously, even though some may be moving in divergent directions. Thus we must seek to understand complexity. The task may be difficult, but the rewards warrant the effort. A true but complicated idea always has less chance of succeeding than does a simple but false one, Alexis de Tocqueville observed long ago. Humankind's ability to free the future from the paralyzing grip of the past may be contingent on its ability to entertain complex ideas for a complicated world.

The framework underlying our examination of world politics in the chapters that follow is designed to facilitate an orderly inquiry into the complex world of world politics. We begin in Chapter 2 with a brief sketch of some of the analytical perspectives through which scholars and diplomats have over the years tried to make sense of world politics. The analysis is designed to show, among other things, how our views of the world are often profoundly shaped by what is happening in the world.

The next fourteen chapters are divided into four parts. In Part II we focus on the actors in world politics. Nation-states are a primary concern here, with attention given to the way in which they decide how to cope with the often hostile international environment in which they find themselves (Chapter 3), and on the conflicts that characterize their interactions with one another (Chapters 4 and 5). The part concludes (Chapter 6) with an examination of the nonstate actors that sometimes challenge nation-states' preeminence in world politics.

Parts III and IV focus on transnational policy issues, but with an important distinction between them. In Part III we focus on the "low politics" of economic and social welfare policymaking. Here questions relating to the global political economy and the impact of national and international behavior on the "global commons" command attention. In Part IV the emphasis shifts to issues of war and peace, those matters of "high politics" that are the essence of the traditional concerns of scholars and diplomats seeking to understand and grapple with trends and transformations in world politics.

We conclude in Part V with two chapters that return to themes examined in detail in preceding chapters and ask how the underlying tendencies in contemporary world politics might enable us to anticipate future trends in world politics. For our concern is not only how best to understand contemporary world politics; it is also how today's world will affect tomorrow's.

SUGGESTED READINGS

Holsti, Ole R., Randolph M. Siverson, and Alexander L. George, eds. *Change in the International System*. Boulder, Colo.: Westview Press, 1980.

Jaspers, Karl. *The Future of Mankind*. Chicago: University of Chicago Press, 1961.

Johnson, Paul. *Modern Times: The World from the Twenties to the Eighties*. New York: Harper & Row, 1983.

Kegley, Charles W., Jr., and Eugene R. Wittkopf, eds. *The Global Agenda: Issues and Perspectives*, 2nd ed. New York: Random House, 1988.

Luard, Evan. *Types of International Society*. New York: Free Press, 1976.

Morse, Edward L. *Modernization and the Transformation of International Relations*. New York: Free Press, 1976.

Parkinson, F. *The Philosophy of International Relations: A Study in the History of Thought*. Beverly Hills, Calif.: Sage, 1977.

Polanyi, Karl. *The Great Transformation: The Political and Economic Origins of Our Time*. Boston: Beacon Press, 1944.

Ruggie, John Gerard. "Continuity and Transformation in the World Polity," *World Politics* 35 (January 1983): 261–285.

TWO

The Study of World Politics: Alternative Perspectives

It's important that we take a hard, clear look . . . not at some simple world, either of universal goodwill or of universal hostility, but the complex, changing and sometimes dangerous world that really exists.

JIMMY CARTER, 1980

Policy-makers are prone to distort reality in accord with their needs even in situations that appear . . . relatively unambiguous.

RICHARD NED LEBOW, 1981

We live in a world defined by our expectations and images. No one really "knows" what that world is like; its nature can be inferred only from how it is perceived. Likewise, because international relations cannot be observed directly, it is possible that many images of the world's political realities are built on illusions and misconceptions. Such images are also likely to become obsolete, because adjustments in the way we think about and visualize world politics tend to lag behind constantly shifting international circumstances.

Because the way we act is shaped so powerfully by what we perceive, we must probe the nature of our images and theories of world politics. That is, the shape of the world's future will be determined not only by changes in the "objective" facts of world politics but also by the meanings that people ascribe to those facts, the assumptions on which their interpretations are based, and the actions that flow from these assumptions and interpretations.

Our purpose in this chapter is to describe some of the major concepts and analytical perspectives through which scholars and diplomats have viewed international relations. Because many of these concepts and perspectives are necessarily influenced by the "realities" of the international phenomena they seek to describe and explain, we shall relate them, where appropriate, to their underlying political and social forces. These concepts and perspectives, essential to the study of international politics, also permit us to outline the intellectual heritage informing *World Politics: Trend and Transformation*. In particular, they enable us to identify the basis for the conceptual distinction between the "high politics" of peace and security and the "low politics" of economic and social welfare issues used to categorize the analyses in Parts III and IV.[1]

We begin with a discussion of individuals' perceptions of and orientations to their social and political environments, ideas that, if transferred to the international level, provide important insight into global disputes on issues of high and low politics alike.

COGNITIVE PSYCHOLOGY: IMAGES OF GLOBAL REALITY

Everyone possesses some kind of mental model of world politics. It may be explicit or implicit, conscious or subconscious. But whichever they are, all models are simplified versions of "reality" that necessarily exaggerate some features of the real world and ignore others.

There is nothing pernicious about simplifying one's view of the world. To make sense out of a confusing abundance of information, "mental maps" of the world must be created. These mental maps are actually conceptual models, inasmuch as concepts are abstractions that organize perceptions.[2] Their importance derives from people's tendency to "respond [not] to the 'objective' facts of the situation . . . but to their 'image' of the situation. It is what we think the world is like, not what it is really like, that determines our behavior. . . . We act according to the way the world appears to us, not necessarily according to the way it 'is' " (Boulding, 1975).

To understand the global system, scholars interested in the psychological dimensions of international relations have found it important to understand the sources of individuals' images of reality. Modes of thinking about politics have been shown to be influenced by many factors, including

❑ psychological needs, drives, and dispositions (for example, trust or mistrust) ingrained in personalities as a result of early childhood experiences.

---

1. The distinction between high and low politics can be traced to the experience of the United States in the years following World War II. With the onset of the Cold War, top-level elected and career officials found that national security issues relating to the East–West struggle dominated their time and attention. In such an environment, nonsecurity issues, especially those pertaining to economic matters, were left to lower-level career bureaucrats. For a variety of reasons (discussed in Chapters 4, 5, 7, and 8), during the 1970s low politics came to compete with high politics for the attention of key policymakers.

2. We use the word *map* to indicate the extent to which mental models are necessarily imperfect replicas of the global realities they are intended to portray. We are referring not only to the kind of world geography that people carry in their heads regarding distance, size, and topography but also to how resources, military capabilities, power, diplomatic influence, and populations, as well as their political meaning, are distributed. Having described mental models in these terms, it is perhaps axiomatic that many such maps may bear little relationship to the realities of a fast-changing interdependent planet (see Sprout and Sprout, 1971).

❑ what we have been socialized into thinking about international relations as children (for example, tolerance of cultural diversity or the fear of it) by parents, teachers, peer groups, as well as the values embedded in our cultural system.

❑ opinions about world affairs articulated by those with whom we routinely associate.

❑ attitudes expressed by authority figures, policymakers, and others respected as experts.

❑ the positions we occupy and the roles we perform: What we see depends on where we sit (child, student, bureaucrat, policymaker, diplomat, and so forth).

These principles from empirical research in cognitive psychology (see Janis, 1982; Jervis, 1969; Singer, 1965) demonstrate that one's perception of the world is not a passive act. The mind is conditioned to select, screen, and filter what is perceived, organizing these sensory sensations by accepting some cognitions (facts) and excluding others from consciousness on the basis of values and beliefs. This means that what we "see" about world politics depends on what we look at, what we look for, and how we react to what we find. The human tendency toward selective perception (and selective recall) suggests that it is true that what we see is what we get. Subconscious predispositions are also central to the formation of thought. What we think about affects what we think. Hence we all are to some extent captives of our perceptual habits. And what we see in and think about the world as a consequence of our selective perception influences our views and corresponding mental images of world politics.[3]

We must be careful not to assume automatically that what applies to individuals applies to nations as well. But there is clear evidence that nations' foreign policies are often shaped by historical circumstances that predispose them, through their leaders, to behave in particular ways toward others, regardless of the "objective" facts of the situation (see Jervis, 1976). The loss of twenty million Soviet soldiers and citizens in the "Great Patriotic War," as the Russians refer to World War II, created an exaggerated fear of foreign invasion and caused a generation of Soviet policymakers to perceive moves by the United States which it considered to be defensive in nature with considerable suspicion and often alarm. Similarly, the long history of America's isolation

---

3. The study of psychology is important to the study of international relations because people differ in their reactions to conflicting or discrepant information. The tendency of most people is to look for information that reinforces preexisting beliefs, to assimilate new data into familiar images, and to distort perceptions so as to deny those data that fail to conform to previous expectations. Tolerance of ambiguity and willingness to consider new ways of organizing our thinking vary among individuals and personality types; some are more "open" and less rigid than others (Rokeach, 1960) and are therefore more accepting of diversity and more able to revise perceptual habits to accommodate new realities. Nevertheless, all individuals are to some extent prisoners of the perceptual predispositions to which they have been conditioned.

from the "dirty power politics" of Europe contributed to the belief that America's democratic political institutions were somehow uniquely virtuous and, ultimately, to the messianic nature of post–World War II American foreign policy. That others might regard the United States as just an "ordinary" great power and see its globalist foreign policy orientation as often ill advised and sometimes threatening is not easily understood by Americans.

What cognitive psychology (and the theory of cognitive dissonance in particular) teaches is that when cognitions are received that run counter to the beliefs and values held by political elites and mass publics, they are often either ignored or interpreted to reinforce rather than restructure preexisting beliefs. The result is that discord in world politics is often fueled by mutual misperceptions. Especially when relationships are hostile, for example, distrust and suspicion between the conflicting parties often arise, as each sees the other as the other sees it. That is, *mirror images* emerge. This syndrome is especially evident in the images of each other maintained by the Soviets and Americans in the East–West conflict. But it applies to many other antagonistic interstate relationships as well. When mirror images develop in international conflicts, self-righteous perceptions often lead to actions and responses deemed by the initiator to be constructive, whereas an adversary's initiatives and responses are perceived as negative and culpable. When this occurs, the resolution of international conflict is extraordinarily difficult. It is not simply a matter of expanding trade and other forms of transnational contact, or of even bringing political leaders together in international summits. Rather, it is a matter of changing deeply entrenched beliefs.[4]

We do not mean to imply by the foregoing that most people are perceptual bigots (although apparently some are). Although images of international relations are resistant to change, they are not incapable of change. Most people have the capacity to refine how they think about the world. Mental maps tend to change when people experience punishment or discomfort as a consequence of clinging to false assumptions. Dramatic events have also been shown to alter international images, sometimes drastically (Deutsch and Merritt, 1965). The dropping of atomic bombs on Japan in 1945, the Korean and Vietnam conflicts, and the Cuban missile crisis in 1962 were learning experiences for many people, alerting them to the vulnerabilities posed by international circumstances and leading them to modify their previous images of international politics (see, for example, Holsti and Rosenau, 1984). Often such consciousness-raising experiences create new mental maps of the globe, new

---

4. The classic empirical examination of the impact of images on foreign policy making is Ole R. Holsti's (1975) study of John Foster Dulles, U.S. secretary of state in the Eisenhower administration. Demonstrating that Dulles operated within the framework of an "inherent bad faith" model of the Soviet Union, Holsti's findings "suggest the fallacy of thinking that peaceful settlement of outstanding international issues is simply a problem of devising 'good plans.' Clearly as long as decision-makers on either side of the Cold War adhere to rigid images of the other party, there is little likelihood that even genuine 'bids' to decrease tensions will have the desired effect."

clusters of perceptual filters through which subsequent events are interpreted, and new criteria for "definitions of the situation" (Pruitt, 1965) when interpreting subsequent events.

Cognitive psychology thus teaches that ideas are resistant to change, but it also teaches that change is possible. People can learn. Evidence for both phenomena can be found in the dominant theoretical perspectives or paradigms[5] used by scholars (and often policymakers as well) to understand the evolving nature of world politics in the face of different historical circumstances. These analytical perspectives thus tell us much about world politics itself, for they flourish in particular international climates, not only because of the persuasiveness of their proponents' message, but also because of their ability to explain why and how particular causal forces affect the course of world affairs.[6] An examination of the various approaches to the study of international relations (in the Western world in particular) and of the competition among them for paradigmatic status illustrates the connection between intellectual images of reality and the phenomena they seek to understand. We shall focus on five perspectives: political idealism, political realism (in both its classical and neorealist forms), behavioralism, transnational relations and complex interdependence, and international regimes. We shall conclude by identifying four additional schools of thought that address particular aspects of world politics.

POLITICAL IDEALISM

The study of international relations as a distinct field of intellectual inquiry is largely a phenomenon of the twentieth century. Its historical roots lie in diplomatic history, an approach to understanding international affairs that

---

5. The word *paradigm* is commonly used to describe the dominant way of looking at a subject of inquiry, such as international relations. It was popularized by Thomas Kuhn's influential book *The Structure of Scientific Revolutions* (1970). Unfortunately, the term has been used in a variety of overlapping ways. But the general idea that thoughts about a particular area of inquiry tend to be structured by the acceptance of particular aspects of the subject's characteristics as more important than others and by agreement about the puzzles to be solved and the criteria that should govern the investigation of them. It has merit if we are to understand how images of world politics are shaped by sociological forces operating within the intellectual community as it seeks to assess the nature and meaning of global political developments.

6. To be sure, there have always been scholars outside the intellectual paradigm dominant during any particular time, challenging it, questioning its relevance to world politics, and proposing alternative conceptions of reality and what knowledge about it should entail. Often those outside the paradigm have come from countries other than those dominant in world politics itself. Marxist thinking has clearly been dominant in the scholarly work of those living in socialist societies, for example, but the ability of Marxist interpretations of reality to attain dominance worldwide has been constrained by the inability of communism as defined by Marx (that is, a classless, stateless society) to become the world's preferred form of political and social organization.

focuses on description and historical detail, not theoretical explanation.[7] The advent of a catastrophic global war in 1914 first stimulated the search for knowledge that could address contemporary policy problems—notably war— in a theoretical context. The search was for sustainable generalizations about the conditions under which war might be avoided and peace maintained. However interesting descriptions of past wars and the individuals who waged them might be, they were of little utility to a world looking for ways to prevent wars of mass destruction. For that purpose, a *theory* was needed that could reliably predict the outbreak of wars and that could tell policymakers what factors could be manipulated or controlled to prevent them.

A number of perspectives on world politics competed for attention in the period of intellectual ferment following World War I. The diplomatic-historical approach continued to claim adherents, and Marxist-Leninist thought became an increasingly controversial paradigm following the Bolshevik Revolution in Russia. Later, with the rise of Adolf Hitler and the Nazis in Germany, national socialism also challenged conventional European thinking about international politics. Nazism, the German variant of national socialism, was particularly provocative. Not only did it glorify the role of the state (as opposed to the individual) in political life; it also advanced a political philosophy that rationalized war as an instrument of national policy. Emerging as dominant, however, was a perspective that came to be labeled *political idealism*. Idealists held widely divergent views of world politics, but what joined them was their shared assumptions about reality and the homogeneity of their conclusions.

Collectively, idealists projected a world view usually based on the beliefs that (1) human nature is essentially "good" or altruistic and people are therefore capable of mutual aid and collaboration[8]; (2) the fundamental human concern for the welfare of others makes progress possible (that is, the Enlightenment's faith in the possibility of improving civilization was reaffirmed); (3) bad human behavior is the product not of evil people but of evil institutions and structural arrangements that motivate people to act selfishly and to harm others—including making war; (4) war is not inevitable and can be eliminated by eradicating the institutional arrangements that encourage it; (5) war is an international problem that requires collective or multilateral rather than national efforts to eliminate it; and therefore, (6) international society must reorganize itself to eliminate the institutions that make war likely.

To be sure, not all advocates of political idealism subscribed to each of

---

7. Not all early treatments were historical or atheoretical. For instance, two of the major writers at the turn of the century, Sir Halford Mackinder and Alfred Thayer Mahan, sought to generate broad theoretical propositions pertaining to the influence of geographic factors on national power and international relations. The efforts of Mackinder, Mahan, and their colleagues laid the foundations for the study of political geography that survives today as an important approach to world politics.

8. The role of human nature in theories of politics is controversial. See Nelson (1974) and Lewontin, Rose, and Kamin (1984) for reviews and critical discussions.

these tenets with equal conviction. Many political idealists would probably disagree with some of them; perhaps all would be uncomfortable with their simplistic wording. Nevertheless, these tenets describe the basic assumptions articulated in one way or another by the leaders and theorists whose orientation toward world affairs captivated the discussion of world politics in the period between the two world wars. The discussion was laced with overtones of moralism, optimism, and internationalism.

Although important differences existed in the idealists' policy prescriptions (see Herz, 1951), their recommended solutions to international problems generally fell into three categories. One called for the creation of international institutions to replace the anarchical and war-prone balance-of-power system composed of independent territorial states. The formation of the League of Nations and an emphasis on international cooperation in coping with social matters were typical of the idealists' institutional solutions to the problem of war.

A second approach emphasized the legal control of war. It called for the use of transnational legal processes such as adjudication and arbitration to settle disputes and inhibit recourse to war. The creation of the Permanent Court of International Justice to litigate interstate conflicts, as well as the ratification of the Kellogg–Briand Pact of 1928, which "outlawed" war as an instrument of national policy (except—note the escape clause—"in self-defense"), were representative of the emphasis placed on legal approaches at that time.

A third approach was to eliminate weapons. The efforts toward disarmament and, less ambitiously, arms control during the 1920s (the Washington and London naval conferences, for instance) are examples of this orientation.

A number of corollary elements of the idealist paradigm supplemented the emphasis that idealists placed on international organization, law, and disarmament. Among them were a belief in the need to substitute attitudes stressing the unity of humankind for narrow, parochial loyalties (under the belief that world public opinion stood behind peace and diplomacy); the removal of barriers to free trade; the replacement of secret diplomacy by a system of "open covenants, openly arrived at"; and, above all, the end to interlocking bilateral alliances and the power balances they were supposed to achieve (but seldom did). Some idealists saw in the principle of self-determination the possibility to redraw the world's political geography so as to make national borders conform to ethnic groupings, under the conviction that a world so arranged would be a more peaceful world. Related to this was the call for democratic domestic institutions. "Making the world safe for democracy," it was believed, would also make it secure and free from war. President Woodrow Wilson's celebrated Fourteen Points speech, which proposed the creation of the League of Nations and, with it, the pursuit of other idealist objectives, expressed the sentiments of the idealist image and program perhaps better than did any other statement.

Although idealist concepts dominated academic discussions and policy rhetoric during the interwar period, much of the idealist program for reform was never tried, and even less of it was ever achieved. And when the winds of international change again shifted and the world was confronted by the German, Italian, and Japanese pursuit of hegemony and world conquest, idealism as a world view receded.

POLITICAL REALISM

The events that led to World War II provoked strong criticism of the assumptions of the idealist paradigm. Many blamed the outbreak of the Second World War on what they believed to be the naive legalistic and moralistic assumptions of the idealists and their neglect of the "realities" of power politics (see Carr, 1939, and Herz, 1951). Consistent with the explanation of image transformation provided by cognitive psychology, critics of the idealists' logic drew "lessons" from their perceptions of events in the interwar period that gave shape to a new set of beliefs.

Calling themselves political realists, advocates of the counterparadigm known as *political realism* coalesced to frame an intellectual movement whose message about world politics reads like the antithesis of the idealists' assumptions.[9] Because that message was—and remains—compelling, it deserves careful scrutiny.

As a theory or, perhaps better, a world view, political realism can be traced to the ancient Greeks and the writings of Thucydides.[10] As applied to world politics in the twentieth century, this world view focuses on the nation-state as the principal actor in world politics and on the way the perceived realities of international politics dictate the choices that foreign policy makers as rational problem solvers must make. Realists share the view that the purpose of statecraft is national survival in a hostile environment. No means is more important to that end than the acquisition of power, and no principle is more important than *self-help*. The concept of state *sovereignty*, a cornerstone of international law, enshrines this perspective and punctuates its necessity by

---

9. Among the principal prophets of this new world view were E. H. Carr (1939), Hans J. Morgenthau (1948), Kenneth W. Thompson (1958, 1960), Reinhold Niebuhr (1947), George F. Kennan (1954, 1967), and, later, Henry A. Kissinger (1964). Readers familiar with the Western intellectual tradition will note that realism drew its inspiration from the classic political philosophies of such theorists as Machiavelli, Hobbes, and Nietzsche, although in a way that bent them to the needs of the time.

10. Although the thinking associated with political realism can be traced to the ancient Greek philosophers, it is more often linked to the political philosophy of the Italian theorist Niccolo Machiavelli, who emphasized in his treatise *The Prince* (1513) a political calculus based on interest, prudence, and expediency above all else (notably morality). The term is often used synonymously with *realpolitik*, as moral crusades are anathema to realist thinking. Moralism is seen as a wasteful and dangerous interference in the rational pursuit of national power. To the realist, therefore, questions about the relative virtues of this or that *ism* (ideological system) are irrelevant and are to be kept outside policy thinking. The ideological preferences of states are immaterial, neither good nor bad—all that really matters is whether one's self-interest is being served.

giving heads of state the freedom to do whatever they perceive necessary to serve their own state's self-interests, by making them alone responsible for ensuring its survival. Accordingly, states are conceived as the superordinate actors on the world's stage, for they answer to no higher political authority. But self-help also means that they must rely exclusively on themselves to protect their interests and ensure their survival.

At the risk of oversimplifying their somewhat discordant message, the classical realists tended to assume that (1) a reading of history teaches that people are by nature sinful and wicked; (2) of all of peoples' evil ways, no sins are more prevalent, inexorable, or dangerous than are their instinctive lust for power and their desire to dominate others; (3) the possibility of eradicating the instinct for power is a utopian aspiration; (4) under such conditions international politics is a Hobbesian struggle for power, a war of all against all; (5) the primary obligation of every state in this environment—the goal to which all other national objectives should be subordinated—is to promote the national interest, defined as the acquisition of power; (6) the nature of the international system necessitates the acquisition of military capabilities sufficient to deter attack by potential enemies; (7) the ability to defend oneself might be augmented by acquiring allies, provided that faith is not placed in their loyalty and reliability; (8) but the task of self-protection can never be entrusted to international organizations or to international law; and, finally, (9) if all states seek to maximize power, stability will result from maintaining a balance of power lubricated by fluid alliance systems.

Realists claim that all states are animated by the same drives and interests: All quest for power and act to benefit themselves at others' expense. The state of international anarchy (with no superior political authority to make, interpret, and enforce compliance with rules), the realists contend, requires governments to act competitively with one another and to resist all challenges to their sovereign power.

The classical realist thinking that came to dominate actual policymaking as well as academic discourse about international politics in the 1940s and 1950s fit the needs of a pessimistic age, in which suspicion of the motives of others was the rule and the prospects for peace seemed remote. The onset of superpower rivalry between the United States and the Soviet Union, the expansion of that Cold War confrontation into a worldwide struggle between the so-called East and West blocs, the development of thermonuclear weapons of mass destruction, the periodic crises that constantly threatened to erupt into global violence—all seemed to confirm the political realists' image of world politics. The realists' belief that the structure of the international system determined the behavior of all nations was particularly convincing. To many, the view that in a threatening international environment foreign policy had to take precedence over domestic problems and policies was also cogent. Above all, stating that the historical imperatives of "power politics" required attention to national security—to arms and influence—*realpolitik* asserted that high politics *was* world politics. States and their incessant competition were the defining elements of global reality—and the superpowers were eventually assigned a preeminent role among them; all other aspects were secondary.

Persuasive though the realists' arguments about the essential properties of world politics may have been, their conclusions were frequently at odds and even contradictory. Once analysis moved beyond the pithy notion that people are wicked and beyond the rhetoric requiring that foreign policy serve the national interest, important questions remained. Do alliances encourage peace or instability? Do arms contribute to security or provoke costly arms races and wars that ultimately undermine it? In advocating that nations preserve peace by preparing for war, do realists ignore the possibility that states are most prone to act aggressively when they perceive themselves to be weak rather than strong? Are international organizations merely another arena for the push and shove believed to characterize world politics, or are they a tool for reforming national instincts for pure self-advantage? And do national interests sometimes converge around the need to agree rather than compete in order to address common problems? If so, is not a sacrifice of sovereign autonomy sometimes warranted?

Such questions are empirical and need real-world evidence and corresponding means of analyzing the evidence for satisfactory answers. In these respects, political realism was found wanting. Possessing a distinctive perspective on international affairs but lacking a methodology for resolving competing claims, the realist paradigm had no criteria for determining which data counted as significant information and which rules were to be followed in interpreting the data. These shortfalls figured prominently in the continuing development of international relations as a distinct field of inquiry during the 1960s and 1970s. As doubts were raised, the criticisms of realism as the dominant paradigm began to mount.

Those critical of the logic of *realpolitik*, as well as some sympathetic to it, began to point to some disturbing deficiencies within the framework itself, and others began to worry about its ethical implications and policy costs (King, 1967; Rothstein, 1972). Included were attacks on the logical consistency of the paradigm's assumptions (if an inexorable law of history is that all actors always seek power, for example, then why is it necessary to advise states that they should quest for power?), challenges to some of the propositions (why is it that nearly every power balance has broken down and eventually resulted in war?), questions about some of the conclusions (in advocating vigilance and military preparedness, did the world view not rationalize perpetuation of arms races in a self-fulfilling manner?), and critiques of the paradigm's description of contemporary realities (was the assumption of the impermeability of the nation-state warranted in an age of nuclear-tipped intercontinental missiles?).

Critics also noted that the paradigm failed to describe accurately some of the major international developments of the post–World War II period. It failed to explain some of the collaborative and integrative associations that were being constructed in Western Europe, for instance, where the coopera- tive pursuit of mutual advantage rather than national self-interest seemed to dominate, at least in economic if not always in military affairs.

The failure of the realist paradigm to provide convincing descriptions of many political events as well as cogent policy prescriptions led to its eventual challenge as the dominant paradigm. Although realism recommended objec- tives that could be achieved through varying means, realists themselves could not agree on which policy alternatives best served the state's needs. Indeed, that their policy recommendations often failed to meet perceived policy needs underscored the uncertainty that realism produced (the same, of course, could often be said of its detractors). But the shadow of political realism is still visible. Much of the world continues to think about international politics in terms of this mental model. Indeed, it has enjoyed a resurgence in the 1980s under the guise of *neorealism*, and we shall therefore return to a further elaboration of the realist perspective. Even without that resurgence, however, the intellectual contributions of realism in its classical formulation provide important insight into the drive for national security that continues to motivate states' foreign policy behavior and thus provides the intellectual foundations underlying our discussion of high politics in Part IV of *World Politics: Trend and Transformation*.

THE BEHAVIORAL APPROACH: A SCIENCE OF INTERNATIONAL POLITICS?

Among its other contributions, classical realism prepared the way for serious theoretical thinking about global conditions and empirical linkages among them. Nonetheless, as dissatisfaction with the shortcomings of classical realism mounted, a counterreaction was set in motion. The counterreaction was largely in terms of method and language, for what emerged to challenge political realism in the 1960s and early 1970s was defined largely by its approach to theory and the logic and method of its inquiry (see Knorr and Verba, 1961; Snyder, 1955; Sondermann, 1957). This new perspective is ap- propriately labeled the *behavioral* approach to the study of international relations, but it is more accurately described as a methodology than as a theoretical perspective.

Behavioralism in international relations was part of a larger movement spreading across the social sciences in general. Often called the *scientific* approach, behavioralism represented a challenge to the preexisting modes of studying human behavior and, more specifically, to the basis on which truth- claims were derived by previous theorists, who came to be called *traditional- ists*. What ensued was an often heated debate among scholars about the principles and procedures most appropriate to investigating international phe- nomena. The debate centered on the meaning of theory, on the requirements for adequate theory, and on the methods best suited to testing theoretical propositions.

Much of the debate between the traditionalists and the behavioralists was strident and was typified as much by "theorizing about theory" (Singer, 1960) as by theorizing about international relations. A reading of the literature of this period attests to the extent to which methodological issues, and not substantive ones, commanded the attention of professional analysts, perhaps reflecting the uncertainty and immaturity of a "new" science in its incipient stages of development, one unsure about itself and its goals.[11]

At the core of the behavioral movement were a number of shared assumptions and analytic prescriptions. The behavioral paradigm sought *nomothetic* or lawlike generalizations about international phenomena, that is, statements about patterns and regularities presumed to hold across time and place. Science, the behavioralists claimed, is first and foremost a generalizing activity. The purpose of scientific inquiry, therefore, is to discover recurrent patterns of interstate behavior. From this perspective (a view incidentally consistent with that of many "traditional" realists and idealists), a theory of international relations should contain a statement of the relationship between two or more variables, specify the conditions under which the relationship(s) holds, and explain why the relationship(s) should be expected to hold. To uncover such theories, behavioralists leaned to comparative cross-national analyses rather than to case studies of particular countries at particular times (as was characteristic of the diplomatic-historical approach). They also acknowledged the necessity of systematically gathering data about the characteristics of nations and how they interacted with one another. Hence, the behavioral movement spawned, and is often synonymous with, the quantitative study of international relations (exemplary are Rosenau, 1980; Singer, 1968).

What made behavioralism innovative was not so much its reliance on controlled comparative techniques and quantitative analyses as its temperament regarding inquiry. Behavioralists sought greater rigor and precision in analysis. They tried to replace subjective belief with verifiable knowledge; to augment impressionism and intuition with testable evidence; and to substitute data and reproducible information for appeals to the allegedly "expert" opinion of authorities in order to acquire knowledge and build on it cumulatively. They aspired to conduct objective or value-free research. They also sought to avoid the tendency of previous scholarship to select facts and cases so as to fit preexisting hunches. Instead, *all* available data, those not supportive of as well as those consistent with existing theoretical hypotheses, were to be examined. Moreover, the behavioralists sought precision by replacing ambiguous verbal definitions of concepts (such as power) with ones on which empirical tests

---

11. For examples of the debate and illustrations of the tone of dialogue, see Hoffmann (1960), Kaplan (1968), Knorr and Rosenau (1969), Knorr and Verba (1961), Tanter and Ullman (1972), and Wright (1955). See also Lijphart (1974) for a review of the issues that this debate entailed.

could be conducted and whose meaning was easily communicated from one analyst to the next. They argued that knowledge would advance best if a cautious, skeptical attitude toward any empirical statement were assumed. "Let the data, not the armchair theorist, speak" and "seek evidence, but distrust it" were slogans representative of the behavioral posture toward the acquisition of knowledge about international affairs.

Armed with new tools for analyzing international relations, with newly generated data for testing competing hypotheses that had been voiced over decades of traditional speculation, and sometimes with generous research support from governments and private foundations, the behavioral approach commanded much of the attention in international relations research. Its early efforts were enthusiastic, and a generation of scholars was trained to study international relations with powerful new conceptual and methodological tools. In the process, some behavioralists addressed empirical questions at the core of the competing ideas concerning the social and political organization of national societies, including Marxist and other ideas regarding the causes and consequences of the inequalities of and between states.

But cumulating verifiable knowledge is a difficult, even tedious, task. The early enthusiasm and optimism of the effort thus began to wane, and voices even within the behavioral movement itself began to ask sometimes embarrassing questions about the approach and its suitability. One of the early proponents of the behavioral movement, David Easton (1969), began to ask—in a self-fulfilling way—if the field was not moving into a *postbehavioral* period. At the heart of this self-scrutiny was a common set of criticisms: that some devotees of behavioralism had become preoccupied with method to the exclusion of real-world problems; that they had focused on testing interesting (and often the most readily quantifiable) hypotheses, but hypotheses that were largely trivial and meaningless to the policymakers responsible for protecting the nation and making the world a better place in which to live; and that the methodology of behavioralism, which sought to ground theories on hard data, necessarily relied on past patterns of human experience that did not describe linkages among variables in a rapidly changing world that would retain their pertinence in the future. Hence the findings might be historically accurate but largely irrelevant to today's world, or to tomorrow's.

Although some behavioral research spoke directly to the moral issues central to the idealist-realist debate (see Kegley, 1988), the behavioralists' relative neglect of many of the ethical questions raised in a world of poverty, hunger, violence, and other forms of malaise was also criticized. Hence the postbehavioral critique called for a new research agenda that would focus on new types of issues and reexamine the underlying philosophical implications of the agenda from a multidisciplinary perspective. Interestingly, however, the advocates of new approaches to studying international relations rarely recommended that scientific methods be discarded. More commonly they advised that such methods be applied to new kinds of problems.

TOWARD AN UNDERSTANDING OF INTERNATIONAL COOPERATION

As we noted, political realism remains an important theoretical perspective underlying analyses of national security affairs. The logic of *realpolitik* retains lasting relevance in part because it captures best the essential nature of the international political system, in which no central institutions manage and resolve conflict among its central actors (of which nation-states remain the most important) and in which the rich and powerful remain dominant. Accordingly, the continuing emphasis on the quest for power and advantage in a competitive system in which states alone are responsible for protection of their welfare and survival is understandable. For scholars and diplomats who seek to understand world politics, power thus remains the key factor in explaining the nature and outcome of conflict at the international level.

Interestingly, scholars have also come to ask whether power may be critical to an understanding of both international cooperation and international conflict. This question motivated much of the theoretical activity that flourished in the 1980s to explain how cooperation could be achieved under anarchy. More specifically, this inquiry sought to understand *international regimes*, a set of interstate collaborative experiences whose intellectual origins as a theoretical perspective stem from an earlier perspective known as *transnational relations and complex interdependence*. A description of the latter will introduce the former theoretical departure, but both require that we return, as an interlude, once more to a discussion of realism.

As in the past, a concern for emergent political problems was a primary motivating force behind the drive to understand international regimes. Oran Young explains:

> [The] burst of work [in recent years] on regimes . . . reflects an emerging sense, especially among Americans, that the international order engineered by the United States and its allies in the aftermath of World War II is eroding rapidly and may even be approaching the verge of collapse. The international trade regime seems incapable of stemming a mounting tide of protectionist pressures flowing from many corners of the world, including the United States itself. The monetary regime is staggering under the impact of a series of debt crises and may go under as these crises become increasingly severe over the next few years. (Young, 1986: 104–105)

Given these global trends and circumstances, how can institutionalized procedures and rules for the collective management of global policy problems—regimes based on coordinated cooperation—be established and preserved? What is the role of power in a cooperative system of interstate interactions? These are questions at the core of recent inquiry.

The continuing centrality of power as an analytical concept in international politics was underscored in Kenneth N. Waltz's influential *Theory of International Politics* (1979). This important and controversial book sought to remedy many of the deficiencies in classical realism as a theory of international politics and thus has become the centerpiece of an ongoing debate about realist theory,[12] which has important ramifications for an understanding of cooperative international interactions.

For Waltz, the distribution of power is the central feature of a theory of international politics. Although states differ along many dimensions, for purposes of understanding international politics the only differences that matter are national capabilities: "States are alike in the tasks that they face," Waltz (1979) argues, "though not in their abilities to perform them. The differences are of capability, not of function." Changes in the distribution of power, in coalitions and alliances, and in patterns of international conflict are explained by changes in the distribution of capabilities among states, which remain the key actors in the system. Further, Waltz, like the classical realists, assumes that states "are unitary actors who, at a minimum, seek their own preservation and, at a maximum, drive for universal domination." From this Waltz concludes that balances of power among states in the international system will necessarily emerge. That is, although states pursue many goals that "fluctuate with the changing currents of domestic politics, are prey to the vagaries of a shifting cast of political leaders, and are influenced by the outcomes of bureaucratic struggles," such factors tell little about the process whereby states come to pursue the goal of balancing power with power. Instead, it is the global system writ large that explains outcomes: "Structural constraints explain why the [same] methods are repeatedly used despite differences in the persons and the states who use them" (Waltz, 1979).

What distinguishes this reasoning from the classical realists' is the claim to account not only for the importance of the balance of power in international politics but also for the processes that lead to its recurrent formation and dissolution. Whereas Hans J. Morgenthau, one of the leading classical theorists, merely pointed to the importance of the balance of power, "Waltz deduces that balances of power must necessarily emerge" (Keohane, 1986b) and, further, that states "will imitate each other and become socialized to their system" (Waltz, 1979). Because Waltz builds on the insights of classical realism in his attempt "to systematize political realism into a rigorous, deductive systemic theory of international politics" (Keohane, 1986b), his ideas lie at the core of what has come to be called *neorealism*.

Neorealism belongs to a body of theory called *structural realism* (Keohane, 1983). Interdependence and regimes are variants on structural realism, as we shall soon make clear. What structural theorists share in common is a

---

12. For a discussion, see the "Symposium on the New Realism" in *International Organization* 38 (Spring 1984), with special attention to the essays by Richard K. Ashley (1984) and by Robert Gilpin (1984), and the collection *Neorealism and Its Critics*, edited by Robert O. Keohane (1986a).

concern for explaining state behavior and system outcomes on the basis of the system, not its constituent units.

> The key distinguishing characteristic of a systemic theory is that *the internal attributes of actors are given by assumption rather than treated as variables*. Changes in actor behavior, and system outcomes, are explained not on the basis of variation in these actor characteristics, but on the basis of changes in attributes of the system itself. (Keohane, 1983: 508–509)

The emphasis that structuralists place on the international system permits us to draw attention to the so-called levels of analysis (Singer, 1961; Spanier, 1987; Waltz, 1954) as they relate to international political inquiry. The term emphasizes the necessity of explaining developments in world politics in terms of the impact exerted by actors at various levels of aggregation, and it draws attention to the implications for understanding world politics that result from emphasizing different levels. These levels range from the system of states interacting with one another (as described by realists), at the broadest level, to individual states and their national foreign policy–making processes at the next level, and finally to the level of the individual policymaker.

Common sense suggests there are interrelationships across all of these levels. Hence, trends and transformations in world politics are unlikely to be explained by changes at only one level. Because there are linkages across levels, this also means that any global development may be traced to forces operating at each level. The behavior of any one nation, for instance, will be affected by the dispositions of its leaders, its domestic political and social conditions, and its external environment and the stimuli it receives from abroad. Similarly, any surge or diminution of global tension tomorrow may be governed in part by how actors at each level choose to behave toward one another today.

Compelling as this commonsense argument may be, no theory has yet been devised that adequately links micro and macro behaviors across levels of analysis and aggregation (see Schelling, 1978, for an insightful discussion of this critical linkage). We compensate for this unfortunate (but significant) theoretical limitation in Chapter 3, in which when describing foreign policy decision making we identify some of the ways that forces operative at the level of the state respond to and, by implication, shape global political relations. But neither realism nor the responses to or variants thereof that fall under the rubric of structural theories are able to account adequately for the impact of domestic politics on international politics; indeed, they dismiss this linkage by ignoring the national sources of international circumstances. Put differently, the domestic and systemic sources of states' foreign policies remain intimately linked, much as two rails of a railroad track are tied together in pursuit of a common goal, but the theoretical linkages that would permit the two to be welded into one have yet to be forged.

Like realism, both the transnational relations and complex interdependence model and the investigation of international regimes embody structural theories of international politics in the sense that they concentrate on the level of the international political system rather than on the units that it contains. But they are variants on structural theories that challenge and extend realism in its classical and neoclassical manifestations because of the somewhat different emphases they place on actors, institutions, and outcomes and on the way that power relates to each, as well as how these relationships may produce cooperation and not just conflict.

Transnational Relations and Complex Interdependence

Nearly all of the global trends that we shall consider in *World Politics: Trend and Transformation* are touched to some extent by the way in which the world's nations find themselves linked to one another in complex, interdependent relationships.

The manifestations of interdependence are most immediate and visible in the international political economy. National economies have become internationalized, as trade and capital flows among them have expanded geometrically. As a result, national political authorities in one nation are no longer able to insulate their jurisdictions from the effects of economic policies engineered by political authorities or private-sector actors located abroad.

Other transnational linkages have also become part of our interdependent world. Military alliances have become entangling and permanent. Heads of state visit one another with such frequency that the practice of summitry is now commonplace. Private citizens increasingly participate in intercultural experiences, whether by mail and telecommunications or through business travel and tourism. And energy resources transferred across borders determine the relative comfort and economic well-being of people residing in widely separated parts of the globe.

As national fates become increasingly interlocked, the incidence and intensity of international conflict may increase because of the disputes that inevitably arise from increasing contact among the parties in interaction. Moreover, interdependence challenges the state system because it directly affects nationalism. Should nationalistic thinking (loyalty to the nation before all else) erode, the climate for the conduct of world politics would be fundamentally altered. Zbigniew Brzezinski, writing before the events with which he had to grapple as national security adviser to President Jimmy Carter, termed the demise of nationalism as a force in world politics *the* major division between the past and the future. Because of this erosion, Brzezinski (1970) saw humankind as being between two ages: "The world is ceasing to be an arena in which relatively self-sustained, 'sovereign,' and homogeneous nations interact, collaborate, clash, or make war. . . . Transnational ties are gaining in importance, while the claims of nationalism, though still intense, are nevertheless becoming diluted. . . . The consequence is a new era—an era of the global political process."

The long-run consequences of global interdependence and its extent are not altogether clear, however. The drive to acquire military capabilities in order to preserve national security, the surge of protectionist sentiment regarding international trade issues, the desire to become independent from foreign sources of critical raw materials, and resurgent nationalism all point to a world characterized by national efforts to minimize the domestic impact that growing international interdependence necessarily expands. Nonetheless, it seems unlikely that nations will be able to extricate themselves easily from their involvement in the affairs of others. Autarky (national self-sufficiency) seems unlikely in a rapidly changing world already suffering from the maldistribution of some goods and resources. And no political system can shield its population from the influence of almost constant communication and information. Few problems, it seems, can any longer be defined as domestic or local, for their characteristics and potential solutions are shaped by conditions transcending national boundaries. Thus, as former Secretary of State Henry A. Kissinger remarked, "We are stranded between old conceptions of political conduct and a wholly new conception, between the inadequacy of the nation-state and the emerging imperative of global community" (cited in Falk, 1976).

As an analytical perspective, the transnational relations and complex interdependence model challenges key assumptions associated with other perspectives, particularly political realism. First, it challenges the assumption that nation-states are the only important actors in world politics. Multinational corporations and transnational banks are examples of other actors that "are important not only because of their activities in pursuit of their own interests, but also because they act as transmission belts, making government policies in various countries more sensitive to one another" (Keohane and Nye, 1984).

Second, the perspective questions whether national security issues must dominate nation-states' decision-making agendas. Under conditions of interdependence, foreign policy agendas necessarily become "larger and more diverse" because a broader range of "governments' policies, even those previously considered merely domestic, impinge on one another" (Keohane and Nye, 1984).

Third, the perspective disputes the notion that military force is the only, even dominant, means of exercising influence in international politics, particularly among the West's advanced industrial and pluralist societies. "Intense relationships of mutual influence exist between these countries, but in most of them force is irrelevant or unimportant as an instrument of policy" (Keohane and Nye, 1984).

The intellectual roots of transnational relations and complex interdependence can be traced to studies of regional integration that began to flourish in the 1950s and 1960s as scholars sought to understand the processes whereby political unification of formerly independent states might be achieved. Collaborative efforts to build new European institutions in Western Europe, historically one of the most war-prone of all world regions, commanded most attention, but the insights gained there were applied to many other world regions (see Nye, 1971). The focus was on the way that institutions, political attitudes, and economic and other forms of transaction flows coalesce to form new political units out of previously separate ones.

Advocates of the transnational relations and complex interdependence perspective extended many of these insights to the range of issues relating to international economic interdependence that came to the fore in the 1970s, especially among the advanced capitalist societies of the West (Keohane and Nye, 1975; Puchala, 1984). International institutions commanded a central place in many of these analyses, as demonstrated in Robert O. Keohane's and Joseph S. Nye's (1977) *Power and Interdependence*, which remains the classic statement on the transnationalism and interdependence perspective. In this sense the perspective embraces idealism.[13]

A careful reading of *Power and Interdependence* indicates, however, that the transnational relations and interdependence paradigm does not reject realism. Instead, the concern of many of those working within it was with "the conditions under which assumptions of Realism were sufficient or needed to be supplemented by a more complex model of change" (Nye, 1987; see also Keohane, 1983). Nye and Keohane in particular sought to devise structural models of international regime change. The *regime* concept, derived and extended from international legal studies generally, eventually became a dominant focus of attention and has been applied broadly in analyses of the international political economy.

International Regimes

Concern for the factors that propel cooperation and collaboration at the international level motivates much of the attention given international regimes. For even though the international system appears to be an "anarchical society" (Bull, 1977), it is ordered anarchy, and international cooperation, not conflict, is often the outcome of relations among states. The interest in regimes is thus "motivated primarily by a desire to understand the extent to which mutually accepted constraints affect states' behaviors" (Zacher, 1987).

Stephen Krasner's definition of a regime has emerged as the most influential:

> Regimes can be defined as sets of implicit or explicit principles, norms, rules, and decision-making procedures around which actors' expectations converge in a given area of international relations. Principles are beliefs or fact, causation, and rectitude. Norms are standards of behavior defined in

---

13. Although international institutions figure prominently in the transnational relations and interdependence perspective, it should be understood that the term implies more than just organizations. Oran Young (1986) underscores the distinction: "Institutions are practices composed of recognized roles coupled with sets of rules or conventions governing relations among the occupants of these roles. Organizations are physical entities possessing offices, personnel, equipment, budgets, and so forth."

terms of rights and obligations. Rules are specific prescriptions or proscriptions for action. Decision-making procedures are prevailing practices for making and implementing collective choice. (Krasner, 1982: 186)

Many other definitions of regimes exist, referring to and emphasizing different aspects of this cluster of interrelated phenomena (for reviews, see Haggard and Simmons, 1987; Kratochwil and Ruggie, 1986; Strange, 1982; Young, 1986). But most converge on the notion of a regime as an institutionalized system of cooperation with respect to a given issue-area. As Krasner (1982) explains, "It is the infusion of behavior with principles and norms that distinguishes regime-governed activity in the international system from more conventional activity, guided exclusively by narrow calculations of interest." Thus an essential feature of a regime is that it constitutes "a system of injunctions about international behavior" (Smith, 1987). Because the regime perspective directs attention to institutions and to the influence of norms on patterns of state behavior, as opposed simply to the pursuit of national interests, it can in some ways be viewed as an attempt to reconcile the idealist and realist perspectives in the study of world politics (Haggard and Simmons, 1987).

The global monetary and trade systems created during and after World War II are clear expressions of international regimes. And both, as well as particular sectors within the trade system, have been the focus of considerable inquiry from the regime perspective.[14] Together the monetary and trade regimes defined a Liberal International Economic Order (LIEO) embracing a combination of principles, rules, norms, and decision-making procedures that limited government intervention in the global political economy and otherwise facilitated the free flow of capital and goods across national boundaries. The International Monetary Fund (IMF) and the General Agreement on Tariffs and Trade (GATT) played important institutional roles in the LIEO, but it was the overarching power of the United States that ensured stability and effective operation of the monetary and trade regimes (see Chapter 7 for elaboration).

What impact has the alleged decline of American power[15] had on the LIEO? Does that decline explain the global economic disorders so prevalent in the 1970s and 1980s? The questions are of special concern to a number of regime analysts concerned with *hegemonic stability*.

Hegemonic stability theorists argue that a preeminent, stability-seeking state (hegemon), such as the United States in the decades following World War II, will promote international regimes that will benefit not only itself but others as well. What the hegemon provides, in which all benefit, is order and

---

14. The literature on international regimes is large and growing. The best single collection remains the special issue of *International Organization* edited by Stephen D. Krasner (1983), which was published in book form by Cornell University Press in 1983. The journal *International Organization* publishes many analyses of issues related to regime dynamics.

15. For one discussion of this thesis, see Paul Kennedy (1988); for a rebuttal, see Bruce Russett (1985).

stability. "The novelty of the theory is that it stands conventional or intuitive logic about hegemony on its head; instead of claiming that hegemony is exploitative and only to the benefit of the hegemon, the theory argues that hegemony is widely beneficial" (Smith, 1987). This runs counter to both the orthodox interpretation and world system theory (as represented by the work of Immanuel Wallerstein, 1980), which predicts that the decline in hegemonic power will be followed by global instability.

Whether the theory of hegemonic stability explains recent economic disorders and the erosion of the Liberal International Economic Order is unclear (see Haggard and Simmons, 1987; Keohane, 1980, 1982, 1984; Rapkin and Avery, 1982; Snidal, 1985; Stein, 1984). But in bringing into perspective a broad range of global political issues destined to dominate the global agenda in the 1990s and beyond, the theory promises to receive continued scholarly attention in the future.

One application of hegemonic stability theory that goes beyond the global political economy is Robert Gilpin's (1981) *War and Change in World Politics*. Gilpin argues that the United States provided order (a public or collective good) that benefited subordinate states but that it did so through coercive rather than benevolent leadership. That is, it enforced regime rules with positive and negative sanctions. In effect the United States acted as "a quasi-government by providing public goods *and* taxing other states to pay for them. Subordinate states will be reluctant to be taxed but, because of the hegemonic state's preponderant power, will succumb. . . . The focus of the theory thus shifts from the ability to provide a public good to the ability to coerce other states" (Snidal, 1985). In the process, the theory begins to look much less like an inquiry into collaborative international behavior and more like an application of classical realism.[16]

Most applications of the regime concept have been in the area of the global political economy; relatively few exist in the national security issue-area or have been extended to relationships, like that between the superpowers, that are marked more by conflict than cooperation. Even the United States and the Soviet Union mix cooperation and conflict, but the risks and costs of cooperation appear to be greater in security than in economic affairs, which is why security regimes are comparatively rare (Lipson, 1984; see also Jervis, 1982). An exception is the nuclear nonproliferation regime (Smith, 1987). It has also been suggested that although regime injunctions do not apply to the overall relationship between the United States and the Soviet Union, the restraining

---

16. In contrast with coercive leadership, the benevolent leadership model sees the hegemon as absorbing the costs of leadership (which, for the hegemon, are greater than the benefits) because it has an independent interest in doing so, regardless of the contributions of others. Others in turn have an incentive to become "free-riders," as they know that the hegemon will provide the collective good with or without their contribution. Thus the benevolent leadership model "turns realism on its head. . . . Rather than the strong exploiting the weak, it is the weak who exploit the strong" (Haggard and Simmons, 1987).

effects of a regime may hold in some sub–issue-areas, particularly those relating to nuclear weapons (Nye, 1987). And there is even some evidence that the superpowers have successfully built the framework of a regime to manage the crises that erupt periodically between them (George, 1986). For the most part, however, realism, which focuses on actors that are independent rather than interdependent, provides greater insight into the high politics of national security affairs.

INTERNATIONAL POLITICS IN A WORLD OF CHANGE

If we are to understand today's changing world and make reasonable prognoses about tomorrow's, we must arm ourselves with an array of knowledge and conceptual tools. What may be termed the *global problematique* is one of vast proportions and complexity—a challenge to insight and understanding. Today's world is divided both ideologically and economically. Its opposing divisions are armed militarily, and they often conflict violently. Yet along with these divisions we also find unprecedented levels of transnational cooperation. And overlaying all of them are a plethora of issues on the global agenda that breed conflict but require multilateral cooperation for their solution; environmental pollution and pressures on the world's delicate life-support systems are but two examples.

The theoretical perspectives discussed in this chapter begin to arm us for the challenge of understanding the changing world around us. We shall draw on them in the chapters ahead. Because this is a book about change in world politics and the forces that promote it, it will be necessary to draw on still other perspectives. Four are identified here and will be discussed in greater detail in the chapters ahead: long-cycle theory, world system analysis, dependency theory, and international political economy.

Long-cycle theory seeks to explain the ebb and flow of world politics, global leadership, and general war over long stretches of history. The literature in this subfield of the discipline is substantial (Goldstein, 1988; Modelski, 1987). One of the reasons for its popularity is the recognition that many features of international politics cannot be understood adequately unless a long-term historical perspective is taken, in which the recurrent appearance and disappearance of important global phenomena might be detected.[17]

World system theory also looks at system dynamics from a long historical perspective. As noted in Chapter 5, it arose in part in response to the theories of national development and nation building that prevailed in the field of comparative politics in the 1950s and 1960s and was motivated by the goal of explaining the rise to dominance of the capitalist societies of the Western

---

17. For a summary and critique of recent contributions to the body of long-cycle theory, which identifies its intellectual antecedents, see Rosecrance (1987).

world and the lack of economic development in many other parts of the world. There are several contending variants of world system theory which stress different factors.[18] Wallerstein's (1980) macrosociological theory of economic change in the world capitalist system and his analysis of the forces driving the formation of world empires through imperialism and their disintegration is the best known.

Dependency theory is sometimes subsumed as a component of either the world system or international political economy perspectives. It seeks to explain the perpetuation of the system of dominance and dependence that characterizes the relationship between the world's rich and poor nations. Its intellectual father is Dr. Raúl Prebisch, an Argentinian economist who directed the United Nations Economic Commission for Latin America in the 1950s. Initially looking at the unfavorable terms of trade (see Chapter 8) alleged to have led to economic stagnation and foreign control of Third World economies, dependency theorists have expanded their analysis in order to construct a model of "dependent development." This seeks to account for such paradoxes as the tendency for Third World economic growth to exacerbate social inequalities and class cleavages, and for urbanization and the expansion of literacy rates to be accompanied by the marginalization of the masses (for illustrative treatments, summaries, and critiques, see Caporaso, 1978, 1980).

Finally, *international political economy* is a diverse perspective that has been broadly applied to various aspects of international politics. Its classical, Marxist, and modern approaches can be distinguished, although these often embrace incompatible assumptions and arrive at divergent conclusions (Caporaso, 1987). In general, the perspective evaluates the sources and consequences of the international division of labor and wealth by examining how politics influences economic outcomes, and vice versa (for overviews, see Sandler, 1980; Strange, 1984).

Armed with these tools, we can begin to address difficult and often disturbing questions: Will the world's complex metamorphoses outrun its ability to devise new mechanisms of political and social control? Will the world be flexible enough to adjust its perceptions to changing global realities? Will we be able to adapt conventional mental habits so as to comprehend unconventional circumstances?

SUGGESTED READINGS

Dougherty, James E., and Robert L. Pfaltzgraff, Jr. *Contending Theories of International Relations*, 2nd ed. New York: Harper & Row, 1981.

Holsti, K. J. *The Dividing Discipline: Hegemony and Diversity in International Theory*. Boston: Allen & Unwin, 1985.

---

18. For a broad reviews and critiques, see Chirot (1986) and Chirot and Hall (1982). For applications to foreign policy behavior, see McGowan and Kegley (1983).

Kelman, Herbert C., ed. *International Behavior: A Social-Psychological Analysis*. New York: Holt, Rinehart & Winston, 1965.

Keohane, Robert O., ed. *Neorealism and Its Critics*. New York: Columbia University Press, 1986.

Keohane, Robert O., and Joseph S. Nye, Jr. *Power and Interdependence: World Politics in Transition*. Boston: Little, Brown, 1977.

Knorr, Klaus, and James N. Rosenau, eds. *Contending Approaches to International Politics*. Princeton, N.J.: Princeton University Press, 1969.

Krasner, Stephen D., ed. *International Regimes*. Ithaca, N.Y.: Cornell University Press, 1983.

Light, Margot, and A. J. R. Groom, eds. *International Relations: A Handbook of Current Theory*. Boulder, Colo.: Lynne Rienner, 1985.

Maghroori, Ray, and Bennett Ramberg, eds. *Globalism Versus Realism: International Relations' Third Debate*. Boulder, Colo.: Westview Press, 1982.

Mansbach, Richard W., and John A. Vasquez. *In Search of Theory: A New Paradigm for Global Politics*. New York: Columbia University Press, 1981.

PART II

Relations among Global Actors

THREE

Foreign Policy Decision Making: Coping with International Circumstances

Foreign policy is the system of activities evolved by communities for changing the behavior of other states and for adjusting their own activities to the international environment.

GEORGE MODELSKI, 1962

Foreign affairs is a complicated and disorderly business, full of surprises, demanding hard choices that must be based on judgment rather than analysis—taking place in a world that changes so rapidly that memory and experience are likely out of date.

THOMAS C. SCHELLING, 1968

Analysts typically use the term *actor* to refer to those collectivities that are the primary moving forces in world politics. The term conjures up the image of the world as a stage on which those most capable of capturing the drama of world politics act out the roles assigned to them. The leading actors dominate the center of the stage, and others cast in supporting roles are less in evidence as they move along the periphery. The actors also seem to be playing their roles under constraints that are not readily visible to the casual observer, much as the actors in a community playhouse production follow their scripts under the guiding hand of the director.

Today the actors on the world stage are many and varied. They include countries, more properly called nation-states (like the United States and the Soviet Union), international organizations (like the United Nations), multinational corporations (such as International Business Machines), and terrorist groups, among others. We shall discuss each of these types of actors in subsequent chapters of this book. Here we focus on nation-states, and in particular on the processes through which they reach foreign policy decisions. This attention is warranted, as nation-states remain the principal repositories of economic and military capabilities in world affairs, and they alone assert the legal right to use force.

Although the terms state, nation, and nation-state are often used inter-changeably, technically they are not the same. A *state* is a legal entity repre-sented by a government empowered to make decisions and enforce rules for the people residing on a particular piece of the global terrain.[1] A *nation* is a collection of people who on the basis of ethnic, linguistic, or cultural affinity perceive themselves to be members of the same group. Thus *nation-states* are polities controlled by members of some nationality recognizing no authority higher than themselves. The term implies a convergence between territorial states and the psychological identification of people with them.[2] (The origins and development of the *state system* are discussed in Chapter 5.)

A primary objective of nation-states' foreign policies is to protect their *sovereignty*, a legal principle that promises freedom from the dictates of others. The international environment often appears hostile because the interests and objectives of other nation-states frequently threaten the freedom that states prize most. As a result, the primary task that decision makers face is to formulate foreign policies to ensure their state's independence and, ultimately, survival. Accordingly, they direct their foreign policies at other actors, whose behavior is an important determinant of their own foreign policy. By implica-tion, from this viewpoint the choices that policymakers make will be shaped by strategic calculations of power, not by domestic politics or the process of policymaking itself.

This view of the sources of nations' foreign policies is the cornerstone of political realism (see Chapter 2). It conceives of the nation-state as the principal actor in world politics and maintains that the realities of international politics dictate foreign policy makers' choices. For many situations, this explanation of how nations decide to act toward others is persuasive. We shall therefore begin our inquiry by studying the model of rational decision making that political realism presupposes. Following this, we shall consider two alternative frame-works: the bureaucratic politics and the hero-in-history decision-making mod-els. We shall conclude by briefly examining the role that national capabilities and domestic politics play in influencing nations' foreign policy decision-making processes.

---

1. As a legal construct, states are assumed to possess a relatively permanent population, a well-defined territory, and a government possessing sovereignty (that is, supreme authority over its inhabitants as well as freedom from interference by others). The properties of states under international law are discussed in Chapter 14.

2. Many states are made up of many nations, not just one, and some nations are not states. These nonstate nations are ethnic groups, such as native American tribes in the United States or Palestinians residing in the Middle East, composed of people without sovereign power over the territory they occupy. See Bertelsen (1977) for a discussion of nonstate nations, and Gastil (1978) for a listing of peoples without nation-states and peoples separated from existing nation-states. Gastil's inventory suggests that perhaps three-quarters of a billion people fall into one or another of these categories.

THE UNITARY ACTOR AND RATIONAL DECISION MAKING

When we speak generically about *foreign policy* and the decision routines that produce it, we are referring to the goals that the officials representing states seek to obtain abroad, the values that give rise to those objectives, and the means or instruments through which they are pursued. Given this definition, the question at issue is how best to describe the processes whereby the choices designed to cope with global circumstances are reached.

The theory of political realism emphasizes that the international environment largely determines state action. Accordingly, it assumes that all states and the individuals responsible for formulating their foreign policies similarly approach the problem of adapting to the challenges posed by the world beyond their borders. Because realism views states' basic motives and the corresponding decision calculus of its policymakers as the same, it assumes that each state makes its choices as though it were a *unitary actor*.

Perhaps the best way of understanding the relationship between states' foreign policy–making processes and their behavior in world politics according to this viewpoint is by visualizing states as billiard balls and the table on which they interact as the state system. This metaphor compares world politics to a game in which states, the billiard balls, continuously clash and collide with one another. The actions of each are determined by the interactions between and among the balls, not by what occurs within them. The leaders who make foreign policy decisions, the type of governments they head, the characteristics of their society, and the internal economic and political conditions of the state they represent are unimportant. Foreign policy decisions are shaped by events and circumstances abroad; what a state does to and with others is determined by their actions and by the dynamic action and reaction of each unit within the system. The system of action and reaction is itself the author of each unit's foreign policy behavior.

If this image derived from the logic of *realpolitik* is accurate, then foreign policy making consists primarily of adjusting the state to the demands of a global environment of strife and struggle and accommodating it to the pressures of a world system that remains permanent in its essential features. The unitary actor assumption maintains that all policymakers follow the same decision calculus to define their country's *national interest*. The overriding concern for the national interest requires the rational calculation of opportunities and constraints so that the state is able to maximize its power and to cope successfully with threats from abroad. The *rational actor* model of foreign policy making presumes that *all* decision makers go through the same processes to make value-maximizing choices designed to pursue the national interest defined in terms of power. In other words, the assumption is that all decision makers are essentially alike.

If they follow the [decision] rules, we need know nothing more about them. In essence, if the decision-maker behaves rationally, the observer, knowing the rules of rationality, can rehearse the decisional process in his own mind, and, if he knows the decision-maker's goals, can both predict the decision and understand why that particular decision was made. (Verba, 1969: 225)

What constitutes "rationality," and how might decision makers go about making "rational" foreign policy? At its core, rationality entails purposeful, goal-directed behavior that is exhibited when "the individual responding to an international event . . . uses the best information available and chooses from the universe of possible responses that alternative most likely to maximize his goals" (Verba, 1969). Scholars who study decision making and advise policy-makers on ways to improve their policy-formulation skills have described perfect rationality as a sequence of decision-making activities involving the following intellectual steps:

1. *Problem recognition and definition.* The necessity for decisions begins when policymakers perceive the existence of an external problem with which they must deal and attempt to define objectively its distinguishing characteristics. They must see the situation as it actually exists and not merely as they assume it to be. Accuracy requires full information about the actions, motivations, and capabilities of other actors as well as the state of the international environment and the transforming trends within it. The search for such information must be exhaustive; all the facts relevant to the problem must be gathered.
2. *Goal selection.* Rational actors must define how they want the perceived problem to be resolved. This disarmingly simple requirement is far from easy to achieve. It necessitates ranking values in terms of the degree to which they are preferred. This can be difficult because many national goals may be incompatible or mutually exclusive and their relative value can vary in different contexts. Yet, to set priorities rationality requires that all goals be identified and ranked in a hierarchy from most to least preferred.
3. *Identification of alternatives.* Rationality requires that an exhaustive list of all available policy options be compiled, which includes an estimate of the costs and opportunities associated with alternative courses of action that may be chosen to realize each goal in the hierarchy of preferences.
4. *Choice.* Finally, rational decision making consists of selecting from among these options the one alternative with the best prospect of achieving the desired goal(s). For this purpose, a rigorous means–ends, cost–benefit analysis must be conducted, informed by an accurate prediction of the likely results or chance of success of each possible option.

Clearly the requirements of perfect rationality are stringent. Decision makers nonetheless often describe their own behavior as resulting from a rational decision-making process designed to reach the "best" decision possible.[3] Moreover, elements of this idealized version of foreign policy decision making have been exhibited in some past foreign policy decisions made in response to threats from abroad. For example, the 1962 Cuban missile crisis reveals several ways in which the deliberations of the key American policy-makers concerned with the issue of Soviet missiles in Cuba conformed to a rational process (Allison, 1971). On recognizing the emergent problem, President John F. Kennedy charged the crisis decision-making group he formed to "set aside all other tasks to make a prompt and intensive survey of the dangers and all possible courses of action." Six options were ultimately identified: Do nothing; exert diplomatic pressure; make a secret approach to the Cuban leader Fidel Castro; invade Cuba; launch a surgical air strike against the missiles; and blockade Cuba. Choosing among these six alternatives required that goals be specified. Was removal of the Soviet missiles, retaliation against Castro, or maintenance of the balance of power the goal? Or did the missiles pose no serious threat to the vital interests of the United States? "Do nothing" could not be eliminated as an option until it was determined that the missiles did indeed represent a real threat to U.S. security. Once it was agreed that the goal was to eliminate the missiles, the discussion turned to evaluating the surgical air strike and blockade options. The latter was eventually chosen because of its presumed advantages, among which were the demonstration of firmness it permitted the United States and the flexibility with respect to further choices it allowed both parties.

Often, however, it would appear that rational decision making is more an idealized standard by which to evaluate behavior than an accurate description of real-world decision making. Theodore Sorensen, himself a participant in the Cuban missile crisis decision process, has indicated how the actual decision making often departed from the idealized version the Kennedy administration aspired to:

> Each step cannot be taken in order. The facts may be in doubt or dispute. Several policies, all good, may conflict. Several means, all bad, may be all that are open. Value judgments may differ. Stated goals may be imprecise. There may be many interpretations of what is right, what is possible, and what is in the national interest. (Sorensen, 1963: 19–20)

Despite the virtues promised by rational choice, it is clear that in general the impediments to rational decision making are substantial. Foreign policy making takes place in an environment that imposes substantial constraints and

---

3. Theodore Sorensen (1963) described an eight-step process for policymaking that the Kennedy administration sought to follow that is consistent with the model we have described: (1) agreement on the facts; (2) agreement on the overall policy objective; (3) precise definition of the problems; (4) canvassing of all possible solutions; (5) listing of the possible consequences flowing from each solution; (6) recommendation of one option; (7) communication of the option selected; (8) provisions for its execution.

burdens. These limits are not just human (deriving from deficiencies in the intelligence, capability, and psychology of those who make decisions on behalf of nation-states). They also derive from circumstantial and organizational obstacles to making sound policy. For example, the setting for foreign policy making reduces the capacity of leaders to decide in ways that clearly promote their nation's interest. A variety of factors interfere with that capacity. Foremost among them is the ever-present ambiguity of most international situations requiring a choice. A complicating factor is that most decisions are reached in a group context, which requires agreement among many people about the wisest course of action. That is not easy, but nevertheless effective policy implementation requires achieving a modicum of consensus. Consequently, the politics of policymaking and the influence of domestic political factors are important facets in the foreign policy–making process.

A close examination of the ways in which decision makers make decisions reveals other behaviors that often depart from the ideal process of rational choice. Problem recognition is often delayed, for example. Moreover, information sufficient to define emergent problems accurately is frequently lacking, with the result that decisions are made on the basis of incomplete information. In addition, the information that is available is often inaccurate because it is screened, sorted, and rearranged by the large bureaucratic organizations on which political leaders depend for information and advice. Goal selection, moreover, is difficult because of ambiguities in defining national interests. Because policymakers work constantly with overloaded agendas and short deadlines, the search for policy options is seldom exhaustive. And in the choice phase of the decision process, goal-maximizing alternatives are rarely selected; instead of choosing the option or set of options that has the maximum chance of realizing desired goals, the typical decision maker evaluates one option at a time but terminates the evaluation as soon as an option is discovered that appears to be superior to those previously considered. Decision makers typically engage in what Herbert A. Simon (1957) has labeled "satisficing" behavior: Rather than seeking to discover optimal alternatives, they are routinely content to select the choice that meets minimally acceptable standards.

Part of the reason for the discrepancy between the theory and practice of rational decision making relates to the assumption that states are unitary actors. In practice, states are composed of individuals with different beliefs, values, and preferences, and these differences produce disagreement over the goals to be pursued and the plans developed to implement them. These disagreements are not resolved in a tidy, orderly, rational process but, as described more fully later, through bargaining and compromise among the key players, with inertia, incremental change, and sometimes unsound policies being common occurrences. "Rather than through grand decisions or grand alternatives, policy changes seem to come through a series of slight modifications of existing policy, with new policy emerging slowly and haltingly by small and usually tentative steps, a process of trial and error in which policy zigs and zags, reverses itself, and then moves forward" (Hilsman, 1967).

Thus, despite the image they seek to project, it is apparent from the ways in which policymakers go about making decisions in real life that foreign policy making is an exercise that lends itself to error, rigidity, bias, miscalculation, mistakes, and fiascoes. The real world of foreign policy making thus warrants the conclusion that the ideal requirements of rational decision making are rarely if ever met in practice.

The discrepancy between the ideal process of rational decision making and actual performance is summarized in Table 3.1. William D. Coplin (1971) captures the discrepancy in this way: "Foreign policy decision makers tend to avoid new interpretations of the environment, to select and act upon traditional goals, to limit the search for alternatives to a small number of moderate ones, and finally to take risks which involve low costs if they prove unsuccessful." Indeed, the degree of rationality in foreign policy decision making "bears little relationship to the world in which officials conduct their deliberations" (Rosenau, 1980).

But knowing that rational foreign policy making is more an ideal than a description of reality, we can assume nevertheless that policymakers aspire to rational decision-making behavior, which they may occasionally approximate. Indeed, as a working proposition, it is useful to accept rationality as a vision of how the decisional process should work and as a description of key aspects of the foreign policy formulation process:

Officials have some notion, conscious or unconscious, of a priority of values; . . . they possess some conceptions, elegant or crude, of the means available and their potential effectiveness; they engage in some effort,

TABLE 3.1 ■ Foreign Policy Decision Making in Theory and Practice

The Ideal Process	*The Actual Performance*
Accurate, comprehensive information about the situation	Distorted, fragmentary information about the situation
Clear definition of national goals	Personal motivations and organizational interests bias national goals
Exhaustive analysis of all options	Limited number of options considered, none thoroughly analyzed
Selection of course of action by rational decision criteria	Selection of course of action by political bargaining and compromise
Instantaneous evaluation of policy consequences followed by correction of errors	Superficial evaluation, imperfect detection of errors, and delayed correction

extensive or brief, to relate means to ends; and . . . therefore, at some point they select some alternative, clear-cut or confused, as the course of action that seems most likely to cope with the immediate situation. (Rosenau, 1980: 304–305)

THE BUREAUCRATIC POLITICS OF FOREIGN POLICY DECISION MAKING

Picture yourself as a head of state charged with managing your country's relations with the rest of the world. To make decisions for your state, you must acquire information and seek advice, and you must see that the policies initiated are properly implemented. To whom can you turn for these functions? Out of necessity, you must turn to many others for the expertise you lack.

In today's world the extensive economic, political, and military relations of states require dependence on large-scale organizations, and it to these that leaders turn to manage foreign affairs. This is more true of great powers than it is of small states, but even states without large budgets and complex foreign policy organizations make most of their decisions in a group or organizational context (Korany, 1986). The reasons stem from the indispensable services these organizations perform, services that enhance the state's capacity to cope with changing global circumstances.

Just as bureaucracy has become a necessary component of modern government, often many different bureaucratic organizations are involved in making and executing a nation's foreign policy. In the United States, for example, the State Department, the Defense Department, and the Central Intelligence Agency are key elements in the nation's foreign policy machinery, but there are many other departments and agencies that also are responsible for various aspects of America's foreign relations, as shown in Table 3.2. The same is true in other nations. Because the government of the Soviet Union faces many of the same kinds of foreign policy problems and issues as does that of the United States, for instance, it likewise relies on a variety of departments and agencies to manage its foreign relations, as illustrated in Table 3.3.

Bureaucratic management of foreign relations is not new. It was in evidence long ago in Confucian China. But it is a peculiarly modern phenomenon. Bureaucratic procedures are relied on throughout the world, in large part because they are perceived to contribute to rational decision making and efficient administration. The intellectual origins of that proposition date back to the seminal theoretical work on bureaucracies by the German sociologist and political economist Max Weber (1864–1920). Bureaucratic decision making produces effective administration and rational choice, Weber argued, because of the ways in which large-scale bureaucracies are organized. In particular, bureaucracy enhances rationality and efficiency by assigning responsibility for different tasks to different people, defining rules and standard operating procedures that specify how tasks are to be performed, relying on a system of records to gather and store information, and dividing authority among different organizations so as to avoid duplication of effort. Ideally the presence of many organizations results in "multiple advocacy" (George, 1972) which enhances the probability that all possible policy options will be considered. In addition to efficiency, bureaucracy allows some specialists the luxury of engaging in forward planning designed to determine in advance the objectives to be accomplished in meeting long-term needs and the means by which they might be attained. Unlike heads of state, whose roles require that attention be focused on the crisis of the moment,[4] bureaucracies can consider the future and not merely the present.

What emerges from this description of bureaucracy is another idealized picture of the policymaking process that appears conducive to the realization of rational choice. Before jumping to the conclusion that bureaucratic decision making is a modern blessing, however, we should emphasize that these propositions tell us how, according to organization theory, decision making through bureaucracies *should* occur. They do not tell us how foreign policy making in bureaucracies *does* occur. The actual practice of bureaucratic decision making and the foreign policy outcomes it produces depict a reality of burdens and not just benefits.

Consider once more the 1962 Cuban missile crisis, probably the single most threatening crisis in the postwar era and one in which American policymakers are often viewed as having very nearly approximated the ideal of rational choice.

From another perspective, however, which is often described as the *bureaucratic politics* model of decision making,[5] the missile crisis reveals some of the ways that decision making by and within organizational contexts compromised rather than facilitated rational choice. As described by Graham Allison (1971) in his well-known book on the missile crisis, *Essence of Decision*, there are really two elements in the bureaucratic politics model. One, which Allison calls *organizational process*, reflects the constraints that organizations place on decision makers' choices. The other, which Allison calls *governmental politics*, draws attention to the "pulling and hauling" that occurs among the key participants in the decision process.

How do large-scale bureaucratic organizations contribute to the policymaking process? One way, as we indicated, is by devising *standard operating procedures* (SOPs) for coping with policy problems when they arise. For

---

4. As Henry A. Kissinger (1979) observed: "There is little time for leaders to reflect. They are locked in an endless battle in which the urgent constantly gains on the important. The public life of every political figure is a continual struggle to rescue an element of choice from the pressure of circumstance."

5. The characteristics of the bureaucratic politics model of foreign policy decision making are elaborated in Allison (1971), Caldwell (1977), C. Hermann (1988), Kissinger (1973), and Townsend (1982); for a critique, see Krasner (1972).

TABLE 3.2 ■ Foreign Affairs Machinery of the United States

National Policy and Leadership	President National Security Council				
Foreign Affairs Function	Political Affairs	Military Affairs	International Commercial and Economic Affairs	Informational and Educational and Cultural Exchange	Intelligence
Foreign Affairs Agency	Department of State	Department of State Department of Defense Arms Control and Disarmament Agency	Departments of State, Agriculture, Commerce, Energy, Labor, and Treasury Export–Import Bank International Trade Commission Overseas Private Investment Corporation U.S. Trade Representative International Development and Cooperation Agency Agency for International Development	Department of State U.S. Information Agency	Central Intelligence Agency (CIA) National Security Agency (NSA) Defense Intelligence Agency (DIA)

Source: Adapted from *Atlas of U.S. Foreign Relations* (Washington, D.C.: U.S. Department of State, 1987), p. 4.

TABLE 3.3 ■ Foreign Affairs Machinery of the Soviet Union

National Policy and Leadership	General Secretary of the Communist Party of the Soviet Union Central Committee (CPSU)			
	Politburo	Secretariat of the Central Committee of the CPSU		Council of Ministers of the USSR
	Defense Council			

Foreign Affairs Function	Political Affairs	Military Affairs	International Commercial and Economic Affairs	Informational and Educational and Cultural Exchange	Intelligence	Relations with Communist Parties and International Fronts
Foreign Affairs Agency	Foreign Ministry	Defense Ministry Defense industry ministries Secretariat[a] • Department of Defense Industry	Foreign Ministry Ministry of Foreign Economic Relations	State Committee for Science and Technology State Committee for Cultural Relations with Foreign Countries Secretariat[a] • International Department • Propaganda Department Union of Soviet Societies for Friendship and Cultural Relations with Foreign Countries	Committee for State Security (KGB);	Secretariat[a] • Department for Liaison with Communist and Workers' Parties of Socialist Countries • International Department

[a]CPSU organization

Source: Adapted from *Atlas of the Soviet Union* (Washington, D.C.: U.S. Department of State, 1987), pp. 5–6; *Atlas of U.S. Foreign Relations* (Washington, D.C.: U.S. Department of State, 1987), p. 4; and Gordon B. Smith, *Soviet Politics* (New York: St. Martin's Press, 1988), pp. 80–81.

example, once the Kennedy administration opted for a naval quarantine of Cuba during the 1962 missile crisis, so as to prevent further shipments of Soviet missiles, the U.S. Navy could be called on to implement the president's decision according to previously devised routines. Curiously, however, these same routines or SOPs effectively limit the range of viable policy choices from which political decision makers might select options. That is, rather than expanding the number of policy alternatives in a manner consistent with the logic of rational decision making, what organizations can and cannot do defines what is possible and what is not. Again in the case of Cuba, a surgical air strike designed to destroy the Soviet missiles then under construction in Cuba was a leading alternative to the blockade but was finally eliminated as a possible policy option when it was discovered that the U.S. Air Force could not guarantee 100 percent success in taking out the missiles. Thus organizational procedures and capabilities profoundly shaped the means from which the Kennedy administration could choose to realize its objective, which was the complete removal of all Soviet missiles from Cuban soil.

What Allison calls governmental politics is related to the bureaucratic character of modern foreign policy making in complex societies. Not surprisingly, the participants in the deliberations that lead to policy choices often define issues and favor policy alternatives that reflect their organizational affiliations. "Where you stand depends on where you sit" is a favorite aphorism reflecting these bureaucratic imperatives. Thus State Department officials would typically be expected to favor diplomatic approaches to policy problems, whereas military officers from the Pentagon would routinely be expected to favor military solutions.

Because the players in the game of governmental politics are responsible for protecting the nation's security, they are "obliged to fight for what they are convinced is right," with the consequence that "different groups pulling in different directions produce a result, or better a resultant—a mixture of conflicting preferences and unequal power of various individuals—distinct from what any person or group intended" (Allison, 1971). Rather than being a value-maximizing choice, then, the process of policymaking is itself intensely political. According to the governmental process paradigm, in other words, an explanation of why nations make the choices they do resides not in their behavior vis-à-vis one another in the global arena but within the governments themselves. And rather than presupposing the existence of a unitary actor, "it is necessary to identify the games and players, to display the coalitions, bargains, and compromises, and to convey some feel for the confusion" (Allison, 1971). From this perspective, the decision to blockade Cuba was as much a product of *who* favored the choice as of any inherent logic that may have commended it. Once Robert Kennedy, the president's brother and the attorney general, Theodore Sorensen, the president's special counsel and "alter ego," and Robert McNamara, his secretary of defense, united behind the blockade, a coalition of the president's most trusted advisers and those with whom he was personally most compatible had formed (Allison, 1971). How could he have decided in favor of any other option?

Quite apart from the influence of bureaucratic organizations on the policy choices of political leaders, a number of other characteristics associated with the way that large-scale organizations affect the decision-making environment in which foreign policy choices are framed warrant scrutiny.

One characteristic derives from the proposition that bureaucratic agencies are parochial. According to this argument, every administrative unit within a state's foreign policy–making bureaucracy seeks to promote its own purposes and power. The agency's needs are put ahead of the state's needs, which sometimes encourages national interests to be sacrificed for bureaucratic interests. As a corollary, bureaucratic parochialism breeds interagency competition and bureaucratic imperialism. Far from being neutral or impartial administrators desiring only to carry out orders from the head of state, bureaucratic organizations comprising a state's foreign affairs government frequently take policy positions designed to maximize their own influence relative to that of other agencies. They seek to expand their size in order to increase their clout and importance. Characteristically they are driven to enlarge their prerogatives and expand the conception of their mission; they seek to take on the responsibilities of other units and to gain the powers that go with those responsibilities. The world is thus increasingly run by bureaucracies whose jurisdictions within states overlap, whose purposes are blurred, and whose capacity for coordinated action are compromised.

Part of the reason for this propensity is that bureaucratic agencies seek to minimize interference from and penetration by those authorities to whom they report as well as other agencies within the government of which they are a part. Because knowledge is power, the common device for promoting organizational exclusivity is to hide inner workings—and policy activities—from others. The "invisible government" operating within the United States National Security Council during the Reagan administration that permitted Lieutenant Colonel Oliver North to orchestrate the arms-for-hostages deal, popularly known as the Iran–*contra* affair, illustrates this syndrome.

The natural tendency of bureaucracies to act as entities unto themselves is reinforced by the proclivity of bureaucrats to adapt their outlook and beliefs to those prevailing in the organizations of which they are a part. Accordingly, every bureaucracy tends to develop a shared "mind set" or dominant way of looking at reality akin to the "groupthink" characteristic of the cohesiveness and solidarity that small groups often develop (Janis, 1982). The development of an institutional mind set discourages creativity, dissent, and independent thinking; it encourages reliance on standard operating procedures and deference to precedent rather than exploration of new options to realize goals.

What these salient characteristics of bureaucratic decision making suggest can be stated in a single general proposition: Decision making by collectivities may reduce (rather than increase, as Max Weber hoped) the degree to which rational choice rules the world.

A second consequence of bureaucratic decision making is that by refusing to act promptly in response to orders issued by a head of state, bureaucracies may serve as a brake on policy innovation. The foreign affairs machinery of governments is often capable of disloyalty to the head of state it ostensibly serves. Bureaucratic unresponsiveness and inaction sometimes manifest themselves as lethargy, but at other times bureaucratic sabotage can be direct and immediate, as vividly illustrated again by the American experience in the 1962 Cuban missile crisis. While President Kennedy sought to orchestrate American action and bargaining, his bureaucracy in general and the navy in particular were in fact controlling events by doing as they wished.

> [The bureaucracy chose] to obey the orders it liked and ignore or stretch others. Thus, after a tense argument with the Navy, Kennedy ordered the blockade line moved closer to Cuba so that the Russians might have more time to draw back. Having lost the argument with the President, the Navy simply ignored his order. Unbeknownst to Kennedy, the Navy was also at work forcing Soviet submarines to surface long before Kennedy authorized any contact with Soviet ships. And despite the President's order to halt all provocative intelligence, an American U-2 plane entered Soviet airspace at the height of the crisis. When Kennedy began to realize that he was not in full control, he asked his Secretary of Defense to see if he could find out just what the Navy was doing. McNamara then made his first visit to the Navy command post in the Pentagon. In a heated exchange, the Chief of Naval Operations suggested that McNamara return to his office and let the Navy run the blockade. (Gelb and Halperin, 1973: 256)

Bureaucratic recalcitrance is a recurrent annoyance to leaders throughout the world and is encountered in authoritarian and democratic political systems alike. Policy implementation and revision in centralized communist societies have been slowed or stopped by bureaucratic resistance (Holmes, 1981; Valenta and Potter, 1984),[6] for example, and in the United States nearly every president has complained at one time or another about how the bureaucracy ostensibly designed to serve him has undercut his policies, as the statements noted in Box 3.1 illustrate. The implementation of foreign policy innovations thus poses a major challenge to most leaders (see Smith and Clark, 1985).

The prospect for change is further discouraged by the dynamics of the governmental politics paradigm described earlier, which sees policy choices as the "political resultant" of a tug of war among competing agencies, a political game with high stakes, in which differences are settled at the minimum common denominator instead of by rational, cost–benefit calculations. As former U.S. Secretary of State Henry A. Kissinger described the process:

> Each of the contending factions within the bureaucracy has a maximum incentive to state its case in its most extreme form because the ultimate

---

6. As Allen S. Whiting (1985) put it in evaluating China's foreign policy, it is "subject to the same vicissitudes of subjective perception, organizational conflict, bureaucratic politics, and factional infighting that bedevil other governments, perhaps more so given its size."

BOX 3.1 ■ Bureaucratic Obstacles to Decisive Foreign Policy Making: Accounts by American Presidents

You should go through the experience of trying to get any changes in the thinking, policy, and action of the career diplomats and then you'd know what a real problem was. But the Treasury and the State Department put together are nothing as compared with the Navy. . . . To change anything in the Navy is like punching a feather bed. You punch it with your right and you punch it with your left until you are exhausted, and then you find the damn bed as it was before you started punching.

Franklin D. Roosevelt

I sit here all day trying to persuade people to do the things they ought to have sense enough to do without me persuading them.

Harry S. Truman

There is nothing more frustrating for a President than to issue an order to a Cabinet officer, and then find that, when the order gets out in the field, it is totally mutilated. I have had that happen to me, and I am sure every other President has had it happen.

Gerald Ford

You know, one of the hardest things in a government this size is to know that down there, underneath, is the permanent structure that's resisting everything you're doing.

Ronald Reagan

outcome depends, to a considerable extent, on a bargaining process. The premium placed on advocacy turns decision making into a series of adjustments among special interests—a process more suited to domestic than to foreign policy. This procedure neglects the long-range because the future has no administrative constituency and is, therefore, without representation in the adversary proceedings. Problems tend to be slighted until some agency or department is made responsible for them. . . . The outcome usually depends more on the pressure or the persuasiveness of the contending advocates than on a concept of over-all purpose. (Kissinger, 1969: 268)

Thus it is perhaps not surprising that bureaucracies throughout the world are frequently the object of criticism by both the political leaders and the citizenry they supposedly serve.

THE ROLE OF LEADERS IN FOREIGN POLICY DECISION MAKING

The course of world history is determined by the decisions of political elites. Leaders—and the kind of leadership they exert—shape the way that foreign policies are made and the consequent behavior of nation-states in world politics.

These simple propositions describe a popular image of the source of states' foreign policies. It is tempting to think of foreign policy as being determined exclusively by the hopes and visions of a head of state, even though as we noted, nations' foreign policies typically result from the efforts of many individuals and organizations. "There is properly no history, only biography," was the way Ralph Waldo Emerson encapsulated the view of individual leaders as movers of history.

This *hero-in-history* model equates national action with the preferences and initiatives of the highest officials in national governments. Leaders are assumed to lead, and new leaders are assumed to "make a difference" (see Bunce, 1981). To reinforce this image, names of leaders are attached to policies as though the leaders were synonymous with the nation itself, and most successes and failures in foreign affairs are attributed to the leader in charge at the time they occurred. By extension, if foreign policy is little more than the predispositions of the leadership, then the Reagan and Brezhnev doctrines, for example, were simply products of the personalities of the leaders who enunciated them.

The mass citizenry is not alone in thinking that leaders are the decisive determinants of a state's foreign policy and, by extension, the course of world history. Leaders themselves seek to inculcate impressions of their own self-importance while attributing extraordinary powers to other leaders. The assumptions they make about the personalities of their counterparts, consciously or unconsciously, in turn influence their own behavior toward them (Wendzel, 1980).[7]

Despite the popularity of the hero-in-history model, we must be wary of ascribing too much importance to the impact of individual leaders. Their influence is likely to be much more subtle than popular impressions would have us believe. Henry Kissinger, himself a highly successful American diplomatic negotiator who has been described as "the most powerful individual in

---

7. This interpretation stresses that the images of leaders determine their actions and decisions (see Kelman, 1965, 1970). Perceptions indisputably shape foreign policy behaviors and actions in a powerful way, which is why political psychology is so important to understanding the origins of human behaviors. Rationality is "bounded" by leaders' assumptions about reality and their expectations. Consider, as an illustration, the roots of antagonism between the United States and the Soviet Union, which may be attributed to the perceptions of both American and Soviet leaders that encompass the assumptions of "the obvious innocence of the national self, the obvious guilt of the enemy, the unchangeableness of the enemy's evil nature, the efficacy of force in dealing with such an opponent, and the inefficacy of anything but force" (White, 1984).

the world in the 1970s" (Isaak, 1975), warned against placing too much reliance on personalities. Discussing Soviet-American relations during a commencement address at the University of South Carolina (1985), he noted:

> [There is] a profound American temptation to believe that foreign policy is a subdivision of psychiatry and that relations among nations are like relations among people. But the problem [of reducing tension with the Soviet Union] is not so simple. Tensions that have persisted for 40 years must have some objective causes, and unless we can remove these causes, no personal relationship can possibly deal with them. We are doing neither ourselves nor the Soviets a favor by reducing the issues to a contest of personalities.

Most leaders operate under a variety of political, psychological, and circumstantial constraints that limit considerably what they can accomplish and reduce their control over events. In this context Emmet John Hughes observed that "all of [America's past presidents] from the most venturesome to the most reticent have shared one disconcerting experience: the discovery of the limits and restraints—decreed by law, by history, and by circumstances—that sometimes can blur their clearest designs or dull their sharpest purposes." "I have not controlled events, events have controlled me" was the way Abraham Lincoln summarized his presidential experience.

The question at issue is not whether leaders lead; nor is it whether they make a difference. They clearly do both. But they are not in complete control, and their influence is severely circumscribed. Personality and personal political preferences do not determine public policy directly. The relevant question is not so much whether leaders' personal characteristics make a difference but, instead, under what conditions their personal characteristics are influential.[8]

In general, the impact of a leader's personal characteristics on his or her nation's foreign policy behavior increases when the leader's authority and legitimacy are widely accepted by citizens. This is especially true in centralized authoritarian or totalitarian governments. Moreover, certain kinds of circumstances tend to enhance the potential impact of individuals. Among them are new situations that free leaders from conventional approaches to defining the situation; complex situations involving a large number of different factors; and situations devoid of social sanctions that permit freedom of choice because norms delineating the range of permissible options are unclear (DiRenzo, 1974).

---

8. As Margaret G. Hermann has observed, the impact of leaders is modified by at least six kinds of characteristics:

    (1) what their world view is, (2) what their political style is like, (3) what motivates them to have the position they do, (4) whether they are interested in and have any training in foreign affairs, (5) what the foreign policy climate was like when the leader was starting out his or her political career, and (6) how the leader was socialized into his or her present position. World view, political style, and motivation tell us something about the leader's personality; the other characteristics give information about the leader's previous experiences and background. (1988: 268)

A head of state's self-image—that person's belief in his or her own ability to control events politically—will also influence the degree to which a leader's personal values and psychological needs will govern decision making (De-Rivera, 1968). Conversely, when such a sense of self-importance and efficacy is absent, leaders governed by self-doubt will undermine their own capacity to lead and implement policy changes. This linkage is not direct, however; it will be affected substantially by the extent of the populace's desire for strong leadership. When public opinion within a nation coalesces to produce a strong preference for a powerful leader and when the state is headed by an individual with an exceptional need to be admired, foreign policy will then more likely be a product of that leader's inner needs. For example, Kaiser Wilhelm II's narcissistic personality is alleged to have met the German people's desire for a symbolically powerful leader, and that public preference in turn influenced the foreign policy that Germany pursued during Wilhelm's reign which ended with the disaster of World War I (see Baron and Pletsch, 1985).

Other factors undoubtedly also influence the degree to which leaders can and do shape how nations decide. For instance, when leaders believe that their own interests and welfare are at stake in a situation, they tend to respond in terms of their private needs and psychological drives, as suggested by the highly personalized policy reactions of the shah of Iran and Ferdinand Marcos of the Philippines when they felt themselves personally threatened by internal insurrections which led to the overthrow of their regimes. But when circumstances are stable and routinized and when leaders' egos are not entangled with policy outcomes, the impact of their personal characteristics is less obtrusive. The amount of information available about particular situations is also important to assessing leaders' impact on policy performance. In the absence of pertinent information regarding a situation, policy is likely to be based on leaders' gut likes or dislikes. Conversely, "the more information an individual has about international affairs, the less likely is it that his behavior will be based upon non-logical influences" (Verba, 1969).

Similarly, the timing of a leader's assumption of power is important. When an individual first assumes a position of leadership, the formal requirements of that role are least likely to circumscribe what he or she can do. That holds true especially for new heads of state who routinely are allowed a "honeymoon" period during which they are relatively free of criticism and unusual pressure. Moreover, when a leader comes to office following a dramatic event (a landslide election, the assassination of a predecessor, or the acquisition of sovereign statehood by a former colony), "the new high level political leader can institute his [or her] policies almost with a free hand. Constituency criticism is held in abeyance during this time" (Hermann, 1976).

Perhaps most critical as a determinant of leaders' control over foreign policy making is the existence of conditions of national crisis. During crises, decision making tends to be centralized and handled exclusively by the top leadership. The situation is ambiguous and threatening. Crucial information is likely to be unavailable. Leaders tend to perceive themselves responsible for outcomes. In a situation that simultaneously challenges the will of a nation and the self-esteem of the decision maker, the decision processes tend to become fused with the personality psychodynamics of the state's leader; and the resolution of a policy crisis under such circumstances could depend ultimately on the outcome of a personal, emotional crisis (DiRenzo, 1974). Not surprisingly, therefore, great leaders in history customarily have arisen during periods of extreme challenge. Leaders appear to be heroes, capable of determining events; the moment may make the person, rather than the person the moment, in the sense that a crisis can liberate a leader from the constraints that normally would inhibit his or her capacity to engineer change in their state's foreign policy.

Compelling as the hero-in-history viewpoint may be, we must be cautious and remember that leaders are not necessarily all-powerful determinants of states' foreign policy behavior. Rather, leaders shape decision making more powerfully in some circumstances than in others. The impact of personal factors varies with the context, and often the context is more powerful than the leader.

Thus, the utility of the hero-in-history model of foreign policy must be questioned. The "great man"-versus-"zeitgeist" debate is relevant here. At the core of this timeless controversy is the perhaps unanswerable question of whether the times must be conducive to the emergence of great leaders or whether, instead, great people would have become famous leaders regardless of when and where they lived (see Greenstein, 1987). At the very least, the hero-in-history model appears much too simple an explanation of how states react to pressures from abroad. Most world leaders follow the rules of the "game" of international politics (Cohen, 1980; Spanier, 1987), which suggests that the ways in which states cope with their external environments are influenced less strongly by the types of people heading states than by other factors. Put differently, states respond to international circumstances in often similar ways, regardless of the predispositions of those who head them, which may account for the remarkable uniformities in state practice in a world of diverse leaders, different political systems, and turbulent change. In this sense, political realists' assumptions about the uniformity of different actors' motives, which are hypothesized to derive from the rational calculation of opportunities and constraints, are both reasonable and compelling.

OTHER DIMENSIONS OF FOREIGN POLICY DECISION MAKING

We have described three general models of how nations reach decisions—a rational actor model, a bureaucratic politics model, and a hero-in-history model. All apply to all countries to some degree, but none is applicable to every country under every circumstance. Situations change in such a way that one model may apply in one circumstance but not another.

Furthermore, the diversity that characterizes the nation-states comprising the contemporary state system makes it difficult to generalize about which circumstances matter most in what situations. History, culture, geography, geostrategic location, perceptions, misperceptions, military might, economic prowess, resource endowments, political system, and position in the international pecking order all are factors that affect how nations decide. The United States, for example, prospered under a fortuitous set of circumstances in which the vast oceans separating it from Europe and Asia combined with the absence of strong, threatening powers on its borders to permit it to develop economically and militarily without any immediate security threat. China, on the other hand, which shares an extended common border with the Soviet Union, much as the United States shares one with Canada, perceives the state on the other side as a security threat, with the location of the border itself partially a product of a long history of "unequal treaties" between China and outside powers that powerfully shapes China's contemporary view of the world.

On the southern side of the U.S. border is Latin America, a region long the object of studied interest and frequent intervention by the giant to the north. Realizing autonomy from its northern neighbor is a continuing theme in many Latin American nations' foreign policy concerns. In this sense they share a concern with other states in world politics that find themselves unable to compete on an equal footing with the world's more advantaged nations, a fact underlying the political division between the world's rich nations, which tend to be concentrated in the Northern Hemisphere, and its poor, which tend to be concentrated in the Southern Hemisphere.

Maintaining autonomy from continental politics is an enduring theme in Great Britain, whose island status, like Japan's, has been a source of both concern about developments abroad and a means of isolation from them. Germany, on the other hand, which sits in the very heartland of Europe, has found its domestic political system and foreign policy preferences profoundly affected by its geostrategic position. "In this century alone, Germany has undergone four radical changes in political personality—from Wilhelm II's empire to the Weimar Republic, from Hitler's *Reich* of the Thousand Years to its two postwar successors, the Federal Republic of Germany (FRG) and the German Democratic Republic (GDR)" (Joffe, 1985). Significantly, the rise or demise of all four, as the case may be, was tied directly to war. France, twice a victim of German aggression in this century, in turn has emerged from World War II as a middle-rank power intent on improving its position in the pecking order of the world's powerful. It has done so by seeking to increase its power base through population growth, rapid industrial development, economic modernization, and the acquisition of the most advanced of modern weapons (Macridis, 1985b).

The quest to modernize not only economically but also socially and politically is an important aspiration of many nations throughout the world. Principal among them are Middle Eastern states, in which the transition from traditional societies to modernity has been a continuing source of domestic unrest and international upheaval during much of the post–World War II era. How those forces have been managed at home and abroad has figured prominently on the global agenda historically and continues to do so today.[9]

As the foregoing examples suggest, trends and transformations occurring in the world today are profoundly affected by a multitude of factors which may explain why nations pursue the kinds of foreign policies they do. How these factors intertwine with issues and situations to create the fabric of contemporary world politics will be examined in the subsequent chapters of this book. As a preface to this inquiry, it is useful to make a few general observations about the way that these factors may affect the decision-making processes in different nations, which then leads to variations in the ways that nations seek to cope with international circumstances.

Level of Development and the Role of Economic and Military Capabilities

Because rationality is a goal to which all nations are hypothesized to aspire and that they may approximate from time to time and under varying circumstances, it is perhaps most relevant to ask under what conditions the bureaucratic politics and hero-in-history models are likely to be most applicable.[10]

All nations are subject to some extent to the vagaries of bureaucratic politics, but bureaucracies are relatively more important in advanced industrial societies whose governments are confronted with exceedingly complex questions requiring multifaceted expertise that only highly developed organizations can provide. In such circumstances, the capacity of individual leaders to rise above the issues that their nations face so as to impose their own hopes and visions on the future is severely circumscribed. Put differently, the hero-in-history model is less applicable as an explanation of foreign policy behavior in

---

9. See Macridis (1985a) for essays that explore ideas related to the historical, strategic, and cultural conditions that affect nations' foreign policy behavior.

10. Such questions lie at the core of the comparative study of foreign policy, a research orientation dedicated to the search for theories that can account for the internal and external sources of foreign policy behavior (see Hermann, Kegley, and Rosenau, 1987). Most of the voluminous literature in this field (see East, Salmore, and Hermann, 1978) has addressed the impact of national attributes on external conduct by examining the relationship between a state's size, wealth, type of government, culture, and the like and its behavior. In the context of our discussion, these factors operate as intervening variables conditioning the kind of decisions that different types of actors are prone to reach. For instance, a state's external orientation is clearly affected by its size: Small states are more vulnerable to the pressures from beyond their borders than are large, wealthy countries, a circumstance that influences fundamentally the way in which they define their foreign policy goals and restricts the range of alternatives available for their pursuit. For this reason most analysts have sought to develop categories or discern types of states and to associate certain decision-making procedures and properties with each of them, as we shall illustrate in the paragraphs that follow.

situations in which the level of economic advancement—by necessity if not design—diffuses responsibility for the control, coordination, and implementation of public policy among multiple domestic political actors. The contrast is especially germane to the Soviet Union, in which both proponents and opponents of the efforts of General Secretary Mikhail Gorbachev to modernize the Soviet politicoeconomic system see the Soviet leader's greatest challenge as his ability to motivate the massive, sluggish, unresponsive Soviet state bureaucracy to share his vision of the future and make the sacrifices required to achieve it.

The converse proposition occurs in states in which bureaucratic restraints are not sufficiently developed as to prevent political leaders from pursuing their personal preferences. Here Libya's leader, the mercurial Muammar Qaddafi, and Idi Amin, the ruthless dictator who formerly ruled Uganda, stand out. Both presumably were given greater opportunities to play the hero-in-history role than were most of their counterparts in North America, Western Europe, and the Soviet Union because their foreign policy whims and wishes were less constrained by large-scale bureaucratic organizations. However, both also doubtlessly felt more constrained by the outside world than did their counterparts in the more economically advanced countries.

What the foregoing suggests is that the degree of economic and industrial development enjoyed by a state greatly affects the nature of its foreign policy–making system. The more advanced that states are in these regards, the more they will develop and depend on bureaucratic decision-making procedures; the less advanced, the greater will be the opportunity for the hero in history to emerge as the decisive force in shaping a nation's foreign policy. As a general proposition, we can suggest that the more developed a state is economically, the more likely it is that bureaucratic rather than leadership performance will determine the way it seeks to cope with external circumstances.[11]

The level of a nation's economic development is also important insofar as it enhances its capabilities to engage in interstate diplomacy and to pursue its goals and interests abroad. Rich nations tend to have interests that extend far beyond their borders and also the means necessary to pursue and protect them. Not coincidentally, political systems that enjoy advanced industrial capabilities also tend to be powerful militarily, in part because military might is a function of economic capacity. Nuclear weapons, regarded by many as the ultimate expression of military prowess, for example, have historically been the product of the most scientifically sophisticated industrial economies in the world. In this sense they are the *result* of being powerful, not its cause (Waltz, 1971).

---

11. Although the hero-in-history decision-making model tends to apply to decision making for most new Third World countries in which governments tend to be led by powerful elites (Calvert, 1986), the model also applies to all states under conditions of crisis or national emergency when those circumstances expand the decision-making power of individual leaders.

The United States and the Soviet Union stand out among all of the world's nations precisely because they enjoy that combination of economic and military capabilities, including extensive arsenals of nuclear weapons and the means to deliver them anywhere, which leads them to have global interests and the capacity to pursue and protect them. Extensive national resource endowments contribute to their capabilities, and their enormous size, with each stretching across an entire continent, contribute to their overwhelming importance in world politics. In fact, size, which is often used in combination with other factors to distinguish great powers from middle-ranked or minor powers, by itself is an important national attribute predicting the extensiveness of states' foreign policy interests. One consequence is that great powers (large states) tend to become involved in foreign conflict more frequently than do minor powers (small states) (Jensen, 1982).

Type of Political System

Besides level of development, a second important dimension affecting state behavior internationally is the nature of its political system. Here the important distinction is between constitutional democracy and authoritarianism and totalitarianism in their various manifestations. Whether the type of political system affects either states' foreign policy performance or the goals and objectives they seek to attain abroad remains a matter of serious dispute among scholars. There is even disagreement among them as to whether the process of policymaking differs significantly between them. This follows naturally from the proposition that decision making in advanced industrial states is driven by essentially similar processes, which suggests that the nature of a state's political system is largely irrelevant to the way it decides.

But there are important differences in the political processes of democratic (open) and authoritarian and totalitarian (closed) political systems. In neither can political leaders long survive without the support of important domestic political interests, but in the former those interests are likely to be dispersed well beyond the government itself and those who benefit (more or less) directly from it. In democratic societies in particular, public opinion and interest groups who seek to represent that opinion are more visibly part of the political process. Similarly, the electoral process in democratic societies typically frames choices and produces results about who will lead more meaningfully than in authoritarian regimes, in which the real choices are made by a select few behind closed doors. In short, democracy promises that public beliefs and preferences matter.

This is not to deny that elitism operates in democratic societies, for it clearly does. According to at least some versions of this model, decisions are typically made by a small ruling elite for purposes designed to serve its own interests (Mills, 1956). The military-industrial complexes obtrusively evident in many countries are examples of groups sometimes believed to exercise disproportionate control over foreign policy making. But pluralism—which sees policymaking as an upward-flowing process in which competitive subnational groups pressure the government for policies responsive to their interests and needs—is a peculiarly democratic phenomenon whose pervasiveness is widespread even if its effects are sometimes difficult to pinpoint.

In the eyes of some observers, the result of the intrusion of domestic politics on foreign policy in democratic political systems is that they are disadvantaged in their ability to deal decisively and promptly with foreign policy issues and to bargain with allies and adversaries (see Kennan, 1951). Authoritarian regimes, according to this argument, enjoy special advantages. They are alleged to be both more effective and efficient in their foreign policy making, because ideally they can "make decisions more rapidly, ensure domestic compliance with their decisions, and perhaps be more consistent in their foreign policy." But there is a cost: "Authoritarian regimes often are less effective in developing an innovative foreign policy because of subordinates' pervasive fear of raising questions" (Jensen, 1982).

These brief comments on the way that attributes of states relate to their foreign policy–making processes highlight the extent to which foreign policy decisions are influenced by conditions internal to states, not just those external causes captured in the realists' billiard ball model. Many developments in world politics examined in subsequent chapters recommend that attention be given to the internal roots of external behavior. As the web of global interdependence among nations has progressively tightened, for example, the internationalization of the global political economy has expanded domestic pressures on the formulation of governments' foreign policies. That trend has blurred the distinction between foreign and domestic politics, heightened the salience of welfare issues, aroused the efforts of private groups to modify national policies, and elevated the participation of domestically oriented government agencies in the foreign policy–making process (see Keohane and Nye, 1977). At the same time, national security issues have gained renewed urgency in the public mind as the capacity for nuclear destruction has grown geometrically. Faced with the threat of catastrophic war, citizens in many different countries have mobilized to pressure their governments to refrain from pursuing policies believed to enhance, not deter, the prospects of a nuclear apocalypse. Arms control has become a domestic political issue; it no longer is confined to government-to-government bargaining. Hence, external behavior increasingly springs from internal roots.

MALFUNCTIONS IN THE POLICYMAKING PROCESS

The proposition that domestic stimuli and not just international events are a source of foreign policy is not novel. In ancient Greece, for instance, Thucydides observed how the external behavior of the Greek city-states was often shaped less by what each was doing toward the others than by what was occurring within them. He added that often the behavior of leaders toward other city-states was undertaken to affect not relations with the targets of the action but, instead, the political climate within the leaders' own city-states. In much the same spirit, Mikhail Gorbachev in 1987 disclosed that the Soviet Union's "international policy is more than ever determined by domestic policy."

Do states have the capacity to respond to the demands that external challenges and internal politics simultaneously place on their leaders? For a number of reasons, that capacity seems increasingly to have been strained.

Foreign policy is made in an environment of uncertainty and multiple, competing interests. On occasion, it is also made in situations in which national values are threatened, at which time policymakers are caught by surprise and a quick decision is needed. The stress produced by these factors impairs leaders' cognitive abilities and may cause them to become emotive rather than analytical thinkers, preoccupied with sunk costs, short-run outcomes, and postdecisional rationalization.

To compound the psychological strains, the small homogeneous groups of advisers that leaders typically rely on for guidance and emotional support also have shortcomings. When cohesive groups in stressful situations lack impartial leadership and are insulated from outside criticism, social pressures for conformity may lead group members to adopt stereotypes of their opponents, take extreme risks, discount warnings, and suppress personal reservations about the moral consequences of their recommendations (see Janis, 1982). Consensus seeking replaces critical thinking, with the result that the full range of alternatives is not surveyed, costs attached to the preferred course of action are ignored, and contingency plans to cope with potential setbacks are not developed.

High-level policymakers are also at the mercy of bureaucratic politics. Because of the competition among rival agencies, a head of state may receive a welter of narrow, biased analyses from these contending bureaucracies. Alternatively, they may obtain a concealed compromise produced by a series of lateral agreements aimed at protecting each bureaucracy's parochial interests. In either case, policymakers will not get the full, balanced information that they need to formulate sound policy.

Finally, a lack of information on the conditions under which different types of policy instruments will be successful in attaining their stipulated goals poses a further problem. Given this lack of information, individuals frequently base their positions on foreign policy issues on general and superficial lessons drawn from historical events they have personally or vicariously experienced. These analogies often are inapplicable.

In conclusion, a variety of impediments stand in the way of making wise foreign policy decisions. Fortunately, policymaking machinery can be designed and managed to reduce their impact. Multiple advocacy, subgrouping, formal options systems, second-chance meetings, and the use of devil's advocates are among the procedural tools that are often recommended for this purpose. However, none of them can transform foreign policy making into a neat, orderly system. Policymaking is a turbulent political process, one that involves complex problems, a chronic lack of information, and a multiplicity of conflicting actors. As President Kennedy summarized it, there will always be "the dark and tangled stretches in the . . . process—mysterious even to those who may be most intimately involved."

The trends and transformations currently unfolding in world politics are the product of countless decisions taken daily in diverse national settings throughout the world. Some of those decisions are more important than others, and some of the actors making them are more important than others. The United States and the Soviet Union stand at the center of the world political stage, for they alone possess the combination of economic capacity, military might, and the means to project power worldwide that earns them the status of superpowers. How the superpowers relate to each other thus has enormous consequences for the entire drama of world politics. It is to the dynamics of their contest on the global stage that our attention now turns.

SUGGESTED READINGS

Allison, Graham. *Essence of Decision*. Boston: Little, Brown, 1971.

Calvert, Peter. *The Foreign Policy of New States*. New York: St. Martin's Press, 1986.

Cottam, Martha L. *Foreign Policy Decision Making: The Influence of Cognition*. Boulder, Colo.: Westview Press, 1986.

DeRivera, Joseph H. *The Psychological Dimension of Foreign Policy*. Columbus, Ohio: Merrill, 1968.

Frankel, Joseph. *The Making of Foreign Policy: An Analysis of Decision-Making*. New York: Oxford University Press, 1963.

Hermann, Charles F., Charles W. Kegley, Jr., and James N. Rosenau, eds. *New Directions in the Study of Foreign Policy*. Boston: Allen & Unwin, 1987.

Hermann, Margaret G., with Thomas W. Milburn, eds. *A Psychological Examination of Political Leaders*. New York: Free Press, 1977.

Jensen, Lloyd. *Explaining Foreign Policy*. Englewood Cliffs, N.J.: Prentice-Hall, 1982.

Korany, Bahgat. *How Foreign Policy Decisions Are Made in the Third World*. Boulder, Colo.: Westview Press, 1986.

Snyder, Richard C., and James A. Robinson. *National and International Decision-Making*. New York: Institute for International Order, 1961.

FOUR

The East–West Conflict: Evolution of a Global Confrontation

I shall never agree . . . that the American people are aggressively disposed toward the Soviet Union. There are people, probably, who are suited to tension, confrontation [and] keen rivalry between our peoples. . . . But such a state of affairs is not in accordance with the big and extensive interests of our peoples.

MIKHAIL GORBACHEV, 1987

We ask ourselves: Are we entering a truly new phase in East–West relations? Is far-reaching, enduring change in the postwar standoff possible? . . . Surely, these are our hopes. But let honesty compel us to acknowledge we have fears and deep concerns as well.

RONALD REAGAN, 1987

As World War II drew to a close in 1945, it became increasingly apparent that one era of international politics was coming to an end and a new one was commencing. Unparalleled in scope and unprecedented in destructiveness, the second great war of the twentieth century brought into being a transformed system dominated by two superstates, the United States and the Soviet Union, whose combined power and resources far surpassed those of all the rest of the world. It also speeded the disintegration of the great colonial empires assembled by imperialist nations in previous centuries, thereby hastening the emancipation of many peoples from foreign rule. Unlike earlier international systems, the emergent one consisted of a large number of sovereign states outside the European core area that were dominated by the two most powerful ones. The advent of nuclear weapons also contributed to a novel system of world politics, for they radically changed the role that threats of force and warfare would henceforth play in world politics.

Of these momentous changes, the number and nature of states and the domination of the United States and the Soviet Union define and delimit much of what we call the contemporary global system. Out of these circumstances have grown the two great conflicts of the second half of the twentieth century—the conflict between East and West and the conflict between the rich

61

nations of the North and the poor nations of the South. Our purpose in this and the next chapter is to describe the foundations of these political contests.

We focus first on the origins and evolution of the East–West conflict. By convention, the labels *East* and *West* are used to differentiate, respectively, the communist nations in general, and the Soviet Union and its political and military allies in Eastern Europe in particular, from the coalition of noncommunist nations led by the United States, whose principal partners are the advanced industrial societies of Western Europe, Japan, Canada, Australia, and New Zealand. The term *free world* is also sometimes used to describe the anticommunist coalition led by the United States, which includes the industrialized West and a number of economically less developed nations linked to the United States in mutual defense arrangements.

By contrast, the *Soviet bloc*, as the East is sometimes called, is confined largely to the Soviet Union and its Eastern European allies. Cuba, Mongolia, North Korea, and Vietnam have also sometimes been regarded as bloc members. Although others, such as China and some African countries, have been regarded from time to time as pro-Soviet in their foreign affairs and socialist in their domestic affairs,[1] there have always been fewer members of the Eastern than of the Western camp.

The dispute between East and West has been persistent and pervasive. To understand its nature and consequences, it is necessary to trace the historical roots and evolution of the Cold War, as the East–West conflict has been known historically.

THE ORIGINS OF THE COLD WAR: ALTERNATIVE PERSPECTIVES

By May 1945 the Third Reich, which Hitler had predicted would survive a thousand years, was in ruins. But the victory by the Soviet, American, and British allies over the fascist threat to world conquest produced not only peace for a system that had been devastated by the ravages of total war but also a world fraught with uncertainty. Political agreements that had been carefully arranged and maintained in order to survive in the common struggle against the Axis powers were quickly suspended. In their place, a chaotic international environment of ill-defined borders, altered allegiances and disentangling alliances, power vacuums, economic ruin, and ambiguous rank and hierarchy emerged. The presumed consensus regarding goals, standards of behavior, and mutual obligations that had governed allied efforts to defeat the common enemy was also suspended. Victory was followed by growing uncertainty and distrust about others' intentions.

---

1. At one time the People's Republic of China was generally regarded as a member of the Eastern camp, but by the 1970s, if not before, China had come to see the Soviet Union as a threat to, rather than a guarantor of, its security. One result has been an increase in cooperative ties between China and various Western nations, including the United States.

Perhaps the most certain feature of this otherwise uncertain environment was the ascendancy of the United States and the Soviet Union as its two greatest powers. World War II left both clearly predominant in resources, military capabilities, and influence; in comparison, all other countries were dwarfed by the two giants. As Alexis de Tocqueville had predicted in 1835, world politics and human destiny came to rest with how the United States and Russia would respond to each other.

A Power Rivalry and Conflict of Interests

The simple fact that the United States and the Soviet Union emerged dominant in the postwar world provides one way of interpreting the origins of the Cold War. According to the logic of political realism, conflict between the emergent superpowers was inescapable as a result of each state's inevitable pursuit of power; the conflict came to be essentially a struggle between those at the top of the international hierarchy for preeminent status, with each side seeking to protect its own position while gaining advantage in its relations with, and often at the expense of, the other.

Rivalry and distrust among great powers have been recurrent themes throughout history. Great powers invariably have found areas of vital interests over which to clash, as well as reasons to fear one another's intentions. They have often perceived efforts by their opponents to resolve conflicts of interest as "aggrandizement." Despite the cooperation between the United States and the Soviet Union necessitated by the world war, it was not surprising, therefore, that in the immediate postwar period the manifest and latent power of the two fueled their suspicions of each other and made them rivals. Thus the Cold War between the two emergent giants could be seen as an inevitable product of the efforts of each to attain global leadership.

Is this conclusion warranted? The question needs to be answered in light of the fact that both the United States and the Soviet Union had demonstrated during World War II an ability to subordinate ideological differences and cravings for power to the pursuit of common interests (Gaddis, 1983). Neither was governed exclusively by a relentless search for unilateral advantage; both practiced accommodation as well as confrontation.

Precisely because the United States and the Soviet Union were willing to pursue common as well as conflicting interests suggests that a Cold War in the immediate aftermath of World War II was neither inevitable nor predetermined and that the emerging superpowers' continued collaboration was by no means precluded. Efforts to relax tensions remained a possible policy option.

Indeed, in the early phases of postwar negotiations, cooperation was envisioned by American and Soviet leaders, at least in their official discourse (Gaddis, 1972). For instance, it was President Franklin D. Roosevelt's hope and expectation that their wartime collaboration would continue after the war. Roosevelt believed that flexible accommodation between the United States and the Soviet Union, based on mutual respect for each other's national interests, was possible. He believed that both nations would enjoy the benefits of power, but each within its own *sphere of influence*. An informal agreement was reached that each power would enjoy dominant influence and freedom in specified areas of the globe (see Morgenthau, 1969; Schlesinger, 1967). As John Foster Dulles, presidential policy adviser and later President Dwight D. Eisenhower's secretary of state, noted in January 1945, "The three great powers which at Moscow agreed upon the 'closest cooperation' about European questions have shifted to a practice of separate, regional responsibility." Also implicit was the agreement not to oppose each other in areas not vital to national security. Rules written into the United Nations Charter that obliged the United States and the Soviet Union to share, through the UN Security Council, responsibility for preserving world peace further symbolized the expectation of continued collaboration.

If these were the superpowers' hopes and aspirations at the end of World War II, why did they fail? The foregoing suggests that these interpretations of the Cold War's inevitability are suspect and that there is an alternative interpretation: that the Cold War was instead a product of the choices made by the two nations' leaders. To understand the Cold War's origins, then, we must consider explanations that go beyond the logic of *realpolitik*.

Ideological Incompatibilities

An alternative interpretation holds that the Cold War's origins were rooted in irreconcilable ideological incompatibilities. Secretary of State James F. Byrnes embraced this thesis at the conclusion of World War II when he stated that "there is too much difference in the ideologies of the U.S. and Russia to work out a long term program of cooperation" (cited in Paterson, 1979). What Byrnes was referring to was the fear that communism was an expansionist ideology intent on converting the entire world to its beliefs. Many Americans assumed that all communists were bound monolithically to the Soviet Union and that all communist movements were controlled by Moscow. This threat was reinforced by the belief that communism was necessarily totalitarian and therefore posed a real threat to freedom and democratic institutions throughout the world.[2] These fears thus called for a combative response. As

---

2. The challenge posed by communist doctrine, as contrasted with the Soviet's global aspirations, is difficult to assess. The threat to national security posed by ideas is unclear, whereas the basis for fearing Soviet expansionist tendencies, where evident, is quite clear. Some of the premises on which ideological interpretations of the Cold War rest may thus be questioned. That communism is a cohesive force, for instance, is debatable. With the passage of time, communism has revealed itself as increasingly polycentric: Communist party leaders have voiced their own disagreements about communism's fundamental beliefs, as evidenced by the differences that separate socialist and communist movements and the differences over policy within the Kremlin itself. The greatest fear of some communist states today appears to be fear of other communist states. The Sino-Soviet split, grounded in national interest, not ideology, is the preeminent case in point. Moreover, if communism is an expansionist ideology, it should be noted that it has shown itself to be more flexible than initially assumed, with no timetable for the conversion of nonbelievers and no requirement that revolution be exported to all quarters.

President Eisenhower explained, "We face a hostile ideology—global in scope, atheistic in character, ruthless in purpose, and insidious in method."

Those who argue that the Cold War originated in ideological differences attribute it to more than just the real or imagined American fears of the theories underlying Marxist doctrine. Consistent with the proposition that every ideological movement breeds its antithesis, they argue that, in reaction, United States foreign policy itself became ideological. That counterideology may be termed *anticommunism*. According to these analysts (for example, Commager, 1983; Morgenthau, 1983), American policymakers embraced a world view that led to the conclusion that successful opposition to communism was the primary purpose of American foreign policy—a preoccupation that turned into an obsession to the point that it became an obstacle to the relaxation of the tension underlying the Cold War. According to this perspective, the United States embarked on a missionary crusade of its own, dedicated to eliminating from the globe this alien set of ideas (see Gardner, 1970; Parenti, 1969). As expected, the policies toward the Soviet Union called for by this orientation were competitive and confrontational.

This interpretation thus sees the Cold War as fueled by historic antagonisms between diametrically opposed systems of belief.[3] Like religious wars in the past, the Cold War is seen as a battle for people's hearts and minds. Historically, ideologically driven conflicts have been exceedingly bitter because their participants recognize no virtue in conciliation with enemies. A conception of the Cold War as a struggle between right and wrong and good and evil eliminates "any thought of accommodation or compromise. It excludes the idea of co-existence. How can [one] compromise or co-exist with evil? It holds out no prospect but opposition with all might, war to the death. It summons the true believer to a *jihad*, a crusade of extermination against the infidel" (Schlesinger, 1983).

If the East–West conflict is, indeed, essentially a conflict between two diametrically opposed ideological systems, then the Soviet-American rivalry can be reduced to a contest over ideas, not power or prestige. Inasmuch as ideologically inspired conflicts are inherently all-consuming and irreconcilable (ideologues are uncomfortable with anything less than universal acceptance of their world view), accommodation is hopeless. Toleration of diversity is not a characteristic of nations whose leaders are driven by ideological passions. Hence, under conditions of holy warfare, real opportunities for peace may be missed, and situations in which the competitors' interests converge may be ignored.

This interpretation of Soviet-American animosity contrasts sharply with the view that their differences stem from discordant interests. Instead, it holds that

---

3. Objectively identifying the premises of ideological systems is difficult because definitions of ideology themselves tend to be ideological. For discussions of the ideological beliefs presumed to influence the foreign policy behavior of the United States and the Soviet Union, see Jönsson (1982), Ulam (1971, 1983) and Nogee and Donaldson (1981).

the real source of superpower tension lies in the power of ideas, not the power of nations. According to this viewpoint, beliefs have colored perceptions, shaped expectations, and influenced conduct. True, the Soviets and Americans may have viewed "ideology more as a justification for action than as a guide to action," but once the interests they shared disappeared, "ideology did become the chief means which differentiated friend from foe" (Gaddis, 1983).

If in the past the ideological rivalry of the United States and the Soviet Union significantly colored each one's foreign policy, then we must also ask whether American and Soviet diplomats, burdened by belief systems that they may not have been able to abandon, were destined to pursue a cold war. The consequences of this viewpoint are disquieting.

> The past decades have revealed increasing discrepancies between reality and the foreign policy ideologies of the superpowers. The world has proved to be politically and ideologically pluralistic, while American and Soviet foreign policies have proceeded from convictions that deny this pluralism. Moreover, whereas both ideologies have prescribed irreconcilable antagonism between the superpowers, the realities of nuclear stalemate have dictated limited détente.
>
> In other words, their ideologies have prepared both superpowers poorly for the contemporary world (Jönsson, 1982: 106).

But before tracing the cause of East–West conflict exclusively to the superpowers' incompatible ideologies, we should entertain still another proposition: that the conflict is the product of mutual misperceptions—of the fundamentally divergent ways in which the superpowers have defined their own national interests and interpreted the foreign policy interests and actions of the other.

Misperceptions

Disputes often are precipitated by misperceptions. This may apply especially to the Cold War. This explanation sees the Cold War rooted not in conflicting interests but in mutual misunderstanding: Soviet-American animosity is accounted for by each party's propensity to see in its own actions only virtue and in those of the adversary only malice. These mirror images lead, of course, to conflict and mistrust. Thus, some have noted the proclivity of both Soviets and Americans to harbor the same perceptions of each other: *they* are bent on world conquest; *they* arm for war, whereas *we* arm for peace; *they* intervene in others' territory to expand influence, whereas *we* do so to preserve the prospects for an acceptable way of life; *their* only reliable allies are governments that depend on their troops to stay in power, whereas *our* friends support us out of conviction; *their* people are good and peace loving, but *their government* exploits its people; the mass of *their people* are really not sympathetic to the regime; it cannot be trusted; its policy verges on madness (Bron-fenbrenner, 1975).

To the extent that such mirror images and "we–they," "we're OK, you're not" outlooks become prevalent, as they probably did in the final stages of World War II and thereafter, cooperation is precluded and hostility inevitable. According to this argument, prophecies are self-fulfilling. This interpretation of the Cold War's origins is difficult to deny, given the perceptions that became accepted as dogma. Let us review briefly the opposing Soviet and American viewpoints.

THE SOVIET IMAGE   To the Soviets, reasons for doubting the intentions of the United States were abundant. They lived with the memory of U.S. soldiers participating in the 1918–1919 Allied military intervention in Russia, which turned from its initial mission of keeping arms from falling into German hands into an effort to overthrow the Bolshevik Revolution. They were sensitive to the fact that the United States did not give diplomatic recognition to the Soviet Union until 1933, in the midst of a depression that was perceived to be a sign of capitalism's weakness and the beginning of its ultimate collapse. The war-time experience did little to remove Soviet suspicions of the United States. The Soviets recalled the United States' procrastination before entering the war against the fascists; the American refusal to inform the Soviets of the Manhattan Project to develop the atomic bomb; the delay in sending the Soviets promised Lend-Lease supplies; the failure to open up a second front (leading Josef Stalin to suspect that American policy was to let the Russians and Germans destroy each other so that the United States could then pick up the pieces[4]); the American failure to inform the Soviets of its wartime strategy to the extent that it informed Great Britain; and the use of the atomic bomb against Japan, perhaps perceived as a maneuver to prevent Russian involvement in the Pacific peace settlement (see Alperovitz, 1970, 1985; Alsop and Joravsky, 1980).

These suspicions were later reinforced by the U.S. willingness to support one-time Nazi collaborators in American-occupied countries, notably Italy and France, and by its pressure on the Soviet Union to abide by its promise to allow free elections in areas vital to Soviet national security, notably Poland. The Soviets were also resentful of the abrupt American decision to cancel promised Lend-Lease assistance to facilitate the postwar recovery of the Soviet Union. (The United States later framed the European recovery program, known as the

---

4. While still a senator, Harry Truman, on July 24, 1941, expressed the hope that after Hitler's invasion of Russia, the Nazis and communists would destroy each other. He stated flatly, "If we see that Germany is winning we ought to help Russia and if Russia is winning we ought to help Germany, and in that way let them kill as many as possible, although I don't want to see Hitler victorious under any circumstances." Although Truman was not speaking for President Roosevelt, such sentiments expressed publicly by a member of Congress were unlikely to reduce Soviet suspicions.

Marshall Plan, in such a way as to prevent Soviet participation.) Thus the Soviet distrust of American intentions was presumed to stem from fears of American efforts to isolate and encircle the Soviet Union, buttressed by a historical record of hostility.[5]

THE AMERICAN IMAGE   To the United States, hostility toward the Soviet Union was justified; Soviet belligerence appeared ubiquitous and had provoked the American response. Examples of Soviet misconduct included the Russians' unwillingness to permit democratic elections in the territories they liberated from the Nazis; their refusal to assist in postwar reconstruction in regions outside Soviet control; their maintenance of an unnecessarily large postwar armed force; their stripping of supplies from Soviet areas of occupation; their selfish and often obstructive behavior in the fledgling new international organizations created during and immediately after the war; their opportunistic disregard for international law and violations of agreements and treaties; their infiltration of Western labor movements; and their blatant anti-American propaganda and espousal of an alien ideology that pledged to destroy the American type of economic and political system. The implied threats provoked more than an imaginary sense of fear in Americans, a fear reinforced by the Soviets' unwillingness to withdraw the Red Army from Eastern and Central Europe. The Soviet Union came to be perceived as a military rival straining at the leash to invade Western Europe and to acquire new satellites under Russian occupation. Whereas Roosevelt had argued previously that postwar peace depended on Soviet-American collaboration, the Soviet leaders' actions and anti-American rhetoric led many to view the Soviet Union as the greatest threat to peace.

What even a cursory inspection of the Soviet and American views makes clear is that the leaders of the two countries saw the world very differently. They imposed on events different definitions of reality and became captives of their respective visions. Hence, even though both countries saw their adversary in remarkably identical and stereotypical terms, the misperceptions became a source of conflict and a barrier to the reduction of tension (see Holsti, 1980). Given their mutual fears and suspicions, it is not difficult to understand why both sides' actions were so often misunderstood. George F. Kennan,

---

5. Secretary of Commerce Henry A. Wallace, in a 1946 memorandum to the president, asked how American actions since V-J Day—especially American weapons production—looked to other nations. "These facts," Wallace concluded, "make it appear either (1) that we are preparing ourselves to win the war which we regard as inevitable or (2) that we are trying to build up a predominance of force to intimidate the rest of mankind. How would it look to us if Russia had the atomic bomb and we did not, if Russia had 10,000 mile bombers and air bases within 1,000 miles of our coastline, and we did not?" (cited in Horowitz, 1971: 68). For an engaging analysis that attributes the Cold War's origins to the planning of American strategists during World War II for the postwar era, which rationalized a global police role for the United States and identified the Soviet Union as the "next" enemy, see Sherry (1977).

American ambassador to the Soviet Union in 1952, noted that misread signals were common to both sides:

> The Marshall Plan, the preparations for the setting up of a West German government, and the first moves toward the establishment of NATO [North Atlantic Treaty Organization], were taken in Moscow as the beginnings of a campaign to deprive the Soviet Union of the fruits of its victory over Germany. The Soviet crackdown on Czechoslovakia [1948] and the mounting of the Berlin blockade, both essentially defensive . . . reactions to these Western moves, were then similarly misread on the Western side. Shortly thereafter there came the crisis of the Korean War, where the Soviet attempt to employ a satellite military force in civil combat to its own advantage, by way of reaction to the American decision to establish a permanent military presence in Japan, was read in Washington as the beginning of the final Soviet push for world conquest; whereas the active American military response, provoked by this move, appeared in Moscow . . . as a threat to the Soviet position in both Manchuria and in eastern Siberia. (Kennan, 1976: 683–684)

Interpreting the Cold War as originating in misperceptions reveals how mutual fears, inherent distrust of others' motives, and insensitivity to the impact of one's own action can breed spiraling and prolonged conflict (see Barnet, 1988). It is therefore plausible to view the Cold War as a lost opportunity for cooperation, with missed signals and misunderstandings contributing to the ensuing friction. And though it may be tempting to attribute the hostile relationship to either Soviet or American bad faith, such a simple explanation is not consistent with the historical evidence. It is inappropriate, in other words, to ask who was to blame for the deterioration of relations between the United States and the Soviet Union. Both were responsible because both were victims of their distorted images and false expectations. The Cold War was not simply an American response to communist aggression, which is the orthodox American view; nor was it simply a product of postwar American assertiveness, as many revisionist historians have argued (see Schlesinger, 1967). Each of the emergent superpowers felt threatened. And each had legitimate reasons to regard the other with suspicion.

Explanations that account for the origins of the Cold War exclusively in terms of perceptual variables are, of course, only partially valid. They illuminate some aspects of Soviet-American rivalry but not all. Indeed, an accurate picture of the conflict's sources must also include reference to the competition inherent in all great power relationships and to ideological incompatibilities as well as misperceptions. All three perspectives—power, ideology, and (mis)perceptions—are relevant, and some combination of them is required to capture the essence of this global confrontation. So, too, may be explanations that focus on other factors such as the perceived emergence of "power vacuums" that may have invited the clash in particular geographic locales, the pressures exerted on foreign policies by each country's domestic interest groups and military planners, the impact of shifts in the climate of domestic opinion on international issues, and the effects of innovation in weapons technology and the shift in strategic balances they introduced.[6] But regardless of its causes, the Cold War rapidly became the central element of postwar international politics.

To understand the Cold War's impact on world politics in the postwar era, it is useful to examine the changing nature of the Soviet-American relationship. For even though it remains a prominent fixture of global politics, modification of this relationship over time attests to the ways in which seemingly permanent conditions in international affairs may change and how those changes may stimulate other changes in global affairs. Indeed, the variation exhibited in the texture of Soviet-American interactions since 1945 has served as a catalyst to change in the world political system generally. Although the diplomatic discourse remains littered with reminders that the Soviets and Americans once might have found the other's obliteration acceptable, even attractive, the emergence of a vocabulary of peaceful coexistence, détente, and constructive dialogue demonstrates the rival superpowers' capacity to collaborate as well as compete. This suggests that Soviet-American relations are not necessarily fated to remain hostile, even if in the last quintile of the twentieth century they appear, as before, to be at a crossroad.

THE EVOLUTION OF THE SOVIET-AMERICAN RELATIONSHIP

Soviet-American relations have fluctuated sharply over time, with periods of heated confrontation followed by periods of renewed efforts at cooperation. They have shifted in response to changing circumstances. Nonetheless, the record from 1949 to 1978 suggests a long-term but unstable trend from confrontation toward greater collaboration. It was followed by a pronounced reassertion of threats, only to be met by a renewed effort to relax tensions through conciliatory bargaining and compromise.

Consider, for instance, the characteristics of Soviet-American interactions since 1948, as shown in Figure 4.1. One of their most striking features is the extent to which the two countries' foreign policy exchanges have been reciprocal. A symmetrical action–reaction syndrome is evident: The kind of actions sent by one protagonist tends to be returned by the other. Periods when the United States directed friendly initiatives toward the Soviets have

---

6. The abundance of authoritative but conflicting interpretations of the Cold War's causes attests to the difficulties of resolving historical controversies. See Welch (1970) for a review and assessment of the controversy in the American academic community and Breslauer (1983) for a criticism of accounts of its evolution. Kennan (1984) offers yet another discussion of the factors that have shaped the relationship.

FIGURE 4.1 ■ American-Soviet Relations, 1948–1988[a]

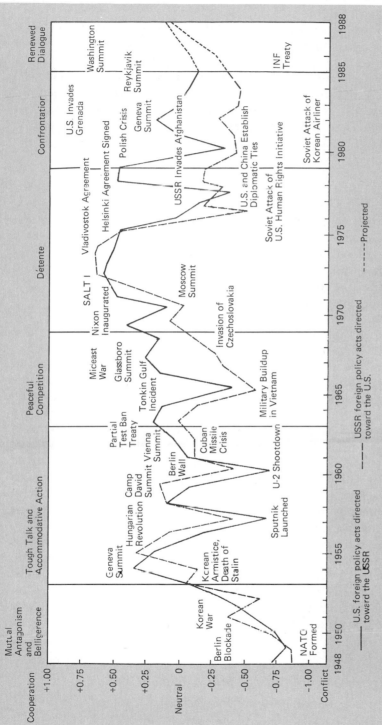

Source: Adapted from Professor Edward E. Azar's Conflict and Peace Data Bank (COPDAB), with data based on Azar and Sloan (1973) as updated through 1978 with data supplied by Professor Azar. Data for 1979–1983 are derived from the World Event Interaction Survey (WEIS), as retrieved and compiled by Frederick A. Rothe. Data for 1984–1985 are provided by Llewellyn D. Howell of Third Point Systems, Inc., of Monterey, California.

[a]The net conflict index is obtained by summing the proportion of cooperative acts (+ %) and conflictual acts (– %). For example, if in a given year, the United States sent 100 acts to the Soviet Union, with 75 being cooperative and 25 conflictual, then the index would be 0.75 – 0.25 = +0.5. If no acts are initiated, or if the cooperative and conflictual acts balanced (i.e., +50% and –50%), the index is zero, indicating a mixed, ambivalent relationship. Data for years prior to 1948 and after 1985 are not available. The trends shown for 1986 to 1988 are estimates derived from reports of major American and Soviet actions toward each other in the *New York Times*. Because these portions of the trend lines are not based on reproducible evidence, they should be interpreted very cautiously.

also been periods when the Soviets acted with friendliness toward the United States; similarly, periods of American belligerence have also been periods of Soviet belligerence.

Following the trends depicted in Figure 4.1, it is possible, for analytical purposes, to divide the history of Soviet-American foreign policy interactions into chronological phases. Although such divisions are necessarily somewhat arbitrary, the diplomatic record suggests that seven distinct phases can be identified.

Wary Friendship, 1945–1946

As previously noted, immediately following the termination of World War II there began a brief but confusing period in Soviet-American relations, which may be labeled *wary friendship*. This was a period characterized by uncertainty of each former ally about the other's intentions. Part of this period reflected the hope that the Soviets and Americans would cooperate to safeguard world peace. Symptomatic of that hope was presidential adviser Harry Hopkins's description of the thinking of the Roosevelt administration: "The Russians had proved that they could be reasonable and farseeing and there wasn't any doubt in the minds of the President or any of us that we could live with them and get along with them peacefully for as far into the future as any of us could imagine" (cited in Ekirch, 1966). The spirit was also evident at the San Francisco conference in the spring of 1945, convened to establish the United Nations.

Doubts began to surface nonetheless and came to dominate discussions in Washington almost as soon as Harry S. Truman assumed the presidency in April 1945. Indeed, it appears in retrospect (Tugwell, 1971) that Truman jettisoned Roosevelt's policies of maintaining postwar harmony with the Soviets. Typical of the shift in mood was Truman's statement that "if the Russians did not wish to join us they could go to hell." The Soviets likewise began to express their suspicions of American intentions. In short, vacillation, ambivalence, and uncertainty marked the behavior of the two powers during this brief interlude. Despite occasional efforts at accommodation (for example, Stalin's advice to Greek insurgents either to stop their insurgency or to carry on without Soviet assistance), both superpowers became increasingly pessimistic about the prospects of avoiding confrontation. This phase lasted for a little over a year, during which time the Soviet-American relationship deteriorated rapidly.

Mutual Antagonism and Belligerence, 1947–1952

The second stage in Soviet-American relations can be characterized as one of mutual antagonism and belligerence. All pretense of collaboration ceased. This was an era in which the Cold War erupted and was in constant danger of becoming hot.[7]

How did Soviet-American relations become so embittered? Some answers to this question have already been suggested. Part of the reason undoubtedly stemmed from how each side interpreted the actions of the other.

Consider, for example, the interpretation of intentions ascribed to the Soviet Union by American policymakers.[8] In February 1946, Stalin gave a speech in which he "spoke of the inevitability of conflict with the capitalist powers. He urged the Soviet people not to be deluded that the end of the war meant that the nation could relax. Rather, intensified efforts were needed to strengthen and defend the homeland" (Lovell, 1970). Shortly thereafter, George F. Kennan, then the second-ranking diplomat in the American embassy in Moscow, sent to Washington his famous "long telegram" assessing the motivations of the Soviet leadership. The conclusions of Kennan's assessment were ominous: "In summary, we have here a political force committed fanatically to the belief that with [the] U.S. there can be no permanent modus vivendi, that it is desirable and necessary that the internal harmony of our society be disrupted, our traditional way of life be destroyed, the international authority of our state be broken, if Soviet power is to be secure."

Kennan's assessment was widely circulated in Washington and presumably had an important bearing on the crystallization of thinking about Soviet postwar intentions. Somewhat later (when he became head of the State Department's policy-planning staff), Kennan's ideas received even wider circulation through the publication of his famous article in the influential journal *Foreign Affairs* (1947), which he signed "X" instead of identifying himself as its author. In it, Kennan argued that Soviet leaders would forever feel insecure about their political ability to maintain power against forces both within Soviet society itself and in the outside world. This insecurity would lead to an activist—and perhaps hostile—Soviet foreign policy. Yet it was in the United States' power to increase the strains under which the Soviet leadership would have to operate, perhaps thus leading to a gradual mellowing or eventual breakup of Soviet power. Hence, Kennan stated what eventually became an often-repeated and accepted view: "In these circumstances it is clear that the main element of any United States policy toward the Soviet Union must be that of a long-term,

---

7. "We are in the midst of a cold war," proclaimed American financier and statesman Bernard Baruch in 1947, thus coining a phrase that was to gain immediate and wide currency.

8. It is easier to describe how American policymakers perceived themselves and the Soviet Union than to make similar statements about Soviet perceptions, because the American record is not shrouded in the same secrecy as is the Soviet record. We must also entertain the possibility, however, that the United States' perceptions of itself and the Soviet Union may in part have been used to justify policies made for other reasons. Therefore, as implied earlier, to suggest that perceptions played a role in the evolution of Soviet-American competition is not to pass judgment on their accuracy.

patient but firm and vigilant *containment* of Russian expansive tendencies" (Kennan, 1947; emphasis added).

It was not long before this intellectual assessment received such wide publicity that Truman made it the cornerstone of American postwar policy. Provoked in part by domestic turmoil in Turkey and civil war in Greece (which he and others believed to be communist inspired), Truman stated: "I believe that it must be the policy of the United States to support free peoples who are resisting attempted subjugation by armed minorities or by outside pressures."

Truman's declaration, eventually known as the Truman Doctrine, was based on the logic of *realpolitik* in view of international politics and was predicated on the belief that the Soviet Union was an imperial power bent on world conquest. This view was made the axiom that soon rationalized a "grand crusade":

> Whenever and wherever an anti-communist government was threatened, by indigenous insurgents, foreign invasion, or even diplomatic pressure (as with Turkey), the United States would supply political, economic, and most of all military aid. The Truman Doctrine came close to shutting the door against any revolution, since the terms "free peoples" and "anti-Communist" were assumed to be synonymous. All . . . any dictatorship had to do to get American aid was to claim that its opponents were Communist. (Ambrose, 1985: 86)

The crusade laid out by the Truman Doctrine was, of course, the Cold War with the Soviet Union, which became a national obsession, demanding the commitment of many of the nation's resources. Containment became the pillar of American foreign policy and colored everything else, including domestic politics, just as it colored all of international politics.

Whether the policy of containment was appropriate or even justified at the time of its promulgation remains a controversial issue among historians. Kennan was chagrined and eventually alarmed at the way his celebrated statement was taken by others out of context and misinterpreted. He noted that after the publication of his "X" article, containment soon became an "indestructible myth," a doctrine "which was then identified with the foreign policy of the Truman administration." But he has also noted the anguish he experienced with the way his assessment was interpreted:

> I . . . naturally went to great lengths to disclaim the view, imputed to me by implication . . . that containment was a matter of stationing military forces around the Soviet borders and preventing any outbreak of Soviet military aggressiveness. I protested . . . against the implication that the Russians were aspiring to invade other areas and that the task of American policy was to prevent them from doing so. "The Russians don't want," I insisted, "to invade anyone. It is not in their tradition. They tried it once in Finland and got their fingers burned. They don't want war of any kind. Above all,

they don't want the open responsibility that official invasion brings with it." (Kennan, 1967: 361)

Ten years after his "containment" metaphor had become American policy, Kennan reiterated that "the image of a Stalinist Russia poised and yearning to attack the West, and deterred only by our possession of atomic weapons, was largely a creation of the Western imagination." But Kennan's disclaimers notwithstanding, the "containment myth," as Kennan called it in his memoirs, "never fully lost its spell." It became, and remained, one of the guiding premises on which American action abroad was based for many years.

The emergence of this world view and its attendant policy prescriptions helped heighten the American tendency to regard instability anywhere as resulting from Soviet conspiracy. It was not only the insurgency in Greece and the domestic strife in Turkey that were interpreted as part of a Soviet offensive; nearly all other crises were attributed to Soviet mischief as well.

Central to the superpowers' propensity to interpret crisis situations as the product of the other's aggressive efforts at global domination was their inability to maintain the "sphere-of-influence" posture tacitly agreed to earlier. When the Soviets moved into portions of Eastern Europe, this was interpreted by the Americans as a manifestation of Soviet ambitions for world conquest. Yet the Soviet Union perhaps had reason to think that the Americans would readily accede to Soviet domination in Eastern Europe. In 1945, for example, Secretary of State James Byrnes had commented that the "Soviet Union has a right to friendly governments along its borders," and Under Secretary of State Dean Acheson had spoken of "a Monroe Doctrine for Eastern Europe." Moreover, during the waning days of the fight against Nazi Germany, General Eisenhower refused to let the American army advance to Berlin and the eastern portion of Germany; instead, the Soviet army was permitted to liberate those areas as a prize for the sacrifices the Soviet Union had made in the war against the Nazis. To some, this decision reflected the American government's naiveté regarding the postwar structure of international politics in Europe that was being built by the way the war against Germany was terminated. But to the Soviet Union it may have reinforced the view that the Western powers would accept legitimate Soviet security needs, particularly the need for a buffer zone in Eastern Europe which had been the common invasion route into Russia for over three centuries. Hence, when the American government began to challenge Soviet supremacy in East Germany and elsewhere in Eastern Europe, the Soviet Union may have felt that previous understandings had been violated and that the West harbored "imperialist designs."

In any event, the results of the emerging view of the Soviet Union were in part self-fulfilling, as a seemingly unending series of situations were defined as Cold War incidents, including the Soviet refusal to withdraw its troops from Iran, the communist coup d'état in Czechoslovakia, the Berlin blockade, the formation of NATO in 1949 and the Warsaw Pact in 1955, and, most importantly, the acquisition of power by the Communist Chinese on the mainland

and the Korean War and Taiwan Straits crises that followed. The Soviets interpreted these same developments through a similar set of perceptual lenses, seeing American actions as a series of attempts to encircle the Soviet Union and eventually to attack it. Hence, the relationship between the two states was not simply "cold"; it was one of open belligerence. Relations became frozen in an embittered quarrel with an ever-present danger of erupting into open warfare. Memoranda later released indicate that in 1952 President Truman twice considered all-out war against the Soviet Union and China (*New York Times*, August 3, 1980).

To be sure, in the heat of confrontation there were moments of cooperation, as concessions, such as the lifting of the Berlin blockade, were interspersed with the hostile actions. But these were more like "cooling" actions for the purpose of preventing the use of armed force rather than true efforts at conciliation. Both the United States and the Soviet Union played the game of power politics with a vengeance, and both pursued the same goal: curtailing the influence of the other and stopping the adversary's presumed effort to conquer the world. The token acts of cooperation represented little more than the kinds of communications between adversaries necessary to continue the contest. Basically, each side saw the world in terms of pure conflict: What one side won, the other necessarily lost. Compromise under such "zero-sum" conditions is impossible. Because each contestant projected a negative image onto its adversary, while maintaining a virtuous self-image, conflict was endemic. The strong element of truth in each other's perceptions of hostility reinforced and sustained the spiral of mistrust and suspicion.

Tough Talk and Accommodative Action, 1953–1962

Although the phase of Soviet-American relations described as mutual antagonism and belligerence was punctuated by the expectation of general war between the two states, it was also a phase during which the United States enjoyed a clear military superiority over the Soviet Union, for it alone possessed the atomic bomb and the means to deliver it. Then, in 1949, the American atomic monopoly was successfully broken by the Soviet Union. Ever since, the evolving strategic strength of the two superpowers has exerted a powerful influence on the entire range of their diplomatic relations, and it ultimately altered their political postures toward each other.

The beginning of the convergence of Soviet and American military capabilities led to a third phase in American-Soviet relations: tough talk and accommodative action. Both nations talked as if war were imminent, but in deeds (especially with the termination of the Korean War) both acted with caution and restraint. President Eisenhower and his secretary of state, John Foster Dulles, promised a "rollback" of the iron curtain and the "liberation" of Eastern Europe, and they criticized the allegedly "soft" and "restrained" Truman Doctrine. They claimed to reject containment in favor of an ambitious "winning" strategy that would finally end the confrontation with godless communism. But communism was not rolled back in Eastern Europe, and containment was not replaced by a bolder American foreign policy strategy. Thus, despite the threatening posture of the United States toward the Soviet Union, more was promised than delivered, and the contradictions between rhetoric and practice were many.

For its part, the Soviet Union, which during this period continued to be in a position of strategic inferiority relative to the United States, advocated "peaceful coexistence" with capitalism, but it also continued, however cautiously, to exploit opportunities for advancing Soviet interests wherever it perceived them to exist, as in Cuba in 1962.

In the midst of the superpowers' rhetorical confrontation, changes in deeds began to take place. A first step toward détente, albeit halting and tentative, was taken with the 1955 Geneva summit, during which the two rivals established a precedent for the mutual discussion of world problems. With hindsight, it is clear that Geneva represented more a pause in hostilities than a fundamental change in the relationship, as throughout the 1950s the Cold War remained an ever-present threat to peace. More symptomatic of this period was Dulles's advocacy of brinkmanship and his threat of "massive retaliation," through which he hoped to force the Soviets into submission. Nonetheless, the first attempts at wider communication between the antagonists were made at the Geneva conference; hostility was endemic and reciprocal, but war did not follow. Although this period was punctuated with a series of Cold War crises and confrontations (as in Hungary, Cuba, and Egypt over the Suez, and over such issues as the downing of an American U-2 spy plane deep over Soviet territory), none of these threats to peace resulted in war, and steps toward improved relations (such as the Camp David meeting of 1959) occurred in their midst.

Peaceful Competition, 1963–1968

A fourth discernible period in Soviet-American rivalry—a phase of intense competition that was nonetheless peaceful—ran from roughly 1963 to 1968. The period began on the heels of the confrontation over missiles in Cuba and included the Vietnam conflict. Moreover, the continuing if restrained hostility coincided with the eruption of a seemingly unrestrained arms race. But amidst these continuing manifestations of Cold War politics were developments that may be interpreted as the origins of détente. All appear to have been tied to the growing parity of American and Soviet military capabilities and to the increasing awareness of the suicidal consequences of nuclear war.

Given what, in the words of Indian prime minister Jawaharlal Nehru, was the apparent recognition that "the only alternative to co-existence is co-destruction," the superpowers searched for ways to coexist. Some of the major issues were resolved with the tacit acceptance by the United States, for example, of a divided Germany and Soviet hegemony in Eastern Europe. The precedents for communication established at Geneva and later at Camp David were followed by the installation of the "hot line" in 1963 linking the White House and the Kremlin with a direct communication line; the Glassboro summit meeting (1967); and several negotiated agreements, such as the Antarctic Treaty (1959), the Partial Test Ban Treaty (1963), the Outer Space Treaty (1967), and the Nuclear Nonproliferation Treaty (1968).

At the American University commencement exercises in 1963, President John F. Kennedy spoke about the necessity of reducing tensions:

> Among the many traits the people of [the United States and the Soviet Union] have in common, none is stronger than our mutual abhorrence of war. Almost unique among the major world powers, we have never been at war with each other. And no nation in the history of battle ever suffered more than the Soviet Union suffered in the course of the Second World War. At least twenty million lost their lives. . . .
>
> Today, should total war ever break out again—no matter how—our two countries would become the primary targets. It is an ironical but accurate fact that the two strongest powers are the two in the most danger of devastation. . . . We are both caught up in a vicious and dangerous cycle in which suspicion on one side breeds suspicion on the other and new weapons beget counterweapons.
>
> In short, both the United States and its allies, and the Soviet Union and its allies, have a mutually deep interest in a just and genuine peace and in halting the arms race. . . .
>
> So let us not be blind to our differences, but let us also direct attention to our common interests and to the means by which those differences can be resolved. And if we cannot end now our differences, at least we can help make the world safe for diversity.

Kennedy did not inaugurate a fundamental change in Soviet-American relations, but in tone and attitude he clearly signaled a shift in how the United States hoped to deal with a hostile adversary. The Soviet Union by this time had also begun to change its political rhetoric. In particular, it increasingly emphasized the necessity of "peaceful coexistence" between capitalism and socialism, a view far different from conventional Marxist-Leninist revolutionary doctrine. Admittedly, these token moves were a far cry from sustained conciliation between the ideological antagonists, but they did represent a significant departure from the confrontational interactions that had previously characterized the Soviet-American rivalry.

Détente, 1969–1978

Continuing a process now well under way, Soviet-American relations took a dramatic turn with the assumption of power in the United States by President

Richard M. Nixon and his national security adviser, Henry A. Kissinger. Their approach to Soviet-American relations was officially labeled *détente* in 1969. The Soviets also adopted the term to describe their policies toward the United States.[9]

As a strategy for peace, détente was designed, in the words of Kissinger, to create "a vested interest in cooperation and restraint," "an environment in which competitors can regulate and restrain their differences and ultimately move from competition to cooperation." As seen from the American view-point, the policy of relaxing tensions with the Soviets and moving toward permanent accommodation and cooperation was based on a "linkage" theory: The development of economic, political, and strategic ties between the two nations, equally rewarding to both, would bind the two in a common fate, thereby lessening the incentives for conflict and war. Soviet global aspirations would be mollified, this view held, because the Soviet Union would be placed in a relationship in which it would be dependent on the continuation of rewarding ties with the United States for peace and prosperity. The linkage theory rested on the premise that the Soviets were no longer militarily inferior to the United States but could nevertheless be managed because they could be made dependent on American goodwill and trade concessions—a dependency that would reduce their incentives for mischief. Furthermore, linkage was designed to make the entire range of Soviet-American relations interdependent so that concessions in any one problem area could and must be compensated for by roughly equivalent concessions in others. For instance, negotiated arms control agreements were linked to acceptance of rules prohibiting military intervention outside the regions defining the superpowers' traditional security interests. Cooperation in one policy area was made contingent on acceptable conduct in other areas.

As a path on the road to peace (indeed, as a policy to avoid nuclear war), détente might be viewed as an abrupt turning point in the institutionalization of peaceful superpower relations. But it was also a product of previous efforts by the superpower adversaries to reduce tensions, diminish mistrust, and increase accommodation. So détente might also be viewed as simply the continuation of a process that was already well under way. As Kissinger himself noted: "America's aspiration for the kind of political environment we now call détente is not new. The effort to achieve a more constructive relationship with the Soviet Union . . . expresses the continuing desire . . . for an easing of

---

9. Kennan (1976) suggests that what became known as détente actually could have commenced as early as 1965, had it not been victimized by Soviet intervention in Czechoslovakia in 1968 and American intervention in Vietnam: "It was not until the first could be forgotten, and the second brought into process of liquidation in the early 1970s, that prospects again opened up for further progress along the lines pioneered by Messrs. Johnson and Rusk some four to six years earlier."

international tensions. . . . What is new in the current period of relaxation of tensions is its duration, the scope of the relationship which has evolved, and the continuation and intensity of consultation which it has produced."

As both a goal of and a strategy for expanding the superpowers' mutual interest in restraint, détente did represent an important shift in a global relationship. In diplomatic jargon, relations between the Soviets and Americans were said to have become "normalized." For the first time in several decades, the expectation of war between the superpowers receded. As demonstrated in Figure 4.1, cooperative interaction became more commonplace than hostile relations, and restraint was exercised. Visits, cultural exchanges, trade agreements, and cooperative technological ventures replaced threats, warnings, and confrontations. Part of the change stemmed from the strategic necessity of avoiding suicidal war; part also presumably stemmed from the awareness of the mutual advantages of collaboration.

The change in this period can also be explained by other factors: the growing sensitivity to and empathy for the other's security needs; the tacit revival of the sphere-of-influence concept and the advantages it could confer on the management of conflicts; the shared concern for the aspirations of a potentially powerful China; and recognition of the need for establishing a crisis-prevention regime (a goal embodied in the Basic Principles Agreement signed at the 1972 Moscow summit). The escalating costs of a continued arms race may also have contributed to the development of détente.

Confrontation, 1979–1984

Despite these precedents and the careful nurturing of rapprochement for nearly a decade, neither the condition nor spirit of détente endured. Although hostile relations waned between 1969 and 1978, competition between the superpowers for advantage and security (at the other's expense) was never wholly absent; as before, a mix of conciliatory and conflictual practices was present throughout the period.

The tendency of the superpower rivalry to oscillate between conciliation and conflict was made especially evident as events unfolded in the late 1970s, when a decided decline from the harmony of détente became evident (see Figure 4.1). To some observers the hardening of relations was interpreted as reaffirmation of their belief that the Cold War had never disappeared, even during the period of normalized relations. From this viewpoint, the struggle had continued during détente, albeit on a new basis and in a new style; the reassuring terminology of détente concealed the unpleasant reality of enduring, fundamental rivalry between the superpowers. More appropriate than the inviting hope that superpower relations could be put on a cordial basis was the entrenched nature of the competition. It was this attribute that led Zbigniew Brzezinski, President Jimmy Carter's national security adviser, to coin the term *contestation* to describe what he believed was the real nature of the relationship between the two powers. Contestation depicts the superpowers' dual compulsion to oppose each other around the globe while also cooperating in order to avoid nuclear annihilation.

Leslie H. Gelb (1976) advanced an analogous argument earlier when he noted that from the American perspective, the Nixon–Kissinger détente strategy sought "to evolve détente into a new form of containment of the Soviet Union—or, better still, self-containment on the part of the Russians." According to Kissinger's conception, détente represented an attempt to devise "new means to the old ends of containment." From this viewpoint, détente became a part of the Cold War; it was not an alternative to it. According to this reasoning, when the United States was in a position of strategic and military supremacy, Cold War politics could be safely practiced by coercion and confrontation. But from a position of strategic parity, confrontation was too risky, and containment had to be practiced only through seduction and collaborative linkages that would tie the Soviets in a web of entangling cooperative arrangements, thereby inhibiting expansionism on their part. Likewise, from the Soviet standpoint, the Soviets saw in the trade, technological, and diplomatic exchanges made possible by détente a way of moderating the U.S. threat, thereby enabling them to concentrate on pressing domestic problems while carrying out competition through nonmilitary means.

At the center of the dialogue of détente was the issue of arms control. The Strategic Arms Limitation Treaty talks (SALT) became the test of détente's viability. Initiated in 1969, the SALT negotiations attempted to restrain the threatening, expensive, and spiraling arms race. Two agreements were eventually concluded, the first in 1972 (SALT I) and the second in 1979 (SALT II). With their signing, each of the superpowers appeared to have gained the principal objective it had sought in détente. Through it the Soviet Union gained recognition of its status as a coequal of the United States. And the United States appeared to gain a commitment to moderation of what it perceived as the Soviet Union's quest for preeminent power in the world.

But the difficulties encountered in bringing the SALT II agreement to fruition (it was signed but never ratified by the United States) underscored the substantial differences that still separated the superpowers. By the end of the 1970s, détente had lost nearly all of its momentum and much of the expectation associated with it only a few years earlier. During the SALT II ratification hearings in the United States Senate the focus was on continued high levels of Soviet military spending, on Soviet "adventurism" in Africa and elsewhere, and on the presence of Soviet military forces in Cuba, all of which spoke to the persistence of the deep-seated American distrust of the Soviet Union.

The Soviet intervention in Afghanistan in 1979 may have prompted the final curtain on the era of détente and the prelude to the resumption of confrontation. President Carter sounded the warning in 1980 by declaring that "Soviet aggression in Afghanistan—unless checked—confronts all the world with the most serious strategic challenge since the Cold War began." By that time the United States had already initiated a series of countermoves, including enunciation of the Carter Doctrine declaring a U.S. willingness to use military force to protect U.S. interests in the Persian Gulf, an effort to organize a worldwide boycott of the 1980 Moscow Olympics, suspension of American grain exports to the Soviet Union, and other limitations of the trade ties between the superpowers that had been nurtured during détente. In the aftermath of Afghanistan, the prospects for Senate ratification of SALT II were also doomed. Antagonism and hostility once more dominated relations between the superpowers.

The departure of Carter from the White House and the death of Soviet President Leonid Brezhnev symbolized the end of one phase and the beginning of another, as Soviet-American relations fell into a deep freeze. The deterioration of relations accelerated, driven by multiple causes. President Ronald Reagan and his Soviet counterparts—first Yuri Andropov and then Konstantin Chernenko—assumed a confrontational posture toward each other's government. The first years of the 1980s were marked by such stridency that prognoses of a new Cold War were commonplace. Talk of war became endemic, as did preparations for it. In terminology redolent of the 1950s, the leaders of each superpower delivered a barrage of confrontational rhetoric. Reagan, for instance, asserted that the Soviet Union "underlies all the unrest that is going on" and described the Soviets as "the focus of evil in the modern world" and their political system as "an evil empire." For its part, Soviet rhetoric was no less restrained or alarmist. The atmosphere was punctuated by Richard Pipes's (a former member of Reagan's National Security Council staff) bold assertion that the Soviets would have to choose either "peacefully changing their Communist system . . . or going to war."

In many respects the early 1980s were like the 1950s, when tough talk failed to be matched by aggressive action. But the 1979–1984 phase also witnessed some match between words and deeds. Resumption of the arms race was the most visible consequence, which was put above all other goals, including competing domestic goals. The confrontation was also extended to new territory (such as Central America) and included renewed propaganda efforts to sell worldwide the alleged virtues of the superpowers' respective economic and political systems. President Reagan also issued a new doctrine that bore his name, in which he pledged U.S. support for anticommunist movements worldwide. Absent was any pretense toward compromise, as the world witnessed "the virtual collapse of détente and, indeed, of most cooperative contacts between the United States and the Soviet Union" (Garthoff, 1985). The East–West conflict thus veered toward patterns evident in the superpowers' rivalry earlier in the postwar era, demonstrating once again the power of domestic and international forces sustaining the East–West conflict. As Arthur Hartman, U.S. ambassador in Moscow during the Reagan administration, observed, "The Soviet Union is our antagonist and will be for the indefinite future."

Renewed Dialogue, 1985–?

It is a popular cliché that the more things change, the more they remain the same. The cliché seems as applicable to Soviet-American relations as it is to many other phenomena. Nearly five decades of superpower relations suggest that the conflict will endure but also that this relationship will alternate between periods of confrontation and periods of accommodation. This cyclical fluctuation predicts that neither confrontation nor détente is permanently precluded.

The turn from hostility toward renewed dialogue as the best description of Soviet-American interactions in the latter half of the 1980s was signaled in early 1984, when Secretary of State George Shultz announced that the United States was "ready for negotiations whenever the Soviet Union is prepared." Shortly thereafter, Konstantin Chernenko expressed his hope for an improvement in Soviet-American relations, declaring, "We are in favor of an active and fruitful dialogue with nations living under a different social system to ours, the United States and Great Britain in particular." President Reagan echoed the hope, asserting in the same year that "we have let [Chernenko] know that we want better relations. We want to sit down and try to resolve some of the problems we have."

Prospects for a more constructive phase in East–West relations became especially positive in March 1985, when Mikhail S. Gorbachev became Soviet general secretary. Gorbachev boldly set out to revise Soviet policy and to improve relations with the United States. His desire for new initiatives was professed in early 1987, when he noted that the prevailing situation "dictates and makes urgent the need for a fundamental break with many customary approaches to foreign policy, a break with the tradition of political thinking and of views on the problems of war and peace, on the defense and security of individual states and international security." The announcement invited renewed dialogue with the United States.

Promoting what he termed *novoye myshleniye* (new thinking), the new Soviet leader seized the public relations spotlight by attacking the supposedly sacred premises of previous Soviet doctrine. Consider four initiatives in particular.

First, Gorbachev challenged the revolutionary mission of Soviet foreign policy, arguing in 1986 that "it is inadmissible and futile to encourage revolution from abroad." This came close to abrogating the long-standing Soviet ideological and national commitment to assist national liberation movements struggling to overthrow capitalism in other countries.

Second, Gorbachev attacked the tendency to rely on belligerent posturing and efforts to bargain through threats and revised the conventional Soviet worship of national security by stressing for the first time *obshchaya bezopasnost* (mutual security). The contention that national security will be diminished, not increased, by reducing the security of its adversary—or, conversely, that American security contributes to Soviet security—was a radical departure from prior thinking. As former Secretary of State Cyrus Vance observed, "The Soviets have made a major change in both rhetoric and doctrine under Gorbachev by adopting mutual security. It runs counter to Leninist doctrine, which was that one had to achieve superiority and threaten others in order to be safe."

Third, Gorbachev placed unprecedented stress on the dangers of nuclear war by recognizing that the destructiveness of nuclear weapons has rendered old assumptions obsolete. That reality required, he radically asserted, abandonment of the cherished Marxist postulate of class confrontation, which he contended must be supplanted by what he termed the "real, not speculative and remote, common human interest" to save all humanity from nuclear annihilation. This viewpoint does not envision the end of economic and ideological competition between socialist and capitalist countries, but it does make it subservient by asserting that competition "can and must be kept within a framework of peaceful competition which necessarily envisages co-operation." This posture conforms to the preface to the 1987 Geneva summit communiqué to which Gorbachev and Ronald Reagan jointly agreed, namely, that "nuclear war cannot be won and must never be fought." Previously, Soviet doctrine had maintained that under certain circumstances a "victory" in a nuclear exchange might be possible.

Fourth, by challenging the Soviet Union's historic obsession with the quest for national security through extraordinarily high expenditures for arms and armies (see Kennedy, 1987b), Gorbachev called for meaningful arms control agreements as a way of reducing the financial burdens of defense and of reducing the dangers of an escalating strategic arms race. "We understand," he lamented, "that the arms race . . . serves objectives whose essence is to exhaust the Soviet Union economically." The pledge to bring the arms race under control represented a break with past policy, as did Soviet willingness to make concessions to achieve this purpose. No longer would the Soviet Union simultaneously pursue guns and butter.

These apparently bold revisions of previous Soviet thinking collectively paved the way for renewed dialogue with the United States across a wide range of issues. In seeking to reduce tensions, Gorbachev seemed to position the Soviet Union to initiate a process designed to abate the most dangerous threats of the Cold War era. "We realize that we are divided by profound historical, ideological, socioeconomic and cultural differences," Gorbachev noted on the occasion of his first visit to the United States in 1987. "But the wisdom of politics today lies in not using those differences as a pretext for confrontation, enmity and the arms race."

The Soviet leader's new posture sought to allay American suspicions while presenting a more positive image of the Soviet Union. The professed changes were greeted in Washington with considerable skepticism. But by presenting proposals clearly in the interests of the United States as well as the Soviet Union, the belief that Gorbachev was motivated by deceit and a desire to lull the West into a false sense of security was somewhat alleviated.[10] Confidence in Soviet motives was reinforced by the first concrete product of the renewed dialogue: the agreement negotiated in 1987 on intermediate-range nuclear forces (INF). As the first postwar arms control treaty to eliminate weapons, the agreement set a historic precedent from which subsequent agreements might evolve.

The United States recognized, however, that the future remained difficult and uncertain. The INF achievement was viewed by many as "easy" compared with the difficult negotiations that limiting intercontinental strategic forces would require, for example. But that cautious skepticism did not preclude subsequent breakthroughs or the continuation of the cordial spirit that prevailed at the Moscow summit in May 1988. In the words of President Reagan (April 10, 1987): "If I had to characterize U.S.-Soviet relations in one word, it would be this—proceeding. No great cause for excitement, no great cause for alarm. And perhaps this is the way relations with one's adversaries should be characterized. We have hopes, and we have determination, and we are proceeding."

Given the past record of the Soviet-American rivalry, perhaps "hope," "determination," and "proceeding" are the best that can be expected of the superpowers' relations. Both superpowers have exhibited a capacity for confrontation and for collaboration, with periodic swings between intensified tension and efforts to relax it. Thus, rivalry and confrontation seem destined to prevail, but pauses in them are also likely to occur, for the overriding need to avoid war requires from each superpower a measure of cooperation. In 1983, Under Secretary of State Lawrence Eagleburger captured the tension that seems destined to characterize the superpowers' contending compulsions: "Our policy toward the U.S.S.R. starts with the fact that both of us have weapons of almost unimaginable destructive force. Each of us can do mortal damage to the other in an afternoon. We have radically different political

---

10. Of interest is why Gorbachev chose to undertake a program so risky to his retention of power, where opposition to it from within his own government was certain. The most compelling answer is that the initiative stemmed from domestic considerations. In February 1987, Gorbachev disclosed that "our international policy is determined more than ever by our domestic policy, by our interest in concentrating on creative work for the perfection of our country. For that very reason, we need a more stable peace, predictability, and a constructive direction of international relations." Perhaps the USSR needed *peredyshka* (a "breathing spell") in the costly competition with the West in order to engineer fundamental reforms necessary to rectify a rapidly deteriorating, desperate domestic condition exacerbated by inefficiency, corruption, and ineptitude (see Kennedy, 1987b, for a vivid description of what Gorbachev is up against). "Take away its 3.7 million men and women under arms and its 25,000-odd nuclear weapons," Strobe Talbott (*Time*, July 27, 1987, p. 29) pointedly observed, "and the Soviet Union would be a Third World country." *Glasnost* (openness), *demokratizatsia* (democratization), and *perestroika* (restructuring) all represent efforts to modernize a malfunctioning system of governance. To rectify these domestic conditions so as to arrest the visible decline of the Soviet Union in the global hierarchy, Third World adventurism, excessive expenditures for arms, and confrontational diplomacy with the United States were precluded. Instead, a peaceful, stable relationship with the United States, based on a new policy, was required.

values, visions of the proper social order and aspirations for the future of the international system. We must steer a middle course between the friendship we cannot have and the war we must not have."

Against this background, confidence in the prospects for a peaceful future may be misplaced, but there is some reassurance in the evidence that "there has been a secular trend toward a more benign and a more, but still modestly, interdependent relationship between the United States and the Soviet Union" (Zimmerman and Jacobson, 1987). Indeed, for all the hostility that has characterized Soviet-American relations since the end of World War II, ironically, that same period is the longest of any in which war between great powers has been averted since the Peace of Westphalia in 1648 (see Gaddis, 1986).[11]

THE IMPACT OF SOVIET-AMERICAN RIVALRY ON OTHER STATES

The prominence of the United States and the Soviet Union in the international hierarchy has made their relationship with each other one of the most pregnant forces for global change. Building new forms of political organization in the world, restructuring the global political economy, and, most importantly, maintaining world peace and order all have been affected by it. Even the prospects for dealing meaningfully with such transnational issues as coping with world population growth and realizing global food and energy security are touched in varying degrees by the conflict. As United Nations Secretary General Javier Pérez de Cuéllar argued in 1983, a prerequisite to the solution of most problems confronting the world today is improvement in the relations between the two superpowers, for without a relaxation of tension, progress on global issues and mediation of conflicts between smaller nations become impossible. In fact, every theme and issue discussed in this book is influenced in some way, directly or indirectly, by the force and fact of the enduring Soviet-American rivalry.

Perhaps the most obvious manifestation of the impact of the United States and the Soviet Union on world politics is in the structural features of the global political system that have come to be tied to, and often defined by, the distribution of economic and military power between the two superpowers. The post–World War II era began with the United States as the preeminent power in the world, but this *unipolar* situation changed quickly. The world power configuration quickly became *bipolar*, with the United States and its allies constituting one pole and the Soviet Union and its allies the other. This

---

11. "Peace is by no means guaranteed," adds William G. Hyland (1987), "but it seems more likely to endure now than 20 or 30 years ago when there were frequent Soviet-American crises. Most strategists believe that a Soviet-American war as a consequence of a deliberate choice is now only a marginal possibility."

power configuration roughly coincided with the periods of Soviet-American rivalry known as mutual antagonism and belligerence and tough talk and accommodative action, which spanned the years from roughly 1947 to 1962.

Periodic crises and the threat of war characterized these phases. By implication, then, we can suggest that the distribution of power between the United States and the Soviet Union not only defined the structural features of the international system; those features also determined Soviet and American behavior. And that behavior was often remarkably similar[12]: Each vehemently attacked the ideological beliefs of the other while perhaps becoming a prisoner of its own; both armed for defense and threatened to use arms to settle the contest; both pursued expansive foreign policies designed to extend their influence into far corners of the globe; and both sought, in an almost predatory fashion, allies who would assist in the struggle.

Europe was the focal point over which the superpowers jockeyed for power and influence. The principal European allies of the superpowers were grouped into the North Atlantic Treaty Organization (NATO) and the Warsaw Treaty Organization (WTO). Both alliances remain cornerstones of the superpowers' external policies, but neither is as cohesive now as it once was.

During the 1950s the European members of the Eastern and Western alliances willingly acceded to the leadership of their superpower patrons. In return, the superpowers extended to their clients security from external threat. As the destructive capacity of American and Soviet arsenals increased, however, and as the strategic doctrines governing the use of weapons of mass destruction changed, the European members of the Cold War coalitions began to question whether their protectors would risk their own destruction in order to save one or more of their allies. The fear that the United States might seek to "decouple" itself from the protection of Western Europe, for example, presents the Atlantic alliance with troublesome issues. Détente further undermined the once cohesive alliances, for it simultaneously laid to rest some of the most contentious issues of the Cold War era that had been left unresolved and reduced the perception of an external threat on which the alliances had been formed in the first place. Interestingly, however, when Soviet-American détente waned in the late 1970s, the superpowers' European allies continued

---

12. Some have alleged that ironically, the Cold War competition made the two countries increasingly alike as a consequence of the kinds of economic demands that the competition has required. Some critics have contended, for example, that the policies of both superpowers have been determined in part by the political power of the respective military-industrial complexes that came into being as a result of the Cold War. A corollary holds that the military establishments of the two societies have become, in a sense, allies, for both need the adversary to justify their demands on their own societies. A further extension of this argument can be found in the "convergence theory"—the argument that the modern process of industrialization will lead developing superstates to possess shared economic and political characteristics—which sees the United States and the Soviet Union becoming more similar than dissimilar across a broad spectrum of socioeconomic and political dimensions. See Brzezinski and Huntington (1964) for an elaboration and critique of the convergence theory.

their search for normalization of relations, for their own interests were served by relaxed tensions and the further expansion of East–West commercial interaction that it implied.

Resurgent nationalism and renewed economic vigor also made the European members of NATO and the Warsaw Pact more assertive on some matters, particularly economic issues. Thus, as the Soviet-American rivalry moved through the stage of peaceful competition to détente, the international power configuration moved from bipolarity to what may be described as a *bipolycentric* distribution of power (see Chapter 13 for elaboration). This concept depicts not only the continued dominance of the United States and the Soviet Union on military matters but also the far greater fluidity that came to characterize interactions between and among Eastern and Western nations on non-military issues.

As diplomatic events between and among East and West unfolded, as the characteristics of the international system were defined and redefined by the converging capabilities of the major actors on the world stage, and as these characteristics in turn influenced American and Soviet behavior, the Third World found itself as both an observer and a pawn in the Cold War contest.[13] On the one hand, it had few capabilities with which to influence the course of the East–West dispute. On the other hand, it found itself as the object of superpower courtship. The courtship assumed the form of competition for allies, of foreign aid flows often designed to serve the donors' political interests more than the recipients' economic development goals, and, frequently, of massive amounts of military assistance. Although the Third World generally pursued a posture of noninvolvement in the East–West conflict, it nevertheless often found itself to be the territory on which some of the most violent conflicts in the postwar period were played out. Not all of these conflicts were immediate products of Soviet-American rivalry, in the sense that the Cold War may have contributed to but did not cause them, but few Third World conflicts have been untouched by the superpowers' rivalry.

Many of these conflicts were related to the decolonization process, which spurred the growth in the number of Third World nations (an important base of the Third World's political power). The decolonization process itself was speeded by the political attacks of the communist countries on Western imperialism and by the political alliance forged between communist countries and the economically less developed nations of the Southern Hemisphere, which effectively condemned colonialism as an acceptable form of political organization and control. It was fed, too, by the support that the United States often provided to decolonization efforts—support that won it friends and influence elsewhere in the world.

---

13. At the first Brezhnev–Nixon summit meeting in May 1972, the arrogance of the superpowers' attitude toward other states, including their allies, was expressed when the Soviet leader "proposed that the two superpowers divide the world and rule it" (Sulzberger, 1987).

Like the European members of NATO (and also Japan) and the Warsaw Pact, the Third World has become more assertive on nonmilitary matters that are otherwise on the periphery of the major political and military issues separating East and West. That they have been able to do so is in part a function of the essential strategic stalemate that emerged between the superpowers (Krepon, 1984), which produced greater fluidity in world politics by enabling the superpowers' allies to escape their strict control. As a consequence, today we find the superpowers acting in many of the same ways they did in the bipolar era of the 1950s and early 1960s: pushing at each other while attempting to pull others into their respective alliance networks. However, unlike that period, in the present phase many allies, who do not always share their patron's image of its adversary's aggressive intentions, have strongly and successfully resisted the superpowers' pressures.

In sum, the East–West conflict has shaped in significant ways the contours of world politics in the postwar era. But this fundamental cleavage is today being crowded by another equally divisive rift on the global agenda, the North–South confrontation. Whereas the East–West competition is essentially a contest between the influential "haves" of the world, the North–South conflict revolves around the political and economic claims of the "have-nots." The problems posed by global disparities in income and wealth, and the North–South confrontation that such disparities have spawned, promise to propel in yet another way the transformation of world politics.

SUGGESTED READINGS

Barnet, Richard J. "An Absence of Trust: Roots of Discord in the Soviet-American Relationship," pp. 127–137 in Charles W. Kegley, Jr., and Eugene R. Wittkopf, eds., *The Global Agenda: Issues and Perspectives*, 2nd ed. New York: Random House, 1988.

Crockett, Richard, and Steve Smith, eds. *The Cold War: Past and Present*. London: Allen & Unwin, 1987.

Gaddis, John Lewis. "How the Cold War Might End," *Atlantic Monthly* 260 (November 1987): 88–100.

Garthoff, Raymond. *Détente and Confrontation: American-Soviet Relations From Nixon to Reagan*. Washington, D.C.: Brookings Institution, 1985.

George, Alexander L., ed. *Managing U.S.-Soviet Rivalry: Problems of Crisis Prevention*. Boulder, Colo.: Westview Press, 1983.

Gorbachev, Mikhail. *Perestroika: New Thinking for Our Country and the World*. New York: Harper & Row, 1988.

Jönsson, Christer. *Superpower: Comparing American and Soviet Foreign Policy*. London: Francis Pinter, 1984.

Nye, Joseph S., Jr., ed. *The Making of America's Soviet Policy*. New Haven, Conn.: Yale University Press, 1984.

Stevenson, Richard W. *The Rise and Fall of Détente: Relaxations of Tension in U.S.-Soviet Relations, 1953–1984*. Urbana: University of Illinois Press, 1985.

FIVE

The North–South Conflict: Roots and Consequences of Global Inequalities

Since the Second World War, the world has undergone a vast transformation as more than 100 new nations have come into being. An international system that had been centered on Europe for centuries, and that regarded all non-European areas as peripheral or as objects of rivalry, has become in an amazingly short span of time a truly global arena of sovereign states.

GEORGE SHULTZ, 1983

While some countries continue in their opulence, there are others in whom the pangs of poverty instill a numbing sense of despair.

HUMAYAN RASHEED CHOUDHURY, 1987

The drums began to roll on schedule when precisely at noon the Portuguese flag was lowered and the red, white, and yellow banner of Lilliput was unfurled to announce the arrival of the newest member of the international community. Visiting dignitaries from the United States, the Soviet Union, Cuba, and elsewhere snapped to attention with the new prime minister as Lilliput's national security forces, a proud if small group of poorly trained and ill-equipped national militia, paraded before the reviewing stand. Over half of Lilliput's 200,000 inhabitants crowded the narrow, poorly paved streets of their nation's capital to cheer the arrival of their new freedom from foreign rule. Little did they know that the prime minister had already scheduled discussions with the visiting American, Cuban, and Russian dignitaries during which he hoped to secure their economic, military, and technical aid in coping with the poverty and squalor as well as military weakness that characterized their country. Perhaps in the process the prime minister would find that overt foreign rule was being replaced by another, more subtle form of foreign dominance.

To most people in the world, the skein of events in Lilliput went largely unnoticed. But their governmental representatives could not be so unconcerned. Already the Soviets and Americans had begun constructing new diplomatic offices in the capital, thus adding another channel to their already complex network of diplomatic linkages with the rest of the world. The decision to establish formal ties was motivated not only by the desire to maintain friendly political relations with Lilliput, whose geographical location made it of potential strategic significance to the major powers. It was also motivated by an economic concern: Lilliput could become a major source of chromium, a mineral of vital importance to industrialized nations.

This scenario is, of course, hypothetical. But the events and the issues are illustrative of real patterns that have been repeated often since World War II. Literally scores of new states have been created during the past four decades. They have frequently been courted by the older, more established nations for political and economic reasons. Yet the new states often share little with those who do the courting. Born legally "sovereign" (though often their sovereign status is politically questionable), they find themselves thrust into an international system that they had no voice in shaping but whose organization and operation they perceive as detrimental to the realization of their own goals. And they are often beset by such overwhelming economic, social, and political problems at home that the likelihood of being able to rise above their under-dog status is remote. We can better understand this as well as other implications contained in the story about Lilliput by examining the characteristics of the many new nations that have been created since 1945 as the global trend toward decolonization unfolded.

WORLDS ONE THROUGH THREE: THE THIRD WORLD IN THE GLOBAL HIERARCHY

The term *Third World* is used to refer to the poorer, economically less developed or developing countries of the world.[1] So numerous are they that it takes less time to list those that are developed than those that are not. The less-developed countries include all of Asia and Oceania except Japan, Australia, and New Zealand, all of Africa except South Africa, and all of the Western Hemisphere except Canada and the United States. Some formulations also include a few European nations in the class of developing economies (Portugal, Spain, Greece, Turkey, Yugoslavia, and Romania). The Third World thus contains more than three-fourths of the world's population, but it accounts for less than a fifth of the goods and services produced in the world (as measured by gross national product [GNP]).

The roughly 25 percent of the world's population that produces more than 80 percent of its economic output is found in the First and Second Worlds. The *First World* encompasses the industrialized nations of Western Europe and North America, plus Japan, Australia, and New Zealand. As members of the

---

1. See Wolf-Phillips (1987) for a discussion of the derivation of the term *Third World* and how it came to be accepted in the development literature.

free-world coalition in the context of the East–West dispute, they share other characteristics, including a common cultural heritage (except Japan), a commitment to varying forms of democratic political institutions and free-market economic principles, and generally high standards of living. Reflecting their common economic characteristics, these nations are known in the idiom of international diplomacy as *developed market economies*. The communist states comprise the *Second World*. Characterized as *centrally planned economies* because of their preference for state-owned and state-managed economic institutions, Second World nations are organized according to socialist principles and share an ideological commitment to the eventual victory of socialism over capitalism.[2]

As described in Chapter 4, the East–West conflict between the First and Second Worlds has focused primarily on political controversies, in particular on military and national security issues. The rhetoric of debate in the North–South conflict, on the other hand, has tended to stress economic issues, even though the issues themselves are often intensely political in nature. The conflict pits the First World nations against the world's "have-not" nations, those characterized by a colonial heritage, relative poverty, a lack of economic development comparable to that of the First and Second World nations, and their location largely in the Southern Hemisphere.

The North–South conflict, in other words, is essentially a struggle by those at the bottom of the international hierarchy to improve their position in the global pecking order, which implies seeking advantage in their relations with the North, often at the North's expense. The North in turn has sought to "manage" the aspirations of the South in such a way as to preserve the advantages that the North now enjoys. (The Second World has largely disassociated itself from the North–South conflict, making it essentially a North/West–South dispute.)

Grouping so many countries under the label Third World can be misleading, as the term masks considerable diversity. The Third World includes, for instance, both huge countries like India and microstates like Tuvalu. Some are desperately impoverished, whereas others are relatively well off economically. Some (notably in Africa) have experienced negative economic growth rates in recent years, whereas others, such as Taiwan, South Korea, and Singapore, have experienced sustained economic growth. Most are recipients of First World economic aid, but others, like the oil-rich nations of the Middle East, have distributed their own largess broadly. Then, too, Third World nations vary considerably in their political institutions, with some monarchies, others

2. Among centrally planned economies, it is possible to distinguish between the developed and the developing. Included in the latter group are Albania, the People's Republic of China, Mongolia, the Democratic Republic of Korea (North Korea), Romania, and the Socialist Republic of Vietnam. The developed centrally planned economies are the Soviet Union and the Eastern European socialist countries other than Romania. The term *Second World* is generally confined to the Soviet Union and Eastern Europe, a group corresponding roughly to the developed centrally planned economies. The People's Republic of China is usually regarded as a Third World country.

dictatorships, and still others democracies. Some of these are stable politically, but many are known for their civil strife and domestic turmoil. The prevailing economic philosophies and systems range from the laissez-faire pursuit of free enterprise under capitalism to central planning and socialist control. And as we shall see, Third World countries sometimes differ in the positions they take on different issues on the global agenda.

Despite this diversity, the label Third World is still useful not only for analytical convenience but also because the countries that make it up often identify themselves as such and behave self-consciously as members of a collective movement in their search for freedom from their economic and political dependence on others.

The emergence of the Third World is primarily a post–World War II phenomenon. Although most Latin American nations were independent before that time, having gained their independence from Spain and Portugal early in the nineteenth century, it was not until 1946 that the floodgates of the decolonization process began to be opened. In the next three decades or so a profusion of new states joined the international community as sovereign entities, comprising by the 1980s a combined population exceeding 3.5 billion people. Nearly all of the new nations were formed from the former British, French, Belgian, Spanish, and Portuguese overseas empires. In many cases the areas granted independence had been colonized only since the late 1800s, when a wave of new imperialism swept the world. In others, the ties had existed for over four hundred years, as in the case of Portugal's colony of Mozambique. Today, relatively few colonies remain. A dozen or so remaining dependent territories may yet someday become independent members of the world community, but most of them have populations of less than 100,000. In short, decolonization is a distinctly contemporary phenomenon, but as a political process it has now largely been completed.

But the vestiges of colonialism remain, with important consequences for world politics. Contemporary world politics is significantly shaped by the needs, circumstances, interests, and objectives of Third World countries, which are often quite dissimilar from those of the older and more established states. For a variety of reasons these dissimilarities stem from and are related to the "gap"—the enormous disparity in wealth and income between the world's rich and poor nations, between those that have advanced economically and those that have remained underdeveloped or only now may have begun to develop economically. Differing perceptions of the gap's causes and correspondingly different prescriptions for its cure also lie at the heart of contemporary world politics. Indeed, the disparity between the rich North and the poor South is often viewed through the nationalistic eyes of Third World leaders as the consequence of "neocolonialism" or "neoimperialism," that is, as mechanisms of unequal exchange that permit the advantaged to exploit the disadvantaged through the institutionalized processes of the contemporary international economic system. Thus the colonial heritage of the Third World is central to many explanations of the South's malaise.

HISTORICAL ROOTS OF THE DIVISION BETWEEN NORTH AND SOUTH: THE RISE AND FALL OF EUROPEAN EMPIRES

As a network of relationships among sovereign entities (and hence the term *international* relations), the *state system* is generally regarded to have been born in 1648 with the Peace of Westphalia, which ended the Thirty Years War in Europe. Thereafter European potentates refused to recognize the temporal authority of the papacy (that is, the Roman Catholic church). A quasi–world polity (bounded, to be sure, by location) was replaced by a system of allegedly independent states recognizing no authority above them. Relations between the sovereign political entities of Europe were to be conducted according to new rules of law, which entitled them to negotiate treaties and settle disputes without recourse to any institution transcending the states. Moreover, all shared equally the same legal rights and duties conferred by their sovereign status: the territorial inviolability of the state, its freedom from interference, its right to conduct foreign relations with other states as it saw fit, and its authority to rule its own population.

Although all states were assumed to be equal in law, they clearly were not equal in capabilities or power. In fact, the international law that emerged in the post-Westphalian state system to regulate behavior legalized the drive for power and created rules by which states could compete with one another for rank in the international hierarchy. Hence, the states that were coequal in law were not coequal in their military and economic capabilities. There were great powers—such as England, France, Russia, Prussia, and Austria—and minor powers—various principalities in Germany and the Italian peninsula. In addition, there existed former great powers, such as the Netherlands, Portugal, and Spain, whose power had diminished greatly by the time the state system was given legal birth in 1648. Collectively, these great and secondary powers carried their competition for territorial control beyond the European area, thereby transforming the European state system into a truly global one. The result was the eventual universalization of the European state system. Europeans controlled a third of the globe by 1800, two-thirds by 1878, and over four-fifths by 1914 (Fieldhouse, 1973: 3).

The first wave of European empire building began during the fifteenth century, as the English, French, Dutch, Portuguese, and Spanish used their military power to achieve commercial advantage overseas. Innovations in a variety of sciences made possible the adventures of European explorers. ''In their wake went Europe's merchants, quickly seizing upon opportunities to increase their business and profits. In turn, Europe's governments perceived the possibilities for increasing their own power and wealth. Commercial companies were chartered and financed, with military and naval expeditions frequently sent out after them to ensure political control of overseas territories'' (Cohen, 1973).

The economic strategy underlying the relationship between colonies and colonizers during this era of classical imperialism was known as *mercantilism*: "the philosophy and practice of governmental regulation of economic life to increase state power and security" (Cohen, 1973). State power was assumed to flow from the possession of national wealth measured in terms of gold and silver. One way to accumulate the desired bullion was to maintain a favorable balance of trade, that is, to export more than was imported: "Colonies were desirable in this respect because they afforded an opportunity to shut out commercial competition; they guaranteed exclusive access to untapped markets and sources of cheap materials (as well as, in some instances, direct sources of the precious metals themselves). Each state was determined to monopolize as many of these overseas mercantile opportunities as possible" (Cohen, 1973).

By the end of the eighteenth century, the European powers had spread themselves, although thinly, throughout virtually the entire world. But the colonial empires they had built had by that time already begun to erode. Britain's thirteen North American colonies declared their independence in 1776, and most of Spain's possessions in South America received their independence early in the nineteenth century. Between 1775 and 1825, ninety-five colonies were terminated (Bergesen and Schoenberg, 1980: 236).

Concurrent with this trend toward the breakup of colonial empires was the waning of the mercantilist philosophy that had sustained the colonial system of classical imperialism. As argued by Adam Smith in his classic *Wealth of Nations*, national wealth was acquired not through the accumulation of gold and silver but, rather, through the capital and goods they could buy. A system of free international trade consistent with the precepts of laissez-faire economics (minimal governmental interference) became the accepted philosophy governing international economic relations. European powers continued to hold numerous colonies, but the prevailing sentiment came to be more anti-imperialist than proimperialist.

Some analysts argue that the European powers' geographic expansion resulted in the creation of a capitalist world-system characterized by an international division of labor among three strata of states: core, semiperiphery, and periphery (Wallerstein, 1974). Northwest Europe first emerged as the core, and as the industrial revolution proceeded, it exchanged manufactured goods for agricultural and mineral products produced in the colonial territories at the periphery. According to this viewpoint, the world economy is overlaid by a political system of competitive states, and state power is sometimes used to perpetuate the international division of labor. Because "in the competitive state system it has been impossible for any single state to monopolize the entire world market, and to maintain hegemony indefinitely . . . success in the capitalist world-system is based on a combination of effective state power and competitive advantage in production" (Chase-Dunn, 1981). By the 1800s, Great Britain emerged as the dominant core state in a succession of global powers.[3] As the hegemonic power in politics and economics, Britain became the chief promoter of free international trade, which had the effect of promoting disproportionate economic growth in the core state, relative to that of the periphery (McGowan, 1981).

Beginning in the 1870s and extending until the outbreak of World War I, a new wave of imperialism washed over the world as new territories were colonized at a rate nearly four times faster than during the first wave of colonial expansion (Bergesen and Schoenberg, 1980). The Western European nations (joined later by the United States and Japan) once more carved the world into a series of overseas empires. By 1914, nearly all of Africa was under the control of only seven European powers (Belgium, Britain, France, Germany, Italy, Portugal, and Spain); in all of the Far East and the Pacific only Siam (Thailand), China, and Japan remained outside the direct control of Europe or the United States. But even China had been divided into spheres of influence by foreign powers, and Japan itself had adopted an imperialist program with the acquisition of Korea and Formosa (Taiwan). In the Western Hemisphere the United States expanded across its continent, acquired Puerto Rico from Spain, extended its colonial reach westward to Hawaii and the Philippines, leased the Panama Canal Zone "in perpetuity" from the new state of Panama (an American creation), and came to exercise considerable political leverage over several Caribbean lands, notably Cuba. The British Empire, built by the preeminent imperial power of the era, symbolized the imperial wave that in a single generation engulfed the world: By 1900 it covered a fifth of the earth's land area and comprised perhaps a quarter of its population (Cohen, 1973: 30). It was an empire on which the sun, indeed, never did set.

In contrast with classical imperialism, the new imperialism of the late nineteenth century was marked by extraordinary competition among the imperial powers, for whom colonies became an important symbol of national power and prestige. In the course of this competition the local inhabitants of the conquered lands were often ruthlessly suppressed. As Benjamin Cohen explained in his book *The Question of Imperialism*:

> The imperial powers typically pursued their various interests overseas in a blatantly aggressive fashion. Bloody, one-sided wars with local inhabitants of contested territories were commonplace; "sporting wars," Bismarck once called them. The powers themselves rarely came into direct military conflict, but competition among them was keen, and they were perpetually involved in various diplomatic crises. In contrast to the preceding

---

3. According to George Modelski (1978), four states have played a dominant role in the management of world affairs since 1500 and therefore fit the description of a world power: Portugal, the Netherlands, Britain, and the United States. Modelski considers Britain to have obtained world power status twice in separate periods during the *long cycle* of the global system. A long cycle describes the rise to the preponderant position of one state and the concomitant decline of its predecessor. Each wave or stage in the cycle of world leadership and governance is estimated to take more than one hundred years (Thompson, 1983).

years of comparative political calm, the period after 1870 was one of unaccustomed hostility and tension. (Cohen, 1973: 30)

Numerous explanations of the causes of the new imperialism have been offered. They include Marxist interpretations, such as V. I. Lenin's famous monograph *Imperialism, The Highest Stage of Capitalism*, which viewed imperialism as the "monopoly stage of capitalism." In general, these interpretations saw capitalism's need for profitable overseas outlets for surplus capital ("finance capital") as a cause of imperialism. From the Marxist perspective, the only way to end imperialism was to abolish capitalism. The Marxists' explanations of imperialism differed from those of the classical or liberal economists, who regarded the new imperialism as "not a product of capitalism as such, but rather a response to certain maladjustments within the contemporary capitalist system which, given the proper will, could be corrected" (Cohen, 1973).

Nonetheless, both the Marxist and liberal economists believed that the new imperialism was based mainly on economic considerations:

The fundamental problem was in the presumed material needs of advanced capitalist societies—the need for cheap raw materials to feed their growing industrial complexes, for additional markets to consume their rising levels of production, and for investment outlets to absorb their rapidly accumulating capital. The rush for colonies was supposed to be the response of these capitalist societies to one or another of these material needs. (Cohen, 1973: 34–35; see this source for an elaboration and critique of various economic interpretations of imperialism.)

More recently, world system analysts have argued that imperialism, specifically the expansion of the British Empire in Africa in the last quarter of the nineteenth century, was encouraged by the need of the hegemonic core state to maintain its privileged position in the international division of labor in the face of growing competition from the newly emerging core states of Germany and the United States (McGowan, 1981).

This new imperialism can also be explained by political factors. In particular, it can be traced to the jockeying for power and prestige characteristic of the balance-of-power international political system that governed relations among the European powers for more than two centuries following the Peace of Westphalia. During the nineteenth century in particular, Britain had ensured the effective operation of the European balance of power by acting as the "balancer," that is, by throwing its superior military power behind one or another of the other European states threatened by conquest so as to guarantee that none would achieve hegemony on the continent.

By 1870, however, Britain's superiority was on the wane. Germany emerged on the continent as a powerful industrial nation, as did the United States in the Western Hemisphere. The rise of modern nationalism—which implied not only a sense of identification with and pride in the nation-state but also the quest for power and national self-fulfillment—further inhibited Britain's balancer role by reducing the flexibility that foreign policy decision makers had traditionally enjoyed in choosing their friends and enemies. The Franco-Prussian War of 1870–1871 symbolized the growing importance of industrial might and nationalistic sentiment. Moreover, Germany's annexation of the French territory of Alsace-Lorraine in 1871 intensified Franco-German antagonisms in a way that prevented the normalization of their relations. The stage was being set for the catastrophe of 1914.

As the European powers competed for power and prestige, not in Europe, but in Asia and Africa, their political domination led to economic domination and exploitation.[4]

> As in the days of mercantilism, colonies were integrated into an international economic system which was designed to serve the economic interest of the metropole [colonial power]. The political victors controlled investment and trade, regulated currency and production, and manipulated labor, thus establishing structures of economic dependency in their colonies which would endure far longer than their actual political authority. (Spero, 1985: 7–8)

Until the outbreak of World War I, the laissez-faire system of free international trade promoted by Britain contributed to rapid economic growth in many colonial territories (Higgins and Higgins, 1979). But Western Europe, North America, Australia, and New Zealand were also able during this period to complete their industrial revolutions and to advance as industrial societies, thus giving rise to the gap between the rich nations of the North and the poor nations of the South so evident today. In the years following World War I the economies of both the North and the South stagnated as all were engulfed in a worldwide depression. But there was an important difference between them, in that most of the countries of the North remained at a high level of income, for already by the time of the Great Depression in the 1930s it was evident that Western Europe, North America, and Australasia were rich and that the rest of the world was poor (Higgins and Higgins, 1979).

On the political front, the period between the First and Second World Wars saw little movement toward the breakup of the colonial empires amassed in previous centuries. The principle of national self-determination, espoused by

---

4. Within the European subsystem itself, the trend was more toward the disintegration of political units into smaller ones than their integration into larger ones, as was occurring elsewhere in the world. (The unification of Germany and Italy are the principal exceptions.) Europe consisted of about fifteen sovereign states in 1871, approximately twenty-five by the outbreak of World War I, and over thirty by the 1930s. The increase in the number of political entities was due partly to the independence movements created by rising nationalistic aspirations and was fueled by the goal of national self-determination, a pattern for expanding the number of states that was emulated worldwide after World War II. See Bergesen and Schoenberg (1980) for an empirical examination of the waves of colonial expansion and contraction between 1415 and 1969.

President Woodrow Wilson in justifying American participation in World War I, was incorporated into the Versailles peace settlement. This principle meant that nationalities would have the right to determine which authority would represent and rule them. This freedom of choice was expected to lead to the formation of nations and governments content with their territorial boundaries and therefore less inclined to make war. In practice, however, the principle was applied almost exclusively to war-torn Europe, where six new states were created from the territory of the former Austro-Hungarian Empire (Czechoslovakia, Romania, Yugoslavia, Poland, Austria, and Hungary). Territorial adjustments were made elsewhere in Europe, many guided by the outcome of popular plebiscites. But the proposition that self-determination ought to be extended to the European colonial empires was not seriously considered.

Interestingly, however, the colonial territories of the powers defeated in World War I were not simply parceled out among the victorious allies. Instead, following the insistence of President Wilson, the territories controlled by Germany and the Ottoman Empire were transferred under League of Nations auspices to countries that would govern them as mandates pending their eventual self-rule. In the Middle East, France was given the mandate for Syria, and Great Britain was given the mandate for Iraq, Transjordan, and Palestine. In Africa, most of the German colony of Tanganyika was mandated to Britain; the West African colonies of Cameroons and Togoland were divided between Britain and France; and the Union of South Africa was given the mandate for German South-West Africa. In the Pacific area, Australia, New Zealand, and Japan were given jurisdiction over the former German colonies.

Many of these territorial decisions were destined to shape political conflicts for the next half-century or more. Principal among them were the decisions relating to the Middle East and Africa, in which the League of Nations called for the eventual creation of a Jewish national homeland in Palestine and arranged for the transfer of control over South-West Africa (now called Namibia) to what was to become the white minority regime of South Africa.

The principle implicit in the mandate system was also significant. The system represented the beginning of the idea that "colonies were a trust rather than simply a property to be exploited and treated as if its peoples had no right of their own" (Easton, 1964). The fact that none of Germany's former colonies or provinces was annexed outright following World War I set an important precedent for the negotiations after World War II, when territories placed under the trusteeship system of the United Nations not only were not annexed but also were given assurances of eventual independence.

In the 1930s and early 1940s the world was challenged by the expansionist drives of Germany, Japan, and Italy. With their defeat in World War II, the threat of worldwide empire building receded (although the threat of worldwide destruction increased with the advent of nuclear weapons), and the trend toward increasing the number of independent political units in the global arena gained momentum. As noted earlier, in the space of a few short decades, more than a hundred new nations, representing perhaps three-quarters of humanity, gained their freedom in a demonstration of political emancipation unprecedented in recorded history.

The postcolonial era began in earnest in 1947, when the British relinquished political control of the Indian subcontinent and India and Pakistan became sovereign members of the international community. War eventually erupted between the new states as each sought to gain control over disputed territory in Kashmir, and it erupted again in 1965 and 1971 (when East Pakistan broke away from West Pakistan to form the new state of Bangladesh). Violent conflict also broke out in Indochina and Algeria during the 1950s and early 1960s, as the French sought to reaffirm political control over colonial territories they had held before World War II. Bloodshed also followed closely on the heels of independence in the Congo (later Zaire) when the Belgians granted their African colony independence in 1960, and it dogged the efforts of Portugal to battle unsuccessfully the winds of decolonization that swept over Africa as the 1960s wore on.

For the most part, however, decolonization was not only a remarkably rapid process, but the actual transfer of political control from the European metropolitan powers to their former colonial territories was also remarkably peaceful. This was arguably due to the fact that the economic and military vitality of many of the colonial powers had been sapped by the ravages of World War II. A growing appreciation of the costs of empire may also have been a contributing factor. More importantly, colonialism became an increasingly unacceptable form of political organization in a world increasingly characterized by rivalry between East and West, in which competition for political allies and fear of large-scale warfare militated against efforts to suppress revolution in the empire. Decolonization "triumphed," Inis Claude (1967) has written, "largely because the West [gave] priority to the containment of Communism over the perpetuation of colonialism."

Claude (1967) has also pointed to the role played by the United Nations in the "collective delegitimization" of colonialism. With colonialism already in retreat, Third World nations in 1960 took advantage of their growing numbers to secure passage of the historic Declaration on the Granting of Independence to Colonial Countries and Peoples. In it the UN General Assembly

> proclaimed that the subjection of any people to alien domination was a denial of fundamental human rights, contrary to the UN Charter, and an impediment to world peace and that all subject peoples had a right to immediate and complete independence. No country cast a vote against this anticolonial manifesto. . . . It was an ideological triumph. The old order had not merely been challenged and defeated in the field—its adherents were no longer willing to be counted in its defense. (Riggs and Plano, 1988: 228)

As the old order crumbled, the North–South conflict between the rich nations of the First World and the newly emancipated nations of the Third World took shape and began to nose its way onto the global agenda as Third World political elites found that political freedom did not translate automatically into political autonomy, economic independence, and domestic well-being.

PROFILES AND PROJECTIONS: GLOBAL DISPARITIES IN INCOME AND WEALTH

The poverty of the South is reflected in and caused by the maldistribution of the world's wealth and its people. As noted earlier, the more than three-quarters of humanity who live in the South account for only about one-fifth of the world's aggregate gross national product, whereas those in the North, making up less than a quarter of the population, account for nearly 80 percent of the world's goods and services. On a per-person basis, this means that the average annual income for the Third World as a whole is less than $3,500 and that the average income for the First (Western industrialized) and Second (socialist) Worlds is well in excess of this amount.

Averages can, of course, be misleading, but differences in wealth are none-theless real. The following describes what these differences mean:

> A child born in the United States will consume thirty to fifty times as many goods in his or her lifetime as one born in the highlands of Bolivia. . . . Rich is what we are when we are consuming thirty times as much as someone else—and that someone is managing to stay alive. Add a grain of salt to the statistics—add enough salt to take care of any quibbles about differing life expectancies or faulty measuring techniques—and say that our wealth exceeds that of the average Bolivian peasant by a ratio of twenty to one. (*New Yorker*, May 16, 1983: 32)

Figure 5.1 and Table 5.1 depict these discrepancies in the distribution of the world's people and its wealth. Figure 5.1 is a particularly compelling illustration of how lopsided the world is, with its greatest mass of people in the South and its greatest concentration of wealth in the North. Yet the actual discrepancies are much greater than either this picture or these numbers suggest. One study puts the average per-capita income in 1985 of thirty-two developed countries (those with both per-capita incomes of at least $3,500 annually and high standards of living[5]), comprising less than a quarter of the world's population, at $10,169. By contrast, the per-capita income of 144 developing countries (those with either per-capita incomes below $4,130 or low standards of living), comprising the rest of the world's population, was only $720 (Sewell and Tucker, 1988: 246).

LEAST-DEVELOPED COUNTRIES Included among these 144 countries are those regarded by the Organization for Economic Cooperation and Development

---

5. Living standards are measured by the Physical Quality of Life Index (PQLI), discussed later in this chapter.

FIGURE 5.1 ■

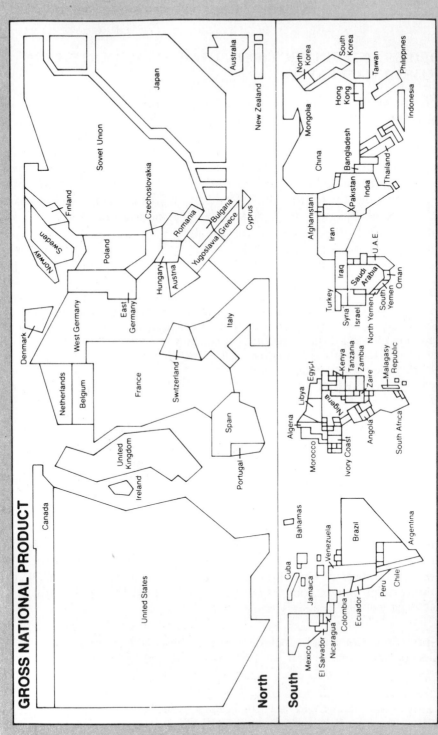

GROSS NATIONAL PRODUCT

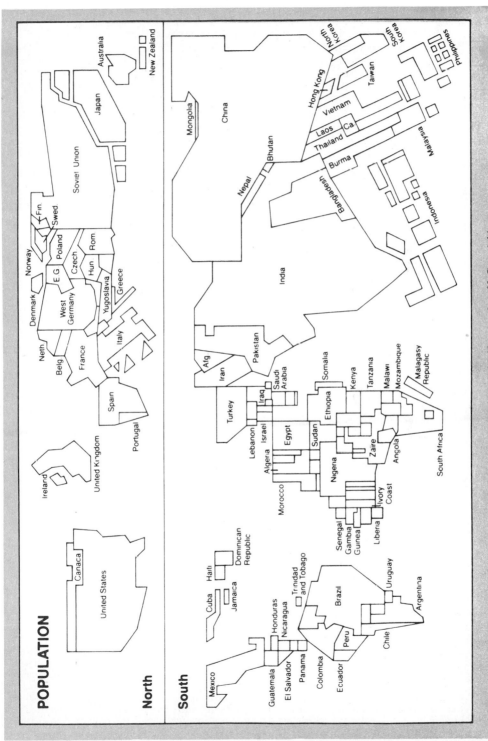

POPULATION

North

South

Source: *Newsweek* October 26, 1981. Charts by Marta Norman, Richard Tringali—*Newsweek* p. 38. Copyright 1981, by Newsweek, Inc. All rights reserved. Reprinted by permission.

TABLE 5.1 ■ The Geographic Distribution of World Population and Per-Capita Gross National Product, 1985

Region or Country[a]	GNP per Capita (U.S. $)[b]	Population (millions)
North America	16,135	264.2
Japan	11,330	120.6
Oceania	8,380	24.0
Western Europe	7,947	377.0
Eastern Europe and the Soviet Union	7,360	390.6
North Africa and the Near East	1,926	218.5
Central America and the Caribbean	1,835	124.6
South America	1,644	265.8
Africa south of the Sahara	570	390.3
Asia (excluding Japan)	382	2,405.0

Source: Adapted from *World Bank Atlas 1987* (Washington, D.C.: World Bank, 1987), pp. 6–9. Data for Eastern Europe and the Soviet Union are adapted from *Handbook of Economic Statistics 1986* (Washington, D.C.: U.S. Central Intelligence Agency, 1986), pp. 35, 55.

[a]Data are not available for the following geopolitical entities: Afghanistan, Albania, Angola, Chad, Cuba, Djibouti, Equatorial Guinea, Iran, Iraq, Kampuchea, Laos, Lebanon, Mongolia, Mozambique, Namibia, North Korea, Reunion, Seychelles, Taiwan, Uganda, Vietnam.

[b]All data are in current dollars.

(OECD) as the "least developed" of the less-developed countries (LLDCs). Nearly two-thirds are in Africa; most of the rest are in Asia. As a group, their average per-capita income in 1985 was only $311.[6] In addition, they tend to

---

6. This figure is based on the thirty-one nations for which data are available, as reported in the *World Bank Atlas 1987* (1987: 6–9). The calculations reported elsewhere in this chapter use data from this source or from previous editions of the *Atlas*, unless otherwise noted.

Caution must be used in interpreting per-capita income figures, because they tend to understate the value of goods and services actually produced and consumed in poorer societies. It is absurd, for example, to think that a Tanzanian could actually live on an income of only $270 a year. Part of the problem is that the GNP measures only those goods and services that enter a society's monetary sector. Yet in many developing societies much economic activity exists outside the exchange economy, particularly in the agricultural sector, where there is much production and consumption that never enter the monetary marketplace (through barter, for instance). The problem is compounded by the fact that gross national products valued in domestic currencies are typically converted for international comparative purposes to a single currency unit, such as the United States dollar, using fixed rates of exchange (the rate at which one currency can be exchanged for another). Because exchange rates do not account for differences in a currency's purchasing power in different countries, cross-national comparisons of income probably overstate the magnitude of the difference between the world's rich and poor. Despite all of these difficulties, per-capita GNP remains the best single indicator available for making intercountry income comparisons.

have only a small amount of manufacturing in their GNP (which means a large agricultural component) and a low literacy level, often with less than a quarter of the adult population being able to read and write. These countries are among the candidates for designation as the *Fourth World*.

OIL-EXPORTING COUNTRIES The poverty of the LLDCs stands in stark contrast with many of the world's oil-exporting nations, whose oil price increases during the 1970s compounded the problems of other developing economies. In 1985 the average per-capita income of eighteen oil-exporting nations stood at $4,086, and the average income of the somewhat smaller group of OPEC nations (Organization of Petroleum Exporting Countries) was $7,015.[7] Even among the OPEC nations, however, there are great disparities in income. Indonesia and Nigeria are at one end of the spectrum, with 1985 per-capita incomes of $530 and $760, respectively, and Qatar and the United Arab Emirates are at the other end, with 1985 per-capita incomes of $15,980 and $19,120, respectively, the latter figure far surpassing even the $16,400 income of the average American citizen. In part the differences among the OPEC nations reflect not only the high concentration of rich oil deposits in the Middle East but also the much larger populations of Indonesia and Nigeria, as compared with those of the Middle Eastern oil-exporting countries. For all the oil exporters, however, perhaps most notable is not how high their incomes are compared with those of other Third World countries but how far they have plunged as worldwide oil prices nose-dived in the mid-1980s. The average income of the members of OPEC dropped some 23 percent between 1981 and 1985, but for particular members, such as Kuwait, for which the drop was nearly 45 percent, the effect of the global plunge in oil prices was even more dramatic.

NEWLY INDUSTRIALIZED COUNTRIES A third important group among the Third World are those countries that have realized very rapid growth in their manufacturing sectors and have become important exporters of manufactures. The composition of this group, known as the *Newly Industrialized Countries* (NICs), varies somewhat depending on the criteria used. Argentina, Brazil, Mexico, South Korea, Taiwan, Singapore, and the British crown colony of Hong Kong are generally included, and Spain, Portugal, Yugoslavia, and Greece are also sometimes included. As a group, the Newly Industrialized Countries are essentially upper-middle-income countries, with annual per-

---

7. OPEC consists of Algeria, Ecuador, Gabon, Indonesia, Iran, Iraq, Kuwait, Libya, Nigeria, Qatar, Saudi Arabia, United Arab Emirates, and Venezuela. The calculations exclude Iran and Iraq, for whom data are not available.

The International Monetary Fund, whose definitions we have adopted for these generalizations, considers countries to be fuel exporters if their fuel exports, on the basis of 1980 data, account for 50 percent or more of their exports. On this basis, the oil exporters consist of the thirteen OPEC members plus Oman, Bahrain, the People's Democratic Republic of the Congo, Mexico, Syria, Trinidad and Tobago, and Tunisia.

capita incomes in 1985 ranging from $1,640 (Brazil) to $7,420 (Singapore). Moreover, they have experienced substantial increases in their annual per-capita incomes, with the growth rate for some of them in excess of 7 percent in real (that is, not inflated) dollars for the 1973–1985 period (*World Bank Atlas 1987*, 1987: 6–9). As a result of their rapid economic growth, the NICs have become not only important exporters of manufactured goods (such as consumer electronics) in the global marketplace but also important markets for the major industrial countries that export capital goods.

The important point about the NICs' rapid economic growth rate is that it means that the economies of many of them have expanded more rapidly than have their populations. This is essential if developing nations are to advance economically and to provide a better standard of living for their people.

The impact of population growth on the economic prospects of developing societies is crucial to understanding the gap between the world's rich and poor. Although developed and developing nations alike have experienced unprecedented economic growth since World War II, the developing nations as a whole have typically had higher growth rates, in part as a consequence of the lower bases from which they began. The average annual growth rate of the developing countries' economic output (as measured by real growth in gross domestic product) between 1965 and 1973, for example, was 6.3 percent, compared with less than 5 percent among the developed nations. The difference was even greater between 1973 and 1980, when the developing countries grew at an average rate of 5.4 percent, compared with the less than 3 percent among the industrialized countries (*World Development Report 1987*, 1987: 16). Despite this dramatic performance (which, incidentally, was sharply curtailed between 1981 and 1985), the gap between the world's rich and poor has continued to widen, largely because of the much higher population growth of the developing nations.

The often untoward economic, social, and, ultimately, political consequences of excessive population growth are explored in detail in Chapter 9. Here we note only the wide diversity in the economic experience and performance of Third World countries, which is often correlated with (but not exclusively so) wide variations in population growth. David Morawetz describes this diversity:

> On one hand nine countries, with a combined population of 930 million people in 1975, grew at an average annual rate of 4.2 percent or better for the full period [1950 to 1975], and a second group of nine countries, with 220 million people, grew at between 3 and 4 percent. On the other hand, the large, poor countries of South Asia and many countries in Africa, with a total of some 1.1 billion people, grew in per capita income by less than 2 percent a year between 1950 and 1975. Thus, although it is true that per capita income has roughly trebled for some 33 percent of the people of the developing world during the past twenty-five years, it is also true that for another 40 percent the increase in per capita income has been only one or two dollars. (Morawetz, 1977: 13–14)

These annual increments of one and two dollars in income for many of the world's poor lie at the heart of the fact that the gap between the world's rich and poor is not only huge but widening. This can be readily understood by contemplating the importance of the differences between the base levels at which the world's rich and poor begin. Consider, for example, the difference between a 5 percent income increase for a person earning $1,000 a year and a person earning $10,000 a year. In the first case, the increase is $50, but in the second it is ten times greater, and the absolute difference between the two has widened by $450. Internationally this means that each year's per-capita income increase in the United States is equivalent to about a *century's* increase in Bangladesh or India (Morawetz, 1977: 29).[8]

The widening absolute gap between rich and poor has become most apparent since World War II. One estimate (Brown, 1972: 42) puts the ratio between incomes in the industrializing societies of Western Europe and the rest of the world in 1850 at roughly two to one. By 1950 the gap had opened to ten to one, and by 1960 to nearly fifteen to one. In more concrete terms, the per-capita income (in uninflated 1980 dollars) of the average American grew from $7,000 in 1955 to $11,500 in 1980. In India, the corresponding figures were $170 in 1955 and $260 in 1980 (McNamara, 1984: 1121). Thus what had been a gap of under $7,000 in 1955 grew to more than $11,000 twenty-five years later. Projected another quarter century hence, we would expect the income of an average American early in the twenty-first century to approach $20,000, but that of an average Indian to be only about $400—a ratio in this particular case of roughly fifty to one. Even though developing nations generally are projected to grow more rapidly between now and the turn of the century, the widening gap between India and the United States will be repeated many times over in other intercountry comparisons.

Narrowing the economic gap between the rich and poor countries requires that the poor continue to grow economically more rapidly than do the rich. Yet only twenty-two developing nations fit this requirement on the basis of their performance from 1960 to 1975. Even if these rates are assumed to remain constant, only a small proportion of these twenty-two nations, as shown in Table 5.2, has a chance of actually closing the gap within a reasonable time. For most the process would take literally hundreds or thousands of years,

---

8. Morawetz also points out, however, that a 1 or 2 percent increase in income in Bangladesh or India probably does more to increase economic welfare than does a similar increase in the United States. This observation reflects the important concept of *marginal utility*, which suggests that at low income levels the net addition to welfare of a given dollar increment is much greater than at higher income levels. More generally, the law of diminishing marginal utility says that each additional unit of income (or unit of resource) will be used to satisfy a less pressing need than will the last unit of income. In other words, people satisfy their most pressing needs first. Because many people in developing societies have not been able to meet many of their pressing needs, a unit increase in income is likely to have a much greater impact on welfare, that is, to have greater marginal utility, than will a similar increase in a developed country. See Russett (1978) for evidence consistent with this argument as it relates to life expectancy and infant mortality within and across nations.

TABLE 5.2 ■ The Gap Between Rich and Poor Nations: Can It Be Closed?[a]

Country[b]	GNP per Capita, 1975 (1974 U.S. $)	Annual Growth Rate, 1960–1975 (%)	No. Years Until Gap Closes If 1960–1975 Growth Rates Continue
OECD countries	5,238	3.7	–
Libyan Arab Republic	4,675	11.8	2
Saudi Arabia	2,767	8.6	14
Singapore	2,307	7.6	22
Israel	3,287	5.0	37
Iran	1,321	6.9	45
Hong Kong	1,584	6.3	48
Korea	504	7.3	69
China (Taiwan)	817	6.3	75
Iraq	1,180	4.4	223
Brazil	927	4.2	362
Thailand	319	4.5	365
Tunisia	695	4.2	422
Syrian Arab Republic	604	4.2	451
Lesotho	161	4.5	454
Turkey	793	4.0	675
Togo	245	4.1	807
Panama	977	3.8	1,866
Malawi	137	3.9	1,920
Malaysia	665	3.8	2,293
Papua New Guinea	412	3.8	2,826
China, People's Republic of	320	3.8	2,900
Mauritania	288	3.8	3,224

Source: From John W. Sewell and Stuart K. Tucker, and contributors, *Growth, Jobs, and Exports in a Changing World Economy: Agenda 1988* (New Brunswick, N.J.: Transaction Books). © 1988 the Overseas Development Council, p. 220. Reprinted with permission.

[a]Absolute gap is the GNP per capita of the OECD countries ($2,378 in 1950, $5,238 in 1975), less the GNP per capita of the individual country.

[b]All developing countries with population of 1 million or more whose growth rate of per-capita income exceeded that of the OECD countries from 1960 to 1975. OECD stands for the Organization for Economic Cooperation and Development. Its members are Australia, Austria, Belgium, Canada, Denmark, Finland, France, Greece, Iceland, Ireland, Italy, Japan, Luxembourg, the Netherlands, New Zealand, Norway, Portugal, Spain, Sweden, Switzerland, Turkey, the United Kingdom, the United States, and West Germany. For purposes of this table, Greece, Portugal, Spain, and Turkey are not considered members of the OECD.

which is obviously not a realistic economic or political goal. But as Morawetz points out:

> Fortunately, there are compelling reasons to believe that most developing countries will not place the closing of the gap at the center of their aspirations. First, not all of them regard the resource-wasting life style of the developed countries as an end toward which it is worth striving; at least some seem to prefer to create their own development patterns based on their own resources, needs, and traditions. Second, when thinking of the per capita income that they would like to attain, most people (and governments) tend to think of the income of a close-by reference group. . . . [Most] people in poor countries do not regard the rich foreigners as part of their reference group and hence are not overconcerned with the gap. They are more concerned, it seems, with their own internal income distributions and their own place within them. (Morawetz, 1977: 30)

Others may dispute this conclusion, particularly given the ability of modern communications systems to bring the enormous international discrepancies in wealth to the attention of the world's poorest people. "What is happening," Indira Gandhi noted in 1982, is that the impoverished "see their poverty . . . with much sharper eyes. Before they tolerated it; today they say 'Why should we tolerate it?' " Moreover, as Morawetz notes, elites in the developing countries are usually more concerned, than are poorer people, with the gap in wealth between nations. Because these elites are the ones with whom the governments of rich nations must deal, this gap cannot be ignored as an international issue.

MEASURING ECONOMIC DEVELOPMENT AND STANDARDS OF LIVING   Gross national product, per-capita GNP, and their growth rates have been the traditional measures used to assess the progress of economic development. It is apparent, however, that these measures offer a far too narrow description of the concept of development. For example, even though developing nations as a whole have realized enormous per-capita income gains since World War II, this indicator fails to show that not everyone has enjoyed the fruits of progress because it cannot tell how evenly or unevenly income is spread among its members.[9] Other factors must therefore be considered in weighing progress

---

9. Widespread poverty within countries tends to be associated with extremely high concentrations of wealth in the hands of a few. In Liberia in the mid-1970s, for example, the richest 5 percent of the population is estimated to have controlled nearly 60 percent of the country's national income, whereas the poorest 20 percent received but 13 percent. This distribution can be compared with that of the United States, in which the richest 5 percent received 13.3 percent of American income and the poorest 20 percent received 6.7 percent (Kurian, 1979: 85–86). More generally, Amin (1987: 1132) estimates that only 10 percent of the population in developing countries disposes of 25 percent of total income, compared with 50 percent of the population in developed nations, and that only a third of the population in developing nations dispose of half of total income, compared with 75 percent of the population in developed nations.

See Lewis and Kallab (1983: 228) and the *World Development Report 1987* (1987: 252–253) for supporting data on the income distribution in selected countries.

toward the reduction of poverty—for example, improving the distribution of income within societies, increasing employment for everyone, and fulfilling basic human needs, including access to food, water, housing, health and health care, education, and employment (see Box 5.1 for a personal perspective on the human dimensions of poverty).

As development strategists shifted their attention in recent years to meeting basic human needs, the need for alternatives to income measures for assessing the standard of living (particularly the level of physical well-being) in different countries became especially compelling. In response to this need, the Washington-based Overseas Development Council (ODC), a private research organization, developed a Physical Quality of Life Index (PQLI) which uses various social indicators to assess progress in meeting basic human needs. The PQLI is based on an average life expectancy at age one, infant mortality, and literacy rates. The higher the score is, the more favorable will be a country's social performance.[10] The Overseas Development Council classifies a *developed* country as one that in 1985 had a per-capita income of at least $4,130 and a high standard of living as indicated by a PQLI of 90 or more.[11] A *developing* country is one with either a 1985 per-capita income below $4,130 or a PQLI score of less than 90. Hence, the oil-rich nations of OPEC are developing societies, for despite their often substantial per-capita incomes, none achieves a PQLI score of 90.

Table 5.3 lists the PQLI scores and the data on which they are based for several different countries falling into different income groups. This information indicates that widely varying levels of social performance are possible, regardless of the income group into which a particular country falls. Sri Lanka is a particularly striking case. In income, it is among the poorest countries in the world, but its standard of living as measured by the PQLI is higher than that of most upper-middle-income countries. Similarly, Cuba's PQLI compares favorably with the world's richest nations, but its GNP per capita places it in the lower-middle-income group. On the other hand, Algeria (a member of OPEC) has a PQLI below that of the low-income countries.

---

10. The PQLI is calculated as follows:
   Each of the components [of PQLI] is indexed on a scale of 0 (the most unfavorable performance in 1950) to 100 (the best performance expected by the end of the century as estimated in 1978). For life expectancy at age one, the most favorable figure expected to be achieved by any country by the year 2000 (77 years) is valued at 100 and the most unfavorable performance in 1950 (38 years in Guinea-Bissau) at 0. Similarly, for infant mortality, the best performance expected by the year 2000 (7 per thousand) is rated 100 and the poorest performance in 1950 (229 per thousand in Gabon) is rated 0. Literacy figures (being percentages) are automatically on a 0 to 100 scale. The composite index, the PQLI, is calculated by averaging the three indexes (life expectancy, infant mortality, and literacy), giving equal weight to each of them. With both the low and the high values stable, movement is toward a fixed rather than a changing target; future improvement or deterioration in social conditions therefore will show up as increases or decreases in PQLI. (McLaughlin, 1979: 132)

11. Although Barbados, Brunei, Hong Kong, Netherlands Antilles, Singapore, and Trinidad and Tobago each have a per-capita GNP in excess of $4,170 and a PQLI of at least 90, the Overseas Development Council considers them to be in a transitional stage of development and therefore classifies them as "advanced developing countries."

BOX 5.1 ■ An American Student Discovers the Meaning of the Third World

"I spent the first 24 years of my life in South Carolina. When I left . . . for Colombia [South America], I fully expected Bogota to be like any large U.S. city, only with citizens who spoke Spanish. When I arrived there I found my expectations were wrong. I was not in the U.S., I was on Mars! I was a victim of culture shock. As a personal experience this shock was occasionally funny and sometimes sad. But after all the laughing and the crying were over, it forced me to reevaluate both my life and the society in which I live.

"Colombia is a poor country by American standards. It has a per capita GNP of $550 and a very unequal distribution of income. These were the facts that I knew before I left.

"But to 'know' these things intellectually is much different from experiencing firsthand how they affect people's lives. It is one thing to lecture in air conditioned classrooms about the problems of world poverty. It is quite another to see four-year-old children begging or sleeping in the streets.

"It tore me apart emotionally to see the reality of what I had studied for so long: 'low per capita GNP and maldistribution of income.' What this means in human terms is children with dirty faces who beg for bread money or turn into pickpockets because the principle of private property gets blurred by empty stomachs.

"It means other children whose minds and bodies will never develop fully because they were malnourished as infants. It means cripples who can't even turn to thievery and must beg to stay alive. It means street vendors who sell candy and cigarettes 14 hours a day in order to feed their families.

"It also means well-dressed businessmen and petty bureaucrats who indifferently pass this poverty every day as they seek asylum in their fortified houses to the north of the city.

"It means rich people who prefer not to see the poor, except for their maids and security guards.

"It means foreigners like me who have come to Colombia and spend more in one month than the average Colombian earns in a year.

"It means politicians across the ideological spectrum who are so full of abstract solutions or personal greed that they forget that it is real people they are dealing with.

"Somewhere within the polemics of the politicians and the 'objectivity' of the social scientists, the human being has been lost."

Source: Brian Wallace, extracted from "True Grit South of the Border," OSCEOLA, January 13, 1978, pp. 15–16.

TABLE 5.3 ■ Economic and Social Indicators of Selected Countries

Income Category[a]	Per-Capita GNP 1985 ($)	Physical Quality of Life Index (PQLI) 1985	Life Expectancy at Birth (years)	Infant Mortality (per 1,000 births)	Literacy (%)
Low-income	279	64	60	73	55
China	310	80	69	35	69
Guinea-Bissau	180	29	39	138	31
India	270	55	56	89	44
Sri Lanka	380	87	70	36	87
Lower-middle-income	724	65	58	84	67
Cuba[b]	960	98	77	16	96
Philippines	580	79	63	48	86
Yemen, Arab Rep.	550	28	45	154	14
Zimbabwe	680	67	57	77	74
Upper-middle-income	2,133	78	66	55	79
Algeria	2,550	62	61	81	50
Korea, Rep.	2,150	88	69	27	92
Mexico	2,080	84	67	50	90
Tunisia	1,190	66	63	78	54
High-income	10,180	95	74	16	97
Czechoslovakia[b]	8,280	93	70	15	99
Kuwait	14,480	84	72	22	70
Sweden	11,890	99	77	6	99
United States	16,690	98	76	11	99

Source: Adapted from John W. Sewell and Stuart K. Tucker, and contributors, *Growth, Jobs, and Exports in a Changing World Economy: Agenda 1988* (New Brunswick, N.J.: Transaction Books). © 1988 the Overseas Development Council, pp. 246–257. Used with permission.

[a]Countries are grouped into income categories according to the following criteria: *low-income*, a per-capita GNP of less than $470; *lower-middle-income*, $470 to $1,189; *upper-middle-income*, $1,190 to $4,129; and *high-income*, $4,130 and up.

[b]Figure is for 1984.

An intriguing question is whether differences in the character of political regimes account for these cross-national variations in individual welfare. There are three basic ways that political processes are believed to affect differences in individual welfare: through the strength of the state apparatus, through democratic political processes, and through the ideological orientation of ruling elites (Moon and Dixon, 1985). Each is in fact related to variations in the welfare of individuals in different national settings as measured by the PQLI. ''Democratic processes are related to positive welfare outcomes irrespective of state strength and ideological norms. For regimes with a roughly centrist ideology, state strength appears to make little noticeable difference one way or another; for those on the left, state strength promotes welfare performance; for those on the right, state strength [inhibits] the provision of basic needs" (Moon and Dixon, 1985).

Overall, however, the strongest association is between wealth and living standards as measured by per-capita GNP and PQLI. This general pattern is illustrated by the PQLI map of the world shown in Figure 5.2. Note in particular that the highest living standards as measured by PQLI tend to be in the Northern Hemisphere, where per-capita incomes are also generally high, whereas the Southern Hemisphere countries generally have lower standards of living, with many appearing at the poverty end of the spectrum (those illustrated in black).[12] This is especially the case for many African nations south of the Sahara and for several South and Southeast Asian nations, including many earlier described as the least developed of the developing nations or Fourth World countries.

The foregoing hints at the complexity of the development process. Raising a people's economic and social well-being involves the interaction of political, social, economic, and cultural factors, ranging from the level of resource endowment and the extent of industrialization to cultural norms regarding family size and the ability and willingness of governments to make difficult and often politically costly decisions. The relations between rich and poor nations within the framework of the international political and economic system also have a bearing on development.

Impediments to Growth in a Typical Developing Country

We can better understand the political dispute between the North and South if we isolate some of the factors underlying the persistent underdevelopment that is today the plight of so many nations. Hans Singer and Javed Ansari (1988) identify high rates of population growth, low levels of income, and technological dependence as salient factors linked to several other considerations.

HIGH POPULATION GROWTH   High population growth was identified as the single most important factor underlying the widening gap between rich nations and poor. Among other things, higher birthrates mean that developing nations generally have a far larger proportion of young people in their societies than do developed nations. "This means that the poor countries have to devote much more of their resources to the task of raising a new generation of

---

12. Social indicators such as the PQLI have been criticized by some because they rely heavily on quantitative data whose quality is often notoriously poor. Reliable statistics on such basics as nutrition, fertility, and even death rates are virtually nonexistent for the rural poor in many developing nations. The problem is compounded in the case of authoritarian and totalitarian regimes, whose governments often hide their domestic situations from outside scrutiny.

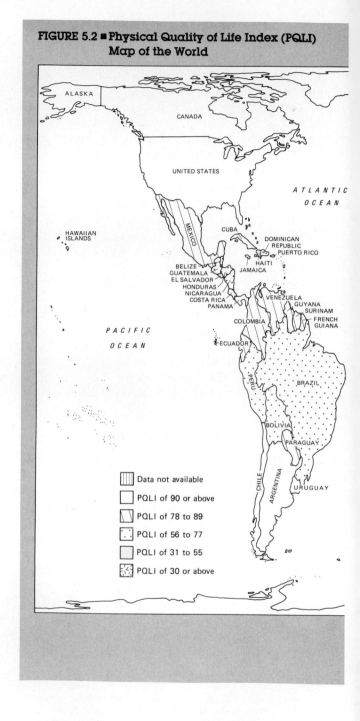

FIGURE 5.2 ■ Physical Quality of Life Index (PQLI) Map of the World

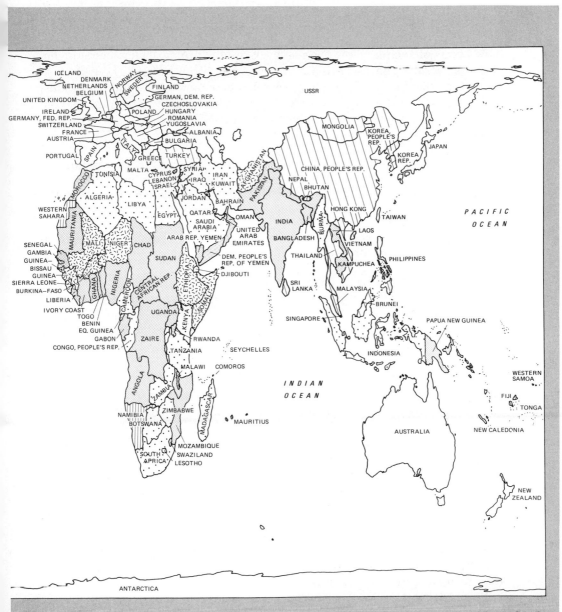

Source: Adapted from John W. Sewell and Stuart K. Tucker, and contributors, *Growth, Jobs, and Exports in a Changing World Economy: Agenda 1988* (New Brunswick, N.J.: Transaction Books. Copyright © 1988 the Overseas Development Council, pp. 258–259. Used with permission.

producers, besides providing services of a given standard to an enlarged and rapidly urbanizing population" (Singer and Ansari, 1988).

LOW LEVELS OF INCOME   Low income levels are the principal characteristic that distinguishes the Third World from the First and Second Worlds. Low levels of income go hand in hand with impoverished economic and social conditions; more importantly, they also prevent poorer countries from generating enough economic surplus to make sizable investments in their future economic growth.

> New sectors of modern economic growth thus remain very small, especially in terms of employment, and are often foreign-controlled. The national economy at large remains deprived of new capital infusion. In the poor countries, agricultural production accounts for about 40–50 per cent of GNP, while in the rich countries the ratio is about 5 percent. Moreover, about three-quarters of the total population of a poor country is engaged in the agricultural sector. (Singer and Ansari, 1988: 42–43)

It is widely assumed that when so many people are engaged in the agricultural sector, many are in fact underemployed, and some perhaps are best classified as unemployed. This means, to use the economist's terms, that labor (which along with land and capital is one of the factors of production) is underutilized. But underutilization is not confined to agriculture. The underutilization of all factors of production "is a central feature of the economy of a poor country" (Singer and Ansari, 1988). Many people in the Third World find themselves deprived of meaningful employment opportunities or, more commonly, find themselves engaged in unproductive labor. Singer and Ansari suggest that the underutilization of labor is "both the cause and effect of a distortion of the consumption and investment patterns and of high and rising inequalities of income distribution." These contribute to inadequate investment in education, health, transportation facilities, credit facilities, and so forth. Without this investment in a country's socioeconomic infrastructure, the poor remain poor, and the gap between them and the rich widens.

TECHNOLOGICAL DEPENDENCE   Developing countries have not proved themselves able to evolve an indigenous technology appropriate to their own resource endowments and are thus dependent on the richer countries to meet their technological needs. This is especially true of the poorest of the poor, but it is also true of the relatively well-off Third World countries, including the oil-exporting countries, whose underdeveloped socioeconomic infrastructures impede economic growth and change.[13]

The imbalance of technological development may be described thus:

---

13. See the extensive study *Appropriate Technologies for Developing Countries*, prepared for the National Academy of Science by Richard S. Eckaus (1977), for an elaboration of some of the alternatives to technology dependence.

Almost all world expenditures on science and technology take place inside the richer countries, and research and development are therefore quite naturally directed towards solving *their* problems by methods suited to *their* circumstances and resource endowments. The problems of the poorer countries, however, are not the same; for instance, they need research to design simple products, to develop production for smaller markets, to improve the quality of and to develop new uses for tropical products, and above all to develop production processes which utilize their abundant labour. Instead, emphasis is placed on sophisticated weaponry, space research, atomic research, sophisticated products, production for large high-income markets, and specifically a constant search for processes that save labour by substituting capital or high-order skills. (Singer and Ansari, 1988: 44)[14]

The causes and especially the consequences of technological dependence are among the principal concerns of Singer's and Ansari's study, *Rich and Poor Countries*. Because developing nations want "to participate in the management of the international economy and to influence the diffusion of technology internationally," they are concerned with finding a strategy for coping with the powerful multinational corporations (MNCs) that have become the principal mechanisms for transmitting technological know-how from rich to poor.

DUALISM IN DEVELOPING SOCIETIES   Overall, the social and economic structure of developing societies is characterized by *dualism* which arises when a society has evolved into two separate sectors. Dual societies have a rural, impoverished, and neglected sector operating alongside an urban, developing, or modernizing sector. There is, however, little interaction between the two:

Most [developing countries] have a large, stagnant, agricultural sector which is linked to the small, modern, large-scale, industrial sector mainly

---

14. The Worldwatch Institute (Norman, 1979) has provided some interesting data on global scientific priorities consistent with the crux of Singer's and Ansari's arguments. The institute has noted that worldwide, $150 billion is spent annually on research and development (R & D). About a quarter of this is spent on military R & D, which is about three times the amount spent on developing alternative energy technologies and more than is spent on energy, health, food production, and environmental protection combined. Moreover, only about $30 million is spent annually on research on tropical diseases, maladies that afflict perhaps a billion people in the Third World, but in the United States alone, nine times this amount is spent on cancer research. This disparity in medical R & D reflects the concentration of such efforts in the developed world. The United States by itself accounts for a third of the world's R & D expenditures, Western Europe and Japan for another third, and the Soviet Union and Eastern Europe for about 30 percent (Norman, 1979: 14). This means that less than 5 percent of the world's R & D expenditures are made in the developing world, in which three-quarters of humanity lives. The Worldwatch Institute's report concludes, "As long as the world's R & D capacity remains highly concentrated in the industrial world, the focus will continue to be largely on the problems of the rich countries, and the developing world will remain dependent on imported—and often inappropriate—technology for its economic development" (Norman, 1979).

through the supply of resources, both labour and capital, from the former to the latter. The growth of the industrial sector neither initiates a corresponding growth process in the rural sector nor generates sufficient employment to prevent a growing population in the stagnant sectors. (Singer and Ansari, 1988: 45–46)

The reason for dualism in the developing countries' economic structures can be found in their colonial past, when the metropolitan powers regarded themselves as the best producers of manufactured goods and their colonies as the best suppliers of basic foodstuffs and raw materials. This resulted in the absence of "spread effects" in the colonial economies' secondary and tertiary sectors. Eventually, rapid population growth overwhelmed the ability of the colonies' rising incomes to produce continued economic growth (Higgins and Higgins, 1979). Yet the hope for a better life in the urban areas has led to a flood of migrants from farm to city, resulting in decrepit urban slums with massive numbers of unemployed seeking work in the small, modern industrial sector.

Historically, population trends in the industrial world suggest that urbanization and industrialization are associated with *declining* rates of population growth. One reason that this pattern is not mirrored in the developing societies is that the death rates in these countries have fallen more precipitously than they have in the industrialized world. This has been caused more by externally introduced measures to reduce death rates than by the changes in attitudes toward family size assumed to be associated with urbanization and industrialization. In addition, the industrialization experienced by colonial economies occurred mainly in the areas of basic foodstuffs and raw materials and therefore may not have altered the traditional colonial societal patterns. "Hence the checks on family size enforced by the urban industrialization of Europe and the New World operated less effectively in the underdeveloped countries" (Higgins and Higgins, 1979).

Estimates of the number of unemployed in the developing nations vary, but the figures all tell essentially the same story of burgeoning numbers of young people entering the labor force far more rapidly than new jobs can be created. The technological dependence of the poor on the rich is related to this dilemma. Because the advanced technology of the industrialized societies is almost always more capital intensive than labor (that is, employment) intensive, it tends to exacerbate rather than alleviate the plight of the jobless.

The persistence of dualism in the economic structures of the developing societies suggests that even in countries with incipient industrial sectors, the benefits will not be widely shared. In fact, "the industrial sector of the poor countries is really a periphery of the metropolitan industrial economies, critically dependent on them for the technology it uses" (Singer and Ansari, 1988). Benefits will be confined to only those groups in developing societies that are able to link themselves to the rich countries:

These will become oases of growth surrounded by a desert of stagnation, thus reinforcing other elements of dualism already present in the poorer countries. The way leads to polarization within the poor country, clashing with the objectives of national planning and national integration. This polarization expresses itself in widening internal income disparities, larger numbers exposed to extreme poverty, and rising unemployment. (Singer and Ansari, 1988: 28)

The problems faced by developing nations can thus be characterized as a series of vicious circles, none of which seems capable of being broken because it is so closely intertwined with so many other intractable problems.

DOMINANCE AND DEPENDENCE IN INTERNATIONAL ECONOMIC RELATIONS The foregoing discussion suggests that the widening gap between the North and the South must be caused by a combination of factors indigenous to Third World nations and inherent in their relationships with First World nations. The developing nations depend on the North not only for technology and manufactured goods but also for markets in which to sell the raw materials and agricultural products that for many are their principal source of the foreign exchange necessary to buy imported goods. In the case of the Newly Industrialized Countries, the North also provides an important market for manufactured goods.

Conventional, Western-oriented theories of economic development traditionally focused on the factors indigenous to Third World nations in their efforts to understand the impediments to Third World development and to recommend ways of overcoming them. Based on the assumption that growth meant increasing increments of per-capita GNP (rather than, say, meeting basic human needs), the task was to identify and remove obstacles to growth and to supply various "missing components," such as investment capital (through foreign aid or private sources) (Todaro, 1981).

Clearly, however, the plight of developing nations is tied not only to the persistence of their domestic economic and social problems but also to their relationships with the rich nations of the North. We shall examine these linkages, as seen by the South, in Chapter 8. Here, what is important to note is that many theorists, particularly from the Third World itself, have contended that the very dependence of the South on the North is responsible for the persistence of the Third World's economic and social ills. This view of the plight of the poor attributes the causes of underdevelopment to the dominance and dependence that typifies the present structure of international economic relationships between the North and the South, rather than to the indigenous characteristics of Third World societies themselves. By extension, this view finds that the global system for distributing wealth is not equitable, that the dependence of the poor on the rich helps explain and perpetuate the differences between the two, and that the poverty of the poor is the result of their exploitation. At the same time, the rich have gotten richer at the expense of the poor.

A number of empirical and normative foci converge on this proposition within the analytical perspective known as *dependency theory*.[15] The argument that the world is divided among "core," "semiperiphery," and "periphery" is central to this perspective. Thus, world system theorists argue that there is only one world system with a top (the core) and a bottom (the periphery) causally connected in a single world division of labor. From this viewpoint, underdevelopment "is not a stalled stage of linear development, a question of pre-capitalism, retarded or backward development, but rather a structural position in a hierarchical world division of labor." Hence, it is necessary only to look "to contemporary relations with other societies to explain underdevelopment" (Bergesen, 1980). This view denies the argument that development is merely a matter of passing through various stages, such as from the traditional society to the mass-consumption society (see Rostow, 1960), for as Andre Gunder Frank (1969), a leading dependency theorist, has argued, "The now developed countries were never underdeveloped, though they may have been undeveloped."

In contrast with the "stages of growth" theory, Frank (1969) attributes "the development of underdevelopment" to the historical expansion of the capitalist system which "effectively and entirely penetrated even the apparently most isolated sectors of the underdeveloped world." The penetration process is viewed as being fueled by capitalism's need for external sources of demand and profitable investment outlets. The agents of penetration are often seen as the overseas branches of the giant multinational corporations (MNCs), whose headquarters are in the North. Foreign investment, whether as private investments by MNCs or public investments in the form of foreign economic and military aid, are the instruments of penetration. Technological dependence and "cultural imperialism" in the form of ideas alien to the indigenous cultures of Third World societies often are the consequence. Ultimately, the MNCs' role is to transfer profits from the periphery to the core, as it is the profit motive that leads to the penetration of peripheral societies in the first place.

Once the periphery has been penetrated by the core, the inherently exploitative linkages that bind them together are sustained by the local elites within the periphery, whose own fortunes are tied to the core and who are co-opted by their desire to maintain their privileged positions in their own societies. One critic of dependency theory describes the role that the Third World's local elites play in the politics of dominance and dependence, by noting that they

---

15. For a sampling of some of the extensive dependency theory literature, see Amin (1974), Baran (1968), Emmanuel (1972), Frank (1969), and the special issue of *International Organization* on dependence and dependency in the global system edited by James A. Caporaso (1978). Todaro (1981) reviews the basic tenets of neo-Marxist views of dependency; Smith (1979, 1981) provides insightful critiques of dependency theory; and Caporaso (1980) discusses prevailing theoretical controversies.

have almost invariably structured their domestic rule on a coalition of internal interests favorable to the international connection. Thus, it is not the sheer economic might of the outside that dictates the dependent status of the South, but the sociological consequences of this power. The result, as most dependency theorists see it, is that the basic needs of the international order must be respected by the South if this system is to continue to provide the services that the local elites need in order to perpetuate their rule in their turn. In other words, a symbiotic relationship has grown up over time in which the system has created its servants whose needs dictate that its survival be ensured, whatever the short-term conflicts of interests may be. (Smith, 1979: 251)

Implicit here is the notion that political repression, applied locally but perhaps with foreign support and assistance, may be necessary to protect the privileges of the few. Finally, dependency theorists reject the concept of dualism to describe the economic and social systems of the Third World countries. Dependency theorists attack the theory of dualism on two major counts:

1. The concept of dualism, with its division into "modern" and "traditional" sectors, suggests that there are two economic systems operating in (nonsocialist) [developing countries], whereas in fact there is only one; international capitalism, which makes the decision for the whole (nonsocialist) world and determines the outcome in social, economic and political terms.
2. Whereas standard or "Dualist" economists tend to suggest that the continuing poverty and growing gaps in developing countries reflect failure of developing policies adopted by governments of developing countries, . . . the truth is that the current situation in [developing countries] reflects the *success* of the policies imposed by international capitalism. The persistence of marginal groups of poor workers and peasants in developing countries reflects a consciously planned system, designed to protect profits by keeping peasant incomes and wages down and reserving for capitalists of advanced countries production requiring advanced technology.[16] (Higgins and Higgins, 1979: 100)

As the foregoing suggests, analysts disagree about many of the propositions central to dependency theory. But what is beyond dispute is that historically, developing nations have directed most of their trade to the industrialized

---

16. Although Singer and Ansari (1988) subscribe to the dualism characterization, it is clear that much of their analysis agrees with the arguments of the dependency theorists. Higgins and Higgins (1979), on the other hand, are critical of the dependency argument, given their analysis of the relationship between the Third World and the capitalist world in terms of trade, foreign investment, and foreign aid, matters that we shall consider in Chapter 8.

economies of the North and have made relatively poor trading partners for one another. From the early 1970s to the early 1980s, the relative importance of Northern markets to Southern exporters declined as Third World countries increased their share of exports to other Third World countries (see Lewis and Kallab, 1983: 246–247). In absolute terms, however, the North remains disproportionately important to the South. Put differently, whereas Northern countries trade primarily among themselves, the South trades primarily with the North. Developing nations have therefore generally been price "takers" rather than setters in the international marketplace, "because in the short run the developing countries need the products and services of the developed countries much more than the latter need the output of the former" (Singer and Ansari, 1988). The developing nations have also inherited rather than initiated trade policy and rules of procedure governing international commerce.

The global disparities in income and wealth that divide North and South— and that in turn seem likely to be perpetuated by that division—have produced a highly stratified international political order. In effect, the international system today is hierarchically organized, with a few top dogs at the pinnacle of the hierarchy and a far larger number of underdogs forming the base. Understandably, Third World nations are not very satisfied with this state of affairs and have therefore pursued a variety of strategies designed to transform the existing order.

BEYOND DEPENDENCE: THE FOREIGN POLICY GOALS OF THIRD WORLD NATIONS

Technological dependence is critical to perpetuating the position of the developing nations at the bottom of the world development ladder. Singer and Ansari (1988) argue, "If the technological gap is not overcome, no form of assistance, trade concessions, aid, grants, technical assistance or fortuitous price rises will prove to be of lasting value. International cooperation policies must be devised which serve to remove this fundamental obstacle in the path of development."

Included in their explanation is a list of elements in the relations among nations in the context of the North–South conflict, including issues relating to trade, aid, and pricing mechanisms.

A New International Economic Order

The developing nations' policy prescriptions for dealing with these issues came to be known collectively in diplomatic circles during the 1970s as the demand for a New International Economic Order (NIEO), that is, an international economic system profoundly different from the Liberal International Economic Order (LIEO) created under the aegis of American hegemony in the decades following World War II. The demand arises from the relative deprivation that Third World nations perceive in their position in the current structure of international economic relations, as well as from the persistence of neocolonial and neoimperial ties between the world's rich and poor. Third World nations see the current system as an instrument of their continued oppression, and they would like to be equal to the more advanced countries in fact, not just in law. Thus Third World nations came to view the NIEO as an alternative to the present exploitative system. Speaking on behalf of the Third World before the United Nations General Assembly in 1979, Cuba's Fidel Castro expressed this view in words commonly used to depict the Third World spirit. He demanded the creation of a "new world order based on justice, on equity, on peace" to replace "the unjust world system that exists today." Under the current system, he said, "wealth is still concentrated in the hands of a few powers" who profit from "exploitation" of the Third World.

The historical roots of the NIEO can be traced to the 1950s and 1960s, when the Third World, with support from the Second World, began forming a united front for dealing with the industrialized West on international economic issues. These efforts resulted in the first United Nations Conference on Trade and Development (UNCTAD), held in Geneva in 1964. The meeting became the forerunner of several conferences held during the next two decades that focused on various aspects of the relations between the world's rich and poor nations.

During the 1964 conference, the Group of 77 (often referred to in diplomatic circles as simply G-77) was formed as a coalition of the world's poor countries to press for concessions from the world's rich. The Group of 77, now numbering over 125 developing countries, continues to act in that capacity today. UNCTAD has also become a permanent organization in the United Nations' family of organizations. Building on the intellectual guidance and aggressive leadership of its first secretary general, Dr. Raúl Prebisch, UNCTAD has effectively become an advocate for the world's less fortunate nations.

The issues addressed in the UNCTAD forum (and in other international bodies) have changed over time in response to changing international circumstances. Among the changes of the post–World War II period has been the ascendance of three independent centers of industrial power in the North: the United States, Western Europe, and Japan. Because each industrial center has different needs and interests, each responds differently to the Third World's demands (Burney, 1979). The United States is essentially a continental power; Western Europe has strong historical ties and cultural bonds with many Third World countries; and Japan, an island nation, is critically dependent on raw-material imports. Conversely, among Third World nations different levels of development, differing degrees of economic and political affiliation with the

North, differing colonial experiences,[17] and differing perceptions of national interests all affected both the stakes in and the positions of individual Third World countries in the outcome of the North–South dialogue.

Political Autonomy

The Third World drive for equality extends beyond economics to politics; equality of dignity and equality of influence are also at issue:

> Many [Third World] leaders are tired of being ignored, of never being invited to the international high table, or of pressing their views and having them regularly rebuffed. More substantially, many are hostile to the notion that the state system should be organized in its present sharply hierarchical fashion, in which a few with wealth, industrial and technological strength, and the capability to apply force regularly make decisions that so profoundly affect the conditions and well-being of even distant states. They are coming to insist upon participating in the making of decisions that affect them. (Wriggins, 1978: 39)

Closely related to the drive for equality is the goal of autonomy or independence: "Each state, it is held, should be able to manage its own political and economic affairs without interference from outside: each should be in a position to decide for itself how its resources should be utilized, what policies industrial and agricultural enterprises operating within its borders should follow, and such economic matters as interest rates for loans, rates of exchange, and export subsidies" (Wriggins, 1978).

Given developing nations' belief that the present structure of international economic relations is responsible for their plight, their drive for independence will require a transformation of the liberal international regimes that condition the international movement of goods, services, capital, labor, and technology (Krasner, 1981). The reason for the drive to transform international regimes is that the developing nations individually are too weak to change the environment that affects them adversely. The widely shared belief in many of the premises of dependency theory facilitates the pursuit of regime transformation, for it galvanizes the developing nations into a collective drive toward goals that they would be too weak to realize by the traditional means of state

---

17. Craig Murphy notes in his discussion of the history of Third World demands for a New International Economic Order that in the early 1970s, the relative immediacy of the colonial experience helped split the South into "moderate" and "radical" camps, with the latter believing that the North owed the South restitution for past colonialism. He further describes the two camps: "The radical camp included mostly Asian and African nations, nonaligned states, states that were recently independent, and other states that supported the restitution ethic. The moderate camp tended to be Latin American, aligned with the West, and included some states that had been independent longer, where people were relatively better off and whose governments rarely talked about the need for restitution for colonialism" (Murphy, 1983).

power in bilateral relations. It also makes it difficult for individual govern-ments to break ranks with other Third World nations without fear of domestic political repercussions (Krasner, 1981, 1985).

Nonalignment

Just as Third World nations have sought to erase the vestiges of dependent relationships implied by the terms *neocolonialism* and *neoimperialism*, most are determined to avoid the East–West conflict because of fear that one form of domination might simply be replaced by another. Hence, they espouse a policy of *nonalignment*.

The nonalignment movement among Third World nations dates from 1955, when twenty-nine Asian and African nations met in Bangdung, Indonesia, to devise a means of combating colonialism. By 1961 the movement had grown into a permanent organization, and since then its membership has expanded from twenty-five to over one hundred, with meetings scheduled every three years.

In 1966, a policy spokesman defined Afghanistan's conception of nonalign-ment at the time by emphasizing the principle of noninvolvement in the controversies dividing the world: "Afghanistan wishes to be on friendly terms with all countries . . . on the basis of mutual respect. It follows a policy of non-participation in political and military blocs. . . . Our country's observance of the principles of neutrality constitutes the basis for the judgment it passes freely on international issues" (cited in Holsti, 1970).

Obviously this statement was made before the internal instability in Afghanistan that arose out of disputes between the pro-Soviet Marxist govern-ment and more traditional political forces in the country and that led to the Soviet military intervention in 1979. The statement nevertheless reflects a conception of nonalignment that sees formal association with any alliance as reducing the freedom of a Third World nation. Zambia's President Kenneth Kaunda elaborated on the virtues of this orientation in 1964 when he asserted, "We will not hitch our carriage to any nation's engine and be drawn along their railway line" (cited in Holsti, 1970). Similarly, King Fahd of Saudi Arabia, discussing his country's decision in 1988 to buy British and Chinese weapons after decades of almost exclusive reliance on American-made arms, captured the motives underlying the policy preference when he declared, "Saudi Arabia is not tied to anyone. . . . So, if things become complicated with a certain country we will find other countries, regardless of whether they are Eastern or Western." (*New York Times*, July 31, 1988: E2)

During its early years some of the world's leading political figures were spokespersons for the nonaligned movement. Over time, however, the move-ment appeared to lose much of its unity and its corresponding political clout as the diversity among Third World nations undermined its cohesiveness. In part, this diversity has found expression in the various foreign policy roles that Third World nations have adopted in efforts to realize their political objectives,[18] even though they have remained committed in principle to nonalignment. Three exemplary, if competing, orientations are captured in the terms of *revolutionary liberator, isolation*, and *ally*.

A *revolutionary liberator* is a foreign policy posture directed toward the external world. The task of the revolutionary liberator state is "to liberate others or to act as the 'bastion' of revolutionary movements, that is, to provide an area which foreign revolutionary leaders can regard as a source of physical and moral support, as well as an ideological inspirer" (Holsti, 1970). Phases of China's and Algeria's post–World War II foreign policies are examples of this role conception. Cuba, under Castro, has been another prominent example, especially since the late 1970s. Others might be found among governing elites who "may find it intolerable to mind their own business when the people in neighboring countries are being systematically oppressed, as in Southern Africa" (Wriggins, 1978).

Elements of the revolutionary liberator role are particularly prevalent among those nations born of a revolutionary experience. In this connection, however, it is interesting to note that Third World leaders' criticism of the existing international order does not necessarily focus on the exclusivity of the global system but on the manner in which the dispossessed are excluded from rank, status, and a fair share of the global pie. This ambivalence finds expression in the posture that Third World revolutionaries sometimes adopt toward international law: The law cannot confer on them the status and rewards possessed by others, but it does help ensure their survival in a threatening international environment in which the power of others could easily overwhelm them. Most are therefore strong supporters of the principle of self-determination and the principle of the inadmissibility of the acquisition of territory by force: One justifies their existence, and the other sustains it (Waldheim, 1984).[19]

Isolation is another orientation to the predicament of economic underdevelopment and political impotence. Isolationism implies that the way to cope with the external world is to avoid contact with it. Instead of trying to reform the global structure, isolationism preaches withdrawal from world affairs.

Isolationism was the United States' dominant foreign policy during its early history. In the political sphere, isolationism was apparent in George Washington's famous advice to "steer clear of permanent alliances with any portion of the foreign world." In the economic sphere, Alexander Hamilton urged the use of tariffs to protect infant industries and to promote national development and self-sufficiency.

---

18. See Hermann (1987) for an application of role theory that links nations' foreign policies to the role orientations and personal characteristics of their leaders.

19. Together these principles help explain the antipathy toward Israel shared by many Third World nations, which is fueled by Israel's policies toward the Palestinian people and its occupation of Arab territory since the June 1967 war in the Middle East.

Under Mao Tse-tung, Communist China isolated itself from foreign contact and concentrated on internal reconstruction. Burma has also pursued a policy of isolationism. Its leader, General Ne Win, spoke of its fears of foreign involvement in Burma and the country's search for autonomy through self-reliance:

> We have got to rely on our own strength in everything. We cannot depend on anybody. We should not try to find fault with anybody. We do not want to quarrel with anyone. . . . Unless we Burmese can learn to run our own country, we will lose it. This kind of aid [bilateral aid to nations in the region] does not help. It cripples. It paralyzes. The recipients never learn to do for themselves. They rely more and more on foreign experts and foreign money. In the end they lose control of their country. (Cited in Holsti, 1970: 270)

Ally is a third orientation that some Third World leaders have adopted. The incentives for association with a superpower patron can be particularly compelling. Such ties may produce not only an enhanced sense of national security but also the foreign aid needed for internal development and perhaps the arms to deal with enemies at home and abroad. Hence, some Third World states may be willing to suffer a partial loss of freedom in return for the material and political compensations offered as an ally of a superpower. Vietnam's embrace of the Soviet Union as a shield from both China and the West may be an example of the kind of incentive that an alliance with a superpower may provide.

Few Third World nations, however, have chosen to take on the role of ally in an open and formal way. This is understandable, as it runs directly counter to the avowed principles of the nonaligned movement. It is nevertheless true that many developing nations have from time to time chosen to associate themselves with one or the other of the superpowers so closely that their status as nonaligned might be questioned. India, for example, whose prime minister Jawaharlal Nehru was one of the early founders and leading spokespersons of nonalignment, chose in 1971 to conclude a "treaty of peace and friendship" with the Soviet Union (presumably as a counterpoise to India's greatest external threat, China). Cuba, too, has closely intertwined its affairs with the Soviet Union, providing a base for Soviet military personnel in the Western Hemisphere and becoming dependent on huge amounts of Soviet economic aid and credits to sustain its socialist economy.

Many African and Asian nonaligned nations have adopted strongly anti-American foreign policy postures (which does not necessarily mean they are inspired by pro-Soviet leanings). Most nations of the Western Hemisphere, on the other hand, have traditionally been closely associated economically and politically with the United States. Nearly all are members of the Organization of American States (OAS), a post–World War II derivative of the Monroe Doctrine with mutual-security implications.

Other Third World countries have also been associated with the United States at one time or another, particularly for purposes of national security. Various Middle Eastern countries that were original members of the non-aligned movement—such as Jordan, Iran, Saudi Arabia, and Egypt—have received, or continue to receive, substantial sums of military aid and perhaps implicit guarantees. Some nations in Asia have been formal treaty partners with the United States in mutual-defense arrangements during portions of the postwar period. Included are Pakistan, Thailand, the Philippines, and the republics of China (Taiwan) and South Korea.

Although members of the nonaligned movement generally shun the kinds of labels that would place them into the camp of one or the other of the superpowers, the term *nonalignment* itself often reflects more myth than reality. Noting that "the movement's claims of unity of purpose and principle have become blurred and less convincing," one observer derided the composition of the nonaligned nations movement at the time of its seventh summit in 1983: "A quarter of its present members are acknowledged dictatorships of one sort or another; about a dozen are openly aligned with the Soviet Union, and ten or eleven are more generally considered pro-Soviet. Perhaps a dozen can be described as more or less pro-American, but these tend to speak with less certain and milder voices" (Shaplen, 1983). Three years later, as the non-aligned movement celebrated its twenty-fifth anniversary, Libya's leader, Colonel Muammar Qaddafi, described the organization as "funny" and "fallacious"—presumably because it did not provide greater material support when the United States launched air raids against Libya in April 1986. There is a sense, nevertheless, in which too close an embrace by a Third World government of either the United States or the Soviet Union can lead to adverse results for both parties. John Kenneth Galbraith has written:

> The will to national independence is the most powerful force of our time. To infringe upon it is to touch the most sensitive of nerves. This has been true for the Soviets; it has been true for Americans. Respecting that independence, one can have friends; impairing it, one can expect only rejection. If the national leadership is strong, effective, and well-regarded, it will not tolerate foreign domination—from anyone. If that leadership is weak, ineffective, unpopular, corrupt, or oppressive, it may accept foreign guidance, support, and a measure of domination. But then it will not be tolerated by its own people. (Galbraith, 1982–1983: 89–90)

THE PRIMACY OF POLITICS: DOMESTIC OR INTERNATIONAL?

Differing interpretations by Third World elites of the foreign policy posture of nonalignment thus appear to reflect the often sharply divergent foreign and domestic situations they face. Varying degrees of industrialization and economic development are among these differences.[20] Different cultures and traditions and varying threats of internal instability arising from religious and ethnic differences must also be weighed—for these, too, are among the numerous dimensions of Third World diversity.

The political elites of Third World countries also have differing perceptions of threats to their physical security or national integrity. For some the principal threat is internal—a lack of identity with the nation, separatism, insurrection, or insurgency. For others, the primary threat is external—a powerful and obtrusive neighbor or one that might become so. Given such threats, the incentives for seeking external military assistance or other forms of external aid are great.

Under such circumstances, the East–West and the North–South conflicts are often not of primary importance to the governing elites. To be sure, either might be used to solidify support at home. As W. Howard Wriggins, formerly American ambassador to Sri Lanka, observed, "When David stands up to Goliath, public, bureaucratic, and often military support at home are quickly generated, even if such actions may provoke certain difficulties in foreign political or even economic relations" (Wriggins, 1978). Still, we must entertain the possibility that for many Third World leaders, foreign policy does not assume primacy. Wriggins maintains that "most Third World leaders do not focus their main attention on North–South relations. For them, such issues are often derivative of other goals and preoccupations" (Wriggins, 1978). It is fair to assume, then, that domestic economic and political issues are among the preoccupations of most Third World governing elites.

Having stressed the Third World's diversity, it is important to reemphasize its common characteristics and experiences. In varying degrees, Third World nations are characterized by poverty, hunger, and a lack of hope. Their societies are vastly dissimilar from the opulent and affluent societies of those nations once—and perhaps still—controlling them. This reality not only defines the Third World's current international position, but it also conditions its efforts to transform the global political order.

The North–South conflict is multifaceted, complex, and potentially explosive. For while the intensity and visibility of the conflict wax and wane, the present and growing disparities between rich and poor nations remain as sources of domestic instability and, eventually perhaps, international violence. Unless and until these disparities are reduced or eliminated, they will ensure that the North–South conflict will continue to figure prominently on the global agenda and to propel the transformation of world politics.

---

20. There are shared patterns in the foreign policy orientations of developing nations and their internal political and economic characteristics. For example, states that tend to be pro-Soviet in their external relations are often one-party states politically, with an orientation toward socialism in their domestic economic systems, whereas those pro-Western in outlook more frequently lean toward capitalism or a mixture of capitalism and socialism. Among both the pro-Soviet and the pro-Western groups, authoritarian governments are often the rule.

SUGGESTED READINGS

Bhagwati, Jagdish N., and John Gerard Ruggie, eds. *Power, Passions, and Purpose.* Cambridge, Mass.: MIT Press, 1984.

Caporaso, James A., ed. "Dependence and Dependency in the Global System." Special issue of *International Organization* 32 (Winter 1978): 1–300.

Chirot, Daniel. *Social Change in the Modern Era.* San Diego: Harcourt Brace Jovanovich, 1986.

Cohen, Benjamin J. *The Question of Imperialism.* New York: Basic Books, 1973.

Faaland, J., and J. R. Parkinson. *The Political Economy of Development.* New York: St. Martin's Press, 1986.

Frank, Andre Gunder. *Latin America: Underdevelopment or Revolution.* New York: Monthly Review Press, 1969.

Moon, Bruce E., and William J. Dixon. "Politics, the State, and Basic Human Needs: A Cross-National Study," *American Journal of Political Science* 29 (November 1965): 661–694.

Singer, Hans W., and Javed A. Ansari. *Rich and Poor Countries: Consequences of International Economic Disorder,* 4th ed. London: Unwin Hyman, 1988.

Walker, Stephen G., ed. *Role Theory and Foreign Policy Analysis.* Durham, N.C.: Duke University Press, 1987.

World Development Report 1987. New York: Oxford University Press for the World Bank, 1987.

SIX

Nonstate Actors in World Politics: The Role of International Organizations and Multinational Corporations

I believe that we are at present embarked on an exceedingly dangerous course, one symptom of which is the . . . erosion of the authority and status of world and regional intergovernmental institutions. . . . Such a trend must be reversed before once again we bring upon ourselves a global catastrophe and find ourselves without institutions effective enough to prevent it.

JAVIER PÉREZ DE CUÉLLAR, 1982

The annual growth rate of IBM . . . at home and abroad for the past decade has been sufficiently great so that, if it continues uninterrupted for another generation, IBM will be the largest single economic entity in the world, including the entities of nation-states.

ROBERT L. HEILBRONER, 1977

Nation-states are the dominant form of political organization in the world, and their interests, objectives, and capabilities significantly shape the contours of world politics. But no mapping of the global political terrain would be complete without locating the role played by the increasing number of nonstate actors. Transnational political movements such as the Palestine Liberation Organization, political parties such as the Social Democrats in the countries of Western Europe, religious groups such as the Roman Catholic church, international governmental and nongovernmental organizations like the United Nations and the International Olympic Committee, and multinational corporations (MNCs) such as Exxon and IBM all have become a significant part of the global topography.

Despite the obvious diversity among these groups, all share a common desire to accomplish their goals by acting transnationally as well as working within the confines of geographically defined national units. This is obviously the case for the Palestine Liberation Organization, whose goal is the realization of a national homeland. But it is also true of the Roman Catholic church, whose transnational links as well as national hierarchies enable it to spread its re-

131

ligious and moral messages. Even multinational corporations such as Ford Motor and British Petroleum, whose goals are profit maximization wherever that might best be accomplished, think of themselves as extraterritorial.

This chapter focuses on the growth of nonstate actors, how they are used by states to realize perceived national interests, and whether these actors have become agents beyond the nation-state propelling the transformation of world politics.

THE GROWTH OF INTERNATIONAL ORGANIZATIONS

There are two principal types of international organizations, those to which governments belong and those to which private individuals and groups belong. Neither type is peculiar to the twentieth century. The first modern international intergovernmental organization (IGO), the Central Commission for the Navigation of the Rhine, was established by the Congress of Vienna (1815), and the Rosicrucian Order established in 1694 fits contemporary definitions of international nongovernmental organizations (INGOs). The number of both types of organizations grew substantially in the half-century before World War I, primarily in response to the growth in transnational commerce and communications that accompanied industrialization. On the eve of World War I, 49 IGOs and over 170 INGOs were in existence (Wallace and Singer, 1970: 272; *Yearbook of International Organizations, 1983*, 1983: 905).

The number of international organizations grew even more quickly after each of the two world wars. In 1940 there were over 80 governmental and close to 500 nongovernmental organizations. By the late 1980s these numbers had increased to more than 300 and 4,200, respectively (Wallace and Singer, 1970: 272; *Yearbook of International Organizations, 1987/88*, vol. 1, 1987: app. 7).[1]

---

1. These figures imply that it is easier to identify international organizations than is in fact the case. In principle, IGOs are defined by a set of formal criteria:

> An international governmental organization is an institutional structure created by agreement among two or more sovereign states for the conduct of regular political interactions. IGOs are distinguished from the facilities of traditional diplomacy by their structure and permanence. International governmental organizations have meetings of representatives of the member states at relatively regular intervals, specified procedures for making decisions, and a permanent secretariat or headquarters staff. In some ways IGOs resemble governments, but they are not governments, for the capacity for action continues to rest predominantly with the constituent units, the member states. IGOs can be viewed as permanent networks linking states. (Jacobson, 1984: 8)

If, however, their permanence, regularly scheduled meetings, or some other criterion were eliminated, the number of IGOs in existence would far surpass the 311 "conventionally defined" organizations just cited, with some 1,300 additional international bodies qualifying for inclusion (see *Yearbook of International Organizations, 1987/88*, vol. 1, 1987: app. 7). Furthermore, some international organizations have been created by others and thus do not fit the preceding definition, although clearly they are international organizations.

In principle, INGOs are easier to define than IGOs are, because the United Nations Economic and Social Council (ECOSOC) has followed the practice of granting these organizations consultative status before the council. Again, however, the Union of International Associations (*Yearbook of International Organizations, 1987/88*, vol. 1, 1987: app. 7) has identified more than ten thousand other nongovernmental entities that share some characteristics with INGOs.

Although more than 90 percent of the present international organizations are nongovernmental, the remaining ones are generally more important because nation-states are the principal centers of authority and legitimacy in the contemporary world. As Harold K. Jacobson explains:

> Authoritative policies are more frequently made in and applied by governmental than by nongovernmental institutions; consequently in most political systems the former are more important than the latter. But the global system accords even greater importance to governmental institutions than is usually the case. States are the primary focal points of political activity in the modern world, and IGOs presently derive their importance from their character as associations of states. (Jacobson, 1984: 7)

Given this distinction, it is useful to think of INGOs as intersocietal organizations that help facilitate the achievement and maintenance of agreements among countries regarding the elements of international public policy (Jacobson, 1984). One indicator of this relationship is that many INGOs interact formally with IGOs. For instance, many INGOs have been granted "consultative status" with various agencies of the United Nations, a status that enables them to work (and lobby) together in pursuit of common programs and policies. The United Nations, on the other hand, often relies heavily on nongovernmental organizations, with the result that the line between governmental and nongovernmental functions can become blurred. Examples can be found in the work of the United Nations Children's Fund (UNICEF), the United Nations Fund for Population Activities (UNFPA), and the United Nations University.

One consequence of the growth of international organizations has been the creation of a complex network of overlapping national memberships in transnational associations. In 1987, for example, the United States had over 1,600 national representations in international organizations, which is nearly double the number it had only two decades earlier. A recent study by the Union of International Associations (*Yearbook of International Organizations, 1987/88*, vol. 2, 1987: app. 3) estimated that the national representatives of some two hundred countries and territories in 4,546 international organizations numbered more than 97,000. These are truly "networks of interdependence" (Jacobson, 1984), even though they often reflect degrees of conflict as well as cooperation.

These networks span the entire panoply of activities associated with modern societies: trade, defense, agriculture, health, human rights, the arts, tourism, labor, education, the environment, telecommunications, science, and refugees, among others. In the twentieth century, transnational associations have also addressed power politics and national security. Each of the world wars was followed by a concerted attempt to create new international institutions and procedures to handle threats to the peace. The first, the League of Nations, was designed to prevent a recurrence of the catastrophe of 1914–1918, by replacing the balance-of-power system with one based on the principle of collective security. When collective security failed to restrain states from waging war unilaterally, the League floundered, and by the end of the 1930s, global conflict had broken out again.

Planning for a new international institution to preserve peace began after the onset of World War II. The primary mission of the new United Nations organization, which came into existence in 1945, was the maintenance of international peace and security.

The United Nations is special among the relatively small group of international governmental organizations. First, its membership approximates universality.[2] Second, partly because nearly all states are members, the United Nations is a multiple-purpose organization. As stated in Article 1 of the United Nations Charter, the purposes of the organization are "to maintain international peace and security"; "to develop friendly relations among nations based on respect for the principle of equal rights and self-determination of peoples"; "to achieve international cooperation in solving international problems of an economic, social, cultural, or humanitarian character, and in promoting and encouraging respect for human rights and for fundamental freedoms for all"; and "to be a centre for harmonizing the actions of nations in the attainment of these common ends." These ideals have carried the United Nations into nearly every corner of the complex network of relations among states. Its conference machinery has become permanent; the organization has provided a mechanism for the management of international conflict; and it has become involved in a broad range of global nonsecurity welfare issues.

No other IGO can claim the same extensiveness of purpose and membership as can the United Nations. In fact, if IGOs are divided along these two dimensions, most are limited-purpose, limited-membership organizations. One study categorized 97 percent of a broadly defined group of 621 IGOs existing in 1980 as specific-purpose organizations. Among them, more than four-fifths were limited-membership, specific-purpose organizations. Only 18 qualified as general-purpose organizations, and of these only the United Nations approximated universal membership (Jacobson, 1984: 48).

Figure 6.1 provides examples of IGOs classified according to criteria analogous to those just described. Clearly there is great variation among the organizations falling into each category, particularly the single-purpose, limited-membership quadrant. The North Atlantic Treaty Organization (NATO), for example, is primarily a military alliance, whereas others in this category (such as the Nordic Council) are concerned with both military security and economic cooperation and hence might be regarded as "political" IGOs. In fact, the majority of IGOs are engaged in a relatively narrow range of social and economic activities, such as trade integration, common functional services,

---

2. North and South Korea are still not members of the United Nations because of the perpetuation of the East–West conflict, which has effectively barred both from membership. Most other states that do not belong, such as Switzerland, are not members by their own choice, although most have joined its specialized agencies and are members of the International Court of Justice.

FIGURE 6.1 ■ A Simple Classification of International Intergovernmental Organizations

		Range of Stated Purpose	
		Multiple purpose	Single purpose
Geographic Scope of Membership	Global	*United Nations*	*World Health Organization International Labor Organization*
	Interregional, regional, subregional	Organization of American States Organization of African Unity League of Arab States Association of Southeast Asian Nations	European Economic Community Nordic Council North Atlantic Treaty Organization International Olive Oil Council International North Pacific Fisheries Commission

and other types of economic and social cooperation. In this sense IGOs are agents as well as reflections of growing social and economic interdependence.

INGOs are even more difficult to classify than are IGOs. The Union of International Associations (itself an INGO) maintains the most comprehensive, up-to-date information about INGOs. Its recent data (*Yearbook of International Organizations, 1987/88*, vol. 1, 1987: app. 7) classify 10 percent of some 4,200 as universal membership organizations, with most of the remaining 90 percent classified as intercontinental or regionally oriented membership organizations. Functionally, the groups span virtually every facet of modern political, social, and economic life, ranging from earth sciences to health care, from language, history, culture, and theology, to law, ethics, security, and defense.[3]

Some data indicate that the INGOs' greatest growth in the postwar period occurred among those organizations involved in activities of direct concern to governments, namely, economic matters such as industry, commerce, finance, and technology, and not among those concerned with essentially non-economic matters, such as sports and religious affairs. INGOs are thus likely to have their greatest impact in advanced industrial states (Feld, 1972), such as the United States and the member countries of the European Community. "This is so because open political systems, ones in which there is societal pluralism, are more likely to allow their citizens to participate in nongovernmental organizations, and such systems are highly correlated with relatively high levels of economic development" (Jacobson, 1984). The membership composition of

3. For a discussion of the problems in classifying international organizations by function, see Bennett (1988), and the *Yearbook of International Organizations, 1986/87*, vol. 3 (1986).

INGOs, therefore, tends to weigh more heavily in favor of the Northern industrialized states than of the Southern developing states.

Before examining further the impact of international organizations on
world politics, we should ask how states have used these institutions to realize
their foreign policy objectives. The history of the East–West and North–South
conflicts as reflected in the United Nations will help us answer this.

THE UNITED NATIONS: BETWEEN EAST AND WEST, NORTH AND SOUTH

The United Nations was originally conceived as an organization of the victorious allies of World War II. The name itself can be traced to the Atlantic
Charter signed by the United States and Great Britain in 1941, which refers to a
postwar international organization, and specifically to the Declaration by
United Nations signed by twenty-six allied nations in January 1942.

Given its wartime origins, it is not surprising that "maintenance of international peace and security" headed the list of the new organization's purposes.
Primary responsibility for this task was lodged in the eleven-member Security
Council, which was expanded to fifteen members in 1965. There has also been
some pressure for further expansion in order to give Japan and the Federal
Republic of Germany permanent membership and to provide for a more
equitable representation of member states. The five major powers allied in war
against Germany and Japan—the United States, the Soviet Union, Britain,
France, and China—were made permanent members of the Security Council
and were given veto power over council actions. This formula reflected the
assumption that the great powers would act in concert to support the principle
of collective security perceived necessary to maintain the postwar peace.
Hence, unanimity was essential, and any disagreement in the Security Council
was viewed as a signal that the ingredient necessary to resolve a particular
conflict was lacking.

However, the Security Council became quickly ensnarled in the emerging
Cold War between the United States and the Soviet Union. Time and again the
Soviet Union, unable to mobilize a majority on its side, exercised its veto
power to prevent council action on matters with which it disagreed. The most
important body within the United Nations, the Security Council, often was
paralyzed, and the new organization's ability to enforce the principle of collective security was severely restricted.

The Security Council is but one of six principal organs established by the
United Nations Charter (see Figure 6.2). Among the others, the General Assembly is the only body in which all the member states are represented, and all
decisions there are made according to majority rule, with no state given a veto.
Unlike the Security Council, which was given the power to take action,
including the use of force, the General Assembly was given only the power to
recommend. But that limited mandate has turned out to be substantial.

FIGURE 6.2 ▪ The United Nations System

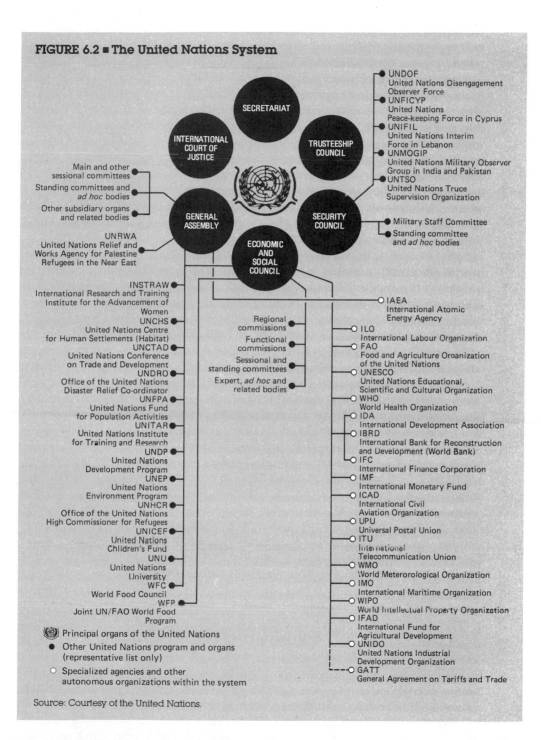

Source: Courtesy of the United Nations.

Unforeseen by the founders of the United Nations, the power to recommend has made the General Assembly a partner with the Security Council in issues of peace and security and has also made it the primary body responsible for social and economic problems. The scope of this involvement is reflected in the complexity of the United Nations itself. The United Nations today is not one organization but a conglomerate of countless committees, bureaus, boards, commissions, centers, institutes, offices, and organizations. Some of these are shown in Figure 6.2, but the United Nations is actually far less orderly.

The proliferation of United Nations bodies and activities paralleled the growth of international organizations generally. It also reflects specifically the way that states have used the United Nations to accomplish their own objectives. Third World nations, who have combined their growing numbers under the one-state, one-vote rules of the General Assembly, have fostered United Nations involvement in areas of particular concern to them. But that was not always the case. The United Nations has evolved from a Western-dominated political organization into a Third World—and a socialist bloc—dominated organization. The forces underlying the transformation are instructive.

Evolving Political Strategies in the Security Council and the General Assembly

In June 1950, North Korea launched a surprise attack against South Korea. The Security Council was called into session and quickly adopted a resolution supporting the use of force by the United Nations to repel the North Korean onslaught.

Because the Security Council authorized military force against the communist aggression, the defense of South Korea technically became a "police action" that bore some resemblance to collective security. Command of the United Nations forces, however, was taken by the United States, which also supplied the bulk of the soldiers, money, and matériel. It did so because combating the North Korean advance was consistent with the American Cold War objective of containing communism. Consequently, the Korean police action came to be regarded as mainly an American military operation aimed against the Soviet Union and the People's Republic of China and not an instance of effective collective security exercised by the world community (although it is true that many United Nations members nominally supported the American action).

More importantly, military actions in Korea were made possible by unique circumstances—the absence of the Soviet Union from the Security Council meeting that voted on the police action, because of a protest against the world body's refusal to seat the Chinese Communist government. Had the Soviet Union been in attendance, it surely would have vetoed any United Nations role in Korea. Before 1950 its vetoes had repeatedly frustrated the United Nations' efforts to deal with emergent Cold War issues, such as the Berlin blockade and the 1948 coup that brought a communist government to power in Czechoslovakia. In fact, during this period the Soviet Union was the most prolific vetoer in the Security Council. It cast 77 vetoes between 1945 and 1955, and it accounted for over 70 percent of the 144 vetoes cast in the first three decades of the United Nations' existence (Riggs and Plano, 1988: 77).

The Western powers began to use their veto more frequently when their ability to command a majority in the Security Council diminished. The United States did not register its first veto until 1970, on the issue of white minority control in Rhodesia (now Zimbabwe) and the extension of economic sanctions to South Africa. Since then it has vetoed measures dealing with such issues as the Middle East, Rhodesia, South Africa, the Panama Canal, and the admissions of Vietnam and Angola to the United Nations.

For years the United States prided itself on never having cast a veto in the Security Council. Having now done so on numerous occasions, it is clear that virtue had little to do with the American position—nor was villainy the primary motivation of the Soviet Union's seemingly obstructionist behavior. Rather, the American and Soviet voting behavior was a product of their differing parliamentary positions in the United Nations. Until 1960 the Soviet Union was clearly a minority power, the United States a majority power. The veto thus was virtually the only effective instrument available to the Soviet Union for protecting its national interests, whereas the United States could assume a more virtuous posture, because it had other devices at its disposal. In this sense the Soviet Union's prolific use of the veto, often exercised in opposition to proposals put forward by the American-dominated majority, was a reflection, not a cause, of the reasons underlying the United Nations' seeming inability to command a more central role in postwar international politics.

Recent United Nations history demonstrates that the United States no longer enjoys majority control and that the Soviet Union no longer clearly is in a defensive minority position. Between 1961 and 1986 the Soviet Union cast only 25 of the 117 vetoes it registered between 1945 and 1986. Between 1971 and 1986 alone, the United States cast 57 (Riggs and Plano, 1988: 77). Thus the two superpowers have come to behave similarly—and in a manner consistent with what the framers of the United Nations Charter had in mind when they adopted the unanimity principle, namely, that agreement among the great powers was essential to the effective maintenance of international peace.

Furthermore, during the United Nations' first years, the United States did not have to veto Security Council actions it opposed because it possessed a "hidden veto," the ability to persuade a sufficient majority of other council members to vote negatively so as to avoid the stigma of the United States having to cast the single blocking vote (Stoessinger, 1977). This ability derived from the composition of the Security Council, among whose nine members the United States could easily count on a pro-Western majority.

The United States enjoyed a similarly commanding position in the General Assembly, in which the Soviet Union frequently derided the Americans' "mechanical majority." Figure 6.3 provides evidence of the dominant American position in the assembly during the early history of the United Nations. It shows the percentage of times the United States and the Soviet Union voted

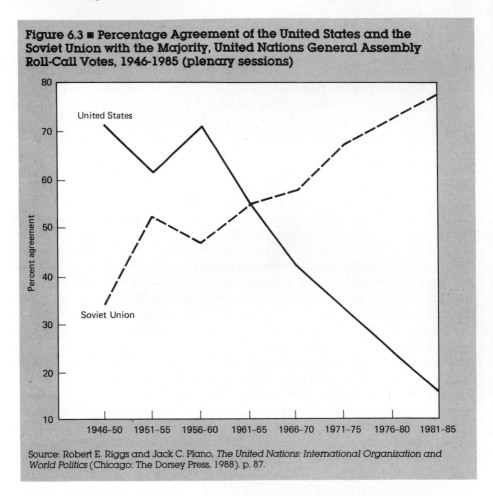

Figure 6.3 ■ Percentage Agreement of the United States and the Soviet Union with the Majority, United Nations General Assembly Roll-Call Votes, 1946-1985 (plenary sessions)

Source: Robert E. Riggs and Jack C. Plano, *The United Nations: International Organization and World Politics* (Chicago: The Dorsey Press, 1988). p. 87.

with the majority on roll-call votes in the General Assembly in each half decade from 1946 to 1986.

These data do not portray the nuances of behavior underlying United Nations' political processes. For example, they do not reflect the compromises that the United States often had to make to garner other nations' support or, indeed, the resolutions that never came to a vote because that support could not be found (Holmes, 1977).[4] Nor do they reveal the different voting patterns

---

4. It is possible to show, for example, that if votes are weighted by how closely contested they were, on the assumption that minimum winning coalitions are more politically important than overwhelming majorities are, then the evidence indicates the United States did not enjoy a commanding position in the General Assembly, even during much of the 1950s. Again, however, this result may reflect not the absence of political clout but the unwillingness of the United States to try to influence the outcome of all issues coming before the assembly (see Wittkopf, 1975).

on different types of issues. The United States, for example, frequently "found itself at odds with the majority in the General Assembly on issues involving decolonization and economic development much more often than on issues concerning security" (Jacobson, 1984).[5] At the same time the Soviet Union found it easy to vote for the positions on decolonization advocated by the United Nations' anticolonial majority.

The overall impression is unmistakable nonetheless. Until the 1960s, the United States consistently enjoyed a majority position in the General Assembly, but since then it has been a member of winning coalitions in the General Assembly less often than has the Soviet Union. Furthermore, the American position has noticeably deteriorated over time, whereas the Soviet position in relation to the majority has improved. Indeed, the relative political success of each superpower as measured by these data has undergone a profound transformation over the past four decades.

The drop in American success in relation to the majority following the Fifteenth General Assembly in 1960 is noteworthy, for it was then that 17 new states were admitted to the United Nations, nearly all of them African. Thereafter the United Nations came to be dominated by the Third World. By the 1980s, well over half of its nearly 160 members came from Africa and Asia. In 1945 less than a quarter of the organization's memberships came from these two regions.

Most of the Third World nations that have joined the United Nations since 1960 have espoused interests and objectives directly related to decolonization and economic development. They did not share the American view that the United Nations was one forum in which to pursue Cold War objectives against the Soviet Union. This did not mean they were necessarily pro-Soviet, for the Soviets, too, had used the United Nations to pursue their Cold War goals. In fact, the Soviet Union's increased voting success after 1960 was less a consequence of Soviet leadership than of its identification with the political priorities of the new Third World majority. But it did mean that the Third World was less than enthusiastic about how the United States and the Soviet Union sought to use the United Nations. Thus the "mechanical majority" presumed to have been enjoyed by the United States came to an end after 1960.

The impact of these developments on the relative position of the United States and the Soviet Union in the United Nations, and on the United Nations itself, can be illustrated with three cases: the question of seating the People's Republic of China, the struggle between the Security Council and the General Assembly for political control of the United Nations' peacekeeping activities, and the closely related struggle among United Nations' members over who pays for what.

---

5. See Rowe (1969) for an analysis of the voting success of the United States and the Soviet Union on various categories of issues discussed by the General Assembly between 1946 and 1966. This study shows that the United States consistently enjoyed greater success on Cold War issues than did the Soviet Union.

The China Question

The "China question" plagued the United Nations for over twenty years—from 1949, when the communists successfully established control over the mainland at the expense of Nationalist Chinese, who retreated to the island of Formosa, until 1971, when the People's Republic of China was finally seated in the world body. The issue was legal but, more so, political: which *government* of China should represent the *state* of China, one of the original members of the United Nations and one of the five great powers with a Security Council veto.

An important background to this issue is the general question of membership, which the United Nations has persistently confronted. Because the United Nations originated as a coalition of victorious wartime allies, the organization faced for roughly a decade the political question of how those "converted" to the antifascist side of peace might be admitted to the club. As the Cold War evolved, both the United States and the Soviet Union approached this issue, not from the viewpoint of who sided with whom during World War II but, rather, who sided with whom in the Cold War. Thus the United States ensured that Soviet protégés applying for membership were denied the necessary Security Council majority, and the Soviet Union used its veto to keep out Western-sponsored applicants. Nearly half of the vetoes cast by the Soviet Union were for this purpose (Stoessinger, 1977).

In 1955, the United States and the Soviet Union negotiated a compromise that resulted in the admission of sixteen new members to the United Nations. The deal permitted the superpowers to support a politically balanced package of applicants, including pro-Easterners, pro-Westerners, and neutrals. The agreement opened the floodgates, and by 1980, the United Nations had more than 150 members, roughly three times the original number.

But mainland China was not part of the 1955 deal. In fact, that matter was the prerogative of the General Assembly, because the issue was not the admission of a new member (an issue subject to veto in the Security Council) but the question of determining which of two governments claiming the right to represent an existing member state should be seated (a matter solely within the jurisdiction of the General Assembly).

The United States sought to prevent the communist government in Peking from being seated at the expense of the Nationalists. The initial American tactic was to avoid direct confrontation. Each year from 1951 to 1960 it proposed that the question be deferred, and year after year it won. Then, in 1961, the United States changed its tactic. Instead of deferring the issue, it proposed that the seating of the People's Republic of China be considered an "important question." This meant that a two-thirds rather than a simple majority was required. Again, the American proposal prevailed.

The China issue was debated in the General Assembly for the next decade. While the debate continued, important developments were occurring outside the United Nations—a growing split between the Soviet Union and China, the emergence of Soviet-American détente, moves toward rapprochement between the United States and China, and increasing public support within the United States for representation of the Peking government in the United Nations. In 1971, the United States finally capitulated; the People's Republic of China was seated; and the Nationalist government of Taiwan, in a face-saving move on the eve of the vote, announced its withdrawal. "After twenty-two years of diplomatic warfare, the United States had suffered its first dramatic parliamentary defeat. Peking was in, and Taiwan was out" (Stoessinger, 1977).

Over the next decade the United States suffered other defeats. In 1983, for example, it was the target of a resolution, approved overwhelmingly, that deplored its invasion of Grenada. In an earlier example, in 1974 it was in a distinct minority in opposing the extension by the General Assembly of permanent observer status to the Palestine Liberation Organization. And in 1975 it lost an important battle when the General Assembly went on record branding Zionism "a form of racism and racial discrimination."[6] The vote outraged the American ambassador to the United Nations, Daniel P. Moynihan, and led him to attack the United Nations bitterly. His view is summed up in the phrase "the tyranny of the UN's 'new majority.'"[7] Times had indeed changed!

From Uniting for Peace to the First Financial Crisis

The political tug of war between the Security Council and the General Assembly for political control of United Nations peacekeeping activities, with the United States and the Soviet Union again the principal players in the contest, also illustrates the impact of member states' foreign policy objectives on the actions of the United Nations.

Following the return of the Soviet Union to the Security Council in 1950, responsibility for United Nations' oversight functions regarding the Korean police action passed to the General Assembly. In an effort to ensure the permanence of this arrangement, the United States sponsored the Uniting for Peace Resolution, which granted to the assembly the power to meet in emergency session and to adopt collective measures to deal with "threats to the peace, breaches of the peace, and acts of aggression" in the event the Security Council was unable to act because of a veto. The Soviet Union strenuously opposed the measure, because it implied that the United Nations might undertake enforcement measures against the wishes of a great power. But the American position prevailed overwhelmingly.

The first time Uniting for Peace procedures were used after the Korean War was in 1956, when the General Assembly authorized the United Nations

---

6. See Stoessinger (1977) for a discussion of the various states' motivations that voted in favor of this resolution.

7. Moynihan's (1975) views of the Third World majority in the United Nations were contained in an article in the March 1975 issue of *Commentary*. Subsequently he wrote a book about his experiences at the United Nations. The title reflects Moynihan's view: *A Dangerous Place* (Moynihan with Weaver, 1978).

Emergency Force (UNEF) to try to restore peace in the Middle East following the eruption of war between Egypt on one side and Israel, Britain, and France on the other. Interestingly, it was not the Soviet Union that cast the negative vote giving rise to the emergency assembly session but, rather, Britain and France. Moreover, the General Assembly did not authorize the use of force in the same way it had in Korea. Instead, it created a "peacekeeping" force whose functions differed substantially from those implied in the principle of collective security. Collective security requires enforcement measures against an aggressor; peacekeeping implies no punishment but, instead, maintenance of the status quo. In short, both the circumstances and the outcome of this first use of Uniting for Peace were substantially different from what the United States had envisioned only six years earlier.

Emergency special sessions of the General Assembly under the Uniting for Peace provisions have been called only sparingly. A second session was called in 1956 to respond to the Soviet intervention in the Hungarian uprising, but no enforcement procedures were adopted. In 1958 the assembly met to consider developments in Lebanon, where American marines had intervened. In 1960, following a Soviet veto in the Security Council, the assembly took over direction of the United Nations Operation in the Congo (ONUC), which had earlier been authorized by the Security Council. And in 1967 the General Assembly met in emergency session in yet another effort to contain the Middle East conflict. More recently, the General Assembly met in emergency session in January 1980 to consider the Soviet intervention in Afghanistan following a Soviet veto in the Security Council.[8] As in the case of the 1956 Hungarian uprising, no enforcement procedures were authorized in a dispute directly involving one of the two most important members of the Security Council.

The use of the Uniting for Peace process in 1980 was somewhat unexpected. The resolution's "transfer" provisions—those moving an issue from the Security Council to the General Assembly—appeared to have become a dead letter by that time. This conclusion is based on the view that, first, the United Nations Congo operation (1960–1964) went too far in opposing the interests of one of the superpowers (the Soviet Union, in that case) and that, second, by the mid-1960s the United States had become as apprehensive about the General Assembly as had the Soviet Union in the 1950s. Its concern was based on the erosion of its ability to command a majority for the positions it espoused in the expanding world forum. It is noteworthy that the Uniting for Peace resolution has never resulted in assembly action in quite the same way that the United States envisioned when it contemplated the lessons of Korea, namely, collective enforcement against aggressive actions initiated or backed by a great power (see Claude, 1971).

---

8. The initiative for an emergency special session was launched by Third World nations. Clearly the United States supported the move, but the fact that it did not have to launch it is reminiscent of the circumstances that led the United States to support the Uniting for Peace procedures in the first place.

Growing American apprehension about the General Assembly was played out in the United Nations' financial crisis. The Soviet Union did not oppose creation of UNEF by the General Assembly in 1956, but it did refuse to pay for the operation, thus exercising a "financial veto." It also refused four years later to share the costs of the Congo operation. The United States built a convincing legal case that the Soviet Union and others who refused to pay were in fact obliged to assume their share of the costs of these operations. The Soviet Union still refused, alleging that the issue was political, not legal. As Stoessinger (1977) observed, "Never had so many people argued so much about so little money. The financial crisis was in reality a political crisis over the proper role for the United Nations to play in the national policies of its member states, particularly the superpowers. Only secondarily was it a crisis over the costs of UN membership."

The crisis peaked in 1964. The United States threatened to deprive the Soviet Union of its vote in the General Assembly, which, according to Article 19 of the charter, could be done by majority vote to any state whose unmet financial obligations to the organization were equal to or greater than its assessments for the preceding two years.[9] In response, the Soviet Union threatened to withdraw from the United Nations. The United States decided to avoid a showdown.

At that time the United States probably had the votes in the assembly necessary to carry out its threat. But the Soviet threat was more credible and, if carried out, would have destroyed the very foundation of the United Nations. Again the political realities of the United Nations that resulted from the changing composition of its membership—and changes in international allegiances throughout world politics—lurked in the background. The United States at one time may have been willing to allow the General Assembly to exercise political control over United Nations peacekeeping activities, but by the mid-1960s it was less certain that such control would not be detrimental to American interests. This view was thus akin to what the Soviet Union had felt in the 1950s, and especially during the Congo operation in the early 1960s.

In acknowledging the American defeat on the issue of collective financial responsibility for United Nations activities, then UN Ambassador Arthur J. Goldberg added that "the United States reserves the same option to make exception [that is, to withhold support from United Nations actions with which it disagrees] if, in our view, strong and compelling reasons exist for doing so. There can be no double standard among members of the Organization." The United States thus signaled that it, too, was coming to view the

---

9. Technically, Article 19 assumes that a state more than two years in arrears would forfeit its vote more or less automatically, following a ruling of the president of the General Assembly, based on a report of the General Assembly's Administrative and Budget Committee. It was determined in 1964, however, that the Soviet Union would challenge such a presidential determination, thus provoking a vote. It should also be noted that countries other than the Soviet Union were also in arrears on the peacekeeping activities, but these states commanded far less attention.

Security Council as the relatively safer haven in which issues of international peace and security should be handled. Since the mid-1960s all questions regarding the financing of peacekeeping activities have been handled by the Security Council, in which the superpowers can protect their interests with the veto.

In the two decades following the financial crisis of 1964–1965, the Soviet Union continued to withhold payments earmarked for certain United Nations activities, the most important of which were its share of the costs of UNEF and the United Nations Interim Force in Lebanon (UNIFIL). Its position on the peacekeeping issue thus has remained the same for decades: that those responsible for creating the need for peacekeeping operations (Israel in the case of Lebanon) should bear the cost and that only the Security Council can apportion the cost of such operations, not the General Assembly (as in the case of UNEF).

Because of these positions, the Soviet Union once more placed itself in a situation in which its financial arrears could put it in violation of Article 19. Then, unexpectedly, the Soviet Union announced in 1987 that it would pay all of its outstanding debts to the United Nations as part of a foreign policy strategy designed to place greater emphasis on the organization. Included in the $245 million debt dating back to the early 1970s was nearly $200 million withheld from UN peacekeeping operations. Soviet officials argued that the move was a logical extension of *perestroika*, or restructuring of the Soviet economy. "To modernize at home, they said, Moscow would have to back away from its costly involvements in the Third World. . . . But rather than simply abandon most of these political investments—which would permit Washington to move into the vacuums and cause a significant loss of face for Moscow—the Soviets hope to neutralize . . . regional disputes by bringing in a strengthened United Nations as buffer and peacekeeper" (Berlin, 1987–1988). What the Soviet move might portend for future UN peacekeeping operations and for involvement of the world organization in disputes between the superpowers remains to be seen, but in some respects the Soviet position harkens back to the concept of the United Nations' founding fathers, "who viewed the Organization as a tool of hegemony—an institution run by the major powers and designed to serve their needs before those of the majority" (Berlin, 1987–1988). But the immediate effect was to alleviate the crisis atmosphere under which the United Nations had operated for some time, as we shall discuss more fully later.

Interestingly, the United States itself now withholds payments to some programs with which it disagrees. The reason is quite clear: "The key to superpower behavior in the United Nations is power and influence. Money is a symbol of that power. States will not oppose policies because they refuse to pay for them; they will refuse to pay for them because they oppose them. In this fundamental respect, the two superpowers remain very much alike" (Stoessinger, 1977).

On the most pressing issues regarding world peace, the United States, the Soviet Union, and the other great powers remain the most important actors in the United Nations. But on other issues, which are probably more numerous, Third World nations command relatively more influence. "When the initiative lies with others, the nonaligned still enjoy collectively a negative veto, because no majority of nine can be mustered [in the Security Council] without them. In the political bargaining process their views must be taken into account even on issues that do not directly interest them" (Riggs, 1978). It seems that the hidden veto once possessed by the United States in the Security Council may have found a new counterpart.

The Third World: From Background to Center Stage

The preceding discussion demonstrates that the superpowers' objectives in the United Nations have been significantly affected by the increasing number of Third World members. Third World objectives have also been affected by the East–West dispute. In many respects, however, the Third World has become relatively more effective than the superpowers in utilizing the United Nations' institutional structures and procedures, especially in the General Assembly, to advance its interests. For example, the General Assembly's one-state, one-vote rule facilitated the Third World's ability to focus global attention on the issue of colonialism and to "delegitimize" it as a form of political organization (see Chapter 5).

Economic development has been another principal Third World objective advanced in the United Nations forum. In the 1950s the then numerically smaller group of Third World nations pressed for organizational responses to their needs and realized some modest (if less than hoped for) results. The United Nations Special Fund, for example, was created as a partial response to Third World pressure for substantial United Nations economic development aid.

As their numbers in the United Nations increased in the 1960s, Third World nations were able to press even more vigorously for economic development and related issues. By the early 1960s the group surpassed the two-thirds mark as a proportion of the total membership. This means that the Group of 77, if and when it can act as a unit, can pass any measure it chooses. In doing so it runs the risk of alienating the minority of industrialized nations, who for the most part pay the costs of United Nations operations. The one-state, one-vote principle in the General Assembly nonetheless accords the developing nations an important measure of political power.

Third World interests have been expressed in a host of world conferences and special General Assembly sessions held since the early 1970s. Among the common characteristics of these conferences is that all were "designed to change attitudes, to stimulate political will, and to raise the level of national and global interest in the subject" (Feld and Jordan, 1983). However, because these conferences frequently become forums for vituperative exchanges between North and South, their contribution to solving—not just articulating—global problems has been minimal. The range of *ad hoc* conferences is significant nevertheless and draws attention to the agenda of issues especially important to the Third World: human environment (1972), law of the sea (1973), population (1974 and 1984), food (1974), women (1975, 1980, and 1985), human settlements (1976), basic human needs (1976), water (1977), desertification (1977), disarmament (1978 and 1982), racism and racial discrimination (1978), technical cooperation among developing countries (1978), agrarian reform and rural development (1979), science and technology for development (1979), new and renewable sources of energy (1981), least-developed countries (1981), aging (1982), the peaceful uses of outer space (1982), Palestine (1982), the prevention of crime and the treatment of offenders (1985), and drug abuse and illicit trafficking in drugs (1987). The subjects covered in the world conferences since 1972 are in effect a list of "the most vital issues of present world conditions," whereas the conferences themselves "represent a beginning in a long and evolving process of keeping within manageable propositions the major problems of humanity. Action plans will have to be revised at later dates, and the evolutionary process will be slow, but momentum has been given to an ongoing set of processes for meeting human demands and aspirations" (Bennett, 1988). In this the United Nations, spurred on by the Third World, can take some credit.

The pervasiveness of the global *ad hoc* conference forum adds to the Third World's ability to use the United Nations' institutional procedures to promote its interests. As the world conference strategy suggests, developing nations prefer broadly based institutional settings in which the one-state, one-vote principle gives them an advantage. Such forums force recognition of the global community's shared stake in the outcome of negotiations on particular issues. In contrast, the First World prefers small, functionally specific forums, generally outside the General Assembly, which, they believe, "are more likely to involve those states that have a real stake in the outcome of the deliberations." According to this viewpoint, "large, general-purpose bodies only encourage ill-informed participation by states uninvolved in the issue at hand and thus increase the likelihood of irresponsibly politicizing the agenda" (Gregg, 1977).

As the preeminent leader of the First World, the United States found itself out of step with majority sentiments in the United Nations during much of the 1970s and 1980s, not only on the issue of the forum in which the North–South dialogue should take place, but also often on the issues discussed in the conferences. It also found itself responsible for much of the escalating cost of running the United Nations that the world conference strategy helped propel. The result was a reinforcement of the United States' growing disenchantment with the world organization. Because the United Nations depends so heavily on the United States, it is useful to examine some of the ways in which the United States has responded to the United Nations' changing political climate.

The United States and the United Nations

A strong case can be made that the policies and programs of the United Nations and the political values and interests of the United States are compatible (Puchala, 1982–1983; see also the essays in Gati, 1983; and Ruggie, 1985). How and why this is the case is not always obvious to a nation that provides the greatest proportion of the money needed to run the United Nations while simultaneously finding itself defending its own interests and values against an antagonistic Third World and Soviet-led socialist coalition.

The growing American disaffection with what it regards as the United Nations' anti-Western bias has manifested itself in several ways. We shall examine two: money and membership.

MONEY   During the 1980s in particular, the United States, not unlike the Soviet Union before it, chose to withhold payment selectively from various UN programs in an effort to register its unhappiness with the organization's activities and, perhaps, to change their direction.

In December 1982, for example, the Reagan administration announced that it would not pay its $1 million annual assessment for implementing the deep-seabed mining provisions of the United Nations–sponsored treaty on the law of the sea. The treaty, concluded in 1982 after a decade of painstaking negotiations, envisions the creation of an international mining company called the Enterprise that would compete with private companies in mining the rich resources of the deep seabed and that would require a mandatory transfer of technology from private companies. In these and other ways, the International Seabed Authority created by the Law of the Sea Treaty, of which the Enterprise is one element, effectively tilts toward the developing nations at the expense of those in the industrial West, where the headquarters of multinational corporations with the technological capability to do the mining are located. Although the negotiations leading to the treaty were premised on the view that the oceans constitute a "common heritage of mankind," the Reagan administration chose instead to protect the interests of the private companies.

At a more fundamental level, the United States has criticized the one-state, one-vote procedures used to allocate the United Nations' expenses among member states and the way those funds are spent. Pressures toward reform of budgetary decision making (mandated by the United States Congress) combined with the slow payment of dues and the selective withholding of funds by the United States and other nations to force a second United Nations financial crisis in 1986. Underlying the crisis was "a tension between the principle of sovereign equality of member states, permitting the more numerous developing countries to wield considerable influence over the kinds of issues on which the U.N.'s attention and resources are focused, and the need to set priorities and manage more effectively the U.N.'s limited monies and manpower, an increasing concern of the developed countries" ("Financing the United Nations," n.d.).

The United Nations' budget consists of three distinct elements: the regular budget (which includes the expenditures of the fifteen specialized agencies of the United Nations, each of which has its own budgetary procedures), the peacekeeping budget, and the budget for voluntary programs. States contribute to the voluntary programs and some of the peacekeeping activities as they see fit. The regular program and some of the peacekeeping activities are subject to assessments.

The precise mechanism by which assessments are determined is complicated (see Lister, 1986), but generally assessments are designed to reflect states' capacity to pay. Thus the United States, which has the greatest capacity to pay, contributes 25 percent of the regular budget of the United Nations, whereas several dozen poor nations pay the minimum, which is 0.01 percent of the regular budget. The United States is also a prime contributor to the United Nations' peacekeeping and voluntary programs. In all, it paid $940 million of the costs of the United Nations in 1985, or 24 percent of the organization's $4 billion budget.[10]

As noted, the first United Nations financial crisis (1964–1965) arose out of the unwillingness of some states to pay for major UN peacekeeping activities. Some continue to refuse to pay for these (even the United States has expressed reservations about continuing its support of the United Nations force in Lebanon [UNIFIL]), but the second financial dispute was a regular budgetary crisis. It arose out of the natural tendency of governments (like individuals) to pay their bills as late as possible and, more importantly, out of the refusal of some to pay for activities that they vigorously opposed as a matter of principle.[11] Such opposition is to be expected in an organization that reflects a world marked by deep-seated antagonisms and often sharply different world views, but it immediately challenges the principle of the United Nations Charter embodied in Article 17, which states that "expenses of the Organization shall be borne by the members as apportioned by the General Assembly."

When the General Assembly apportions expenses, it does so on the basis of one-state, one-vote majority rule. The problem is that those with the most votes—the Third World nations—do not have the money, and those that do—the industrialized nations of the First and Second Worlds—do not have the

---

10. For comparative purposes, it is useful to note that the U.S. contribution to the United Nations in 1985 was roughly the same as the expenditures of the state of Rhode Island, whereas the budget of the entire United Nations system was roughly equal to the budget of the state of Louisiana. Outlays for U.S. national defense in 1985 were more than three hundred times greater than its expenditures on the United Nations.

11. The following refuse to pay for regular budget activities that they do not support or feel were improperly imposed: Bulgaria, Bylorussian SSR, China, Czechoslovakia, East Germany, France, Hungary, Israel, Kampuchea, Mongolia, Poland, Romania, South Africa, Ukrainian SSR, USSR, United States, and Vietnam. In addition to some of these, nine others refuse to pay for some major peacekeeping operations: Algeria, Benin, Cuba, Democratic Yemen, Iraq, Laos, Libya, Syria, and Yemen (Lister, 1986). As noted, the Soviet Union agreed in 1987 to pay its debts to the United Nations.

Figure 6.4 ▪ Relationship between UN Budget Assessments and Voting Strength in the General Assembly

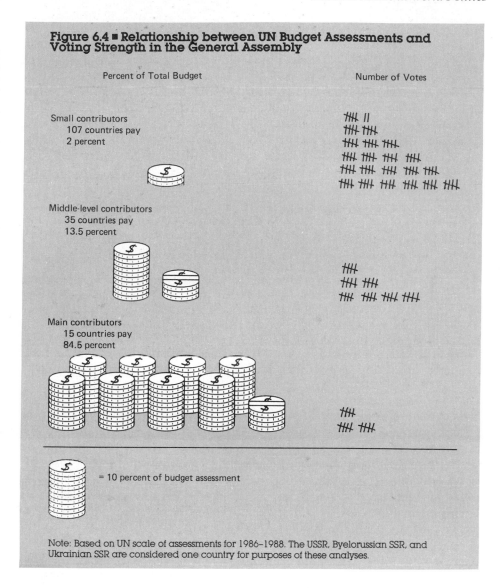

Percent of Total Budget

Number of Votes

Small contributors
 107 countries pay
 2 percent

Middle-level contributors
 35 countries pay
 13.5 percent

Main contributors
 15 countries pay
 84.5 percent

= 10 percent of budget assessment

Note: Based on UN scale of assessments for 1986–1988. The USSR, Byelorussian SSR, and Ukrainian SSR are considered one country for purposes of these analyses.

votes. These vast disparities are illustrated in Figure 6.4. It shows that the main contributors to the United Nations command only fifteen votes, even though they pay nearly 85 percent of its costs. At the other end of the spectrum, the poorer members of the United Nations, who collectively pay only about 2 percent of the organization's costs, command over one hundred votes.

At issue, of course, is not simply money—which remains, as in the crisis of the 1960s, a comparatively paltry sum—but political influence. The 144 states that do not have the money vigorously embrace the principles embodied in the

United Nations Charter, arguing that program needs should determine expenditure levels, rather than the other way around, whereas the fifteen major contributors have been sensitive to the amount they are asked to pay and the purposes for which they are providing funds (Lister, 1986). In many cases these are purposes that are embraced by Third World nations but that fail to enjoy broad political support among the other diverse groups of states making up the United Nations. Thus, demands on the budget reflect the interests of the developing nations in such areas as disarmament, economic development, the Middle East, and Southern Africa.

Consider, for example, the many world conferences held during the past decade and a half:

> Although some of the international colloquies enjoyed Western backing, such as the conferences on the environment, food, population, water sources, and the Law of the Sea, the driving force behind most of them came from the developing nations.
>
> Far from being isolated events, major international conferences are usually stages along a sort of evolutionary ladder. After a particular world problem is acknowledged in a General Assembly resolution, it is often investigated by a United Nations study. The study leads to a conference and the conference to a follow-up action, usually involving an intergovernmental committee with its own mini-secretariat, until—by a series of gradual steps—an institution is created to deal with the problem. ("Financing the United Nations," n.d.: 5)

This evolutionary development has contributed to the sharp increase in the costs of the United Nations since the 1970s, a major concern of the major budget contributors.

It is against this background of endemic cash-flow problems caused by often principled opposition to the sharply increased cost of the work of the organization that the United States precipitated a UN financial crisis in 1986. Owing to several actions by Congress, the United States withheld over half of its roughly $200 million regular-budget contribution. Principal among the congressional actions was the so-called Kassebaum amendment, which effectively cut the United States' contribution from its assessed level of 25 percent to 20 percent pending the development of a system of weighted voting for financial decision making. Other congressional actions mandated across-the-board cuts in the United States' support of the United Nations, as well as cuts targeted at specific items.

The Kassebaum amendment challenged the principle on which the General Assembly makes its budgetary decisions. It effectively asked the United Nations either to adopt a system of weighted voting, in which those that pay more have more votes (as is done in other international organizations, like the International Monetary Fund and the World Bank), or to reduce the United States' assessment. The former is virtually impossible, as it would require an amendment of the UN Charter, whereas the latter would require other states to pay more of the United Nations' costs, which they have indicated they are unwilling to do. The result, then, would be a reduction in the United Nations' activities.

Progress was made during 1987 in devising a political solution to the United Nations' financial crunch that would avert insolvency, on the one hand, and placate the concerns of those that have to pay the most, on the other. Although weighted voting cannot realistically be contemplated, procedures were devised whereby budget recommendations would be made by committees containing a disproportionate number of the major budget contributors.[12] Whether such procedures will mollify congressional critics in the United States remains to be seen. As the United States copes with severe budgetary stringency at home, the retreat from multilateralism, of which its outward criticism and reluctant financial support of the United Nations are symbolic, can be expected to continue, not abate. One thing that might push the United States toward a more moderate position on some of these financial issues is the surprising change in the posture of the Soviet Union toward the United Nations under the innovative leadership of General Secretary Mikhail Gorbachev.

MEMBERSHIP   A second way that the United States has registered its dissatisfaction with what it sees as the anti-Western drift of many United Nations bodies has been to terminate its membership in them. In the 1970s, for example, in an effort to shift the direction of its policies, the Carter administration withdrew for a time from the International Labor Organization. Similarly, the Reagan administration withdrew from the United Nations Educational, Scientific and Cultural Organization (UNESCO) in response to what it regarded as the politicization of UNESCO and its hostility toward Western values, thereby depriving it of a quarter of its budget.[13]

The feud between the United States and UNESCO is long-standing. In the mid-1970s the United States withheld payment of its UNESCO dues in response to an Arab-led effort to oust Israel from the organization. A more recent issue of concern to the United States is UNESCO's efforts to promote a New World Information and Communication Order (NWICO).

Third World nations, together with the Soviet Union and the other communist states, began pushing for a new global information order in UNESCO at the same time that the Group of 77 launched its drive for a New International Economic Order in the General Assembly. The effort stems from the Third

---

12. Granting some members of the United Nations special status in its deliberative bodies is commonly used to secure the political support of more powerful states and is one way in which the organization mirrors the structural inequalities found elsewhere in world politics. The special status (permanent membership) enjoyed by only five members of the Security Council is the clearest expression of these inequalities, but they apply to other limited-membership organs of the United Nations as well (see Jacobsen, 1969, 1978; Volgy and Quistgard, 1974). A weighted voting scheme would formalize these inequalities, although the precise ways in which they would reflect the "real world" would vary, depending on the weighting scheme chosen.

13. Ironically, the U.S. withdrawal from the UNESCO came after most observers felt UNESCO had conformed to U.S. demands (Coate, 1988). The fact that the United States did not alter its decision to withdraw can be attributed to the Reagan administration's urge during its early years to reduce United States involvement in multilateral organizations generally.

World's dissatisfaction with the media coverage it receives from Western news agencies and from its resentment of Western domination of other forms of communication, ranging from radio, television, and films to book publishing and satellite transmissions. At present, virtually all of the world's means of communication are controlled by First and Second World nations.

> There is concern on the part of many Third World countries that, at home, the one-way inward flow of information will encourage consumerism and perpetuate economic dependency. Third World leaders also worry that imbalanced communication adversely will affect northern decisions on the south's economic development. Instead of a free flow of news which the U.S. and other Western countries vigorously defend, the developing countries insist on creation of a free and balanced flow. (Mowlana, 1983: 44)[14]

The situation facing the Third World today is, ironically, not unlike what the United States itself faced before it was a part of the international news monopoly.

> At that time, a European news cartel—composed of the English Reuters, French Havas, and German Wolff agencies—controlled all foreign news sent into the U.S. and all American news to the world. Kent Cooper, then executive manager of the Associated Press, led the crusade to break up the European cartel. "Reuters decided what news was to be sent from America," he wrote. "It told the world about Indians on the warpath in the West, lynchings in the South, and bizarre crimes in the North. The charge for decades was that nothing creditable to America was ever sent. American businessmen criticized the Associated Press for permitting Reuters to belittle America abroad." Cooper pointed out that Havas and Reuters always glorified their own countries. Today, the ironic parallel, as it is perceived, has not been missed by the Third World. (Mowlana, 1983: 43)

What concerns the United States today is the meaning of a "balanced" flow of communication. Although it recognizes that currently there is an imbalance between the North and the South (and it has therefore helped develop communications infrastructures in the Third World), it fears any move toward government controls and the censorship to which they may lead. Indeed, the opinion of the United States is "that no communication system in which the government has a share can truly be free" (Mowlana, 1983). This view places the United States in a rather peculiar situation in the NWICO debate, as even other Western countries have various forms of direct government involvement in their communications industries. But the importance of the United States is nevertheless great, for it is a massive supplier of media products to the rest of the world but consumes almost nothing produced abroad. At stake, therefore, is not only the issue of freedom of the press but also millions of dollars.

Whenever economic interests are at stake, domestic political considerations can be expected to bear on states' foreign policy choices in ways that

---

14. The discussion of the NWICO draws on this source.

may not always appear compatible with long-range foreign policy objectives. In the United States, the Reagan administration's drive to cut government spending resulted in efforts by the United States Congress to curtail the United States' contribution to various multilateral programs. Congress also approved a bill in 1983 that sought to tie the allocation of American foreign aid to the willingness of Third World nations to support the United States in United Nations voting on issues that the United States regarded as important to its interests.

But one must be careful not to assume that these maneuvers are the reactions of a nation otherwise without influence in the United Nations. As Donald J. Puchala (1982–1983) has pointed out, "Little of substance can happen in the U.N. system without American cooperation—and little happens without American resources—so that it is not very surprising that negotiators often defer to United States preferences." Gone, however, is the idealism about the United Nations that was once widespread in the United States. In its place have arisen resentment at the United Nations' seeming inability to act and disillusionment with the attitudes of many of its members toward the United States. Gone too are the days when the United States could use the United Nations to realize its own foreign policy objectives without serious challenge from others. In this sense the transformations in the United Nations mirror the relative decline of American power which is so closely related to the transformation of world politics.

The political tug of war in the United States over how international institutions should serve national interests is an indication of an important fact—that the United Nations, and international organizations generally, are products of the interests of the nation-states that comprise them. In the words of Inis Claude (1967): "The United Nations has no purposes—and can have none—of its own."

International organizations are also capable of adjusting to changing political realities, but it is probably unrealistic to expect great adaptations by them. The ability of the United Nations in particular to rise above the conflicts between states and pursue an independent role in world politics is severely circumscribed. Instead, the United Nations is more often either the *instrument* of states' foreign policies or the *arena* within which states debate issues than it is an independent *actor* in world politics (Archer, 1983). Various secretaries general have achieved some degree of autonomy and pursued quasi-independent roles in world politics. But such activities are more the exception than the rule.

Although the United Nations is rarely able to behave as an independent international actor, it has surely shaped the behaviors of states.[15] Individuals

---

15. Finkelstein (1980) challenges the view that IGOs are merely tools of states and forums for the conduct of interstate bargaining. He argues that "IGOs assert independence. . . . They compete for resources and over turf. They behave in ways which are hard to reconcile with the belief that the diplomacy of member states is the sole determinant of IGO behavior, unless one is prepared to argue also that governments want IGOs to behave that way. . . . IGOs do have purposes of their own."

who have participated in its affairs may also have had their nationalistic perceptions broadened (Alger, 1965; Riggs, 1977). And although the United Nations' ambitious purposes have not been fulfilled, the organization's contribution to the alleviation of human suffering is undeniable. Because it generally cannot act autonomously, however, the United Nations lacks the legitimacy to serve as an independent force capable of powerfully influencing the course of world affairs.

OTHER IGOs: THE EUROPEAN COMMUNITY AND REGIONAL ORGANIZATIONS

The meaning of *autonomy* and *legitimacy* can be illustrated by contrasting the United Nations with the European Community (EC). The latter is made up of three organizations: the European Coal and Steel Community (ECSC, created in 1952), the European Atomic Energy Community (Euratom, 1958), and the European Economic Community (EEC, 1958). The immediate purpose of these institutions (which were first formed by France, West Germany, Italy, Luxembourg, Belgium, and the Netherlands) was the promotion of broad economic integration among the six. But some were also hopeful that the institutions might eventually lead to a United States of Europe.

Since 1967 the three communities have shared common organizational structures (see Figure 6.5), the most important of which is the Council of Ministers. As the name implies, the council consists of cabinet ministers drawn from the European Community's member states. The foreign ministers participate in the council when the most important decisions are made. In this respect the European Community as an association of nation-states is little different from the United Nations. But the EC is also a *supranational* entity empowered to make decisions binding on its national members without being subject to their individual approval. An important instrumentality in making these decisions is the commission and its thousands of European technocrats who, in principle, owe loyalty to the European Community, not to its national constituents. Furthermore, since the mid-1970s the community has had access to sources of revenue independent of its member states, and in 1979 the European Parliament began to be chosen by direct election. (Previously its members had been chosen by the member states' national parliaments.)

None of this means that the European Community will automatically become an integrated political entity approximating a United States of Europe, for integration can be halted or even reversed as a consequence of decisions made by nation-states. As the EC expanded from six members to twelve two decades later,[16] it has found it difficult to ameliorate differences between its more industrialized northern members and those in Southern Europe.

---

16. The European Community was expanded from six to nine members in 1973 with the addition of Denmark, Ireland, and the United Kingdom, from nine to ten in 1981 with the addition of Greece, and from ten to twelve in 1986 with the addition of Spain and Portugal. Turkey applied for membership in 1987.

FIGURE 6.5 ▪ Institutions and Decision-making Process of the European Community

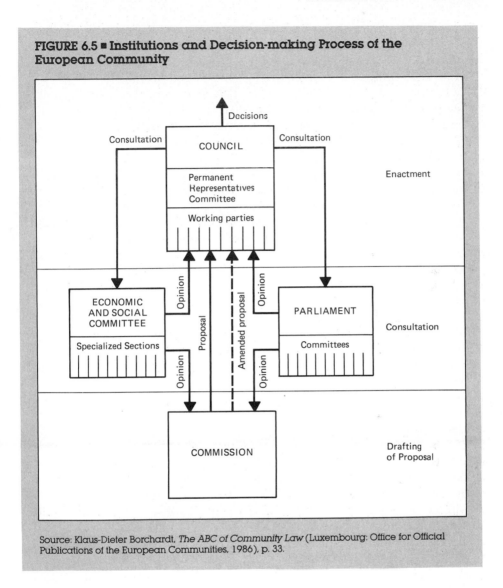

Source: Klaus-Dieter Borchardt, *The ABC of Community Law* (Luxembourg: Office for Official Publications of the European Communities, 1986), p. 33.

Even without such regional differences between the community's richer and poorer members, it has found it difficult to move from a customs union, in which customs duties have been eliminated, and from the free movement of workers, which the EC also enjoys, to a genuine common market, in which the frontiers between member states have been completely abolished. In a genuine common market, a number of inhibitions still apparent in Europe would not exist, including exchange controls, restraints on the movement of goods (many of which are nontariff barriers to trade, discussed in Chapter 7) and the absence of harmonization of product standards (for example, uniform socket sizes for electrical appliances), variations in rules governing taxation and capital movements, regulations on transport standards (such as rules governing truckers' driving hours, rest periods, and the makeup of teams of drivers), and the like (see "Progress Report on Europe's Single Internal Market," 1987). All of these inhibitions serve to safeguard national interests and autonomy. Europe has a long way to travel before it will be able to remove these and to transfer sovereign control to community institutions.

In an apparent effort to infuse the community with new purpose, the EC in 1987, in its first major revision of the Treaty of Rome which established the six-member EEC in 1957, adopted the Single European Act, in which the members of the EC committed themselves to the realization of a single, internal European market by 1992. An important element of the Single European Act is a commitment to majority rule rather than the previously common practice of consensus decision making in the Council of Ministers. Such a procedure should restrict the ability of individual member nations to veto key decisions with which they might disagree.

Despite setbacks in the realization of the optimistic goals embraced by many of its founders, and even without full realization of the promises of the Single European Act, the European Community as an international institution has characteristics that clearly distinguish it from most other international organizations, and in particular from the United Nations. Whereas the United Nations remains almost wholly dependent on its members and therefore does little more than reflect the political reality of the international political system in which it resides, the European Community has a much greater capacity to shape independently its regional subsystem and perhaps the global system as well. In addition to the characteristics of its internal structures, for example, community members have on occasion assumed a common position on important global issues (such as the Arab-Israeli conflict). European political cooperation has in fact materialized in a number of ways not anticipated when the common market was first formed (see Knudsen, 1984).

In the decades following Europe's initiatives, a dozen or so regional economic schemes were created in various other parts of the world, notably among Third World nations.[17] Few achieved anything approaching the same level of economic integration and supranational institution building as in Western Europe, however. Although the reasons underlying the generally modest success of such attempts vary, they boil down to the reluctance of national political leaders to make the kinds of choices that would undermine their sovereignty. At the same time, these attempts at regional cooperation demonstrate the inability of nations to resolve individually the problems confronting them collectively. In this sense, the nation-state seems both ill suited for managing transnational policy problems and for being an agent of organized efforts to do so. The ultimate effect of the collective problem-solving institutions on world politics is therefore problematic. Before probing

---

17. Most of these are designed to stimulate economic growth among its regional members. Regional organizations exist in a variety of forms for different purposes, which makes their characterization and classification difficult. For a discussion of major regional organizations, see Taylor (1984).

this matter further, however, let us first examine another transnational man-ifestation of the transformation of world politics, the multinational enterprise.

THE RISE OF MULTINATIONAL CORPORATIONS: CURSE OR CURE?

Over the past four decades the multinational corporation (MNC) has grown dramatically in size and influence in the expanding world economy. Conse-quently, the MNC has become the object of considerable discussion and animosity: Richard J. Barnet and Ronald E. Müller (1974) refer warily to the "global reach" of the MNC; George W. Ball (1971) coined the term *cosmocorp* to suggest those entities' increasing power in the international arena; Robert Gilpin (1975) has attributed U.S. power to the MNC; David H. Blake and Robert S. Walters (1987) ask the often-posed question whether the MNC is a source of growth or underdevelopment for host countries; and Anthony Sampson (1975) has exposed the oligopolistic aspirations of the major oil companies known as the Seven Sisters. Operating at times in seeming autonomy with resources that often exceed the GNP of its host country and, in certain industries (notably oil), participating in cartels designed to control prices and production internationally, the MNC is both a source of capital investment and a threat to the nation-state.

The growing number and economic clout of MNCs contribute to the controversy surrounding their impact. It has been estimated that in the early 1980s, about eighteen thousand MNCs worldwide controlled assets in two or more countries and that these corporations were responsible for marketing roughly four-fifths of the world's trade (excluding that of centrally planned economies). Between 1960 and 1980, the revenues of the top two hundred multinational firms escalated as their combined share of the world's gross domestic product increased from 18 to 29 percent (Clairmonte and Cavanagh, 1982: 149, 152, 155).

The MNC has become so powerful and its tentacles so far-reaching that it is appropriate to inquire whether it has undermined the ability of ostensibly sovereign nation-states to control their own economies and therefore their own fates. Is it possible that MNCs are undermining the very foundations of the present international system? Or is this question perhaps based on exaggerated expectations of the MNCs' influence and therefore unwarranted?

The benefits and costs ascribed to MNCs in the debate about them are many and complex, as the summary provided in Box 6.1 makes clear. Here we focus on four major issues in the ongoing debate about multinationals: the global reach of multinational corporations, their impact on host and home countries, their involvement in politics, and the question of control.

The Global Reach and Economic Power of Multinational Corporations

What is an MNC? Definitions differ, but they all agree that it is a business enterprise organized in one society with activities abroad growing out of direct

BOX 6.1 ■ The Multinational Corporation in World Politics: A Balance Sheet of Claims and Criticisms

There are many views of the MNC. Its contributions seen as "positive" are listed on the left side, and those considered "negative" are listed on the right. Whether one classifies a contribution as positive or negative will depend largely on one's ideological perspective. Although the arguments for and against MNCs are not as simple as the characterization and classification given here suggest, they may be classified and summarized by noting that proponents and opponents have asserted, in one fashion or another, that multinational corporations . . .

Positive

- increase the volume of world trade.

- assist the aggregation of investment capital that can fund development.

- finance loans and service international debt.

- lobby for free trade and the removal of barriers to trade, such as tariffs.

- underwrite research and development that allows technological innovation.
- introduce and dispense advanced technology to less-developed countries.

- reduce the costs of goods by encouraging their production according to the principle of comparative advantage.
- generate employment.

- encourage the training of workers.
- produce new goods and expand opportunities for their purchase through the internationalization of production.

Negative

- give rise to oligopolistic conglomerations that reduce competition and free enterprise.
- raise capital in host countries (thereby depriving local industries of investment capital) but export profits to home countries.
- breed debtors and make the poor dependent on those providing loans.

- limit the availability of commodities by monopolizing their production and controlling their distribution in the world marketplace.
- export technology ill suited to underdeveloped economies.
- inhibit the growth of infant industries and local technological expertise in less-developed countries while making Third World countries dependent on First World technology.
- collude to create cartels that contribute to inflation.

- curtail employment by driving labor competition from the market.
- limit wages offered to workers.
- limit the supply of raw materials available on international markets.

(continued)

160

BOX 6.1 ■ Continued

Positive	Negative
■ disseminate marketing expertise and mass-advertising methods worldwide.	■ erode traditional cultures and national differences, leaving in their place a homogenized world culture dominated by consumer-oriented values.
■ promote national revenue and economic growth; facilitate modernization of the less-developed countries.	■ widen the gap between the rich and poor nations.
■ generate income and wealth.	■ increase the wealth of local elites at the expense of the poor.
■ advocate peaceful relations between and among states in order to preserve an orderly environment conducive to trade and profits.	■ support and rationalize repressive regimes in the name of stability and order.
■ break down national barriers and accelerate the globalization of the international economy and culture and the rules that govern international commerce.	■ challenge national sovereignty and jeopardize the autonomy of the nation-state.

investment (as opposed to portfolio investment through shareholding). Typically, MNCs are hierarchically organized and centrally directed. "A distinctive characteristic of the transnational organization is its broader-than-national perspective with respect to the pursuit of highly specialized objectives through a central optimizing strategy across national boundaries" (Huntington, 1973). Ford Motor Company's global manufacturing network that produces the Ford Escort, illustrated in Box 6.2, is a graphic example of the transnational character of a multinational manufacturing firm.

The creation of the European Economic Community (EEC) in 1958 gave impetus to this form of business organization. Because the six EEC members anticipated a common external tariff wall around their customs union, it made economic sense for American firms to establish production facilities in Europe. In this way they could remain competitive by selling their wares as domestic products rather than foreign products with their added tariff costs.[18]

---

18. The reasons for direct investments overseas are more complex than this simplified explanation suggests. The product-cycle theory is one example. According to this view, overseas expansion is essentially a defensive maneuver designed to forestall foreign competitors and hence to maintain the global competitiveness of domestically based industries. The theory views MNCs as having an edge in the initial stages of developing and producing a new product and then having to go abroad to protect export markets from foreign competitors that naturally arise as the relevant technology becomes diffused or imitated. In the final phase of the product cycle, "production has become sufficiently routinized so that the comparative advantage shifts to relatively low-skilled, low-wage, and labor-intensive economies. This is now the case, for example, in textiles, electronic components, and footwear" (Gilpin, 1975). See this source and especially Vernon (1971) for an elaboration of the product-cycle theory. Noteworthy is Gilpin's (1975) conclusion after examining several theories of foreign direct investment: "The primary drive behind the overseas expansion of today's giant corporations is maximization of corporate growth and the suppression of foreign as well as domestic competition."

Box 6.2 ■ Global Manufacturing: The Component Network for the Ford Escort (Europe)

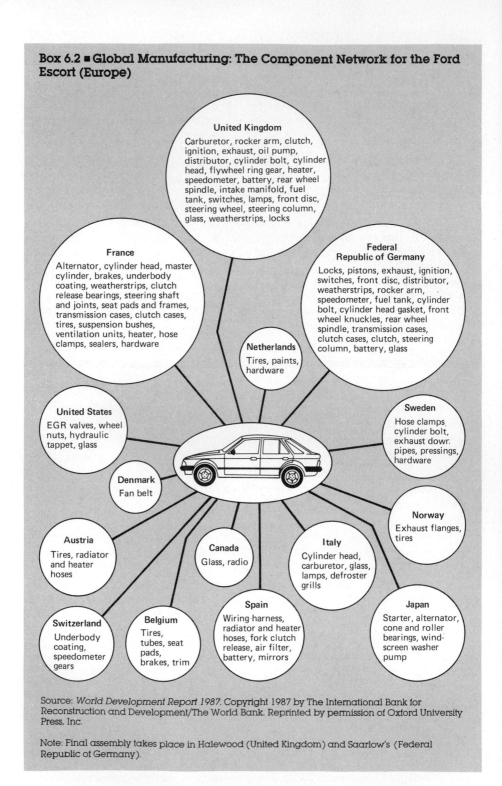

United Kingdom

Carburetor, rocker arm, clutch, ignition, exhaust, oil pump, distributor, cylinder bolt, cylinder head, flywheel ring gear, heater, speedometer, battery, rear wheel spindle, intake manifold, fuel tank, switches, lamps, front disc, steering wheel, steering column, glass, weatherstrips, locks

France

Alternator, cylinder head, master cylinder, brakes, underbody coating, weatherstrips, clutch release bearings, steering shaft and joints, seat pads and frames, transmission cases, clutch cases, tires, suspension bushes, ventilation units, heater, hose clamps, sealers, hardware

Federal Republic of Germany

Locks, pistons, exhaust, ignition, switches, front disc, distributor, weatherstrips, rocker arm, speedometer, fuel tank, cylinder bolt, cylinder head gasket, front wheel knuckles, rear wheel spindle, transmission cases, clutch cases, clutch, steering column, battery, glass

Netherlands

Tires, paints, hardware

United States

EGR valves, wheel nuts, hydraulic tappet, glass

Sweden

Hose clamps, cylinder bolt, exhaust down pipes, pressings, hardware

Denmark

Fan belt

Norway

Exhaust flanges, tires

Austria

Tires, radiator and heater hoses

Canada

Glass, radio

Italy

Cylinder head, carburetor, glass, lamps, defroster grills

Switzerland

Underbody coating, speedometer gears

Belgium

Tires, tubes, seat pads, brakes, trim

Spain

Wiring harness, radiator and heater hoses, fork clutch release, air filter, battery, mirrors

Japan

Starter, alternator, cone and roller bearings, windscreen washer pump

Source: *World Development Report 1987.* Copyright 1987 by The International Bank for Reconstruction and Development/The World Bank. Reprinted by permission of Oxford University Press, Inc.

Note: Final assembly takes place in Halewood (United Kingdom) and Saarlow's (Federal Republic of Germany).

Since the impetus given by the EEC to this new form of investment by individuals in one country in the economic system of another, the MNC has become the agent of the internationalization of production. The United Nations Centre on Transnational Corporations has identified the host-country location of some 104,000 MNC affiliates (Centre on Transnational Corporations, data tapes, July 29, 1987). (*Host country* refers to the country where a corporation headquartered in another country conducts its business activities.) Historically, the United States has been the home country for the largest proportion of parent companies, followed by Britain and West Germany. Furthermore, although the growth of multinational firms is a global phenomenon, if the magnitude of foreign direct investment is used to measure their global reach, it is apparent that the major part of all transnational business is located in the developed areas making up the First World: Practically all foreign direct investment originates in developed market economies, which also absorb more than three-quarters of all investment flows (Commission on Transnational Corporations, 1986: 5). The developing countries' share of foreign direct investment grew in the 1970s, but it plummeted during the debt crisis of the 1980s (see Chapter 8).

The importance of the economic characteristics of the world's giant producing, trading, and servicing corporations is illustrated in Table 6.1, which ranks billion-dollar-or-more firms and nations by the size of their gross economic product. The profile shows that over forty of the world's top one hundred economic entities are multinational corporations. Among the top fifty entries, multinationals account for only nine, but in the next fifty, they account for thirty-two.

Although historically the greatest number of MNCs have been American, the U.S. share in the outward stocks of foreign investment has declined steadily since 1973 (to 38 percent in 1983 from 48 percent in 1973), while the shares of Canada, West Germany, Japan, and Switzerland have risen substantially (Centre on Transnational Corporations, 1985b: 15). Similarly, in 1987 only 77 of *Fortune* magazine's top 200 industrial firms in the world were American, compared with 127 in 1960.

Although the outward stocks and flows of foreign direct investment from the United States have declined, the inflow of funds into the United States is one of the most striking recent developments related to foreign direct investment. During the 1960s the United States received about 10 percent of all foreign direct investment; this proportion rose to about 30 percent by the late 1970s and reached 40 to 50 percent by the mid-1980s, or $22.6 billion in 1984–1985 (Centre on Transnational Corporations, 1987: 5–6). Much of the inflow of investments has taken the form of acquisitions by European and Canadian firms that already had some presence in the U.S. market, and the building of new production facilities by Japan (a trade-replacing form of foreign direct investment) in an effort to establish itself in a market in which it had little presence before 1970. Japanese investments in banking and real

TABLE 6.1 ■ Countries and Corporations Ranked According to Size of Annual Product, 1985

Rank	Economic Entity	Dollars (billions)
1	United States	3915.35
2	Soviet Union	2062.60
3	Japan	1366.04
4	Federal Republic of Germany	667.97
5	France	526.63
6	United Kingdom	474.19
7	Italy	371.05
8	Canada	347.36
9	China	318.92
10	Poland	240.60
11	Brazil	222.01
12	India	194.82
13	East Germany	174.40
14	Australia	171.17
15	Spain	168.82
16	Mexico	163.79
17	Czechoslovakia	135.60
18	Netherlands	132.92
19	Romania	123.70
20	Switzerland	105.18
21	Saudi Arabia	102.12
22	Sweden	99.05
23	**GENERAL MOTORS**	96.37
24	Korea, Republic of	88.44
25	**EXXON**	86.67
26	Indonesia	86.59
27	Belgium	83.23
28	**ROYAL DUTCH/SHELL GROUP**	81.74
29	Hungary	80.10
30	Nigeria	75.94
31	Austria	69.06
32	South Africa	65.32
33	Argentina	65.08
34	Bulgaria	57.80
35	Norway	57.58
36	Denmark	57.33
37	Turkey	56.06
38	**MOBIL**	55.96
39	Algeria	55.23
40	Venezuela	53.80
41	Finland	53.45
42	**BRITISH PETROLEUM**	53.10
43	**FORD MOTOR**	52.77
44	**INTERNATIONAL BUSINESS MACHINES**	50.06
45	Yugoslavia	47.90
46	**TEXACO**	46.30
47	Thailand	42.10
48	**CHEVRON**	41.74
49	Colombia	37.61
50	Pakistan	36.23
51	Greece	35.25
52	**AMERICAN TEL. & TEL.**	34.91

(continued)

TABLE 6.1 ◼ (continued)

Rank	Economic Entity	Dollars (billions)
53	Hong Kong	33.77
54	Philippines	32.63
55	Egypt, Arab Republic	32.22
56	Malaysia	31.93
57	**E. I. DU PONT DE NEMOURS**	29.48
58	**GENERAL ELECTRIC**	28.29
59	**STANDARD OIL**	27.22
60	Libya	27.00
61	**IRI**	26.76
62	United Arab Emirates	26.40
63	**TOYOTA MOTOR**	26.04
64	Kuwait	24.76
65	**ENI**	24.46
66	New Zealand	23.72
67	**ATLANTIC RICHFIELD**	22.36
68	**UNILEVER**	21.63
69	**CHRYSLER**	21.26
70	Israel	21.14
71	**MATSUSHITA ELECTRIC INDUSTRIAL**	20.75
72	**HITACHI**	20.53
73	**PEMEX (PETRÓLEOS MEXICANOS)**	20.38
74	**SHELL OIL**	20.30
75	Portugal	20.14
76	**ELF-AQUITAINE**	20.11
77	**FRANÇAISE DES PÉTROLES**	19.27
78	Singapore	18.97
79	**U.S. STEEL**	18.43
80	**NISSAN MOTOR**	18.23
81	**PHILIPS' GLOEILAMPENFABRIEKEN**	18.08
82	Peru	17.83
83	**SIEMENS**	17.83
84	**VOLKSWAGEN**	17.83
85	**DAIMLER-BENZ**	17.80
86	Ireland	17.25
87	Chile	17.23
88	**NESTLÉ**	17.16
89	Syrian Arab Republic	17.06
90	**PETROBRÁS (PETRÓLEO BRASILEIRO)**	16.05
91	Puerto Rico	15.94
92	**UNITED TECHNOLOGIES**	15.75
93	**PHILLIPS PETROLEUM**	15.68
94	**BAYER**	15.60
95	**TENNECO**	15.40
96	**BASF**	15.07
97	Bangladesh	14.77
98	**OCCIDENTAL PETROLEUM**	14.53
99	**HOECHST**	14.51
100	**FIAT**	14.19

Source: Gross national product data are from *World Bank Atlas 1987* (Washington, D.C.: World Bank, 1987), pp. 6–9. Gross national product data for Bulgaria, Czechoslovakia, East Germany, Romania, and the Soviet Union are from *Handbook of Economic Statistics 1986* (Washington, D.C.: U.S. Central Intelligence Agency, 1986), pp. 35. Sales of industrial firms are from *Fortune*, August 4, 1986, p. 171. *Fortune*, © 1986 Time Inc. All rights reserved.

estate, such as hotels and office buildings, have also been substantial. The growing importance of the United States as a host country is related to national differences in interest rates and variations in the exchange rates among various national currencies experienced during the 1980s, which helped push the value of the U.S. dollar to historic highs at mid-decade (see Chapter 7).

A second major recent development in the global pattern of foreign direct investment is the emergence of Japan as a major home country. The outflow of Japanese foreign direct investment increased nearly fourfold between 1975 and 1985, moving from $3.3 billion to $12.2 billion during that period (Centre on Transnational Corporations, 1987: 9). A primary motivation, as noted, has been penetration of the U.S. market. Western Europe has also been the target of Japanese investments, for similar reasons. Together, Western Europe and North America accounted for three-fifths of Japanese foreign direct investment in 1985 (Centre on Transnational Corporations, 1987: 9). Developing nations accounted for most of the rest. Historically, Japan has invested in Third World nations to secure access to critical raw materials and to take advantage of lower labor costs in developing countries.

The MNCs' expansion could not have occurred on the scale achieved without the financial contribution of the world's international banks. Indeed, the transnational bank (TNB) has itself also become a major actor and force in the global political economy. In 1985 the combined assets of the world's twenty-five largest banks had grown to $2.6 trillion—a figure nearly triple the combined sales of the twenty-five largest industrial firms. Reflecting trends elsewhere in the transforming global political economy, in 1985 five of the ten largest banks were Japanese, whereas in 1978, only one of the ten largest was Japanese (Centre on Transnational Corporations, 1987: 40).

Impact on Home and Host Nations

In addition to its global reach, the domestic impact of the MNC on both home and host countries is a topic of heated debate.

The MNCs' power is often alleged to be exercised at great cost to their home or parent countries. MNCs are charged with shifting productive facilities abroad to avoid demands by powerful labor unions for higher wages. According to this view, because capital is more mobile than labor, the practice of exporting production from industrially advanced countries to industrially backward countries, where labor is cheap and unions weak or nonexistent, is the cause of structural unemployment in the advanced countries. Others contend, however, that especially in the case of the United States, MNCs help reduce the nation's balance-of-payments deficit, create new employment opportunities, and promote competition in both domestic and foreign markets.

If home countries have incurred both costs and benefits, have host countries shared a similar experience? "As privileged organizations," David E.

Apter and Louis W. Goodman (1976) note, MNCs "hold a unique position among growth-inducing institutions able to affect the direction of development." This implies that MNCs may benefit development as much as they impede it. It is nonetheless true that Third World nations have historically viewed multinationals with considerable suspicion. And because they are generally more important to the developing nations' overall GNP and to their most advanced economic sectors than they are to the developed states' economies, Third World views of MNCs have been more emotionally charged.

From one perspective, the movement of capital and production from the First World to the Third has produced net gains for the latter:

> For all the talk (and the reality) of imperialist domination, most of the underdeveloped nations want domestic foreign investment, European and/ or American, for a variety of reasons. The multinationals pay higher wages, keep more honest books, pay more taxes, and provide more managerial know-how and training than do local industries. Moreover, they usually provide better social services for their workers, and certainly provide fancy career opportunities for a favored few of the elite. They are, in addition, a main channel through which technology, developed in the West, can filter into the backward nations. To be sure, the corporations typically send home more profits than the capital that they originally introduce into the "host" country; but meanwhile that capital grows, providing jobs, improving productivity, and often contributing to export earnings. (Heilbroner, 1977: 345–346)

These reasons may explain the widespread quest for multinational investment. As one observer explains,

> . . . a nearly universal demand for substantial MNC activity remains. In many fields the most attractive technology and expertise does not come in "unbundled" form; the advantages in foreign market access that are inherent in most manufacturing MNCs often cannot be duplicated except at a very high price. A rapid and premature jettisoning of the MNC—even in natural resource industries—has led some countries to economic disaster. (Kudrle, 1987: 241)

Interestingly, the developing nations themselves have begun to spawn multinational firms. In 1986, for example, 11 percent of the industrial corporations outside the United States were headquartered in the developing world (*Fortune*, August 4, 1986, pp. 186–203). Wells (1983: 2) has also identified nearly 2,000 overseas subsidiaries of 963 parent firms based in developing countries. Thus, the multinational corporation, "long regarded by its opponents as the unique instrument of capitalist oppression against the impoverished world, could prove to be the tool by which the impoverished world builds prosperity. . . . Third World multinationalism, only yesterday an apparent contradiction in terms, is now a serious force in the development process" (Heenan and Keegan, 1979).[19]

From another Third World perspective, however, the costs associated with MNCs have been excessive. "The capital, jobs and other benefits they bring to developing economies are recognized, but the terms on which these benefits come are seen as unfair and exploitive and as robbing the new nations of their resources" (Cutler, 1978).

One of the alleged costs is technological dependence. According to one argument, technology imported from the North impedes local development: What is transferred to the Third World is often not appropriate to the local setting, and the diffusion effects of industrial activity within the developing nations in particular are limited (see also Chapter 5).

Another argument suggests that because MNCs seek to maximize profits for their shareholders, who more often than not reside in the parent state rather than in the host state, capital is not reinvested in the country of production but instead finds its way into someone else's hands. Moreover, the returns are often described as excessive. Between 1975 and 1978, for example, the profit on American direct foreign investment in the First World averaged 12.1 percent, but in the Third World it averaged nearly 26 percent (Spero, 1985: 276; compare Drucker, 1974).

Critics also charge that profits represent only a small part of the effective return to parent companies. "A large part of the real return comes from licensing fees and royalties paid by the subsidiary to the parent for the use of technology controlled by the parent" (Spero, 1985). Admittedly, parent companies must absorb the costs for research and development through which new technologies are developed, and these are used abroad. Nonetheless, it is argued that

> subsidiaries in underdeveloped countries pay an unjustifiably high price for technology and bear an unjustifiably high share of the research and development costs. The monopoly control of technology by the multinational corporation enables the parent to exact a monopoly rent from its subsidiaries. And the parent chooses to use that power and to charge inordinately high fees and royalties to disguise high profits and avoid local taxes on those profits. (Spero, 1985: 276)

---

19. The emergence of MNCs spawned by Third World nations must be viewed against the evidence demonstrating the continued dominance of the Northern nations. Commenting on the location (in 1980) of some 98,000 MNC affiliates, the UN Centre on Transnational Corporations noted that "the developed market economies account for practically the entire stock of foreign direct investment. Although corporations from some of the more industrialized developing countries have become significant investors abroad in recent years, transnational corporations domiciled in the developed market economies still account for 97% of the recorded flows of foreign direct investment" (Centre on Transnational Corporations, 1985b: 15).

Critics point to the *transfer-pricing mechanism* as another device used by MNCs to increase their profits and minimize their tax burdens. The raw, semi-processed, or finished materials produced by a parent's subsidiaries located in different countries are in effect traded among the subsidiaries. Because the same company sits on both sides of the transaction, the sales or "transfer" prices of these import–export transactions can be manipulated so as to benefit the parent firm. According to Cutler (1978), "Some firms do this as objectively as they can, without regard to tax considerations. But there are also some who exercise this discretion so as to minimize their global taxes and maximize their after-tax earnings. Since tax rates vary around the world, they accomplish this by recording profits in jurisdictions where taxes are relatively low" (see also Centre on Transnational Corporations, 1985a). The net effect is increased capital flow from South to North. Poverty in the host country is said to be the primary product (Müller, 1973–1974).

Although much of the critical literature considers "the remission of 'excessive' profits the key mechanism by which the host country's balance of payments is adversely affected by multinational corporations," Raymond Vernon argues instead "that the annual income remissions are insignificant compared to the local value added annually by such corporations" (cited in Bierstecker, 1978). Vernon also challenges the capital-outflow and technology dependence arguments, alleging that the former "is fallacious because of its failure to measure the implications of changes in domestic output" (cited in Bierstecker, 1978), whereas the latter is subject to "an overwhelming propensity on the part of well-trained and well-informed critics to oversimplify the issue and to disregard the nonconforming evidence" (Vernon, 1975). In a similar vein, Charles Kindleberger (1969) contends that despite MNCs' monopolistic and exploitative tendencies, multinationals as a whole have, paradoxically, expanded competition and enhanced world economic efficiency.

In sum, then, the economic consequences of MNCs' activities are not always discernible or easily agreed upon, which is perhaps why evaluations do not point to consensus. In Spero's (1985) words, "It is impossible to reach any general or definitive conclusion about the overall effect of multinationals on development. The influence of foreign investment varies from country to country, from firm to firm, and from project to project. Some case studies demonstrate the beneficial impact of direct foreign investment; others, the detrimental effects" (see also Blake and Walters, 1987).

Politics and Multinational Corporations

Another aspect of the debate over MNCs concerns their involvement in political activities. The chief area of concern from the perspective of Third World nations is the obtrusive involvement of MNCs in local (host country) politics. MNCs have also been involved in the domestic politics of their home country, lobbying home governments for policies that will enhance the profitability of their business activities abroad. And they have been used by both host and home governments as tools in international politics, especially with respect to issues involving the oil industry.

Perhaps the most notorious instance of an MNC's intervention in the politics of a host state occurred in Chile in the early 1970s. There, International Telephone and Telegraph (ITT) attempted to protect its interests in the profitable Chiltelco telephone company by seeking to prevent Marxist-oriented Salvador Allende from being elected president and subsequently by seeking his overthrow. ITT's efforts to undermine Allende included giving monetary support to his political opponents and, once Allende was elected, attempting to induce the American government to launch a program designed to disrupt the Chilean economy.

On other occasions, multinationals have used bribery to influence key foreign officials. The extent of such activity by American firms was unearthed in the aftermath of the Watergate scandal in the United States in the early 1970s. The Securities and Exchange Commission and later a congressional inquiry disclosed improper foreign payments totaling more than $100 million made by one hundred American firms (Cutler, 1978: 18). Under usual circumstances, however, MNCs engage in direct political action or bribery less often than they use advertising and practice legitimate lobbying of the host government's legislators to influence public attitudes.

MNCs also often lobby their home governments for policies that back the MNCs in disputes with host governments, though they are not always successful in these endeavors (see Rawls, 1986; Spiegel, 1985). The stipulation, made in the early 1970s by the U.S. Congress, that American foreign aid would be cut off from any country that nationalized American overseas investments without just compensation is exemplary of the tendency for home-state governments to support their own MNCs' overseas activities. More generally, MNCs assisted in the creation of the Liberal International Economic Order that had been a prominent postwar goal of the United States, and MNCs, in turn, have helped shape the specific policies regarding trade and taxation that contributed to the realization of that goal. In this sense, MNCs may influence the process by which governments have reached agreement on the rules for the international monetary and trade regimes.

In addition to direct political roles, MNCs indirectly serve as instruments through which national governments pursue their foreign policy objectives. The United States, for example, has sought to use the foreign affiliates of American-based MNCs to extend to other jurisdictions its policies regarding trade embargoes against other nations. This occurred in 1982, for example, when the Reagan administration sought to prevent the French subsidiary of Dresser Industries of Dallas, Texas, from exporting energy-related technology to the Soviet Union. (Interestingly, the United States subsequently "blacklisted" the subsidiary when, acting under orders from the French government, it exported the technologies in question despite American pressures to prevent it.) Similarly, the governments of the Organization of Petroleum Exporting Countries (OPEC) effectively used the multinational oil companies in 1973 and 1974 to achieve OPEC's goal of using oil as a political weapon against the West.

MNCs have also been used to enhance U.S. intelligence-gathering capabilities in other societies. In these cases it almost seems that the MNC is the captive of governments and not an autonomous political actor on the world stage. Perhaps the conclusion that "the multinational is actually a stimulant to the further extension of state power in the economic realm" (Gilpin, 1985), rather than a potential supplanter of the sovereignty of the nation-state, is the best way to characterize the domestic impact of MNCs. Nonetheless, the blurring of the boundaries between internal and external affairs adds potency to the political role that MNCs unavoidably play as actors at the intersection of foreign and domestic policy.

Controlling Multinational Corporations

It is clear that multinationals have become important actors in world politics in that decisions critical to nation-states (especially those in the Third World) are now made by entities over which those nations may not have control. Thus, the question of control of MNCs constitutes a fourth significant issue in the debate about the costs and benefits of multinational corporations.

The question of control is not confined to the Third World, for the international interests of MNCs are not necessarily more compatible with the interests of their home governments than with those of their hosts. As one senior foreign policy official in the United States declared at the time of the Dresser Industries controversy, "Basically we're in an impossible situation. You don't want to get rid of the advantages of this international economic system, but if you try to exercise control for foreign policy reasons, you cut across sovereign frontiers." Furthermore, the MNCs' complex patterns of ownership and licensing arrangements mean that it is often difficult to equate the MNCs' interests with particular national jurisdictions. General Electric, for example, one of the most "American" of all American MNCs, has granted licenses for the production of energy-related equipment to Nuovo Pignone of Italy, Mitsubishi Heavy Industries and Hitachi of Japan, Mannessmann and AEG Telefunken of West Germany, John Brown Engineering of Great Britain, and Thomassen Holland of the Netherlands (U.S. Office of Technology Assessment, 1981). Controlling such a complex pattern of interrelationships, joint ventures, and shared ownership for any particular national purpose is nearly impossible. "The internationalization of the economy—which the U.S. spearheaded—has rendered obsolete old ideas of economic warfare," Richard J. Barnet, coauthor of *Global Reach*, observed in 1982. "You can't find targets any more, and if you aim at a target you often find it's yourself."

The potential long-run importance of MNCs for transforming world order is also depicted in *Global Reach*:

> The global corporation is the most powerful human organization yet de-
> vised for colonizing the future. By scanning the entire planet for oppor-
> tunities, by shifting its resources from industry to industry and country to
> country, and by keeping its overriding goal simple—worldwide profit
> maximization—it has become an institution of unique power. The World
> Managers are the first to have developed a plausible model for the future
> that is global. . . . In making business decisions today they are creating a
> politics for the next generation. (Barnet and Müller, 1974: 363)

Whether the corporate visionaries who manage the MNCs will contribute
to the creation of a more prosperous, peaceful, and just world—as some hope,
and others, whose interests are threatened by a new world political economy,
fear—is questionable. "For some, the global corporation holds the promise of
lifting mankind out of poverty and bringing the good life to everyone. For
others, these corporations have become a law unto themselves; they are
miniempires which exploit all for the benefit of a few" (Gilpin, 1975).

Those who view the MNC favorably see national competitiveness giving
way to a supranational world order in which welfare issues will be more
important than narrow ideological or security contests. From this perspective,
the MNC, which knows no national boundaries or national loyalties and whose
profits (except for the arms manufacturers) are threatened by national aggressiveness and militarism, plays the role of a "peacemonger" in world politics (Ewing, 1974).

Those more negatively disposed toward MNCs maintain that because of
their desire for political stability in order to realize maximum profits, MNCs
are often prone to align with repressive political regimes and "powerfully
oppose the kinds of revolutionary upheavals that in many backward areas are
probably the essential precondition for a genuine modernization" (Heilbroner,
1977). Furthermore, multinationals may be the agents of a worldwide dispersion of economic benefits, but the distribution of these benefits is likely to be
very uneven. Hence, multinationals perpetuate and deepen global inequality;
because they threaten national autonomy, the rise of independent, transnational corporations challenges to some degree the governments of all countries.

Given the global reach, economic power, and ostensible autonomy of the
MNCs, efforts by nation-states to strengthen their bargaining positions vis-à-vis
the MNCs are to be expected. Through the United Nations Commission on
Transnational Corporations, the less-developed countries have sought a code
of conduct to govern the activities of transnational corporations. In 1986 the
commission put forward a proposal that sought to cope with the legitimate
interests of both host countries and multinational corporations in such matters
as transfer pricing, taxation, ownership and control, and environmental protection.

Other attempts to control the MNCs include the Convention on the Settlement of Investment Disputes, negotiated under the auspices of the World

Bank, and the Declaration on International Investment and Multinational Enterprises, embraced by the Organization for Economic Cooperation and Development.

In recent years the developing nations have become less strident in their demands for controls on multinationals and more pragmatic in dealing with them, largely because of a more realistic recognition of the role that MNCs play as agents of investment, trade, and technology transfer in today's interdependent global political economy, and perhaps because they believe that the risks can be managed.[20] Whether such a change in attitude will be conducive to moving those codes of conduct already devised for controlling MNCs toward an effective international regulatory regime, or whether they will sap the impetus and political will to do so, remains to be seen. In either case, contention over the role of multinational corporations in national and international affairs will remain, for states often view the costs and benefits of MNCs quite differently.

NONSTATE ACTORS, INTERNATIONAL REGIMES, AND THE TRANSFORMATION OF WORLD POLITICS

Because multinational corporations challenge the nation-state, they also challenge the very foundations of the contemporary global system. But states will not disappear quickly. Conflict between them and the MNCs is therefore to be expected. As Robert Heilbroner (1977) has argued, "what we seem to be witnessing . . . is a conflict between two modes of organizing human affairs—a 'vertical' mode that finds its ultimate expression in the pan-national flows of production of the giant international corporation, and a 'horizontal' mode expressed in the jealously guarded boundaries of the nation-state."

In the meantime, the rise of multinational corporations and the prodigious growth of other types of nonstate actors challenge the traditional state-centric theory of international politics, which holds that nation-states are the primary actors on the world's political stage. Because the state has "purposes and power," according to this view, it "is the basic unit of action; its main agents are the diplomat and soldier. The interplay of governmental politics yields the pattern of behavior that students of international politics attempt to under-

---

20. The industrial accident in 1984 in Bhopal, India, in which over two thousand people died from a poison gas leak at a Union Carbide pesticide plant suggests that the risks growing out of foreign direct investment may be substantial. The accident seemed to confirm the argument that firms operating in Third World countries often follow less stringent safety standards than would be required of them in an advanced industrial country.

The political fallout from the Soviet Union's nuclear accident at Chernobyl in 1986 may likewise contain lessons for Third World nations that pursue the nuclear option as an alternative to dependence on oil to fuel their economic development. The Chernobyl incident and its implications are examined in detail in Flavin (1987).

stand and that practitioners attempt to adjust or to control" (Nye and Keohane, 1971; see also Mansbach et al., 1976).

Clearly such a view no longer adequately depicts the complexity of world politics. As described in Chapter 2, the behaviors of state and nonstate actors sometimes converge to form *international regimes*. Sovereign states are important members of international regimes. Oran R. Young (1980) argues, in fact, that "the members of international regimes are always sovereign states." Significantly, however, he quickly adds that "the parties carrying out the actions governed by international regimes are often private entities." In this sense the nonstate actors discussed in this chapter—IGOs, INGOs, MNCs, and TNBs—are often the key participants in the regularized conduct of contemporary international relations encompassed by international regimes in such diverse areas as the law of the sea, nuclear nonproliferation, the global monetary and trade systems, and the global food system.

Moving from the level of cooperative international interactions to the level of foreign policy making within nation-states, an adequate conceptualization of contemporary world politics must also acknowledge the influence of nonstate actors on a government's ability to formulate public policy and on the ties among them. Nonstate actors help build and broaden the foreign policy agendas of national decision makers by serving as transmission belts through which one nation's policies become sensitive to another's (Keohane and Nye, 1975). At the same time, some nonstate actors are capable of pursuing their interests largely outside the direct control of nation-states while simultaneously involving governments in particular problems as a result of their activities (Nye and Keohane, 1971).[21]

These reflections invite this conclusion:

> There has developed on the global level an interconnected and intensified . . . complex of relationships . . . in which demands are articulated and processed through formal as well as informal channels, governmental as well as non-governmental organizations, national as well as international and supranational institutions. These processes of interaction are interdependent . . . and they perform a variety of functions, most prominently those of welfare and security. They are the structures through which governments perform a variety of functions; they are the way in which state and society seek to arrange their domestic and foreign environment. (Hanrieder, 1978: 1278)

The transformation of world politics is being played out in these complex, interdependent relationships among diverse national and transnational actors.

---

21. An example of the often relative autonomy of nonstate actors was provided by the international response to the American effort to organize a worldwide boycott of the 1980 Summer Olympics in Moscow. For the American policy position, it was important that West Germany and Japan were among those who decided not to participate. However, several national Olympic committees voted to participate, even though their governments had favored a boycott. Included among them were the national Olympic committees in Britain, France, Italy, and Australia.

This by no means indicates that the nation-state is dead, however. Governments still retain the capacity to influence, indeed to shape, transnational interactions. It is not accidental that supranationalism (as in Western Europe) has been confined largely to economic interactions and that matters of national security are confined largely to government-to-government interactions.

Thus it is important not to exaggerate the importance of nonstate actors and their impact on nation-states. Nation-states retain a (near) monopoly on the use of coercive force in the international system. The majority of new international governmental organizations founded in the 150-year period since the Congress of Vienna (1815) were established *after* the most warlike periods, but there is almost no association between the number of IGOs in the international system and the incidence of interstate war during the 150-year period (Singer and Wallace, 1970).[22] The nation-state cannot be lightly dismissed, therefore; it still molds the activities of nonstate actors more than its behavior is molded by them. Hence it would be premature to abandon the focus on the nation-state in international politics, just as it would be inadequate to regard the state as the only relevant actor or the sole determinant of its fate.

SUGGESTED READINGS

Barnet, Richard J., and Ronald E. Müller. *Global Reach: The Power of the Multinational Corporations.* New York: Simon & Schuster, 1974.

de Cuéllar, Javier Pérez. "The United Nations and World Politics," pp. 178–185 in Charles W. Kegley, Jr., and Eugene R. Wittkopf, eds., *The Global Agenda: Issues and Perspectives*, 2nd ed. New York: Random House, 1988.

Franck, Thomas M. *Nation Against Nation: What Happened to the U.N. Dream and What the U.S. Can Do About It.* New York: Oxford University Press, 1985.

Gati, Toby Trister, ed. *The US, the UN, and the Management of Global Change.* New York: New York University Press, 1983.

Hanson, Eric O. *The Catholic Church in World Politics.* Princeton, N.J.: Princeton University Press, 1987.

Jacobson, Harold K. *Networks of Interdependence.* New York: Knopf, 1984.

Kerr, Anthony J. *The Common Market and How It Works.* Oxford, England: Pergamon Press, 1983.

Khan, Jushi M., ed. *Multinationals of the South. New Actors in the International Economy.* New York: St. Martin's Press, 1986.

---

22. Because this conclusion contradicts other findings regarding IGO involvement in conflict management, perhaps we should ask whether the data and analysis from which it derives might be interpreted differently. The conclusion is based on the assumption that there should be an association between the amount of war and organization within closely constrained time periods (five years). If, however, the data are arranged into twenty-five rather than five-year periods (which is perhaps a reasonable length in which to expect institutional developments to have an impact on the international system), then "the data would appear to support the argument that as the number of IGOs has grown, the amount of violence in the global system has decreased" (Jacobson, 1984: 199, n. 1).

Riggs, Robert E., and Jack C. Plano. *The United Nations: International Organization and World Politics*. Chicago: Dorsey Press, 1988.

Taylor, Phillip. *Nonstate Actors in International Politics: From Transregional to Substate Organizations*. Boulder, Colo.: Westview Press, 1984.

PART III

Low Politics: Transnational Policy Issues

The Transformation of the International Political Economy: Perspectives from the First World

If the peoples of the West lose faith that democratic governments have control over their economic destinies, the economic crisis could become a crisis of Western democracy. . . . In a world of many perils, continuing economic weakness is likely to undermine the democracies' ability to conduct an effective foreign policy or to maintain their collective defense.

HENRY A. KISSINGER, 1983

We have come to a divide. The economic changes we are watching will reshape the international security system. They are fundamental shifts of the power relations among nations.

JOHN ZYSMAN, 1987

Transnational economic developments are among the most important factors transforming world politics, for today the political controversies that comprise the "high politics" of great power struggles are often rooted in the quiet world of "low politics"—the world of economic and social welfare policy. The undercurrents of low politics force the struggle for national security and political power into new shapes by constraining the use of political power and by influencing how and when such power may be used.

It is at the intersection of politics and economics that some of the most significant controversies in world politics occur. The contests between rich and poor, supplier and producer, importer and exporter, and advantaged and disadvantaged all are affected by the interplay of political and economic forces. Moreover, from a national perspective, the balance of fiscal power now seems as important to national security and the quality of life as does the balance of military power. The term *political economy* (and the analytical perspective that underlies it) highlights the intersection of politics and economics, whose importance derives from the proposition that politics (the exercise of power) determines economics (how things of value are distributed).

The potential importance of economic factors as they relate to political circumstances is suggested by the dramatic increase in international trade that the world has experienced since World War II. In the mid-1980s, world exports were valued at nearly $2 trillion annually, more than ten times greater than two decades earlier. World exports now account for roughly 17 percent of all the nations' combined gross national products, more than double what it was little more than a decade earlier.

The growing importance of trade in nations' economic life portends the emergence of an interdependent global economic system. *Interdependence* is a term widely used to describe the interlocked natures of the world's economies. Because the extent of interdependence among nations varies greatly, some analysts (such as Waltz, 1970, 1979) have questioned whether it is appropriate to regard the world today as more interdependent than in previous periods.[1] But if we think of interdependence as *mutual sensitivity* and *mutual vulnerability* (Keohane and Nye, 1977), from a global perspective there is little question that nations' economic fates have today become intertwined at unprecedented levels.

Interdependence does not automatically confer mutual benefits. National responses to the stall in the growth of world trade experienced in the early 1980s after several decades of steady increases illustrate the dilemmas that interdependence often poses. As the volume of world trade leveled off, competition for control of existing markets intensified as a consequence of the growing need for most countries to acquire and retain export-generated revenues. As a result, the world marketplace became more politicized, as governments sought to protect their national economies from foreign competition while trying to help their own industries penetrate others' economies. Such political activity for economic motive has challenged the norms and rules that heretofore have governed the conduct of international commerce, and its intensity is partly why trade and related economic policy issues now figure so prominently on the global political agenda. The suitability of conventional institutions for coping with these issues, including the nation-state itself, often lurks in the background. Indeed, the eminent international economist Charles P. Kindleberger (1969) has declared that "the nation-state is just about through as an economic unit. . . . The world is too small. It . . . [does] not permit the sovereign independence of the nation-state in economic affairs." Changes within the global political economy thus challenge the entire texture of world politics, for under conditions of interdependence, the boundary between market and state has become increasingly blurred.

The purpose of this and the next chapter is to explore the sources of these developments and to assess their implications. We shall concentrate on four

---

1. Part of the difficulty arises out of the multiple meanings of interdependence. For a sampling of empirical studies using quantitative indicators to assess trends in various aspects of global interdependence, see Katzenstein (1975), Krasner (1976), "The Realities of Economic Interdependence" (1984), Rosecrance et al. (1977), and Rosecrance and Stein (1973).

interrelated aspects of the international political economy: (1) the international monetary system, (2) the system of international trade as conducted among the industrialized nations of the First World, (3) the international trade between them and developing nations of the Third World, and (4) the economic linkages between the First World and the planned economies of the Second World.

NATIONAL ECONOMIES IN THE GLOBAL POLITICAL ECONOMY

As the principal actors in world politics, nation-states alone are responsible for ensuring their citizens' capacity to acquire desired economic goods, for enhancing the general economic welfare, and for protecting economic gain (and the political status achieved as a consequence of past economic success) from encroachment by others.

Domestically, states organize themselves for these purposes quite differently. Some have *open* economic systems. Open systems allow the "invisible hand" of the marketplace to determine the flow of economic transactions within and across the state's borders. Such countries are commonly known as *market* economies.

At the opposite end of this spectrum are *closed* systems. Because closed systems rely on government intervention to regulate and manage the economy, they are also called *centrally planned* or *command* economies. Taxes, wage and price controls, monetary regulations, tariffs, and other policy instruments are used in closed systems to prevent competitive market forces from becoming determinants of economic transactions.

Where a nation falls along the open-closed continuum is an important factor in helping its policymakers decide how the nation might adjust imbalances in its economic transactions with the rest of the world.[2] For many states, trade is the most important international economic transaction. A deficit in a state's *balance of trade* results from an imbalance between exports and imports, from more being purchased abroad than is sold. The *balance of payments* is a more inclusive summary statement of a state's financial transactions with the rest of the world. The balance-of-payments figure comprises items not included in trade, such as foreign aid transfers and the income of citizens employed abroad who send their paychecks home. If more money

---

2. Open and closed are useful conventions for classifying differences between economic systems, but they are relative terms. No economy is completely open or closed, as every system has, to a greater or lesser extent, ingredients of both types. Which political model for the management of national economies is most conducive to growth and welfare is the subject of much controversy (see Lindblom, 1977; Olson, 1982; Reich, 1983).

Cameron (1978) argues that increased collectivism at home is a consequence of vulnerability to international economic forces. This conclusion raises the question of whether increased international interdependence will necessarily lead to a further concentration of economic as well as political power in the hands of national governments, which implies that all national economies will be pushed in the direction of closed economic systems.

flows out of the country than comes in, then the country will suffer a balance-of-payments deficit. When this happens, some kind of corrective action must be taken.

For countries with closed economies, the process of adjusting international income to international expenses is comparatively easy. The government can simply mandate an increase or decrease in the importation of certain commodities, for example. Countries with relatively open economic systems can use similar devices to restrict imports or capital flows in order to balance their international payments, but such measures would make their economies less open and are therefore seldom employed.

More often, nations committed to maintaining an open economy cope with balance-of-payments problems by trying to reduce the level of their economic activity at home or to adjust their currency's exchange rate. The latter action will affect the relative attractiveness of the country's exports to foreign buyers and its imports from abroad to domestic buyers. A currency *devaluation*, for example, will make exports cheaper and imports more expensive. Neither of these techniques alters the market, but each can change the quality of social life. For instance, if a country has a balance-of-payments deficit, lowering either the level of economic activity (deflation) or the exchange rate (devaluation) will reduce the country's international expenditures while increasing its international revenues. However, deflating the economy means putting people out of work and reducing real wage levels. Similarly, devaluation will also reduce real wage levels. In short, these adjustment techniques work by lowering the level of employment and the level of income.

In addition to these two, states can also finance balance-of-payments deficits if they have access to financial assets (liquidity) in the form of accumulated reserves of foreign currency or loans from multilateral agencies or other countries. The International Monetary Fund (IMF) has become a particularly important source of funds for states experiencing temporary shortfalls in their balance of payments. Often, however, the IMF will provide assistance only if the borrowing state promises to undertake domestic reforms to correct the economic problems that may have caused the deficits. These reforms are often usually difficult to institute politically, because they frequently require domestic sacrifices that affect employment opportunities and the standard of living. Indeed, whether a state's economic system is open or closed, the adjustment of its international economic transactions has important domestic consequences. For this reason, states are sensitive to how international commercial relations are organized and conducted.

In principle, economic relations between states are voluntary exchanges that nations, either through private entities or public enterprises, enter into freely for mutual benefit. Indeed, the *raison d'être* of foreign trade is that it offers advantages to both parties in the exchange. According to the principle of *comparative advantage*, any two nations will benefit if each specializes in those goods that it can produce relatively cheaply and acquires, through trade, goods that it can produce only at a higher cost. Trade will be encouraged because those countries most efficiently producing cars, textiles, wines, or whatever will be able to export them, because their relatively lower cost to foreign consumers will make them attractive. Those same countries will also have incentives to import other goods that may be acquired at lower cost from foreign sources. Specialization therefore permits each to enjoy a higher standard of living than would be possible without it (and without international trade). Thus, when trade is unfettered by nonmarket forces or politically imposed barriers, all nations stand to share in the benefits. This simple conclusion—that the net gain in welfare to most countries is greater as a consequence of their exchange of goods with one another—is the basis of classic (liberal) international trade theory. The process whereby trade produces gains in welfare is illustrated in Box 7.1.

The actual operation of the international economic system is, of course, far more complicated than this simple illustration suggests. Nations routinely interfere with free trade. Political considerations thus interrupt the free flow of goods across national boundaries. And because states are not equal economically (some are endowed with greater resources and productive capacities than others are), the international economy is shaped by political motives among unequals. Such motives include the search for self-benefit instead of mutual benefit, for self-advantage at the expense of others. *Beggar-thy-neighbor* policies—in which states seek to promote domestic welfare by promoting trade surpluses and other measures that can be realized only at the expense of foreign nations—are commonplace, not the exception.[3]

All nations, whether they are relatively open economic systems or relatively closed ones, seek simultaneously to maximize the beneficial effects of international economic transactions on national conditions and to minimize their adverse effects. The variation evident in national postures toward international economic issues is closely linked to countries' positions in the international pecking order. Rules governing international commerce (like rules governing international politics) often evolve according to the wishes of the stronger players. Historically, these have been the advanced capitalist societies of the Western industrialized world, particularly Britain in the nineteenth century and the United States in the twentieth. Both used their military superiority and economic advantage to create international economic regimes in which market forces play a more powerful role and are accorded more legitimacy than are state intervention and control. The Liberal International

---

3. *Beggar-thy-neighbor* is a term associated with politicoeconomic strategies that seek to promote domestic welfare at the expense of other nations. In general, the term refers to efforts by one country to reduce its unemployment in such a way as to adversely affect its neighbors. Currency devaluations, tariffs, quotas, and export subsidies are strategies associated with beggar-thy-neighbor strategies. Many of these were tried during the 1930s, and the term therefore is commonly associated with national economic strategies pursued at that time, when currency devaluations and foreign exchange controls were used by various nations to improve their domestic economic conditions at the expense of others. In the end, the effort of all countries to generate a trade surplus by cutting exports led to a breakdown of the entire international trade system.

BOX 7.1 ■ Comparative Advantage and the Gains from Trade

Start with two countries, for example, the United States and the United Kingdom. Each produces steel and cloth. The hypothetical figures below show output per hour for workers in each country. It's clear that the U.S. has an absolute advantage; American workers are more productive in turning out both products than the British workers.

WORKER PRODUCTIVITY

	U.S.	U.K.
Steel, units of output/hour	9	4
Cloth, units of output/hour	3	2

Does this mean that there is no possibility for trade between the two countries? If the U.K. wants to trade with [the U.S.], should it try to produce something else in which it has an advantage? And if trade occurs, should the U.S. continue to allocate its scarce resources in the same way it has done? The answer to all these questions is no.

Each country should specialize in those items in which it has the best comparative cost advantage or least comparative cost disadvantage, and trade with others. Here's why.

Since the U.S. is three times more productive in steel than cloth, it should direct more of its resources into steel. One cost of producing more steel is lost cloth output. But the U.S. can turn out three additional units of steel for every unit of cloth production given up, while the U.K. can obtain only two units of cloth.

In the U.K. workers are also more productive in steel than in cloth making. But greater emphasis should be placed on cloth production because Britain is at a smaller disadvantage, compared with America, in this area. If the U.K. specializes in cloth and the U.S. in steel, and they trade, each will benefit.

The chart shows that by moving resources in the U.S. to steel production and in the U.K. to cloth production, the same total inputs will cause steel and cloth output to rise 10 units each. This gain indicates a more efficient allocation of resources. Benefits to both countries can be realized when the U.S. trades its extra steel for British cloth. Indeed, the U.S. ends up with more steel than before specialization and trade and with the same quantity of cloth. The U.K. finds itself with more cloth and the same amount of steel. More output in both countries means higher living standards.

(continued)

Economic Order (LIEO) created under the aegis of United States hegemony following World War II is variously described as an "open" and "liberal" international regime for precisely the reason that it minimized the role of government in its effective operation.

Powerful capitalist states prefer open systems because their relatively greater control of technology, capital, and raw materials gives them more opportunities to profit from a system that operates according to the principle of comparative advantage. At the same time, however, they also have special responsibilities. They must ensure that those nations facing balance-of-pay-

184

BOX 7.1 ■ Continued

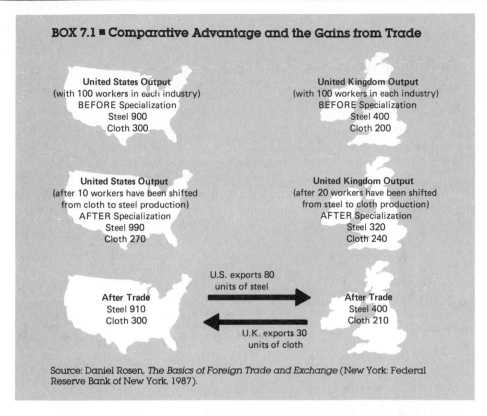

BOX 7.1 ■ Comparative Advantage and the Gains from Trade

United States Output
(with 100 workers in each industry)
BEFORE Specialization
Steel 900
Cloth 300

United Kingdom Output
(with 100 workers in each industry)
BEFORE Specialization
Steel 400
Cloth 200

United States Output
(after 10 workers have been shifted
from cloth to steel production)
AFTER Specialization
Steel 990
Cloth 270

United Kingdom Output
(after 20 workers have been shifted
from steel to cloth production)
AFTER Specialization
Steel 320
Cloth 240

U.S. exports 80
units of steel

After Trade
Steel 910
Cloth 300

After Trade
Steel 400
Cloth 210

U.K. exports 30
units of cloth

Source: Daniel Rosen, *The Basics of Foreign Trade and Exchange* (New York: Federal Reserve Bank of New York, 1987).

It's clear that if all countries produce those things which they are most efficient in producing, then the world's output and income would be increased, and everyone's standard of living would rise.

Source: Daniel Rosen, *The Basics of Foreign Trade and Exchange* (New York: Federal Reserve Bank of New York, 1987).

ments deficits will be able to obtain the credits necessary to finance their deficits. If the powerful states cannot do this, they are likely to move toward more closed domestic economies, which may undermine the open international system otherwise advantageous to them (Block, 1977). Generally, the powerful states must make certain that the system's liquidity (the reserve assets held by states for settling their international accounts) is sufficient to carry on international financial transactions. In short, those states most able to influence the system also have the greatest responsibility to ensure its effective operation.

The ability of powerful states to manage the international economic system can change. In the twentieth century, the United States assumed the managerial role played by the British in the nineteenth century. This shift, particularly obvious by the end of World War II, reflected the new pecking order of the powerful in world politics. And if such a shift occurred once, it could occur again. Indeed, most observers agree that the international political economy has been undergoing a profound transformation for a decade or more as the power of the United States relative to others has declined. Where that transformation may be taking us remains uncertain, but understanding its nature and sources must begin with an examination of the role of the United States in the creation and management of the Liberal International Economic Order in the post–World War II period and the challenges to that role. We begin with the international monetary system, for as Charles P. Kindleberger (1977b) pointed out, it is here that we shall find "the primary unraveling of the American . . . hegemony . . . in the world economic system."

THE TRANSFORMATION OF THE INTERNATIONAL MONETARY SYSTEM

An important difference between the operation of a domestic economy and that of the international economy is that the nations making up the latter do not use the same currencies. If nations are to trade or otherwise engage in financial transactions with one another, they must devise a means to determine the value of their currencies relative to one another so that they can carry out their exchanges. It was this task, among others, that the World War II allies faced as they began planning for the postwar world, even as they continued their struggle against the Axis powers.

The allies' deliberations were influenced by the lessons drawn from the experiences of the interwar years, particularly the Great Depression of the 1930s. The main lesson derived was that the United States could no longer isolate itself from world affairs, as it had tried to do after World War I. As a result, the United States actively led in the creation of the various rules and institutions that were to govern post–World War II international relations.

In the economic sphere these rules and institutions came to be known as the Bretton Woods system, named for the New Hampshire conference site where the agreements were negotiated. As envisioned in the Bretton Woods agreements of 1944, they sought a postwar international monetary regime characterized by stability, predictability, and orderly growth. Governments would have the primary responsibility for enforcing the rules and otherwise making the regime work effectively. They would be assisted by the International Monetary Fund (IMF), created at Bretton Woods as a formal mechanism to assist states in dealing with such matters as maintaining equilibrium in their balance of payments and stability in their exchange rates with one another. The International Bank for Reconstruction and Development (IBRD), now commonly known as the World Bank, was also designed as a vehicle to facilitate recovery from the war, although its role today relates primarily to promoting economic development in the Third World (see Box 7.2).

The postwar economic structure rested on three political bases: "the concentration of power in a small number of states, the existence of a cluster of important interests shared by those states, and the presence of a dominant power willing and able to assume a leadership role" (Spero, 1985).[4]

Power was concentrated in the developed countries of Western Europe and North America. Neither Japan nor the Third World then posed an effective challenge to Western dominance, and the inclusion of the communist states of Eastern Europe and the Soviet Union in the international economy was limited (see Chapter 8). The concentration of power thus minimized the number of states whose agreement was necessary in order to make the system operate effectively.

The regime's operation was facilitated by the shared interests of these states, including a preference for an open economic system combined with a commitment to limited government intervention, if this proved necessary. The onset of the Cold War was a powerful force cementing Western cohesion on economic issues. Because the West saw itself as having a common external enemy, economic cooperation came to be perceived as necessary, not only for prosperity, but also for national security. The perception contributed to a willingness to share economic burdens. It was also an important catalyst to the assumption of leadership by only one state and to the acceptance of that leadership role by others. The leader was, of course, the United States.

The Role of the United States in Managing the International Monetary System

Although the International Monetary Fund and the World Bank have become important instruments for the effective operation of the international economic system, in the immediate postwar period they proved insufficient for managing the postwar economic recovery because they were given too little authority and too few financial resources to cope with the enormous economic devastation suffered by Western Europe during the war. The United States stepped into the breach.

AMERICA'S ROLE UNTIL THE 1960s   The United States dollar became the key to America's managerial role. Backed by a vigorous and healthy economy, a fixed relationship between gold and the dollar (that is, $35 per ounce of gold), and a commitment by the government to exchange gold for dollars at any time (known as *dollar convertibility*), the dollar became as good as gold. In fact, it was preferable to gold as the liquid investment for other countries' balance-of-

---

4. Our discussion of the international monetary system draws on this source. See also Blake and Walters (1987).

BOX 7.2 ■ The Bretton Woods Conference and Its Twin Institutions

The International Monetary and Financial Conference of the United and Associated Nations was convened in Bretton Woods, New Hampshire, on July 1, 1944. By the time the conference ended on July 22, 1944, based on substantial preparatory work, it had defined the outlines of the postwar international economic system. The conference also resulted in the creation of the International Monetary Fund (IMF) and the International Bank for Reconstruction and Development (IBRD, or the World Bank)—the Bretton Woods twins.

The World Bank was to assist in reconstruction and development by facilitating the flow and investment of capital for productive purposes. The International Monetary Fund was to facilitate the expansion and balanced growth of international trade and to contribute thereby to the promotion and maintenance of high levels of employment and real income. Also discussed at Bretton Woods were plans for an International Trade Organization (ITO). This institution did not materialize, but some of its proposed functions are performed by the General Agreement on Tariffs and Trade (GATT), which was established in 1947.

The discussions at Bretton Woods took place with the experience of the interwar period as background. In the 1930s every major country sought ways to defend itself against deflationary pressures from abroad—some by exchange depreciation, some by introducing flexible exchange rates or multiple rates, some by direct controls over imports and other international transactions. The disastrous consequences of such policies—economic depression with very high unemployment—are well known. The participants in the Bretton Woods conference were determined to design an international economic system where "beggar thy neighbor" policies, which characterized the international economic community when World War II began, did not recur. There was also a widespread fear that the end of World War II would be followed by a slump, as had the end of World War I.

Thus the central elements of the system outlined at Bretton Woods were the establishment of convertibility of currencies and of fixed but adjustable exchange rates, and the encouragement of international flows of capital for productive purpose. The IMF and the World Bank were to assist in the attainment of these objectives. The economic accomplishments of the postwar period are in part the result of the effectiveness of these institutions.

Source: *World Development Report, 1985*. Copyright 1985 by The International Bank for Reconstruction and Development/The World Bank. Reprinted by permission of Oxford University Press, Inc., p. 15.

payments surpluses and savings. Dollars earned interest, which gold did not; they did not entail storage and insurance costs; and they were needed to buy imports necessary for survival and postwar reconstruction.

Thus the postwar economic system was not simply a modified gold standard system; it was a dollar-based system. Dollars became a major component of the international reserves used by national monetary authorities in other countries and of the "working balances" used by private banks, corporations, and individuals for international trade and capital transactions. Moreover, the dollar became a "parallel currency"; that is, it was universally accepted as the "currency against which every other country sold or redeemed its own national currency in the exchange markets" (Triffin, 1978–1979). In order to maintain the value of their currencies, central banks in other countries either bought or sold their own currencies, using the dollar to raise or depress the currencies' value. Such intervention was often necessary, because under the Bretton Woods agreements states were committed to keeping fluctuations in their exchange rates within very narrow limits. In other words, the Bretton Woods system was based on *fixed exchange rates* (as opposed to floating rates, in which market forces are the primary determinants of currency values).

A central problem of the immediate postwar years was how to get American dollars into the hands of those who needed them most. One vehicle was the Marshall Plan, which provided Western European nations with the resources to buy the American goods necessary to rebuild their war-torn economies. Eventually $17 billion in Marshall Plan assistance flowed to Western Europe. The United States also encouraged deficits in its own balance of payments as a way of providing international liquidity in the form of dollars.

In addition to providing international liquidity, the United States supported European and Japanese trade competitiveness and condoned certain forms of protectionism (such as Japan's restrictions against products imported from the United States) and discrimination against the dollar (such as the European Payments Union, a multilateral European group that promoted intra-European trade at the expense of trade with the United States). These short-run costs were willingly incurred because the growth that they were expected to stimulate in Europe and Japan would in time provide widening markets for American exports. The perceived political benefits of strengthening the Western world against the threat of communism were also considerable.

"The system worked well. Europe and Japan recovered and then expanded. The American economy prospered in spite of, or partly because of, the dollar outflow which led to the purchase of American goods and services" (Spero, 1985). Furthermore, the "top currency" role of the dollar facilitated the globalist foreign posture pursued by the United States (Strange, 1971). Indeed, U.S. foreign economic and military aid programs were made possible by acceptance of the dollar as the means of paying for them. Business interests could readily expand abroad because American foreign investments were often considered desirable, and American tourist dollars could be spent with few restrictions. In effect, the United States operated as the world's banker. Other countries were required to balance their financial inflows and outflows. In contrast, the United States enjoyed the advantages of operating internationally without the constraints of limited finances. The dominant position of the United States also meant that its internal economic circumstances affected other nations in significant ways. Through the ubiquitous dollar, the United States thus came to exert considerable influence on the political and economic affairs of most other nations.

Yet there were costs. The United States' influence on others required that it be sensitive to what was happening elsewhere. Massive private investments overseas, which came to be linked to domestic prosperity, were exposed to the threat of nationalization. The enormous number of dollars held by others also made the American domestic economy vulnerable to financial shocks abroad. Decision makers therefore sought to insulate the American economy from these shocks, but their task was made more difficult because some tools available to others were proscribed by the status of the dollar as a reserve currency.

For most countries an imbalance between financial inflows and outflows could be corrected most readily by raising or lowering the rate of exchange of its currency, that is, the value of its currency in relation to that of other nations. A country with an adverse balance of trade (one that imports more from other nations than it exports to them) could devalue its currency. That would have the effect of making its exports more attractive to foreign buyers, because the exports would become less costly in relation to the goods of other countries. At the same time, imports from other countries would become relatively less attractive to domestic consumers. The consequent improvement in the balance of trade—caused by promoting exports and curtailing imports by redirecting domestic demand from foreign to domestically produced products—would contribute ultimately to a favorable balance-of-payments position by increasing financial inflows and reducing outflows. Reducing domestic unemployment by promoting exports would be an additional benefit realized by devaluing one's currency. But this simple mechanism—devaluation (and revaluation) of currency exchange rates, which lies at the heart of international financial adjustments—was made more difficult for the United States because of the dollar's pivotal role. Devaluation, for example, would adversely affect political friends and military allies who had chosen to hold large amounts of dollars. Accordingly, the United States was reluctant to devalue its currency, especially so in an environment marked by competition with Soviet communism. Furthermore, because of the importance of the dollar in other countries' reserve assets, a devaluation of the dollar by the United States could easily be offset by a subsequent devaluation of the currencies of the countries adversely affected by American action—which would effectively restore the status quo before the U.S. action.

In 1959, Robert Triffin, a long-time advocate of world monetary reform, suggested that the dollar-based international monetary system was inherently unviable. Triffin (1978–1979) predicted, correctly, that eventually a means of feeding world reserves other than through dollar-linked gold would have to be found and that the number of foreign-held dollars would overwhelm the ability of the United States to convert them into gold. The latter circumstance contributed to an erosion of the confidence that others had in the soundness of the American dollar and its economy, and it led the United States to sever the link between the dollar and gold.

THE DEMISE OF AMERICAN DOMINANCE, 1960–1971 By as early as 1960 it was apparent that the dollar's top currency status was on the wane. Thereafter, the dollar-based international monetary system unilaterally managed by the United States became a multilaterally managed system under American leadership. There are several reasons for the dollar's declining position.

If too few dollars were the problem in the immediate postwar years, by the 1960s the problem became one of too many dollars. The costs of overseas military activities, foreign economic and military aid, and massive private investments produced increasing balance-of-payments deficits, which earlier had been encouraged but later reached unmanageable proportions. Furthermore, American gold holdings in relation to the growing number of foreign-held dollars fell precipitously. Given these circumstances, the possibility that the United States might devalue the dollar led to a loss of confidence by others and hence an unwillingness to continue to hold dollars as reserve currency. The French under the leadership of Charles de Gaulle even went so far as to insist on exchanging dollars for gold.

Along with the glut of dollars, the increasing monetary interdependence of the advanced industrial societies of the First World led to massive transnational movements of capital. The internationalization of banking, the internationalization of production via multinational corporations, and the development of a Eurocurrency market outside direct state control all strengthened this interdependence.[5] An increasingly complex relationship between the economic policies engineered in one country and their effects on another was the result. This in turn spawned a variety of more or less formal groupings of the central bankers and finance ministers from the leading economic powers who devised various *ad hoc* solutions to their common problems. The decision was also made to create a form of "paper gold" known as Special Drawing Rights (SDRs) in the IMF to facilitate the growth of international liquidity by means other than increasing the outflow of dollars.[6]

Although the United States was the chief proponent and supporter of the various management techniques devised during the 1960s, none proved sufficient to counter the dollar crises that began in the late 1960s and early 1970s. An important reason underlying these crises is that the Bretton Woods regime never operated in quite the way it was intended. Under Bretton Woods, each state was obligated to maintain the value of its currency in relation to the

---

5. Eurocurrencies are dollars and other currencies held in Europe as bank deposits and lent and borrowed outside the country of origin.

6. SDRs are reserve assets that nations' central banks agree to accept to settle their official financial transactions. Because their value is set in relation to a "basket" of major currencies, SDRs tend to be more stable than either gold or a single currency.

American dollar (and through it to all others) within the confines of the agreed-upon exchange rate. In this way the value of the currencies needed to carry on international financial transactions would remain stable and predictable. If it proved difficult to maintain the agreed-upon rate of exchange because of persistent structural weaknesses in a nation's economy, then a currency de-valuation was in order and was supposed to be carried out only after consulta-tions with others through the IMF. But this did not happen.

> Exchange rate alterations proved to be traumatic politically and econom-ically under the Bretton Woods system. Devaluations were taken as indica-tions of weakness and economic failure by states and, thus, were resisted. Exchange rates became more rigid than the founders of the IMF had anticipated. When states, nevertheless, were compelled to devalue their currencies, it was usually done without consultation with the IMF, because negotiations prior to the fact invited heavy speculation against the weaken-ing currency in international money markets. (Blake and Walters, 1987: 62)

Changes in the international political economy undermined the willingness of others (possibly including the monetary authorities in other countries) to continue to hold American dollars. By the 1960s the European and Japanese recovery from World War II was complete, which meant that American mone-tary dominance and the dollar's privileged position were no longer acceptable. In a sense, however, the rejuvenated economies were still subject to the wishes of the wealthy United States—an unwelcome circumstance that may have been perceived as a loss of sovereignty. For its part, however, the United States was not always receptive to criticism of its policies and the privileges conferred on it by its top currency status. Instead, having enjoyed that position for years, it came to see its own economic health and that of the international economy as one and the same. Any attack on the dollar was therefore "viewed instinctively by Americans as an attack on international economic stability" (Blake and Walters, 1987).

The reasons for the United States' inability to control its balance-of-pay-ments deficits are many, including an unwillingness to pull back from its costly, globalist foreign policy posture and a lag in the modernization of its economic productive facilities, growing out of American-based multinational firms' decisions to build branch plants abroad rather than new facilities at home. Fred L. Block elaborates:

> The exercise of American political and military power on a global basis has been designed to gain foreign acceptance of an international monetary order that institutionalizes an open world economy, giving maximum op-portunities to American businessmen. It would be absurd for the United States to abandon its global ambitions simply to live within the rules of an international monetary order that was shaped for the purpose of achieving these ambitions. So it is hardly surprising that the United States continued to pursue its global ambitions despite the increasing strains on the interna-

tional monetary order. The fundamental contradiction was that the United States had created an international monetary order that worked only when American political and economic dominance in the capitalist world was absolute. That absolute dominance disappeared as a result of the reconstruction of Western Europe and Japan, on the one hand, and the accumulated domestic costs of the global extension of U.S. power, on the other. With the fading of the absolute dominance, the international monetary order began to crumble. The U.S. deficit was simply the most dramatic symptom of the terminal disease that plagued the postwar international monetary order. (Block, 1977: 163)

The Europeans and Japanese especially came to resent the prerogatives that the United States derived from its position as the world's banker and from its ability to determine the level of international liquidity through its balance-of-payments deficits. Not only did these prerogatives affect the economies of Europe and Japan; they also gave the United States the ability to make foreign expenditures for political purposes that came to be less and less acceptable to others.

Among the United States' political pursuits with which many European nations disagreed was the Vietnam War. And among the economic conditions that they came to share was inflation, which in the United States was stimulated by President Lyndon B. Johnson's unwillingness to raise taxes to finance either his Great Society domestic programs or the Vietnam War. In this sense Europe was forced to pay for another country's foreign policy adventures, about which they had great reservations.

Détente between the United States and the Soviet Union also had an impact on the Western-based economic system. The decline in fear of and hostility toward the Soviet Union as an external threat carried with it a decline in the willingness of others to accede to American leadership. The changing international political environment thus combined with the changing international economic environment to militate against continued American hegemony in international monetary matters.

The deteriorating U.S. domestic economic situation also began to erode its leadership position, particularly as inflation reduced the competitiveness of American goods overseas. Historically, the United States had enjoyed favorable balances of trade. This was important, because its favorable trade balances were used to offset its unfavorable payments balances, which by the end of the 1960s had become chronic. The favorable trade situation itself disappeared by 1971, however, when for the first time in the twentieth century the United States suffered a trade deficit of $2 billion, and it worsened thereafter. The result was a growing demand by industrial, labor, and agricultural interests for protectionist measures designed to insulate them from foreign economic challenges and threats.

Part of the blame for the trade deficit was laid at the doorstep of America's major trading partners. In particular, Japan and West Germany were criticized for maintaining undervalued currencies (that is, currencies that did not accurately reflect the cost of goods in those countries). This made their goods attractive internationally (and to the American consumer), which in turn enabled these countries to generate balance-of-payments surpluses by selling more overseas than they bought. At the same time, the relative position of the United States in international trade was deteriorating, as America's share of international trade declined and Europe's and Japan's increased.

Faced with these circumstances, President Richard M. Nixon undertook a number of steps in 1971 designed to shore up the United States' sagging position in the global political economy, the most important of which severed the link between gold and the dollar. The decision marked the end of the Bretton Woods system of fixed exchange rates. In its place a system of free-floating currency values emerged, one in which currency values were to be determined primarily by market forces rather than governmental interventions. The theory underlying the new system was that a country experiencing adverse economic conditions would see the value of its currency in the marketplace decline in response to the preferences of its traders, bankers, and business people. This would make its exports cheaper and its imports more expensive, which would then move the value of its currency back toward equilibrium—all without the need for central bankers to support their currencies. In this way, it was hoped, the politically humiliating devaluations of the past could be avoided. What was not foreseen was that the floating-exchange rate system would introduce an unparalleled degree of uncertainty and unpredictability in international monetary relations.

The strident actions of the United States in 1971 came as a shock to the other Western industrialized nations. They perhaps represented America's reaction to its growing dependence on the rest of the world and its realization that the United States alone could no longer determine the course of international monetary matters. The result was that the political bases on which the Bretton Woods system had been built lay in ruins. American leadership was no longer accepted willingly by others or exercised willingly by the United States. Power had come to be more widely dispersed among the states making up the system, and the shared interests that once bound them together had dissipated.

International Monetary Disorder: The "OPEC Decade"

Formal negotiations on reform of the international monetary system were begun in the summer of 1972. Before anything could be decided, however, the world economy suffered yet another shock—a massive increase in the price of oil effected by the Organization of Petroleum Exporting Countries (OPEC) shortly after the 1973 Yom Kippur War in the Middle East. In the months that followed, the price of a barrel of Saudi Arabian benchmark crude skyrocketed from $2.10 to $10.24. Then, in 1979–1980, the world suffered a second oil shock when oil prices jumped even more dramatically. Together, the two oil shocks seriously challenged the international monetary system; indeed, they threatened to shatter the entire global political economy.

The high cost of energy following the first oil shock resulted in worldwide recession. Paradoxically, however, worldwide inflation also persisted. *Stagflation*—the term coined to describe a stagnant economy accompanied by rising unemployment and high inflation—entered the economic lexicon. Inflation persisted despite the return to economic growth in 1976 and contributed to OPEC's desire to continue to increase the price of oil so as to maximize the return on its resources. But not until the price of oil began in 1979 to rachet upward from $20 a barrel did the real price to OPEC rise.

Following the second oil shock, the world plunged into what became the longest and most severe economic recession since the Great Depression of the 1930s. In response to the first energy-related recession, the leading industrial powers (which were also the largest importers of oil) chose conventional fiscal and monetary expansion to reflate their economies. During the second recession they shifted their priority to controlling inflation. Their strict monetarist policies were accompanied by large fiscal deficits and sharply higher interest rates, both of which were particularly apparent in the United States. In an era of complex interdependence, none could escape the consequences of these developments, as we shall note in more detail later.

The high cost of energy caused substantial dislocations in many nations' balance-of-payments positions, as billions of "petrodollars" flowed to the oil-producing states. The initial problem posed by the massive energy-induced shift in wealth was how to recycle the petrodollars from the oil producers to the oil consumers. Although some observers had predicted that the magnitude of the recycling problem would lead to the collapse of the international economic order, recycling did occur, even after the oil price increases imposed by OPEC in 1979 and 1980. In addition to the IMF, the World Bank, and individual nations, private banks in the capitalist world proved particularly effective in managing the flow of funds. In the process, however, the debt burden of many nations, particularly in the Third World, assumed ominous proportions. The threat of massive defaults by countries unable to service their debts pushed the international monetary order to the brink of crisis in the early 1980s, thereby challenging in yet another way the viability of the established global political economy. (See Chapter 8 for a discussion of the debt crisis.)

The combination of the dollar's importance to the international monetary system and the sheer magnitude of American energy consumption during the OPEC decade ensured a special role for the United States in the global energy picture. Throughout the decade following OPEC's initial price hikes, the United States consumed between 25 and 30 percent of all the oil produced in the world. Furthermore, American dependence on foreign sources of oil began to grow at precisely the same time that the per-barrel cost of oil first shot upward. Massive amounts of dollars were therefore spent overseas, over $40 billion for petroleum and petroleum products in 1977 and then a record $74 billion in 1980.

The massive influx of dollars into the international monetary system meant that someone had to be willing to hold them. During much of the 1970s, however, it appeared as though the dollar was no longer attractive, as demonstrated by the substantial drop in its value. Then, following the second oil shock and the Reagan administration's shift toward monetarist policies designed to curb inflation, the dollar reversed its decline and rose to record highs on foreign exchange markets. Figure 7.1 illustrates the shifting fortunes of the dollar by tracing its value in relation to other major currencies. The trough in the value of the dollar between roughly 1978 and 1980, its marked upward trend until 1985, and its downturn thereafter are particularly noticeable.

The coincidence of the declining value of the dollar and the rising cost of foreign-oil imports during the 1970s suggests that America's seemingly insatiable energy appetite was an important underlying cause of the dollar's decline toward the end of the decade. Persistent inflation in the United States—itself fed by rising fuel costs, the cumulative costs of past wars and present defense expenditures, and federal budgetary increases in the public sector generally— was also a factor. Ironically, the decline in the dollar's value internationally may also have fed domestic inflation, as the dollar cost of foreign-produced goods increased. The importance of this fact is heightened by the growing proportion of imports in America's national product. In the decade ending in 1980, American imports as a proportion of its GNP more than doubled, from 4.5 percent in 1971 to 9.6 percent in 1980. Because total American imports in 1980 were in excess of $250 billion, the potential impact of foreign goods on domestic prices was substantial.[7]

From the perspective of foreign countries, the United States' persistent economic problems made it less desirable to hold dollars, which, of course, caused the value of the dollar to fall even farther. As noted earlier, this trend was reversed in the early 1980s when a combination of renewed economic growth in the United States and a sharp reduction in inflation seemed to

---

7. The inflationary impact of more costly foreign goods may be compounded by domestic producers, who, when faced with reduced competition, may increase their own prices in order to maximize their profits. Similarly, workers may seek to boost their wages to maintain their real incomes in the face of rising costs of foreign-produced goods. But domestic price and wage inflation eat up the positive effects of American trade and payments balances that derive from the greater competitiveness abroad of American goods made possible by the devaluation of the dollar. Appreciation of the dollar also reduces its competitiveness and increases the attractiveness of foreign imports. This is what happened when the dollar's decline reversed itself in the 1980s, thereby encouraging an even greater increase in imports as a proportion of GNP.

Policymakers in the United States worried again in the late 1980s about the inflationary impact of the declining dollar, which, as discussed later in this chapter, skidded downward from its peak in early 1985 in an almost uninterrupted trend for nearly three years. During the first part of this fall, however, the inflationary effect of the dollar's decline was cushioned by other factors, including the surge of foreign investment into the United States noted in Chapter 6 and again later in this chapter. Stephen Marris explains:

First, the sharp drop in oil prices more than offset the inflationary impact of the declining dollar on US import prices through most of 1986, so that for over a year US inflation declined, even though the lower dollar was pushing other import prices up. Second, a remarkably strong bull market on Wall Street meant that, for most foreign investors, exchange rate losses were offset by capital gains on stocks and bonds. . . . (Marris, 1987: 14)

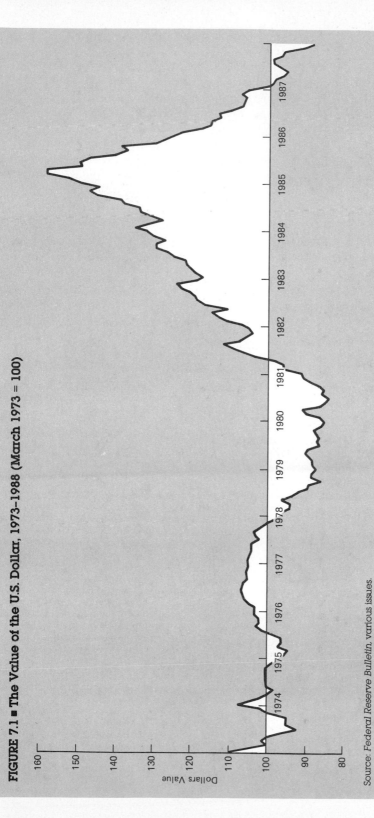

FIGURE 7.1 ■ The Value of the U.S. Dollar, 1973–1988 (March 1973 = 100)

Source: *Federal Reserve Bulletin,* various issues.

Note: The index is the weighted average value of the U.S. dollar against the currencies of the other nine major industrialized nations plus Switzerland.

restore faith in the dollar (which rose over 20 percent in value between 1981 and 1983). More importantly, interest rates in the United States remained high relative to interest rates in other countries, and the United States was seen as a safe haven for financial investments in a world otherwise marked by political instability and violence. Foreigners therefore rushed to acquire the dollars necessary to take advantage of profitable investment opportunities in the United States. The increased demand for dollars thus drove up the exchange rate. This situation contrasted sharply with that in the 1970s, when the United States' overwhelming foreign indebtedness, often called the "dollar overhang," was a principal fear.

For the United States, the appreciation of the dollar was a mixed blessing. On the one hand, it reduced the cost of imported oil.[8] On the other hand, it increased the cost of American exports to foreign buyers, thereby reducing the competitiveness of American products in overseas markets. This meant the loss of tens of thousands of jobs in American industries that produced for export. It also meant a record trade deficit in excess of $160 billion in the mid-1980s, as imports from abroad became relatively cheaper and hence more attractive to American consumers.

In a normally functioning market, this situation would set in motion self-corrective processes that would return the dollar to its equilibrium value. Growing American imports, for example, though beneficial to United States trade partners in generating jobs and thus stimulating their return to economic growth, should create upward pressure on the value of others' currencies. Conversely, a drop in American exports should ease the demand for dollars, thereby reducing the dollar's value in exchange markets. Most analysts agree

---

8. Because oil is not only priced in dollars but is also typically paid for with dollars, appreciation of the dollar reduces the cost of oil to the United States but increases it for others, because it requires more foreign currency (such as yen, marks, or francs) to acquire the dollars necessary for an equivalent amount of oil than when the dollar was "worth less." The reverse, of course, is also true. Thus, when the dollar declined relative to other currencies between 1978 and 1980, this reduced the cost of oil to much of Europe and Japan, which depend heavily on imported oil. The cost increased following the reversal of the decline of the dollar in 1980 and may have contributed to the lag in the other industrial countries' economic recovery, compared with that of the United States.

The cycle reversed itself again in the late 1980s, when the declining value of the dollar pushed up the cost of oil to the United States. Members of OPEC were among the major losers at this time, as the dollars they received for their resources were able to buy fewer goods than previously. That realization contributed to continuing disarray in the oil cartel as it sought to manage global prices and production to its own advantage in the post-OPEC decade.

What applies to oil applies to other commodities as well. Commodities like sugar, rubber, and silver, on which Third World nations depend to earn foreign exchange, are also priced in dollars, so as the dollar declines, the revenues that Third World nations receive for their products (necessary to repay foreign loans as well as to promote economic development at home) are reduced. At the same time, of course, American products needed for development become less expensive. Currency fluctuations thus have both positive and negative effects, and how they are evaluated therefore depends in part on where one sits. But part of the message also is that fluctuations in the U.S. dollar are especially important because of the pivotal role of the dollar in the global political economy.

that in the early 1980s these mechanisms did not work as they should have because of the persistently high interest rates in the United States. These were sustained in large measure by the federal government's huge budget deficits—which themselves were sustained by unparalleled military spending. Eventually, however, the United States' deficits were deemed the culprits as a renewed sense of global economic uncertainty plagued decision makers in such widely separated yet economically intertwined places as Tokyo and London, Washington and Sydney, Hong Kong and Bonn.

International Monetary Disorder: Beyond the OPEC Decade

October 19, 1987, came to be known on Wall Street as "Black Monday." On that date the Dow Jones index of the value of thirty U.S. industrial stocks sustained a 508-point drop, its biggest in history. The 22.6 percent loss—which translated into hundreds of billions of dollars in lost equity—followed plunging stock prices in Tokyo, where the stock market had opened hours earlier. In the next several days, stock prices tumbled worldwide as falling prices in Asia were followed by falling prices in Europe, then in the United States, and then in Asia again. Figure 7.2, which shows the value of stocks on the Tokyo, London, and New York markets during these fateful days, illustrates how interdependent the world's financial centers had become. Just as the multinational corporation earlier had propelled development of a global system of production, Black Monday demonstrated the existence of a global market.

What caused Black Monday? The search for answers produced many complex explanations, but there is general agreement that an important precipitating cause was the continued decline in the value of the dollar. As shown in Figure 7.1, the dollar began to slip in early 1985 and continued a long decline thereafter, losing nearly 60 percent relative to the currencies of the other major industrialized countries by mid-1987. Against certain currencies, especially the Japanese yen, the decline was even more pronounced.

What caused the decline? Again, the answers are complex but generally reflect a loss of confidence in the dollar analogous to the loss of confidence that produced the dollar's decline in the 1970s. But whereas the seemingly insatiable U.S. energy appetite explained the loss of confidence in the 1970s, deficits explained it in the 1980s—U.S. trade and government budget deficits in particular.

To understand the relationship between deficits and the dollar, it is useful to examine briefly why fluctuations occur in a nation's currency rate of exchange.[9]

---

9. The following description applies only to those currencies that are "convertible" into other currencies. Generally this means that the description applies only to First World nations, because the currencies of Second and Third World nations are usually insufficiently attractive internationally to be traded outside their own borders.

FIGURE 7.2 ▪ Daily Closing of Major World Stock Indexes, September 28 to October 26, 1987

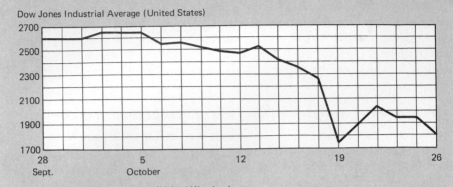

Dow Jones Industrial Average (United States)

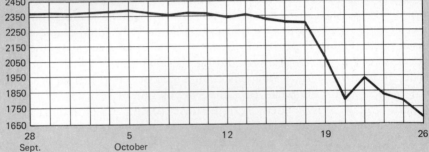

Financial Times 100-share Index (United Kingdom)

Note: No official close due to storm on Friday October 16.

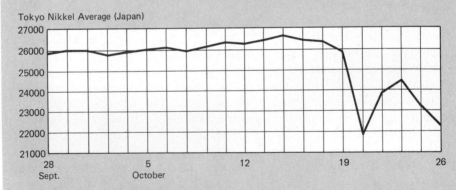

Tokyo Nikkel Average (Japan)

Source: *Wall Street Journal,* October 27, 1987, p. 51. Reprinted by permission of *The Wall Street Journal* © Dow Jones and Company, Inc. 1987. All Rights Reserved.

Money works in several ways and serves different purposes: It must be acceptable, so that people earning it can use it to buy goods and services from others. It must serve as a store of value, so that people will be willing to keep some of their wealth in the form of money. And it must be a standard of deferred payment, so that people will be willing to lend money knowing that when the money owed them is repaid in the future, it will still have purchasing power.

Inflation occurs when too much money is created in relation to the goods and services produced in an economy. In such an environment, money becomes more plentiful and hence less acceptable, which means that it cannot serve well as a store of value or a medium of exchange to satisfy debts. Governments work to ensure that their currencies do the jobs intended for them, which means, among other things, trying to maintain an inflation-free environment.

In the international monetary system, movements in a nation's exchange rate occur in part when assessments of the underlying economic strength of a country or the ability of its government to maintain the value of its money change. A deficit in a country's balance of payments, for example, would likely cause a decline in the value of its currency relative to others, because the supply of the currency would be greater than the demand for it. Similarly, when those engaged in international economic transactions change their expectations about the future value of a currency, they might reschedule their lending and borrowing; fluctuations in the exchange rate could follow.

Speculators—those who buy and sell money in order to make it—may also affect the stability of a nation's currency internationally. Professional speculators make money by making guesses about the future. If, for example, they believe that the Japanese yen will be worth more in, say, three months than it is now, they can buy yen today and sell them for a profit three months hence. Conversely, if they believe that the dollar will be worth less in ninety days, they can sell some number of yen today for a certain number of dollars and then buy back the same number of yen in ninety days for fewer dollars, thus making a profit.

On what basis do speculators make these kinds of decisions? One is their reading of the health of the currency in which they are speculating. If they believe the U.S. dollar is weak because the American economy itself is weak, they may conclude that the American government will permit a devaluation of the dollar. Another, closely related consideration is whether a government is believed to have the political will to devise effective policies to ensure the value of its money, particularly against inflation. If speculators think that it does not, they would again be wise to sell dollars today and buy them back tomorrow at the (anticipated) lower price. In the process, of course, speculators may create self-fulfilling prophecies: They may "prove" that the dollar needs to be devalued simply because of the volume of seemingly unwanted dollars that are offered for sale.

Just as governments seek to protect the value of their currencies at home, they seek to protect them internationally by intervening in the marketplace. Their willingness to do so is especially important to importers and exporters, who depend on orderliness and predictability in the value of the currencies they deal in to carry on their transnational exchanges. Governments intervene when nations' central banks buy or sell currencies to change the value of their own currencies in relation to others. But unlike speculators, they are pledged not to manipulate exchange rates so as to gain unfair advantage.

In the latter half of the 1980s the enormous trade and federal government budget deficits of the United States combined to erode confidence in the U.S. dollar. This then contributed to its decline internationally, for the deficits demonstrated to many the inherent weaknesses in the American economy and the inability of its political system to cope with these and other problems. The growing magnitude of each is illustrated in Figures 7.3 and 7.4. The first shows the steady growth of the U.S. trade deficit to its record-setting peak of $169.8 billion in 1986. The second shows the steady rise in the government's deficit until it peaked at $212 billion in 1985.

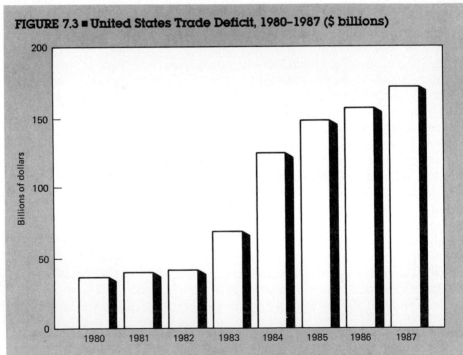

FIGURE 7.3 ■ United States Trade Deficit, 1980–1987 ($ billions)

Source: 1980–1985 adapted from U.S. Bureau of the Census, *Highlights of U.S. Export and Import Trade,* Report FT 990, December 1984, 1985, and 1986; 1986–1987 adapted from U.S. Bureau of the Census, *United States Foreign Trade, Summary of U.S. Export and Import Merchandise Trade,* Report 900, December 1987.

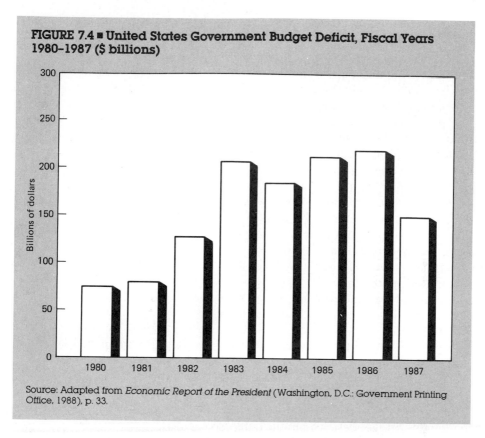

FIGURE 7.4 ▪ United States Government Budget Deficit, Fiscal Years 1980–1987 ($ billions)

Source: Adapted from *Economic Report of the President* (Washington, D.C.: Government Printing Office, 1988), p. 33.

The burgeoning trade deficit experienced by the United States in the 1980s was a product of several factors, not least of which was the extraordinarily high value that the dollar attained in mid-decade. As the value of the dollar soared, the competitiveness of American producers overseas plunged. Consider, for example, the plight of American farmers. In 1981 their exports were valued at $43.3 billion. Five years later, in 1986, agricultural exports stood at $26.3 billion, a nearly 40 percent drop that contributed directly to the devastating, depression-like loss of income that drove tens of thousands from their farms forever.

In addition to the value of the high-flying dollar, declining productivity was another factor that contributed to the U.S. trade deficit. The American farmer is extraordinarily productive. But many other American workers are not, at least when compared with their counterparts overseas. Declining American productivity has been attributed to a loss of the technological edge to Japan and others that the United States enjoyed in the 1950s and 1960s. Insufficient domestic savings and insufficient investment in civilian research and development as well as basic education contributed to the decline (see Thurow, 1988), as did the widespread perception that "made in America" no longer meant superior quality.

Persistent budget deficits by the U.S. federal government exacerbated the American economic malaise. As noted earlier, the deficits were driven in large part by unprecedented military expenditures that drove up interest rates and contributed thereby to the persistence of the overvalued dollar. Even though they promoted economic growth domestically, many analysts felt that continued high levels of defense spending were counterproductive in the long run. Because dollars spent on research and development for defense tend to steer scientists and engineers away from civilian applications, opportunities to close the technological gap with Japan and others in the development of consumer products are lost (Kennedy, 1988; see also Rosecrance, 1988).

High levels of defense spending also contributed to making the United States a debtor nation for the first time in half a century, meaning that it owes more money abroad than others owe the United States. In fact, by 1988 the United States owed $1,250 billion to others, making it the world's largest debtor nation (Rothstein, 1988: 20). Going into debt by borrowing from others does not necessarily mean problems today, as explained in the excerpt in Box 7.3. But to many it represents yet another ominous symbol of the inability of the United States to set its financial house in order. And in the long run, the growing national debt means that tomorrow's money spent to pay today's bills will not be available to meet future problems.[10] The likely result will be a decline in the unusually high standard of living Americans have come to enjoy.

Congress and the president sought in the waning days of the Reagan administration to realize legislatively mandated targets for reducing the continuing U.S. budget deficits, but the behavior of financial and capital markets at home and abroad suggested that there was little confidence worldwide that the United States had embarked on a meaningful path toward resolving its politicoeconomic problems.

The wide gyrations in the value of the U.S. dollar since the Nixon administration unilaterally terminated the Bretton Woods international monetary regime pointed to the need to devise alternatives to Bretton Woods, but none has been successful. During the 1970s, proposals were made to create in the IMF a "dollar substitution" account that would enable nations to trade unwanted dollars for IMF-backed funds rather than dumping them on the open market, but nothing came of them. Later, French President François Mitterrand called for a formal alternative to the defunct Bretton Woods regime, noting that "monetary disorders fuel economic wars between friends." President Ronald Reagan seemed to share that sentiment when he acknowledged in his

---

10. The U.S. national debt rose from $914.3 billion in 1980 to $1,823.1 billion in 1985. Interest on the debt rose from $52.5 billion to $129 billion during this same period. A simple projection of these trends would push the debt to $13 trillion by the year 2000, which is fourteen times the debt in 1980, and the interest on the debt would mount to $1.5 trillion, which is twenty-nine times the 1980 figure (Kennedy, 1987a: 30).

BOX 7.3 ■ The United States As a Debtor Nation

. . . U.S. public and private investments abroad no longer [exceed] the value of foreign holdings of this country's public and private assets. In that sense the U.S. has become a debtor nation.

Joining the ranks of the world's Micawbers has no immediate consequence for people in this country. There is no debtor's prison for nations. The change in status should not cause this country to hold its head less high in the councils of nations even [though the United States has become] the world's largest debtor. Nor will foreign investors suddenly liquidate their U.S. holdings, leaving this country scrambling to pay off its foreign debts.

The significance of the debt measure is that it takes broad account of this country's economic position vis-à-vis the rest of the world. . . . [T]he merchandise trade deficit, the focal point of recent concern, doesn't tell the whole story. The United States could afford to go on importing far more goods than it is able to export as long as that merchandise imbalance was offset by surpluses in service exports or returns from U.S. investments abroad. The trouble . . . is that the huge merchandise deficits the country has been running have overwhelmed surpluses in the service accounts. As a result, the country has been amassing foreign debt. The cost of paying interest and other returns to the foreign holders of that debt further aggravates the balance-of-payments problem, since the United States can no longer depend on net returns from its foreign investments to help offset trade deficits. And in the long term, that means this country may have to sacrifice some of its own standard of living to finance its foreign obligations.

. . . [T]he United States grew and prospered as a debtor nation during the 19th century. In those years it imported huge amounts of foreign capital and labor to exploit its enormous resource base—an investment that paid off handsomely both here and abroad. The difference now is that capital formation in this country has not, at least so far, been commensurate with the inflow of foreign capital. Instead, much of our recent foreign borrowing has gone to finance private consumption through tax cuts and public consumption through government spending. In a very real sense, the country is borrowing from its future.

Source: © *The Washington Post*, September 19, 1985.

1986 State of the Union message the U.S. need to begin "coordinating economic and monetary policy among our major trading partners." But no permanent institutional procedures were forthcoming.

The one concrete change in the outward manifestations of the international monetary system in the post–Bretton Woods period has been the European Monetary System (EMS), launched by the European Community in 1979 to stabilize the currency values of the European Community's member nations against one another and against the dollar. As with other initiatives of the European Community, the EMS's promise and performance have diverged (see

Cohen, 1979; Ungerer, 1983). Nevertheless, the system may still contain the seeds of a regionalized international monetary system. The scenario envisions the European Community emerging dominant in Western Europe and in those areas of Africa and the Caribbean linked by treaty to the European Community, with Japan dominant in the Far East and Southeast Asia, and the United States remaining dominant elsewhere, notably in the Western Hemisphere.

Pending these developments, periodic meetings of heads of state, financial ministers, and other important officials designed to achieve macroeconomic policy coordination among the principal economic powers of the Western industrialized world remain the most visible institutionalized mechanism for managing the international monetary system in the post–Bretton Woods era. For the most part, however, they have proved insufficient to the tasks at hand. The reason is clear: Policymakers are uncertain how to maximize their interests in an interdependent global context while simultaneously minimizing the domestic economic and political costs of their foreign entanglements. The "monetary" dilemma faced by the United States and its major economic partners and politico-military friends and allies as they sought to cope with the multiple deficits plaguing the American economy and government in the waning days of the Reagan administration illustrates the problems: Europe sought a cut in U.S. budget deficits and an increase in U.S. interest rates so as to prop up the dollar by attracting foreign investment, but the United States hesitated for fear of causing a recession (in a presidential election year). Instead, the United States sought a decrease in its allies' interest rates so as to stimulate their economies and, with that, their demand for U.S. products (but at the risk of inflation in the importing economies) and looked to their central banks for support in shoring up the value of the faltering dollar. Both positions and the many embellishments they entail demonstrate the perils as well as the promises of interdependence in today's global political economy. They also underscore the continuing decline of American economic power vis-à-vis others, which contributed measurably to the turbulence and uncertainty of the post–Bretton Woods international monetary system.

THE TRANSFORMATION OF THE INTERNATIONAL TRADE SYSTEM

The volume and value of international trade has grown exponentially since World War II. Because the postwar period has also witnessed an unprecedented increase in world production, international trade arguably has been one of the great engines driving economic growth and raising living standards worldwide to levels never before achieved. But increased trade protectionism threatens to halt this process by lowering trade growth globally as well as nationally. In fact, the (real) value of world trade declined between 1980 and

1985, when world exports stood at roughly $150 billion below their 1980 level of more than $2 trillion.

Many of the same forces that nudged the crisis-prone international monetary system away from the precepts of the postwar Liberal International Economic Order induced states to adopt protectionist and beggar-thy-neighbor trade policies so as to obtain the foreign exchange necessary to pay for their imports, service their debts, and otherwise meet their domestic economic goals while simultaneously deflecting the impact of external developments on their domestic political economies. Beggar-thy-neighbor strategies cannot work for every country, however; not everyone can run a balance-of-trade surplus. As in the case of balances of payments, when one country is in a surplus position, another must have a deficit. Nonetheless, the growing prevalence of protectionism has dealt yet another blow to the Liberal International Economic Order.

The predominant political rationale underlying trade protectionism is clear. With an estimated 30 million people in the industrial world looking for jobs during the recession of the early 1980s, it was easy to conclude that foreign imports were responsible for the loss of domestic jobs. According to classic international trade theory, however, cutting off imports denies the benefits that comparative advantage and free trade promise (see Box 7.1). It has been estimated, for example, that restrictions placed on the export of Japanese automobiles to the United States increased the average cost per car in 1984 by $640, for a total cost to the American consumer of some $6.6 billion (Boonekamp, 1987: 4).

Protectionism may also postpone needed structural changes in national economies, as technological changes alter the relative efficiencies of different industries. As explained by one leading international economist:

> Import protection is like the toadstool—superficially attractive but potentially deadly. What protectionists prefer to ignore is that while individual industries might well profit from protectionism, at least for a time, the economy as a whole will suffer as increasingly more resources are locked into inefficient, low-growth activities. A healthy economy must be capable of adapting continuously to changes in the competitive environment. Capital and labor must be able to shift readily into growing, high-productivity sectors. Otherwise overall economic growth—the ultimate guarantor of jobs—gradually will be stifled. History is replete with tragic examples of economies that have choked on a diet of protectionism. (Cohen, 1983: 10)

Growing protectionism thus entails a move away from the open or liberal multilateral trading system that has been painstakingly nurtured during much of the post–World War II period. The forces currently militating against the preservation of the system can be better understood by examining its postwar history and the role played by the United States in shaping it.

Creating the Liberal Trade Regime: America's Leadership Role

The importance of the United States to the international trade system derives from the size of its economy and the value of its production sold abroad. In 1985, for example, U.S. exports equaled 5 percent of its gross national product. This contrasts sharply with the exports of many other countries that are relatively more "involved" in the world economy. Japan's exports-to-GNP ratio in the same year, for example, was 13 percent, Britain's 21 percent, West Germany's 29 percent, Norway's 34 percent, and Taiwan's 51 percent. Despite these higher ratios, however, only West Germany's exports rivaled in value the more than $213 billion of United States production sold abroad. In fact, the ranking among these seven countries according to their exports-to-GNP ratio is nearly the opposite of their ranking according to the size of their economies. In 1985 the United States' gross national product was nearly six times that of West Germany and more than sixty times greater than that of Taiwan. Generally, therefore, and despite the relative decline in American economic dominance, the United States' economy and its policies relating to foreign economic matters are much more important to other nations than their economies and policies are to the United States. As the then United States trade representative, Reuben Askew, put it in 1980, "True, we are no longer the single, pre-eminent economic power in the world. But we are still the strongest."

The importance of the United States to the world economy was even more pronounced in the immediate postwar period. Today the United States accounts for less than a quarter of the world's aggregate GNP; in 1947 it accounted for half of all world production. It is not surprising, therefore, that the United States became the dominant voice in matters of trade as well as monetary affairs.

The liberal trading system that the United States promoted, like the position it took toward international monetary matters, was once again informed by the lessons that the 1930s seemed to suggest. The zero-sum, beggar-thy-neighbor policies associated with the intensely competitive economic nationalism during the interwar period were a major cause of the worldwide economic catastrophe of the 1930s that ended in global warfare. In the postwar period, priority was assigned to removing barriers to trade, particularly tariffs, whose purpose as an instrument of international economic policy is "to alter the structure of production by expanding the output of the protected goods" (Kindleberger, 1977a).

Management responsibilities for the postwar economic system as envisaged during World War II were to be entrusted to the International Trade Organization (ITO), which was to seek lower restrictions on trade and to set rules of commerce. It was hoped that the ITO, together with the IMF and World Bank, could assist in avoiding a repetition of the international economic breakdown that followed World War II. But the ITO was stillborn.

The United States was the prime mover behind all three of these specialized international agencies. The ITO failed when the liberal trading system envisioned in the Havana Charter was so watered down by demands from other countries for exemptions from the generalized rules that the United States government deemed the document worthless. In its place, the United States sponsored the General Agreement on Tariffs and Trade (GATT). In a sense, GATT, which is now an established international agency, became the cornerstone of the liberalized trade regime originally embodied in the ITO.

The *most-favored-nation* (MFN) principle became the mortar of the effort to promote free international trade. According to this principle, the tariff preferences granted to one nation must be granted to all other nations exporting the same product. The principle seeks elimination of preferential treatment in the granting of trade concessions; every nation is to be treated the same as the most favored one is (provided, of course, that the trading partners have previously agreed to grant one another MFN status). Thus the principle stands for nondiscrimination in the way that nations treat one another.

Under GATT and the most-favored-nation principle, a series of multilateral trade negotiations aimed at tariff reductions with broad national participation was undertaken. The seventh of these sessions, the Tokyo Round of Multilateral Trade Negotiations (MTN), so named because the basis for the negotiations was established in Tokyo in 1973, was concluded in Geneva in 1979 after nearly five years of bargaining. An eighth, the Uruguay Round, was launched in 1986.

The high point of postwar momentum toward a liberalized trading system—insofar as tariff reductions on industrial products goods is concerned—was the Kennedy Round of negotiations, which actually took place during the Johnson administration (1964–1967). In this, as well as in all previous multilateral trading conferences, the United States was the principal mover. As "leadership" implies, the United States was willing to accept fewer immediate benefits than were its trading partners in anticipation of the longer-term benefits of freer international trade. In effect, the United States was the locomotive of expanding world production and trade. By stimulating its own growth, the United States became an attractive market for the exports of others, and the outflow of United States dollars stimulated the economic growth of other nations in the "American train." Evidence supporting the wisdom of this strategy, particularly the association between tariff reductions and export growth, is provided in Figure 7.5. The average duty levied on imports to the United States was reduced by more than half between the late 1940s and the early 1960s. Correspondingly, world exports nearly tripled during this period.

The Kennedy Round did not deal successfully with tariff barriers on agricultural products, however. Lack of progress on this issue, and subsequent disagreements over it, began to raise doubts among American policymakers about the wisdom of America's expansionary policies. The immediate challenge was posed in 1966 in the Common Agricultural Policy (CAP) instituted by the European Economic Community (EEC). Toward outsiders, the CAP was

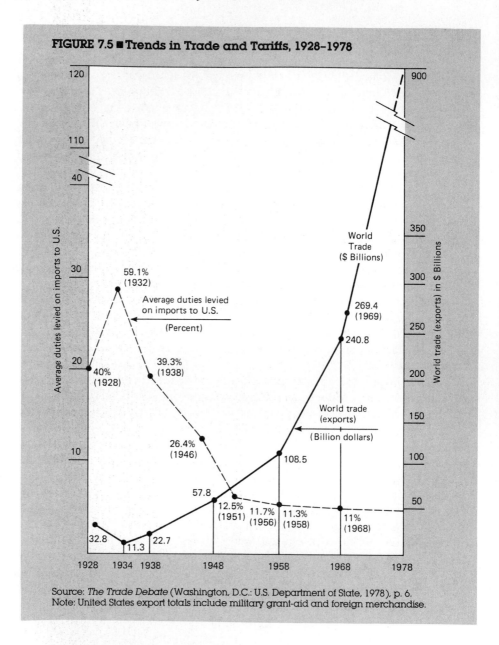

FIGURE 7.5 ■ Trends in Trade and Tariffs, 1928–1978

Source: *The Trade Debate* (Washington, D.C.: U.S. Department of State, 1978), p. 6.
Note: United States export totals include military grant-aid and foreign merchandise.

a protectionist tariff wall designed to maintain politically acceptable but artificially high prices for farm products produced within the EEC. The effect
was to curtail American agricultural exports to the EEC, which by the 1960s
had become a principal trading partner of the United States.

The Kennedy Round was based on the Trade Expansion Act of 1962, passed by the United States Congress in an effort to improve the United States' competitive trade position in relation to that of the European Economic Community. The president's authority to negotiate trade matters under the Trade Expansion Act expired with the end of the Kennedy Round. Thereafter, Presidents Johnson and Nixon fought a rearguard action against the rising protectionist forces that bombarded Congress with trade-restriction demands.

The challenge of an economically revitalized and politically united Europe was among the factors that led to the waning of American support for a multilateral free-trade regime. Other factors that began to erode the foundations of the liberalized trading system included the extension by the European Community of preferential trade treatment to nations in Africa, the Mediterranean, and the Caribbean; the expansion of the Common Market from six members to nine in 1973; the extension of associate status to others; and the feeling by many Western nations that Japan was continuing to pursue highly protectionist trade policies, in contrast with the liberalized trading scheme that the others were seeking to create (Spero, 1985). Generally, the forces undermining the postwar trade regime were much the same as those that undermined the international monetary system, the collapse of which itself contributed to the lack of progress on trade matters. The shifting constellation of political forces within the Western world and between it and the communist world was also important. The consequence was a loss of American leadership in the system.

In much the same way that the monetary disorder of the 1970s reflected the inability of the Bretton Woods system to master the international economic forces that had been unleashed, the erosion of the liberal trade regime of the 1950s and 1960s reflected the inability of GATT and the most-favored-nation principle to keep pace with the new developments. As described by a former counsel to the United States special trade representative:

GATT was formed to promote free-market competition among a maximum number of countries under a relatively few simple rules: nondiscrimination (the United States must treat Japanese and European products equally, for example); no barriers to imports other than declining tariffs; and no protection of faltering industries from import competition except through temporary measures taken publicly in emergency cases. These were rules for a simpler era, when trade was a fraction of its present volume, tariffs were the main trade barrier, a few Western countries dominated international trade and postwar optimism for international free enterprise was high—at least in the United States, which was the pre-eminent economic superpower. Although by the 1970s all of these circumstances had changed drastically, the GATT rules remained substantially the same and, as a result, were widely ignored. Without viable international rules, trade relations quickly revert to the law of the jungle. (Graham, 1979: 52)

Challenges to American Leadership and the Liberal Trade Regime

The political necessity of maintaining product prices above their economically justifiable levels, exemplified by the European Community's agricultural policies, reflects an important underpinning of protectionist logic: It appeals to powerful domestic political interests that perceive the costs of free trade as greater than its benefits.

The *infant industry* argument is a well-known rationale used against free trade. According to this argument, tariffs or other forms of protection are necessary to nurture young industries until they can mature and until their eventually lower-cost production enables them to compete effectively in the world marketplace.

The infant industries argument is often articulated by Third World countries, for whom the absence of protection from the more efficient Western firms prohibits the realization of their domestic industrialization goals. Among the developed countries, the argument against free trade is more commonly rationalized by the perceived need for protection from cheap foreign labor, or perhaps from more technologically sophisticated producers. Already established industries may, for example, seek safeguards in the form of government assistance or trade restrictions targeted at specific foreign producers so as to protect domestic producers.

Techniques affording protection through nontariff mechanisms are many and varied. *Import quotas*, for example, specify the quantity of a particular product that can be imported from abroad. In the late 1950s, for example, the United States established import quotas on oil, arguing that they were necessary to protect the nation's security. The economic effect was that the government, rather than the marketplace, determined how much would be imported and by whom. Sugar is another commodity that the United States has subjected to quotas in pursuit of its foreign policy objectives, particularly in the Caribbean (see Krasner, 1978). The effect of quotas is to protect domestic producers, regardless of their efficiency relative to foreign producers. Often this means that the consumer either pays higher prices or must settle for commodities inferior to those that could otherwise be obtained from abroad.

Export quotas also impose barriers to free trade. Export and import quotas are similar, but the two differ in that import quotas are unilateral instruments of policy, whereas export quotas are imposed pursuant to negotiated agreements between producers and consumers.[11] The United States and the European Community, in particular, have pressed other countries to accept *Orderly Market Arrangements* (OMAs) and *Voluntary Export Restrictions* (VERs) in

---

11. Import quotas differ from voluntary export restraints (VERs), discussed later, in that the former are normally applied on a global, nondiscriminatory basis, whereas the latter are negotiated bilaterally.

order to protect domestic industries threatened by foreign imports.[12] Of the roughly one hundred major known VERs in operation, fifty-five restrict exports to the European Community, and thirty-two restrict exports to the United States (Boonekamp, 1987: 3). Sectors subject to OMAs and VERs include automobiles, footwear, steel, ships, electronic products, and machine tools. In some cases there are even networks of agreed-upon export restrictions. The classic example is in textiles and clothes, which has a long history.

> In the 1950s, when domestic interests began putting pressure on the U.S. Government for protection against cheap cotton-textile imports from the Far East, Washington negotiated several informal VERs with Japan and, later, Hong Kong. Ostensibly "temporary," they soon were imitated by major European importers; and in 1961 all were formally consolidated into the first of a series of multilateral cotton-textile agreements later expanded to include woolens and synthetic fibers as well. Now called the Multifiber Arrangement [which was renegotiated in 1986], and involving some forty countries in all, the scheme has evolved into an elaborate international market-sharing agreement that allows virtually no room at all for significant structural adjustment. Importing countries troubled by excess domestic capacity and deteriorating demand are determined not to allow lower-cost Third World exporters to threaten employment at home. Consequently, a disproportionate fraction of their workers remain tied to a stagnant industry. (Cohen, 1983: 10)

It has been estimated that some 10 percent of total world trade is subject to the distorting effects of OMAs and VERs (Boonekamp, 1987: 3). Moreover, their prevalence has grown substantially in the 1980s, particularly as they apply to the exports of Japan and the Newly Industrialized Countries of Far East Asia. Although these restrictions on exports are arguably not illegal under GATT's rules, which are concerned with governmental actions affecting trade, they certainly are in contravention of its broad goal of trade liberalization.

Import and export quotas are two examples of a class of trade restrictions known as *nontariff barriers* (NTBs). NTBs have become more important forms of protection than tariffs are (in the area of industrial products, at least, tariffs are now relatively unimportant inhibitions against the free flow of goods and services across national boundaries). With the rise of the welfare state, some types of NTBs have become particularly ubiquitous. As advanced industrial societies seek to ensure the welfare of their citizens through numerous and

---

12. Voluntary export restriction (or restraint) is a generic term for all bilaterally agreed restraints on trade. It usually arises from pressure on an exporting country by an importing country and can be thought of as "voluntary" in the sense that the exporting country may prefer it to other trade barriers that the importing country might impose. An OMA is a voluntary export restriction that involves a government-to-government agreement and often specific rules of management and consultation rights and calls for monitoring trade flows (Boonekamp, 1987). Boonekamp (1987) discusses the nature of VERs, why they were introduced, and their economic effects.

often complex government regulations regarding health and safety, foreign-produced goods frequently cannot compete. Examples are the emission-control and safety standards imposed on the auto industry by the United States government in order to reduce air pollution and the risk of serious injury. When initiated, these standards, although meeting domestic needs, put burdens on certain foreign auto producers.

Health and safety standards have come to be regarded as necessary and legitimate forms of government regulation. They have no necessary bearing on international trade, but if they are imposed to limit external competition—and only secondarily, if at all, to safeguard domestic welfare—then they become legitimate objects of attack by free-trade advocates. The problem lies in the difficulty of distinguishing legitimate NTBs from regulations designed primarily to limit foreign competition. The French and British, for example, suspect that American noise regulations imposed to restrict the supersonic Concorde passenger plane were really an attempt to limit competition in the aircraft industry after the United States' decision not to produce the Boeing SST.

The range and variety of NTBs are extensive. Just as health and safety regulations may be legitimately designed to protect a nation's citizens, the measures often taken to limit foreign imports in contravention of what liberal trade theory would otherwise see as mutually beneficial to all—a liberal multilateral trade regime—are often deemed justified (see Box 7.4 for an amusing illustration). Even though the goods produced by one country may be superior in quality and cheaper in price than are those produced in another country, the latter may still use import quotas, export quotas, and other nontariff barriers to keep out the superior, less expensive, foreign-produced goods. It will do this if it perceives the foreign goods' superior performance as resulting not from purely market forces but from government subsidies granted to the export industries in the producing country. Such subsidies reflect a *neomercantilist* posture, a term that specifically refers to "a trade policy whereby a state seeks to maintain a balance-of-trade surplus and to promote domestic production and employment by reducing imports, stimulating home production, and promoting exports" (Blake and Walters, 1987). Generally, neomercantilism refers to state intervention in economic affairs in order to enhance the state's economic fortunes.[13] Japan is frequently described as a neomercantilist power, having achieved tremendous export growth in the postwar years as a consequence of an intimate government–business alliance. Some argue it is appropriate for countermercantilist policies to be adopted against such a country. The protectionist urge is not the exclusive preserve of any one state, however, but is a reminder of the political foundations of policies that might otherwise seem purely economic in origin.

The case for protection is often compelling. Free trade may promise bene-

---

13. See Chapter 4 for a discussion of classical mercantilism.

BOX 7.4 ■ The "Poitiers Effect"

The "new protectionism" usually refers to the use of nontariff barriers such as VERs and orderly marketing arrangements. But it only takes a little ingenuity to introduce an administrative regulation which can be an effective barrier to trade.

In October 1982, citing a "Japanese invasion" in consumer electronics, the French government decreed that all imports of videocassette recorders (VCRs) would have to pass through Poitiers. Although not the most obvious point of entry, Poitiers could hardly be better suited to the purpose. It is a town hundreds of miles inland from France's northern ports where the VCRs are landed. It has a tiny customs crew that is obviously inadequate to the task of clearing hundreds of thousands of VCR imports. As the town where the French repelled an earlier invader, the Moors, Poitiers seemed an apt choice.

Moreover, a particularly long and tedious set of customs regulations were strictly enforced at Poitiers. All the accompanying documents were thoroughly examined and each container opened. A large number of VCRs were taken out of their boxes by the customs inspectors, who carefully checked their serial numbers and made sure that the instructions were written in French. Finally, a number of VCRs were dismantled to make sure that they were actually built in their reported country of origin. The regional customs director responsible for Poitiers said of the new regulations: "Before the new policy, it took a morning to clear a lorry-load of video recorders. Now it takes two to three months. We are still clearing consignments that arrived here [three months ago] when the policy went into effect. . . ."

As planned, the "Poitiers effect" severely limited VCR imports into France. Before the use of Poitiers, more than 64,000 VCRs, mostly from Japan, entered France each month for the first ten months of 1981. Afterward, less than 10,000 VCRs cleared the customs point at Poitiers each month, while the rest of the supply waited in bonded warehouses throughout the town. Exporters did not passively concede to the French barriers. Denmark, the Federal Republic of Germany, and the Netherlands, which also export VCRs to France, filed a complaint with the EC Executive Committee in Brussels, which in turn brought charges against France at the European Court of Justice for breach of EC free trade rules. Japan brought its complaint to the GATT and then suspended or curbed VCR shipments to France.

It is not clear what the French hoped to gain from the use of the Poitiers weapon. The French electronics firm Thomas-Brandt did not make its own VCRs, but sold Japanese VCRs under its own label. It experienced a shortage of these when the government required all the imports to go through Poitiers. Shortly after the establishment of Poitiers, the EC Commission negotiated a VER limiting Japan's exports to the entire European Community. This was followed by an agreement between Thomas-Brandt and Japan's JVC to manufacture component parts in France and later the lifting of the Poitiers restrictions. It is likely that several complex issues concerning intragovernment and government-industry relations played a role in the Poitiers scheme. Yet, although the motives remain somewhat obscure, the protective effect of it is clear.

Source: *World Development Report 1987*. Copyright 1987 by The International Bank for Reconstruction and Development/The World Bank. Reprinted by permission of Oxford University Press, Inc., p. 141.

fits to all, but the costs are often substantial to particular domestic groups confronting adverse economic circumstances as a result of free trade. To workers standing in an unemployment line because the factory in which they worked was forced to close because it could no longer compete with foreign producers, the fact that other consumers are able to buy a cheaper product matters little. Business and labor alike are therefore prone to argue for protection. And because they are politically powerful, they frequently get it. Foreign economic policy, in these circumstances, is motivated primarily by domestic political considerations.

Consider, for example, the position of the United States, the world's preeminent trading nation, in the steel and automobile industries. In 1955 the United States produced 39 percent of the world's steel, but by 1981 that proportion had slipped to 15 percent. In the same year, employment declined 25 percent compared with its level twenty years earlier. In the case of autos, the American proportion of world production declined from 68 percent in 1955 to only 21 percent in 1981. Between 1978 and 1981 alone, 275,000 jobs were lost in the American auto industry (Walters, 1983: 27). It is perhaps circumstances such as these that led Emil Van Lennep, secretary general of the OECD, to assert in 1982 that "the danger of a chain reaction of beggar-thy-neighbor policies with potentially disastrous consequences is now greater than at any time since World War II."

The Multilateral Trade Negotiations conducted in Geneva between 1975 and 1979 were initiated against the background of a growing incidence of neomercantilist challenges to the liberal trading system that the United States and others had espoused and promoted for decades. Lowering tariffs on industrial commodities remained a concern in the Tokyo Round of negotiations, but there was more emphasis on reducing barriers to the free flow of agricultural products. The question of how to deal with nontariff barriers also assumed new importance. Thus the negotiations not only took place in an atmosphere of increased international interdependence but also were significantly colored by it.

The Tokyo Round produced new international rules to deal with subsidies and countervailing duties, dumping, government purchasing, product stands, custom valuation and licensing, agriculture, aircraft, and developing nations.[14] Its relation to and impact on the precepts underlying GATT and the liberal

---

14. Graham (1979) provides a useful discussion of the new rules in each of these areas. He concludes that "the Tokyo Round agreements effectively replace the GATT rules. While remaining on the books, the old rules will be largely ignored when they conflict with new agreements. The GATT rules, for example, require that all imports from all sources be treated equally. The Tokyo Round agreements, by contrast, condone discrimination by stipulating that only signatory countries are to enjoy the benefits" (Graham, 1979). As we shall see in Chapter 8, the departure from GATT's rules regarding nondiscrimination among trading partners is an issue of particular importance to Third World countries.

trade regime created in the aftermath of World War II are more difficult to describe. As Stephen D. Krasner explains:

> The outcome of the Tokyo Round does not accord with any general principle. In some areas the agreements closely conform with liberal ideals of increasing trade, enhancing the autonomy of the market, and upholding nondiscrimination. In other areas the agreements fail to expand trade, legitimate state intervention, and endorse discriminatory practices. The underlying rationale for this outcome was not general principle but particularistic interests. In areas where there are not significant import-competing industries or where there are crosscutting cleavages within sectors, steps were taken which move the international trading system closer to the liberal ideal. In areas where import-competing industries dominate national political decisions, the MTN agreements endorse existing discriminatory and restrictive practices. (1979: 524–525)

Although the United States no longer appears willing to exercise the kind of leadership in international trade matters or to absorb the costs of leadership that it once did, it was a primary force prodding members of GATT to try again to negotiate multilateral solutions to the many problems confronting international commerce in a rapidly changing, complex, interdependent global political economy. As in the past, the new effort, the Uruguay Round, seeks to cope with agricultural trade. The marked change in the global food regime during the past decade (explored in more detail in Chapter 9) requires attention to the issue even while making the resolution of its diverse, contentious elements more difficult.

At the core of differences on the issue of agricultural trade is the enormous subsidies that the governments of the leading producer countries in the First World pay farmers to keep them competitive in the international marketplace, where prices are often much lower than in Europe or North America. In 1986, for example, the European Community spent over $20 billion dollars, or more than two-thirds of its budget, on agricultural subsidies. The United States, for its part, spent about $30 billion in farm support programs, an amount exceeding the net income of U.S. farms (Wallis, 1986: 2).

The perceived need for such subsidies reflects fundamental structural changes in the global system of food production which, as with textiles, are difficult to manage because of the potentially adverse domestic political consequences in those countries of Western Europe and North America for which the global market is an outlet for surplus production. The difficulty arises from the emergence of new competitors among Third World producers and from the shrinkage of traditional markets as technological innovations permit expanded agricultural production in countries previously experiencing food deficits.

A second major area for negotiation in the Uruguay Round is trade in services (such as insurance and data processing) and intellectual property rights (such as books and computer software). World trade in services is estimated to exceed $370 billion annually (*Gist*, May 1987), and the United States ranks as one of its largest exporters. But few rules exist to govern it. As the comparative advantage in the production of manufactured goods, such as consumer electronics and automobiles, moves toward advanced developing nations like the Newly Industrialized Countries, the importance of trade in services and intellectual property, in which the now developed countries already enjoy comparative advantages, will become even more important to them. The task, as seen by the advanced industrial societies like the United States, is to develop rules that protect their present or potential advantages so as to enable them to yield the production of manufactures to developing countries. From the point of view of the developing countries, on the other hand, severe impediments to the enhancement of their advantages in manufactured products already exist in the form of nontariff and other barriers to access to markets in the First World. That perception will doubtlessly harden their bargaining position on issues salient to the industrialized societies of the North.

Because of the increasingly complex issues that the transformation of the global political economy portends, the Uruguay Round of negotiations promises to be long and difficult, with no assurance that contentious issues will be resolved to anyone's satisfaction. The relative decline of the United States' economic power and leadership capacity adds uncertainty to an already uncertain environment. Against this background, the prospects for the world economy—if the lessons of the 1930s remain relevant to the 1990s—will depend in part on the ability of the countries of the world to construct a trade regime to serve the world's collective interest in preserving a system of free trade.

THE FUTURE: FROM "FREE TRADE" TO "FAIR TRADE"

GATT has estimated that close to half of all world trade is now subject to some form of quantitative restraint (Lighthizer, 1983). Clearly, the promise and practice of free trade are now widely divergent. Part of the reason is that states differ in their assessment of the role that government should play in regulating economic behavior—where, in other words, they fall along the continuum between an open and a closed economic system and what they view as appropriate government intervention in market-oriented economies. The United States, for its part, is unlikely to assume the costs of leadership in an environment in which others are perceived to be playing by a different set of rules. Lee Iacocca, the president of the Chrysler Corporation, reflected popular sentiment in 1983 by charging that "because the U.S. government still clings to free trade rules, America lacks a trade policy responsive to new realities of international competition. For American businessmen and workers—sent out into the global marketplace to compete without government help—the playing field is not level; it's tilted against them."

Iacocca stressed not the issue of free trade, but *fair* trade. Ironically, the Chrysler Corporation was able to survive in the face of stiff foreign competition only with billions of dollars in government-backed loans, a glaring example of the extent to which even in the United States the government has intervened in economic life.[15] There is nevertheless a feeling in the United States that American business enterprises are at a competitive disadvantage when dealing with others. As the focus of American trade policy shifts from free trade to fair trade, explains Robert Walters (1983), it is apparent that there is "an insistence that other states stand aside to permit market forces to operate in as non-discriminatory a fashion between domestic and foreign interests as Americans *perceive* these forces to operate in the U.S." But other First World countries do not share these perceptions. Elsewhere in the industrialized world and in Third World countries,

> the state has traditionally assumed important entrepreneurial and developmental roles in economic affairs—most unlike the laissez-faire and arms' length regulatory concepts of the state's role in America. If greater international agreement on fair trade principles depends upon securing acceptance abroad of the role of the state as advocated in mainstream American economic thought, this approach to contain protectionism in the 1980s must certainly fail. (Walters, 1983: 31)

GATT may also prove ineffectual as a mechanism for dealing with the trade issues of the 1980s. In a sense GATT has run its course; it "is unable to contribute much more to world trade growth merely by performing the tasks it has done so well in the past" (Blake and Walters, 1987), for tariff barriers no longer pose a significant inhibition to international trade.

Trade issues promise to occupy a pivotal place on the global agenda, as well as on national agendas, as we move toward the 1990s. International trade has become an important domestic political issue, even at the level of local politics, and an interdependent world ensures that the choices made to deal with those issues in one national setting will surely affect others in another setting. In this sense, interdependence is, paradoxically, a force promoting economic nationalism. And economic nationalism in the long run is destined to undermine the overall prospects for the world economy's growth and to encourage states to focus on short-term issues rather than to confront long-term problems (see Stewart, 1984). Thus the rules, norms, and international institutions that comprise the existing trade regime are being tested by the very First World nations whose interests they have most clearly served. "The industrial countries," Henry A. Kissinger (1982) has noted, "are still groping to reconcile the imperatives of their domestic policies with the realities of interdependence."

---

15. Vernon (1982) points out that the United States continues to preach free trade even though it has knowingly violated the rule of nondiscrimination because "it has had trouble envisaging a coherent world trading system without such a rule."

SUGGESTED READINGS

Avery, William P., and David P. Rapkin, eds. *America in a Changing World Political Economy*. New York: Longman, 1982.

Blake, David H., and Robert S. Walters. *The Politics of Global Economic Relations*, 3rd ed. Englewood Cliffs, N.J.: Prentice-Hall, 1987.

Block, Fred L. *The Origins of International Economic Disorder*. Berkeley and Los Angeles: University of California Press, 1977.

Cline, William R., ed. *Trade Policy in the 1980s*. Washington, D.C.: Institute for International Economics, 1983.

Gilpin, Robert. *The Political Economy of International Relations*. Princeton, N.J.: Princeton University Press, 1987.

Gray, H. Peter. *Free Trade or Protection?* New York: St. Martin's Press, 1985.

Hormats, Robert D. *Reforming the International Monetary System: From Roosevelt to Reagan*. New York: Foreign Policy Association, 1987.

Marris, Stephen. *Deficits and the Dollar: The World Economy at Risk*, 2nd ed. Washington, D.C.: Institute for International Economics, 1987.

Olson, Mancur. *The Rise and Decline of Nations: Economic Growth, Stagflation, and Social Rigidities*. New Haven, Conn.: Yale University Press, 1982.

Spero, Joan Edelman. *The Politics of International Economic Relations*, 3rd ed. New York: St. Martin's Press, 1985.

EIGHT

The Transformation of the International Political Economy: Second and Third World Perspectives

The years immediately ahead will reveal whether the will exists to meet head-on the problems faced by a quarter of the human race. The task is to help raise the productivity of hundreds of millions of people who, by their own efforts alone, are unable to break out of the grip of absolute poverty. If we fail, the world faces a perilous era.

ROBERT S. McNAMARA, 1979

We do not want to undermine the interests of Americans in the world nor to disrupt the existing world economic ties. Mutual understanding should develop and deepen normally. It requires, therefore, the development of trade. This would be normal, too.

MIKHAIL GORBACHEV, 1987

The international monetary and multilateral trading systems that evolved during the postwar decades were built primarily under the aegis of the Western industrialized nations whose interests they served. The Soviet Union and its Eastern European allies chose to create an economic order with only minimal linkages with the First World. Developing nations on the periphery of the First World were also outside the privileged circle; yet the remaining vestiges of colonial economic linkages entangled the Third World in Western systems over which they had little control. Many Third World nations thus viewed the international economic structure as a source for the perpetuation of their underdog status. From their perspective, the end of colonialism merely ushered in a period of more subtle and devious exploitation.

The most strident effort by developing nations to alter their position in the global political economy resulted during the 1970s in their call for a New International Economic Order (NIEO). The debate that ensued over such a new order has been an issue largely between the First and the Third Worlds. The communist countries have formed political alliances with one side or the other from time to time and on a variety of issues, as their political advantage

221

dictated. But in part because of their own lack of economic ties with the South (as well as the West) and in part because they believe that they are not responsible for the consequences of colonialism suffered by the Third World, the Second World has not been an active participant in some of the most intense debates between the North and the South about the structure and operation of the global political economy.

Over time the Second World has gradually become more closely linked to the First World economically. The socialist world's planned or command economies have experienced chronic problems, which the Soviet Union and its allies have sought to alleviate through greater contacts with the West. But the West has not always been uniformly receptive to these overtures, and differing views of the political interests of the East and West have affected their economic interactions. Moreover, the expansion of East–West commercial interactions has been constrained by the difficulties that the West's market economies have had in managing their relations with the East's command economies. The Soviet Union has expressed interest in joining the General Agreement on Tariffs and Trade, for example, but it seems unlikely the United States will agree to accession to the liberal international trade regime by such a large planned economy until issues important to the United States have been addressed in the Uruguay Round of trade negotiations.[1] Against this background, expanding commercial ties between East and West remains a comparatively less important issue in the global political economy than the dispute between North and South, which continues to command considerable attention.

THE NORTH–SOUTH DIALOGUE: AN OVERVIEW

The historical roots of the developing nations' demands for a new order can be traced to the 1964 United Nations Conference on Trade and Development (UNCTAD), at which a number of nations banded together to form the Group of 77 as a coalition of the world's poor to press for concessions from the rich. The G-77, as the group is often called in diplomatic circles, effectively joined the nonaligned movement during the 1973 Algiers summit of nonaligned nations when issues relating to economic as well as political "liberation" came to the fore. Algeria, then the spokesperson for the nonaligned countries, led the call for what became in 1974 the Sixth Special Session of the United Nations General Assembly. Using their superior numbers, the Group of 77 secured passage at that time of the Declaration on the Establishment of a New International Economic Order.

---

1. The international monetary order remains a preserve of the First World, although its ability to operate effectively has certainly been shaped by demands and expectations emanating from outside this charmed circle.

It is significant that both the special United Nations session and the declaration on the NIEO occurred during the worldwide food and energy crises of the 1970s, for not until the OPEC cartel successfully raised petroleum prices were the demands of the Third World nations of the South given serious consideration by the Western industrialized nations of the North. OPEC's success also augmented the stridency of the developing nations' demands, for whom the phrase "New International Economic Order" became a rallying cry for their drive for a basic restructuring of the existing global political economy.[2]

The Third World's demands challenged the Liberal International Economic Order (LIEO) and the processes that sustained it, which had been created during the 1950s and 1960s under the aegis of the United States, the hegemonic power of the postwar years. Inspired by the belief that "commodity power" endowed the Third World with the political strength necessary to challenge the advanced industrial nations of the North, the developing nations felt that their superior numbers could yield influence in the United Nations, UNCTAD, the IMF, the World Bank, the Third United Nations Law of the Sea Conference, and various other global and regional forums in which a North–South dialogue was sought. In these institutions the Third World called for more rapid economic development, increased transfers of resources from industrialized to developing nations, and a more favorable distribution of global economic benefits. Other issues addressed included aid, trade, foreign investment, foreign ownership of property, multinational corporations, debt relief, commodity price stabilization, compensatory financing mechanisms to stabilize export earnings, and price indexation designed to tie the prices that developing nations received for their exports to the prices that they paid for their imports.

Collectively, the demands for a New International Economic Order sought a redistribution of income and wealth from rich nations to poor. In addition to that motivation, at a more fundamental level what was sought was a transfer of political influence to Third World nations through a substantial alteration of the rules and institutional structures governing the transnational flow of goods, services, capital, and technology. Simply put, the Third World sought *regime change*—a revision of the rules, norms, and procedures of the Liberal International Economic Order to serve the interests of the Third World rather than the industrialized North (Krasner, 1985).

The desire for regime change is driven by the Third World's belief that the global political economy is structured so as to perpetuate developing nations'

---

2. The developing nations did not challenge the state system itself, only the way in which it currently functions. Thus, the choice of the word *international* rather than *global* or *world* is significant. "The growing assertiveness of the developing countries cannot be found to herald the beginning of a new world," declared Robert W. Tucker (1980). "It is not the state system per se that is condemned, but the manner in which the system operated in the past and presumably continues to operate even today. It is primarily through the state that the historically oppressed and disadvantaged nations seek to mount a successful challenge to what governing elites of developing countries view as persisting unjust inequalities."

subordinate position. Many Third World nations contend that existing international economic institutions, such as the IMF and GATT and the political processes they govern, are "deeply biased against developing countries in their global distribution of income and influence" (Hansen, 1980). The perception is buttressed by a legacy of colonial exploitation and the continued existence of levels of poverty and deprivation unknown in the North. "Equity" is therefore a driving force behind Third World demands for regime change. At a more specific level, many Third World leaders find particularly irksome four items in their economic relationships with the North. W. Arthur Lewis, the Nobel Prize–winning economist, summarizes them as follows:

> First, the division of the world into exporters of primary products and exporters of manufactures.
> Second, the adverse factoral terms of trade for the products of the developing countries.
> Third, the dependence of the developing countries on the developed for finance.
> Fourth, the dependence of the developing countries on the developed for their engine of growth. (Lewis, 1978: 3)

The North rejects the view that the economic woes of the developing nations are a product of the current international order; instead, it locates the causes (and potential cures) of those problems in the domestic systems of Third World countries themselves. Accordingly, proposals to radically alter existing international economic institutions as well as the more modest elements of the Third World program have met with resentment and resistance. Intransigence was especially apparent during the 1980s in the United States, as the Reagan administration approached the Third World primarily from the vantage point of its role in the East–West conflict, with little interest shown in those aspects of Southern interests and objectives related to the transformation of the Liberal International Economic Order.

Because UNCTAD has long served as a spokesperson of the world's poor, it has been a central stage on which the North–South conflict has been played. Ever since the G-77 was first formed, the periodic meetings of UNCTAD have focused attention on Third World problems and priorities. Box 8.1 summarizes the principal issues addressed during the seven UNCTAD meetings held since 1964.

This brief summary illustrates the extent to which the demands and concerns of the Third World nations have changed over time. For instance, UNCTAD VI and VII exhibited greater concern with immediate issues than with the long-term goals of structural reform and regime change that had dominated the agenda in earlier meetings. The new mood was summarized by Farouk Sobhan of Bangladesh, chairman of the Group of 77, in 1983: "We cannot change institutions overnight. We have to do this gradually with a sense of purpose and pragmatism."

What accounts for the Third World's apparent retreat from its earlier, militant posture toward regime change?

First, the economic climate faced by most Third World nations changed sharply. North and South alike experienced a general and prolonged economic slump in the early 1980s, but for many Third World nations the consequences were especially damaging. Economic growth rates deteriorated in many of them, and in some, particularly in Africa, they actually reflected "negative growth." The prices of many of the commodities exported by Third World nations fell sharply compared with the prices they had to pay for their imports. Faced with reduced export earnings and higher interest rates, the debt burdens of many Third World nations assumed ominous proportions. Thus acute economic problems at home caused many Third World leaders to focus pragmatically on immediate policy problems rather than ideologically on the longer-term drive for structural reform that had been launched a decade or more earlier. A corollary view that seemed to pervade both UNCTAD VI (1983) and UNCTAD VII (1987) was a growing recognition that the interdependence of North and South required cooperation rather than confrontation if the economic health of both, on which each depended, was to be restored and maintained.

Second, the erosion of the Third World's bargaining leverage contributed to the softening of its militancy. OPEC's successful cartelization of the oil market in 1973–1974 served as a rallying point for the entire Group of 77 and gave rise to the belief that "commodity power" could be used to break the North's resistance. But the denouement of the OPEC decade in the face of a worldwide oil glut in the 1980s removed any reason the North might have had to make major concessions to Southern demands. Thus the Third World may have come to the realization that among all the obstacles to the establishment of the NIEO, "the principal factor which impedes progress is the lack of will on the part [of the] powerful, and the lack of power on the part of the willing" (Laszlo et al., 1980).

As the unifying force of commodity power recedes, perhaps indefinitely, differences among the Group of 77 can be expected to surface. Differences in the past colonial experience of Third World members move them in different directions, and differences in economic circumstances today become more divisive. The differences between the more advanced of the developing nations, on the one hand, of which the Newly Industrialized Countries (NICs) stand out, and the less well-off, especially the least developed of the less-developed countries (LLDCs), on the other, become especially clear.

The New International Economic Order may come to be seen in the decades ahead as little more than the rhetoric of debate in the period from roughly 1973 to 1981, with new phrases yet to be found to inform the future of North–South politico-economic relations. But until the problems of the poor and their related perceptions are addressed, the developing nations can be expected to continue to press for an overhaul of the system they had little or no voice in creating. The reasons underlying these problems and perceptions

UNCTAD I, Geneva 1964

■ The creation of a forum to attract attention to issues supporting the developing countries, not covered by existing institutions.

■ The formalization of the Group of 77 and beginning of discussion on a few issues such as terms of trade, resource gap, and Generalized System of Preferences (GSP).

UNCTAD II, New Delhi 1968

■ Between 1964 and 1968 the UNCTAD secretariat focused more seriously but still sporadically on GSP, the needs of the developing countries for assistance, terms of trade, technology transfer, and selected development policies.

■ The Conference led the OECD to initiate work on a scheme of preferences.

■ Dr. Raúl Prebisch retired in 1969 as the Secretary-General of the UNCTAD.

UNCTAD III, Santiago 1972

■ Unlike the Geneva and New Delhi meetings, where these issues were considered separately, UNCTAD III saw discussion on interrelationships between trade, money, finance, and development at a technical level.

■ Initiation of an effort by Mr. Robert McNamara, President of the World Bank, to mobilize global support for the poor, suggesting ways to integrate the bottom 40 percent of the population in the development process.

UNCTAD IV, Nairobi 1976

■ Stocktaking of progress in various forums (CIEC, GATT) on decisions taken at the Sixth and Seventh Special Sessions of the UN General Assembly in 1974 and 1975, respectively, particularly in the light of the oil price increase, monetary instability, recession, inflation, increased balance of payments gap of the non-oil developing countries, decline in commodity prices, and the uncertainty that the minimum development needs in many developing countries would be met.

■ Main emphasis on commodities (Integrated Programme for Commodities—Common Fund) and to a lesser degree on external debt.

■ Resolution on a Common Fund symbolized G-77 unity.

(continued)

---

derive, of course, from the enormous inequities between the North and the South, discussed in Chapter 5. Until these and the causes that animate them are removed, the conflict between the rich nations of the North and the poor of the South will persist.

The pages that follow address the issues relating to trade, aid, and debt that fuel the Third World drive for structural reform and on which its future prospects in an interdependent global political economy depend. In Chapter 9

BOX 8.1 ■ Continued

UNCTAD V, Manila 1979

■ Emphasis on trade and financial flows aspects of the relationships between developed and developing countries.
■ Emphasis on growing interdependence between different parts of the world economy.
■ Efforts to bring socialist countries into the dialogue on economic issues.
■ Emphasis on trade liberalization and concern about expanding protectionism.

UNCTAD VI, Belgrade 1983

■ Movement by G-77 toward immediate issues relating to the global economy and Third World development and away from demands for structural reform.
■ Emphasis on a common analysis of the world economic situation and an agreed strategy for economic recovery and development.
■ Continued concern for the issue of trade protectionism.
■ Recognition of the important role of the World Bank and International Monetary Fund as multilateral development institutions.

UNCTAD VII, Geneva 1987

■ Broad agreement on the need for macroeconomic policy coordination among major industrial countries.
■ Acceptance of the need for growth-oriented adjustment among developing countries, including the need for adequate external support.
■ Focus on four substantive issues: resources for development, including the Third World debt problem; commodity prices; the role of trade in economic development; and the problem of the Least Developed of the Less Developed Countries (LLDCs).

Sources: Summary description of UNCTAD I through UNCTAD V from Mahmud A. Burney, "A Recognition of Interdependence: UNCTAD V," *Finance and Development* 16 (September 1979): 18; summary description of UNCTAD VI and UNCTAD VII adapted from Shahid Javed Burki, "UNCTAD VI: For Better or for Worse?" *Finance and Development* 20 (December 1983): 18–19; and Carlston B. Boucher and Wolfgang E. Siebeck, "UNCTAD VII: New Spirit in North–South Relations?" *Finance and Development* 24 (December 1987): 14–16.

we shall examine the role that population growth plays in affecting many Third World goals domestically, and in Chapter 10 we shall explore the sources of OPEC's resource power and evaluate the utility of commodity power as a policy instrument in the future. The nature of global inequalities described in Chapter 5 and the role that multinational corporations (treated in Chapter 6) play in perpetuating or alleviating conditions related to the issues that Third World nations find most irksome bear on the discussion throughout.

LINKAGES BETWEEN NORTH AND SOUTH: TRADE AND AID

Trade-related issues are at the core of many of the Third World's demands. The structure of the trade relationships between many developed and developing nations was formed during the age of imperialism, when colonies existed for the presumed benefit of their colonizers.[3] Frequently this meant that the colonies were sources of primary products, such as agricultural commodities and mineral resources, and markets for the 'finished manufactured goods produced in the metropole. This pattern persists today as a general description of the structure of trade ties between developed and developing nations. As shown in Table 8.1, in 1985 the developing countries as a whole relied on primary products (including fuels) for two-thirds of their export earnings (the money necessary to buy goods from abroad), and more than 60 percent of their imports were in the form of manufactures. The developed countries in the First World, in contrast, relied on primary products for less than a quarter of their earnings, with manufactured products accounting for over 75 percent.

Commodity Exports and the Terms of Trade

Over the past two decades, the developing nations as a whole have substantially increased the proportion of manufactures in their trade, an important development to which we shall return later. It nevertheless remains true that primary products continue to dominate the exports of many developing nations, particularly the poorest of them. And in many cases it is a single export commodity that prevails. Coffee, for example, accounts for nearly 90 percent of Burundi's exports and two-thirds of Colombia's. It is alumina and bauxite in Jamaica (52 percent), fish and iron ore in Mauritania (59 and 41 percent, respectively), and copper in Zambia (86 percent). These examples are included in Figure 8.1, which graphs the often excessive dependence of Third World nations on a limited number of primary products for foreign exchange earnings.

The developing nations' dependence on a narrow range of primary product exports places the argument over the *terms of trade* at the center of the debate between North and South. This phrase refers to the ratio of export prices to import prices. The developing nations believe that the prices they receive for their exports vary erratically in the short run and fall in the long run, whereas the prices of the manufactured goods that they import increase steadily.

The developing nations' terms of trade are alleged to have deteriorated because of their position in the international economic structure (Pirages, 1978). The South remains critically dependent on the North not only for

---

3. See Boulding and Mukerjee (1972) for evidence that the acquisition of colonial empires did not benefit the imperialist powers economically. Recognition of this was a factor in the imperial powers' willingness to liquidate their empires (sometimes readily and sometimes reluctantly).

TABLE 8.1 ■ Composition of World Exports and Imports, by Groups of Countries, 1985 (percentages)

Products	Developed Market Economies (First World)	Developing Market Economies (Third World)	Centrally Planned Economies (Second World)	World
Exports				
Primary Products	22.3	65.6	35.0	34.3
Food, beverages, and tobacco	8.7	12.7	.1	9.4
Crude materials (excluding fuels); oils and fats	5.7	7.7	6.2	6.2
Mineral fuels and related materials	8.0	45.2	28.1	18.6
Manufactured Products	75.4	33.2	50.4	63.0
Chemicals	10.0	2.5	6.4	7.9
Machinery and Transport Exports	39.1	10.7	26.1	31.1
Other Manufactured Goods	26.4	20.1	17.9	24.0
Miscellaneous	2.2	1.1	14.6	2.6
Total	100.0	100.0	100.0	100.0
Imports[a]				
Primary Products	34.2	34.9	32.6	34.3
Food, beverages, and tobacco	8.9	10.2	11.6	9.4
Crude materials (excluding fuels); oils and fats	6.2	5.9	6.3	6.2
Mineral fuels and related materials	19.1	18.7	14.3	18.6
Manufactured Products	63.9	62.3	63.6	63.0
Chemicals	7.8	8.7	7.4	7.9
Machinery and Transport Exports	30.7	31.8	34.4	31.1
Other Manufactured Goods	25.3	21.8	21.9	24.0
Miscellaneous	1.9	2.9	4.2	2.6
Total	100.0	100.0	100.0	100.0

Source: Adapted from United Nations, *Monthly Bulletin of Statistics* 41 (May 1987): Special Table C.

[a]Based on world trade data valued f.o.b. (free on board). Data do not include trade between the Federal Republic of Germany and the German Democratic Republic.

FIGURE 8.1 ■ Developing Country Dependence on Primary Products for Foreign Exchange Earnings, 1986

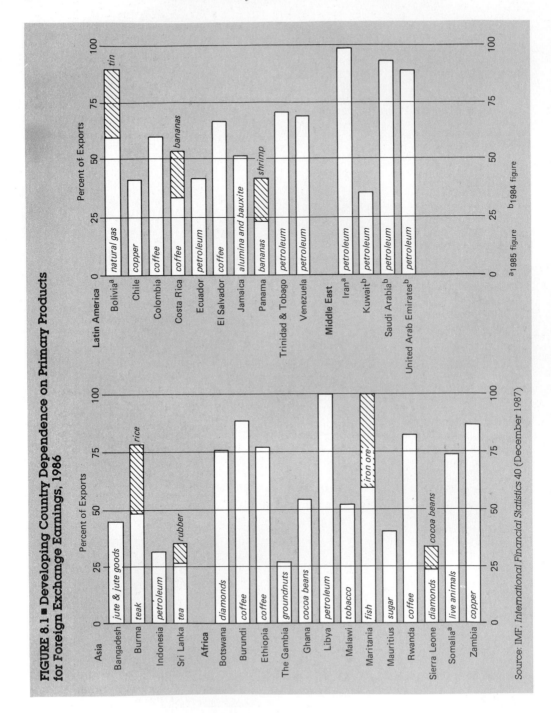

Source: IMF, *International Financial Statistics* 40 (December 1987)

^a1985 figure

^b1984 figure

manufactured goods but also for technology. Natural resources flow into Northern markets where sophisticated Northern technology can convert them into finished goods more efficiently. Through wage and fringe benefit programs, powerful labor unions and giant corporations institutionalize the comparatively high cost of the technologically sophisticated products produced in the North, the demand for which is sustained by worldwide advertising campaigns.

The developing nations are unable to compete on similar terms with the North, the argument continues. The South cannot bid up the prices for the materials produced in the developing nations, which are set by the North rather than the exporting countries of the South. Organized labor in the developing countries is also unable to effect higher prices for commodity exports, because there are alternative sources of supply, whose extraction in any event is energy rather than labor intensive—and the supply of labor relative to demand for it in most developing nations is overwhelming. In a system in which those with the most money determine prices, Third World nations find themselves unable to determine the terms of trade for their products.

There is no question that the developing nations' primary product exports are subject to sharp price fluctuations. As noted earlier, for example, non-oil commodity prices dropped sharply in the early 1980s during the recession induced by the second oil shock, when they reached a lower level in real terms (after adjusting for the rise in prices of manufactured goods imported by developing nations) than at any time since World War II (*World Development Report 1983*, 1983). Prices rebounded somewhat between 1984 and 1986, as shown in Figure 8.2, only to continue their fall thereafter. The near free-fall of oil prices between 1985 and 1986 is also shown in Figure 8.2, which charts the downward trend of the terms of trade for the developing nations during this decade.

Other evidence can be marshaled that is consistent with the developing nations' argument that they face adverse terms of trade. Whether such trends are due to a long-term structural deterioration or are the product of short-term perturbations related to changes in the business cycle remains a matter of controversy among analysts.[4] Regardless, the policies pursued by Third World leaders are influenced by such perceptions, which are related to their belief that dominance and dependence characterize the economic relationship between North and South. As Robert L. Rothstein notes (1979), "Many economists doubt that there has been a secular decline in the terms of trade for commodities, but what is believed or assumed—taken on faith—is more important here than analytical argument."

---

4. Streeten (1974) offers a useful discussion of the terms-of-trade debate. See also Blake and Walters (1987) and Singer and Ansari (1988). A critical view of the debate is given in Higgins and Higgins (1979).

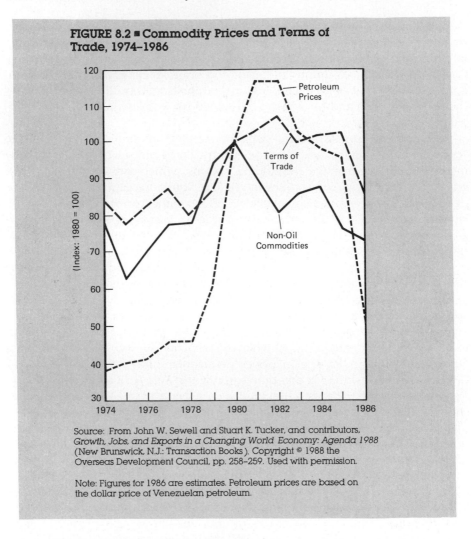

FIGURE 8.2 ■ **Commodity Prices and Terms of Trade, 1974–1986**

Source: From John W. Sewell and Stuart K. Tucker, and contributors, *Growth, Jobs, and Exports in a Changing World Economy: Agenda 1988* (New Brunswick, N.J.: Transaction Books), Copyright © 1988 the Overseas Development Council, pp. 258–259. Used with permission.

Note: Figures for 1986 are estimates. Petroleum prices are based on the dollar price of Venezuelan petroleum.

Price Stabilization

Reversing the unfavorable terms-of-trade pattern is a long-term objective of the Third World nations. A more immediate goal is reducing the fluctuations in the prices that they receive for their commodities.

Commodity trade is important to North–South relations because many developing nations derive the bulk of their export earnings from commodity exports and because most commodity exports are consumed by the First World (Rothstein, 1979). Exports to the Second World are insignificant, and domestic consumption within the producing nations is very low. "Consequently, the developing countries may suffer severely—and proportionately more than their developed trading partners—from instabilities in commodity trade, and they normally lack the resources and the flexibility to diversify or to save in the good years in order to cushion the bad" (Rothstein, 1979). Further-more, "it is the rich countries which determine the terms, because in the short run the developing countries need the products and services of the developed countries much more than the latter need the output of the former" (Singer and Ansari, 1988).

Creation of a new commodities regime was a principal objective of the Group of 77 and UNCTAD during much of the 1970s. It was the central issue during the UNCTAD IV meeting in Nairobi, Kenya, in 1976, when the G-77 secured the adoption of the proposed Integrated Programme for Com-modities. As originally formulated, the Integrated Programme called for a revolutionary approach to international decision making and management of trade in commodities (see Rothstein, 1979).

Proposals for a Common Fund designed to finance buffer stocks in a number of commodities in an effort to stabilize their prices eventually became the focus of attention.[5] The Group of 77 pushed for a $6 billion fund and a significant voice in its management.[6] The developed nations opposed both the amount, most of which they would have to finance, and the management proposals, which were heavily weighted in favor of the South.

What finally emerged was a far cry from the ambitious goals that the Group of 77 and the UNCTAD secretariat had originally set out to achieve. An agree-ment was reached in 1979 to create a $750 million arrangement consisting of a kind of bank to assist individual commodity organizations in purchasing buffer stocks of raw materials, which would be used to keep commodity prices within predetermined ranges, and an international aid organization designed to help poorer developing nations expand, diversify, and market their com-modity exports.

The ninety signatories to the Common Fund required to bring it into operation were finally gathered in 1986, but the fund remained short of the necessary financial contributions, in part because the United States had signed but not yet ratified the agreement. The socialist countries of the Second World had also until then remained aloof from the fund, but in 1987, at the UNCTAD VII meeting in Geneva, the Soviet Union with great fanfare signed the Com-mon Fund agreement.

Soviet support will likely enable the Common Fund to become operational, but the fund's ability to help restore commodity prices so critical to Third World nations remains doubtful. Its successful operation is hampered because only individual international commodity agreements involving producers and consumers may be parties to it, but agreements do not exist in all of the commodities envisaged by the fund, and concluding new ones has proved

---

5. As originally envisaged, eighteen products were to be covered by the Common Fund: bananas, bauxite, cocoa, coffee, copper, cotton, hard fibers, iron ore, jute, manganese, meat, phosphates, rubber, sugar, tea, tropical timber, tin, and vegetable oils.

6. See Rothstein (1979) and Schechter (1979) for examinations of objectives and the evolution of strategies regarding the Integrated Programme and the Common Fund in particular.

difficult. In addition, many existing commodity agreements have been relatively ineffective.

Other avenues are available for dealing with the developing nations' commodity problems. Associations of producing countries, for example, avoid the difficulties inherent in international commodity agreements, which require balancing consumer and producer interests. Compensatory financing arrangements, which seek to stabilize export earnings through financial assistance rather than through buffer-stock manipulation of prices, are another alternative. The International Monetary Fund, for example, maintains a Compensatory Financing Facility designed to assist Third World nations with balance-of-payments difficulties caused by shortfalls in their export earnings.

The European Community operates a compensatory financing scheme known as STABEX. It is part of the Lomé Convention, concluded in 1975 (and renegotiated twice since) between the European Community and sixty-six African, Caribbean, and Pacific nations (the so-called ACP nations), mostly former European colonies, which in some respects can be interpreted as the intellectual inspiration for UNCTAD's proposal for an integrated commodity program (Hart, 1978). Through the convention the EC granted the ACP nations preferential trade access to the European market without the requirement of reciprocity for the EC nations. It also increased the amount of foreign aid available to the ACP countries while giving them a voice in the management of aid projects. But the centerpiece of Lomé is STABEX, a compensatory financing arrangement designed to stabilize ACP export earnings in forty-eight agricultural products (mineral exports are covered in a separate agreement[7]). It was described shortly after its inception as "ground-breaking" and "politically genuinely significant" (Gruhn, 1976).[8]

Despite this initial optimism, the contribution of STABEX to the goal of commodity price stabilization is unclear. As the World Bank (*World Development Report 1986*, 1986) put it in commenting on both STABEX and the IMF Compensatory Financing Facility (CFF): "To be successful, compensatory schemes must have clear objectives, permit quick identification of shortfalls, and provide prompt payments without complicated conditions. Neither the CFF nor STABEX has been ideal in these respects." Furthermore, it became apparent at the time Lomé was renegotiated that the very economic problems that make compensatory financing mechanisms attractive to producing countries can breed conflict between producing and consuming countries over the coverage and operation of the scheme (Islam, 1982).

Thus, just as the Common Fund seems unlikely to have the measurable impact on commodity trade once sought by advocates of the New Interna-

---

7. The minerals scheme is known as MINEX. It was negotiated in 1979 and designed to give mineral producers the same benefits that STABEX earlier granted to producers of agricultural commodities, principally tropical products. See Shonfield (1980).

8. See also Bywater (1975) and Ravenhill (1984) for further discussions of the Lomé Convention and STABEX.

tional Economic Order, the STABEX experience suggests that alternative approaches to Third World goals regarding commodity price stabilization are also unlikely to produce quick or easy solutions to Third World problems. The reason is simple: "Supporting and stabilizing the prices of commodities and providing compensatory financing for Third World exporters both require that resources be transferred from consuming to producing countries, which invariably means from developed to developing countries. Here the major obstacle has been, and remains, Northern unwillingness to make the required transfers" (Puchala, 1983).

Trade, Not Aid: Developing Nations As Exporters of Manufactured Products

Although developing nations continue to depend heavily on primary product exports, notably fuels, during the past two decades their export composition has shifted sharply away from agricultural products. In 1965 these commodities accounted for half of the developing nations' exports, but by 1980 their share had dropped to 23 percent (*World Development Report 1983*, 1983: 10). Manufactured products, on the other hand, have grown in importance, accounting for nearly half of the non-OPEC developing countries' exports in 1985 (United Nations, *Monthly Bulletin of Statistics 41 [May 1987]: Special Table C*). Thus, "developing countries can no longer be caricatured as exporters of primary products and importers of manufactures" (*World Development Report 1983*, 1983).

The shift in the composition of Third World exports challenges empirically the rhetoric of the North–South dialogue. As a World Bank official observed, "The developing countries have persistently argued their case for changing the structure of a global economic order on the grounds that at present they are unequal partners with the industrial nations. While this concept may be politically attractive, it is increasingly inaccurate as a framework for analysis of the dynamics of current world economic development" (Burki, 1983). Thus a "new international division of labor" may be replacing the one characterized by the terms *core* (the industrial world) and *periphery* (the developing world). In this new international division of labor, the developing nations, traditionally the suppliers of primary and semiprocessed goods, provide a substantial portion of the First World nations' manufactured and processed goods, and the latter provide the developing nations with raw materials and agricultural products (Sanderson, 1984).

The growing share of manufactures in Third World exports attests to the success that some have achieved in developing their own industrial base. At one time the preference of many Third World nations was to achieve "import-substitution industrialization" so as to be able to produce domestically goods otherwise purchased overseas (such as gasoline, pesticides, or other refined petroleum products). More recently, the preference has been the development of export industries capable of competing in overseas markets so as to stimulate "export-led growth" at home. The remarkable strides achieved by the Newly Industrialized Countries that have pursued this strategy have served as a standard for others.

Because of the importance of trade to the realization of Third World economic goals, gaining access to the market economies of the industrialized world has figured prominently on the Third World's agenda. Indeed, "trade, not aid" has been a persistent Third World plea, for many developing nations believe that they have been systematically denied access to markets in developed countries through both tariff and nontariff barriers.

To overcome the obstacles that Third World nations face in their drive to gain access to First World markets, developing nations have sought preferential, as opposed to most-favored-nation, trade treatment. Preferential treatment, they believe, would enable them to build diversified export industries capable of competing on equal terms with those of the North.

In partial response to that view, the industrialized nations established a system of nonreciprocal and nondiscriminatory tariff preferences for developing nations, known as the Generalized System of Preferences (GSP) which, following codification during the Tokyo Round of multilateral trade negotiations, has enabled developed nations to grant trade preferences to developing nations without violating GATT's rules regarding most-favored-nation trade treatment. The extension of preferential treatment is a significant departure from the nondiscrimination principle that dominated the Liberal International Economic Order throughout the Bretton Woods period.

Despite this apparent Northern concession, its effects have been disputed. For example, as initially designed, the GSP of the United States covered only a limited number of products,[9] and the Tokyo Round of multilateral trade negotiations included a "graduation clause," insisted on by the United States, which would eliminate GSP preferences as Southern countries reach higher levels of development, or "graduate" from the need to compete on something other than an equal footing with industrialized nations (Spero, 1985). With the U.S. GSP set to expire in 1985, Congress wrote the "graduation principle" into law by denying future GSP benefits to countries with per-capita incomes over $8,500. It also tied the preferences to steps by the beneficiaries to open their markets to U.S. exports and to other issues of importance to the United States, such as the protection of intellectual property rights. Thus "reciprocity" came once again to be a principle emphasized in a program initially designed to be a unilateral commitment by the United States and other industrialized nations to help developing nations (Pease and Goold, 1985). And the United States in fact in early 1988 revoked the GSP privileges (effective in 1989) enjoyed by South Korea, Taiwan, Hong Kong, and Singapore and moved to impose barriers on various Brazilian products. The action against these Newly Industrialized

9. See Cohen and Meltzer (1982) for an examination of the American domestic context within which the United States' GSP program was formulated.

Countries was deemed especially significant, because it was the first time that trade preferences were denied to *countries* (none of which, incidentally, had reached the automatic cutoff of $8,500 in per-capita income) rather than to specific products.

In addition to strong objections to the "graduation clause," the developing nations felt that the Tokyo Round of multilateral trade negotiations did little to cope with the rising protectionist sentiments in the North which they perceived to have been directed against them. As shown in Table 8.2, there appears to be some basis for that belief: According to data from the World Bank, some 20 percent of the exports of developing countries to industrialized countries are subject to nontariff barriers, compared with only 11 percent of industrial countries' exports to these same markets. Moreover, the proportion of Third World trade subject to trade restraints appears to be growing, especially in the United States, where the percentage increased from less than 13 percent in 1981 to more than 16 percent in 1984.

Because of their belief that the Tokyo MTN did not address protectionist sentiments in the North, the developing nations, many of which do not belong to GATT, generally shunned the accords. However, the Uruguay Round of negotiations' greater focus on nontariff barriers sparked considerable interest among the developing nations and drew some of the most important of them into fuller participation in the GATT deliberations. Whether those deliberations ultimately prove beneficial to the interests and objectives of Third World nations remains problematic, but the process, as in the UNCTAD forum, draws attention to the proposition that the economic health of rich and poor in an

TABLE 8.2 ■ Shares of Imports Subject to Nontariff Barriers in Industrialized Countries, 1981 and 1984

	Percentage of Imports from:			
	Industrialized Countries		*Developing Countries*	
Market	*1981*	*1984*	*1981*	*1984*
European Community	10.3	10.7	21.1	21.7
Japan	12.3	12.4	14.5	14.5
United States	7.2	9.2	12.9	16.1
All industrial countries	10.5	11.3	19.5	20.6

Source: *World Development Report, 1986.* Copyright 1986 by The International Bank for Reconstruction and Development/The World Bank. Reprinted by permission of Oxford University Press, Inc., p. 23.

Note: Data are based on 1981 weighted averages for all world trade in all products except fuels. Nontariff barriers do not include administrative protections such as monitoring measures and antidumping and countervailing duties.

interdependent global political economy requires sensitivity to the politico-economic problems of each.

Foreign Aid

The developing nations may prefer trade to aid, but aid has a long heritage in the relations between rich and poor nations. And although foreign aid, like the principle of free trade, is now under considerable attack in many of the most important donor countries, it remains in many ways a preferred weapon in the developed nations' arsenal for coping with the South, in part, perhaps, because it is more easily tailored to the pursuit of specific foreign policy objectives.

The developing nations, for their part, often view aid as a moral obligation of the rich to the poor necessary to redress the injustices of the imperial past. Against this background, they have charged in the course of their drive to restructure the global political economy that "the volume and value of foreign aid flowing from North to South have been unjustifiably low" (Hansen, 1979).

Certainly, by some empirical standards, the volume of aid has been substantial. The United States alone has granted over $175 billion in economic aid since the end of World War II. Other developed nations have since joined in the effort, and various multilateral institutions (such as the World Bank, the United Nations Development Program, the Inter-American, Asian, and African Development banks, the European Community, and various OPEC and Arab institutions) have channeled significant amounts of resources to the Third World. Collectively, the total volume of bilateral and multilateral resources flowing to developing countries in the mid-1980s was more than $35 billion annually. If private resource transfers are counted, including private investments, loans, and credits, and grants by private voluntary agencies, in most years the overall level has been more than twice this.

Historically, the United States has been the most prominent aid donor, with official development assistance ranging from $3 billion to nearly $10 billion annually over the past two decades. Beginning in the 1960s, other Western nations began to contribute significant amounts of aid. These nations, together with the United States, make up the Development Assistance Committee (DAC) of the Organization for Economic Cooperation and Development (OECD).[10]

In 1984–1985 the DAC accounted for $28.9 billion, or 79 percent, of the world's development assistance (that is, funds allocated on concessional terms) flowing to developing nations and multilateral institutions (see Table 8.3). Aid from the communist countries has been much less significant in volume. Less than $4 billion of communist aid was granted in 1984–1985, representing only about 9 percent of the total worldwide.

---

10. DAC members are Australia, Austria, Belgium, Canada, Denmark, Finland, France, West Germany, Italy, Japan, the Netherlands, New Zealand, Norway, Sweden, Switzerland, the United Kingdom, the United States, and the Commission of the European Community.

TABLE 8.3 ■ Trends in Aid by Major Donors, by Volume, Share of World Total, and Percentage of GNP, 1970–1985

	Volume of Aid ($ millions in 1984 constant dollars)				Share of World Aid (percent)				Aid as Percentage of GNP			
	1970–71	1975–76	1980–81	1984–85	1970–71	1975–76	1980–81	1984–85	1970–71	1975–76	1980–81	1984–85
DAC Countries	17583	20111	24738	28924	78.2	63.8	67.7	78.7	.34	.35	.36	.36
United States	7313	7304	7745	8907	32.5	23.2	21.2	24.2	.31	.26	.23	.24
Other Western Europe	196	57	202	173	.9	.2	.5	.5	.33	.34	NA	NA
OPEC Countries	1018	8609	8429	3986	4.5	27.3	23.1	10.8	.78	2.61	1.66	.75
Saudi Arabia	476	3943	5249	2911	2.1	12.5	14.4	7.9	5.3	6.78	4.16	3.00
Centrally Planned Economies	2541	2112	2771	3360	11.3	6.7	7.6	9.1	.15	.14	.2	.23
Soviet Union	1983	1731	2242	2840	8.8	5.5	6.1	7.7	.15	.16	.22	.28
Developing Nation Donors[a]	1149	636	387	300	5.1	2.00	1.1	.8	NA	NA	NA	NA
Total	22487	31525	36527	36743	100	100	100	100	NA	NA	NA	NA

Source: Development Cooperation: 1986 Report (Paris: Organization for Economic Cooperation and Development, 1987), p. 49.

Note: Aid is official development assistance (ODA). NA indicates not available.

[a]China, India, Israel, and Yugoslavia.

During the 1970s, the OPEC nations became a significant new addition to the world's list of aid donors. In 1980–1981 OPEC's $8.6 billion in aid topped the United States' bilateral aid and represented nearly a quarter of the world's development assistance. With the sharp decline of worldwide oil prices in the mid-1980s, however, OPEC's oil revenues declined sharply, and this curtailed the ability of the cartel's members to sustain aid flows to others. In fact, many OPEC countries found themselves seeking external sources of funds to cope with the balance-of-payments deficits they themselves suddenly faced.

Against this background, what is the basis for the have-nots' charge that the volume and value of aid have been inadequate? Any number of yardsticks can be used to measure how far aid has fallen short of what the developing nations perceive their needs to be and the donors' abilities to meet them. The generally agreed-upon standard for measuring the burden of aid has been the donors' GNPs, and the usual formula is to transfer resources equivalent to 0.7 percent of the GNP. As Table 8.3 indicates, the OPEC nations have consistently exceeded this target, but the DAC donors and particularly the communist countries have fallen far short of it. Furthermore, the trend has been flat rather than upward, which is largely a consequence of the downward trend in the relative aid effort of the largest donor country, the United States. Between 1965 and the mid-1980s, U.S. development assistance as a proportion of its GNP declined by more than half—plummeting from 0.49 percent in 1965 to 0.24 percent in 1985. The United States now ranks at the bottom of the list of DAC donors in the proportion of its production that it allocates to foreign aid.

The rapid decline in the *relative* volume of American aid reflects a failure to increase aid commensurately with real increases in GNP or with rising prices. A combination of "donor fatigue" with the seeming intractability of the development process, a conviction that domestic needs should take priority over foreign ones, and, from time to time, disenchantment with the performance of the multilateral lending agencies explains the failure. The consequence has been a sharp decline in the purchasing power of the aid that is granted. Although the annual net flow of official U.S. development assistance doubled between 1967 and 1980, for example, when inflation is taken into account, the value of American aid was actually less in 1980 than it had been in the 1960s (Lewis and Kallab, 1983: 284). The developing nations have experienced tremendous population increases in the past two decades, and most aid donors have "tied" their aid to purchases in the donor country (even though the donor country may not be the lowest-cost producer of the goods that the developing nations need).[11] When these two facts are added to the picture, it

---

11. Tying means that the aid recipients are required to spend their aid dollars to purchase goods produced in the donor country. C. Fred Bergsten (1973: 104) argues that "tying alone reduces the real value of aid by 10 to 30 percent below its nominal value." It should also be clear that tying aid to the products of donor countries effectively makes aid a subsidy for the domestic producers of those products.

becomes clear that the per-capita volume of foreign aid among Third World countries is small and that its value is shrinking.

Finally, the relative insignificance of foreign aid can be seen in comparisons between aid and other expenditures. Global military expenditures, for example, are more than twenty times greater than official government-to-government economic aid flows. The disparity is even greater in the United States. Furthermore, Americans in 1986 spent nearly seven times as much on tobacco products and more than ten times as much on alcoholic beverages as their government spent on official development assistance (Sewell and Tucker, 1988: 242).

Beyond criticism of the meager volume and value of aid, the developing nations often complain about the political strings attached to foreign aid grants and loans. For example, the United States, like many other donors, has used its foreign aid to woo friends and potential allies (especially in its competition with the Soviet Union). Although such practices are no longer as blatant as they once were, the United States still continues to concentrate its aid in those countries in which it perceives the maximum political payoff. Indeed, the allocation of American foreign assistance has been guided especially by security interests. Israel and Egypt in particular have been singled out as major recipients of American aid because of their critical role in furthering U.S. political and security goals in the Middle East.[12] Assistance to other states in that region and in the Caribbean and Central America has also been determined by security considerations. Overall, two-thirds of American aid in the second Reagan administration was in the form of security assistance, compared with less than 50 percent in 1980 (Sewell and Contee, 1987: 1022; see also Kegley and Wittkopf, 1987: 136). The United States has also gone on record declaring that those states seeking American assistance will be appraised on the basis of their willingness to support American positions on resolutions before the United Nations. A congressional mandate in 1984 in fact required foreign assistance funding to take into account individual states' speaking and voting practices in the United Nations: Thereafter, no aid was to be granted to a country that the president found to be "engaged in a consistent pattern of opposition to the foreign policy of the U.S." This policy underscores the fact that states often use economic instruments for the purpose of exercising political leverage.

The behavior of the United States is not exceptional. Although OPEC sprinkled its lavish resources among a relatively large group of nations, the largest percentage of its aid has been allocated to Arab countries (*World Development Report 1985*, 1985: 102–103), with much of the rest spread among

---

12. In fiscal 1987, Egypt and Israel received $6.1 billion of total U.S. military and development aid, or 49 percent of the total U.S. aid budget. Included was some $5.1 billion in security aid (60 percent of the total) which included military aid and a type of security supporting assistance known as "economic support funds" (Sewell and Contee, 1987: 1022–1023, 1030).

Asian and African nations with sizable Muslim populations (Poats, 1982: 248–250). Britain and France have also given much of their aid to their former colonies. Noting the failure of many recipients of foreign aid to improve their economies, some observers (Hayter, 1971, for example) have even suggested that foreign aid is often a tool used by the North to perpetuate neocolonial and neoimperial ties, thus further subordinating the weak and poor while contributing to the welfare of those already strong and rich.

Ironically, however, many Third World countries seem unable to live without foreign aid, even though they may be unhappy about living with it. The "debt crisis" of the early 1980s bears this out. The causes of the crisis and the preferred remedies promoted to resolve it weave together many of the strands of the tapestry of North–South perceptions and preferences regarding the New International Economic Order.

THIRD WORLD DEBT AND THE CHALLENGE OF INTERDEPENDENCE

OPEC's success in cartelizing the global oil regime during the 1970s was important in galvanizing the non-oil-producing developing nations into the belief that commodity power would enable them to "force" the North into replacing the Liberal International Economic Order with a new order more amenable to their interests and objectives. Ironically, however, the two oil shocks of the 1970s created an environment in which many Third World nations deemed it prudent to borrow heavily from abroad, and the second shock simultaneously eroded the economic bases on which the repayment of those loans depended. The result was a debt crisis that first erupted in 1982 and continued thereafter, although with varying degrees of urgency.

In 1985 the United States proposed an approach to the debt crisis, popularly known as the "Baker initiative," which seemed to signal a change in the attitude of the United States, a critical player in the debt game, toward its solution. "For the first time the [Reagan] Administration officially recognized that the debt crisis is here to stay, and that austerity has to give way to growth" (Bogdanowicz-Bindert, 1985–1986). Analytically, then, 1985 might be thought of as the dividing point between two approaches to the debt problem. In the first phase, the International Monetary Fund played a critical role in inducing Third World nations to undertake reforms at home that would enable them to meet their obligations abroad. In the second, there seemed to be a greater appreciation not simply of the mutual peril of debtors and creditors but also of the critical role that creditors play in ensuring the financial—and ultimately political—solvency of the debtor nations. As we trace developments in these two phases of the debt crisis, the complex linkages between North and South, and between politics and economics, that give meaning to the concept of interdependence, will become apparent.

Averting Disaster, 1982–1985

As it first emerged in the early 1980s, the debt crisis spread to a broad group of countries, ranging from Poland in Eastern Europe to Brazil in Latin America, from the Philippines in the Far East to Nigeria in West Africa. It grew out of a combination of heavy private and public borrowing from private and public sources during the 1970s that led to an accumulated debt estimated to have been over $600 billion by 1980 and nearly twice that amount seven years later (see Figure 8.3). Many debtor nations found that they needed to borrow more money not to finance new projects but simply to stay even. That is, they needed new loans to meet their debt service obligations (interest and principal payments) on previous loans. Some with the largest debts—including Poland, Mexico, Argentina, and Brazil—required special treatment to keep them from going into default when they announced they did not have the cash necessary to pay their creditors. Eventually the Third World debtor nations, especially those in Latin America, received the most attention. Although the debt obligations of many Eastern European nations remained perilously high, their improved trade status with the West eased concern about their ability to meet their debt obligations.

The foreign debt accumulation of the 1970s was part of a process that saw private loans and investments and official nonconcessional loans become more important than public foreign aid to all but the poorest of the poor countries.[13] During the 1960s, official development assistance represented about 60 percent of the total capital flows to developing nations; by 1982 this proportion had been cut to 28 percent (Burki, 1983: 17; also Lewis and Kallab, 1983: 275, 282). Among the many results was a greater sensitivity to the interdependence of North and South as "the financial solvency of a great number of developing and some developed countries became a major preoccupation of the commercial banks and other developed country investors" (Burki, 1983). Governments in turn became concerned because many of the world's major private banks had significant exposure in these countries. "Default by the debtor nations thus could have had several serious consequences for the international monetary system: a collapse of confidence in the international banking system, possible illiquidity or insolvency of the banks, dangerous disruption of the financial markets and—in a worst-case scenario—world recession or depression" (Spero, 1985).

---

13. During the 1970s, private financial institutions surpassed not only official aid but also multinational corporations as the principal source of financial capital available to Third World countries. The result in many cases was a condition of "indebted industrialization" (Frieden, 1981) as governmental institutions in state-capitalist regimes became actively involved in promoting industrial growth. A decade later many observers (see, for example, Kuczynski, 1987) as well as some state-capitalist regimes (such as Mexico) concluded that disengagement of the state from direct involvement in industrialization activities, often through a process of "privatization," was a necessary component of the internal reforms needed to cope effectively with the debt crisis. See Young (1987) for a discussion of privatization around the world.

FIGURE 8.3 ▪ External Debt of Developing Countries, 1970–1986 (billions of U.S. dollars)

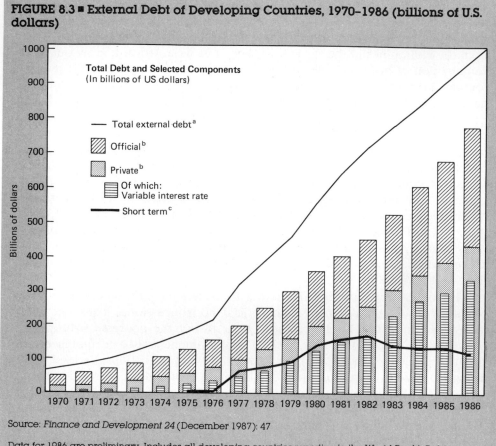

Source: *Finance and Development 24* (December 1987): 47

Data for 1986 are preliminary. Includes all developing countries reporting to the World Bank's Debtor Reporting Service. Includes data for Poland from 1984–86 only.

[a]Includes public and publicly guaranteed debt, private nonguaranteed debt, short-term debt, and use of IMF credit.

[b]Public and publicly guaranteed debt only.

[c]Short term is defined as debt with original maturity of one year or less. Data were unavailable for 1970–74.

The first oil shock gave impetus to the "privatization" of Third World capital flows. As dollars flowed from oil consumers in the West to oil producers in the Middle East and elsewhere, the latter, unable to invest all of their newfound wealth at home, "recycled" their "petrodollars" by making investments in the West. In the process the funds available to private banks for lending to others increased substantially.

Many of the non-oil-exporting developing nations became the willing consumers of the private banks' investment funds.[14] The fourfold rise in oil prices effected by the OPEC cartel hit these nations particularly hard. Thus to pay for the sharply increased cost of imported oil along with their other imports, they could either tighten their belts at home so as to curb their economic growth or borrow from abroad so as to sustain that growth and pay for needed imports simultaneously. Many chose the latter. Private banks for their part were willing lenders, as "sovereign risk"—the risk that governments might default—was believed to be virtually nonexistent (see Box 8.2).

Just as the United States was a net borrower from the world when it was building its own economy in the past, countries seeking today to industrialize must often rely on external capital. As long as the exports needed to earn the money to pay back the loans grow at the same rate, the accumulation of further debt is no problem. Moreover, there can be long-run payoffs in that investments made today in development projects, such as roads, hydroelectric dams, and steel plants, may eventually more than make up the cost of the original loans by providing new income and exports.

Whether developing nations always spent their borrowed money wisely can be questioned. Argentina, for example, is reported to have spent an estimated $6 billion on sophisticated military equipment between 1978 and 1982 which it used against Britain during the Falkland Islands (Malvinas) war (*Washington Post*, September 13, 1982, p. A18). Brazil, the largest debtor, used foreign loans to finance a number of "white elephants," including three nuclear power plants built at a cost of over $5 billion—of which only one works; the world's largest hydroelectric dam—which still was not operational after thirteen years of construction and $15.2 billion of investment; and a never-completed railroad—which cost $1.2 billion (Henry, 1987: 29).

Others have alleged that the capital flight from debtor nations was in many instances as great or greater than the amount of new loans made to them, with much of the money flowing from unscrupulous political leaders into private accounts in the very banks extending the loans to the governments in the first place (Ayittey, 1986; Henry, 1986). Whether caused by corrupt officials (the wealth of the Marcoses when they left the Philippines in 1986 for refuge in the United States was estimated to be $10 billion) or middle-class entrepreneurs seeking a safe haven for their profits, the outflow of money reduces that available for the investments that create new jobs and new wealth.

At the same time that the developing nations' debt grew substantially during the 1970s, however, so did the resources needed to service it. Consequently, the burden of the growing debt—whether measured by the ratio of the debt to exports or by the ratio of debt service payments to export earn-

---

14. Many actually preferred to borrow from private banks rather than other governments or multilateral agencies, because the banks generally placed fewer restrictions on the use of the borrowed money than did the public sources.

BOX 8.2 ■ Sovereign Risk and Its Implications for International Lending

When a government borrows from abroad or guarantees a loan, the legal status of the contract is unlike that between two private companies. It is much harder to enforce, since a sovereign borrower may reject a claim against it within its own territory. The problems arising from this limited enforceability are complicated by the fact that governments have considerable discretion over policy choices that affect their own ability to fulfill a contract. Many of these policies—shifts in monetary policy, limits on exchange remittances, changes in competition policy, changes in taxes—could not be deemed a breach of contract, even though their effect might be to negate the substance of the loan.

The ability of governments to influence economic outcomes, coupled with a lender's limited scope for imposing legal sanctions, means that contracts between developing countries and the private market have little economic value unless both parties feel it is in their long-term interest to honor their obligations. This means that the (present discounted) economic value to a borrower of meeting its obligations must be equal to or greater than the present value of not meeting them. In short, the countries that are most likely to service their debts are those that would suffer most if they did not do so.

To a borrower, the cost of possible sanctions depends on the importance of its future trade and finance with the lender (and its sponsoring government). Countries that are heavily involved in international trade depend on a continual flow of finance, the use of transport facilities, smooth customs clearance, and so on. They are therefore very open to sequestration orders and to a cutoff of trade credits. Their past success has been made possible by the network of trade and finance. They are unlikely to choose to jeopardize the chances of future success by excluding themselves from that network.

The major international banks have a comparative advantage in dealing with sovereign risk because they are closely involved in a number of facets of a developing country's international business. This helps explain the growth in importance of banking intermediation during the 1970s.

Source: *World Development Report, 1985*. Copyright 1985 by The International Bank for Reconstruction and Development/The World Bank. Reprinted by permission of Oxford University Press, Inc., p. 92.

ings—was essentially the same in 1980 as it was in 1970 (*World Development Report 1983*, 1983).

But the picture changed sharply after 1980. The drop in commodity prices associated with the worldwide recession caused the ratio of Third World debts to exports to rise markedly between 1980 and 1982. Economic growth slowed as the prices of the commodities needed to pay for the debt dropped and the money needed to pay off the loans simply failed to materialize. The appreciation of the dollar in foreign exchange markets added to the debt burden, as many of the loans held by developing nations are denominated in dollars. The ratio of debt service obligations to export earnings rose sharply, moving from 12.9 percent in 1980 to 19.5 percent in 1982 as a consequence of rising interest rates (International Monetary Fund, 1987: 180). The magnitude of the debt also grew to staggering proportions, increasing from $634 billion, or 82 percent of exports in 1980, to $850 billion, or 120 percent of exports, two years later (International Monetary Fund, 1987: 181, 186). For countries in the Western Hemisphere the ratio of debt to exports jumped from 184 percent in 1980 to 274 percent in 1982 (International Monetary Fund, 1987: 186).

The linkage between interest rates and Third World debts illustrates clearly how interdependent North and South had become. The banks lending to developing nations began to make variable-rate loans (that is, loans whose interest rates rise and fall with market conditions) so as to ensure their own profitability in a period of uncertainty. The Western industrialized nations at the same time adopted strict monetarist policies as a way of coping with their persistent inflation. Thus, as interest rates climbed in the West, the developing nations found that their external debt obligations marched higher. In Brazil, for example, each percentage point increase in interest rates is estimated to have cost the country an additional $700 million annually (*New York Times*, April 12, 1984, p. A27).

Not all of the debtor nations were hit equally hard by these difficulties, but many found themselves severely strained, as indicated by the fact that in 1983 more than twenty debtor nations negotiated to *reschedule* more than $51 billion in debts, that is, to stretch out the original repayment schedules so as to ease the immediate debt burden. Both the number of debtors and the dollars involved far surpassed anything witnessed in the previous decade. Yet in 1985, over $116 billion in debt held by some two dozen debtor nations had to be rescheduled (*World Development Report 1985*, 1985: 28).

The specific event that triggered the debt crisis was the threat in August 1982 that Mexico would default on its loans. The United States was instrumental in averting the disaster, and it urged at that time that the International Monetary Fund (IMF) assume a leadership role in securing debt relief for many Third World countries. The IMF did so not only by providing access to its own resources but also by inducing private lenders to make even more credit available to their debtors.

But IMF aid comes with strict conditions that the organization monitors to ensure compliance. When the IMF makes a loan to a country, it imposes programs designed to curb inflation, limit imports, restrict public spending, expose protected industries, and the like. At the same time the loan recipient is urged to increase its exports (which is why this approach is often regarded as an "export-led adjustment" approach to the debt problem). The fact that the "conditionality" of the IMF's aid adds so clearly to the strains on the political and social fabric of debtor nations led some commentators to ask whether IMF's policies might not be self-defeating. As one caustically observed, "The I.M.F. is probably the most effective neocolonialist instrument the modern world has yet devised" (Krauthammer, 1983).

Economic austerity caused by demands for drastic economic reforms were blamed for the overthrow of the Sudanese government of President Jaafar Nimeri in 1985. "The aid from western donors was not flowing," lamented Sudan's ambassador to Washington shortly before the military coup that ousted Nimeri. "The Sudan was down to rationing gasoline to two liters a week trying to meet IMF demands," he continued. "Do you pay the IMF back or buy gas for your country? Where do we get the money from unless we suspend all imports into the country?"

The prospect of domestic turmoil existed elsewhere, as the debt and related financial issues inflamed domestic political conflict in many of the most heavily indebted nations, including Brazil, Argentina, Mexico, Chile, and Nigeria, among others. Fidel Castro sought to capitalize on the situation and to assume a leadership role among the nations of the crisis-ridden Western Hemisphere in their confrontation with U.S. banks. Espousing a view widely shared in Latin America—that the huge debt is "unpayable" anyway—Castro repeatedly urged that the debt simply be "erased." He warned in a June 1985 speech that the alternative to a political solution that would somehow cancel the debt was "revolutionary social explosions." In a similar vein, Peru's new president, Alan Garcia, announced during his inauguration speech in the summer of 1985 that he would limit debt repayments to 10 percent of Peru's export earnings, thereby serving notice of his intention to keep from diverting all of Peru's resources to debt servicing. Later in the year he declared in a dramatic speech before the United Nations General Assembly that "it is either debt or democracy. . . . We believe the objective must be the unity of debtor countries and a radical change of the current situation." He elaborated in 1987, proclaiming, "Each of us has the right . . . to not pay more than what its economy can pay. . . . That is the moral law of the debtors."

It was in this emotionally charged atmosphere that the United States assumed a leadership role in seeking to devise a long-term solution to the debt issue. In the fall of 1985 Secretary of the Treasury James A. Baker unveiled a $29 billion plan that would use resources from both the World Bank and the private sector in a new effort to stimulate Third World economic growth. According to the Baker plan, new loans would still be made only if debtor nations undertook domestic economic reforms, and it emphasized a "market approach" to the debt problem that fit well with the Reagan administration's conservative philosophical belief that stimulating the world economy was the only viable way out of the problem. But in part because it demonstrated a preference for the World Bank over the IMF as the multilateral forum through which to push for resolution of the debt crisis, the initiative was regarded as a signal that the United States had concluded that IMF conditionality and related short-term fixes were no longer appropriate to resolve a long-term adjustment problem.

The Search for Long-Term Solutions, 1985–?

Although the Baker initiative was heralded as an important shift in the United States' attitude toward the debt problem, for a variety of reasons it failed to elicit much enthusiasm. Among other things, its market- and reform-oriented orientation angered many debtor nations that did not share the Reagan administration's ideological orientation (Amuzegar, 1987) and that resented being told that the poor should not borrow more money than they could repay.[15] But radical solutions fared no better. Despite repeated calls for a "debtors' cartel," for example, none emerged. As with other cartels, the widely varying circumstances of individual debtor countries plus the incentive each might have to "cheat" by striking a separate bargain with banks, creditor governments, or international organizations undermined the debtor nations' ability to act effectively as a collectivity (Aggarwal, 1987).

Two events in 1987 added renewed urgency to the continuing debt crisis and to the imperative of finding long-term solutions: In February, Brazilian President José Sarney announced that his country was suspending interest payments on the bulk of its $108 billion debt, declaring, "We cannot pay the debt with our people's hunger"; and in May, Citicorp Chairman John Reed astonished the financial world with the announcement that the giant American bank would take a billion-dollar loss in 1987 by setting aside reserves to cover its shaky international loans. Chase Manhattan, Bank of America, Chemical Bank, and Manufacturers Hanover quickly followed with similar actions. Meanwhile, hard-pressed debtors were kept afloat by piling more debt on existing debt—even though private commercial lending slowed to a trickle after 1982—resulting in a record debt in excess of $1.1 trillion by 1987 and a ratio of debt to exports that grew from 120 percent in 1982 to 169 percent in 1987. For the fifteen most heavily indebted nations (twelve of which were in Latin America), the figure reached 350 percent (International Monetary Fund, 1987: 186).[16]

As debtors and creditors positioned themselves to protect their own interests, recriminations over responsibility for the crisis flourished.

---

15. It is interesting to recall in this context that by this time the United States had become the world's largest debtor, with debt obligations in early 1988 exceeding those of Argentina, Brazil, and Mexico combined (Rothstein, 1988: 20).

16. The nations classified by the IMF as "heavily indebted" are Argentina, Bolivia, Brazil, Chile, Colombia, Ecuador, Mexico, Peru, Uruguay, Venezuela, Côte d'Ivoire (Ivory Coast), Morocco, Nigeria, the Philippines, and Yugoslavia. In addition to these, the World Bank includes Costa Rica and Jamaica in its classification of "highly indebted" countries.

> [Officials in less-developed countries] blame the outcome principally on adverse developments in the world economy—the deflationary and protectionist policies of the industrial countries and the asymmetry of the global adjustment process under which the International Monetary Fund (IMF) asked [less-developed country] debtors to deflate their economies to reduce their trade deficits, but did not ask creditor countries to inflate their economies to reduce their trade surpluses. [Less-developed country] officials emphasize sharp increases in their import prices, rising real interest rates after 1979, unfavorable terms of trade, reduced exports caused by shrinking industrial markets, and the developed countries' failure to coordinate economic policies, reduce their budget deficits, and eliminate trade restrictions. Creditors and industrial-country officials, by contrast, trace the genesis of the crisis to the [less-developed countries'] domestic policies—unbridled fiscal and monetary expansion, overvalued exchange rates, rigidity in prices and interest rates, excessive use of short-term private credits for long-term development and defense projects, refusal to adopt adjustment measures, and capital flight. (Amuzegar, 1987: 142–143)

Partial blame for the debt crisis might also be attributed to the commercial banks, who willingly made sometimes questionable loans in the 1970s in search of easy profits, only to become perhaps overly cautious in the 1980s at precisely the time that Third World nations depended on a continued infusion of new resources to service old obligations.

Underlying the often acrimonious debate about culpability are widely varying viewpoints about the best way to manage the debt burden without risking national or international disaster. The IMF austerity program pushed vigorously between 1982 and 1985 could claim considerable success from a strictly financial viewpoint. Third World balance-of-payments deficits were trimmed sharply; trade deficits were transformed into surpluses; and the debt was regularly serviced. "Thus the purely financial aspects of the debt problem were largely overcome by a minimum of financing and a maximum of adjustment" (Amuzegar, 1987).

Unanswered by the IMF strategy was the more difficult question of how Third World nations were to expand productive capacity and exports, not just cut their imports. Moreover, the strategy was politically unpalatable: "Bent on disinflation and demand control, [it] ran afoul of national sensitivities and desire for growth" (Amuzegar, 1987).

Innovative solutions to the debt crisis have been sought (see Kuczynski, 1987). Among them have been "debt-equity" swaps. These arrangements permit a nation's debt to be bought (usually by a multinational corporation) at current market prices, that is, at discounted rates, and then converted to the local currency of the debtor nation, where it is reinvested in stocks or in other productive assets in anticipation of long-term returns. The International Finance Corporation, an arm of the World Bank, has actively promoted such arrangements.[17]

Innovations are doubtlessly important, but most long-term solutions to the debt crisis invariably turn to the interdependent trade linkages between North and South (Brock, 1984), and in particular to the way that the resultant domestic welfare of each has become linked to the prosperity of the other. The United States, for example, saw its $42 billion in farm product exports to Latin America in 1981 fall by nearly one-third four years later. "Even moderate growth in Latin America, instead of depression, might have pushed those sales to perhaps $50 billion [by 1987], making a measurable contribution to reducing the U.S. trade deficit and helping some of the distressed areas in the Midwest" (Kuczynski, 1987). "About one-third of America's annual trade deficit is attributed to the shift in U.S. trade balances with Latin American debtors. By one estimate, every dollar of interest collected by the United States involved a loss of one dollar in trade" (Amuzegar, 1987: 146).

From the viewpoint of many Third World nations, revitalizing the market for primary products is critical. This, in fact, was part of the thinking underlying the "export-led" scenario for resolving the debt problem that motivated much of the IMF-led austerity approach in the first phase of the debt crisis. According to this approach, the revival of economic growth in the industrialized nations, with the United States as the locomotive pulling the rest of the Northern train forward, would revive the demand (and hence the price) for the South's commodities and other exports, thus enabling the Third World nations to service their debts and return to economic growth.

Because of the importance of Third World markets to many Northern producers, some economists questioned whether it was possible to sustain economic growth in the long run using a "North first, South later" strategy. In 1985, for example, a third of the exports of the United States went to developing nations. Reduced economic growth in Third World nations combined with IMF-led efforts to reduce imports thus adversely affected Northern producers and placed a potential brake on further economic output. The persistence of a strong dollar in international exchange markets also inhibited the export of American products by reducing their competitiveness. The paradox of reduced competitiveness is that it is the recipe for neomercantilist protectionism as American workers seek to protect their jobs from the threat posed by less expensive foreign products.

---

17. A novel variant on the debt-equity arrangement was put together by the United States and Mexico late in 1987. According to the plan, commercial banks would cancel some of their existing loans to Mexico in return for smaller Mexican government bonds that would pay an attractive rate of interest. The bonds would be backed by U.S. Treasury bonds that the Mexican government would purchase at market rates. The U.S. bonds would ensure repayment to those holding the Mexican bonds. Mexico in turn would receive the money it invested in U.S. bonds, plus interest, when the bonds mature (say, in twenty years) if it is able to meet its obligations to the private banks (see Rothstein, 1988).

Clearly, weakness in the prices of the commodities that many Third World nations export has been a major factor contributing to the persistence of their debt problems. Whether long-term improvements in the market offer realistic solutions is, however, problematic. Commodities have increasingly become "uncoupled" from industrial economies as the material intensity of manufacturing has steadily diminished (Drucker, 1986). Gaining access to First World markets nonetheless remains critical.

Just as Northern markets are important to the South, the growing importance of Southern markets to Northern producers places a premium on positive economic developments in both hemispheres. Neither augurs well for the future. As hostility toward the North engendered by the burdens of the oppressive debt grows (the level of domestic welfare in Latin America in the 1980s was measurably less than in the 1970s), the South is increasingly unlikely to continue to accommodate Northern solutions to the debt crisis. Conversely, as the North perceives itself as threatened by Southern imports with which it seemingly cannot compete, powerful domestic interests will demand "protection" from "unfair" foreign competition. Threatened is the principle of free trade, which, as we described in Chapter 7, has been an important concept underlying the unparalleled growth in global economic well-being experienced since World War II.

What, then, are the long-term solutions to the debt crisis? Making interest payments bearable so as to avoid near-term disasters and providing more funds for development of Third World economies so as to ensure sustained economic growth in the long term are general prescriptions (Kuczynski, 1987; also Amuzegar, 1987). Filling in the specific blanks is more difficult—all the more so because an interdependent world binds all in a common fate whose control eludes each. But the design of an effective strategy for coping with the debt crisis is all the more urgent because of its complexity, for if the lessons of the 1930s are a guide, not only economic well-being but also international peace may hang in the balance.[18]

THE EVOLUTION OF EAST–WEST ECONOMIC LINKAGES

"In foreign economic relations, politics and economics, diplomacy and commerce, industrial production and trade are woven together. Consequently, the approach to them and the management of them must be integrated, tying into

---

18. Pfister and Suter (1987) examine international financial relations since about 1800 in the framework of cycles and trends of the world system. Noting that there have been four international debt crises during this period (1826–1842, 1875–1882, 1932–1939, and 1982–), they conclude that the most recent may not end with a collapse of international financial relations, as occurred in the 1930s, despite similarities between the two crises, because greater institutionalization in the 1980s (as manifested in multilateral debt rescheduling and development finance) may enable the financial system to withstand challenges to it. Pfister and Suter explain the greater institutionalization of international relations in part by hegemonic cycles of the world system.

one knot . . . our political and economic interests.'' This observation by Soviet President Leonid Brezhnev underscores the extent to which politics and economics in the command or planned economies of the Soviet Union and Eastern Europe are purposefully intertwined. Production and distribution decisions thus are made by the government. In contrast, in the market economies of the First World, prices are allowed to play a decisive role in encouraging production and regulating the distribution of goods and services.

This is not to say, however, that Western governments have embraced free enterprise and laissez-faire philosophies without reservation. They, too, manage their economies and seek to regulate them through interventionist practices. The resurgence of neomercantilism in their foreign economic policies attests to their departure from the principle of permitting market forces to shape freely economic conditions. Still, the differences between the planned economies of the East and the market economies of the West are fundamental. They represent opposing approaches to the problem of stimulating economic growth and distributing its product.

The differences between planned and market economies have an important bearing on commercial relations between them. "For the West, the underlying rule would still be that any trade can take place unless a government prevents it; while for members of COMECON [Council for Mutual Economic Assistance], and especially for the U.S.S.R., the rule would be that no trade takes place unless the state initiates it'' (Vernon, 1979). Differing perceptions of how gains are realized from international commercial transactions flow from this distinction. "The Soviet system is based on the proposition that social gain is maximized by the state's commands. The American system, like the system of most Western countries, is fashioned on the proposition that as individuals pursue their private gain, the benefits for the country will exceed its costs, yielding a social gain'' (Vernon, 1979).

The ideological postures distinguishing the capitalist West and the socialist East regarding the role of government in economic affairs have remained throughout the post–World War II period. Experimentation with profit incentives in Hungary and China[19] and the flirtations with deregulation in the Soviet Union under Gorbachev's *glasnost* (openness) reform plans in the 1980s do not substantially move those states away from their commitment to socialism or to a planned economy. The fundamental differences in the philosophies of the East and West thus remain. The nature and volume of East–West commer-

---

19. Because China is properly regarded as a Third World rather than a Second World country, it is beyond the purview of our analysis here. However, it should be noted that trade between the United States and China has increased measurably since the early 1970s, when the two countries began the process of normalizing relations between them, following more than two decades of U.S. policy designed to isolate China from the rest of the world. As rapprochement proceeded, Washington often actively sought to increase commercial ties with China as a counterpoint to the Soviet Union. In each year from 1980 through 1985, U.S. trade turnover (exports plus imports) with China approximated or surpassed its trade turnover with the Soviet Union and Eastern Europe combined.

cial interactions, however, have not, as both have changed materially since World War II.

The evolution and expansion of economic ties between the First and Second Worlds can best be attributed to the changing perceptions of the costs and benefits that such ties produce. Not surprisingly, this evolution closely parallels the seven periods used to describe the evolution of the superpowers' diplomatic and political relationship in Chapter 4: (1) wary friendship (1945–1946); (2) mutual antagonism and belligerence (1947–1952); (3) tough talk, accommodative action (1953–1962); (4) peaceful competition (1963–1968); (5) détente (1969–1978); (6) confrontation (1979–1984); and (7) renewed dialogue (1985–?).

From Wary Friendship to Mutual Antagonism

During World War II, Western planners anticipated the participation of the Soviet Union in the postwar international economic system, just as they originally anticipated Soviet cooperation in maintaining the postwar political order. Although economic ties between the Soviet Union and the West before the war had not been extensive, the war itself, through American Lend-Lease assistance, had led to closer links. Moreover, the Soviet Union had participated in the Bretton Woods negotiations.

There was little question in the West that Eastern Europe would be an active partner in the postwar economic system. Trade between Eastern and Western Europe had been extensive before the war, and even as late as 1947 it was assumed that these ties would eventually be reestablished (Spero, 1985).

But 1947 was a critical year in the political struggle between East and West, for it was then that President Harry S. Truman effectively committed the United States to an anticommunist foreign policy. In June 1947 Secretary of State George C. Marshall outlined an American commitment to aid in the economic recovery of Europe. The European Recovery Program, as the Marshall Plan was formally called, was put in place the following year. It was framed in such a way as to make Soviet participation possible, but unattractive. Although its immediate objectives were couched primarily in economic terms, the Marshall Plan was conceived as a political weapon in the United States' increasingly anti-Soviet orientation. Revealingly, much of the debate in Congress over the plan was framed in terms of "stopping the onslaught of communism" (see Berkowitz et al., 1977). This kind of rhetoric certainly did not make the recovery program inviting to Soviet policymakers. The Soviet Union accordingly rejected the American offer of aid and also refused to permit Poland and Czechoslovakia, both of which had been offered Marshall Plan assistance, to accept it.

Under Soviet hegemony the nations making up the Council for Mutual Economic Assistance (CMEA or Comecon, created by the Soviet Union in 1949 to carry out what was known at the time as the Molotov Plan for the economic integration of Eastern Europe[20]) became remarkably inward looking. In 1938 over two-thirds of East European exports went to Western Europe; only 10 percent went to the Soviet Union or other Eastern countries. But by 1953 these proportions were nearly reversed: 64 percent of Eastern exports were traded among the Eastern European countries and the Soviet Union; less than 15 percent went to Western Europe; and only a trickle found their way to the Western Hemisphere (Spero, 1985: 347). More importantly, the Soviet Union was able to use its superior political and military capabilities to force its weaker neighbors to pursue economic policies clearly advantageous to the Soviet Union. The result was the creation of a regional economic system isolated from the West, one designed to augment the Soviet Union's capability to compete politically and militarily with the West.

The West did little to inhibit the economic isolation of the East. Under American leadership, economic ties between the socialist and capitalist worlds were actively discouraged. In particular, the United States sought to curtail trade in so-called strategic goods, items that might bolster Soviet military capabilities and thus threaten Western security, and sponsored the Coordinating Committee (Cocom) in order to induce America's allies to join in a unified embargo effort. However, the allies' response to this drive to use economic instruments to fight the Cold War was never enthusiastic:

> For the United States, the strategic embargo was intended to impair not only Eastern military strength but also Eastern political and economic power. The U.S. embargo therefore was directed at military capability in its largest sense, that is, at nonmilitary goods which would enhance economic performance and development as well as at military goods. On the other hand, the Europeans and Japanese, who had a greater economic stake in trade with the East than the United States did, felt that a broad embargo would simply encourage greater Eastern solidarity without hindering military and political capability. Thus they advocated a more limited definition of strategic goods, namely, those with direct military implications. As a result of allied resistance, the international list was always less comprehensive than the U.S. control list. (Spero, 1985: 349)

The United States also placed more restrictions on granting financial resources to the communist countries than did its allies, and in 1951, during the Korean War, it moved to strip the Soviet Union and other communist countries of any trade preferences. Thus the East was denied markets for its own products as well as access to Western goods and finances (see Spero, 1985, for

---

20. The Eastern European members of Comecon are Bulgaria, Czechoslovakia, the German Democratic Republic, Hungary, Poland, Romania, and the Soviet Union. Albania was expelled as a member following the split between China and the Soviet Union. Since 1962, membership in Comecon has been available to non-European countries, and Outer Mongolia, Cuba, and Vietnam are its three non-European members.

details). Economics thus joined hands with politics in creating and perpetuating the Cold War.

Toward Peaceful Competition

With Nikita Khrushchev's ascension to power in the Soviet Union in the mid-1950s and the formation of the European Economic Community in Western Europe in 1958, elements of polycentrism began to appear in the East and the West as both began to make initiatives toward accommodation. The atmosphere, to be sure, remained hostile, but at least in the economic sphere some thawing of the Cold War was in the offing.

Khrushchev tried to rejuvenate the moribund CMEA as an instrument for promoting intra-Comecon trade. Greater policy coordination, standardization of industrial products, emphasis on long-term trade agreements, establishment of an international bank for socialist countries, and increased specialization and division of labor among Comecon countries were sought as accompaniments to the expansion of trade. The results, however, were disappointing because of the persisting bias toward economic self-sufficiency, a scarcity of goods, and the poor quality of those goods available (Korbonski, 1973). These factors, combined with the growing demand of their economies, led the communist countries to increase substantially their trade with the noncommunist world. "In time, member states [of Comecon] were openly urged to acquire modern technology in the West instead of trying to develop it at home in order to accelerate the process of development" (Korbonski, 1973). Western Europe was a willing participant in the expansion of trade, and between 1958 and 1971 the value of trade between the CMEA and the EEC increased fivefold (Kuhlman, 1976).

Access to Western technology led to increased East European interest in more trade with the West. Eventually, the Soviet Union itself, whose planned economy failed to generate the economic growth and technological improvements necessary to meet production goals, began to seek greater trade ties with the capitalist world. This desire for trade with the West has persisted, fed in no small measure by the continuing inability of the Soviet command economy to produce the technology required for its growth rate to increase.

During the 1960s the rising demand in the socialist countries for consumer goods and the continued failure of the Soviet agricultural system to meet its production goals also contributed to an increased interest in greater trade with the West. In 1964, Khrushchev made the Soviet Union's first major purchase of Western grain. The combination of production, consumer, and agricultural demands in the East and the general receptiveness in the West led to a $6.4 billion increase in East–West trade between 1960 and 1968 (Nove, 1978: 16).

Nevertheless, as long as the Cold War continued, East–West trade remained unimportant, as a percentage of both world trade and the total trade of East and West. Although both East and West Europe favored greater commerce and took steps in that direction, the United States and the Soviet Union continued, for political reasons, to reject any major change in East–West economic relations. The superpowers' large self-sufficient economies enabled them to be less influenced by the potential economic advantages of interaction than their smaller and more trade-oriented partners were and more influenced by overriding political and security concerns. . . . Not until the late 1960s and early 1970s . . . did the policies of the superpowers change. Political tensions decreased, and forces encouraging East–West economic interaction were able to come into play. (Spero, 1985: 351)

From Détente to Confrontation

Détente became the official policy of both the United States and the Soviet Union with the inauguration of President Richard M. Nixon in January 1969. Expanded trade relations coincided with the improved diplomatic relations that détente enabled.

Two related political factors contributed to the Soviet desire for increased commercial ties. The first was the growing tension between the Soviet Union and China. This conflict placed a premium on the Soviets' establishing relatively stable relations with the West, a stability that trade might encourage. The second factor was the Soviets' growing perception, even without their rivalry with China, of the desirability of reducing tensions with the United States, presumably as a way of reducing the threat of war and the cost of armaments. Moreover, the drive for economic advancement was motivated by the Soviets' desire "as a superpower . . . to fly its flag in the entire world's economy, not merely that of its own bloc" (Yergin, 1977).

To fly its flag, the Soviet Union had to move from the "extensive" mode of economic development ("growth based upon increases in the labor force and the capital stock") to an "intensive" mode ("growth resulting from improved technology leading to higher productivity") (Yergin, 1977). To rejuvenate the sluggish Soviet economy, access to Western technology and the credits necessary to buy it were required, and to supplement the shortfalls in Soviet agricultural production, grain imports were necessary.

American interests in expanded commercial ties, on the other hand, were principally political—they would contribute to what Secretary of State Henry A. Kissinger described as a "vested interest in mutual restraint" by the superpowers and would give the Soviets "a stake in international equilibrium." What the Soviets wanted from détente (of which expanded commercial intercourse was only one element) therefore converged with what the United States wanted, namely, "a scheme to moderate the Soviet world revolutionary thrust by increasing Soviet dependence on stable relationships with the United States and other Western nations" (Brown, 1977). Kissinger's "linkage" strategy for the containment of Soviet influence and expansionism was predicated on this logic.

However, the United States also had economic incentives for expanding its trade with the East. Over time, the willingness of other industrialized nations to restrict trade with the communist world had waned, with the result that they had captured the major share of communist trade with the West.[21] This is shown in Figure 8.4, which illustrates the growth in East–West trade between 1969 and 1987, as well as the United States' small portion of the total volume.

The agreements reached at the 1972 Moscow summit which grew out of the superpowers' negotiations on strategic arms (SALT) were the cornerstone of détente, but expanded East–West trade was part of the mortar. A joint commercial commission was established at the summit, whose purpose was to pave the way for the granting of most-favored-nation (MFN) status to the Soviet Union and the extension of American government-backed credits to the Soviet regime.

The Nixon administration also expressed interest in selling greater quantities of American grain to the Soviet Union. During the Moscow summit Nixon commented several times to Brezhnev and Premier Alexei Kosygin that grain sales to the Soviet Union would have a beneficial impact on American public opinion, symbolizing to the American public the tangible rewards of the waning of the Cold War and the advent of détente (Kissinger, 1979). At the time the Soviet leadership expressed little interest in a formal response to the proposal. But shortly thereafter the American government negotiated an agreement offering the Soviet Union $750 million in credits with which to buy American agricultural products.

Unknown to the administration at the time, the Soviet Union was facing a catastrophic crop failure and desperately needed American grain. Hence, borrowing the tenets of "state capitalism,"[22] the Soviets set about putting together one of the largest commercial transactions in history, one that led to a sharp increase in the world price of grain. Thus, what was to have produced a positive impact on American public opinion turned into a blunder, casting a shadow over the entire question of expanded East–West trade. Kissinger recounts the effects of the Soviet grain deal in his memoirs:

> [The Soviets] gave us a lesson in the handicaps a market economy has in negotiating with a state trading enterprise. Each of our grain companies, trying to steal a march on its competitors, sold the largest amount possible and kept its sale utterly secret, even from the US government. Not for several weeks did we realize that the Soviets had, by a series of separate transactions, bought up nearly one billion dollars' worth of grain in one year—nearly our entire stored surplus. And we had subsidized the deals at a

---

21. By 1976 other Western industrialized nations accounted for 29 percent of communist trade, whereas the U.S. share was only 2.5 percent (U.S. Department of Commerce, 1978: v).

22. Governments sometimes act as transnational business enterprises, thus shifting their roles from that of landlord to that of entrepreneur (see Klapp, 1982). The Soviet Union is an interesting example. By operating in the international capitalist marketplace as an independent actor, its practice of socialism at home but capitalism abroad runs counter to the role deemed appropriate to the state in Marxist ideology. Its involvement in the capitalist marketplace thus portends the nightmare that Karl Marx feared—"state capitalism" by a communist society.

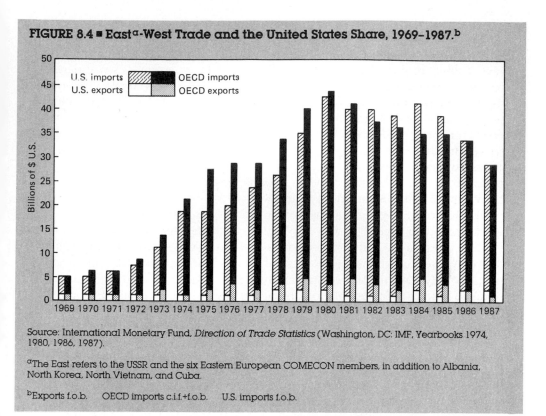

FIGURE 8.4 ▪ East[a]-West Trade and the United States Share, 1969–1987.[b]

Source: International Monetary Fund, *Direction of Trade Statistics* (Washington, DC: IMF, Yearbooks 1974, 1980, 1986, 1987).

[a]The East refers to the USSR and the six Eastern European COMECON members, in addition to Albania, North Korea, North Vietnam, and Cuba.

[b]Exports f.o.b.   OECD imports c.i.f.+f.o.b.   U.S. imports f.o.b.

time when the Soviet Union quite literally had no other choice than to buy our grain at market prices or face mass starvation. . . . At first the sale was hailed as a political masterstroke. It led to the usual maneuvering as to who should get credit. . . . Soon, however, no one wanted any credit; the grain sale rapidly became a political scandal; Nixon was accused of selling at bargain rates to our adversaries and driving up the price to American consumers. (Kissinger, 1979: 1270)

Eventually an agreement providing for the more orderly entry of the Soviet Union into the American grain market was negotiated, but the political damage wrought by the "Great American Grain Robbery" was substantial. "The sale turned from a step toward détente and a boost to the U.S. economy into a political threat to the policy of détente and an economic debacle" (Spero, 1985).

Even more damaging was the fate of most-favored-nation status and in-creased credits for the Soviet Union. Most-favored-nation treatment was to have been granted by the U.S. Trade Act of 1974, which provided MFN status for the Soviet Union and other communist countries in fulfillment of the 1972

Trade Agreement between the United States and the Soviet Union. But a congressional amendment (known as the Jackson–Vanik amendment) made MFN status contingent on the liberalization of communist policies relating to Jewish emigration. Although the Soviet Union did tacitly signal its willingness to permit freer emigration of Soviet Jews, early in 1975 it reversed its position on the understandings, labeling them a violation of the 1972 Trade Agreement (which had called for an unconditional elimination of discriminatory trade restrictions and reaffirmed the principle of noninterference in domestic affairs). Hungary and Romania were eventually granted most-favored-nation status, subject, however, to annual review by Congress of each country's emigration policy, which became an impediment to better relations, especially between the United States and Romania.[23]

Denial of MFN status for the Soviet Union was a slap in the face, for it symbolized the Soviet Union's "exclusion from the international economic system, whereas the restoration of most-favored-nation status symbolized the end of Western discrimination" (Spero, 1985). The slap became a black eye when in early 1980 the United States played its "China card" and granted MFN status to the People's Republic of China, the Soviet Union's principal communist rival.

More significant than symbolic was the issue of American government-backed credits. Because Soviet and Eastern European currencies are not convertible (that is, they are subject to government controls and therefore are not easily exchanged for Western currencies) and because the exports from which they earn hard (Western) currencies have been relatively limited, the communist economies generally have lacked the foreign exchange necessary to buy the goods from the West that they desire.[24] During the 1970s this situation changed as a consequence of heavy borrowing from the West. By 1982, the East's debt to the West stood at $80 billion (*Washington Post*, December 13, 1982, p. A22), up from only a few billion dollars at the beginning of the 1970s. The debt itself created the need for greatly increased export earnings by the

---

23. The United States also granted Poland and Yugoslavia most-favored-nation status. In these cases, however, the grants were made before passage of the 1974 trade act and are therefore not subject to annual review by Congress before extension of MFN status by the president.

24. Comecon countries typically seek to balance their trade on a bilateral, rather than a multilateral, basis. Thus, the Soviet Union will seek to balance its trade with each of the Eastern European nations rather than with all of them collectively, as is the case in the Western multilateral trading system. Consistent with this strategy, barter trades with the West can be used to circumvent the constraints of limited availability of hard currencies. "These swaps take a number of different forms. One consists of straight barter of specific quantities of goods, such as American soft drinks for Russian vodka; another more generalized form allows the Western partner to choose from a shipping list; a third consists of barter that pays off the Western partner with future output from a specified plant—so-called compensation deals" (Vernon, 1979). Compensation deals are particularly attractive as a means through which Western firms might gain access to the Soviet Union's extensive reserves of raw materials, including oil and natural gas. In return for "paybacks" in raw materials, the Soviet Union gains Western technology, equipment, and managerial skills.

Comecon nations or the extension of government-backed credits by the West, particularly the United States.

American policy regarding credits to the Soviet Union evolved in a manner similar to that regarding the MFN-status question. In late 1974, Congress limited American credits to the Soviet Union to $300 million over a four-year period, which was actually less than had been granted previously. Its action appears to have been motivated by a desire to assert legislative control over the activities of the Export–Import Bank as well as concern growing out of the 1972 grain deal and the abuses unveiled by the Watergate scandal. But the impact on expanding East–West trade was devastating.

> From [the Soviet Union's] point of view, . . . the need for most-favored-nation status was (and is) primarily theoretical. Credits, on the other hand, were of immediate importance and utility. If trade were to expand substantially, credits were required. But [Congress] said, in effect, that after having made an important concession [regarding the emigration of Soviet Jews], the Soviets would be eligible for less in credits over the subsequent four years than had already been received over the previous two, before they had made any concession. It looked very much as though the Congress were putting a ceiling over trade rather than a floor under it. (Yergin, 1977: 532)

Upon assuming office, President Jimmy Carter committed himself to the policy of détente and apparently to the principle of normalizing East–West commercial relations. But because of congressional constraints, East–West trade stagnated in the second half of the 1970s.

Furthermore, the Carter administration's commitment to a worldwide campaign on behalf of human rights often led to American attacks on the Soviet Union's human-rights policies. Commercial relations with the Soviets (particularly their desire to acquire high-technology goods from the United States) were seen as a source of leverage to realize American foreign policy objectives in the human-rights area. As Soviet-American relations deteriorated, the administration pursued economic instruments to counter the continued high levels of military spending by the Soviet Union, its overseas military buildup and arms transfers to the Third World, and its backing of Cuban intervention in Angola, Ethiopia, and elsewhere in Africa. As Carter national security staffer Samuel P. Huntington (1978) argued, "Economic détente and military adventurism cannot go hand-in-hand for long. At some point the Soviets will have to make a choice."

President Carter eventually made the choice himself. As a reprisal for the trials of Soviet human-rights dissidents in 1978, Carter imposed new controls on the sale of a computer to the Soviet news agency TASS that was to have been used at the 1980 Summer Olympics in Moscow. Later, additional punitive measures were instituted: a partial grain embargo and further restrictions on American exports following the Soviet military intervention in Afghanistan in late 1979. The commercial ties that a decade earlier had been built to cement détente became the victim as well as the instrument of Soviet-American rivalry. Détente faded, and in its place arose a phase of intense superpower confrontation.

The Future of East–West Commercial Interactions: From Confrontation to Renewed Dialogue

The words of Allen Wallis, under secretary of state for economic affairs in the Reagan administration, show how radically American attitudes and perceptions shifted between the early 1970s and the early 1980s and how the broader context of Soviet-American relations frames the way in which commercial ties came to be viewed:

> The theory underlying détente was that a web of economic, scientific, cultural, and political relationships would so interlink Soviet and Western societies that their views on security and other core issues would tend to converge. It was believed that the tangible benefits flowing from economic and other interchanges would encourage Soviet restraint in foreign policy. . . . We all know how the hopeful views of East–West relations spawned early in the decade soured at the end of the decade, especially after 1979. Détente, with its web of relationships and incontestible economic benefits to Soviet society, was no barrier at all when Soviet decisionmakers saw opportunities to advance their strategic position through overseas adventurism or outright military aggression. Any one who had illusions that fundamental Soviet views had changed during détente was quickly disabused of those notions. . . . [The Soviets'] sponsorship of Cuban adventures in Africa, their continuing activities in Indochina, their invasion of Afghanistan, their crackdown in Poland, and their involvement in Central America were visible indications that their fundamental values and policies had not been changed at all by a more lenient, friendly, and cooperative attitude on the part of the West. Underlying these aggressive acts, of course, was the massive and unrelenting Soviet military buildup that went far beyond any reasonable notion of what would be needed to defend the U.S.S.R. (Wallis, 1983: 1–2)

The denouement of détente between 1980 and 1985 might have set the stage for a complete rupture of commercial ties between East and West. But in fact it did not. The United States did place restrictions on the export of energy technology to the Soviet Union in the early Reagan presidency as the United States sought, first, to punish the Soviets for their presumed complicity in the imposition of martial law in Poland and, second, to win cancellation of the planned Soviet–Western European pipeline that would eventually bring natural gas from Soviet Siberia to markets in Western Europe. At the same time, however, Reagan lifted Carter's ban on grain sales to the Soviet Union. Eventually, in 1983, Washington and Moscow concluded a new long-term grain sales agreement. The accord—the first major bilateral pact negotiated since the Soviet invasion of Afghanistan—contained language that effectively pledged the United States not to interrupt future grain shipments in pursuit of its self-defined national security policy goals.[25] Efforts to halt completion of the trans-Siberian pipeline were also eventually dropped—but not before they had produced a serious split in the Atlantic alliance.

Serious intra-NATO fissures appeared when the United States tried not only to persuade other Western nations to embargo the sale of energy technology to the Soviet Union but also to require foreign subsidiaries of American-based multinational corporations to conform to the dictates of American policy. Supporters of a hard-line policy cited Lenin's prophecy that the capitalists would gladly sell the rope with which they would be hanged—and contended that the Siberian pipeline was such a rope, as it provided high-technology equipment to the Soviet "military machine." Many European allies of the United States simply did not share this view. Nor did they share with the United States the belief that completion of the trans-Siberian pipeline would make Western Europe unduly dependent on Soviet sources of energy. What they did was to point to the inconsistency in American policy that attempted to pressure the Western Europeans into not selling the Soviets energy technology at the same time the United States was selling them grain.

The pipeline fracas cast in sharp relief the differences on the issue of East–West trade that often separate the United States from its allies in the industrialized world. For Europe and Japan, the tradition of trade with Eastern Europe and the Soviet Union, the fact of their geographical proximity to them, the differences in their import needs, and their perceived marketing possibilities lead them to place a premium on commercial ties between East and West. For a more self-sufficient and security-conscious United States, commercial concerns are less important. As shown in Figure 8.4, U.S. trade with the East is small, and as a proportion of total U.S. trade with the world, it is minuscule.

Henry Kissinger argues that the failure of the policies that he had once championed in fact lay in the inability of the United States and its allies to act in concert on trade-related issues:

> In a crisis, we thought, the fear of losing markets or access to raw materials, Western technical innovations or bank credits would produce Soviet caution. But this assumption presupposed a Western willingness to use its economic strength in the service of overall strategy. This clearly has not happened. On the contrary, so many Western nations have let themselves become dependent on Soviet trade that a trade cut-off is more likely to turn

---

25. A week after the Soviet-American grain agreement was signed, the Soviet Union shot down a Korean civilian airliner, killing all of its nearly three hundred passengers. Despite clamors by some members of Congress to abrogate the new grain agreement in retaliation for the Soviet attack, it was permitted to stand.

into a Soviet weapon against the West. (*New York Times*, January 18, 1982, p. A19)

A major conclusion about East–West trade that can be drawn from Figure 8.4 is that there have been fluctuations in the level of trade associated with swings in the overall superpower political relationship: Trade has tended to expand during periods in which tensions have relaxed and to contract during periods of superpower animosity.

To be sure, the Western propensity to use trade as a political instrument of influence will remain; but the record also indicates a prudent Western readiness, even on the part of the United States, to jettison this practice and reduce restrictions if and when economic conditions make them excessively costly. The willingness of the United States to sell grain and permit technology transfers to the Soviet Union so as to satisfy politically important domestic groups, and the revision of Soviet trade policy under Gorbachev to support economic reforms at home (see Vanous, 1986), are exemplary of this adaptive flexibility. The gas pipeline issue likewise speaks to the pull of economic interests over immediate political objectives among at least some members of the Western alliance.

It is instructive that in the mid-1980s the superpowers' renewed dialogue once more paved the way for the negotiation of expanded trade between the West and East.

Since 1985 . . . governmental and nongovernmental trade talks have resumed. The new Soviet leadership has introduced trade and economic reforms, sought affiliation with the major Western economic institutions, and, in the eyes of some analysts, launched a strategy to acquire Western technology and capital—not only to secure the economic benefits, but also to weaken the [NATO alliance] and U.S. military effort and widen differences between Europe and the United States. U.S. government actions have . . . abetted Soviet initiatives by offering to subsidize grain sales to the Soviet Union . . . and, in early 1987, removing controls on energy equipment and technology sales to the Soviet Union. . . . And the Reagan administration . . . announced measures in February 1987 to reexamine U.S. export controls in light of U.S. competitiveness needs. (Nau, 1987: 48)

These signs of improved East–West relations are not without precedent. They inspire a sense of *déjà vu*, recalling the hopeful mood and expectations that prevailed during the period of détente. Some of that experience was bitter, however, which reminds us that each superpower is driven by the complex demands of domestic politics, the requirements of intra-alliance cohesion, and the dual compulsion of competition and cooperation with the other. As each seeks to balance and manage these demands, either one may appear predominant at any particular time.[26] In the long run, however, neither the dictates of consumerism in Kiev nor the perquisites of politics in Iowa will be permitted to determine the course of superpower relations. Instead, as the deterioration of the superpowers' political relationship in the early 1980s illustrates, East–West economic collaboration and political-military confrontation are incompatible—the latter must recede before the former can advance.

THE FIRST, SECOND, AND THIRD WORLDS IN THE 1990s

The ebb and flow of East–West commercial interactions during the past two decades indicate how fragile and subject to political considerations these ties are. The critical question for the 1990s is whether the Soviets and Americans can resolve the political and military issues that divide them. A major lesson of the past is that the state of political relations will more readily shape economic affairs between East and West than the latter will affect the former, especially in the short run.

Continued Soviet hegemony in Eastern Europe will enable the Soviet Union to impose its will regarding East–West commercial interactions on its Eastern European allies more easily than the United States will be able to convince its allies in Western Europe to share its fears and support its policies. The difficulties that both the Carter and Reagan administrations experienced in persuading the United States' NATO partners to impose sanctions on the Soviet

---

26. Consider the constraints posed by groups in both societies holding diametrically opposed views on East–West collaboration, and their influence on the potential for change. In the Washington policymaking community, for example, there exists, Daniel Yergin (1977) persuasively argues, two basic images of the Soviet Union. One sees the Soviet Union "as a revolutionary state, single-mindedly geared to expansion. . . . For those who hold this view, détente is not merely a fraud, but a danger, a relaxation less of tension than of the American guard so enabling the Soviet Union to take advantage of American goodwill." This is the image that was dominant during the height of the Cold War. In contrast, the image dominant during the early 1970s "views the Soviet Union less as a world revolutionary state than as a conventional great power. While obviously possessing vast military strengths and not lacking in imperialist drives, it is still a cautious power, concerned with protecting what it has, and with much to gain from stability" (Yergin, 1977). These images in turn lead to quite different views of Soviet-American trade. The first sees "trade [as] one of the major items of transport on the 'one-way street.'" For those subscribing to the second image, "trade is one of the major means of encouraging a détente, establishing mutually advantageous relations, and strengthening the Soviet stake in international stability."

Finally, Yergin contends that the image of the Soviet Union dominant at any particular time is directly related to Soviet behavior—if Soviet behavior reflects adventurism, this will strengthen the political hand of those subscribing to the Cold War image; if an effort to reduce tensions is more apparent, this will bode well for those subscribing to the détente image. Commercial interactions between the United States and the Soviet Union will be affected accordingly. Developments in American policy in the 1980s suggest that the Cold War image reemerged as dominant in American policymaking circles in the early 1980s but then receded in the late 1980s during the phase of Soviet-American relations known as *renewed dialogue*.

Union for its invasion of Afghanistan and its presumed complicity in thwarting the Solidarity labor movement in Poland are illustrative. More significantly, perhaps, trade between East and West is generally more important to the superpowers' European allies than it is to the superpowers themselves. Continued trade in the European context may therefore give impetus to domestic lobbies in Europe supporting its perpetuation. Such a development could contribute to the weakening of ties between the United States and Europe and facilitate the creation of regional economic systems. Meanwhile, the effort of the Soviet regime under Gorbachev to use innovative foreign policy proposals to cope with domestic difficulties may move it toward greater involvement in the Liberal International Economic Order, particularly the multilateral trade system. Under the leadership of the United States, the Northern countries would then face the task of devising institutional rules to cope with the challenges that planned economies pose to the liberal system in which market forces play a central role.

Any move toward increased involvement in the global political economy by the command economies of the East could be significant to the Third World nations, for it implies that the Second World could come to identify its interests more closely with the First World on issues comprising the North–South agenda. At present, the Second World as a whole has established only modest economic ties with the Third World. And these appear dictated more by political expediency than by such liberal economic principles as comparative advantage. But should the ties between the First and Second Worlds become closer, the polarization between North and South may become more pronounced. This is all the more likely if the Soviet Union, as the Gorbachev regime has pledged, retreats from actively seeking to create opportunities to advance its interests and extend its influence among Third World nations.

The South can be expected to continue to press its interests by seeking some kind of restructuring of the international economic order. The demands for a new order will likely remain muted as immediate challenges require pragmatic policies—mainly to deal with the Third World debt situation—and the diversity inherent in the Third World may permit separate bargains to be struck between the North and factions in the South on certain issues. But the Third World nations' perception that the present structure of the international economic order preserves its dependent and unequal position in the international hierarchy is likely to fuel for some time their desire for a radical transformation of the international division of labor, the structure of world industry, and the global trading system.

How might Third World demands and aspirations be satisfied and properly managed? Despite the contentious rhetoric surrounding the North–South debate in the past and the persistent global inequalities on which it has been based, it is clear that the South cannot force the North to submit to its demands, nor will the North do so voluntarily. More reasonable is a scenario in which the North makes piecemeal concessions to Third World demands out of self-interest borne of the realization that the North and the South are interdependent, and hence the well-being of each is dependent on the health of the other. But because interdependence entails costs as well as opportunities for powerful domestic interests, the future will continue to be shaped by perceived differences in the interests and experiences of rich and poor nations as they maneuver for influence and advantage in the global political economy.

SUGGESTED READINGS

Bhagwati, Jagdish N., and John Gerard Ruggie, eds. *Power, Passions, and Purpose: Prospects for North–South Negotiations.* Cambridge, Mass.: MIT Press, 1984.

Brandt, Willy. *Common Crisis: North–South, Cooperation for World Recovery.* Cambridge, Mass.: MIT Press, 1983.

Cline, William R. *International Debt and the Stability of the World Economy.* Washington, D.C.: Institute for International Economics, 1983.

Franklin, Daniel. "Soviet Trade with the Industrialized West," *SAIS Review* 8 (Winter–Spring 1988): 75–88.

Murphy, Craig N. *The Emergence of the New International Economic Order Ideology.* Boulder, Colo.: Westview Press, 1984.

National Academy of Sciences. *Balancing the National Interest: U.S. National Security Export Controls and Global Economic Competition.* Washington, D.C.: National Academy of Sciences, 1987.

Nossiter, Bernard D. *The Global Struggle for More: Third World Conflicts with Rich Nations.* New York: Harper & Row, 1987.

Sewell, John W., and Christine E. Contee. "Foreign Aid and Gramm–Rudman," *Foreign Affairs* 65 (Summer 1987): 1015–1036.

Sewell, John W., and Stuart K. Tucker. *Growth, Exports, and Jobs in a Changing World Economy: Agenda 1988.* New Brunswick, N.J.: Transaction Books, 1988.

Wright, Moorhead, ed. *Rights and Obligations in North–South Relations.* New York: St. Martin's Press, 1986.

NINE

The Global Commons: Population, Food, and the Environment

The final binding thought is to shape a more satisfying future for the coming generations, a global society in which individuals can develop their full potential, free of capricious inequalities and threats of environmental degradation.

RAFAEL M. SALAS, 1984

What's happening today has never happened before. It will dramatically change the U.S. and the world in which we live. . . . For about a decade and a half, the people of the free, modern, industrial world . . . have not borne enough children to reproduce themselves over an extended period of time.

BEN J. WATTENBERG, 1987

Interdependence is a key to understanding the transformation of the Liberal International Economic Order. Because the concept challenges the suitability of national solutions to global problems, it has also been used to address the relationship between humankind and the biological and geophysical environments within which human interactions occur.

The ecological perspective on world politics (Pirages, 1978, 1983; Sprout and Sprout, 1968, 1971) views the global environment as a unified ecosystem of delicately and tightly integrated components. Its emphasis is on the interrelatedness of biological, economic, political, social, technological, geographic, and other elements of the globe's subsystems. The ecological perspective thus commands appreciation of the extent to which the fate of humankind is contingent on the viability of the earth's ecosystem that makes life itself possible. This obvious but often ignored principle underscores the fact that nature imposes limits, that the planet's *carrying capacity*—its ability to support human and other life forms—is not infinite.

How many people can the earth support? What is its ultimate carrying capacity? No one knows for sure, in part because human ingenuity and rapidly advancing technology keep stretching the boundaries. Thus the growth projected for today's more than five billion inhabitants into the next century will

268

doubtlessly be accommodated. But at what cost—to human freedom, human welfare, and ultimately to the environment necessary to sustain humankind?

The *tragedy of the commons* is a compelling metaphor widely used to examine these questions. It was first articulated in 1833 by the English political economist William Foster Lloyd and was popularized and extended to contemporary world problems by the human ecologist Garrett Hardin in an article appearing in *Science* magazine in 1968.[1] The commons metaphor envisions human behavior driven by the search for self-advantage and personal benefit. Because it stresses the importance of individual action and personal motivations, it applies well to the evolution of systems (like the global one) in which formal government is minimal and individual (national) choice unregulated.

The central question asked through the analogy is, What is the likely human approach to resources held in common in an unregulated environment? If individuals are interested primarily in advancing their personal welfare, what consequences should be anticipated for the finite resources held in common, and hence for all?

Consider, as Hardin did, what occurred in nineteenth-century English villages where the village green was typically common property and all herdsmen were permitted to graze their cattle on it. Sharing the common grazing area worked well as long as the number of cattle did not exceed the land's carrying capacity, for if that occurred, the pasture would be ruined, and the number of cattle it could support would decline drastically. But the incentives were powerful for individual herdsmen to increase the size of their herds as much as possible, because only in this way could they maximize their individual gain. If pushed, individual herdsmen might concede that the collective interest of all would be served if each reduced the size of his herd, so that the commons could be preserved. But self-restraint—voluntary reduction by one herdsman of the number of his own cattle to relieve the pressure on the common village green—was not popular. Indeed, there was no guarantee that others would follow suit. On the other hand, the addition of one more animal to the village green would produce a personal gain whose costs would be borne by everyone. Hence, rational economic behavior encouraged all to increase indiscriminately the size of their herds, and it discouraged self-sacrifice for the common welfare. Ultimately, the collective impact of each effort to maximize gains was to place more cattle on the village green than it could sustain. "Ruin is the destination toward which all men rush, each pursuing his own best interest in a society that believes in the freedom of the commons" (Hardin, 1977).

The tragedy of the commons has become a standard concept in environmental politics and ecological analyses because it illuminates so well the sources of many human problems and predicaments. It is particularly appro-

---

1. For elaborations on the interpretation provided here, see Hardin and Baden (1977), Hardin (1977), Soroos (1977, 1984, 1988), and Schelling (1978).

priate when the English common green can be compared with planetary "common property," such as the oceans, fisheries, and the atmosphere, from which individual profit is maximized on the basis of a first-come, first-serve principle. Overuse of common property is also highlighted, as when the oceans and atmosphere become sinks for environmental pollutants perpetrated by a few but whose costs are borne by many. The task becomes one of devising regulations for an ecopolitical environment that thrives on freedom of choice (see Soroos, 1988).[2]

A major unregulated freedom of choice on which Garrett Hardin focused in his well-known article is the human freedom to propagate. "The most important aspect of necessity that we must now recognize," he wrote, "is the necessity of abandoning the commons in breeding. Freedom to breed will bring ruin to all. . . . The only way we can preserve and nurture other and more precious freedoms is by relinquishing the freedom to breed, and that very soon. . . . Only so, can we put an end to this aspect of the tragedy of the commons."

Not everyone will agree with the moral and ethical implications of Hardin's arguments. Few decisions, in fact, are more intensely personal or more intimately linked to the social and cultural fabric of a society than those of individual couples relating to marriage and the family. Furthermore, just as the ultimate carrying capacity of the global ecosystem has proved elastic, the impact of unregulated population growth on environmental quality remains unclear (see Repetto, 1987). Nonetheless, the balance of both theory and evidence points to a world in which unrestrained population growth will result in environmental degradation and lost economic opportunities that will, in turn, create incentives—perhaps imperatives—for governmental restraints on individual choice (McNamara, 1984). Political conflict is sure to follow. A world interdependent ecopolitically as well as economically is certain to share those consequences. It has been shown that demographic changes fuel domestic conflict and contribute to lost economic opportunities (Choucri and North, 1972, 1975; Diaz-Briquets, 1986). Even those not experiencing excessive population growth contribute to the problem and share in its consequences by placing a disproportionate strain on global resources. As the world approaches its (unknown but finite) ultimate carrying capacity, life as we know it will become increasingly difficult to sustain.

Our purpose in this chapter and the next is to focus attention on population, resources, and the environment as they relate to world politics. Here we focus on demographic variables, their correlates, and their implications. Par-

---

2. Thomas Schelling (1978) observes that the commons image has become widely used as a kind of shorthand "for situations in which people so impinge on each other in pursuing their own interests that collectively they might be better off if they could be restrained, but no one gains individually by self-restraint." He goes on to point out that "the commons are a special but widespread case out of a broader class of situations in which some of the costs or damages of what people do occur beyond their purview, and they either don't know or don't care about them."

ticular attention is given to growth in the Third World countries and to the impact of population pressures and rising affluence on the global food regime. This sets the stage for a discussion in Chapter 10 of the political role of resources in today's global political economy, with particular attention given to the implications of global patterns of the production and consumption of oil and other nonrenewable and renewable commodities for world politics.

TRENDS IN WORLD POPULATION GROWTH

Today's world population of more than five billion people constitutes a significant proportion of all the people who have ever lived, and it continues to grow. If present population trends are projected ahead eight centuries, ours will be a standing-room-only planet, with land surface of only one square foot per person. No one can seriously regard such a world as likely. Nor are the other images that have been conjured up to shock the public consciousness realistic portraits of the future. But what they do tell us is that the pressures of population growth pose a serious threat to the human condition, one unprecedented in scale. The relevant questions, therefore, are, At what level will the world's population be stabilized? and How will that stability be achieved?

The rapid growth of world population today is described by a simple mathematical principle articulated in 1798 by the Reverend Thomas Malthus, namely, that population when unchecked increases in a geometric or exponential ratio (1 to 2, 2 to 4, 4 to 8, and so forth), whereas subsistence increases in only an arithmetic ratio (1 to 2, 2 to 3, 3 to 4). When population increases in such an accelerating fashion, the compound effect can be staggering.

Consider, for example, the consequences resulting from the simple decision of whether to have two children or three. If parents decide to have three children and if each of their children and their children's children make the same decision, by the third generation thirty-nine people will have been born—three in the first, nine in the second, and twenty-seven in the third. If, however, the initial decision is to have two children instead of three and if each child makes the same choice, over three generations only sixteen people will have been born (two in the first, four in the second, and eight in the third). Projecting these same patterns to whole societies, the cumulative consequences can be enormous. For example, the population of the United States in 1968 was 200 million. Assuming two-child families, the population will grow to 300 million by the year 2015. However, if we assume three-child families, 300 million will be reached before the turn of the century, and the population will have doubled to over 400 million by 2015. Extending these same projections over a century, the population of the United States in 2068 will exceed 800 million if three-child families are the rule but will remain well under 400 million with two-child families.

Another way to contemplate how sensitive the world population is to even small, incremental changes in its rate of growth (the difference between births

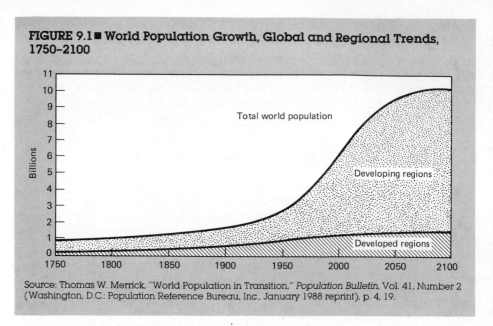

FIGURE 9.1 ■ World Population Growth, Global and Regional Trends, 1750–2100

Source: Thomas W. Merrick, "World Population in Transition," *Population Bulletin*, Vol. 41, Number 2 (Washington, D.C.: Population Reference Bureau, Inc., January 1988 reprint), p. 4, 19.

and deaths) is to consider how long it will take the population to double given a particular growth rate. Just as money deposited in a savings bank will grow more rapidly if interest is paid not only on the original investment but also on interest payments, population increases are a function not only of increases in the original number of people but also of those increases accruing from past population growth. Thus a population growing at a 1 percent rate will double in sixty-nine years, whereas a population growing at a 2 percent rate will double in only thirty-five years.[3]

The explosive proportions of today's population growth are illustrated in Figure 9.1, which indicates that it took from the beginning of time until the early 1800s for world population to reach one billion people. Because of substantial declines in death rates, the world population reached two billion about 130 years later, around 1930. Since then, additional billions have been added even more rapidly: Three billion was reached by 1960, four billion in 1975, and 5 billion in 1987. As present trends unfold, the world will reach the six-billion figure before the turn of the twentieth century and ultimately stabilize at something over ten billion by the twenty-first century.

How rapidly the world adds billions to its number is predicted by its growth rate. Worldwide, the rate of population growth peaked at just over 2

---

3. This is merely another way of saying that the population grows exponentially rather than arithmetically. The impact of different growth rates on doubling times can be calculated by dividing sixty-nine by the percentage of growth. Thus a population growing at 1 percent will double in sixty-nine years, but a population growing at 3 percent will double in twenty-three years.

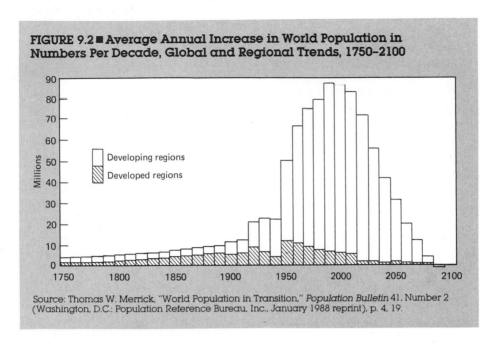

FIGURE 9.2 ■ Average Annual Increase in World Population in Numbers Per Decade, Global and Regional Trends, 1750-2100

Developing regions
Developed regions

Source: Thomas W. Merrick, "World Population in Transition," *Population Bulletin* 41, Number 2 (Washington, D.C.: Population Reference Bureau, Inc., January 1988 reprint), p. 4, 19.

percent in the late 1960s and then declined to 1.7 percent by the 1980s. Even this small slowing of the global rate of population growth is consequential, for it means that world population in the year 2000 will be 20 percent less than the 7.5 billion people that the birth and death rates of the 1950s would have produced had they continued uninterrupted.

Whatever the ultimate rate of growth, the trends are apparent and the consequences inevitable; it is not a question of whether the world will become more crowded but of how crowded it will become. In 1986 the world grew by more than 83 million people, an amount equivalent to adding the entire population of France and Colombia to the world or populating New Zealand again every other week or the Bahamas each day. Even more will be added each year in the future. As illustrated in Figure 9.2, more people will be added to the globe's population in the last fifth of the twentieth century than at any other time in history—even though the world's population growth rate has slowed markedly and will continue downward in the years ahead. We can better understand why this result is inevitable if we go beyond the simple arithmetic of population growth and explore its dynamics.

Factors Affecting National and Regional Variations in Population Growth

The rate of natural population increase in the United States in 1987 was 0.7 percent. This is an annual rate typical of industrialized nations today, where births and deaths have nearly stabilized. Hence, the difference between a typical industrialized nation and the world population growth rate of 1.7 percent is largely attributable to a population surge in the Third World, where sharply lower death rates since World War II have resulted from advances in medical science, agricultural productivity, public sanitation, and technology. The paradox posed by reduced death rates is that this favorable development has contributed to an accelerating rate of population growth in precisely those nations least able to support a burgeoning number of people.

Variations in national and regional population growth virtually ensure that today's demographic division of the world will persist into the future. In fact, it will widen. As shown in Figure 9.1, the 3.7 billion people who inhabited the Third World in 1985 will have grown to 4.8 billion by the year 2000, whereas the comparable increase among the developed nations will be only from 1.2 billion to 1.3 billion (Merrick, 1986: 13).

The developing countries' high fertility rates (which measure the number of births by women in their prime reproductive years) derive from a variety of sources. Apart from the pleasures that children provide, entrenched religious norms often sanction and encourage parenting, prescribing the bearing of children (particularly male offspring in some cultures), as both a duty and a path to a rewarding afterlife. In addition, many societies' cultural traditions ascribe prestige and social status to women according to the number of children they bear. But most importantly perhaps, high fertility rates are affected by economic factors. Large families add more hands to a family's labor force today and may be a future source of social security for parents who live in societies that have no public programs to provide for the elderly. Under such conditions, parents usually try to have as many children as possible so that they can earn more today and be cared for in their old age. When the infant mortality rate is high, the incentives for creating many offspring are even greater—the more children that are produced, the higher the probability is that some will survive. Twenty percent of the children of parents in developing countries die before their fifth birthday (Sivard, 1987: 3), and in some of them, half of all deaths occur before the age of five (U.S. Department of State, 1978b: 5). Thus the logic underlying high fertility rates is often most compelling where poverty in all its manifestations is most widespread; the tragedy is that such high rates often reinforce the persistence of poverty.

The Momentum Factor

Even more important to understanding the implications of today's population surge in the Third World (which is a result of high, but declining, birthrates and rapidly falling death rates) for tomorrow's world is the "momentum" factor. Like the momentum of a speeding train, population growth simply cannot be brought to an immediate stop even with an immediate, full application of the brakes. The momentum factor helps explain why in the last quintile of the twentieth century more people will be added to the globe's population than at any other time in history.

Population momentum is especially great in societies with high proportions of young people. In these societies, families are formed and babies produced at a rate faster than older persons die. Even if these young people choose to have only two children, large numbers of young couples can still produce extremely large numbers of total births and hence a continuing momentum of growth. This process will continue until the age structures shift toward equal numbers of people in each age group.

Consider, for example, the three age and sex population profiles shown in Figure 9.3. Mexico's profile shows an "expansive" population, because each new age group or cohort contains more people than did the one before it. In contrast, the United States has a "constrictive" profile, because recent cohorts have been smaller than preceding ones, and Sweden's profile is of a "stationary" population, because it has roughly equal numbers of people in each cohort.

Although most nations of the developed world have moved toward Sweden's "zero-population growth" profile, developing nations generally mirror

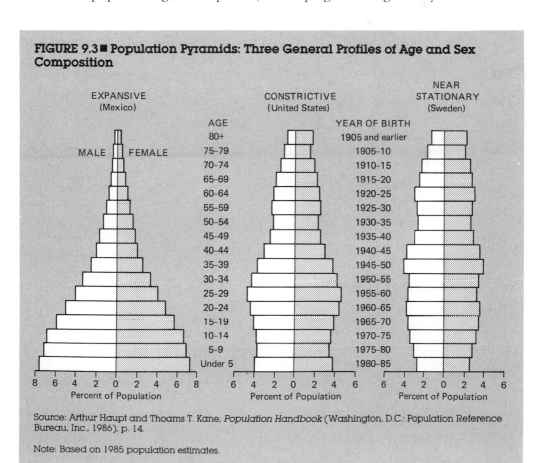

FIGURE 9.3 ■ Population Pyramids: Three General Profiles of Age and Sex Composition

Source: Arthur Haupt and Thoams T. Kane, *Population Handbook* (Washington, D.C.: Population Reference Bureau, Inc., 1986), p. 14.

Note: Based on 1985 population estimates.

the Mexican pattern. The sheer momentum of population growth in the Third World is thus linked to the developing nations' age profiles. Because each cohort is typically larger than the one before it, the number of young men and women entering their reproductive years will also grow. Figure 9.4 demonstrates the importance of this momentum by projecting into the future the larger proportion of fertile age groups in the developing world. It also demonstrates how different the population growth of the developed and the developing worlds is likely to be, which is, of course, partly a consequence of the different age structures of the two worlds' populations. The predictable consequence will be the rapid emergence of a world in which only a tiny fraction of its population will reside in developed countries.

Slowing expanding population implies that the Third World must move toward a replacement-level rate of fertility—that is, two children to replace two parents—as many industrialized nations have already done. Even then, momentum will continue to fuel an expanding population. In general, population growth will continue for as many as fifty to seventy years after replacement-level fertility is achieved. This startling fact underscores the urgency of grappling with the population problem; for every decade of delay in achieving replacement-level fertility, the world's peak population will be some 15 percent greater (U.S. Department of State, 1978b: 49).

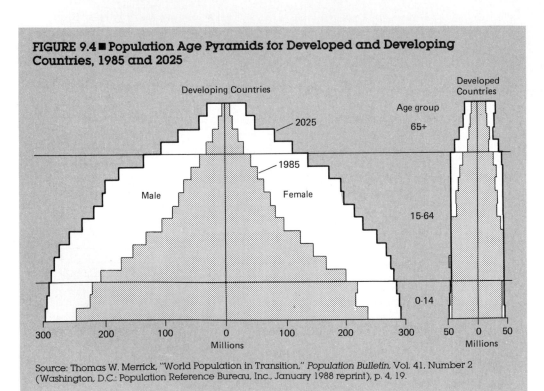

FIGURE 9.4 ■ Population Age Pyramids for Developed and Developing Countries, 1985 and 2025

Source: Thomas W. Merrick, "World Population in Transition," *Population Bulletin,* Vol. 41, Number 2 (Washington, D.C.: Population Reference Bureau, Inc., January 1988 reprint), p. 4, 19.

The consequences of population momentum for the world are illustrated in Figure 9.5. If the world were to reach the goal of replacement-level fertility around the year 2020, some seventy years later this would lead to a steady-state population of around eleven billion people. If replacement-level fertility were not reached by this time, of course, the world's ultimate population size would be much greater. Conversely, if replacement-level fertility could be reached earlier, the impact would be equally substantial. As Robert S. McNamara, former president of the World Bank, pointed out, "if the date at which replacement-level fertility is reached could be advanced from 2020 to 2000 . . . the ultimate population would be approximately 3 billion less, a number

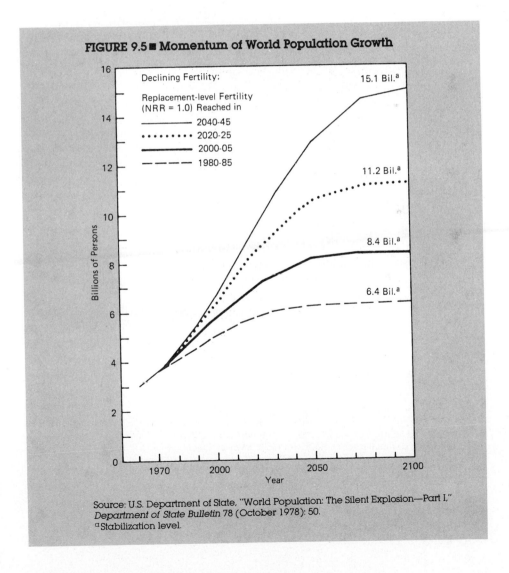

FIGURE 9.5 ■ Momentum of World Population Growth

Declining Fertility:

Replacement-level Fertility
(NRR = 1.0) Reached in
———————— 2040-45
• • • • • • • • 2020-25
━━━━━━ 2000-05
— — — — 1980-85

15.1 Bil.[a]

11.2 Bil.[a]

8.4 Bil.[a]

6.4 Bil.[a]

Billions of Persons

Year

1970　　2000　　2050　　2100

Source: U.S. Department of State, "World Population: The Silent Explosion—Part I," *Department of State Bulletin* 78 (October 1978): 50.
[a]Stabilization level.

equivalent to 75 percent of today's world total. This reveals in startling terms the hidden penalties of failing to act, and act immediately, to reduce fertility.''

The obvious question, then, is how to achieve replacement-level fertility. Important insights can be found in the demographic transition theory, which is the most widely accepted explanation of population changes over time.

The Demographic Transition Theory

The demographic transition theory seeks to explain the transition that Europe and later North America experienced between 1750 and 1930, when a condition of high birthrates combined with high death rates was replaced by a condition of low birthrates and low death rates. The transition started when death rates began to fall, presumably because of economic and social development and especially because of rising standards of living and improved control of disease. In such circumstances, the potential for substantial population growth was, of course, great. But then birthrates also began to decline, and during this phase population growth slowed. Such declines occur, according to the theory, because economic growth alters attitudes toward family size. In preindustrial societies, children are economic bonuses. As industrialization proceeds, children become economic burdens as they inhibit social mobility and capital accumulation.[4] The transition from large to small families, with the associated decline in fertility, is therefore usually assumed to arise in industrial and urban settings. This fourth stage in the demographic transition was achieved when both the birth and death rates reached very low levels. With fertility levels near the replacement level, the result was a very low rate of population growth, if any at all. The panel on the left in Figure 9.6 depicts the demographic transition experienced by most nations in the developed world.

By contrast, the panel on the right in Figure 9.6 makes clear that the developing nations have not yet experienced the rapidly falling birthrates following the extraordinarily rapid increase in life expectancy that occurred after World War II. In fact, the precipitous decline in death rates has largely been the result of more effective "death-control" measures introduced by the outside world.[5] The decline in the developing nations' death rates thus differs sharply from the long-term, slow declines that Europe and North America experienced. They have been the result of externally introduced and rapid

---

4. In the United States, for example, the cost of raising a child in an urban setting was estimated in the early 1980s to range from $83,000 to $93,000, depending on the region of the country (*Family Economics Review*, 4 [1983]: 30).

5. Sri Lanka is frequently cited as an example of the effect of public-health measures on the developing nations' death rates. Malaria and malaria-related diseases were a major cause of the historically high death rates in Sri Lanka, which in 1945 stood at twenty-two per one thousand. In 1946 the insecticide DDT was introduced in an effort to eradicate the mosquitoes that carry malaria. In a single year the death rate dropped 34 percent, and by 1955 it had declined to about half the 1945 level (Ehrlich et al., 1977: 197).

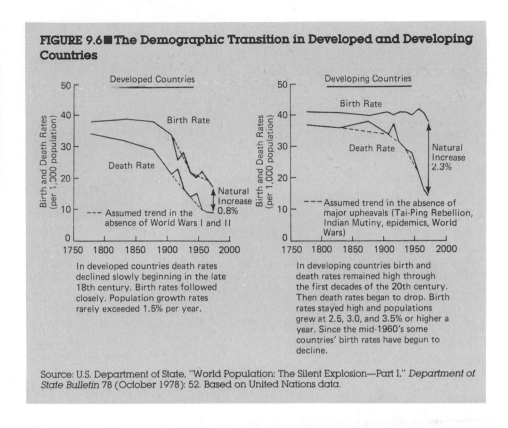

FIGURE 9.6■ The Demographic Transition in Developed and Developing Countries

In developed countries death rates declined slowly beginning in the late 18th century. Birth rates followed closely. Population growth rates rarely exceeded 1.5% per year.

In developing countries birth and death rates remained high through the first decades of the 20th century. Then death rates began to drop. Birth rates stayed high and populations grew at 2.5, 3.0, and 3.5% or higher a year. Since the mid-1960's some countries' birth rates have begun to decline.

Source: U.S. Department of State, "World Population: The Silent Explosion—Part I," *Department of State Bulletin* 78 (October 1978): 52. Based on United Nations data.

environmental changes rather than the fundamental and evolutionary changes that affect a nation's policies, institutions, or ways of life (Ehrlich et al., 1977). In particular, the developing nations have failed to record the more or less automatic decline in fertility rates that follows the decline in the rate of mortality that, according to the demographic transition theory, is assumed to be associated with economic development. A population "explosion" is the inevitable result.

Although developing countries have yet to move toward replacement-level fertility, demographers generally expect that this will happen. This is the assumption underlying the projections in Figures 9.1 and 9.2, which anticipate that the transition to low fertility and mortality will occur by the year 2025 and that fertility will decline to replacement level by 2040. Given the assumption, it is possible to foresee a stable global population of just over ten billion people early in the twenty-second century.

Projections so far into the future are inevitably subject to error for a number of reasons, not least of which is uncertainty about death rates. A large-scale conventional war or a limited nuclear war that could induce a climatic catastrophe through "nuclear winter" (see Sagan, 1983–1984), for example, could dramatically alter long-term population projections. A more populous world is also a more vulnerable one. Consider, for example, the difference in population density in Bangladesh and the state of Louisiana in the United States, two delta lands of similar size. Four and a half million people lived in Louisiana in 1986; 104 million populated Bangladesh. A natural disaster in Bangladesh—where typhoons are commonplace—carries a proportionately greater threat to life.

Death due to malnutrition and starvation may also affect the long-term growth of the world population. Twice in recent years, in the 1970s and again in the 1980s, broad stretches of the Sahel area in Africa experienced life-threatening drought and famine. Africa as a continent is also (for the time being) more threatened than others by AIDS (acquired immune deficiency syndrome), a mysterious, frightening, and fatal disease that threatens to become the plague of the twenty-first century, comparable to the Black Death of the Middle Ages.[6] The World Health Organization estimates that fifty thousand Africans have symptoms of AIDS and that another two million or more are infected with the virus (Harden, 1987: 16). The threat posed by the fatal disease knows no national boundaries and has in fact spread epidemically to virtually every quarter of the world. But it is a particular threat to Africa because "it appears to have spread among its limited pool of professional and technical elite. . . . AIDS could, in a sense, decapitate some African countries. The growing epidemic . . . aggravates an already severe shortage of skilled people and raises the prospect of economic, political and social disorder" (Harden, 1987; see also R. J. McCartney, 1987, for a discussion of the spread of AIDS to Western Europe).

Turning from deaths to births, the demographic transition theory, which is essentially based on the European experience prior to World War II, may be incomplete. It envisages four phases: (1) high birthrate, high death rate; (2) high birthrate, falling death rate; (3) declining birthrate, relatively low death rate; and (4) low birthrate, low death rate. The experience in Western Europe since the 1970s suggests a possible fifth phase: low death rate, declining birthrate. Some have called this Europe's "second" demographic transition (van de Kaa, 1987).

The total fertility rate in Europe during the past two decades has failed to stabilize at the replacement level (which is 2.1 births for every woman, roughly what is required for two children to replace two parents), as the demographic transition theory seems to predict. Instead, the total fertility rate for Western Europe as a whole stands at 1.8, with the highest rate in Ireland (2.6) and the lowest in West Germany (1.3) (in most of Africa, by comparison, it

---

6. In the words of John Platt (1987), "By the end of this century, AIDS could have the impact of a world war, producing recession and a stay-at-home society at the same time that it transforms world health and demographics." These dire predictions are the epigraph to Platt's article, "The Future of AIDS," part of a series begun in late 1987 in the World Future Society publication *The Futurist*.

is over 6) (*Population in Perspective*, 1986: 7). As a result, a secular decline of Europe's population has been set in motion. Put differently, a West German population half its current size is now in view. We shall return later to some of the policy implications associated with this startling fact.

A second puzzle that the theory of demographic transition does not solve applies to developing nations: some seem to be stuck somewhere between the second and third stages of the transition. In such widely separated places as Costa Rica, Korea, Sri Lanka, and Tunisia, for example, death rates have fallen to very low levels, but fertility rates seem to have stabilized well above the replacement level (Merrick, 1986). Perhaps the reason lies in the absence of change in social attitudes toward family size of the sort Europe and North America have experienced.

Changes in cultural attitudes toward limitations on family size have been shown to be an important ingredient in environments where social and economic improvements are taking place (Population Reference Bureau, 1981). Research also shows that the education and status of women in society combine to have a great influence on family size preferences.

Women who have completed primary school have fewer children than those with no education. Having an education usually means that women delay marriage, seek wage-paying jobs, learn about and have more favorable attitudes toward family planning, and have better communication with their husbands when they marry. Educated women have fewer infant deaths; high infant mortality is associated with high fertility. Similarly, when women have wage-paying jobs, they tend to have fewer children (and conversely, women with few children find it easier to work). Unfortunately, as women in developing countries attempt to move into the paid labor force, they will be competing with men for scarce jobs. (Population Reference Bureau, 1981: 5; see also *State of World Population 1985*, 1984)

Despite the questions that the demographic transition theory leaves unanswered and the puzzles that remain to be solved, the theory underscores the critical linkages between demographic changes and changes in the larger socioeconomic environment within which they occur. Government policies often seek to change the former through the latter.

In 1974, the United Nations sponsored a World Population Conference to address the population "problem," which essentially meant population growth in Third World countries. The lessons of the demographic transition theory informed the view of many of the delegates from the Third World. If declining fertility follows more or less automatically from improvements in the standard of living, the appropriate approach to the population problem is first to attack the problems of economic and social development that inhibit improvements in the quality of life. The population problem will then take care of itself. The slogan "development is the best contraceptive" reflects this view, which is consistent with the early European experience, when industrialization and the wealth it promoted coincided with rapid declines in fertility rates.

Other views were apparent among Third World countries, including, for example, various Marxist propositions that ascribed the lack of economic progress not to population growth but to the absence of equitable income distributions globally as well as nationally.

Many First World nations, on the other hand, sought a more direct attack on the population problem than the protracted solution implied by the "development is the best contraceptive" approach. Led by the United States, they conceded that economic development could contribute to declining fertility rates, but they advanced the view that the control of birthrates could itself substantially address the immediate problem and thereby contribute to subsequent economic development. The policy position was consistent with the emphasis on family planning programs placed until that time by the United States, other governments, international organizations, and various nongovernmental organizations (with U.S. support) through their foreign aid and development assistance programs.

A decade later, in 1984, a second World Population Conference was held in Mexico City. By that time a new consensus had emerged around the proposition that family planning could make an important contribution to the realization of other goals. Curiously, it was now the United States, previously a major advocate of this viewpoint, that found itself out of step with global sentiments. Reflecting the conservative political sentiments of the Reagan administration, the delegation from the United States adopted the general viewpoint that free-market principles ought to take precedence over government intervention in economic and population matters. It also vigorously opposed abortion as an approach to family-planning programs.

Although the views of the United States in 1984 were clearly in the minority, they reflected a growing sense of dissatisfaction with the conclusions and policy prescriptions of earlier analyses of the global ecopolitical implications of population growth, especially *The Limits to Growth*, published in 1974 by a private group known as the Club of Rome, and *The Global 2000 Report of the President*, published by the United States government in the last year of the Carter administration. Both came to be characterized as products of "growth pessimists." The position of the U.S. delegation in Mexico City, on the other hand, was consistent with that of "growth optimists" (see, for example, Simon, 1981; Simon and Khan, 1984), who criticized the earlier limits-to-growth analyses. They argued that the earlier models "ignore the role of markets in bringing population, resources, and the environment back into balance. . . . [Growth optimists] point out that human ingenuity has developed resource-saving (or substituting) inventions in response to shortages created by population growth. In their optimistic view, population growth is a stimulus, not a deterrent, to economic advancement" ("Global Population Trends," n.d.).

The debate between optimists and pessimists carries with it important policy implications. But as is often the case in dealing with complex social scientific questions, determining who is right is difficult. We can appreciate this by considering some of the correlates of these demographic changes.

CORRELATES OF DEMOGRAPHIC CHANGES

The composition and distribution of societies' populations significantly affect how demographic variables relate to other sociopolitical phenomena. For example, the high proportion of young people in developing countries places strains on certain social institutions, whereas the higher proportion of older people in the developed countries creates other problems.

Generally the impact of population growth on economic development is the most immediate and important question facing developing countries. In contrast, the main issues for developed nations tend to focus more on the impact of affluence on global resources and the global commons. The growing imbalance of the world population between the have and the have-not nations as played out in global patterns of emigration and immigration bridges the two viewpoints.

The Impact of Population Growth on Economic Development

Growth pessimists place considerable emphasis on the adverse effects of population growth on economic development. Clearly, population growth has contributed to the widening income gap between the world's rich nations and its poor (as discussed in Chapter 5). At the individual level, population growth also contributes to lower standards of living, as poor people tend to have more children to support than do those who are relatively better off. "Also, by depressing wages relative to rents and returns to capital, rapid population growth devalues what poor households have to sell—their labor. Property owners gain relative to wage earners when the labor force grows quickly" (Repetto, 1987).

It is also true, however, that "politics and economic policies influence the distribution of income within countries far more than population growth rates do" (Repetto, 1987). This fact lies close to what is emerging as the conventional view among demographers and development economists of the effects of population growth on economic development. Contrary to the view of growth pessimists, the emerging consensus casts population "not as the sole cause of underdevelopment, but an accomplice aggravating other existing problems" (*The New Population Debate*, 1985; see also *World Development Report 1984*, 1984, esp. chap. 5).

THE THIRD WORLD   Consider, for example, the relationship between the age structures of developing societies and other socioeconomic variables. In developing countries, dependent children (those younger than fifteen years old) typically comprise 40 to 45 percent of the total population (compared with 25 percent in the developed world). This means there is only about one working-age adult for each child under fifteen in the Third World, compared with nearly three working-age adults in the developed countries (U.S. Department of State, 1978b: 47). Such a large proportion of dependent children places a heavy burden on public services, particularly the educational system, and encourages the immediate consumption of economic resources rather than their reinvestment to promote future economic growth.

As these same children reach working age, they also contribute to the enormous unemployment and underemployment problems that the developing nations typically face. Yet countries whose populations grow faster than their economies do cannot absorb increasingly large numbers of working-age people into the productive mainstream of their societies. According to the International Labor Organization, "the total labor force of the Third World Countries will be 600 million to 700 million larger in the year 2000 than it was in 1980. To employ all those additional workers, the developing countries would have to create more jobs than now exist in Western Europe, Japan, the United States, the Soviet Union, and the other industrialized nations combined" (Fallows, 1983: 45).

The impact of rapid population growth on subsequent unemployment is dramatized further by the situation in Latin America, whose combined population in the early 1950s stood at about 150 million. It is projected to soar to 845 million by the year 2025. Half of the population of Latin America in 1983 was eighteen years old or younger and about to enter the labor force (Fallows, 1983: 45). This presents Latin America with a labor problem that is, in the words of Robert Fox of the Inter-American Development Bank, "intractable." "[The problem] is based on a population already born. Latin American countries would have to create an average of 4 million new jobs each year until 2025 [to accommodate the growth]. The U.S., with an economy five times larger, averages 2 million new jobs per year" (cited in Fallows, 1983: 45–46).

Furthermore, the search for jobs contributes to the rapid growth of already massive urban areas.

> Living in Mexico City, they say, gives you the pollution equivalent of forty cigarettes a day—that's just one person's share of the six thousand tons of gas and soot that fall daily on the sprawling metropolis.
> Why would anyone want to live there? The straight answer is the chance of a job in one of the 300,000 factories that belch out the smoke in the first place. They might not comply with the anti-pollution legislation, but they do obey the laws of supply and demand: people want work and factories want workers. ("State of World Population '82," 1982: 79)

Globally, urbanization is proceeding at a rapid pace, but increasingly the world's largest cities will be in the Third World. Thirty-eight percent of the world's people were estimated to be living in cities in 1983, a figure projected to reach 52 percent by the end of the century (Mayur, 1984: 22). Worldwide, by the year 2000 there will be fifty-eight cities of over five million people, compared with half that number in the early 1980s ("State of World Population '82," 1982: 79). More than half of these will be in the Third World, where a combination of natural growth and a desire to escape poverty in the countryside will fuel the expansion of the megalopolises. In many instances the estimated rates of growth and the numbers involved are astounding. Lagos, Nigeria, a city of 800,000 in 1960, will be a city of 9.4 million in 2000; Cairo, with 5.7 million inhabitants in 1970, will grow to more than 13 million by then; and Mexico City, with 10.9 million inhabitants in 1975, will become a massive urban center of some 31 million people.

Urbanization places added pressures on the need for expanded social services associated with rapid population growth, because urban development requires more investment in infrastructure than does rural development. It also increases the pressures on local agricultural systems, because there are fewer hands in the countryside to feed the growing number of mouths in the city. Urbanization thus contributes to the need to import food from abroad, thereby further straining already limited resources. And within the urban areas themselves, the often deplorable living conditions contain the seeds of social unrest and political turmoil. Already many urban areas are better termed agglomerations than cities, "where people, other than the urban elite and middle classes, are without adequate water, sanitation, health, education, and other social services; where people are often living five or six in a room, acutely aware of the great disparity in wealth and poverty about them. All this contributes to alienation and frustration on a massive scale" (U.S. Department of State, 1978b).

Ironically, as present trends unfold, Third World countries will bear not only the greatest burden of a burgeoning population of young people but also, eventually, of older people as the enormous number of today's youth grow to maturity and old age fifty years hence. Although the Third World today contains three-quarters of the world's people, it contains only half of those over sixty. By 2025, the population pyramid for developing regions shown in Figure 9.4 will begin to turn upside down because of declining birthrates and increased longevity, and the Third World will increase its share of the "gray generation" to three-quarters ("The Age of Aging," 1982: 82). It is a generation with which the advanced industrial societies of the West are beginning to grapple now.

THE FIRST WORLD   For developed countries, the move toward zero-population growth has resulted in a gradually aging society, as comparatively fewer babies are born and life expectancy increases. Some gerontologists (those who study aging and its consequences) have speculated that a gradually aging society will tend to be a more conservative one politically. Others have argued that the move toward zero-population growth will have untoward effects on the economic systems of advanced industrial societies, which seem to thrive on the growth in aggregate demand. There is evidence to refute both of these views (see Weller and Bouvier, 1981). But what is beyond dispute is that older people will increasingly comprise a social and potential political force worldwide: In 1975, there were only six countries with an over-sixty generation of more than ten million people; by 2025, there will be more than three times as many ("The Age of Aging," 1982: 82).

Already in developed nations, the proportionately larger number of older people has created a dependency problem that will be greatly magnified after the turn of the century. "The [International Labor Organization] predicts that there will be 270 million 'economically inactive' over 55-year olds in industrialized countries by 2020. That will mean 38 older dependents for every 100 workers—twice as many as in 1950" ("The Age of Aging," 1982: 84). More generally, by the year 2025 there will be a billion people over sixty—one person in seven, compared with only one in twelve in 1950, but there will be comparatively fewer people of working age to support them as a result of today's declining population growth rate. As we noted, Third World countries will experience the greatest increase in these numbers. North and South will thus face a common demographic problem: "Only by harnessing the skills of the elderly alongside the strength of the young can we prevent the aging [from] becoming an ever-increasing burden to us all" ("The Age of Aging," 1982).

Coping with a gradually aging population is a necessary consequence of the move toward zero-population growth. Providing for the increasing number of dependent elderly relative to the number of productive workers is already a matter of political concern in Europe, Japan, and North America, where fertility levels are already below replacement. In Western Europe in particular, two other concerns have joined with this one to form the basis of an intense political debate about the wisdom of pursuing pronatalist policies (designed to raise fertility) and the consequences of failing to do so. Much of the debate turns on questions of individual versus collective welfare (van de Kaa, 1987; see also Wattenberg, 1987).

Proponents of pronatalist measures are concerned with the "continued vitality of national populations that do not replace themselves: no children, no future, is the key phrase" (van de Kaa, 1987). National pride, concern for the nation's place among the world powers, and sensitivity to the vitality of European culture in a world where non-European countries grow much faster are also at issue. Military planners in the NATO alliance, for example, already worry about West Germany's ability to perform its critical role on the central front in the face of a diminishing pool of military manpower.

On the other hand, opponents of pronatalist measures "dismiss as exaggerated the specter of Europe as a decrepit society of ruminating octogenarians." They "attach no special value to their own cultures" and tend to oppose stimulating population growth in a world where this is already a serious problem. They believe that "economic resources rather than military resources or population size determine a country's international standing" and that "economic integration is a much more effective way to maintain Europe's international position than stimulating the birth rate." Finally, they question whether it makes sense to stimulate births when Europe already suffers from high levels of unemployment. "With modern technology eliminating jobs, workers are encouraged to work shorter hours, part-time, or retire early and immigration is halted," the argument continues, "so why should we have more people?" (van de Kaa, 1987).

The Impact of Population Growth on the Global Commons

The untoward effects of population growth on economic development often play themselves out through excessive pressures on natural resources and the desecration of the delicate life-support systems on which humankind depends. Worldwide, there is mounting evidence of rapid deforestation, desertification, and soil erosion (see *World Resources 1986*, 1986, esp. chap. 5). It is most acute where population growth and poverty are most apparent.

> Growing populations without access to farmland push cultivation into hillsides and tropical forests, with destructive effects on the soil. The demand for firewood is a primary reason for massive deforestation. Twenty percent of household income is spent on firewood in Addis Ababa. In the Gambia and Tanzania, wood has become so scarce that each household spends more than two-thirds of worker days per year gathering needed wood. (Murray, 1985: 10)

In the case of the Sahel in Africa, growing populations of livestock as well as humans hastened the conversion of productive land into a desert that ultimately led to famine (*The New Population Debate*, 1985). Nowhere is the tragedy of the commons illustrated more graphically.

The process of desertification demonstrates how overshoot of the carrying capacity of biological systems multiplies.

> Once the demand for fuelwood exceeds the sustainable yield of local forests, it not only reduces tree cover but also leads to soil erosion and land degradation. When grasslands deteriorate to where they can no longer support cattle, livestock herders often take to lopping foliage from trees, thus putting even more pressure on remaining tree cover. Both contribute to a loss of protective vegetation, without which both wind and water erosion of soil accelerate, leading to desertification—a sustained decline in the biological productivity of land.
>
> A decline in the diversity of plant and animal communities marks the onset of desertification. This in turn leads to a reduction of soil organic matter, a decline in soil structure, and a loss of water retention capacity. It also lowers soil fertility, reduced further by increasing wind and water erosion. Typically the end result is a desert: a skeletal shell of soil consisting almost entirely of sand and lacking in the fine particles and organic matter that make soil productive. (Brown et al., 1987: 26)

According to Lester Brown and his associates at the Washington-based Worldwatch Institute,

> In countries where rates of population growth remain high, a three-stage "ecological transition" emerges that is almost the reverse of the demographic transition in that its end result is disastrous. In the first stage, expanding human demands are well within the sustainable yield of the biological support system. In the second, they are in excess of the sustainable yield but still expanding as the biological resource itself is being consumed. And in the final stage, human consumption is forcibly reduced as the biological system collapses. (Brown et al., 1987: 26–27)

Excessive population growth doubtlessly strains the environment and contributes to destruction of the global commons. But so does excessive consumption. In this respect it is not the poverty-stricken, growing masses of the South who place the greatest strains on the global habitat, but the affluent, consumption-oriented minority in the North, where one person consumes forty times what the average person in Somalia consumes. The United States heads the list; comprising but 5 percent of the world's population, Americans consume 40 percent of world resources every year ("Global Population Trends," n.d.: 3). Consider the following: "Every 7 1/2 seconds a new American is born. He is a disarming little thing, but he begins to scream loudly in a voice that can be heard for seventy years. He is screaming for 26,000,000 tons of water, 21,000 gallons of gasoline, 10,150 pounds of meat, 28,000 pounds of milk and cream, 9,000 pounds of wheat, and great storehouses of all other foods, drinks, and tobacco. These are the lifetime demands on his country and its economy." (Rienow and Rienow, 1967: 3)

The disproportionate impact of the world's rich is especially apparent in the demands they place on global supplies of food and energy. We shall therefore examine these issues later in this chapter and in the next. Here we shall note only briefly some of the issues related to the global commons that are linked to the energy-intensive, consumption-oriented life-styles of those making up the First World.

One is deforestation. In the South it is occurring as expanding populations search for fuelwood. In West Germany and elsewhere in Europe it is occurring for reasons that remain uncertain, but the belief is that chemical changes in the atmosphere are responsible for killing the forests (see Postel, 1986).

Acid rain is a common atmospheric consequence of burning fossil fuels. The burning of coal in particular produces sulphur and nitrogen oxides in the atmosphere which, after traveling long distances, return to the earth in rain or snow, thus contributing to the acidification of lakes, the corrosion of materials and structures, and the impairment of ecosystems. Acid rain has fallen in measurable amounts in the Scandinavian countries, the United States, and Canada. In recent years Canada has alleged that it suffers adversely from the failure of the United States to curb atmospheric pollution, which causes the acid rain that kills aquatic life and damages crops and forests in Canada.

The burning of fossil fuels has produced another environmental condition known as the *greenhouse effect*. Combustion, especially the burning of coal, releases carbon dioxide into the atmosphere. As the concentration of carbon dioxide increases, it could cause the average temperature of the earth's surface to rise by several degrees, with an even greater increase in the now-frigid polar regions. In a controversial study released in 1983, the U.S. Environmental Protection Agency (EPA, 1983) projected that the climatic changes associated with the greenhouse effect would begin to be felt as early as 1990. Eventually, shifts in the world's climatic patterns could have political, social, and economic consequences, as the world's traditional food-producing areas are affected, its rainfall patterns are altered, and its coastal waters rise. Disturbingly, the EPA report concluded that even a total ban on the burning of fossil fuels would do little more than delay the inevitable warming effect.

First World countries have also contributed disproportionately to the destruction of the ozone layer that protects the earth from dangerous, cancer-producing ultraviolet rays from the sun. The damage occurs when artificial chemicals known as chlorofluorocarbons are released into the atmosphere. The chemicals are widely used in refrigerators and air conditioners as refrigerants, in styrofoam cups, in cleansers for computer components, and as aerosol propellants for such things as deodorants. Currently, nearly a million tons of the destructive chemicals are released into the atmosphere every year, where they can remain active for more than a century (*The Inter Dependent*, October–November, 1987, p. 1). Recognizing the problem, a major agreement was concluded among twenty-four nations in 1987, whose purpose is to reduce drastically the amount of the dangerous chemicals released into the atmosphere.

Other examples of environmental stress associated with affluence can be added to this brief list. They include soil erosion caused by the expansion of energy-intensive, mechanized agriculture to marginal lands; water shortages caused by the massive requirements of modern agriculture, industry, and residential living; and depletion of ocean fisheries caused by technology-intensive overfishing and pollution of spawning beds. Together they reinforce a fundamental point: The belief that there are "too many people" ultimately has meaning only in relation to something else, such as the availability of food and renewable and nonrenewable resources and pressures on the global commons. Measured against any of these yardsticks, it is not the world's less-developed nations of the South that exert the greatest demands and pressures on the global carrying capacity; it is the advanced industrialized societies of the North.

Global Patterns of Emigration and Immigration

Fertility, mortality, and migration are the three basic demographic variables that determine all population alterations. Migration has been especially important, indeed, an increasing source of concern in Europe, the Middle East, and the United States, and, promises to become even more so as population growth in the Third World over the next several decades creates pressures toward outward movement. Major cultural changes can be expected in the receiving countries of the North where fertility levels are already below the replacement level, with the result that a larger proportion of their populations in the future will be made up of recent immigrants from nations culturally different from their descendants.

Immigration is now the primary demographic variable in U.S. population growth. With fertility in the United States below the replacement level since the early 1970s, immigration accounted for more than a quarter of the nation's population growth between 1980 and 1985, and the proportion is growing (Bouvier and Gardner, 1986: 4). Even more important is the dramatic shift in the origins of the immigrants over the past two decades.

> Europeans made up 90 percent of immigrants 100 years ago when the Statue of Liberty was dedicated and more than half still in 1965 when a new influx was prompted by the law change that lowered barriers that had been based largely on race. Only 11 percent of the 570,000 legal immigrants recorded in 1985 came from Europe. Asians accounted for 46 percent of the legal total and Latin Americans—mainly Mexicans and almost all Spanish-speaking—made up 37 percent. (Bouvier and Gardner, 1986: 4)

In addition to legal immigrants, the United States has absorbed large numbers of illegal immigrants, variously estimated to be somewhere between 200,000 and 500,000 per year, most of whom entered through Mexico.

Migrants are of two types: political refugees who move because of threats to their convictions or fear for their lives and those who move for economic reasons. The United Nations High Commission for Refugees keeps tabs on about eleven million refugees worldwide, a number that more than doubled in less than a decade (*New York Times*, February 16, 1986, p. E3). More than half are concentrated in the Middle East, and about a third are in Africa. Refugees are often by-products of war. For example, many of the Asian immigrants to the United States in the early 1980s were victims of the Vietnam War. Political turmoil and civil strife in El Salvador, Nicaragua, Guatemala, and elsewhere in Central America and the Caribbean have caused an influx of migrants from these areas.

Other than refugees, migrants, both domestically and internationally, typically are in search of a better standard of living and way of life. Internationally, migrants are often willing to take jobs in faraway lands shunned by local people. Typically this means they earn less than the natives do but more than they would earn in their homelands, even doing the same thing. From the point of view of the host countries, migrants often are welcomed, not only because they are paid low wages for tasks that natives do not want to perform, but also because the country accepting migrants pays little if anything for their health, education, and welfare needs.[7] The home countries for their part sometimes encourage people to emigrate as a way of reducing unemployment and because migrants can be counted on to return considerable portions of their income to their families at home.

Although the United States is a nation born of immigrants, public attitudes in recent years have clearly indicated a preference for limiting the number of legal immigrants and preventing the influx of illegal aliens into the country. Such attitudes reflect a growing concern about the impact of immigrants on traditional American values, not unlike that raised in Europe in the context of the debate over the wisdom of pursuing pronatalist government policies.

In Europe, immigrants came to be especially important after World War II when they provided much of the unskilled labor needed to assist in reconstruction. Others migrated from former colonies, notably the British Commonwealth, to settle in the "mother" country. The mid-1970s was the peak of the "guest worker" era, when one of every seven manual workers in Germany and Britain was a migrant, as were a quarter of those in France, Belgium, and Switzerland (Barnet, 1980b: 56). However, with unemployment now the primary economic problem in Europe, migrants are no longer as welcome. In West Germany, for example, where the government once offered incentives to entice foreigners to emigrate to the Federal Republic and which in the early 1980s was the home of some four million guest workers, the government now offers incentives to leave. Many, however, in Germany and elsewhere, prefer to stay but have found assimilation into the local society and culture difficult. Clashes between Germans and Turks, between Britons and Indians and Pakistanis, and between French people and migrants from North Africa are recurrent (*Population in Perspective*, 1986).

The Middle East is also the scene of migrant-related tensions. Here oil money attracted foreigners, where in many of the receiving countries they now constitute two-thirds of the labor force (*Population in Perspective*, 1986: 27). Many came from other Arab countries, but large numbers also came from outside the region, mainly from India, Pakistan, Thailand, and South Korea. Echoing a now familiar theme, there is concern for the impact of non-natives on Arab culture and religion, but here the large majority of aliens who are not citizens can never hope to be. The question is whether foreigners will be able to stay in the oil-rich countries as revenues from oil recede. The question portends controversy among the nations and peoples concerned.

---

7. Foreign workers are also likely to be the first victims of bad economic conditions. In early 1983, for example, Nigeria expelled upwards of two million foreign workers. The official reason was the alleged involvement of alien workers in bloody religious riots that earlier had rocked sections of the country. But others viewed the expulsion as a response to the growing unemployment problem in Nigeria, as its economic development projects were curtailed following the loss of oil revenues caused by the worldwide oil glut of the early 1980s (see *Washington Post*, January 31, February 2, and February 4, 1983).

The foregoing demonstrates how critical international immigration has become to today's transforming global political economy. In many Northern nations in particular, migration, not population growth, is *the* population problem. Nevertheless, the two problems are linked and promise to become inseparably so as environmental degradation and lost economic opportunities in the South arising from a rapidly expanding population prompt the search for a better way of life in the North.

THE TRANSFORMATION OF THE GLOBAL FOOD REGIME

A green revolution, wars on hunger, and a flotilla of ships carrying "food for peace" have failed to win the battle against world hunger. According to the World Bank, half a billion people in the poorest countries of Africa, Asia, and Latin America suffer from chronic undernourishment. The problem goes far beyond the sporadic pictures of starving babies on the evening news. Famine victims can be aided in the short term by infusions of emergency food aid. Victims of chronic hunger are not so easily helped.

Such hunger is not caused by worldwide food shortages. In fact, the world is awash in unsold grain. Spectacular and continuing advances in agricultural research have helped to transform countries once dependent on food aid into net exporters. Yet mass hunger persists. Poor people and poor nations in much of the world are unable either to purchase the surplus food stored throughout the world or to produce adequate food for themselves. (Spivack and Florini, 1986: 1–2)

The foregoing statement summarizes the key parameters defining the current global food situation. The elements warrant repeating: Chronic hunger still exists; it persists in the face of dramatic advances in agricultural productivity; it persists despite international efforts designed to alleviate food shortages; it persists even in otherwise poor countries that have become net exporters of food; and it persists in a world awash in grain. We shall touch on all of these elements in the remaining sections of this chapter, when we examine the factors giving rise to the current situation and the way in which national and international factors have combined to propel the transformation of the global food regime.

Population Growth and Food Supplies

The gloomiest of Thomas Malthus's predictions made nearly two centuries ago was that the world's population would eventually outstrip its capacity to produce enough food to sustain its growing numbers. Malthus's prognosis was based on what he regarded as the simple mathematical fact that population grows exponentially, whereas agricultural output grows only arithmetically.

What Malthus did not foresee was that agricultural output would also grow at an increasing rate, largely as a consequence of technological innovations.

Increases in the world's food output have been particularly impressive since World War II. In the thirty-five years from 1950 to 1985, world grain harvests increased from less than 750 million tons to 1.7 billion tons (O'Brien, 1988: 395). Even though the world experienced unprecedented population growth during this period, the growth in food production was so spectacular that it permitted a 25 percent increase in per-capita food supplies and a corresponding increase in meeting minimum nutritional standards (O'Brien, 1988: 395).

The greatest increases in food production occurred as a result of the increased productivity of farmers in the developed world, but impressive gains were also recorded in many countries of the Third World as a result of expanding acreage devoted to agriculture and, later, the Green Revolution (the introduction of new high-yield strains of wheat and rice) in such countries as Mexico, the Philippines, India, Indonesia, Pakistan, and Bangladesh. As a consequence, by the 1980s, Indonesia, once a massive importer of food, had largely been removed from the import market, and India, once regarded as a permanent candidate for the international dole, had actually become a modest grain exporter.

Despite these impressive gains, however, increases in the per-capita availability of food have been spread unevenly. In the developing nations, the increased output per person continues to lag behind that of the developed nations. Figure 9.7 records the different experiences of North and South. Among the former, increases in per-capita food production since the 1950s have generally moved upward in tandem with increases in total food production, but among the latter—whose percentage increases in total food production have actually been greater than the developed world's—per-capita food production throughout the past several decades has generally lagged behind. The difference between total and per-capita production of food is what is eaten up in population growth. Moreover, even in countries where the Green Revolution has produced spectacular gains in food production, its rewards are often distributed quite unevenly (R. Hopkins et al., 1982; Wolf, 1986).

Nowhere does Malthus's grim prediction that population growth would outstrip food production appear more apt than in Africa. During the 1970s, Africa's food production increased by only 1.8 percent annually, but its population grew at a rate of 2.8 percent. Per-capita food production actually declined in thirty-five African countries during the decade and increased in only six ("Food 1983," 1983: 72). Starvation and death became daily occurrences in broad stretches of the Sahel, ranging from Ethiopia in the east to Mauritania in the west. The situation was repeated a decade later, when in Ethiopia in particular, world consciousness was awakened by the tragic specter of tens of thousands suffering from malnutrition and dying of famine at a time of unprecedented food surpluses worldwide. The lives of some 35 mil-

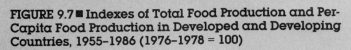

FIGURE 9.7 ■ Indexes of Total Food Production and Per-Capita Food Production in Developed and Developing Countries, 1955–1986 (1976–1978 = 100)

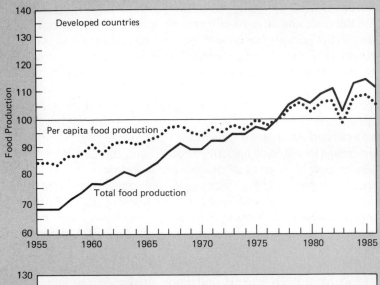

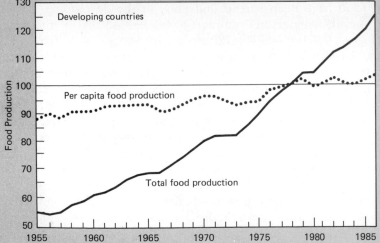

Source: Data for 1955–1979 adapted from *World Indices of Agricultural and Food Production, 1975–85* (Washington, D.C. U.S. Department of Agriculture, 1985), pp. 12–17. Data for 1980–1986 adapted from *World Food Needs and Availabilities, 1987/88* (Washington, D.C.: U.S. Department of Agriculture, 1987), p. 13.

lion were in danger during the famine of 1983–1985; 10 million "fled from their homes, farms, and countries in search of food and water"; and an estimated million died (Spivack and Florini, 1986: 23).

Population growth and environmental degradation are critical factors explaining the continuing human tragedy in Africa. Indeed, Africa is a clear instance in which the tragedy of the commons has been played out in all of its most tragic manifestations. But intranational and international conflict also reinforce and contribute to the continent's problems. A third of the countries in sub-Saharan Africa have been ravaged by continuing civil unrest and major armed conflict in recent years. In all, perhaps 90 million people have been affected by conflict and drought (Spivack and Florini, 1986: 20–21). Moreover, there is clear evidence that food has become a weapon in Africa's civil conflicts. In Ethiopia, for example, both the government and Eritrean rebel forces wage battle for the peasantry with the promise of food (Harden, 1988). In the words of Shun Chetty of the United Nations High Commission for Refugees, "He who controls roads controls food. He who controls food controls the people."

Africa has also suffered because of its position in the global political economy. The decline of commodity prices worldwide, discussed in Chapter 8, has severely affected Africa, because many African countries are among those that depend most on commodity exports to generate foreign exchange earnings. Many African nations also suffer from a crushing debt burden. The result is that Africa has become a continent of acute concern. "Bleak for the remainder of the decade" is the way that a 1985 U.S. Central Intelligence Agency report put it, in characteristic bureaucratic understatement.

What makes the African dilemma of special concern to policymakers is that the policies of both African and Western governments may have contributed to it. African governments promoted policies that kept food prices low so as to promote domestic tranquility and prevent political turmoil but that in turn reduced farmers' incentives to produce food and encouraged migration from farms to cities. Western countries contributed to the problem by providing food imports at subsidized prices.

Ensuring Global Food Security

Africa's food needs (and the reasons for them) have come to be a special concern, but as the foregoing makes clear, Africa's problems are not solely domestic in nature but also have to do with its place in the larger global food regime. Ensuring global food security has become a goal of the world community, and the attention it has received, though varied, attests to the importance of food as an issue on the global agenda.

Food security is usefully defined as the "access by all people at all times to enough food for an active, healthy life."

Its essential elements are the availability of food and the ability to acquire it. Conversely, food insecurity is the lack of access to sufficient food and can be either chronic or transitory. Chronic food insecurity is a continuously inadequate diet resulting from the lack of resources to produce or acquire food. Transitory food insecurity, on the other hand, is a temporary decline in a household's access to enough food. It results from instability in food production and prices, or in household incomes. The worst form of transitory food insecurity is famine. (Reutlinger, 1985: 7)

Achieving food security became an item on the North–South agenda during the 1970s when at about the same time as the first OPEC-induced oil crisis, the ability of the multitude of nationally based agricultural systems to produce sufficient food for the world's growing billions was severely challenged.

The particulars surrounding the food crisis of the 1970s, which saw world grain reserves (defined in terms of days of worldwide grain consumption) drop from over a hundred days in 1968 to only forty days in 1974 (Sewell, 1980: 178), included a series of weather-induced crop failures in China, the Soviet Union, and Africa; the boost in oil prices that added to the cost of fuel and fertilizer used in agricultural production; and the decision of the Soviet Union to enter world grain markets in an unprecedented way to make up for shortfalls previously absorbed by the Soviet economy. The combined impact of all of these factors was a 300 percent increase in the price of grain in the face of what worldwide was only a 3 percent shortfall in grain production (Sewell, 1979: 60–61). The result was that "rising food prices added as much to . . . global inflation as did rising petroleum costs" (Sewell, 1979). It was in this context that Africa was struck with the first of the two famines it would face in the 1970s and 1980s.

In addition to those suffering transitory food insecurity, as were many during the African famines, the Food and Agriculture Organization of the United Nations estimated in 1974, at the time of the World Food Conference in Rome, that 460 million people in the developing world suffered from malnutrition, a number that grew by 1980 to perhaps 730 million (Reutlinger, 1985: 7).[8] These—about two-thirds of whom live in South Asia and another fifth in sub-Saharan Africa—are among the victims of chronic food insecurity because they do not have incomes sufficient to buy food, even if it is available. The victims of chronic food insecurity have probably declined as a proportion of

---

8. Malnutrition refers to a deficiency in the *quality* of food eaten, that is, in its protein, vitamin, and mineral content. It is often difficult to distinguish malnutrition from undernutrition, which implies a deficiency in the *quantity* of food eaten measured in terms of calories. Hence, the term *protein-energy malnutrition* is sometimes used to refer to both undernutrition and malnutrition (Food and Agriculture Organization, n.d.). Malnutrition—particularly in the form of protein deficiency in infancy—can lead to permanent brain damage as well as retard normal growth and invite debilitating disease. The physical problems persist often after the food deficiency is corrected; permanently disabled people are left to then propagate still another generation of malnourished and disabled children.

the total population in developing countries, but their numbers have increased owing to population growth (Reutlinger, 1985).

Poverty is an important cause of the perpetuation of millions of chronically hungry people in a world of plenty. According to the microeconomic principle known as Engel's law, poorer families typically spend a much greater percentage of their budget on food than do higher-income groups. Thus, as Richard Barnet (1980a) has observed, "Most people who stop eating do so not because there is insufficient food grown in the world but because they no longer grow it themselves and do not have the money to buy it." This is what is meant by the concept of *effective demand*, which says that the ability to acquire more food depends on having the income necessary to buy more food. Many people in the developing countries simply are not capable of registering an effective demand for food because they do not have the purchasing power necessary to secure an adequate diet.

Given the causes of widespread chronic food insecurity, addressing its deleterious effects requires more than simply increasing food production or imports. It requires attacking the very causes of poverty. As one analyst put it: "Social, political, and economic forces working outside agriculture skew income distribution across and within countries and in the process skew food-buying power. Without faster, broader-based economic growth to boost income and buying power, as many as 1 to 1.5 billion people could be locked out of sharing in future food gains" (O'Brien, 1988: 408).

Another factor coloring the early 1970s' world food picture was a change in the growth pattern of the world's supply of fish. Fish had by then become an important ingredient in the world food supply, particularly protein consumption. Between 1950 and 1970 the world's fish catch increased steadily at an average annual rate of 5 percent, far in excess of the population growth during this period. Then in 1970, after reaching an annual catch level of 70 million tons, these trends were abruptly reversed, and the world's fish catch stabilized at sixty-five million to seventy million tons annually.

Overfishing results from the technology-intensive fishing methods used by some countries, notably the Soviet Union and Japan, for whom fish are an important dietary component, and is a major factor contributing to the deterioration of the world's fish catch and its fisheries. The stabilization of the fish catch is not due to any lessening of demands on fisheries but because the maximum sustainable yield of many table-grade fish has been reached or exceeded. The result is a classic illustration of the tragedy of the commons.

Catch of species such as cod, halibut, herring, anchovy, and the California sardine have dropped dramatically because not enough fish were left to regenerate the stock for the future. Depletion of these fisheries came about for essentially the same reasons that the herdsmen added cattle to an already overgrazed pasture in Hardin's English village. Operators of fishing fleets receive all of the profits from the sale of their catch while dividing the costs associated with overfishing with all others harvesting the same fishery. Further, fugitives that they are, fish passed up by one fleet in the interests of conservation are likely to turn up in the nets of others, who as free riders continue to deplete the fishery. (Soroos, 1988: 349)

Fortunately, in the case of the world's fisheries there is some reason for optimism. The United Nations Convention on the Law of the Sea, adopted in 1982, resolved a host of issues relating to the management of the world's fisheries. Coastal states now impose two-hundred-mile exclusive economic and fishing zones in which they determine the sustainable fish catch. Within these zones they take what they want and then parcel out the remainder to foreign fishing vessels. The global fishing regime is thus effectively moving toward a managed commons arrangement in which short-term benefits and long-term costs are more nearly matched for everyone.

Development of a Global Market

Population growth is one of the principal forces driving the increased demand for food; wealth is another.[9] It is important in part because of the demand it generates for agricultural products on which many Third World nations depend to earn the foreign exchange needed to buy capital equipment or other goods from abroad. Frequently these export products are dietary supplements for people in wealthier countries.

> This has a number of important consequences. First, many export products such as sugar, tea, coffee, cocoa and sisal, have limited nutritional value, and hence cannot be directly "diverted" from the international marketplace to meet pressing domestic needs. Second, there are limited internal markets for most traditional export crops, and larger domestic markets are unlikely to develop until income increases. To the extent that internal markets develop, they are most likely to reflect the tastes of the wealthier portions of the domestic population. Such patterns of export agriculture can easily lead to a sharp and direct trade-off between foreign exchange earnings . . . and the production of basic foodstuffs. (Christensen, 1978: 758–759)

The tragic irony is that cash crops are often exported at the same time that domestic food needs are unmet.

Wealth also affects dietary habits. As personal income rises, individuals tend to move away from the direct consumption of grain and toward its indirect consumption, with substantial increases in beef and poultry consumption most evident. Thus, as global patterns of grain consumption indicate, one

---

9. The Food and Agriculture Organization (n.d.: 14) estimates that population growth accounts for 70 percent of the increase in the demand for food in the developing countries, but only 55 percent in the developed countries. Rising incomes account for the remaining portions.

of the characteristics of social and economic development is that people climb the *food ladder* as well:

> In the poorer countries the average person can get only about 180 kilograms of grain per year—about a pound per day. With so little to go around, nearly all grain must be consumed directly if minimal energy needs are to be met. But as incomes rise, so do grain consumption levels. In the wealthier industrial societies such as the United States and the Soviet Union, the average person consumes four-fifths of a ton of grain per year. Of this, only 90 to 140 kilograms is eaten directly as bread, pastries, and breakfast cereals; most is consumed indirectly as meat, milk, and eggs.
>
> In effect, wealth enables individuals to move up the biological food chain. Thus, the average Russian or American uses roughly four times the land, water, and fertilizer used by an Indian, a Colombian, or a Nigerian. (Brown, 1978: 134)

The changing consumption patterns described by the food ladder concept have had an important impact on the overall food picture since World War II. "While fewer than 200 million people had made the transition to diets with a quarter or more of their calories from livestock products by the mid-1950s, more than 600 million people had made the transition by the early 1980s. An added 650 million consumers in the middle-income countries had also begun the transition" (O'Brien, 1988: 398). Whether the world will be able to sustain a similar transition up the food ladder for billions more in the future is, however, problematic.

The ability of people in various parts of the world to move from the direct to the indirect consumption of grain via poultry and livestock was made possible in part by the emergence of a global food market. As shown in Figure 9.8, world trade in food products actually increased more rapidly in the decades following World War II than did food production itself. Correspondingly, the world divided into two types: net food exporters, of which until recently there were a declining number, and net food importers, whose numbers have grown dramatically.[10] Eventually North America became both the "breadbasket" and the "feedbag" for virtually the entire world. By 1980, Latin America, Western Europe, Eastern Europe and the Soviet Union, Africa, and Asia all had become net importers of grain (see Table 9.1). Australia and New Zealand were alone among the non–North American world regions in being net exporters. The Soviet Union and several of the Newly Industrialized Countries registered sharp increases in both wheat imports and coarse grains, whereas most First World countries increased only their imports of feed grains (Food and Agriculture Organization, 1982; Hathaway, 1983). In all cases, how-

---

10. Three cereals—wheat, rice, and corn—make up the bulk of cereal production in the world, with a number of minor grains, such as oats, rye, barley, millet, and soybeans, making up the remainder. Of the three most important cereals, wheat and corn are the principal export products.

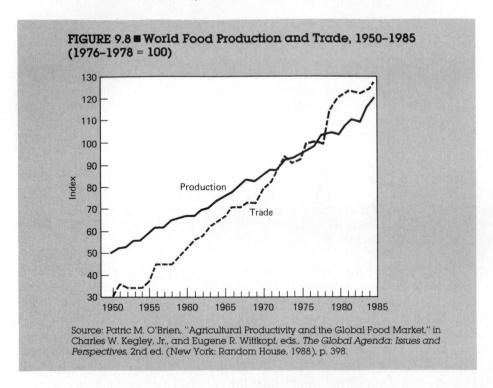

FIGURE 9.8 ■ World Food Production and Trade, 1950–1985 (1976–1978 = 100)

Source: Patric M. O'Brien, "Agricultural Productivity and the Global Food Market," in Charles W. Kegley, Jr., and Eugene R. Wittkopf, eds., *The Global Agenda: Issues and Perspectives,* 2nd ed. (New York: Random House, 1988), p. 398.

ever, food imports permitted the enhancement of both the quality and variety of the importing nations' dietary intake.

As the world came to depend on Canada and the United States to meet its food needs, North American farmers enjoyed an unprecedented level of export-led prosperity. Furthermore, their future looked bright, as present and projected economic growth trends forecast a vastly increased world demand for food between 1980 and the year 2000 as well as sharply higher real food prices. *The Global 2000 Report to the President* (1980a, 1980b), based on the best projections of the United States government, advanced such forecasts. *Global 2000* also warned that the projected demand for food would require substantial increases in Third World agricultural productivity. And although ecologists worried that the projected demand would result in environmentally hazardous soil erosion and deforestation and outstrip the ability of improved farm technology to meet the increase in demand, for North American farmers the future was bright, not gloomy.

This situation changed radically in only a half-decade. As described by an agricultural analyst in the U.S. Department of State, "the world of the American farmer lies in disarray, with mounting surpluses, heavy farm debt, and massive farm subsidy costs. Demand for U.S. farm products is weak, land values are down, and farm policy seems to be at a dead end" (Avery, 1985). The reasons underlying "the bad news for the American farmer," he continued, "is

TABLE 9.1 ■ World Net Grain Trade by Regions, 1950–1986 (million metric tons)

Region	1950	1960	1970	1980	1985	1986
North America	23	39	56	131	103	102
Latin America	1	0	4	– 10	1	– 4
Western Europe	– 22	– 25	– 30	– 16	11	14
U.S.S.R. and Eastern Europe	0	0	0	– 46	– 35	– 37
Africa	0	– 2	– 5	– 15	– 29	– 22
Asia	– 6	– 17	– 37	– 63	– 72	– 73
Australia and New Zealand	3	6	12	20	21	20

Source: Lester R. Brown, Edward C. Wolf, Linda Starke, William U. Chandler, Christopher Flavin, Cynthia Pollock, Sandra Postel, and Jodi Jacobson, *State of the World 1987* (New York: Norton, 1987), p. 46. Data for 1985 are from Lester R. Brown, Edward C. Wolf, Linda Starke, William U. Chandler, Christopher Flavin, Sandra Postel, and Cynthia Pollock, *State of the World 1986* (New York: Norton, 1986), p. 16.

Note: Data for 1985 and 1986 are preliminary.

that the global bad news is wrong. The world is not on the brink of famine or ecological disaster brought on by desperate food needs.'' The ecological and other ''constraints that were expected to limit food production during the 1980's and 1990's have been far less severe than almost anyone foresaw,'' whereas the productivity of farmers in the developing nations has grown rapidly in response to ''improved technology and stronger incentives to use it'' (Avery, 1985). Additional near-term constraints that eroded the export competitiveness of American agricultural products included the rise in the value of the dollar, global economic recession, and increased competition from others. The result was a sharp decline in the value and volume of U.S. agricultural exports (see Table 9.1).

The most spectacular increases in productivity since the late 1970s have occurred in China, which has become the world's second largest food producer. In 1978 the Chinese government shifted from a commune-organized to a market-based agricultural system that offered more financial incentives to farmers to produce. The reform seems to have been the missing piece in China's agricultural puzzle:

> From 1978 to 1984 grain production rose by nearly 5 percent a year (from 1957–78 grain output had risen at an annual rate of about 2 percent), cotton production almost tripled, and China reversed its position on the world market to become an overall exporter of several agricultural products. The real gains, though, have been accrued by the rural population through substantial increases in farm income. (Spivack and Florini, 1986: 34)

In terms of competition in the export market, the most important change in recent years has been the emergence of the European Community, notably

France, as a net food exporter. The development is clearly a product of the European Community's Common Agricultural Policy (CAP), which subsidizes farm production by maintaining product prices above world levels. The United States pursues similar "production-oriented" policies, which have the effect of encouraging farmers to produce as much as possible. In fact, as noted in Chapter 7, the European Community in 1986 spent two-thirds of its budget on agricultural subsidies, and the United States' expenditures on farm support programs exceeded the net income of its farmers (Wallis, 1986: 2). Food surpluses have been the predictable result. Thus Europe now exports many of the products that only recently it imported. Like the United States, it also stockpiles production that cannot be sold. A world awash in (unsold) grain is a second predictable result.

With the addition of Western Europe to the roster of food exporters and the removal of China and India from the list of major food importers, the global food regime in the late 1980s finds three geographic regions still dependent on imported grain, much of it from North America: Asia (other than China and India), Africa, and Eastern Europe and the Soviet Union. Interestingly, the Soviet Union, which previously entered the international grain market only to make up temporary shortfalls in Soviet agricultural production, now appears likely to remain a food importer, with Argentina a major supplier. The need to import is the result of continuing mismanagement of the Soviet agricultural system and the apparent inability of its planned approach to agricultural production to meet the demands of Soviet citizens for a better and more varied diet (see Brown, 1982).

As in the Soviet Union, food imports are needed elsewhere to feed growing urban populations. Leningrad, Moscow, Cairo, Lagos, Dacca, and Hong Kong all depend on food imports to feed their millions (Brown et al., 1987). The dependence of these large and growing urban agglomerations on imported food has forged an unlikely transnational political alliance between food producers and consumers. Because Third World urban dwellers are typically more influential politically than are their rural counterparts, urban residents form a kind of de facto political alliance with Northern food producers that, on the one hand, demonstrates the interconnectedness of the global political economy but that, on the other hand, has helped produce "a world food system less stable than could otherwise be imagined" (Paarlberg, 1982). As noted earlier, in many food-producing countries of the North, farm prices have been subsidized, resulting in an artificial stimulation of production, whereas in many Southern countries, farm prices have been maintained at artificially low levels, which reduces production incentives. "By controlling the food policies of their respective governments, a powerful minority in the North (rural producers) has joined in a curious alliance with a powerful minority in the South (urban consumers), the result being a 'North-to-South' flow of food that misrepresents production efficiencies and drags against the urgent task of agricultural development in poor countries" (Paarlberg, 1982). Nowhere is the impact of domestic politics on the global food regime more apparent.

Toward the Future: National and International Responses to Global Challenges

Viewed from a long-term perspective, many of the pessimistic, neo-Malthusian projections regarding the impact of population growth and rising affluence on world food supplies have proved wrong because of more rapid advances in agricultural technology than thought possible even a decade ago. Debate persists among analysts about the kinds of economic and ecological demands that can be expected to exert pressure on the global food regime as the world moves toward the twenty-first century and about the prospects for producing enough food for the generations who will live in that century. But from the viewpoint of ensuring global food security,

> the main issue is not the worldwide availability of food, but the capacity of nations, groups within nations, and individuals to obtain enough food for a healthy diet. . . . Ultimately it is not countries but individuals who suffer from a shortage of food—not because of fluctuations in national production but because of higher food prices, which they cannot afford, or because of inadequate arrangements for marketing food. Their diet will improve only when their general economic state does. (*World Development Report 1984*, 1984: 91)

Coping with the causes of underdevelopment has a long history in the relations between developed and developing nations, as described in previous chapters. Among them, a number of institutions can be cited whose task is to cope with transitory and chronic food shortages and to direct development assistance efforts in agricultural production.[11]

At the international level, the United Nations Food and Agriculture Organization (FAO) provides technical assistance for agricultural projects and rural development. The World Food Program also provides support for development projects and has been an important vehicle for the transfer of food aid designed to cope with transitory food shortages. IFAD, the International Fund for Agricultural Development, provides low-cost loans to help the poorest among the developing countries. An outgrowth of the 1974 World Food Conference, IFAD's governing board is composed of equal numbers of members from Western industrialized nations, OPEC nations, and developing nations—a decision-making structure designed to ensure that no one group of nations will dominate the organization. The World Food Council is also an outgrowth of the 1974 World Food Conference. Its primary task is to provide a forum for discussing policy issues relating to food and agricultural development. Finally, the World Bank figures among the international organizations concerned with food and agriculture, as many of its loans are directed toward agricultural projects. Evaluating the impact of these organizations is difficult, but they do represent a collective sensitivity to the global dimensions of agricultural issues.

---

11. Our discussion here draws on Spivack and Florini (1986), where additional details can be found.

At the national level, many individual nations, and private groups within them, have actively promoted research on agricultural problems affecting the Third World, with a view toward increasing productivity. The Green Revolution, for example, is the product of research originally begun in the 1940s under the sponsorship of the Rockefeller Foundation. More broadly, it is the product of the transfer of Western agricultural technology to Third World nations.

As in other areas, the United States is prominent among those nations that have directed resources to the tasks of providing humanitarian relief in emergencies and long-term agricultural development assistance. Not infrequently and not surprisingly, a combination of domestic and international political considerations motivate its behavior.

Public Law 480, the "Food for Peace" program, is the most ubiquitous and time-worn mechanism whereby the United States brings "agripower" to bear on its foreign policy objectives while simultaneously meeting domestic needs. Through PL-480, credit sales of U.S. government–owned agricultural surpluses are channeled to other countries. The program's political character is underscored by the fact that priority is given to nations considered friendly to the United States,[12] even though its primary objective is to generate overseas markets for U.S. grain (Insel, 1985). Analysts dispute whether in creating dependence on imported grain, Food for Peace shipments may not in the long run be detrimental to Third World countries, by eroding the incentives to develop their own agricultural capabilities. Beyond question is that the surplus-disposal program ensures American farmers of a "market" for their products. In this way PL-480 serves the interests of America's domestic agricultural industry as well as the nation's foreign economic and security policy.

The United States' most celebrated effort to brandish the "food weapon" occurred in 1980, when the Carter administration sought—unsuccessfully—to punish the Soviet Union for its 1979 invasion of Afghanistan by placing an embargo on grain sales to the Soviet Union (above amounts previously agreed to). Although the United States had before used its position as a primary food supplier to pursue foreign policy objectives, the Soviet grain embargo was the first American attempt to use its food power on such a massive scale and for so blatantly political an objective.[13]

The failure of the American experiment can be attributed to many factors

---

12. The political character of the Food for Peace program is underscored by the fact that of the sub-Saharan African nations most vulnerable to the drought and famine of 1984–1985, only the Sudan and Zaire were included on the list of congressionally approved PL-480 beneficiaries (Insel, 1985).

13. A more recent example of the use of the "food weapon" by the United States and part of an economic sanctions program concerned Nicaragua.

In January 1981, the United States terminated its bilateral aid program, including "Food for Peace" shipments and suspended a $10 million wheat sale. Later that year, the United States blocked a $30 million credit from the Interamerican Development Bank for a fisheries project. In May 1983, the U.S. import quota for Nicaraguan sugar was cut 90 percent and subsequently terminated in May 1985 when a total bilateral trade embargo was imposed. (Hufbauer and Schott, 1985b: 732)

(Paarlberg, 1980), including the manner in which domestic political considerations reduced the effectiveness of the embargo. The critical factor, however, was "leakage" in the embargo caused by the willingness and ability of other states to make up the difference in Soviet food imports caused by the American action. In particular, Argentina greatly expanded its exports to the Soviet Union, thus largely negating the intended effects of the American embargo. Thus the grain embargo predictably failed because others were willing and able to divert production of a supply-elastic resource to the highest bidder (see also Chapter 10). In the meantime, critics argued, the image of the United States as a reliable trade partner was tarnished, causing buyers to go elsewhere in search of reliable grain suppliers.

The United States will continue to play an active role in efforts to realize global food security through its food aid and agricultural development assistance program and through its domestically managed system of grain reserves that can be used to cushion year-to-year fluctuations in grain production. It will doubtlessly also play a critical role in meeting the increased demand for food that rising population and income will inevitably generate. From a near-term perspective, however, U.S. foreign agricultural policy will be directed primarily by the challenge of coping with increased foreign competition. From this perspective, the image of the United States as an unreliable trading partner that may have been created by the Soviet grain embargo may have adverse long-term consequences.[14]

Like the United States, the European Community uses "food aid" to dispose of surplus commodities produced under the protective umbrella of its Common Agricultural Policy; and both have used export subsidies to capture overseas markets and to protect domestic producers. Many of the newcomers to the agricultural export business are motivated less by domestic interests and more by foreign economic objectives. Among those objectives is export growth so as to expand foreign exchange earnings and debt-servicing capacity. Ironically, the economic well-being of the United States and other First World nations has become tied to the Third World nations' success in realizing that objective, even though Third World exports increasingly challenge First World preeminence in the global marketplace.

TOWARD A MANAGED COMMONS ARRANGEMENT

Domestic politics often dominates agricultural policymaking in North and South alike, demonstrating how marginal global values, such as the goal of

---

14. In 1983 the United States and the Soviet Union reached a long-term grain agreement under which the United States pledged not to interrupt future grain shipments in pursuit of its self-defined foreign or national security policy goals. The pledge was a particular application of the principle that American agricultural policy generally has been "driven more by the need to protect a major domestic economic, social and political interest than by the need for foreign exchange produced by [agricultural] exports, no matter how significant those trade earnings may be" (Insel, 1985).

global food security, often are in an international political system that encourages nation-states to act in terms of their own self-interests. The simple truth is that governing elites' political fortunes rise and fall on the basis of what happens to their constituents at home, not what happens to others abroad. Furthermore, many of the global problems touched on in this chapter will fundamentally affect the welfare of yet unborn generations, but they typically have few or no advocates in the councils of government.

To avoid the desecration and ultimate destruction of properties held in common, Garrett Hardin (1968) recommended the construction of a system in which those who make decisions and reap the benefits would also bear the costs and consequences of their actions; that is, they would be "intrinsically responsible" for their behavior, as in a system based on private property. Especially pessimistic about voluntary restraints on exploitative behavior, Hardin advocated building accountability into decision making. At the international level, this would imply that states would have responsibilities as well as (sovereign) rights.

Efforts to induce states to behave in an ecologically responsible way generally have not fared well, and the record does not inspire optimism. Some success has been realized when states have negotiated specific obligations and rules with respect to particular issues. Law of the sea is a case in point. A measure of success has also been realized in devising a regulated commons arrangement for dealing with marine pollution (Soroos, 1988). However, many other areas of international public policy, in which the behavior described by the commons metaphor may predictably lead to tragic consequences, remain outside international control.

Despite all of the transnational dimensions of population and food policy, both remain outside international regulation. The population "problem"—whether defined as excessive growth in the South or as insufficient growth in the North—will eventually move toward equilibrium, but at different levels that imply radically different consequences. Public policy can steer the direction ultimately taken. In this respect the widespread agreement internationally that excessive population growth retards the realization of economic and other welfare objectives bodes well for national and international efforts to reduce fertility rates in the world's most rapidly growing countries.

In contrast, with the exception of the rules constructed to regulate fisheries, no such minimal agreement on principles exists within the global food regime. The regime is fragmented and unsettled, and it invites intense competition for export markets. In the North, the competition for export markets is driven by the maintenance of costly domestic subsidy programs that serve the interests of a political minority. Among a growing number of agricultural exporters in the South, the effort to penetrate Northern markets with agricultural products is motivated, as with manufactured products, by the adage "trade is better than aid." But here, as elsewhere in the global trade regime, protectionist sentiments in the North militate against Southern desires.

Tragically, in an unmanaged system such as this, the number of people experiencing chronic and transitory food insecurity grows even while agricultural surpluses pile up in national warehouses.

SUGGESTED READINGS

Brown, Lester R., et al. *State of the World 1988*. New York: Norton, 1988.

Lappé, Frances Moore, and Joseph Collins. *World Hunger: Twelve Myths*. New York: Grove Press, 1986.

Meken, Jane, ed. *World Population and U.S. Policy: The Choices Ahead*. New York: Norton, 1986.

Repetto, Robert. "Population, Resources, Environment: An Uncertain Future," *Population Bulletin* 42 (July 1987): 1–44.

Simon, Julian L. *The Ultimate Resource*. Princeton, N.J.: Princeton University Press, 1981.

Soroos, Marvin S. *Beyond Sovereignty: The Challenge of Global Policy*. Columbia: University of South Carolina Press, 1986.

Spivack, Neal, and Ann Florini. *Food on the Table: Seeking Global Solutions to Chronic Hunger*. New York: United Nations Association of the United States of America, 1986.

Tullis, F. LaMond, and W. Ladd Hollist. *Food, the State, and International Political Economy*. Lincoln: University of Nebraska Press, 1986.

Wattenberg, Ben J. *The Birth Dearth*. New York: Pharos Books, 1987.

World Commission on Environment and Development. *Our Common Future*. New York: Oxford University Press, 1987.

TEN

Oil, Energy, and Resource Power

Clearly, OPEC will be back in the driver's seat in the 1990s. Since most oil that can be produced by non-OPEC countries already is being produced, each additional barrel of oil needed to meet rising world demand will come from OPEC. . . . And we will be confronting a new, truncated OPEC in the 1990s. . . . The locus of power in OPEC will switch back to the Persian Gulf states. . . .

CHARLES EBINGER, 1985

Whoever controls world resources controls the world in a way that mere occupation of territory cannot match.

RICHARD J. BARNET, 1980

Like the global food regime, the principles and rules governing energy are in disarray. Great uncertainty prevails about the probable role that energy supplies will play in world politics in the 1990s and about the energy policies and programs that can enhance the performance of the international political economy and promote the security of nations. During the 1970s countless predictions were made about increases in future energy prices and the dangerous consequences that would likely result. However, these forecasts have proved incorrect; instead of increasing, the price of oil worldwide eroded considerably in the 1980s. In part those predictions were wide of the mark because they underestimated how adaptive people and nations would be in response to the extraordinary rise in the cost of energy during the 1970s and early 1980s. The unexpected price decline that occurred in the mid-1980s and the changes that have followed in its wake, however, may set the stage for another energy crisis in the 1990s. As before, the future cannot be predicted with confidence, but the dramatic changes in the global oil regime during the past two decades portend further adjustments in the 1990s that will doubtlessly have global ramifications.

Our primary concerns in this chapter are with the causes of and lessons to be drawn from the two "oil shocks" of the 1970s whose reverberations figure so prominently in understanding the trends and transformations in the international political economy elaborated in Chapters 7 and 8 and elsewhere in this book. Developments since the 1970s related to energy have profoundly altered the character of world politics. Indeed, the process of adjusting to those developments continues to influence the contours of world politics and promises to do so for years to come (as, for example, through adjustments required to address the Third World debt problem).

These profound changes in world politics occurred within a comparatively short period of time, which might be called the *OPEC decade*. It began in October 1973, when members of the Organization of Petroleum Exporting Countries (OPEC), in response to the outbreak of war in the Middle East, imposed an embargo on the supply of oil and cut overall production levels. Immediately thereafter, OPEC elected to raise the price of its oil—a decision that precipitated the first of two oil shocks during the 1970s. The OPEC decade ended in March 1983 when in response to a worldwide oil glut, OPEC for the first time in its history agreed to cut its official price of oil and set a ceiling on its aggregate production levels. Since then, the production, price, and supplies of energy have exhibited much variation, making the future problematic and reducing policymakers' ability to make decisions based on reliable forecasts.

The onset of the OPEC decade in 1973 represents a watershed in the post–World War II world; the changes wrought during the subsequent decade are destined to continue to shape world politics throughout the remainder of this century and may set in motion forces that could coalesce to produce another, equally destabilizing period of crisis driven by changes in energy politics. For that reason we must study the role of oil and energy in world politics by examining the lessons suggested by this traumatic experience.

THE MAKING OF THE OPEC DECADE: HISTORICAL PATTERNS OF ENERGY PRODUCTION AND CONSUMPTION

Before the onset of the OPEC decade, energy had been relatively cheap and available in seemingly limitless quantities, especially in the United States, the world's largest consumer of energy resources. But since 1973, energy has been dear and, for at least a time, in relatively short supply.

The dynamics that govern supply and demand, price and production are influenced by the ways in which individuals in different national settings behave. Just as people in the world's rich nations place a disproportionately large burden on the global commons, they also consume a disproportionately large share of its energy resources. The enormous gap between the energy consumed in the developed and the developing nations is illustrated in Figure 10.1, which compares the rate of per-capita energy use in the United States, Western Europe, and Japan to that used in the centrally planned economies (including China) and the developing nations. The differences—which show energy consumption in Europe and Japan as four or five times that of Third World countries, or more than fifteen times as great in the case of the United

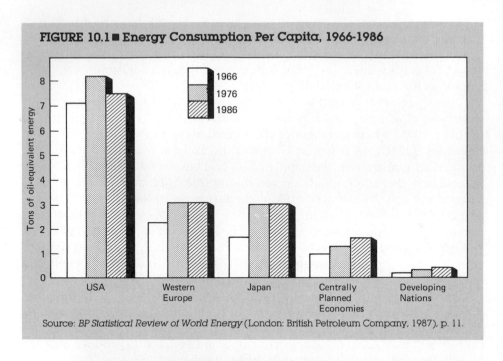

FIGURE 10.1 ■ Energy Consumption Per Capita, 1966-1986

Source: *BP Statistical Review of World Energy* (London: British Petroleum Company, 1987), p. 11.

States—parallel the gap between the world's rich and poor nations apparent in so many other dimensions of contemporary world politics.

Energy consumption is closely associated with the production of goods and services as measured by gross national product (GNP). During the roughly fifty years from the 1930s to the 1980s, the world's demand for energy increased at almost the same rate as did the aggregate world gross domestic product (GDP) (International Energy Agency, 1982: 69), reflecting in important ways the substitution of energy for labor in the industrial societies of the North. In industrial production, in transportation, and in the distribution of goods and services, intensive uses of energy have become the hallmark of the modern industrial society. Not surprisingly, therefore, the developing nations of the South, which have not yet become mechanized to the extent characteristic of industrial societies, see higher rates of energy use as the key to more rapid economic development and higher standards of living.

Although the correlation between income and energy use is high, wide differences exist in the energy consumption associated with given levels of economic output for different countries. Pakistan and Sri Lanka, for example, had the same per-capita incomes in 1985, but Pakistan used over 50 percent more energy per capita than did Sri Lanka; Argentina used nearly twice as much energy per capita as did Uruguay but had less than a third higher per-capita GNP (*World Development Report 1987*, 1987: 202–203, 218–219). Even more striking are the differences among developed nations. In 1985, for example, the United States used more than twice as much energy per capita as did prosperous Japan, whose economy enables its citizens to rival the living standards enjoyed by Americans.

Several reasons account for the high level of energy usage in the United States. Historically, energy has been abundant and cheap in the United States, a circumstance that removed incentives to develop efficient energy practices and conservation programs. Americans' personal preferences for automobiles and trucks as their principal modes of transportation also contributed to the rate of consumption.[1] Given the enormity of overall U.S. energy consumption, the policies and practices of the United States exert a powerful influence over the entire global energy picture.

Historical Trends in Fossil Fuel Usage

Rapid increases in the rate of energy usage in general and petroleum in particular are primarily post–World War II phenomena. In 1950, when the world population was about 2.5 billion people, world energy consumption was 2.5 billion tons of coal-equivalent energy. Population increased rapidly during the next quarter century, but energy use increased even more rapidly. By 1979 the world's 4.4 billion people were consuming 8.7 billion tons of coal-equivalent energy (Sivard, 1981: 6). This increase was closely tied to the unprecedented level of economic growth that the world experienced in the postwar era. From 1950 to 1973, the world economy expanded at a rate of 4 percent annually, spurred by the 7 percent growth in world oil output during this period (Brown, 1979: 17). On a per-capita basis, this meant that the amount of oil available increased from an average of 1.5 barrels per person in 1950 to over 5.3 barrels in 1973 (Brown, 1979: 18). (One barrel of oil equals forty two U.S. gallons.) This dramatic rise in production has made oil and, somewhat less so, natural gas, the principal sources of commercial energy in the world today.

The historical transition to oil and gas dependence worldwide followed the experience of the United States. Little more than a century ago, fuelwood was the principal energy source. As the mechanical revolution altered the nature of transportation, work, and leisure, coal began to replace fuelwood. Early in the twentieth century, coal became the dominant source of energy worldwide, and by 1913 it accounted for 75 percent of the world's energy consumption (Sivard, 1979a: 7).

The subsequent shift from coal to oil and natural gas was spurred by new technological developments, particularly the internal combustion engine. The

---

1. In 1986 transportation accounted for 63 percent of the petroleum used in the United States (U.S. Department of Energy, 1987a: 9, 29).

United States, which was well endowed with petroleum resources, was a leader in the development of oil-based technologies, above all in the automotive and petrochemical industries. Although oil accounted for less than a third of world energy production in 1950, by 1965 it equaled coal production, and in the next decade oil rapidly outpaced coal as the main energy source. Everywhere the reasons were the same. Energy derived from oil and gas was cleaner and less expensive than coal. (Coal had also been inexpensive, but effective labor demands for higher wages, rules to protect the environment, and more costly safety standards had increased its relative cost.) From the end of the Korean War until the early 1970s, oil prices actually declined worldwide compared with the prices of other commodities, with natural gas prices showing a similar decline in the United States where it was more extensively consumed than in other parts of the world (Willrich, 1975). The long-term stability of world oil prices is striking. As shown in Figure 10.2, World Wars I and II each produced small, step-level increments in the price of oil, but essentially it remained stable. As the price of other commodities as well as manufactured goods rose, oil became relatively cheaper. It therefore made good economic sense to use it in large quantities. The result was that by 1979—the peak year of global oil consumption since the first well was drilled in the middle of the nineteenth century—the world was using over 31,000 gallons of petroleum every second. The United States alone was consuming

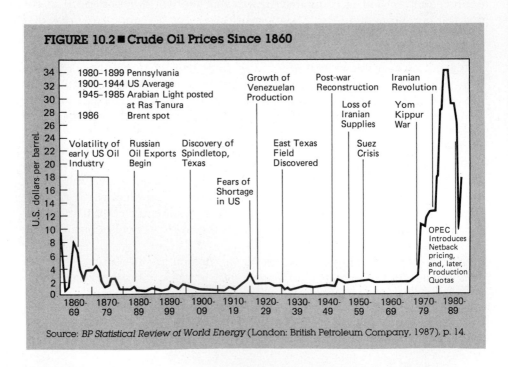

FIGURE 10.2 ■ Crude Oil Prices Since 1860

Source: *BP Statistical Review of World Energy* (London: British Petroleum Company, 1987), p. 14.

more than a fourth of this amount. Not until the onset of the OPEC decade was a continuation of this upward trend in consumption challenged.

The Rise of OPEC

The chief actors propelling the worldwide shift from coal to oil were eight multinational corporations known as the "majors"—Exxon, Gulf, Mobil, Standard Oil of California, Texaco (all American based), British Petroleum, Royal Dutch Shell, and Compagnie Française des Petroles. In the mid-1970s these eight firms (the first seven of which are often referred to as the *seven sisters*) controlled nearly two-thirds of the world's oil production (Abrahamsson, 1975: 80). Their operations encompassed every aspect of the business from exploration to the retailing of products at their gas stations.

The majors were largely unhindered in their search for, production of, and marketing of low-cost oil. They had easily obtained concessions from nations in such oil-rich areas as the Middle East, and the communist countries were virtually the only states from which the majors were barred. A buyer's market existed, which meant that the majors had to control production output so as to avoid glut and chronic oversupply. They did this by keeping other competitors, known as *independents*, out of the international oil regime, by engaging in joint ventures and otherwise cooperating among themselves to restrict supply, and by avoiding price competition (Spero, 1985). The oil companies were thus able to manage the price of oil at a level profitable for themselves even while the price of oil relative to other commodities declined.

An abundant supply of oil at low prices facilitated the recovery of Western Europe and Japan from World War II and encouraged consumers to adopt energy-intensive technologies, such as the private automobile. The overall result was an enormous growth in the worldwide demand for and consumption of energy.

To sustain these high growth rates, the continual discovery and extraction of new oil deposits were required. But because the real cost of oil did not increase commensurately with the cost of other commodities, goods, and services, the incentives for developing petroleum reserves outside the Middle East waned. And incentives for developing new technologies for alternative energy sources, such as coal, were virtually nonexistent. This meant that when OPEC increased the price of oil fourfold in the winter of 1973–1974, oil consumers had no recourse but to absorb the costs because of the absence of energy alternatives.

In addition to the growth of global demand for oil, another factor that facilitated OPEC's success was the growing dependence of much of the world on Middle Eastern oil. By 1979, the Middle East accounted for one-third of the world's oil supplies (production) but less than 3 percent of its demand (consumption). Before the 1979 Iranian revolution, Iran and Saudi Arabia alone accounted for nearly a quarter of the entire world's production of oil.

In contrast, Japan and Western Europe accounted for over 30 percent of the world demand for oil but produced less than 4 percent domestically. American dependence on foreign sources was somewhat less, but as domestic supplies of American oil were depleted during the OPEC decade, the United States increasingly turned to OPEC to provide the needed oil. The resultant shortfalls in the noncommunist nations of the industrialized world were met by increased production by OPEC.

Besides the absence of energy alternatives and worldwide dependence on Middle Eastern oil, OPEC's takeover of control of production and pricing policies from the multinational oil companies also contributed to its success. This occurred over a period of several years, as the bargaining advantages enjoyed by the multinationals vis-à-vis the host governments of the producing countries deteriorated. OPEC's formation in 1960 was part of the process whereby the oil-producing nations sought to increase their own economic returns as well as their leverage with the majors. Their efforts were given a boost by the increase in the number of independents in the oil field between the 1950s and the 1970s, whose presence made for a more competitive market that reduced the bargaining power of the majors vis-à-vis the host states.

Libya provided the catalyst for the first oil shock. Following a coup in September 1969 that brought to power a radical government headed by Colonel Muammar Qaddafi, Libya cut production and increased the price for its oil. Several factors contributed to Libya's success, but the important point is that other oil-producing states quickly learned from Libya's experience, which "revealed the vulnerability of the companies and the unwillingness of the Western consumers to take forceful action in their support. It also led to a major conceptual change in the minds of oil producers by demonstrating that government revenues could be raised not only by increasing exports but also or instead by increasing price" (Spero, 1985).

For the Arab members of OPEC, the possibility of using oil as a political weapon to affect the outcome of the unsettled Arab-Israeli dispute was a matter of keen interest. Their common desire to defeat Israel was in fact one of the main elements uniting them. Thus when the Yom Kippur War broke out between Israel and the Arabs on October 6, 1973, the stage for using the oil weapon was set.

Less than two weeks after the outbreak of that war, the OPEC oil ministers seized the right to determine prices unilaterally, and the Arab producing countries decided to reduce their production levels. Control over production and prices—which quadrupled between October 1973 and January 1974—thus was transferred from the oil companies to the host governments. Furthermore, the political goals sought by the Arab members of OPEC regarding the Arab-Israeli dispute were pursued by cutting back oil production and imposing an embargo on exports to consuming countries considered too pro-Israeli, principally the Netherlands and the United States.

The events of 1973–1974 suggested several lessons. One was that the oil weapon, having been used successfully once, could be used again.[2] The inability of the major multinational oil companies to control the international oil regime, as they had done for decades, was a second.[3] A third important lesson was that even the world's most powerful nation, the United States, had become vulnerable to economic pressures exerted by foreign powers as it moved away from relative self-sufficiency in oil production.

Shaping the OPEC Decade:
The Role of the United States

The rise of OPEC as a significant international actor was facilitated by the United States' growing vulnerability to OPEC's production and pricing actions and by the shift from a buyer's to a seller's market.

Historically, the United States has been a major producer as well as consumer of oil. In 1938 the United States accounted for nearly two-thirds of the world's crude oil production and over 70 percent of production in the non-communist world (Darmstadter and Landsberg, 1976: 33). By 1973, however, these proportions had slipped to 16 and 19 percent, respectively (*BP Statistical Review of World Energy*, 1984: 5).

American oil production began to decline precipitously in the early 1970s at the same time that domestic demand increased. The need to import oil from abroad to balance consumption and production grew correspondingly. By

---

2. For reasons elaborated later in this chapter, many analysts believe that the oil weapon, defined as an instrument for the realization of political objectives, has largely been defused. During much of the OPEC decade the oil cartel in fact appeared to be less a politically cohesive organization than a collection of states motivated simply by economic gain. OPEC's continuing difficulties in coordinating the price at which its members sell oil or the volume of their production illustrate the point. However, there are instances in which the oil weapon appears to have been brandished. In the summer of 1979, for example, Saudi Arabia increased its oil production by one million barrels a day to ease supply shortages caused by the Iranian production cutback. The move was widely interpreted as an inducement to Washington to adopt a more pro-Arab posture in its efforts to secure a comprehensive Middle Eastern peace settlement.

The Nigerian government also brandished its oil weapon in 1979 when it nationalized British Petroleum. In explaining its action, Nigeria accused the oil company of shipping British North Sea oil to the white minority regime in South Africa.

A third example is perhaps the $2-per-barrel price hike announced by Saudi Arabia in May 1980. The increase came shortly after the American Public Broadcasting System showed a film entitled *Death of a Princess*, regarded by the Saudi regime as an unfair portrayal of Saudi society and Islamic law. Some news commentators therefore interpreted the price increase as a reprisal against the United States for its refusal to block public viewing of the film.

3. During the crisis, in fact, the oil companies responded "with the conditioned reflexes of entrepreneurs minimizing their risks at the margin." As Raymond Vernon (1976), an expert on multinational corporations, explained: "The patterns of oil distribution in the crisis, dictated by the principles of greatest prudence and least pain, were curiously non-national. Anyone looking for confirmation of the view that it paid a country to have an oil company based within its own jurisdiction would have found scant support for such a hypothesis in this brief episode in the oil industry's history."

1973, imports accounted for over a third of American consumption (compared with about 20 percent in the mid-1960s) (Darmstadter and Landsberg, 1976: 31). Growing American oil import dependence thus helped make possible the OPEC price hikes and production controls of 1973–1974.[4]

Despite the adverse economic consequences of the first oil shock, petroleum consumption in the United States continued to grow between 1973 and 1978, while domestic production declined further. This made the United States increasingly dependent on foreign sources of oil and especially vulnerable to the pricing decisions made by exporters. This set the stage for the second "oil shock," which came in 1979–1980 in the wake of the Iranian revolution that ousted the government of Shah Muhammad Reza Pahlavi and led to the creation of the revolutionary Islamic republic headed by the Ayatollah Khomeini. As Iranian oil production dropped, the short-term price of oil increased sharply (see Figure 10.2). The longer-term consequence was a second oil-induced global economic recession whose effects continue to ripple through the global political economy (see Chapters 7 and 8).

Oil and National Security During the OPEC Decade

Important national security issues were also raised by the decade of challenges to the power of the strong by the power of the weak. The principal security problem derived from a simple fact: OPEC—in particular its Middle Eastern members—accounted for a disproportionate share of the oil produced and traded internationally. What happened within and among the OPEC nations had enormous consequences for the rest of the world, particularly the Western industrialized world. In 1974, for example, OPEC accounted for two-thirds of world oil production outside the communist world, and much of this had to pass out of the geopolitically sensitive and politically volatile Middle East before it could reach oil-short markets in Western Europe, Japan, and elsewhere. Concern for ensuring Western oil supplies was heightened in 1979, when the Soviet Union intervened militarily in Afghanistan, which poised it perilously close to the Middle Eastern oil lifeline to the West.

Against this background, President Jimmy Carter in 1980 enunciated the doctrine bearing his name, in which he pledged that "an attempt by an outside force to gain control of the Persian Gulf region will be regarded as an assault

---

4. Several factors contributed to this increased dependence, including an "accelerated demand for energy in the aggregate; a dramatic falling off of reserve additions of oil and natural gas; severe constraints, largely for environmental reasons, on the use of coal; lags in the scheduled completion of nuclear power plants; and protracted delays in oil and gas leasing" (Darmstadter and Landsberg, 1976).

The growing demand for oil, particularly gasoline, was the core of the problem. The demand for oil in turn was related to price, which, as noted earlier, actually declined relative to other commodities from the 1950s to the 1970s. Hence, there was little incentive for, or public interest in, conservation measures. On the supply side, however, American domestic oil production did not keep pace with trends in consumption, and U.S. reserves of oil relative to total world reserves declined steadily (Darmstadter and Landsberg, 1976).

on the vital interests of America and such an assault will be repelled by any means necessary, including military force." The Reagan administration subsequently reaffirmed the Carter Doctrine, and it carried forward its predecessor's efforts to develop a rapid-deployment military force with skills peculiarly suited for intervention in the Persian Gulf area. The Reagan administration also implied that it might be willing to move against an *internal* threat when in 1981 it asserted, "Saudi Arabia we will not permit to be an Iran" (*New York Times*, October 7, 1983).

The United States also responded to its growing oil import dependence by developing a strategic petroleum reserve from which stockpiled oil could be drawn to replace imported oil in the event of a supply interruption, and it led the creation of the International Energy Agency which is designed to oversee the sharing of oil among the Western industrialized nations in the event of an emergency.

During the OPEC decade many analysts concluded that the most likely threat to Middle Eastern oil supplies was that posed by internal instability in a key oil-producing country. The events in Iran leading to the second oil-price shock in 1979 reinforced this belief. As noted earlier, domestic political turmoil there led to oil production cutbacks and a sharp upturn in the price of oil (fed by consumers' anticipation of severe supply shortages). The subsequent new round of OPEC-mandated price increases underscored the Western countries' new levels of vulnerability to disruptions in prices and supplies from abroad.

The Iranian situation was particularly troublesome for the United States. For years before the Iranian revolution the United States had pumped billions of dollars worth of sophisticated military equipment into Iran—transfers premised on the belief that the shah's government would use Iranian military might to protect the oil-rich Persian Gulf area from outside—namely, Soviet—interference, thus ensuring a continual flow of Persian Gulf oil to the West. Similar motivations were behind the massive American arms shipments sent to Saudi Arabia both before the Iranian revolution and since. The revolutionary government that came to power in Iran in 1979, however, was resolutely anti-American. With Iran removed from the ranks of pro-Western nations in the region, Saudi Arabia's position as a politically Western-oriented oil supplier gained added significance.

The fact that Saudi Arabia possessed huge oil reserves and was the largest producer in OPEC placed it center stage in the maintenance of Western energy security. At issue was not only Saudi Arabia's ability to protect its vast oil fields from terrorist or other attacks but also the task of averting a repetition of the internal political disruptions that Iran experienced. Robert Stobaugh and Daniel Yergin describe the uncertain scenario in early 1979:

> Too little is known about internal relations in Saudi Arabia to make any solid predictions. What is obvious, however, is that a pre-modern social structure, based upon kinship, has been catapulted into the modern age. No

one, not even members of the royal family, can guess how successfully the present system will adjust to the new world—or for how long. No one who has assimilated the lessons of Iran can confidently assess what the corrosive effects of instant wealth will be, and how suddenly they will bubble to the surface. And Saudi Arabia is surrounded by rivals and enemies—Iran, not only unstable but with a rising influence of Sh'a [Shi'ite] Islam, antithetic to the Sunni Islam of Saudi Arabia; South Yemen, with a Marxist government aided by Cuban and Soviet military elements; Iraq, with a Soviet military presence. (Stobaugh and Yergin, 1979: 839)[5]

The threat of internal upheaval that came to preoccupy Western policy-makers was intensified by the related threat of regional conflict, two phenomena that are often indistinguishable. Following the Israeli invasion of southern Lebanon in 1982, for example, a multinational peacekeeping force of American, French, Italian, and British soldiers was placed in Lebanon. As it became embroiled in Lebanon's continuing political and religious strife, the peacekeeping force eventually found itself the target of not only political opposition by some Arab governments but also terrorist attack by pro-Iranian Shi'ite militants. At the same time, the protracted Iran–Iraq war threatened to engulf other oil-producing states in the Persian Gulf area in a wider war.

The threat presented by the broader geopolitical dimensions of Middle East conflict to the maintenance of global energy security has also been a matter of concern. Ensuring an adequate supply of oil requires not only access at the wellhead but also secure routes to refiners and consumers.[6] The two most important of these routes are from the Persian Gulf area to the Cape of Good Hope at the tip of Africa and from there to Europe and North America, and eastward from the Persian Gulf through the Strait of Malacca to Japan. The importance of the African route grew just before and during the OPEC decade. In 1965 most of the crude oil going to Europe traveled through the Suez Canal, but after its closure during the 1967 Arab-Israeli War (it was reopened in 1975), the canal receded in importance and, a decade later, became less critical as a sea-lane with the creation of supertankers too large to pass through it. Thus the African route became far more important and remains so today.

---

5. The seizure of the Grand Mosque in Mecca in late 1979 by hundreds of militants led Stobaugh and Yergin (1980) to conclude that the event "seemed to say—and this, no doubt, was an intention of its perpetrators—that the great stabilizer of the world oil market is itself not stable. That such a conspiracy could go undetected is deeply disturbing." Interestingly, however, eight years later, in 1987, Iranian "pilgrims" who traveled to Mecca broke out in riotous demonstrations against the United States, only to be dealt with quickly by Saudi security forces. The Saudi government also dealt with the incident more effectively than it had in 1979, leading some observers to conclude that Saudi Arabia was more stable politically in the late 1980s than it had been in the late 1970s (Hamed, 1987).

6. It is interesting to note that in 1986, Canada, the United States, and Western Europe accounted for over 40 percent of the world's crude oil-refining capacity. The Middle East, in contrast, accounted for only 5 percent. The discrepancies were even more striking a decade earlier, when the Western nations accounted for 53 percent of the world's refining capacity and the Middle East only 4 percent (*BP Statistical Review of World Energy*, 1987: 16).

As a result of these developments, America's Middle Eastern policy came to be guided by the goal of ensuring the flow of oil to the West.[7] Although some Western policymakers interpreted the Soviet invasion of Afghanistan in 1979 as a prelude to a major invasion of the Persian Gulf area, that view eventually gave way to one that saw Moscow's aims "not at getting Middle East oil for itself, but at making Western access more tenuous and dependent on Soviet forbearance" (Gelb, 1983) so that the Soviets could be assured of a greater voice in the Middle East.

This assessment was grounded in part on projections that the Soviet Union's domestic supplies of oil would be sufficient to meet demand for the foreseeable future. In fact, the largest oil producer in the world throughout the OPEC decade and since is not Saudi Arabia or any other member of OPEC; it is the Soviet Union. Even though its domestic consumption is high, the Soviet Union is also a net exporter of oil. Many of its exports are funneled to the Soviet Union's Eastern European allies, where they comprise a significant part of the overall economic linkages among the Comecon nations. Thus the Warsaw Pact countries are jointly self-sufficient in energy. The communist countries as a group have also exported modest amounts of oil to the West, which it uses to earn "hard" (that is, Western) currency with which to purchase imported goods.

Whether the Soviet Union would be able to sustain its enviable position as a net oil exporter became questionable during the OPEC decade. In 1977 a U.S. Central Intelligence Agency (1977) report predicted that the Soviets' productive capacity would peak in the early 1980s and then fall sharply, and that by 1985 the Soviet Union and Eastern Europe would be required to import several million barrels of oil daily; further, it speculated that this might cause the Soviet Union not only to reduce its exports but also to compete for OPEC oil for its own use. Later analyses indicated that Soviet oil production did, indeed, begin to slow in the early 1980s and that it actually declined between 1984 and 1985 (which was the first time that had happened since World War II); they also revealed that its production of natural gas (of which the Soviet Union has the world's largest reserves) had grown. Eventually gas will become an important export commodity and source of foreign exchange to the Soviet Union. This is ensured by the trans-Siberian pipeline, which when made fully opera-

---

7. Many of the most important political and military allies of the United States are much more dependent on oil imports than is the United States. In 1981 the United States depended on imports to meet 36 percent of its oil needs. The comparable figure for West Germany was 94 percent, for France 99 percent, and for Italy and Japan 100 percent. The United States is also relatively more self-reliant for its total energy needs than are many of its allies. Domestic sources met 87 percent of total American energy use in 1981. By contrast, domestic sources provided only about a third of total energy use in West Germany, and less than 10 percent in Italy, France, and Japan (Darmstadter et al., 1983: 181). The fact that the United States' allies are so dependent on foreign sources of energy contributes to the salience of energy issues in American policymaking circles. However, as we shall show later, the different relative vulnerabilities of the United States and its allies are related to different perceptions of the role of energy as it pertains to national security.

tional by the 1990s will provide much of Western Europe access to Soviet energy supplies.

The trans-Siberian pipeline project produced a serious split between the United States and some of its NATO allies over the question of granting the Soviet Union access to Western technology. The United States in the early 1980s imposed stiff controls on the export of oil and gas technology to the Soviet Union in an effort to punish it for its role in imposing martial law in Poland as well as to dissuade Western Europe from completing the pipeline that would bring Soviet natural gas into Western European markets. To the United States, Western European dependence on Soviet energy supplies would compromise Western security by making Europe subject to Moscow's dictates and by providing the Soviet Union with much-needed hard currency. European leaders did not agree and argued that Soviet gas would ultimately account for a relatively small proportion of total energy use and, further, that the alternative was greater dependency on politically insecure sources of gas and oil in Africa or the Middle East (Ebinger, 1982).

The pipeline debate illustrates how the interrelated issues of energy and national security are often viewed differently by Washington and its NATO allies. The priorities established by the United States are simply not shared by the other Western industrialized nations. Differences among them arise in part from their relative positions as consumers and producers of energy (for example, Britain and Norway, as producers of North Sea oil, take a view of production and pricing policies different from that of other Western European countries). Differences also derive from varying perceptions of the Soviet threat to the Middle East and of the relative importance of regional conflict and internal instability as threats to the oil lifeline to the West (Lieber, 1982). As Charles Ebinger (1982), director of Georgetown University's Energy and Strategic Resources Program, put it, "Europe sees Middle Eastern politics as the paramount threat to oil supplies. The United States too often perceives energy as tangential to national security, the chief threat to which it views as the Soviet challenge."

THE UNMAKING OF THE OPEC DECADE: ENERGY PRODUCTION AND CONSUMPTION IN THE 1980s AND BEYOND

Reducing dependence on foreign supplies of oil became a major policy preoccupation for all of the Western industrialized nations during the OPEC decade. By the early 1980s, conservation measures, economic recession, and a shift to alternative sources of energy combined to push down the demand for oil. As shown in Figure 10.3, the consumption of oil by the United States, Western Europe, and Japan declined to 53 percent of the world total in 1986, compared with two-thirds of consumption in the early 1970s. The figure also documents

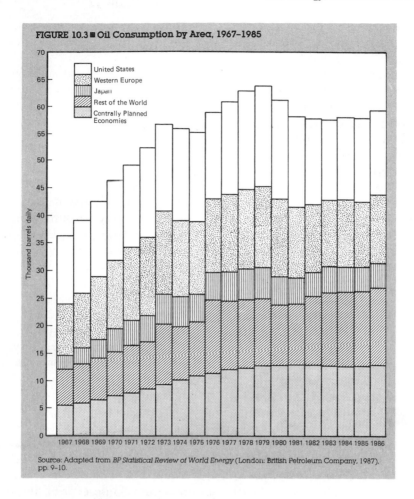

FIGURE 10.3 ■ Oil Consumption by Area, 1967–1985

Source: Adapted from *BP Statistical Review of World Energy* (London: British Petroleum Company, 1987), pp. 9–10.

how the aggregate demand for oil had grown during the OPEC decade to its peak in 1979 and how it declined subsequently.

The Decline of OPEC

It is difficult to estimate the relative contribution of conservation measures and reduced economic growth to the softening demand for oil in the 1980s. Both made an impact, the latter through *income effects* (that is, as reductions in energy use caused by recession-induced reductions in national incomes), the former through *price effects*, which can be broken down into *irreversible* and *reversible* conservation measures (Mossavar-Rahmani, 1983). Irreversible measures translate into improved energy efficiency resulting from the turnover of capital stock or from retrofitting, such as driving automobiles with improved mileage standards, building more energy-efficient commercial buildings and industrial plants, and improving the insulation in existing residential buildings.

Reversible conservation measures derive from behavioral changes, such as turning the thermostat lower in the home or office during the winter or driving in a commuter car pool.

Without a doubt, conservation measures reduced the energy-intensiveness of the industrialized nations' economies during the OPEC decade. As we noted, increases in demand for energy were associated closely with increases in economic output. This linkage was particularly evident before the first oil shock, where among the industrialized nations of the West a nearly one-to-one relationship existed. That is, from 1960 to 1973 every 1 percent increase in energy consumption was associated with the same percentage increase in gross national product (International Energy Agency, 1982: 69). Since 1973, however, this correspondence has declined greatly. In the United States, for example, the number of BTU's (British thermal units) of energy consumed per GNP dollar in 1986 was only three-quarters of the level in 1973 (U.S. Department of Energy, 1987a: 14). For the Western industrialized nations as a whole, the efficiency with which energy was used rose by 34 percent during the OPEC decade (*New York Times*, September 28, 1983, p. 27). The effect of these changes will be to stretch out the available supplies of petroleum for many additional years. At the same time, however, worldwide economic growth can be expected to stimulate further demand for energy in the future. In an environment of healthy economic growth, income-induced conservation measures will, by definition, disappear, and the behavioral changes induced by high energy prices may be reversed. In the United States, for example, the return to economic growth following the recession precipitated by the second oil shock stimulated increased demand for oil as consumption rose by more than 800,000 barrels per day between 1983 and 1986 (*BP Statistical Review of World Energy*, 1987: 9).

In addition to the reduced demand for oil, a second important development since the OPEC decade has been reduced dependence on OPEC. As shown in Figure 10.4, OPEC in 1973 accounted for 53 percent of the world's oil output, but by the mid-1980s this proportion dropped to less than a third. Although the proportion remained substantial, in effect OPEC moved from being a principal supplier of oil to being a *residual supplier*, as consumers first sought energy resources elsewhere.

Several factors account for the shift away from OPEC. One, of course, is the reduced demand for oil, as discussed. A second is the discovery during the 1970s of new sources of oil outside the OPEC framework. The development of the North Sea oil fields by Britain and Norway, the completion of the Alaskan pipeline by the United States, and Mexico's increased oil output were essential elements underlying the changing global oil environment. As shown in Figure 10.4, one consequence of these new sources was that the share of the world's oil output outside OPEC, the United States, and the centrally planned economies rose between 1973 and 1986 from 11 percent of the world total to 25 percent. By the mid-1980s, China also was poised to become a net oil supplier.

FIGURE 10.4 ■ Oil Production by Area, 1967-1986

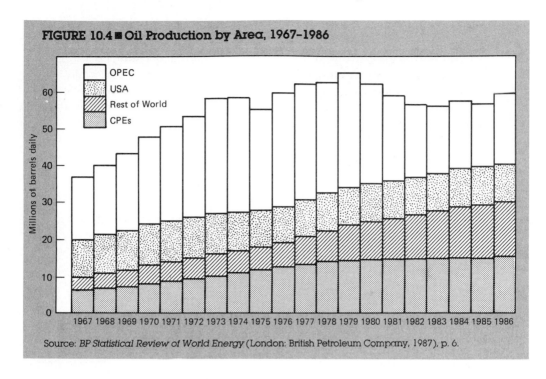

Source: *BP Statistical Review of World Energy* (London: British Petroleum Company, 1987), p. 6.

A shift to alternative energy sources is a third factor contributing to the reduced reliance on OPEC oil. Coal, for example, again became a major source of energy in the United States. Coal's share of energy used to generate electricity increased from 44 percent in 1973 to 54 percent in 1986, whereas the share of petroleum dropped from 18 percent to less than 6 percent (U.S. Department of Energy, 1987a: 31). (The proportion of natural gas used to generate electricity also fell, while the proportion of nuclear energy increased.)

The shift away from oil was evident elsewhere as well. The French, for example, increased their electrical generation through nuclear power more than seventeenfold between 1973 and 1986 (U.S. Department of Energy, 1987a: 118) as part of an ambitious nuclear energy program designed to help reduce dependence on imported oil. Japan raised its imports of coal to meet a growing proportion of its electrical generation and industrial needs. Brazil invested heavily in the generation of fuel ("gasohol") extracted from agricultural products. And the West German government encouraged a shift from oil to natural gas, facilitated by the anticipated completion of the trans-Siberian gas pipeline.

In addition to the reduced demand for oil and a lessening of dependence on OPEC, a third outgrowth of the OPEC decade was a shift in the character of the international oil market (see Morse, 1986). Completing a process set in motion more than a decade ago, the major multinational oil companies are no longer the linchpins of a global oil regime. Rather, control of the pricing and production decisions has shifted to the oil-producing countries themselves. Although the major multinational oil firms continued in the wake of the second oil shock to control the "downstream" activities of transporting, refining, and marketing petroleum and petroleum products, the oil-producing countries seem likely to win control of this aspect of the petroleum industry as well. The major oil multinationals thus have become little more than contractors to the oil-producing countries.[8]

Winners and Losers in the Denouement of the OPEC Decade

Oil prices began to soften following their 1981 peak and went into a near free-fall in 1986. This was accelerated by many pressures (see Morse, 1986), but the single most potent reason can be attributed in large measure to the worldwide oil glut resulting from the decision of key members of OPEC, notably Saudi Arabia, to increase their output in an effort to regain the market share lost to others during the OPEC decade. In a world characterized by *mutual vulnerability* and *mutual sensitivity*—in short, interdependence—some were sure to win, and others to lose.

American consumers were among the sure winners. Declining oil prices were the major factor lowering inflation in the United States during the first half of the 1980s. As inflation abated, economic growth proceeded. To the extent that the American "locomotive" was able to pull the rest of the world economy in its train in promoting economic growth (see Chapters 7 and 8), others became beneficiaries of America's improved economy. Certainly American consumers dependent on gasoline, heating oil, and natural gas shared in the benefits of reduced oil prices, as did American industries dependent on fossil fuels, such as truckers, airlines, and the chemical industry. Other import-dependent countries, such as Brazil and Chile, benefited similarly. Furthermore, as inflation declined, interest rates also eventually declined, reducing the burden of many debt-ridden Third World countries whose obligations were tied directly to the cost of borrowing.

But there were losers. At the same time that American consumers as a whole benefited from oil price reductions, for example, oil producers in the states of Texas, Oklahoma, and Louisiana suffered severely. So too did many of

---

8. The expansion of the producing countries' downstream activities may give them a greater stake in preventing supply disruptions. In early 1988, for example, Saudi Arabia and Texaco Oil Company sought a billion-dollar deal whereby Saudi Arabia would buy into some of Texaco's oil refineries in the United States. Industry analysts saw the proposed move as increasing Saudi Arabia's financial stake in the United States as an oil consumer, which would give incentive to Saudi Arabia to avoid future supply disruptions, as these would impair its own economic well-being.

the banks that had invested heavily in the domestic oil industry during the OPEC decade. Others who had staked resources in the development of unconventional energy technologies also found themselves among the losers.

Much the same occurred internationally. For example, Third World debt (examined in Chapter 8) is tied directly to the way that international bankers and national decision makers responded to the costs and opportunities presented during the OPEC decade. The OPEC nations themselves were among the principal victims of the decline in oil prices, as the revenues on which they had staked important domestic development objectives disappeared. Saudi Arabia, for example, saw its oil income plummet from $113 billion in 1981 to only $28 billion in 1985 (Morse, 1986: 796). Non-OPEC oil exporters suffered similarly. Mexico, an emergent oil exporter, for example, lost considerable revenue on which it depended to pay its enormous foreign debt (but it benefited from interest rate reductions made possible in part by the reduced cost of oil internationally). Multinational oil companies suffered commensurately.

The soaring value of the U.S. dollar between 1981 and 1985, which was stimulated in part by the direct and indirect effects of the erosion of energy prices worldwide, also led to untoward consequences. As noted in Chapter 7, oil is typically priced and paid for in dollars. Thus, as the value of the dollar rose, other nations, as Western Europe and Japan, found that their oil import bill grew even as the American consumers' bill declined. And Americans who produced for the export market, mainly farmers, found it increasingly difficult to compete overseas.

Alternative Energy Sources

Just as the OPEC decade and its denouement created winners and losers domestically and internationally, the search for substitutes for oil and efforts to sever dependence on it as an energy source carries with it important global ecopolitical and economic implications.

Estimates of the world's reserves of fossil fuels are imprecise; yet all agree that coal is vastly more abundant than is either oil or natural gas. In the United States, for example, where domestic energy resources have always been abundant, the ratio of domestic reserves to production indicates that the amount of available crude oil will run out sometime during the 1990s and that gas reserves will be depleted shortly thereafter. The reserves of coal, however, will last for centuries.

Similar disparities exist in the worldwide distribution of proved and estimated reserves of coal, oil, and natural gas. This means that the resources currently in the shortest supply are those being depleted most rapidly. On the basis of current ratios of production to known reserves, oil can be expected to last only until about the year 2020 (*BP Statistical Review of World Energy*, 1987: 2).

Declining oil supplies will not lead to declining energy supplies if economically and politically viable energy alternatives are found and utilized. In addition to increased reliance on coal and natural gas, greater use of nuclear and hydropower could ease the transition to a non-oil-based energy system. Oil derived from unconventional sources such as tar sands and shale could also become economically viable, and renewable forms of energy might also become feasible, such as solar, tidal, and wind power, geothermal energy, and bioconversion.[9] Unfortunately, one of the major consequences of the smaller demand for fossil fuels in the post-OPEC era has been the reduction of incentives to develop these unconventional energy sources. Therefore, coal, natural gas, and nuclear power are likely to figure even more prominently as alternatives to oil. But each is beset with a range of economic, technical, and political uncertainties.

COAL   The world's most abundant energy resource is coal, but the feasibility of greatly expanding its use as an alternative to oil is circumscribed by the environmental hazards it poses. As described in Chapter 9, one of these is *acid rain*, which contributes to the acidification of lakes, the corrosion of materials and structures, and the impairment of ecosystems. A second is the *greenhouse effect*, which is believed likely to cause the average temperature of the earth's surface to rise by several degrees which would seriously damage much of the global environment. These and other social costs or "externalities" associated with a more widespread use of coal are difficult to measure, but they lay the basis for sustained political opposition to this energy source.

NATURAL GAS   Natural gas is cleaner and more convenient to use than is either oil or coal, and estimates of proven reserves indicate it is a viable energy source for at least the next half-century. Unlike coal, however, it is distributed very unevenly on a regional basis, which means that its continued development will depend on export trade. However, problems related to storage and transportation have yet to be resolved (Sivard, 1981).

The two largest natural gas markets are the United States and the Soviet Union, which consumed, respectively, 28 percent and 34 percent of the total world production in 1986 (*BP Statistical Review of World Energy*, 1987: 24). The Soviet Union is also a major producer of gas and possesses the largest reserves, with 43 percent of the world's proven reserves in 1986 (*BP Statistical Review of World Energy*, 1987: 23). The United States, on the other hand, has only about 5 percent of the world's gas reserves. Historically the United States has met from domestic sources virtually all of its need for gas, but it seems likely that it will increasingly have to look to imports to sustain its high

---

9. Stobaugh and Yergin (1979) provide a useful discussion of the economic and political factors associated with alternative energy strategies. A somewhat more technical discussion can be found in Ehrlich, Ehrlich, and Holdren (1977).

demand. As with oil, the Middle East is a likely source, as it holds over a quarter of the world's proven reserves but consumes only 3 percent of world production.

Getting gas from the wellhead to consumers is the primary problem. Assuming that environmental constraints can be overcome, pipelines are the preferred method of transport. But they are expensive and massive engineering projects (the 3,700-mile pipeline being built from the Soviet Union to Western Europe is a good example). Liquefied natural gas is an alternative, perhaps the only one for transshipment from the Middle East to North America or to the growing Western European and Japanese markets. But experts disagree as to the safety of liquefied natural gas. Because the liquefaction of gas permits a 1/600th reduction of its volume, "a tank of [liquefied natural gas] contains 600 times as much energy as the same size tank of natural gas. If it should spill, it would vaporize and become highly inflammable and explosive. In a densely populated area, such an accident could result in catastrophe" (Sivard, 1979a). Concern for safety has thus combined with cost considerations and sensitivity to dependence on OPEC sources to limit the development of new liquefied natural gas projects, at least in the United States (Stobaugh and Yergin, 1979).

NUCLEAR ENERGY   Among the known technologies, nuclear energy is seen by many as the leading alternative to dependence on fossil fuels. In 1986 nuclear power accounted for 5 percent of worldwide energy usage, and the demand for nuclear energy continued to grow at an annual rate of 7.1 percent. The United States is the single largest consumer of nuclear energy, but France is the country that uses it most intensively, deriving some 27 percent of its total energy use in 1986 from nuclear power (*BP Statistical Review of World Energy*, 1987: 7, 34).

Worldwide, some projections indicate that by the year 2020, nuclear power could account for a third of the world's energy needs. This assumes, however, that conditions will be favorable to its continued development. Currently they are not, with safety being the principal obstacle. Two well-publicized nuclear accidents, one at the Three Mile Island nuclear power plant in Pennsylvania in 1979, and a second at Chernobyl in the Ukraine in 1986, dramatized the risks and seemed to vindicate the skeptics who had warned about the dangers posed by nuclear energy. Catastrophe was averted at Three Mile Island, but even without the threatened meltdown of the reactor core, the accident released the largest-ever level of radioactive contamination by the American commercial nuclear industry. At Chernobyl, however, catastrophe did strike.

A few days [after the Chernobyl nuclear power plant exploded on April 26], much of Europe was experiencing the highest levels of radioactive fallout ever recorded there, and within two weeks, minor radioactivity was detected throughout the northern hemisphere. . . .

Chernobyl is the world's most serious nuclear power accident so far. The direct costs include 1,000 immediate injuries, 31 deaths, 135,000 people evacuated from their homes in the Ukraine, and at least $3 billion in financial losses. But the long-term implications are far more troubling and uncertain. It may not be possible simply to "remove the consequences of the accident," as Soviet officials put it. The health of Europe could be affected for decades. Estimates of resulting cancer deaths by researchers in the field range from less than 1,000 to almost 500,000. . . .

Rarely have so many countries been so affected by a single event. Chernobyl has tested the ability of East and West to cooperate, the public's confidence in government authorities, and society's faith in technology. And since Chernobyl, nuclear power has become a contentious international issue, particularly for neighboring countries with differing nuclear policies. (Flavin, 1987: 5)

Even before the first of these two nuclear accidents in 1979, the place of the nuclear industry in the world's energy future had begun to be scaled down from previous plans. Although virtually all of the industrial world, including the Soviet Union, determined in the wake of the first oil shock that a rapid buildup of nuclear power was necessary, only in France did the nuclear industry develop as planned (Stobaugh, 1982). In the United States, in contrast, many of the earlier orders for nuclear power plants were either canceled or deferred, and since 1978 no new plants have been ordered by the utilities industry. Faced with soaring costs, regulatory logjams, and political opposition, the industry also halted construction of numerous plants already under way. Elsewhere, the growth of West Germany's nuclear industry came to a virtual standstill, and earlier ambitious plans to develop nuclear power in Norway, Denmark, Austria, Australia, and New Zealand were postponed indefinitely. Nuclear power did continue to be developed in the Soviet Union, the United Kingdom, and Japan, but not at the pace once anticipated. The number of nuclear power plants that the Third World developing countries had planned to build was cut to half or less than the number expected in the mid-1970s (Stobaugh, 1982).

Reduced demand for electricity in the wake of the OPEC decade, rising political opposition to the nuclear industry in the wake of the Chernobyl accident, and concern for the safety of nuclear installations generally have combined to build resistance to the further development of nuclear energy. The safety issue has been especially prominent in the United States and Western Europe. Although there has not yet been a major accident in North America, the potential for widespread death and damage cannot be dismissed. A United States Nuclear Regulatory Commission study of nuclear safety, for example, concluded that a worst-case accident could result in more than 100,000 deaths and $300 billion in damage at certain locations in the United States (*Washington Post*, November 1, 1982, p. 1). Predictions such as these have made the mere siting of nuclear installations a contentious political issue in many countries. In West Germany the environmentalist Green Party has received substantial support, with the call to abolish nuclear energy high on its list of priorities.

How and where to dispose of highly radioactive nuclear wastes is another contentious issue, one that has been prominent in Europe and Japan as well as the United States. Spent fuel from nuclear-generating facilities must be removed periodically. It is then "cooled" in water to remove some of the most intense radioactivity before being reprocessed, a procedure that separates still-useful uranium and plutonium from other waste materials. No safe procedure for handling nuclear waste—some of which remains dangerous for hundreds of thousands of years—has yet been devised. In the meantime, large quantities of nuclear waste have accumulated, representing a substantial threat to environmental safety.

A related fear is that nuclear know-how might be acquired by countries that do not already possess it, thereby giving them the means to develop nuclear weapons. Proliferation is essentially a national security issue. Nuclear-generating facilities produce weapons-grade material, specifically highly enriched uranium and plutonium. Neither of these materials, which can be used to create a nuclear explosive device, is used commercially as fuel in the current generation of nuclear power reactors.[10] Yet at current and projected rates of production, the amount of such material created will eventually make available enough weapons-grade material to place within reach the construction of tens of thousands of nuclear bombs every year. Preventing the spread of nuclear weapons is therefore tied to the development of safeguards in the commercial nuclear industry.[11] Often, however, the strict enforcement of safeguards by the now-nuclear states is lax because other foreign and economic policy objectives have taken priority over nonproliferation. The result is a "silent spread" of nuclear know-how to large numbers of non-nuclear states (Spector, 1985, 1986; see also Chapter 11). The quest by additional nations to acquire a nuclear power capability for essentially political or even national security purposes thus complicates the question of how to maximize the use of nuclear power in an oil-dependent world.

In the final analysis, then, the factors that have crippled the nuclear power industry have reduced the ability of nuclear-generated power to compete with power generated from fossil fuels. If nuclear power is to be a viable energy

---

10. Commercial generating facilities generally use natural uranium, in which the fissile isotope U-235 occurs in low concentrations (less than 1 percent), or slightly enriched uranium (3 to 4 percent). Nuclear weapons, by contrast, require highly enriched uranium, which at present can be produced by only a few states.

Plutonium is an artificial element produced as a by-product of uranium-burning reactors. If separated from spent fuel by chemical reprocessing, it can be used to produce additional electrical generating capacity. However, only about ten kilograms of plutonium are needed to make a nuclear weapon (U.S. Arms Control and Disarmament Agency, 1979: 23).

11. See Kegley, Raymond, and Skinner (1980) for a cross-national empirical study suggesting the close linkage between the transnational commerce in uranium fuels, the diffusion of nuclear energy technology, and the enhanced probability of nuclear weapons dispersion.

alternative in the future, a number of potent political controversies that have yet to be confronted must be resolved.

This brief exploration of alternatives to energy derived from oil demonstrates that the "energy problematique" is in fact a complex mixture of technical, economic, environmental, political, and military issues. Preparing for a postpetroleum world therefore requires a frontal attack on a multitude of well-entrenched challenges, not the least of which is preservation of the standard of living to which much of the developed world has grown accustomed and to which others aspire. Mustering the political will to address constructively the problems posed may prove the most formidable task. Yet the need is clear, even if it is less compelling today than in the recent past. As Denis Hayes (1977) states, "Most energy policy is still framed as though it were addressing a problem that our grandchildren will inherit. But the energy crisis is *our* crisis. Oil and natural gas are our principal means of bridging today and tomorrow, and we are burning our bridges."

A COMING CRISIS?

Hayes's analysis of the requirements for converting to a postpetroleum world was completed in the immediate aftermath of the first oil shock. Describing the energy problem as a crisis was fashionable then. Today it is more meaningful to ask if there is a coming crisis, for the concern for oil, energy, and resource power are not regarded as the salient issues on the public policy agendas of most countries as it was during the crisis atmosphere between 1973 and 1983.[12]

Lower oil prices have contributed to the reduction of perceived threats. In the near term (three to five years) these reductions will benefit consumers and nations worldwide. But they will also undermine the prospects for realizing the long-term goal of achieving national and global energy security. Therein lies the paradox.

> Lower oil prices, even if they persist for only a few years, will stimulate growth in total energy and oil demand, discourage oil production from high-cost reserves, slow down gains in efficiency and conservation, reduce the incentive to develop alternative fuels, and lead to rising dependence on imported oil. At the same time, lower oil prices promote economic growth, increase GNP, and have a net beneficial effect on the economies of the United States and other oil-importing countries. (U.S. Department of Energy, 1987b: 223)

Despite the adverse consequences of lower oil prices, immediate alarm is probably unwarranted because, as the U.S. Department of Energy (1987b)

---

12. See Renner (1987) for a critical appraisal of the energy policies (or lack thereof) of the Reagan administration and of the need to devise a strategy whose "short-term task is to avoid the recurrence of another oil crisis in the 1990s" and whose "long-term task is to manage the transition from the present heavily oil-reliant energy system to a future system based on renewable energy sources."

predicted, "World oil consumption is expected to grow more slowly than total energy demand despite falling oil prices" and "the ability of importing nations to respond to oil supply disruptions . . . is improving." That assessment also predicted that the cost of U.S. oil imports will rise from $28 billion in 1981 (in 1986 dollars) to $80 billion, with a similar pattern for other countries likely. Forecasts beyond the near term are difficult; nonetheless, warns this report, the possibility exists that under certain circumstances "a politically inspired oil embargo similar to the one organized among suppliers in 1973–74 . . . could become [a significant threat] as oil imports increase and excess production capacity declines."

Other estimates are even less sanguine about the future. One well-known futurologist sees a striking similarity in the developments leading to the two oil shocks of the 1970s and the 1980s:

> The contemporary era has been dominated by two complete cycles of energy trauma and . . . a third cycle is now possibly in its early stages. The first cycle began with a worldwide economic and commodity boom and related tightening of the world petroleum market in the late 1960s and early 1970s. Political-military events precipitated the crisis of 1973–74, which was then followed by a period of recession and basically flat oil prices in the mid-1970s. The second cycle began with an economic boom and a related increase in petroleum consumption in the late 1970s resulting, once again, in a tightening of the petroleum market. Political events in Iran triggered a second crisis in 1979–80 which culminated in another, deeper, recession that lasted through the early 1980s. With the petroleum price collapse of 1986, there is increasing evidence of developments indicative of the early stages of a third cycle, but the length of time it will take the global economy to create another tight oil market remains a matter for analysis. (Pirages, 1986: 32)

The lingering effects of the deep economic recession of the early 1980s will doubtlessly inhibit any rapid movement toward another tight oil market. Similarly, the irreversible income effects of higher oil prices in the 1970s and early 1980s will continue to pay dividends in the future as a result of energy-efficiency programs previously put into place. But other factors that may influence the future energy situation and thereby affect the foregoing projections and prognoses deserve additional attention.

Oil, OPEC, and the Future

The World Bank (*World Development Report 1983*, 1983: 29–30) estimated in the early 1980s that by 1995 petroleum will account for only 35 percent of global energy consumption, compared with 46 percent in 1980, even though total energy consumption will grow from 135 million to 191 million barrels of oil-equivalent energy during this same time. Coal is expected to supply the largest portion of the projected increase in global energy demand, followed by nuclear and hydroelectric power.

Despite petroleum's declining share of world energy consumption, it will still play a key role in the global energy picture for the remainder of this century and perhaps beyond, particularly if reduced oil prices continue to undermine incentives to develop high-cost oil deposits or alternative energy sources, and with them the security that diversified energy sources provide (see Jessup, 1988). OPEC's continued importance is thereby also ensured. Although its share of world oil production declined from almost half in 1979 to less than a third in 1986, it continues to control over two-thirds of the world's proven reserves of oil. The Persian Gulf members of OPEC are especially important, because they control over 80 percent of OPEC's reserves, with Saudi Arabia alone accounting for more than a third (*BP Statistical Review of World Energy*, 1987: 2). The Persian Gulf members of OPEC also account for nearly two-thirds of OPEC's current (1986) production.

These statistical data alone underscore how important OPEC oil in general, and Persian Gulf oil in particular, are to the world's future energy security. Whether OPEC as an organization will be able to regain the cohesion necessary to act as a potent political and economic force in directing the world energy market is, however, problematic. The members of the already fragile organization differ widely in their financial needs, oil reserves, political regimes, foreign policy objectives, and political aspirations. They are also geographically distant, with widely disparate sociocultural systems, population sizes, levels of income, internal problems, and external challenges.[13] Increasingly,

---

13. Moreover, they have been affected differently by the shifting character of the international oil regime set in motion by the OPEC decade. Some members of OPEC, for example, who used their oil revenues to invest heavily in domestic development projects during the OPEC decade may not have the financial reserves necessary to ride out even a short-run decline in oil income. For these producers, higher prices and increased production are in their domestic political interest. For others, who were able during the OPEC decade to amass large reserves of cash or to invest their newfound wealth in productive assets overseas, it may be possible to withstand reduced oil income and to await the day when their resource will once again generate handsome returns. In the meantime, however, many of these same states that invested heavily in the Western industrialized nations find themselves, paradoxically, "hostage" to the economic and political fortunes of those in which the investments were made. Luke (1983), for example, argues that the economic modernization of the Arab members of OPEC has unfolded in such a way as to keep those states dependent on Western industrialized nations. In such an environment of "mutual vulnerability," there is little prospect that the supply or price of oil will be manipulated to achieve short-run political objectives.

A question of related interest is how the depletion of their oil reserves will affect the different OPEC members. Some can expect to find themselves little better off than they were before the oil bonanza. As one well-known oil expert commented, "the odds at this time are that when the oil revenues begin to peter out, a number of the OPEC countries will find themselves not too much better off than before—like Spain, after it had been inundated by gold and silver from its Latin American empire in the late sixteenth and early seventeenth centuries" (Levy, 1978–1979).

Others have found their hopes for modernization and industrialization via oil-induced investments tempered by the realization that "the injection of oil money will not by itself bring about rapid development. Self-sustained growth is an evolutionary process and for this reason the life span of the oil revenues must be extended to ensure a continuous flow of foreign exchange" (Fesharaki, 1981). Saudi Arabia perhaps falls into this category. The Saudis spent literally tens of billions of dollars during the OPEC decade to seize a unique historical opportunity to move their desert kingdom into the ranks of the industrially prosperous. The effort required herculean efforts to build everything from new highways and port facilities to sophisticated petrochemical plants and even entire new cities. Yet their ability to manage and operate these new facilities effectively and efficiently may be years in coming.

however, the six Persian Gulf members of the thirteen-member organization will be the only ones that matter.

One factor that will enhance the position of the Persian Gulf states is closely related to the rapid growth in recent years of the demand for energy in the Third World countries generally.

> In low-income developing countries, rising energy demand is the result of continued urbanization—which creates a shift from reliance on traditional fuels (such as wood) to greater reliance on commercial fuels (such as oil, gas, and coal). In the higher-income, newly industrializing countries, the relocation of some energy-intensive industries, such as steel, away from the [Western industrialized nations] to these countries has caused energy demand to rise rapidly.
>
> Rising incomes and an increase in the transportation sector's use of energy have caused the demand for oil to rise even faster than overall energy demand in many developing countries. (U.S. Department of Energy, 1987b: 225)

As these developments take place in the oil-producing countries themselves, some of them—such as Ecuador, Gabon, Algeria, Nigeria, and Indonesia—will need to direct their production to domestic needs rather than the export market (Ebinger, 1985).

Second, as the North Sea and Alaskan oil finds of the 1970s reach their maximum production levels and then begin to drop in the years ahead, the enormous concentration of oil in the Middle East will loom larger in importance. The process, which is strikingly similar to the developments giving rise to the OPEC decade, is already discernible in the United States, as illustrated in Figure 10.5. Domestic production in the United States has fallen since 1984, but demand has grown as a consequence of lower oil prices and continuing economic growth. Imports have thus been needed to fill the gap. These imbalances are expected to accelerate in the years ahead, with the United States importing perhaps as much as 70 percent of its oil by 1996 (compared with 27 percent in 1985 and 47 percent at the peak in 1977) (*The Oil Rollercoaster*, 1987: 8). "During times of significant excess supply and declining prices, dependence may involve acceptable risks to national security. However, if supply becomes as tight as it did in the early 1970s, OPEC will wield enormous economic and political power over consuming nations" (*The Oil Rollercoaster*, 1987). Even in the absence of cohesion among OPEC's key members, individual members of the cartel will be profoundly important, and maintaining access to Middle East oil will remain a critical issue on most nations' foreign policy agendas.

As oil prices rise in the 1990s, as they are expected to do, the escalating cost of oil growing out of increased dependence on foreign suppliers will have repercussions for the entire world economy. Furthermore, the preceding scenario, which sees rising oil consumption and declining reserves among the Western industrialized nations leading once more to dependence on OPEC

FIGURE 10.5 ■ Trends in U.S. Oil Production, Consumption, and Imports, 1970–1987

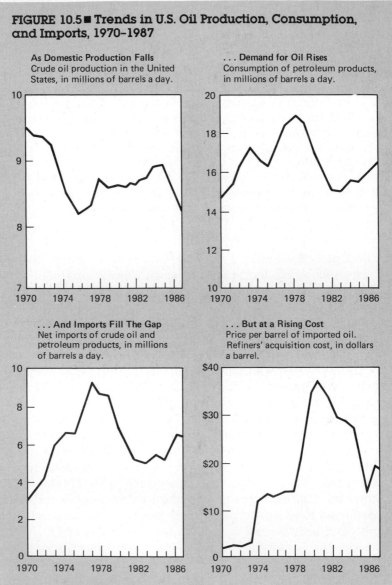

As Domestic Production Falls
Crude oil production in the United States, in millions of barrels a day.

. . . Demand for Oil Rises
Consumption of petroleum products, in millions of barrels a day.

. . . And Imports Fill The Gap
Net imports of crude oil and petroleum products, in millions of barrels a day.

. . . But at a Rising Cost
Price per barrel of imported oil. Refiners' acquisition cost, in dollars a barrel.

Source: "Growing U.S. Dependence on Imported Oil," *New York Times*, November 19, 1987, p. D1. Copyright © 1987 by The New York Times Company. Reprinted by permission.

Note: 1987 production and consumption data are estimates; 1987 import data are through November; 1987 cost data are through July.

producers, could push oil prices much higher than currently anticipated. Under these conditions, "the perceptions in the oil markets would change overnight. Uncertainty over assured supplies again would haunt the oil consuming nations; competition among the major oil importers surely would follow. History warns us that when uncertainty over assured supplies begins, upward pressure of oil prices is close behind" (Jessup, 1988).

Oil and National Security (Again)

In 1987, in response to the fear that the continuing war between Iran and Iraq might widen and thereby threaten the continued flow of oil from the Middle East, the United States substantially increased its naval presence in the Persian Gulf region and made the controversial decision to escort Kuwaiti oil tankers through the Persian Gulf and the perilous Strait of Hormuz, where oil tankers had become routine targets in the war. Nothing could have underscored more dramatically the importance that the United States attaches to the Middle Eastern oil lifeline to the West.

It warrants reiterating that the Middle East is a highly volatile region where the threats of internal conflict and war are ever present, from which a politico-military event might erupt to trigger a future energy crisis once trends in production and consumption converge to create a tighter oil market. Various national and subnational groups in the region also harbor deep-seated hostility toward the United States. The possibility that the Soviet-American rivalry might spill into the region is thus a continuing danger. The Soviet Union, for example, has historically been a major arms supplier for Syria and Iraq, and the United States has been the principal supplier of Saudi Arabia and Israel. For the Soviet Union, the Middle East is an area of immediate security concern, as it shares an extended border with Iran and otherwise finds the area in its own backyard.[14] At the same time, however, Soviet leaders seem to understand that the United States defines the area as critical to its national security, but they fear that instability there might be used as a pretext for American military intervention, which would be inimical to Soviet national security (Bohi and Quandt, 1984).

The superpowers' competition for influence and allies through arms exports, military advisers and other forms of military presence, and economic and military aid extends beyond the Middle East to Africa and Asia, with much of it taking place in areas adjacent to, and often parallel to, the major oil sea-lanes of transportation from the Middle East to Europe, North America, and Japan. As noted earlier, there is no apparent reason to believe that the Soviet Union has consciously sought to extend its influence among Third World

14. See Gawad (1986) for an interpretation that sees Persian Gulf oil and Islamic fundamentalism in Iran as factors enhancing the Soviet Union's ability to gain economically from the Middle East at the same time that its own domestic oil sector deteriorates.

countries so as to be able to interdict the supply of Middle East oil to Western markets.[15] It is true nonetheless that the Soviet Union today has power-projection capabilities far greater than it had ten or twenty years ago, putting it in a position to strike at Western interests in ways and in places not previously possible.

What about the energy future of the Soviet Union itself? As noted earlier, some Western analysts question the Soviet Union's ability to maintain its own output. As evidence mounts that it has had difficulty meeting its production targets (whether because of mismanagement, outmoded technology, or a decline in the productivity of the most easily accessible oil fields), the Soviet Union may find compelling reasons to expand its influence in the Persian Gulf area. But its inclination to do so by force is marginal because its overall energy resources (particularly its vast reserves of natural gas, whose production continues to expand) promise to remain substantial well into the future (Hewett, 1984).

> If the Soviets were ever to see a strategic advantage in controlling Gulf oil, it would be not because of their own needs but because of the leverage it would give them over Europe and Japan. The offsetting consideration would obviously be the risk of global war that would lie behind any Soviet threat to the Gulf. Deterrence of an overt military move by the Soviets toward the Gulf will depend on both the regional balance of forces, which favors the Soviets—but not overwhelmingly—and the global balance of power that would come into play in any superpower confrontation in the Gulf. (Bohi and Quandt, 1984: 42)

The apparent inability of the Soviet Union to maintain domestic oil production could adversely affect its other foreign policy objectives. Oil exports to the West are a major source of its "hard" (convertible) currency earnings, accounting for some 55 percent of such earnings in 1985 and 40 percent in 1986 (the sharp decline is due largely to the drop in world oil prices) (U.S. Department of Energy, 1987b: 227). If the amount of Soviet oil available for export to the West continues to decline in the 1990s as projected (U.S. Department of Energy, 1987b; see also Gawad, 1986), Soviet leaders may face a difficult choice—cutting exports to the West, which would curtail their ability to obtain needed imports from abroad; or cutting exports to Eastern Europe, which could provoke social unrest. Already, differences between the Soviet Union and Eastern Europe over energy policy issues are a serious source of discord in the socialist camp (Volgyes, 1988). Faced with this predicament, the Soviet Union's future is brightened by the fact that its huge reserves of fossil fuels as well as its vigorous nuclear energy program give the Soviet leaders "considerable flexibility in substituting other energy sources for its domestic oil use" (U.S. Department of Energy, 1987b).

---

15. For assessments of Soviet Third World objectives, see Halliday (1987), Papp (1986), Shulman (1986), and Whelan and Dixon (1986).

ON THE (DIS)UTILITY OF RESOURCE POWER

The tremendous impact of OPEC on the international political economy during the OPEC decade, whose effects continue to be felt, derived from the fact that oil was in high demand but unevenly distributed throughout the world. Scenarios of a coming crisis likewise project an imbalance between world production and consumption of an essential resource. This does not necessarily mean that the OPEC cartel will be able to realize its political goals, as that would depend on a degree of cohesion in regulating prices and production in pursuit of a common objective that may be impossible to achieve. In fact, since its rise to prominence in the early 1970s, OPEC has rarely been able to agree to act in concert in pursuit of specific political objectives. Instead, its impact derived essentially from price-oriented actions characteristic of a classic oligopoly. Its behavior nevertheless has had important political ramifications in consuming countries, and the fact that most of the cartel's most important members were located in the politically sensitive Middle East added special urgency to the maldistribution of global oil production and consumption.

Are there other commodities with these same characteristics? Are other OPECs therefore possible? Might they, too, become vehicles for enhancing the economic welfare of their members at the expense of others or for realizing the long-term political aspirations for a restructuring of the Liberal International Economic Order that so many Third World countries find disadvantageous?

The data displayed in Table 10.1 seem to support the proposition that the developing nations already hold substantial commodity power. Note, for example, that in the 1981–1983 period they accounted for 98 percent of the world's exports of rubber, 92 percent of its exports of coffee and cocoa, 85 percent of its exports of tea, and 75 percent of its exports of tin. Such an apparently high degree of global dependence on a few exporters of commodities, some of which are regarded as "critical" or "strategic" resources, has been a matter of serious concern among policymakers in many importing countries, especially after their experiences with the OPEC cartel. In the early years of the Reagan administration, for example, American policymakers frequently talked about an impending "resource war" as resource-dependent industrial nations clamored to ensure secure access to resources vital to their advanced economies. Yet no resource war has broken out, and none of the commodities that seem so firmly in the control of Third World producers has come under monopoly control in the same way that oil did during the OPEC decade—even though producers' associations have at one time or another been formed in many of these commodity markets.[16] Why not? And what do these apparently failed prognoses regarding impending war and dashed hopes about commodity power portend for the future?

---

16. Several studies have considered the possibility of other resource markets becoming cartelized, and most agree that oil is unique. Among them are Arad and Arad (1979), Krasner (1974), Pirages (1978), Smart (1976), Spero (1985), Stern and Tims (1976), and Varon and Takeuchi (1974). Other studies relevant to this topic are by Chouchri (1972), Connelly and Perlman (1975), Paarlberg (1984), Russett (1984), Schneider (1976), Winberg (1979), and Wu (1973).

TABLE 10.1 ■ Major Primary Commodity Exports of Developing Countries, 1981–1983 ($ billions and percentages)

	Developing-Country Exports		Major Developing-Country Suppliers 1981–83 (Percentage of World Exports of Commodity)							
	($ Billions)	(Percentage of World Exports of Commodity)								
Petroleum	$216.5	81.0	Saudi Arabia	26.8	Mexico	5.8	U.A.E.	5.7	Iran	5.6
Sugar	8.5	69.1	Cuba	36.6	Brazil	5.9	Philippines	3.5	Thailand	3.5
Coffee	8.3	91.6	Brazil	20.0	Colombia	16.4	Ivory Coast	4.8	El Salvador	4.6
Copper	5.1	63.8	Chile	22.1	Zambia	12.2	Zaire	7.3	Peru	4.8
Timber	4.6	27.8	Malaysia	11.0	Indonesia	3.8	Ivory Coast	1.9	Philippines	1.7
Iron ore	3.2	46.8	Brazil	24.9	India	5.2	Liberia	4.4	Venezuela	3.3
Rubber	3.0	98.3	Malaysia	47.0	Indonesia	24.8	Thailand	15.4	Sri Lanka	4.2
Cotton	2.9	43.4	Egypt	6.5	Pakistan	5.5	Turkey	5.5	Mexico	4.2
Rice	2.5	55.0	Thailand	22.5	Pakistan	9.2	China	5.5	India	3.0
Tobacco	2.3	51.3	Brazil	9.8	Turkey	7.4	Zimbabwe	6.0	India	4.6
Maize	2.0	19.2	Argentina	8.7	Thailand	3.5	Yugoslavia	1.2	Zimbabwe	0.5
Tin	1.9	74.7	Malaysia	28.6	Indonesia	13.4	Thailand	12.7	Bolivia	10.0
Cocoa	1.9	92.1	Ivory Coast	26.4	Ghana	16.3	Nigeria	12.2	Brazil	11.8
Tea	1.5	84.6	India	26.6	Sri Lanka	18.2	China	12.8	Kenya	8.9
Palm oil	1.4	81.6	Malaysia	70.1	Indonesia	7.0	Ivory Coast	1.7	Papua New Guinea	0.5
Beef	1.3	16.7	Argentina	5.4	Uruguay	2.5	Brazil	2.2	Yugoslavia	1.3
Bananas	1.2	86.7	Costa Rica	16.7	Honduras	14.2	Ecuador	13.8	Colombia	10.2
Wheat and meslin	1.2	6.9	Argentina	5.7	Turkey	5.7	Uruguay	0.4	Yugoslavia	0.1
Phosphate rock	1.1	62.9	Morocco	34.1	Jordan	8.5	Togo	4.8	Senegal	3.0

Source: Published by permission of Transaction Publishers, from *Growth, Jobs, and Exports in a Changing World Economy,* by John W. Sewell and Stuart K. Tucker. Copyright © 1988 by Transaction Publishers.

Resource Dependence and Commodity Power

The ability of Third World producers to wield commodity power—and the incentives that the First World importing countries might have to use force of arms to ensure their access to vital resources—depends on a peculiar combination of circumstances. Dependency is the critical factor, but it can take on various manifestations. As Bruce Russett observes:

> Fears of dependence in industrialized economies arise from several different economic and political possibilities. The first involves changes in market conditions that suppliers impose deliberately, for economic reasons: in effect, the possibility of significant price increases imposed by a single supplier or, more likely, by a cartel in order to reap monopoly (or oligopoly) profits. . . .
>
> A second possibility concerns changes in market conditions imposed deliberately, but for political purposes, by suppliers or hostile third parties. Here we refer chiefly to embargoes, boycotts, or trade sanctions, such as the American economic sanctions against the Soviet Union for its action in Poland and Afghanistan [described later in this chapter]. . . . (Russett, 1984: 483)

As we noted, OPEC's behavior during the OPEC decade reflected political and economic motives, both of which created fears of resource dependence in the North. The oil embargo against the United States and the Netherlands in the immediate aftermath of the Yom Kippur War was clearly politically motivated to affect the importance that each attached to its support of Israel. Thereafter, most of OPEC's efforts to coordinate pricing and production policies were motivated to maximize economic returns to its members. To understand the elements that allowed these actions to succeed and to predict whether they can be repeated in other commodity markets in the future, several factors critical to the exercise of a commodity power need to be evaluated.

ECONOMIC FACTORS   The two market conditions necessary for effective monopoly power are (1) a lack of responsiveness to prices by consumers and (2) a lack of responsiveness in the supply of the commodity growing out of increases in its price. These two conditions are known technically as the *price inelasticity of demand and supply*.

The demand for a commodity is price inelastic if the amount consumed changes little even if its price increases substantially. The price inelasticity of demand is essential to a producers' cartel whose goal is to maximize the amount of foreign exchange it earns from its product. If the demand is price elastic, the total amount of money earned by producers will be less at the new, higher price than at the old, lower price, because of reduced consumption. But if the demand is price inelastic, the total revenues will be greater at the higher prices.

The price inelasticity of supply operates in much the same way. If the supply of a commodity is price inelastic, this means that new producers will not (or cannot) enter the market to take advantage of the higher rates of return associated with higher prices. If new producers do enter the market, which means that the supply is price elastic, the increased supply will likely drive prices back down, making the foreign exchange earned no greater and perhaps even less than before prices were increased. Even if prices do not return to previous levels, the reduced market share that the individual producers will control will reduce their monetary receipts. Clearly, then, the price inelasticity of supply is also essential.

The experience of OPEC illustrates how important these economic factors are to commodity producers. The crucial role that oil had come to occupy in the world energy picture by the onset of the OPEC decade was made apparent by the near absence of any change in global demand following the fourfold increase in the price of oil during the winter of 1973–1974 (Smart, 1976). On the supply side, the long lead time required to develop new petroleum sources (demonstrated by the time required to bring the Alaskan and North Sea finds into production) combined with the absence of energy alternatives to preclude rapid movement away from dependence on OPEC oil. Eventually both the demand for and supply of oil proved to be more price elastic than most analysts had predicted, as consumers responded to higher prices by reducing consumption and as potential new energy producers entered the marketplace more rapidly than most analysts anticipated. Both forces contributed substantially to the denouement of the OPEC decade. But in the immediate aftermath of the first oil shock, supply, like demand, generally proved price inelastic.

How do other commodities compare with oil? In the near term it would appear that many commodity producers could enjoy the benefits of monopoly control, as both demand and supply are sufficiently price inelastic that the producers could enjoy the benefits of increased export earnings if they could cooperate to control prices and output (Krasner, 1974). In the long term, however, the price elasticity of demand for many of the major commodities traded internationally, particularly minerals, is clearly not conducive to effective cartelization (see Varon and Takeuchi, 1974). Three factors capable of altering market conditions are important to explaining this: stockpiles, recycling, and substitutes.

Many commodities are easily stockpiled. The United States, for example, has maintained since 1939 large "strategic stockpiles" of certain minerals, and in response to the oil shocks of the 1970s it now maintains a strategic petroleum reserve as well. All of these strategic inventories are designed to give the United States a cushion against the actions of foreign producers.

Recycling is another means of affecting commodities supplies. Recovering metal from scrap material is one example; recycling aluminum soft-drink cans is another. Augmenting recycling capacity may take time, and the resultant product may be relatively expensive, but the important point is that in many cases minerals are not completely used when they are consumed.

Substitution is a third way that producers' cartels can be undermined. If aluminum becomes too expensive for making cans, tin can be substituted. If tin becomes too expensive, glass or plastic might be used. Even oil has its substitutes in coal, hydropower, and nuclear energy. In the long run, then, there appear to be few commodities produced and exported by Third World nations whose potential for market control are not undermined by simple economic forces.

POLITICAL FACTORS   What about political factors? Is there some combination of these that might enhance the poor nations' bargaining power by increasing the rich nations' fear of them?

Several "political" factors appear to be necessary for translating control over the supply of a commodity (especially nonrenewable resources compared with renewable resources, such as agricultural products) into effective political power, that is, the use of resource power for realizing political returns, not simply economic or commercial benefits. Three are especially important: (1) *scarcity*—"the global, physical availability of the raw material in question, relative to other natural resources as well as possible substitutes"; (2) *distribution*—"the political and economic character of the market for the specific raw material, its existence in reserve form among the consuming nations, and its pattern of consumption"; and (3) *essentiality*—"the intrinsic importance of the raw material . . . either in security or in economic terms" (Arad and Arad, 1979).

One survey of the applicability of these prerequisites to a range of nonrenewable natural resources concluded that oil was the only resource that met all three criteria (Arad and Arad, 1979; see also Russett, 1984). As we have seen, during the 1980s even oil did not meet these three basic requirements. Several circumstances explain why.

First, many First World countries are clearly dependent on foreign imports of mineral and other products to sustain their sophisticated economies, but this does not mean they are dependent on Third World exports. Canada is a principal source on which the United States relies heavily for many of its mineral imports, for example. Similarly, other developed nations are often important sources of commodities that enter world trade. Australia is an important producer of bauxite and alumina; South Africa is an important source of manganese, chromium, platinum, and gold; and the Soviet Union is an important producer of these same four minerals. In fact, the major exporters of most minerals in the world today generally include developed as well as developing countries. An examination of the distribution of world mineral reserves indicates this situation is unlikely to change. The producers of many agricultural commodities that are traded internationally so as to enhance the dietary intake of people in the world's rich nations are concentrated in the Third World, but their products fail to meet the criterion of product essentiality.

Second, because the producers of many important products traded internationally are so diverse economically, the prospects of building effective producers' cartels among them are diminished. When we add to this the fact that many of the principal producers of the minerals traded internationally consist of such politically antagonistic states as South Africa and the Soviet Union, the possibility that effective producers' cartels might be created becomes remote indeed.

Finally, just as many First World nations are dependent on foreign imports to sustain their economies, many Third World commodity producers are dependent on exports to sustain theirs. For example, our examination of the debt situation in Chapter 8 made clear that many Third World countries have become extremely sensitive in recent years to the need for export earnings to maintain their economic health. Few, therefore, can afford the financial and potential political risks that efforts to cartelize export markets may entail. Indeed, one of the striking lessons from the OPEC experience is that its success depended in large part on the ability of the cartel's key members to bear the brunt of production reductions so as to maintain higher oil prices. This meant that the "swing producers," mainly Saudi Arabia and, less so, Kuwait, had to have enough money (foreign exchange) "in the bank" so as to absorb the costs of production cutbacks.

But the second lesson is more important: OPEC's success as a political force depended on shared political values (at least among its most important members, the Arab ones) that enabled it to be transformed at least for a short time from simply another commodity producers' association into an effective political force. The shared value was antipathy toward Israel, combined with the desire by the most important members of OPEC to use the oil weapon to affect the outcome of the long-standing and bitter Middle East conflict. Perhaps more than anything else, it was this political factor that distinguished OPEC from other producers' cartels.

Economic Sanctions As Instruments of Foreign Policy

OPEC's oil embargo against the United States and the Netherlands in 1973 in an effort to force them to revise their policies toward Israel is a prime example of economic sanctions, which can be defined as "deliberate government actions to inflict economic deprivation on a target state or society, through the limitation or cessation of customary economic relations" (Leyton-Brown, 1987). International economic sanctions are part of the broad array of instruments of economic statecraft available to governments (see Baldwin, 1985); their general purpose is to demonstrate resolve and to exercise influence in a manner short of the actual use of military force. The widespread use of economic sanctions as instruments of foreign policy is documented in the 103 cases since the beginning of World War I in which sanctions have been deployed in pursuit of particular foreign policy objectives (Hufbauer and Schott, 1985a).

Despite their frequent use, most efforts to apply economic sanctions have failed. This record has led many policy analysts to conclude that economic sanctions are not very useful instruments of policy (see, for example, Knorr,

1975, 1977). Why is this the case? And why, then, do policymakers continue to rely on economic sanctions as instruments of influence? Let us address each question in turn.

Three conspicuous cases of the application of economic sanctions in the context of the Soviet-American rivalry illustrate their shortcomings: those applied against Castro's Cuba beginning in 1960; against the Soviet Union following its intervention into Afghanistan in 1979; and against Poland and the Soviet Union between 1981 and 1982 following the imposition of martial law in Poland in December 1981.

The United States instituted sanctions against the Castro regime shortly after it assumed power in 1960. The sanctions themselves began with a cut in the amount of sugar permitted to enter the United States under the quota system maintained by the United States but eventually were extended to a ban on all U.S. trade with Cuba, combined with an effort to induce other nations to follow suit. Two objectives were sought. Initially, the goal was the overthrow of the Castro government. Failing that, from about 1964 onward the goal was containing the Castro revolution and Cuban interventionism in Central and South America and Africa (Roca, 1987).

Clearly the United States was unsuccessful in securing Castro's overthrow, and it was only marginally successful in containing Cuba's ability to pursue its own revolutionary brand of foreign policy abroad. "The major accomplishment of the US economic embargo . . . consisted of increasing the cost to Cuba of surviving and developing as a socialist country and of pursuing an international commitment" (Roca, 1987). That it was able to do so was largely due to the willingness of the Soviet Union to support Cuba economically, to the inability of the United States to persuade other Western nations to curtail trade and financial relations with Cuba, and to Castro's charismatic leadership and the Cuban government's domestic political control at home (Roca, 1987; see also Schreiber, 1973).

Following the Soviet Union's intervention in Afghanistan in 1979, the United States imposed several economic sanctions on the Soviet Union and undertook other measures, such as a boycott of the 1980 Summer Olympics, which were scheduled to be held in Moscow. Among the most celebrated of U.S. efforts was a partial embargo on the sale of grain to the Soviet Union. Among other things, the actions sought "to punish the Soviet Union while at the same time limiting the damage to the economic interests of important domestic groups" (Falkenheim, 1987; see also Paarlberg, 1980).

The embargo on grain sales did not stop the flow of grain to the Soviet Union in large measure because, as noted in Chapter 9, other nations (principally Argentina) increased their exports to make up the shortfall in American exports. What the (partial) embargo and the other sanctions were intended to accomplish remains a matter of dispute, however, in part because the reasons for the Soviet intervention in Afghanistan were themselves open to conflicting interpretations. If the goal was "to punish the Soviet Union for its invasion of

Afghanistan in order to moderate future Soviet foreign policy behaviour" (Falkenheim, 1987), it may have been appropriate if the Kremlin's intention was to push into the remote Southwestern Asian land as a prelude to a further advance toward the rich oil fields in Iran and elsewhere in the Persian Gulf. But if its behavior was merely the defensive reaction of a great power seeking to maintain a client regime in a bordering state, thereby preventing its neutralization or fall into the "enemy camp," U.S. sanctions may have been quite irrelevant to the task.

In any event, the evidence suggests that the sanctions imposed by the United States extracted a cost on Soviet society but did not have a great impact on its foreign policy, in part because the Soviet economy is largely self-sufficient, which minimizes the impact of external events on its economic system, and in part because Soviet leaders were determined to resist external pressures on their foreign policy behavior. Economic sanctions thus served to increase the resolve of Soviet leaders to do as they please rather than to diminish it (Falkenheim, 1987).

Similar lessons apply to Poland. Following the imposition of martial law by the Polish government in 1981 to forestall continued labor and related unrest, the Reagan administration imposed a series of sanctions against both Poland and the Soviet Union, including, among others, restrictions on U.S. government credits for the purchase of food and other commodities by Poland, restrictions on high-technology exports to Poland, and suspension of its most-favored-nation status with the United States (Marantz, 1987). In the case of the Soviet Union, one goal was to restrict the flow of Western goods and technology necessary to proceed with the trans-Siberian gas pipeline designed to bring Soviet energy resources into Western European markets.

As in the other cases of imposing economic sanctions to prosecute the East–West contest, the Polish sanctions were motivated by several objectives. Among them was the hope that the severity of Polish martial law might be lessened, the beliefs that "doing nothing" was morally reprehensible and that the United States had to stand up to the Soviet Union, and the expectation that economic pressure on the Soviet Union would increase the economic strains under which the Soviet system would have to operate (Marantz, 1987). As in the case of imposing sanctions in the aftermath of the Soviet invasion of Afghanistan, by "doing something" in response to the Polish crisis, the Reagan administration's sanctions enabled it to satisfy domestic constituencies with measures short of more forceful actions that some of the more conservative critics of America's Soviet and Eastern European policies might have preferred (see Marantz, 1987).

In the end, the Reagan administration was forced to seek a face-saving compromise with its European allies on the pipeline issue which permitted its construction to proceed as they wished. The compromise was necessary to preserve a degree on unity in the Atlantic alliance in the face of the inability of the sanctions imposed by the United States (and others in varying degrees) to alter the behavior of either the Soviet Union or Poland.[17] The absence of consensus among the NATO allies was itself a factor contributing to the sanctions' failure. But other factors were also at work, including the Soviet Union's ability and willingness to support its client, namely, Poland, and the relative invulnerability of the Soviet economic and political systems to external pressures (Marantz, 1987).

Even without the special circumstances involved in Western efforts to impose economic sanctions on the Soviet Union and its allies, the utility of economic sanctions as instruments of foreign policy enjoys a checkered history at best. Notable in this regard is the long history of efforts by various nations and groups of nations to impose international economic sanctions on South Africa in an effort to influence the Pretoria regime to liberalize its policies regarding racial separation, known as *apartheid*, with a view toward its eventual elimination. For example, at the behest of Third World nations, the United Nations imposed a voluntary arms embargo against South Africa in 1963, which became "mandatory" in 1977, and more recently South Africa has been the object of an oil embargo.

The attitude of the United States toward South Africa has been of special concern to the opponents of *apartheid*, because the United States has major investments in South Africa and is a primary importer of the many critical minerals of which South Africa enjoys vast reserves. A frequent argument in the United States during the long years of debate about the appropriate response of the United States to *apartheid* focused on who would be the victims of internationally applied sanctions: South African blacks, already the victims of a policy of systematic racial discrimination, or the white minority regime who perpetuated it? Upon assuming office in 1981, the Reagan administration adopted a policy of "constructive engagement" toward South Africa, whose broad purpose was a diplomatic approach to the Pretoria regime on the *apartheid* issue. But in 1985, in an unusual domestic political development, the Congress of the United States legislated, over a presidential veto, mandatory sanctions against South Africa in an effort to modify the policies that Congress found objectionable.

The long and generally unsuccessful history of international economic sanctions led many observers to conclude that the actions mandated by the U.S. Congress would have little material impact on the South African govern-

---

17. "Don't bite off more than you can chew" is one of the conclusions of a study of more than eighty attempts in the twentieth century to use economic sanctions in pursuit of foreign policy goals:

> Countries often have inflated expectations of what sanctions can and cannot accomplish. At most, there is a weak correlation between economic deprivation and political willingness to change. The *economic* impact of sanctions may be pronounced, both on the sender and the target country, but other factors in the situational context almost always overshadow the impact of sanctions in determining the *political* outcome. (Hufbauer and Schott, 1983: 76)

ment (cf. Minter, 1986–1987). One reason is that a typical response to economic coercion in the sanctioned society is a heightened sense of nationalism, a *laager* mentality (circle the ox wagons to face oncoming enemies), which stimulates resistance in the target state. Another, perhaps more important reason in the South African case is that although governments may impose sanctions publicly, they nevertheless interact in many ways to support the sanctioned state covertly.

If the sanctions against South Africa, like the sanctions imposed by the United States in pursuit of its Cold War goals, are ineffective, which seems likely given the general inability of economic sanctions to realize preferred foreign policy goals, why do governments continue to use economic sanctions in pursuit of foreign policy objectives?

In a provocative study that focuses not on the broad array of economic sanctions employed by states during the past half-century but on a narrower number that focus on the use of trade sanctions as instruments of policy, James M. Lindsay (1986) argues that the objectives sought by the sanctioning countries fall into five basic categories: *compliance* ("to force the target to alter its behavior to conform with the initiator's preferences," as in the case of the 1982 U.S. embargo of Libya designed to force it to end its support of terrorism), *subversion* ("to remove the target's leaders . . . or overthrow the regime," as in the case of the early U.S. trade embargo of Cuba), *deterrence* ("to dissuade the target from repeating the disputed action in the future," as in the case of the Soviet grain embargo by the United States), *international symbolism* ("to send messages to other members of the world community," as in the case of the British sanctions against Rhodesia following its unilateral declaration of independence in 1965), and *domestic symbolism* ("to increase its domestic support or thwart international criticism of its foreign policies by acting decisively," as in the case of U.S. sanctions against Iran following its seizure of U.S. diplomats in 1979).

The cases described earlier suggest that *symbolism* is a primary motivation behind the use of international economic sanctions. In fact, it is likely to be the most important motivation underlying the choice of sanctions over other policy options, particularly military force. "When military options are not feasible or desirable and the initiator wants to respond forcefully to the target's behavior, sanctions provide a means of 'doing something'" (Lindsay, 1986). Whether the "symbolic utility" of economic sanctions in the face of their otherwise "apparent disutility" is a cause for applause or concern may be disputed. "Critics may deride the symbolic uses of trade sanctions as empty gestures, but symbols are important in politics. This is especially so when inaction can signal weakness and silence can mark complicity" (Lindsay, 1986). Thus economic sanctions may often fail to achieve the most visible objectives for which they are implemented, but they serve important functions nonetheless, including providing a policy alternative to the use of force to publicize and condemn another's unacceptable behavior.

LOOKING AHEAD

Even though economic sanctions often fall short of the objectives their proponents seek, they will continue to be used as instruments of foreign policy
when states seek to register protest and force compliance by means short of
military force. In this sense, resource power remains one of the means
whereby nations seek to influence one another in international politics. A
world interdependent economically in fact multiplies the opportunities to use
economic instruments of influence. But because interdependence implies
mutual sensitivity and vulnerability, those choosing to use resource power will
incur domestic costs as well.

Among Third World countries, the euphoria that once greeted OPEC's
efforts to convert resource power into political leverage has dissipated. The
Third World nations that previously had thought of reliance on commodity
exports as a form of dependence found through OPEC's experience that
commodity cartels might enable them to use their very dependence as a form
of strength. But that idea has proved illusory. Commodity associations of one
form or another may nevertheless still be pursued by developing nations as a
means of coping with their underdog status in the global pecking order.
Although it is doubtful that any will be able to achieve very ambitious goals,
commodity associations may cause disruptions in various national economies
as well as the international marketplace (Spero, 1985). The experience of the
OPEC decade suggests that if a future crisis in the global energy regime
unfolds, the disruptions could be great. Thus the transformation of global
political economy from today's future into tomorrow's present remains fraught
with uncertainty.

SUGGESTED READINGS

Arad, Ruth W., et al. *Sharing Global Resources*. New York: McGraw-Hill, 1979.

Darmstadter, Joel, Hans H. Landsberg, and Herbert C. Morton, with Michael J. Coda.
    Energy Today and Tomorrow: Living with Uncertainty. Englewood Cliffs, N.J.:
    Prentice-Hall, 1983.

Ebinger, Charles K. *The Critical Link: Energy and National Security in the 1980s*.
    Cambridge, Mass.: Ballinger, 1982.

Gever, John, et al. *The Threat to Food and Fuel in the Coming Decades*. Cambridge,
    Mass.: Ballinger, 1986.

Hewett, Ed A. *Energy, Economics, and Foreign Policy in the Soviet Union*. Washington,
    D.C.: Brookings Institution, 1984.

Leyton-Brown, David, ed. *The Utility of Economic Sanctions*. New York: St. Martin's
    Press, 1987.

Morse, Edward L. "After the Fall: The Politics of Oil," *Foreign Affairs* 64 (Spring 1986):
    792–811.

Odell, Peter R. *Oil and World Power*. New York: Penguin, 1983.

Pirages, Dennis. "World Energy Crisis 1995," *Futures Research Quarterly* 2 (Fall 1986): 31–47.

Yergin, Daniel, and Martin Hillenbrand, eds. *Global Insecurity: A Strategy for Energy and Economic Renewal*. New York: Penguin, 1982.

PART IV

High Politics: National Security, Arms, and War

ELEVEN

The Quest for National Security: Trends in Military Capabilities

The adversaries of the world are not in conflict because they are armed. They are armed because they are in conflict and have not yet learned peaceful ways to resolve their conflicting national interests.

RICHARD M. NIXON, 1969

Up to the present, we are told that nuclear arms are a force of dissuasion which have prevented the eruption of a major war. And that is probably true. Still, we must ask if it will always be this way.

POPE JOHN PAUL II, 1980

High politics deals with issues of peace and security. Hence the term describes the behaviors of global actors seeking to reduce their fears, in contrast with their efforts to increase their standards of living. In an unsafe world the search for national security has become almost synonymous with world politics. The pervasive sense of threat explains states' preoccupation with and extensive preparations for war.

Because the international system's present structure requires that nations rely on little more than themselves for their own protection, national security frequently is assigned the most prominent place on their foreign policy agendas, with low politics secondary to it. National security—the psychological freedom from fear—is a supreme value. Without the state's capacity to ensure its survival, all other values and goals are threatened.

What breeds the competition that propels the search for security through preparations for war?

All nations want many of the same things—self-preservation, national identity, sovereign freedom, status, and wealth. These are sought, however, in an anarchical system affording no state protection from the hostile designs of others; each can be made secure only by its own strength. To ensure their own protection, most are therefore motivated to acquire as much military might as their resources allow.

The predicament that such behavior creates is the *security dilemma*: Arms acquired for defensive purposes are perceived by others as threatening, which then provokes similar behavior by those threatened (Herz, 1951). The syndrome has also been described as the *spiral model* (Jervis, 1976), which explains that one country's efforts to enhance its own defense has the effect of alarming its opponents, which then react similarly, with the result that an escalating arms race is produced that reduces the security of all parties. The process was described well by Sir Edward Grey more than half a century ago:

> The increase in armaments, that is intended in each nation to produce consciousness of strength, and a sense of security, does not produce these effects. On the contrary, it produces a consciousness of the strength of other nations and a sense of fear. Fear begets suspicion and distrust and evil imaginings of all sorts, til each government feels it would be criminal and a betrayal of its own country not to take every precaution, while every government regards every precaution of every other government as evidence of hostile intent. (Grey, 1925: 92)

The unintended consequence of an arms race, which no one consciously sought, is diminished security for all. But it is important to emphasize that the security dilemma results because

> even when no state has any desire to attack others, none can be sure that others' intentions are peaceful, or will remain so; hence each must maintain power for defense. Since no state can know that the power accumulation of others is defensively motivated only, each must assume that it might be intended for attack. Consequently, each party's power increments are matched by the others, and all wind up with no more security than when the vicious cycle began, along with the costs incurred in having acquired and having to maintain their power. (Snyder, 1984: 461)

This predicament explains the absence of security in the world. All nations search for strength; all cherish national advantage; none willingly accepts vulnerability. Preparation for war and mutual insecurity are the consequences. Accordingly, it is understandable why, when contemplating the subject of world politics, many peoples' visions tend to be dominated with images of armies marching and bombs exploding.

Underlying the security dilemma are two important but largely unchallenged assumptions that policymakers habitually make: (1) Security is a function of power, and (2) power is a function of military capability. The undesired, costly, and deadly results that typically derive from these assumptions have been widely acknowledged. But the anarchical conditions in which world politics unfolds invite their acceptance nonetheless. By definition, there are no escapes from a dilemma, and that includes the security dilemma. Much as the "tragedy of the commons" accounts for the failure of the world to manage its ecological resources responsibly, the security dilemma explains why states sharing a common interest in security nonetheless engage in individual actions that prevent them from obtaining it. One nation's security can be attained only by jeopardizing another's; the equation converts the pursuit of national security into world insecurity.

To understand better the sources of the security dilemma, we begin with a brief inquiry into the nature of power and its relation to military preparedness and the quest for national security. We then consider the practices in which states engage to diminish threats to their national security, specifically trends in their expenditures for and transfer of arms across national borders. Together, these trends frame the global circumstances defining the environment in which national security is pursued.

POWER IN INTERNATIONAL POLITICS

What is this entity called *power* that political realists and others regard as the central element in international politics and whose quest they depict as states' primary motive? Power, when attained, is assumed to confer on its possessor the ability to promote national interests. But definitions of power abound, and the concept is used ambiguously to refer to disparate phenomena (see Claude, 1962; Wolfers, 1952).

In essence, power manifests itself in the ability of one actor to persuade another to do what it otherwise would not do. Power is the exercise of influence over another. Thus power is a political phenomenon. It is the ability to coerce or to obtain what one wants through manipulation (which is perhaps why politics is often regarded as "dirty"). Indeed, to say that nations pursue power is to say that they seek the ability to control others. Accordingly, power is a measure of the relations among nations that reflects which dominates and which is subservient.

When power is viewed in this way, the following question arises: What enables states to achieve their goals? That is, what kinds of capabilities or resources are necessary to attain power over another? Many factors simultaneously enhance a state's ability to achieve its goals vis-à-vis others, and these multiple factors, or some combination of them, provide a composite measure of states' relative *power potential*. If we could weigh comparatively each state's total capabilities, the world's nations could be ranked according to their capacity to draw on resources to exercise influence. Such a ranking would reveal the system's hierarchy of power or dominance, differentiating the strong from the weak, the great from the nongreat.

Of all the resources that make for national power, military force and economic resources are usually regarded as the most important, with the former providing the basis for the acquisition of the latter. Economic resources enable the development of military capabilities with which states can project their power abroad; they enhance a state's political leverage in its dealings with others and provide the means to the end of military power. The assumption that the capacity to destroy is crucial to calculating power ratios derives from the widespread belief that it leads to the capacity to influence. The belief rests in turn on the corollary that to make others behave according to one's will, the ability to inflict punishment is critically important, more so than the ability to offer rewards. Whether these propositions, which are consistent with the logic of *realpolitik*, are valid is not certain, but regardless, most national security planners proceed on the basis of them.

In addition to military capability, other factors or combinations of them presumably contribute to national power (and to disparities among nations' capacity to exert political leverage on the world's stage). Power differentials are thought to spring also from relative differences in societies' population and territorial size, geographic location, raw materials, degree of dependence on foreign supplies of materials, technological capacity, national character, ideology, efficiency of governmental decision making, industrial productivity, volume of trade, savings and investment, educational level, and national morale.

However, there is no consensus on how these factors can best be weighed, what their relative importance should be in making comparisons across nations, or what conditions modify the contribution that each factor may make to the equation. Many agree that nations are not equal in their capacity to influence others, that the power capabilities of some greatly exceed those of others, but few agree on a list of the most powerful nations, let alone a ranking of the nations in terms of their power potentialities.

Part of the difficulty of defining what constitutes power is that the potential impact of these contributing factors depends on the circumstances obtaining in a bargaining situation between actors, and these are subjective rather than concrete. Power ratios are not products of measured capabilities; they are influenced fundamentally by how these concrete resources are perceived. In addition, power is necessarily relational—a state can have power over some other actor only to the extent that it can get its way with that actor. The outcome of a political confrontation between two actors is influenced by both actual and perceived strength as they relate to the particular issue over which the dispute is fought. To make a difference, adversaries must take cognizance of the enemy's capabilities and perceive it willing to mobilize them for coercive purposes. They must, for example, regard as credible their adversary's threat to use military capabilities—they must believe that their opponent can and will use its strength to influence militarily the outcome of a conflict. Intentions—and especially perceptions of them—thus matter greatly. As we shall see, the possession of weapons does not necessarily increase a nation's power if its adversaries do not believe that it is committed to use them to defend its national interests.

In this context, it is noteworthy that historically those with the greatest arsenals have not necessarily gotten their way in political conflicts. If the relations between strong and weak nations as measured by their relative military capabilities are examined closely, an unexpected pattern emerges. Weaker states often have successfully exercised political influence against their military superiors and resisted pressure from them. A Vietnam that was weak in the conventional military sense succeeded against a vastly more militarized France, and later, the United States, despite the superiority of its adversaries' weapons. An armada of missiles and bombers capable of inflicting horrendous destruction did not enable the United States to prevent the emergence of a communist government in Cuba only ninety miles from its shores. Similarly, vastly superior military power did not prevent seizure of the USS *Pueblo* by North Korea in 1968 or the taking hostage of American diplomatic personnel by Iran a decade later. The Soviet Union's inability to influence by force the course of political events in Afghanistan also suggests that the impotence of military power is not peculiar to the United States. In these and other important instances, so-called second-rate military powers appear at times to have exerted more influence over great powers than great powers have over them. In fact, against certain forces—such as politically mobilized populations— military force has proved ineffectual. "Real power—the ability to affect others —seems in fact more widely dispersed than perhaps at any time in the world's history" (Bundy, 1977).

Although the energetic quest for power through military force remains, its realization has proved elusive. Sir Oliver Wright, British ambassador to the United States in 1982, defined a superpower as "a power no one else can push around." But because all are vulnerable to being pushed around, could it be that superpowers do not exist? The superpowers may be muscle-bound, confined by their own strength and exposed to challenges from abroad with which their military resources cannot cope.

A related lesson of recent years is that influence may derive as much from economic power as from military might, especially with respect to some issues. The capacity of the state to compete successfully in world markets through the development of new products and to mobilize the acquired capital and resources may confer great political clout, as the example of postwar Japan illustrates (Rosecrance, 1986). The distribution of relative monetary strength and economic resources generally may have become as influential as has the distribution of arms and armies. These not only provide the foundation from which a strong defense capability may be created but also are among the primary values that military might is designed to protect. The ascendance of economic power relative to military power represents a profound transformation (Morse, 1976). This proposition is supported by the continuing importance of the United States in the postwar international system, which derives from its economic strength as well as from its military might. The same holds true for other nations, as was glaringly evident in 1973 and 1974 when the oil-producing nations were able to bring the militarily superior nations of the Western world to their knees.

Alternatively stated, force ratios may no longer translate into power in the way that they once did. The nature of military capabilities has so changed that military inferiority may no longer undermine the state's bargaining leverage as it did in the past, although subordinate capabilities certainly remain a liability for purposes of deterrence and defense (see Schelling, 1966). Today, in part because of the destructiveness of weapons, some of the countries that have spent the least for weapons may paradoxically be as secure as are their heavily armed counterparts. Relevant in this context is President John F. Kennedy's warning that in the event of another total war, regardless of how it might begin, the most heavily armed superpowers would automatically become the primary targets of destruction.

Reformers in the idealist tradition (recall Chapter 2) have questioned the logic that causes states to emerge in the behavior that creates and sustains the security dilemma that dominates contemporary world politics. To them "the central theme of international relations is not evil but tragedy. States often share a common interest, but the structure of the situation prevents them from bringing about the mutually desired situation" (Jervis, 1976). To escape the predicament, the reformers have called for a change in the way that the problem of national security is typically approached and how the elements of national power have been defined (for example, see Brown, 1986). They see weapons as "indefensible" (see Lifton and Falk, 1982). Unarmed or defenseless countries, they argue, would be able to practice a flexibility in their foreign policies that their armed neighbors could not, as they would be freed from the responsibilities that the possession of (military) power requires and would not have to devote their energies to controlling its use. Although such countries would have to live in the constant shadow of others' missiles, they could nonetheless live in the comfort that those missiles were not directed at them. Disarmed nations may have more actual political troubles, but they are likely to have fewer imaginary ones, or so this reasoning holds. They could also live in the knowledge that the absence of a military capability does not preclude them from exercising influence by other means.

But these are speculative, even utopian, thoughts. The meek have not inherited the earth. The belief embraced enthusiastically worldwide is that arms make nations powerful and, hence, secure. The quest for security through arms thus continues unabated. Nations continue to negotiate in the language of military power and to seek peace through military strength. Three sets of indicators support this conclusion: trends in military spending, military capabilities, and the global arms trade.

THE QUEST FOR MILITARY CAPABILITIES

People's values are revealed by how they spend their money. Similarly, how governments allocate their revenues reveals their priorities. Examination of national budgets discloses an unmistakable pattern: Nearly all states seek security through substantial outlays of national revenues for arms.

Trends in Military Spending

Not only is the commitment to purchase military protection nearly universal; it is also growing, as nations often spend increasing proportions of their income for arms and armies. Globally, the aggregate annual outlays of revenues for weapons was estimated in 1985 at $900 billion, a figure that tripled the amount spent in 1972 (U.S. Arms Control and Disarmament Agency [hereafter, ACDA], 1984: 1; 1987: 1). Another way of stating this is to note that in 1985 the world spent $1./ million every minute for military purposes. Moreover, the amount of money spent annually on arms and armies has risen almost constantly in this century, with only intermittent periods of modest reductions. Even when stated in terms of constant prices, this pattern persists, for military spending has increased at a rate faster than has the rise in prices, something that makes the thirteenfold increase in world military expenditures between the mid-1930s and the mid-1980s all the more impressive.

The developed nations spend by far the most for military preparedness, as Figure 11.1 shows. As traced in constant 1983 dollars so as to take the effects of inflation into account, in 1984 the developed nations spent $643 billion for defense, and the developing nations spent $165 billion (ACDA, 1987: 59). This distribution is described better by referring to the percentage share of total world military expenditures attributed to different nations and groups of nations. In 1984, the United States and the Soviet Union accounted for 60 percent of all the dollars spent for arms in the world.[1] Next in order were the United Kingdom (3 percent), China (2.9 percent), France (2.7 percent), and West Germany (2.7 percent). Hence, the top six spenders accounted for over 70 percent of all military expenditures in the world. The dominance of NATO and the Warsaw Pact in the global picture is also noteworthy: NATO in 1984 comprised 41 percent of the world share, and the Warsaw Pact accounted for 37 percent (ACDA, 1987: 2).

Although historically the rich nations have been the most apt to allocate substantial portions of their budgets to acquire arms, with military expenditures usually rising in periods of peace as well as war, the desire to arm is now widespread. In fact, one of the major trends in today's transforming world is found in the extent to which the poorer nations have mimicked the budgetary habits of the rich (Mullins, 1987). Trends in Third World military spending since 1960 reveal a sixfold increase (in constant dollars), which exceeds the pace at which world military expenditures have risen generally (Sivard, 1987: 42). At the same time, the developing countries' military expenditures, which represented less than 5 percent of the world's total in 1960, grew by 1984 to 20 percent (Luckham, 1984: 355; ACDA, 1987: 1). Those that can least afford weapons have made the greatest sacrifices to obtain them, it seems. Only the lack of economic growth in recent years appears to have restrained this momentum.

---

1. "Between 1979 and 1986, U.S. military spending rose by an average of 5.8 percent each year. By contrast, American intelligence agencies have estimated that Soviet military spending rose at an average annual rate of 2.1 percent during this period." In the space of these seven years, "preparations for war have cost the United States $2 trillion. . . . This amounts to $21,000 for each American household" (*The Defense Monitor* 16, No. 7 [1987]: 3, 1).

FIGURE 11.1 ■ World Military Expenditures, 1974–1984[a]

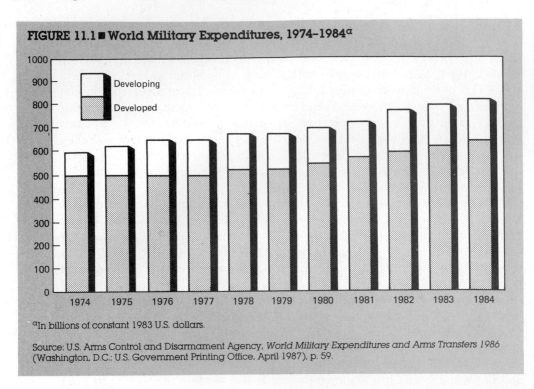

[a]In billions of constant 1983 U.S. dollars.

Source: U.S. Arms Control and Disarmament Agency, *World Military Expenditures and Arms Transfers 1986* (Washington, D.C.: U.S. Government Printing Office, April 1987), p. 59.

Money spent is one indicator of the propensity to seek security through arms. Another perhaps more meaningful measure is the *relative burden* of military spending. This is usually calculated as the ratio of defense spending to gross national product, which increased for both developed and developing countries in the 1980s (ACDA, 1987: 5). For comparative purposes, it is useful to examine the variations among different states' burdens. Table 11.1 illuminates the pattern by grouping the world's nations according to their share of GNP devoted to the military on the vertical axis and their GNP per capita on the horizontal axis. The data show wide variation among countries. Some wealthy countries (for example, the United States, the United Arab Emirates) bear a heavy burden for defense, but others (Japan, Finland) do not. Likewise, some very poor countries (Cambodia, Laos) are burdened heavily by defense, whereas other impoverished countries (Nepal, Chad) are not. In general, however, it is clear that many of the world's poor countries are the most burdened by the costs of defense. This pattern may be interpreted as an indication that the share of resources devoted to national security is determined less by the average wealth of states' citizens than by their governments' perceptions of security needs, which may be shaped by local and historical circumstances, not just international ones.

The level of military expenditures may also be influenced by domestic factors (for example, to satisfy the perceived requirements of public opinion, fiscal policy, or internal security) or psychological motives (such as the need for status and prestige). The relationship between wealth (and wealth per person) and military spending is thus far from a direct one. This in turn suggests that a more complicated explanation of military spending is necessary than the simple formula that the availability of money exerts pressure for military preparedness.

Global expenditure patterns testify to the acceptance worldwide of the proposition that power can be purchased. Aside from the fundamental question of whether these purchases enhance or reduce national security, there exists a related question: What are the effects on national well-being?

The Social and Economic Consequences of Military Spending

The money devoted to military spending affects how the earth's five billion people live. Military preparedness commands relatively more resources than do other global problems requiring resources for their solution. Consider the following (Sivard, 1987: 3, 5–6):

❑ Defense spending worldwide since 1960 has consumed over $15,200,000,000,000 (in 1984 U.S. dollars) and has risen at a rate that far outstripped the growth of the world's combined product per person.
❑ The two superpowers together spent about $1.5 billion a day on defense (in 1986), yet seventeen nations performed better than the United States in reducing their infant mortality rate, and forty-five performed better than the Soviet Union.
❑ The world's defense budgets together are equal to the combined income of 2.6 billion people in the world's forty-four poorest nations.
❑ Third World defense budgets have increased sixfold since 1960, but half the populace in those countries did not have safe water to drink.
❑ In developing countries as many as twenty percent of children born die before their fifth birthday; yet those countries spend almost four times as much on arms as they do on health care.
❑ The world spent 2,900 times as much on armed forces (in 1986) as it did on peacekeeping activities.

These comparisons show clearly that most countries are more concerned with defending their citizens from foreign attack than they are with protecting them from deprivation through social, educational, and health expenditures. Worldwide military spending cannot be said to cause directly a decline in the standard of living of the earth's population, but military spending and global poverty appear to be closely linked: When expenditures for arms go up, so do disease, illiteracy, and suffering.

Consider how the United States and the Soviet Union, first in military spending, ranked (in 1984) among all nations across various social indicators— in reducing infant mortality, eighteenth (United States) and forty-sixth (Soviet

TABLE 11.1 ■ Relative Burden of Military Expenditures, 1984

ME/GNP[a] (%)	GNP per Capita (1983 dollars)					
	Under $200	$200–499	$500–999	$1,000–2,999	$3,000–9,999	$10,000 and over
10% and over	Cambodia[b] Laos		Yemen (Aden) Egypt Yemen (Sanaa)	Iraq Korea, North Syria Jordan Nicaragua Mongolia[b]	Oman Israel Saudia Arabia Libya Soviet Union	Qatar
5–9.99%	Ethiopia	Cape Verde[b] China Vietnam[b] Zambia Somalia	Angola Lesotho Zimbabwe El Salvador	Lebanon[b] Peru Taiwan	Bulgaria Greece Iran Germany, East	United Arab Emirates United States
2–4.99%	Burma Burkina Faso Equatorial Guinea[b] Guinea-Bissau[b] Mali	Pakistan Afghanistan[b] Mauritania[b] Mozambique[b] India Burundi Kenya Tanzania Guinea[b]	Morocco Guyana Honduras Thailand Botswana[b] Bolivia	Cuba Korea, South Turkey Albania[b] South Africa Chile Malaysia Argentina Yugoslavia	Czechoslovakia Poland Singapore United Kingdom Romania France Hungary Bahrain Netherlands	Kuwait Germany, West Sweden Norway Denmark Canada Switzerland

	Senegal	Central African Republic[b]	Cameroon		Portugal	Guatemala	Belgium	New Zealand	Finland
	Madagascar	Haiti	Papua New Guinea		Tunisia	Paraguay	Australia	Ireland	
	Indonesia	Sri Lanka	Nigeria		Uruguay	Ecuador	Italy	Venezuela	
	Benin	Sao Tome & Principe[b]	Swaziland		Algeria	Colombia	Trinidad and Tobago	Cyprus	
	Togo	Zaire	Ivory Coast		Congo	Fiji	Spain	Austria	
	Liberia	Uganda	Philippines		Suriname	Dominican Republic	Gabon		
	Rwanda[b]				Panama	Costa Rica			
	Sudan								
1–1.99%	Bangladesh								
	Malawi								
	Chad								
	Nepal								
Under 1%	Niger				Brazil		Barbados		Japan
	Sierra Leone				Jamaica		Malta		Luxembourg
	The Gambia[b]				Mexico		Ghana		Iceland
					Mauritius				

Source: U.S. Arms Control and Disarmament Agency, *World Military Expenditures and Arms Transfers 1986* (Washington, D.C.: U.S. Government Printing Office, April 1987), p. 5.

[a] Countries are listed within blocks in descending order of ME (Military Expenditures)/GNP (Gross National Product).

[b] Ranking is based on a rough approximation of one or more variables for which 1984 data or reliable estimates are not available.

Union); in school-age population per teacher, twentieth and twenty-fifth; in physicians per population, eighteenth and first; in literacy rate, fifth and fifth (tie); in public-health expenditures per person, eighth and twenty-fourth; and in life expectancy, eighth and forty-fourth (Sivard, 1987: 46–47). These rankings lead to the conclusion that high military spending is associated with relatively poor performance in social indicators. They suggest that when security is defined in the broadest sense of the term—security in the expectation that one will live a full life—then security is not being purchased by the acquisition of arms. High rates of military spending thus appear to reduce social welfare, not enhance it (see Nincic, 1982; Russett, 1982; Wolpin, 1983).

A trade-off between guns and economic growth also has been suspected. For example, Ruth Sivard (1979b) observes that "no analytical studies . . . have yet established a positive link between military expenditures and economic development in the broad sense. There is, in fact, a growing body of evidence pointing to retarding effects through inflation, diversion of investment, use of scarce materials, misuse of human capital. . . ." One econometric study found that every additional dollar spent on arms in the Third World reduced domestic investment by 25 cents and agricultural output by 20 cents (see Klare, 1987: 1279–1280). For most developing countries, it appears that the net effect of military spending has been to retard the rate of growth (Deger and Smith, 1983).

Despite the existence of a voluminous literature on the subject, however, the guns-versus-growth issue remains controversial because "previous research on the impact of military spending on the economy has produced disparate, inconsistent, and unstable results" (Chan, 1987). A strong correlation that holds for all countries simply has not been established. "The effects of monetary expenditure on the economy," conclude Smith and Georgiou (1983), "depend on the nature of the expenditure, the prevailing circumstances, and the concurrent government policies."

Even if linkages cannot be shown to hold across all countries, there is reason to believe that the strain of military spending on economic growth may be especially severe in the most advanced industrial societies. It may be questionable to assume a direct causal connection between increases in military spending and retarded economic growth rates, rising unemployment, reduced productivity, balance-of-payments deficits, the national debt, and the like. But if a causal connection is dubious in the short run (when military spending can mean new jobs, for example),[2] in the long run it can be compel-

---

2. Even this fact is itself open to challenge from the viewpoint of public policy:
   Former Defense Secretary Caspar Weinberger has argued for higher military spending, saying that it will help create jobs. Each billion dollars spent for military purposes creates an estimated 28,000 jobs. But he failed to mention that the same billion spent for education could create 71,000 jobs. Each billion diverted from education to military purposes therefore eliminates 43,000 jobs. (Fischer, 1987: 11)

ling.[3] As Richard J. Barnet (1979) found, "Mounting evidence appears to confirm what common sense would suggest: A country [the United States] which, year after year, spends more than $100 billion annually to support a bureaucracy of four million people who produce nothing, and which buys hundreds of thousands of machines that make nothing, is not on the road to prosperity." "The problem in defense spending," President Dwight D. Eisenhower observed in 1956, "is to figure how far you should go without destroying from within what you are trying to defend from without."

THE PARADOX OF THE POWER OF THE POWERFUL   Analogously, a price tag is associated with a global or imperial foreign policy. A superpower's hegemonic aspirations and worldwide involvements may stretch its capacity to maintain economic growth. Thus the military spending necessary for imperial power may lead only to imperial failure (Jacobs, 1984).

This conclusion is affirmed in Paul Kennedy's (1988) influential book, *The Rise and Decline of the Great Powers*. Comparing the performance of great powers over a period of five centuries, Kennedy discerned a recurrent pattern: Dramatic economic growth has propelled a number of states to hegemonic status, but once achieved, each great power was then irresistibly driven to expand its military commitments worldwide to protect its enlarged interests. The economic resources required to maintain this presence and position ultimately undermined the strength that the military investments were designed to preserve: "The difficulties experienced by contemporary societies which are militarily top-heavy merely repeat those which, in their time, affected Phillip II's Spain, Nicholas II's Russia and Hitler's Germany. A large military establishment may, like a great monument, look imposing to the impressionable observer; but if it is not resting upon the firm foundation . . . [of] a productive national economy, it runs the risk of a future collapse" (Kennedy, 1988).

To avert a replay of this pattern, Kennedy warns that the United States and the Soviet Union must "balance the short-term security afforded by large defense forces against the longer-term security of production and income" (Kennedy, 1988). Maintaining this balance poses a challenge to the superpowers, but the dismal historical record underscores the incompatibilities of tractors and tanks, economic productivity and military superiority, and prosperity at home and power abroad. Kennedy's arguments are especially appro-

---

3. Nowhere, perhaps, is the negative impact of military spending on economic growth more dramatic than in the Soviet Union. Between 1960 and 1981 the Soviet Union spent $1.3 trillion in pursuit of military power. This investment has been extremely costly (see Rothschild, 1980). By 1987 the Soviet Union ranked no higher than twenty-third in economic and social performance among 142 countries (Sivard, 1987: 5), and it faced declining productivity (Kennedy, 1988). Over the long term, investments in military goods and services have not proved economically beneficial.

priate to the relative decline of the economic prowess of the United States compared with that of Japan, West Germany, and the Newly Industrialized Countries. As research and development funds are concentrated in the military rather than the civilian sector, the best scientists and engineers in the United States focus their energies on military applications rather than on the development of new consumer products (Kennedy, 1987a). The result is that the United States will lose its competitive edge in one product after another, as has already happened with automobiles and consumer electronics.

Richard Rosecrance (1986) argues similarly in his comparison of military-political and trade strategies as alternative means to national advancement. "Since 1945 a few nations have borne the crushing weight of military expenditure," he observes, "while others have gained a relative advantage by becoming military free-riders who primarily rely on the security provided by others. While the United States spent nearly 50 percent of its research and development budget on arms, Japan devoted 99 percent to civilian production." In addition to sacrificing other economic opportunities, Rosecrance continues, military spending has direct costs in the form of extraordinarily expensive equipment that rapidly becomes dated in the face of rapid innovations in weapons technology. Tanks routinely cost $2 million or more per copy, for example, and fighter planes cost upwards of $10 million each. But even these demands pale in comparison with the cost of missiles and ships. It was perhaps this realization that led President Eisenhower to caution Americans so often about the dangers of living beyond the country's means.[4]

Trends in Military Capabilities

The world currently spends nearly $1 trillion a year in preparations for intimidation and war (Sagan, 1988: 4). The growth in military spending worldwide has altered the environment in which the world's nations reside as their feverish spending for national security has led to a world in which many nations possess more weapons of ever more destructiveness.

MODERN WEAPONS TECHNOLOGY   The technology associated with modern weapons has radically transformed the nature of warfare. The largest "blockbuster" bombs of World War II delivered a power of 10 tons of TNT; the atomic bomb that leveled Hiroshima had the power of over 12,000 tons of TNT; less than twenty years later the Soviet Union possessed a nuclear bomb with the explosive force of 57 megatons (million tons) of TNT. Today, the

---

4. This possibility was also once acknowledged by Caspar Weinberger (in 1972, well before he became secretary of defense and began to see things in a different light): "The identification of a threat to security does not automatically require an expenditure in the defense budget to neutralize it. . . . The defense budget . . . must be seen not only in terms of what we must defend ourselves against but what we have to defend. The more we take from the commonwealth for its defense the smaller it becomes" (cited in Fallows, 1982).

world's nuclear arsenals contain the equivalent of well over 1 million Hiroshimas. "They contain 2,667 times the explosive energy released in World War II, and carry the equal of 3.2 tons of TNT for every individual on earth" (Sivard, 1987: 16). The use of such weapons could destroy not only entire cities and countries but, conceivably, the world's entire population.[5] Albert Einstein dramatically described the threat posed when he observed that he did not know what the weapons of a third world war would be but that in a fourth world war they would be "sticks and stones."

More bucks have led to more bombs with more bang, making ours an age of overkill. The warheads on one American Poseidon submarine are capable of destroying 160 cities in the Soviet Union; a single American bomber can deliver a force level equal to nearly twice the tonnage delivered by all of the participants in World War II. The combined nuclear stockpile of the two superpowers, with explosive power equivalent to 16 million kilotons or 1.3 million Hiroshima-sized bombs, are able to destroy every city on earth seven times over. Moreover, refinements in military technology enable the super-powers to deliver these weapons within a few hundred feet of their targets as far away as nine thousand miles in less than thirty minutes.

The world, in short, has been revolutionized by the changes in the military capabilities that military spending has purchased. Today's weapons are increasingly destructive, deadly, and accurate. As Figure 11.2 demonstrates, the first generation of atomic bombs (like the single device that reduced Hiroshima to rubble) could destroy an area of three square miles, and the delivery systems then available limited the destruction to a single target. The United States' MX missile has the capacity to destroy an area seventy-eight times as extensive as the area leveled in Japan—and it could devastate ten targets at once. (The reason for this is that missile systems may be "MIRVed"—in which case each *multiple independently targetable reentry vehicle* carried by a ballistic missile can be directed to a separate target.) As *Washington Post* correspondent Richard Harwood notes,

> Our young pilots today . . . could fly over Leningrad some morning and with a single bomb, exploded at 3,000 feet, kill perhaps 900,000 people and seriously injure another 1,225,000. It would create winds of a velocity of 470 miles an hour—far greater than any hurricane. These winds would hurl people through the air at high speeds smashing them into buildings. Air pressures from the explosion would strike houses with the force of 180 tons. All that from one bomb. It would have a yield of 1 million tons of TNT. (Harwood, 1979: 1)

---

5. Estimates of the number of people who would perish in the event of a nuclear clash vary (see Chapter 12, especially Figure 12.2). Former Secretary of Defense Harold Brown (1983) predicted that the "destruction of more than 100 million people in each of the United States, the Soviet Union, and the European nations could take place during the first half-hour of a nuclear war." For other estimates and scenarios, see Sagan (1983–1984) and Schell (1982).

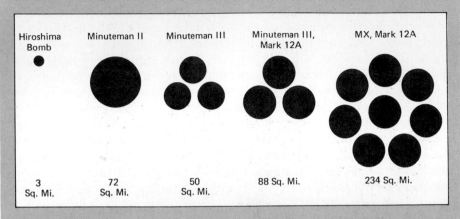

FIGURE 11.2 ■ Number of Targets That Can Be Attacked and Area That Can Be Destroyed by Different U.S. Strategic Weapon Systems

Hiroshima Bomb	Minuteman II	Minuteman III	Minuteman III, Mark 12A	MX, Mark 12A
3 Sq. Mi.	72 Sq. Mi.	50 Sq. Mi.	88 Sq. Mi.	234 Sq. Mi.

Source: *The Defense Monitor* (September–October, 1978), p. 3. Published by the Center for Defense Information, Washington, D.C.

Laser weapons, "hunter-killer" satellites, and antisatellite (ASAT) weapons that can project force in and wage war from outer space have also become a part of the military landscape. Furthermore, technological improvements enable adversaries to target their existing weapons systems with increasing precision. During the Falklands War, the world was given a chilling view on television of the efficiency of today's weapons technology. Viewers were able to witness an Exocet missile, launched by another ship that had already turned back home, speed forty miles exactly six feet above the sea and hit its target, square amidship.

The growing numbers of strategic weapons can be added to the picture of their increasing accuracy and destructiveness. When World War II came to an end, there was but one atomic bomb still in existence. By 1988 the United States was estimated to have stockpiled 13,134 strategic nuclear warheads (weapons designed for use against an adversary's homeland) and the Soviet Union 10,664 (Arms Control Association, Fact Sheet, May 1988). In addition, the United States and the Soviet Union have each deployed somewhere between 10,000 and 20,000 tactical nuclear weapons, perhaps even more.[6] (Tactical nuclear weapons are designed for the direct support of combat operations.) "Mini-nukes"—nuclear weapons small enough to be carried in a suitcase—are also now in existence. In 1987, the superpowers increased their

6. The exact number remains a closely guarded secret, and estimates vary widely. *The Defense Monitor* in February 1979 estimated then that "the United States has as many as 30,000 nuclear weapons (including about 20,000 tactical weapons) and the Soviet Union has about 20,000 nuclear weapons." Later, in 1988, *The Defense Monitor* (vol. 17, no. 3, p. 7) put the number of U.S. intermediate-range and battlefield nuclear weapons in Europe alone at just over 4,500, and the number of similar Soviet weapons at nearly 6,000.

supply of nuclear bombs at the rate of sixteen each week (Sivard, 1987: 5). "The United States and the Soviet Union together still somehow manage to build enough new nuclear weapons *each year*," Carl Sagan (1988: 4; emphasis added) notes, "to destroy every sizable city on the planet."

THE PROLIFERATION PROBLEM   The quest for nuclear weapons has not been confined to the two superpowers. The balance of terror has been exacerbated by the decision of others to develop nuclear weapons of their own, decisions that have produced the so-called proliferation problem. *Proliferation* refers to the probability that more and more nations will become members of the "nuclear club."[7] Consistent with the choices that produce the security dilemma worldwide, the decision of one nation to acquire nuclear weapons encourages others to take that step. The dreaded possibility is a chain reaction leading to the appearance of weapons of mass destruction in the arsenals of many countries—a situation no one desires, given the possibility either that one or more of them eventually will choose to use them or that they will be used accidentally.

The fact that the American acquisition of nuclear capabilities in 1945 was followed in succession by that of the Soviet Union (1949), Great Britain (1952), France (1960), China (1964), and India (1974) supports the view that further proliferation is likely if not inevitable. Estimates vary, but experts agree that perhaps as many as thirty other states now have the economic and technological potential to become nuclear powers.[8]

India's successful nuclear explosion in 1974 elevated apprehensions that other near-nuclear states would follow its example. This has not yet happened overtly (although the U.S. Central Intelligence Agency believes that both Israel and South Africa have clandestinely acquired nuclear weapons). The nuclear powers have sought to limit nuclear weapons to those powers that already have them and have supported the Nuclear Nonproliferation Treaty (NPT) for that purpose. The 128 non-nuclear states that were party to the treaty in 1988 have adhered to its provisions, keeping membership in the nuclear club to six. Even the forty-some states that have refused to sign the treaty have not openly violated its main provisions.

---

7. The addition of new nuclear states is commonly referred to as the Nth country problem. The increase in the number of states possessing nuclear weapons is called *horizontal proliferation*, in contrast with increases in the capabilities of an existing nuclear state. The latter is often referred to as *vertical proliferation*.

8. Among those widely regarded to be "threshold" states, Israel, South Africa, and Pakistan are often cited. Others perceived as potential proliferators are Argentina, Brazil, South Korea, and Taiwan. To these some authorities add Cuba, Libya, Iraq, and Egypt. Still others have made the acquisition of a nuclear bomb a goal but are far away from realizing it. Iran under Khomeini is exemplary. A high Khomeini adviser stated, "Our civilization is in danger, and we have to do it [build a bomb]. . . . It is our duty to start" (cited in Segal, 1987). Furthermore, a host of other states are clearly capable of producing nuclear weapons but are unlikely to violate the terms of the Nuclear Proliferation Treaty (see Gauhar, 1985).

But the incentives for joining the nuclear club are powerful, and the obstacles to the proliferation of nuclear powers are fragile and weak. Indeed, proliferation is spreading silently and rapidly "when measured in terms of countries that have the capability to produce nuclear weapons and that might be prepared to do so in a major conflict or in response to other pressures" (Spector, 1985). Many states are motivated to follow the lead of the nuclear states and justify that pursuit with the same kind of rationale that the nuclear states previously voiced. French President Charles de Gaulle averred that without the bomb France could not "command its own destiny," and Britain's Labour party member Aneurin Bevan asserted that without the bomb Britain would go "naked into the conference chamber." Many non-nuclear states may conclude that they have little incentive to be bound by an NPT agreement that dooms them to superpower domination and requires them to entrust their security to superpower protection (see Bull, 1984).

The widespread use of nuclear technology and expertise for generating electricity, which by 1987 had spread to fifty-seven countries (Sivard, 1987: 17), reinforces this prognosis, because the uranium and plutonium produced as waste by the nuclear industry in generating electrical power can be reprocessed and used as an ingredient to create nuclear weapons (see also Chapter 10). The material generated by nuclear reactors can be put into military production, either overtly or, as in the case of India, covertly. Either path will result in the further growth of nuclear weapons as fuel for their manufacture becomes more readily available. As President Jimmy Carter observed, "We know that by the year 2000 nuclear power reactors could be producing enough plutonium to make tens of thousands of bombs every year."

The accessibility of nuclear know-how and the failure to prevent its dispersion were illustrated by the ease with which Pakistan in 1979 made a successful end run around the technology-export controls of the United States and several Western European governments when it quietly bought all the basic parts—allegedly with funds supplied by the radical government of Libya—necessary for a uranium-enrichment plant. That experience demonstrated how existing political barriers to proliferation can be transcended. Since then, the United States has lifted its restrictions and has ceased to absorb the political costs of vigorously preventing allies from developing their nuclear weapons programs (Ottaway, 1987; Spector, 1985). Should Pakistan choose to convert its uranium-enrichment laboratory into a bomb-producing facility, it is probable that this would touch off a nuclear arms race between it and India, two traditional enemies in an already volatile area of the world. The feared chain reaction that would induce other nations to engage in the nuclear game might then be set off. If the good news is that the nonproliferation regime has thus far kept the chain reaction from being set in motion, the danger is that either complacency or the vertical proliferation by those otherwise voicing support for nonproliferation will undermine the regime. Nuclear weapons, like gods of old, have become symbols of limitless power to which qualities of awe and omnipotence are attributed and for which material sacrifices are made (Chernus, 1987).

THE RACE FOR CONVENTIONAL ARMS AND ARMIES If most nations have hitherto refrained from joining the nuclear club, nearly all have participated in the race to acquire conventional weapons. The developing nations in particular have sought energetically to obtain armaments commensurate with those of the industrialized nations. They are "born arming" (Mullins, 1987). As Kenneth N. Waltz (1975) observes, "States imitate the military innovations contrived by the country of greatest capability and ingenuity. And so the weapons of major contenders, and even their strategies, begin to look much the same all over the world." The result is that the weapons of war are no longer concentrated in selected countries or regions; rather, the nearly universal drive for military power has led to the diffusion of arms throughout the world.

Changes in weapons technology have been extraordinary and promise to continue, thereby threatening to render obsolete both orthodox ways of classifying weapons systems and prior equations for evaluating power ratios. As an influential U.S. strategic report predicted:

> Dramatic developments in military technology appear feasible over the next twenty years. They will be driven primarily by the further exploitation of microelectronics, in particular for sensors and information processing, and the development of directed energy. These developments could require major revisions in military doctrines and force structures. . . . The much greater precision, range, and destructiveness of weapons could extend war across a much wider geographic area, make war much more rapid and intense, and require entirely new modes of operation. Application of new technologies to both offensive and defensive systems will pose complicated problems for designing forces and assessing enemy capabilities. (The Commission on Integrated Long-Term Strategy, 1988: 8)

As a result, the distinction between conventional and strategic weapons has become increasingly blurred.

The transformation of conventional weapons systems represents one dimension of global militarization. Another face of the competitive quest for security is the number of men and women in the armed forces of national governments. Worldwide, the number of military personnel has grown steadily since 1960. At that time there were 18.5 million people in uniform; by 1986 there were 25.6 million (Sivard, 1987: 42).

It is noteworthy that a substantial proportion of these personnel are stationed on the territory of other states (either by invitation or as a result of intervention). In 1985 an estimated two million soldiers served abroad, and ninety-one countries and territories had foreign forces on their soil (Sivard, 1986: 10). The available data show an average ratio worldwide of one serviceman abroad to every fourteen stationed within the borders of their own country; for the superpowers, the ratio is almost one abroad to four at home (Sivard, 1987: 13).

Most of the growth of the armed forces has occurred in the Third World. Between 1960 and 1986, the armed forces of the developed world remained constant at 10.1 million, although the total in the developing world almost doubled, growing from 8.4 to 15.6 million—or over 60 percent of the world total (Sivard, 1987: 42). The global rise in military personnel thus is attributable almost entirely to the militarization of the Third World.

For relatively poor nations to subsidize the growth of their military establishments at such rates constitutes a considerable financial burden. Part of the reason that they support their military establishments rests with the developing nations' use of military personnel for nonmilitary, nation-building purposes. But when the costs of equipping such armies with weapons are added, it is clear that the sacrifice is often enormous. Indeed, the question raised is how countries with underdeveloped industrial bases are able to acquire the weapons that their soldiers are presumably trained to use, particularly because the manufacture of those weapons often requires sophisticated technologies. A major part of the answer is that the great powers either give or sell them arms. Let us therefore consider the ways that arms are being dispersed worldwide.

Trends in the Arms Trade

As the demand for arms in an insecure world has grown, the sale of weapons has expanded substantially. The transfer of arms across borders has assumed such proportions that it has been labeled a form of "foreign policy writ large" (Pierre, 1982).

Trends in global arms trafficking are suggested by the value of arms sales. The world's trade in arms has increased steadily since 1960, when the dollar value of weapons sales worldwide was $2.5 billion, or less than 1 percent of world military expenditures. In contrast, between 1982 and 1985, agreements to transfer arms had risen to an annual average of $37 billion, or over 6 percent of total military expenditures (Sivard, 1987: 42; ACDA, 1988: 6).

However, noticeable in recent years has been a reduction in the rate at which aggregate arms purchases have grown. Arms imports worldwide grew by 17.5 percent between 1975 and 1979, but only 1.9 percent between 1979 and 1984 (ACDA, 1987: 7). Contributing to this downturn were the global economic recession of the early 1980s, budgetary constraints, the crush exerted by debt servicing, and the diminished demand for expensive new weapons as a result of previous purchases. Well-stocked, saturated inventories have decreased governments' interest in and ability to absorb additional equipment. The reduced growth rate may be temporary (or even artificial, owing to the failure to incorporate in the standard export estimates black-market sales of $5 billion to $10 billion annually) (Klare, 1987: 1274), but it may portend a future restriction of the growth of the arms trade after many years of increases.

The developing nations have been the leading market for the traffic in arms, accounting since the mid-1960s for three-fourths of all trade (ACDA, 1988: 7). An estimated $258 billion in armaments were ordered by the developing countries between 1978 and 1985, sales that provided, among other equipment, nearly 14,000 tanks and self-propelled cannon, 28,000 armored personnel carriers, 4,000 supersonic combat aircraft, and 35,000 surface-to-air missiles (Klare, 1987: 1257).

An unmistakable characteristic of this quantitative increase has been a corresponding qualitative increase in the sophistication of the weapons being purchased. In an earlier period, arms sales to the Third World were confined largely to primitive, often obsolete equipment; today, when competition among an expanding number of suppliers of arms has become fierce, some of the most advanced weapons produced have entered the trade.

The pattern of longer-term change in worldwide arms imports and exports is captured in Figure 11.3, which shows the distribution of arms transfers by supplying countries and recipient regions in 1967 and 1984.

Particularly noteworthy is the sharp increase in arms imports by nations in the Middle East (and, secondarily, Africa); purchases by countries in the Middle East "accounted for 43% of the world total in 1984 [and] had been on a generally rising trend that had sustained the world total" (ACDA, 1987: 7). This increase can be attributed to both security and economic developments. Strategically, the Middle East was, and remains, the locus of intense strife, and the countries in the region continue to face chronic national security problems. The two superpowers have found the region an arena in which to compete for allies and influence and, as the world's largest arms merchants, have used arms grants and sales as policy instruments. The Middle Eastern countries have been eager consumers of the arms made available; in 1984 five of the world's top six arms-importing states were in the Middle East, with Iraq, Saudi Arabia, and Iran leading the pack (ACDA, 1987: 8). But economics has also played a significant role. The influx of arms was heavily influenced by the OPEC oil price increases in the 1970s which enabled many Middle Eastern countries to pay for the military hardware they sought. The extraordinary drop in oil revenues (from about $280 billion in 1981 to $80 billion in 1986) has eroded the basis for these countries to maintain the pace of their previous arms purchases (Cody, 1987: 22; ACDA, 1987: 7).

Finally, changes have also occurred in the composition of the arms suppliers. Between 1973 and 1980, six states—the United States, the Soviet Union, France, Great Britain, West Germany, and Italy—together accounted for nine of every ten dollars in the arms trade; of these, the two superpowers supplied two-thirds of the arms shipped to the Third World (Klare, 1986: 3). The globalist policies and productive capacities of the superpowers have combined to encourage both to use arms sales as an instrument of influence in their continuing rivalry. The United States, which President Carter once labeled "the arms merchant of the world," has since 1960 been the greatest supplier of

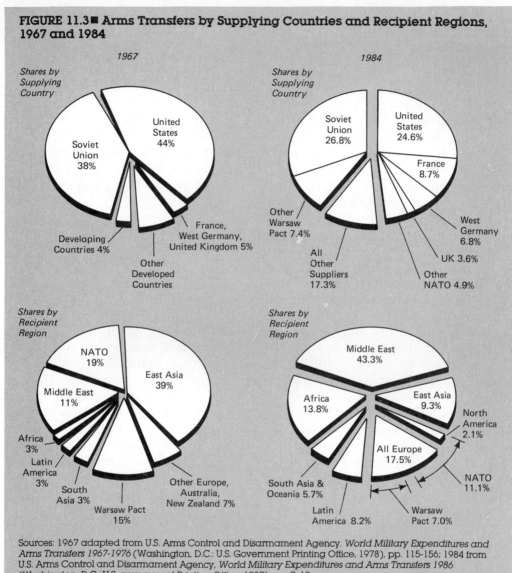

FIGURE 11.3■ Arms Transfers by Supplying Countries and Recipient Regions, 1967 and 1984

Sources: 1967 adapted from U.S. Arms Control and Disarmament Agency, *World Military Expenditures and Arms Transfers 1967-1976* (Washington, D.C.: U.S. Government Printing Office, 1978), pp. 115-156; 1984 from U.S. Arms Control and Disarmament Agency, *World Military Expenditures and Arms Transfers 1986* (Washington, D.C.: U.S. government Printing Office, 1987), pp. 7, 10.

Note: 1967 figures based on constant 1975 U.S. dollars; 1984 figures based on constant 1983 U.S. dollars.

arms to the world. But the Soviet Union has been close behind (and in 1987 slightly ahead). Although the superpowers' share of worldwide arms exports has dropped significantly from the combined 82 percent of the market they controlled in 1967, they continue to be the source for nearly two-thirds the weapons supplied (ACDA, 1988: 10). Neither has seriously sought to reduce this activity (although the Carter administration issued in 1977 Presidential Directive 13 for this purpose, but it was later rescinded). Clearly, the superpowers value arms sales and grants as tools for strengthening their allies and winning the political support of the uncommitted.

The dominance of the superpowers in the world arms market, however, has eroded. Between 1979 and 1984 some newly industrialized and even developing countries entered the arms market, aggressively selling their own specialized military equipment. In that brief period alone, the number of new-country suppliers grew dramatically, and they increased their share of world arms exports from 6 percent in 1975 to 17 percent in 1984 (ACDA, 1987: 9). After the top six suppliers of conventional arms, Spain, Poland, Czechoslovakia, Bulgaria, Yugoslavia, South Korea, Brazil, East Germany, North Korea, and Belgium each ranked next in order (ACDA, 1987: 16).

A subsidiary result of the intensified competition among suppliers for a share of the arms market has been a reduction in the price that weapons systems command (a deflation that may conceal the consistently high volume of military equipment shipped abroad). Purchasers have been able to negotiate more favorable terms, including attractive credit arrangements to finance purchases (for example, to facilitate sales the United States agreed in 1986 to postpone interest payments on loans for weapons purchases). Another consequence of supplier diversification has been a relaxation of the restrictions that suppliers formerly had placed on sales, as in the conspicuous cases of France in 1981 and West Germany in 1982 (see Klare, 1986). Diversification has also ended many of the patron–client diplomatic relations that previously had cemented the supplier–customer bond.

Cash also has become an increasingly important economic rationale for foreign military sales, especially for countries that are experiencing chronic balance-of-payments deficits, like the United States, and others that are driven to sell arms abroad in order to subsidize arms production at home, such as Israel (Frankel, 1987).[9] Because other nations need cash too (to pay for oil or food imports, for example, or to obtain foreign exchange for other needs), the competition for revenue has rationalized the pursuit of commerce in arms. Moreover, because the sale of weapons constitutes big business, the companies in the business comprise a powerful domestic lobby for the continuation of arms transfers abroad.

The arms trade is also fostered by its utility in pursuit of other policy goals. To support friendly governments, to honor the requests of one's allies, and to buy the loyal political friendship of the recipient or, more probably, to acquire political influence over it—all are compelling rationales.

---

9. Arms manufacturing is, by its very nature, an expensive proposition. One way to reduce the per-unit cost of a particular weapons system is to produce weapons for foreign consumption as well as for the immediate security needs of the producing state. Selling weapons abroad in order to amortize the cost of developing new ones thus becomes an attractive incentive.

Whether the arming of other nations has accomplished all of its intended foreign policy objectives is open to dispute. For example, one of the propositions on which the United States and the Soviet Union seem to have based their policies is that peace can be maintained by spreading arms to politically pivotal recipients. Yet because many of the arms recipients are Third World nations in which the frequency of interstate war and domestic political instability is very high, it is not surprising to find that violence has often occurred in precisely those countries that have armed themselves the most. Worth noting in this context is that all wars since 1945 have been fought with an unknown amount but high percentage of conventional weapons that were acquired through arms transfers. The toll in lives from these wars is an estimated twenty million people (Sivard, 1986: 13).

Equally troublesome are the nature of the regimes that suppliers have often chosen to arm and the undesired consequences that have sometimes resulted from those choices. For instance, the United States has armed both sides in several Third World conflicts, such as in the Indo-Pakistani clash (see Simpson, 1967); so on occasion have the Soviets. And because loyalty is often a fragile commodity, the supply of weapons can sometimes backfire. The Falklands War in 1982 is one example; Great Britain found itself shipping military equipment to Argentina just eight days before Argentina's attack on the British-controlled islands off the Argentine shore (Sivard, 1982). Similarly, Libya found its ability to confront the United States militarily strengthened by arms it received from South Korea, itself supplied by the United States. The problem with the transfer of arms is that the uses to which they are put are often beyond the control of the supplier. Betrayal can result when arms sold to an ally, or by an ally to a third party, are subsequently used for purposes that challenge the national interests of the supplier. For example, the supply of arms to Iran by Portugal and China in 1987 proved diplomatically costly to both (De Young, 1987; McCartney, 1987).

From the viewpoint of the recipient nations, however, the reasons for seeking weapons are not hard to identify. Recipients are often willing to pay the price because they feel threatened by others, a proposition given credence by the tendency for arms shipments to gravitate to regions (for example, the Middle East and Africa) where the potential for or existence of armed conflict is high. It is the absence of security in these trouble spots, and not solely the suppliers' greed and the recipients' modernization plans, that whets states' appetites for more efficient weapons systems. Through arms, threatened states hope to protect their national security. For others, the drive to acquire arms may be related to the desire to obtain military tools to deal with internal opposition. Expanding military capability is also important to many Third World leaders, who prize a strong national army as a symbol of statehood and independence and who hope to attain prestige in the world's pecking order.

It is tempting to assume that the dispersion of large numbers of advanced weapons systems necessarily has made the globe more war-prone. But this assumption can be questioned, for as Michael Klare notes (1987), "It would be foolish to argue that increased arms transfers automatically increase the risk of war—the decision to wage war is determined by numerous factors. [On the other hand,] there is no doubt that the widespread availability of modern arms has made it *easier* for potential belligerents to choose the military rather than the diplomatic option when seeking to resolve local disputes.'' The arms trade does not make the world more secure, even if it also does not necessarily make it more violent.

Although arms transfers have increased many nations' capacity to wage war, the military might of the superpowers remains in a category by itself. For that reason, it is necessary to give special attention to the superpowers' military approach to each other.

DETERRENCE AND STRATEGIC DOCTRINE: THE SOVIET-AMERICAN CASE

The dropping of the atomic bomb in the closing days of World War II is the most important event distinguishing prewar from postwar international politics. In the blinding flash of a single weapon and the shadow of its mushroom cloud, the international arena was transformed from a ''balance-of-power'' system to one more akin to a ''balance of terror.'' Even since, the central policy questions have been what to do with atomic (and later thermonuclear) weapons and what to do about them: (1) Should they be used and, if so, how? and (2) how can their use by others be prevented? Indeed, no country from 1945 to the present has failed to appreciate the dangers (or, to some, the opportunities) of such weapons of mass destruction.

Although the existence of incredible weapons of mass destruction has been a constant throughout the postwar period, the United States and the Soviet Union have taken varying postures toward their use. For analytic convenience, their policy postures can be broken into two periods: (1) the era of American monopoly or superiority in strategic weapons, beginning in 1945, and (2) the subsequent period, roughly since 1960, when the United States no longer stood alone in its capacity to annihilate another nation without fear of its own destruction.

Views of Strategic Doctrine
During the Period of American Superiority

When nations enjoy military superiority vis-à-vis their principal adversaries, they tend to think of weapons as instruments in diplomatic bargaining, that is, as tools to be used for the political purpose of changing others' behavior. The United States is no exception. The concept of compellence (Schelling, 1966) describes American strategic doctrine with respect to nuclear weapons during the period of American nuclear superiority. *Compellence* refers to the use of nuclear weapons as instruments of influence to get others to do what they might not otherwise do. At the height of the Cold War, the United States sought repeatedly to gain bargaining leverage by conveying the impression that it was willing to use nuclear weapons against the Soviet Union. Political victories could be won through intimidation, it was felt. Symptomatic of this thinking was Secretary of State John Foster Dulles's practice of what he termed *brinkmanship*—the strategy of backing adversaries into the corner and taking them to the brink of war by threatening them with nuclear destruction in order to force their accommodation.[10]

From a position of strength, the U.S. threats of *massive retaliation* against Soviet population and industrial centers were deemed an appropriate way of deriving from the possession of superior destructive force the realization of American foreign policy objectives. This strategy of intimidation was labeled *countervalue* because it proposed to target American weapons on objects that the Soviets presumably would most value, industrial and population centers, and thereby maximize the bargaining leverage of the United States. The alternative is a *counterforce* strategy, in which destructive capability is targeted against the enemy's military forces and weapons rather than its industrial and population centers, thus sparing the general civilian population from immediate destruction.

From the Soviet Union's perspective, the doctrine of massive retaliation was highly threatening. Its response was twofold. Following Nikita Khrushchev's assumption of power, peaceful coexistence came to dominate Soviet rhetoric. *Peaceful coexistence* presumed that Soviet-American rivalry would continue but that communism's allegedly inevitable victory over capitalism could be won without the necessity of armed conflict; it would be a battle between economic systems and the political ideologies underpinning them. Perhaps this posture reflected the Soviets' fear that a nuclear exchange would destroy them but that the United States would survive. In any event, the second Soviet response to the American doctrine of massive retaliation entailed an intensified effort to build its own nuclear force and to develop sophisticated means of delivering nuclear weapons against the United States. The successful launching of the world's first space satellite (Sputnik) in 1957, which proved as well the Soviet capability to deliver a nuclear warhead, demonstrated its technological advances since breaking the American monopoly on atomic weapons in 1949.

Views of Strategic Doctrine
Since the Waning of American Superiority

American strategic superiority eroded steadily during the 1950s and thereafter. During the shift toward parity (equality) in the Soviet-American strategic balance, the assumption that weapons of mass destruction could actually be used

---

10. Dulles's practice of this strategy was more rhetorical than real. It is important to consider as well the important differences between Dulles's rhetoric and the actual practices of the Eisenhower administration.

began to be challenged. Awareness of the dangers of threatening the use of the U.S. nuclear arsenal prompted a doctrinal shift away from strategies of confrontation and compellence. The idea that nuclear weapons could be employed in diplomatic bargaining was dealt a death blow by the nearly suicidal Cuban missile crisis of 1962. Since then, nuclear weapons have been used primarily to deter aggression. *Deterrence* is the reliance on strategic capabilities to prevent others from attacking. The doctrinal shift from offense by compellence to defense by deterrence is important, for it marked the end of a period in which leaders perceived weapons as useful for coercion and the beginning of another in which weapons of mass destruction have been used defensively by threatening to impose unacceptably high costs on an adversary contemplating aggression.[11]

Ironically, confining the uses of nuclear weapons to retribution in order to prevent a Soviet attack served to stimulate the arms race rather than to inhibit it. A deterrent strategy depends on the ability to deliver without question unacceptable damage on the opponent. To ensure an ability to inflict such high costs, a second-strike capability is necessary. A *second-strike capability* requires a country to be able to withstand an initial strike by an adversary and still retain the ability to retaliate with a devastating second blow. In this way the adversary will be assured of destruction, thus deterring the initial preemptive attack. In order to ensure that a second-strike capability has been acquired and that an adversary is aware of it, deterrence requires a seemingly almost unlimited search for sophisticated retaliatory capabilities. As President Nixon stated in 1971, "Potential enemies must know that we will respond to whatever degree is required to protect our interests. They must know that they will only worsen their situation by escalating the evil of violence."

The United States and the Soviet Union have maintained an approximate balance or equivalence in their strategic levels since the mid-1970s (although political leaders and experts in both societies have sometimes sounded the alarm that the adversary had achieved a critical edge). The "stalemate" was summarized by Soviet Premier Leonid Brezhnev's assertion in 1978 that the Soviet Union "considers that approximate equilibrium and parity are enough for defense needs. We do not set ourselves the goal of gaining military superiority. We also know that this very concept loses its meaning with the present enormous stockpiles of nuclear weapons and systems for their delivery." By 1988 some observers felt that the acceptance of equivalence had become institutionalized: "Tacitly, the superpowers have agreed to stop comparing their overall national power in terms of the size of their respective nuclear arsenals" (Hunter, 1988).

---

11. The view prevalent since 1962 is that nuclear weapons cannot safely be used to compel an adversary into doing something it would not otherwise do, because the threatened state might react irrationally and thereby initiate a mutually suicidal nuclear exchange. There are, however, some strategists in both the United States and the Soviet Union who continue to advocate nuclear blackmail for political goals and who advance the view that it might be possible to fight, survive, and even win a nuclear war (Gray and Payne, 1980; for a critique, see Howard, 1981).

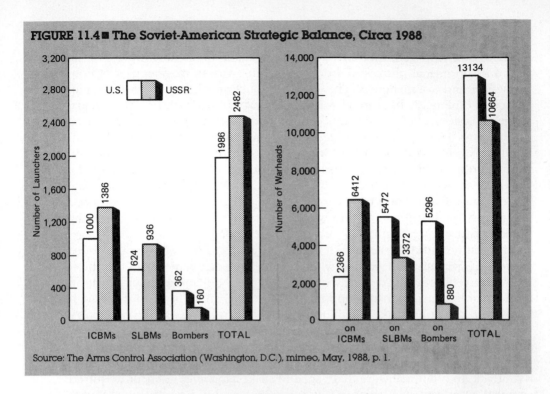

FIGURE 11.4 ■ The Soviet-American Strategic Balance, Circa 1988

Source: The Arms Control Association (Washington, D.C.), mimeo, May, 1988, p. 1.

Nonetheless, insecurity is bred by the difficulties in comparing military power quantitatively. Different perceptions of the same evidence can lead to different conclusions and hence to controversy and fear that the adversary has gained a decisive edge. One view of the strategic balance between the United States and the Soviet Union is provided in Figure 11.4. Based on U.S. government estimates, it demonstrates that the Soviet Union has gained numerical advantages over the United States in missile launchers, whereas the United States has maintained its traditional advantage in the number of warheads able to be delivered. Missile *throw-weight* (one measure of deliverable destructive power) is another calculation traditionally used to make comparisons, but its relevance has declined in the face of both superpowers' urge to reduce the megatonnage of their warheads' yield in favor of more "efficient" (read smaller but more destructive) warheads.[12] These aggregate comparisons must also be weighed against the relative technological sophistication of the superpowers' delivery capabilities, in which the United States has consistently maintained a decisive edge.

The comparative data on the superpowers' arsenals summarized in Figure

---

12. "The total explosive power of U.S. weapons today [1988] is only one quarter of the peak reached in 1960," noted the Commission on Integrated Long-Term Strategy (1988: 39–40). In addition, "The average warhead yield of U.S. nuclear weapons today is only one-fifteenth its 1957 peak. Even on the Soviet side, while the total number of nuclear weapons has been steadily increasing, the total explosive power and average warhead yield have both been declining since the mid-1970s."

11.4 make it strikingly clear that even without strict equivalence in the super-powers' destructive capacity in some categories of weapons, each is unquestionably capable of devastating the other. Mutual vulnerability is the result. Thus, insofar as each maintains a relatively invulnerable second-strike capability (which itself, however, has become a matter of controversy as technological developments render land-based missiles increasingly vulnerable to a devastating first strike), it is able to destroy every identifiable target of the other many times over, even after absorbing the enemy's most damaging first strike. Each is thereby restrained from attacking the other. "[What] is significant about nuclear weapons is not overkill, but mutual kill," observes Robert Jervis (1986). "The result is what can be called, without exaggeration, the nuclear revolution." Mutual deterrence has led to an uneasy but nonetheless prolonged period of superpower peace. However, as Jervis (1986) notes, "Nuclear weapons have brought the superpowers both great security and enormous insecurity."

MUTUAL ASSURED DESTRUCTION During the 1960s and 1970s, the phrase *mutual deterrence*, based on the principle of *mutual assured destruction* (MAD), gained currency as officially backed concepts used to characterize the strategic balance. The term *balance of terror* accurately described the essential military stalemate between the superpowers, for mutual deterrence was based on the military potential for and psychological expectations of widespread death and destruction for both combatants in the event of a nuclear exchange. Peace, in short, came to be the product of mutual vulnerability: If one attacked the other, it would do so at the price of its own destruction. Nuclear deterrence thus "is like a gun with two barrels, of which one points ahead and the other points back at the gun's holder. If a burglar should enter your house, it might make sense to threaten him with this gun, but it could never make sense to fire it" (Schell, 1984).

The relative mutual invulnerability of the superpowers' retaliatory forces led the United States during the Nixon administration to opt for a strategy of *sufficiency*, meaning that assured destruction was to be maintained but that no longer would the United States seek to retain superiority over the Soviet Union. At the same time, given that the superpowers' strategic capabilities were roughly equivalent, an effort was made to keep the Soviet Union from attaining superiority over the United States. This emergent balance in the two superpowers' strategic arsenals laid the basis for SALT (Strategic Arms Limitations Talks), a cornerstone in the détente phase of the Soviet-American rivalry, in which both sides sought to prevent the collapse of the fragile balance of terror that supports mutual assured destruction. The SALT negotiations attempted to guarantee each superpower's second-strike capacity and thereby to preserve the fear of retaliation on which stable deterrence presumably rests. Although the pursuit of this shared goal has not been without difficulties, a precarious peace has persisted, predicated on the precarious existence of mutual assured destruction.

The evolution of Soviet-American military competition and doctrine suggests a number of general patterns: that arms races are fed by mutual fears; that national security is believed to be strengthened by the acquisition of arms; that each partner to the competition is extraordinarily sensitive to the other's advances in military capabilities; and that technological advances might undermine the fragile strategic balance by making one partner vulnerable to attack by the other.

A characterization of the forces governing Soviet-American military competition must also highlight the tendency of each to pursue an arms race and arms control simultaneously, the propensity of each to seek peace while preparing for war, and the inclination of each to regard the price of national security as never too high.

Underlying these matters are inherently psychological and subjective factors; perceptions, not military hardware, technology, and destructive capabilities, are what ultimately matter most. As President Reagan's Commission on Strategic Forces observed, "Deterrence is not an abstract notion amenable to simple quantification. . . . Deterrence is a set of beliefs in the minds of . . . leaders, given their own values and attitudes, about capabilities and will."

The assumptions underlying the superpowers' quest for national security have influenced their force postures and doctrines. In particular, in much the same way that their diplomatic and political interactions have been characterized by reciprocity (recall Figure 4.1), the superpowers' development of their arsenals have exhibited reciprocity as "American and Soviet actions [have] helped to stimulate each other's nuclear weapons development" (Holloway, 1983). In the course of this symmetrical competition, the strategic systems of the competitors have come to resemble one another.

Box 11.1 documents the syndrome by tracing the dynamics of the Soviet-American nuclear competition and demonstrates the extent to which the strategic choices of each nation have predicted the subsequent choices of the other.[13] Every weapons procurement initiative by one side has been followed by a compensatory response by the other. A convergence in the superpowers' strategic levels has been the product. There is an element of irony in the fact that as a consequence of the action-and-reaction cycle to their strategic competition, the superpowers face essentially similar threats to their own survival. The strategic security dilemma confronts each competitor.

FROM MAD TO NUTS   The superpowers' doctrines and the policies for dealing with the use of their arsenals have not exhibited the same close level of

---

13. An example: In 1983, when President Reagan pushed for the deployment of one hundred MX missiles in order to "catch up" with the Soviets, Soviet Defense Minister Dimitri Ustinov was asked what the Soviets would do while the United States played catch-up—call a halt of their own arms building until the United States declared that parity had been achieved? His instructive reply: "If the present leadership of the White House . . . challenges us by beginning deployment of the MX missile, then the Soviet Union will respond to this by developing a new intercontinental ballistic missile of the same class, and its characteristics will in no way be inferior to the MX."

BOX 11.1 ■ Convergence in the Superpowers' Weapons Systems: A Chronology of Reciprocal Developments

Action ⇄ Reaction
In the Superpower Competition

Conventional Weapons

USSR **1949**	main battle tank	**1952** US
US **1955**	nuclear-powered submarine	**1958** USSR
US **1955**	large-deck aircraft carrier	**1975** USSR
USSR **1955**	wire-guided anti-tank missile	**1972** US
US **1959**	photo reconnaissance satellite	**1962** USSR
US **1960**	supersonic bomber	**1975** USSR
US **1960**	computer-guided missle	**1968** USSR
US **1961**	nuclear-powered aircraft carrier	**1992** USSR
USSR **1961**	surface-to-air missile	**1963** US
US **1962**	long-range fighter bomber	**1973** USSR
US **1964**	air-to-surface missile	**1968** USSR
USSR **1970**	high-speed attack submarine	**1976** US
US **1972**	television-guided missile	**1987** USSR
USSR **1972**	heavy attack helicopter	**1982** US
US **1975**	jet-propelled combat aircraft	**1983** USSR
US **1976**	large amphibious assault ship	**1978** USSR
USSR **1978**	multiple-launch rocket system	**1983** US
US **1987**	binary (chemical) weapons	**199?** USSR

Nuclear Weapons

US **1945**	atomic bomb	**1949** USSR
US **1946**	electronic computer	**1951** USSR
US **1948**	intercontinental bomber	**1955** USSR
US **1952**	thermonuclear bomb	**1953** USSR
USSR **1957**	intercontinental ballistic missile (ICBM)	**1958** US
USSR **1957**	man-made satellite	**1958** US
USSR **1958**	early-warning radar	**1960** US
US **1960**	submarine-launched ballistic missile (SLBM)	**1968** USSR
US **1966**	multiple warhead (MRV)	**1968** USSR
USSR **1968**	anti-ballistic missile (ABM)	**1972** US
US **1970**	multiple independently-targeted warhead (MIRV)	**1975** USSR
USSR **1971**	sea-launched cruise missile	**1982** US
US **1983**	neutron bomb	**199?** USSR
US **1985**	new strategic bomber	**1987** USSR
USSR **1987**	single warhead, mobile ICBM	**1992** US
US **1990?**	stealth bomber	**199?** USSR

Source: Ruth Leger Sivard, *World Military and Social Expenditures 1987–88* (Washington, D.C.: World Priorities, 1987), p. 14.

381

similarity but, on occasion, have moved closer to each other. The super-powers' doctrines during the period of confrontation between 1980 and 1985 provide a recent example of this convergence. The Carter administration announced a shift from the traditional American countervalue strategy toward a posture resembling the Soviets' presumed counterforce strategy. For the first time, Carter declared, American nuclear missiles would be targeted more toward military facilities, command posts, and political centers and less toward Soviet population and industrial centers.[14]

This doctrinal departure set the stage for a new debate about the role of nuclear weapons and the purposes that should guide their use. At issue are the intentions underlying the superpowers' arsenals. Were they designed for pur-poses of defense and deterrence? Or were they designed to wage war, perhaps by seeking to attain a first-strike capability? Neither adversary has reason to trust the other, and hence both are motivated to base their evaluations of intentions on capabilities. Each assumes that unless deterred, its opponent might be tempted to use its arsenal for attack. Inherent bad faith and "worst case" assumptions govern the formulation of doctrine. These fears were exac-erbated, not alleviated, by the new talk in the early 1980s that surfaced about the practicability of preemptive strikes and the "winability" of a nuclear exchange. For example, the concept of *damage limitation* was given atten-tion, which suggests that one way to avoid the destructive effects of nuclear weapons is to use them first, thereby destroying a portion of the adversary's weapons before they can be used. Debate about such a concept heightened perceptions of threat and stimulated the search for better ways to protect national security with nuclear weapons.

In this heated atmosphere, there arose in the United States (and perhaps also in the Soviet Union) intense debate about the principles governing strate-gic weapons. The positions can be dichotomized, for purposes of discussion, by differentiating between the advocates of the *nuclear utilization theory*, or a NUTs approach, and those embracing the concept of *mutual assured destruc-tion*, or MAD. For the proponents of NUTs, nuclear weapons are seen not only to play a deterrent role but also to be utilized in war. For some, such a posture was necessary because the Soviet Union was believed to be preparing to fight—and win—a nuclear war (Pipes, 1977; see Holloway, 1983, and Kennan, 1984, for contrasting views of Soviet thinking about nuclear weapons). Fur-thermore, the advocates of NUTs argued that it was possible to fight a pro-tracted nuclear war (that is, any use of nuclear weapons would not necessarily

---

14. For some time it has been part of the U.S. strategic doctrine not to target civilian population centers per se, but the Carter administration shifted the focus more specifically to Soviet war-supporting industries and economic recovery capabilities (Ball, 1983). In practice, however, the distinction may be largely meaningless, as military and industrial sites are often co-located with population centers. "Simply by virtue of associated industrial and military targets, all of the 200 largest Soviet cities and 80% of the 866 Soviet cities with populations above 25,000 are included in U.S. war plans" (Ball, 1983: 33). *Collateral damage* is the concept that war planners use to talk about damage inflicted on the nontargeted surrounding human and nonhuman resources as a result of military strikes on enemy forces or military resources.

escalate to an unmanageable, all-out nuclear exchange) and that by making nuclear weapons more usable, they would enhance deterrence rather than detract from it, by making the nuclear threat more credible.

The proponents of MAD, on the other hand, held that deterrence remained the only sane role to which to assign nuclear weapons, because the use of nuclear weapons of even limited capabilities would surely escalate to an unrestrained exchange. "It is inconceivable to me," former Secretary of Defense Robert McNamara reflected, ". . . that limited nuclear wars would remain limited—any decision to use nuclear weapons would imply a high probability of the same cataclysmic consequences as a total nuclear exchange" (cited in Rhodes, 1988). According to this view, the technical requirements and human capacity to wage a protracted limited nuclear war would surely be strained beyond the breaking point. Furthermore, because the threatened use of even tactical nuclear weapons would lower the nuclear threshold, many believed that a nuclear strategy premised on the usability of nuclear weapons in war would in fact make war more likely, not less, and thereby diminish the weapons' deterrent capability. From this viewpoint, both superpowers were destined to live in a MAD world, even if, ironically, this meant that they would remain in the "mutual hostage relationship" in which their earlier weapons decisions had imprisoned them (see Kecny and Panofsky, 1981).

In addition to their own continuing quests of greater military capabilities, both superpowers sought to extend their deterrent capabilities to their principal allies, thereby entrapping them in this same hostage relationship. (This is sometimes termed *extended deterrence*, the goal of which is to prevent an attack not only on oneself but also one's allies.) Thus, deterrence is seen as necessary not just to guard the country's homeland but also to prevent the enemy from attacking targets outside the country's own defense perimeter and alliance network.[15]

As the nuclear debate raged, political leaders in the United States and the Soviet Union both professed their commitment to avoiding nuclear war because it was "unthinkable." Both sought ways to prevent a nuclear exchange, for the United States by relying on MAD[16] and for the Soviet Union by

---

15. The credibility of the American extended deterrent guarantee to the NATO countries has been questioned by both American allies and by U.S. strategic theorists since its inception. Henry Kissinger punctuated the doubt when in 1979 he noted that the promise involves "strategic assurances that we cannot possibly mean or if we do mean, we should not execute because if we should execute, we risk the destruction of civilization." This circumstance has led some critics to advocate "decoupling" Europe from the American strategic security umbrella and encouraging the NATO countries to develop for themselves a credible deterrent capacity.

16. Modifications in strategic doctrine have been proposed to enhance the adversaries' awareness that destruction in response to its attack would be ensured. For instance, to address potential uncertainties about whether fixed-site ICBMs could survive an attack in sufficient numbers to guarantee retaliation, a "launch-on-warning" doctrine was advocated. This calls for the automatic release of bombers and missiles upon early warning that the enemy had initiated an attack, under the conviction that the threat of the preemptive strike would successfully deter the adversary. Critics regard the doctrine as extremely destabilizing in crisis situations, as it calls for the creation of a doomsday instrument outside human control.

expanding the capabilities of both its defensive and offensive systems. At the same time, however, each superpower continued to develop and deploy the kinds of weapons that NUTs required—so-called discriminating low-yield nuclear weapons made possible by new technologies in guidance and precision. These prepare the contestants for warfare short of a massive all-out nuclear attack and are viewed by advocates as effective deterrents against a conventional war (in Europe in particular). But given the possibility that the use of even these smaller weapons could escalate to an unlimited war, the purposes that NUTs' strategists assign them appear highly dangerous. As the Commission on Integrated Long-Term Strategy (1988) concluded, keeping a limited war within bounds "involves a reckless gamble with fate." "In the last analysis . . . the deterrent against the massive conventional attack is the same as the deterrent against the all-out nuclear attack."

FROM OFFENSE TO DEFENSE   The shift in strategic thinking from offense to defense likewise has been viewed by some experts as a challenge to the principle of mutual assured destruction, because a defensively oriented doctrine conceivably could remove the incentives for restraint on which stable deterrence presumably depends. President Reagan's Strategic Defense Initiative (SDI), proposed in 1983 as a means to provide a defensive shield against ballistic missiles, was criticized on these grounds. To free the world from the threat of nuclear war, SDI calls for the development of and reliance on a high-tech "Star Wars" ballistic missile defense (BMD) system using advanced space-based technologies to destroy Soviet offensive weapons launched in fear, anger, or by accident. Reagan claimed that these technologies could make nuclear weapons "impotent and obsolete." Thus the Strategic Defense Initiative represented a profound shift in U.S. nuclear strategy away from reliance on offensive missiles to deter an attack—that is, from dependence on mutual assured destruction, which President Reagan deemed "morally unacceptable."

Considerable uncertainty surrounds Star Wars. Official statements about the program raise expectations that doubtlessly will not be met until well into the next century, if ever. The ability to end the balance of terror through technological fixes has been doubted by scientists, many of whom question the feasibility of doing so (see Slater and Goldfischer, 1988). The program is fraught with ambiguities and uncertainties, raising questions as to whether the effort to construct an effective defense against strategic weapons is feasible or foolish (see Haley and Merritt, 1986). Risked is not just investment in an extraordinarily expensive system that, in the last analysis, might induce an unwarranted sense of safety because it might not work, but one that could provide an incentive for the development of a new generation of offensive weapons designed to overwhelm the defensive ones.

While each superpower continued to engage in a massive arms buildup, each also tried to extricate itself from the costs (financial and psychological) that the new arms race entailed, by negotiating new arms control agreements (see Chapter 13). Included in these efforts were proposals for an arms *build-down* (permitting both superpowers to modernize their arsenals, so that as less-threatening new warheads were built, more-threatening, older warheads could be destroyed) and START negotiations (Strategic Arms Reduction Talks) aimed at decreasing significantly the number of U.S. and Soviet missiles instead of merely preserving the balance, as SALT had sought. Other arms control endeavors (especially those relating to intermediate-range nuclear forces [INF]) figured prominently in the dialogue. Whether all this strategic posturing would lead to nuclear war or to nuclear peace remained, as ever, a subject of intense debate. The "search for a variant of, or substitute for, strategic nuclear war, in the form of counterforce strategy and tactical nuclear war which would avoid indiscriminate nuclear destruction and thereby restore the traditional distinction between victory and defeat" appears to remain a primary goal (Morgenthau, 1983).

To be militarily invulnerable, to contain an escalating and costly arms race, to remain prepared to meet any military challenge, to maintain an invincible deterrent capability, and to preserve peace—these are the primary goals of both superpowers. And to see one's nation as the best hope for peace and the strongest voice for restraint characterizes the self-image of both countries.

ESCAPING THE SECURITY DILEMMA?

The search for national security through preparation for war is understandable in a world in which states perceive themselves as ultimately responsible for their own self-defense. As President Dwight D. Eisenhower once noted, the view is compelling that "until war is eliminated from international relations, unpreparedness for it is well nigh as criminal as war itself." The belief prevails that peace is a product of strength and that security can be obtained by the possession of as much or more firepower than that of one's enemies. Security thus rests on the strength of each state relative to others. Hence the security dilemma has been a feature of the international system confronted by diplomats throughout history. The philosopher Jean-Jacques Rousseau, for example, argued in the eighteenth century that "the state . . . always feels itself weak if there is another that is stronger. Its security and preservation demand that it make itself more powerful than its neighbors. It can increase, nourish and exercise its power only at their expense. . . . Because the grandeur of the state is purely relative it is forced to compare itself to that of the others. . . . It becomes small or great, weak or strong, according to whether its neighbor expands or contracts, becomes stronger or declines."

The fears engendered by visions of nuclear devastation and by the cognizance of a nation's vulnerability to physical destruction also contribute to the belief that these perils might be avoided by the attainment of a sufficient deterrent capacity. Defense planners often base their plans on "worst-case" analyses that intensify the perceived need for more military preparation to avoid these nightmares. The urge to arm is further stimulated by the ubiquitous influence of defense planners in the policymaking process of most countries. The policies proposed by defense planners have an uncanny, if understandable, habit of reflecting military thinking, and foreign policy decision makers have a penchant for adopting the vocabulary and concepts of their military advisers.[17]

To ask whether national security is risked rather than ensured by military preparedness is to raise an uncomfortable question that challenges the orthodox approach to national security prevalent throughout much of the world's history. But it is required if the ultimate questions are to be answered—Can the security dilemma be escaped and the vulnerability of the world to annihilation be removed? Less apocalyptically, how can new conceptions of national security, which incorporate awareness of the threats posed to well-being by the erosion of states' economic and ecological foundations (see Brown, 1986), be brought before policymakers for serious consideration?

Since the advent of nuclear weapons, most nation-states' security has clearly receded. Today nearly all states are "conditionally viable" (Boulding, 1962) because they are dependent on other states for their survival. The superpowers are especially vulnerable as a result of the instruments of destruction they have created to protect themselves—a realization that led George Kennan to conclude in 1986 that "what most needs to be contained, as I see it, is not so much the Soviet Union as the weapons race itself." The exposure to destruction and the concomitant presence of fears too horrible to contemplate were noted by former Secretary of Defense Harold Brown who in 1983 observed, "If one takes as a measure of national security the ability of the people of the United States to determine their own future without being influenced by what happens outside their own borders, the threat of nuclear destruction means that U.S. national security has deteriorated markedly and probably irreversibly since the early 1950s."

If militarization does, indeed, lead to a decrease in national and global security, how then can states escape this dilemma and free themselves from the prospect of destruction?

As the preceding discussion suggests, the predicament currently affords little room for maneuver. Security rests on the preservation of deterrence—an uncertain theory based on a peculiar, almost illogical premise that security depends on the continuing vulnerability of each state. Safety requires everyone to remain endangered. The threat system must be preserved in order to counter the threat: No sane actor will attack if attack ensures self-destruction.

---

17. Recall the discussion of bureaucratic politics in Chapter 3. In this context, Carl Sagan has observed:

> Each nation has military and intelligence establishments that evaluate the danger posed by the other side. These establishments have a vested interest in large military and intelligence expenditures. Thus, they must grapple with a continuing crisis of confidence—the clear incentive to exaggerate the adversary's capabilities and intentions. When they succumb, they call it necessary prudence; but whatever they call it, it propels the arms race. (Sagan, 1988: 7)

The theory of deterrence is open to criticism. And yet regardless of its deficiencies, it is the policy on which most of the militarized world relies. Plausible alternatives that can be implemented without encountering strong resistance do not appear available. As Harold Brown lamented, there is no choice but to continue to depend on deterrence to prevent destruction. Hence, human destiny may be becoming, as H. G. Wells long ago prophesied it would, more and more a race between self-restraint and survival. Security may depend as much on the control of force as on its pursuit.

SUGGESTED READINGS

Brown, Lester R. "Redefining National Security," pp. 371–381 in Charles W. Kegley, Jr., and Eugene R. Wittkopf, eds., *The Global Agenda: Issues and Perspectives*, 2nd ed. New York: Random House, 1988.

Buzan, Barry. *People, States & Fear: The National Security Problem in International Relations*. Chapel Hill: University of North Carolina Press, 1983.

Dewitt, David B., ed. *Nuclear Non-Proliferation and Global Security*. New York: St. Martin's Press, 1987.

Jervis, Robert, Richard Ned Lebow, and Janice Gross Stein. *Psychology and Deterrence*. Baltimore: Johns Hopkins University Press, 1985.

Keeny, Spurgeon M., Jr., and Wolfgang K. H. Panofsky. "MAD vs. NUTS: Can Doctrine or Weapons Remedy the Mutual Hostage Relationship of the Superpowers?" *Foreign Affairs* 60 (Winter 1981): 287–304.

Kegley, Charles W., Jr., and Eugene R. Wittkopf, eds. *The Nuclear Reader: Strategy, Weapons, War*, 2nd ed. New York: St. Martin's Press, 1989.

Klare, Michael. "The Arms Trade: Changing Patterns in the 1980s," *Third World Quarterly* 9 (October 1987): 1257–1281.

McNeill, William H. *The Pursuit of Power: Technology, Armed Force, and Society Since* A.D. *1000*. Chicago: University of Chicago Press, 1982.

Mullins, A. F., Jr. *Born Arming: Development and Military Power in New States*. Stanford, Calif.: Stanford University Press, 1987.

Wolfers, Arnold. "National Security As an Ambiguous Symbol," *Political Science Quarterly* 67 (December 1952): 481–502.

TWELVE

Resort to Force: Armed Conflict and Violence in World Politics

In my opinion the world is moving ineluctably towards a third world war—a strategic nuclear war. I do not believe that anything can be done to prevent it. The international system is simply too unstable to survive for long.

HANS J. MORGENTHAU, 1979

Mankind must put an end to war or war will put an end to mankind.

JOHN F. KENNEDY, 1963

Every day, newspapers and television news programs remind us that we live in an age of violence. Their reports document states' habitual reliance on force to settle disputes. Preparing for and making war looks like a major national preoccupation. Indeed, it has been estimated that not a single day has been free of war since 1945 (Kidron and Smith, 1983) and that on any given day "an average of twelve wars [is] going on somewhere in the world" (Sampson, 1978: 60).

The actual amount of past and present armed conflict is difficult to measure. But although estimates vary considerably,[1] all demonstrate the continuing willingness of people to fight for what they want or to repel what they reject. It is little wonder so many people seem to equate world politics with war.

---

1. Estimates depend on the criteria used to define war. For example, Norman Cousins speculates that since 3600 B.C. there have been over 14,500 major and minor wars which have taken the lives of over 3.5 billion people (cited in Beer, 1974: 7). Another inventory recorded 14,531 wars over 5,560 years of history, which translates into an average of over 2.5 wars a year (Grieves, 1977: 7). Other, less speculative accounts support this estimate. Quincy Wright (1942) documented 278 wars from 1480 to 1940; Lewis Fry Richardson (1960b) identified over 300 wars between 1820 and 1949; and Pitirim Sorokin (1937), perusing human history from approximately 1100 through 1925, records 862 wars. (In the process he found that his native Russia had experienced over a thousand-year span only one-quarter of a century without a war.) Additional evidence reports 510 wars between 1700 and 1987, distributed with 68 in the eighteenth century, 205 in the nineteenth, and 237 in the twentieth (Sivard, 1986: 26). Perhaps the most rigorous scientific effort to explore the historical incidence of war is the Correlates of War project (Small and Singer, 1982), which identifies 118 interstate wars between 1816 and 1980.

To understand better the role of armed conflict in the contemporary world, its various forms must be distinguished and their frequency measured. Criteria for differentiating war from other forms of international conduct that result in death must also be specified.

In this regard, *war* and *conflict* are different. War cannot be considered mere conflict. Conflict occurs when two or more parties perceive differences between or among them and are committed to resolving those differences to their own satisfaction. Conflict is an intrinsic product of communication and contact between peoples; when people(s) interact, some conflict is inevitable. As an essential part of all social interaction, therefore, conflict should not be regarded as either infrequent or abnormal.

Nor should conflict necessarily be regarded as undesirable. Conflict performs many positive functions (such as promoting social solidarity, clarifying values, stimulating thinking and creativity, and encouraging learning) which, if managed properly, are constructive to human progress. Paradoxically, close contact leads to both friendship and enmity: Cooperation may produce conflict, and conflict may promote cooperation (see Coser, 1956).

But when international conflicts are not managed properly, the potential arises for resort to force as a method for its resolution. Karl von Clausewitz's famous dictum that war is merely an extension of diplomacy by other means underscores the fact that force is an instrument through which nations may seek to achieve their political objectives. But it is also the deadliest. War's onset means that persuasion did not work and that negotiations were unsuccessful. War is, in this sense, as Clausewitz stated, "a form of communication between nations," albeit an extreme form.

The foregoing conceptualization defines war as the use of organized military force against an adversary to achieve political objectives. It differentiates conflict from armed conflict. With this in mind, this chapter considers the different ways in which both forms of conflict are manifested globally, but with special attention to armed conflict. For purposes of presentation, five modes of armed conflict will be examined: wars in general (and their causes), military confrontations short of force (crises), "low-intensity conflict," civil wars, and terrorism. Although these five types of armed conflict can be distinguished analytically, they in fact overlap, are interrelated, and contribute to one another's onset.

WAR: SOME EMPIRICAL EVIDENCE

An examination of the frequency of war through time permits inferences to be made about changes in it. To trace changes in war's incidence, the state system since 1815 can be broken into five historical periods, with 1848, 1881, 1914, and 1945 demarcating the significant "turning points" between them. These divisions conform to what many scholars and policymakers conventionally regard as major transition points in contemporary history; they also permit

TABLE 12.1 ■ Frequency with Which 118 Wars Have Begun over Five Historical Periods, 1816–1980

Period	Number of Wars	Average Number of States
1816–1848	20	29
1849–1881	28	39
1882–1914	24	40
1915–1944	20	60
1945–1980	26	116

Source: Calculated from data in Melvin Small and J. David Singer, *Resort to Arms: International and Civil Wars, 1816–1980* (Beverly Hills, Calif.: Sage, 1982), p. 131.

comparisons in the amount of war begun across five successive periods of approximately thirty-two years' duration each. When considered in this fashion, it becomes possible to gauge whether the total number of wars begun in international history has changed. Table 12.1 summarizes the relevant information.

The evidence summarized in Table 12.1 measures only wars *between* states, and it relies on a definition of war that counts only sustained military conflicts involving at least two sovereign states resulting in at least one thousand battle deaths (see Small and Singer, 1982). When measured in this restricted way, the data show that war has been a recurrent phenomenon, with some 118 interstate wars between 1816 and 1980. Its frequency has fluctuated only moderately; the incidence has been fairly stable over time, and no linear trend in the outbreak of wars is evident.[2] Furthermore, if the expanding number of countries in the system is taken into account, it can even be said that a modest decline has occurred in the outbreak of wars between states since 1816. Thus, when we adjust for the number of nations, the post–World War II era has been relatively more peaceful than were the periods that preceded it.

Or has it been? A somewhat different picture of the historical record emerges when attention focuses on the number of wars *under way*, rather than on the number of wars between states that start. The onset of war may be largely stable, but the annual amount of war under way shows both greater fluctuation and greater magnitude. Interstate war has been under way almost continuously over the past 165 years of international history—a constant feature of an otherwise transforming world political system. Although there

---

2. This finding is supported by Lewis Fry Richardson's (1960b) data and is reinforced by K. J. Holsti's (1988: 410) inventory, which identified thirty-eight instances of military force in the twenty-year period between 1919 and 1939, as compared with fifty-nine in the forty-one years between 1945 and 1986.

were eighty years between 1816 and 1980 in which no wars began, there were only twenty in which none was under way (Small and Singer, 1982: 149).

Of particular interest is the global pattern of warfare since 1945. Here we shift our focus from wars between states to consider the occurrence of war generically, that is, all international armed conflicts in which foreign overt military actions were undertaken by one or more states within one or more foreign territories. Defined broadly in these terms, the available evidence indicates that between September 1945 through 1986, 269 such incidents of international armed conflicts have occurred (Tillema, 1987). Thus, the extent of wars commencing and under way worldwide has remained high since World War II and has risen since the mid-1970s. Figure 12.1 portrays the pattern between 1945 and 1985, an era in world politics unlike all others—the nuclear era.

These data demonstrate how widespread war has remained since 1945. This does not necessarily mean that all nations have experienced wars; the rate of war involvement varies considerably for different countries. In fact, at the level of the nation-state rather than the system as a whole, there has been an actual decrease over time in the average number of wars in which nations

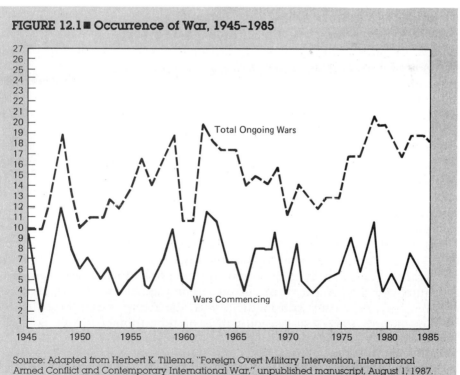

FIGURE 12.1 ■ Occurrence of War, 1945–1985

Source: Adapted from Herbert K. Tillema, "Foreign Overt Military Intervention, International Armed Conflict and Contemporary International War," unpublished manuscript, August 1, 1987.

participate (see Small and Singer, 1982). This has been especially evident in the experiences of the great powers since 1945. But because some nations repeatedly have been at war, warfare has been a persistent component of the global environment in which states interact.

THE DESTRUCTIVENESS OF MODERN WARFARE

If the good news is that wars have not increased in frequency in association with the growth of the number of nation-states, the bad news is that wars are becoming more deadly. One of the clearest long-term trends in the global system is the dramatic increase in the intensity and severity of war. Its destructiveness can be measured by the most important statistic: the loss of human life.

> Wars in the 20th century so far have killed 99 million people, 12 times as many as in the 19th century, 22 times as many as in the 18th century. The increasing scale of the slaughter has reached incredible proportions. While in the 19th century there were 14 wars with deaths of 100,000 or more, in this century there have been three times as many. In the last century there were two wars with deaths over 1 million; in this century 13 such wars, including World War I, which took 20 million lives and World War II, 38 million. (Sivard, 1986: 26)

The fact documented by these statistics is that wars have taken increasing numbers of lives, both absolutely and relative to population size. The overall trend in casualties has risen most rapidly since World War I. "On average," Ruth Sivard (1986: 7, 13) records, "there have been ten times as many deaths per war in the 20th century as in the 19th. . . . Conventional weapons [killed] an estimated 20 million people between 1945 and mid-1986."[3] More apocalyptically, Bruce Russett (1965: 12–13) observed that death from war has increased tenfold every fifty years and that "if this growth rate . . . were to continue, wars by around the end of this century would kill the equivalent of the present population of the globe." Thus a significant aspect of the overall casualty rates is that they have risen in conjunction with technological developments, a factor that we shall consider in more detail.

As overall casualty rates have gone up, their costs have increasingly been borne by civilians and noncombatants; the casualty rates of the soldiers doing the fighting have actually gone down. In the 1960s, for example, civilians accounted for 52 percent of the deaths from war; by the 1970s, they accounted for 73 percent; and in the 1980s, the figure mushroomed to 85 percent (Sivard, 1987: 28). The growth is partly attributed to the fact that

---

3. The deaths resulting from war have risen rapidly since the turn of the century. Pitirim Sorokin (1937) estimated that in Europe the casualty rate in the first quarter of the twentieth century "exceeded the total casualties for all the preceding centuries taken together."

civilian populations have increasingly become the targets of destruction, as in the aerial bombardment of cities.

The introduction of nuclear weapons creates new dangers that threaten to exacerbate this trend exponentially. As noted earlier, today's nuclear weapons are far more destructive than those used against Japan during World War II. Consequently, the prospect of waging even a "limited" nuclear war with today's weapons is traumatic to visualize. It is conceivable that in the event of a nuclear holocaust, life as we know it would cease. The catastrophic proportions of nuclear destruction are illustrated in Figure 12.2, which shows that the expected death toll resulting from a nuclear exchange between the superpowers would be nearly nine times greater than the number of deaths suffered by Soviets and Americans in previous wars. And these figures do not include the tens of millions more who would suffer the ravaging effects of radiation. Studies of the immediate and delayed effects of nuclear war (see Dyson, 1984; Ehrlich et al., 1983; Katz, 1982; Lewis, 1979; Sagan, 1983–1984; Schell, 1982) picture a postnuclear environment that is repugnant to contemplate (see Box 12.1).

How has the increasing destructiveness of modern weapons changed the nature of contemporary warfare? Indications of change are easy to detect. The length of interstate wars steadily increased between 1816 and World War II, for example, but then began a drastic decline (Small and Singer, 1979). Wars since 1945 have simply been shorter. Similarly, the average number of nations participating in major wars (which had been rising steadily since 1815) has fallen sharply since World War II. Wars are also more geographically confined. In fact, wars today are usually local wars involving small countries and conventional weapons: Since 1945 about 58 percent of wars have been between minor states (Holsti, 1988: 399). Hence, major wars have ceased to occur, but the number of smaller ones has expanded. This reverses the historic pattern that characterized the previous century when war between the major powers was frequent and took a large toll in human lives. These changes suggest that warfare between and among states is undergoing a substantial transformation in the contemporary international system.

Paradoxically, the world's most powerful nations are among the most constrained in their use of their military strength against one another. The destructiveness of modern weapons seems to have reduced their practical utility. This thesis was articulated by Winston Churchill in 1953, when he inquired whether weapons might breed restraint. He confessed that on occasion he had "the odd thought that the annihilating character of [nuclear weapons] may bring an utterly unforeseeable security to mankind. . . . It may be that when the advance of destructive weapons enables everyone to kill anybody else no one will want to kill anyone at all." Again in 1955 Churchill speculated: "After a certain point has passed, it may be said, the worse things get the better. . . . Then it may be that we shall, by a process of sublime irony, have reached a stage in this story where safety will be the sturdy child of terror, and survival the twin brother of annihilation."

FIGURE 12.2 ■ Estimated Soviet and American Deaths in a Nuclear War

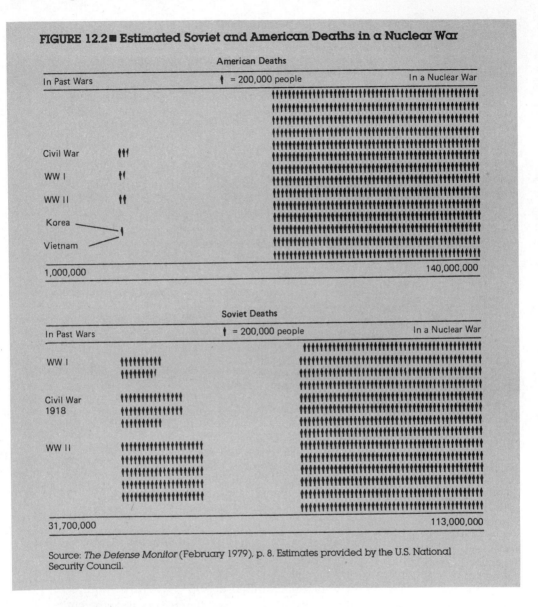

Source: *The Defense Monitor* (February 1979), p. 8. Estimates provided by the U.S. National Security Council.

This predicament is a good explanation for the sharp decline since 1945 in wars among the major powers.[4] In fact, general war among the great powers has not occurred since World War II (although wars by proxy, such as China's

---

4. And it fulfills a prediction made by Alfred Nobel (the Swedish armaments manufacturer whose endowments fund the Nobel Peace and other prizes), who speculated in 1892 that "perhaps my dynamite plants will put an end to war sooner than your congresses. On the day two army corps can annihilate each other in one second, all civilized nations will recoil from war in horror."

BOX 12.1 ■ Three Views of the Aftermath of a Nuclear Attack

A Physician's View

A 20-megaton nuclear bomb . . . would create a fireball 1½ miles in diameter, with temperatures of 20 million to 30 million degrees Fahrenheit. . . . All living things would be vaporized within a radius of "ground zero." Six miles from this point, all persons would be instantly killed by a huge silent heat flash traveling at the speed of light. . . . Within a 10-mile radius, the blast wave would slow to 180 mph. In that area, winds and fires would probably kill 50 percent of the population, and injure another 40 percent. . . . Within 20 miles of the center, 50 percent of the inhabitants would be killed or injured by the thermal radiation and blast pressures, and tens of thousands would suffer severe burn injuries. . . . Medical "disaster planning" for a nuclear war is meaningless.[a]

A Biologist's View

It is clear that the ecosystem effects *alone* resulting from a large-scale thermonuclear war could be enough to destroy the current civilization in at least the Northern Hemisphere. Coupled with the direct casualties of perhaps two billion people, the combined intermediate and long-term effects of nuclear war suggest that eventually there might be no human survivors in the Northern Hemisphere.[b]

An Astronomer's View

A nuclear war, even a fairly modest one, now seems likely to trigger a period of hemispheric, and possibly global, sub-freezing cold and dark that would have catastrophic consequences for our planetary civilization and perhaps for our species. The cause would be absorption of sunlight at altitude by dust from high yield ground bursts and, particularly, by soot from the burning of cities and forests. . . . This effect [has been called] Nuclear Winter. . . . A quite "small" nuclear war, involving 1,000 weapons, each of 100-kiloton yield, all exploded over cities, could produce virtually the full Nuclear Winter effects. . . . Vast numbers of survivors would soon starve to death.[c]

[a]International Physicians for the Prevention of Nuclear War, "The Medical Consequences of Nuclear War," as reported by the Associated Press, March 8, 1980.
[b]Paul R. Ehrlich et al., "Long-Term Biological Consequences of Nuclear War," *Science*, December 23, 1983, p. 1299.
[c]Carl Sagan, from the *Wall Street Journal*, February 16, 1984, p. 35, and "Nuclear War and Climatic Catastrophe," *Foreign Affairs* 62 (Winter 1983–1984): 271.

and the Soviet Union's support for opposing sides in the 1977–1978 Vietnam–Cambodia conflict, have been chronic). It was perhaps the incredible costs and risks of fighting that led President Nixon to say, in the context of the Vietnam War and implicitly in reference to wars between major powers, "I seriously doubt that we will ever have another war. This is probably the very last one.'' This sentiment has been shared by others. Writing ''On the Obsolescence of War,'' John Weltman (1974) asserted, for instance, that ''violence as an instrument of foreign policy has increasingly become highly inefficient, if not counterproductive.'' Even more confidently, Werner Levi (1981) predicts in *The Coming End of War* that the day is nearing when ''weapons [will] wipe out war.''

Although the possibility of nuclear war certainly lingers, and although the superpowers continue to stockpile the weapons of war, warfare is not the intended purpose (see Kegley and Wittkopf, 1989). As Melvin Laird, secretary of defense in the Nixon administration, observed, ''Nuclear weapons . . . are useless for military purposes.'' In fact, the goals have changed from winning in war to deterring an adversary from initiating it: Each player wants not so much to win as to avoid loss. To deter an attack, some advocates, such as former U.S. Defense Secretary Caspar Weinberger, insist that the option of an early first use of nuclear weapons must be preserved. Others, such as Robert S. McNamara (1983), also a former defense secretary, reject this view, contending that ''to the extent that the nuclear threat has a deterrent value, it is because it in fact increases the risk of nuclear war.''

A rival explanation for the world's ability thus far to avoid nuclear war is also worth contemplating. This is the pessimistic view that humankind has escaped nuclear devastation largely by sheer luck. By the laws of probability, so this reasoning goes, the longer that nuclear arsenals continue to exist, the more likely it is that human miscalculation will inevitably trigger a nuclear exchange. According to probability theory, in other words, any event that can possibly happen will happen; the question is not if but when. From this perspective, deterrence is inherently unstable—it cannot be perpetual. The odds for nuclear holocaust through a fatal error, whether of judgment, performance, miscalculation, or accident, are great.[5] Moreover, the limits to rationality under conditions of crisis, the obstacles to effective interstate communication, and the risks associated with competitive confrontations all heighten the potential dangers (see Carnesale et al., 1985).

---

5. Although most analysts believe that a nuclear war would most probably begin through the escalation of a conventional war, the danger of war occurring through miscalculation or accident cannot be discounted. *New York Times* correspondent Tom Wicker illustrates the dangers thus:

> More than 100,000 American military personnel have some form of access to or responsibility for nuclear weapons. A House subcommittee has reported that in 1977—a typical year—1,219 of them had to be removed from such duty because of mental disorders, 256 for alcoholism and 1,365 for drug abuse.
>
> There's every reason to suppose that the Soviet Union, with more or less equal nuclear force, has at least as severe a problem. Because their technology is not as advanced as that of the U.S., the Soviets may have a worse record of malfunctioning by the computers that control missile firings.
>
> That's a scary thought, since on our side the North American Defense Command reported 151 computer false alarms in an 18-month period. One had American forces on alert for a full six minutes before the error was discovered. (Wicker, 1982: E19)

These apocalyptic thoughts suggest that the destructiveness of nuclear weapons will lead not to their nonuse but, rather, to annihilation—later if not sooner. At best, nuclear weapons produce a precarious stability in the absence of real security. The ostensible peace between the superpowers since 1945 may, indeed, be the product of luck rather than a *pax atomica*. The idea that holding more and more powerful weapons will make nations more and more safe may thus be questioned.

These speculations lead to a related set of questions—those dealing with the causes of war and the factors and forces that promote and inhibit its occurrence. Accordingly, it is appropriate to review contending ideas about the sources from which wars originate.

THE CAUSES OF WAR: ALTERNATIVE PERSPECTIVES

The resort to force has prompted efforts throughout history to understand its causes. Inventories of the causes of war invariably conclude that the list of factors noted is incomplete (see Blainey, 1973; Howard, 1983; Pruitt and Snyder, 1969; Waltz, 1954), in part because most agree that the causes of war are rooted in multiple sources.

In the final analysis, wars originate from the decisions of national leaders, and the choices they make for war or peace collectively determine the direction of global trends. It is therefore common in discussions of the roots of war to consider the relationship of war to individuals and human choice. For this, the question of the role of human nature is central.

Is War Rooted in Human Nature?

The repeated outbreak of war has led some to conclude that humankind's inherent and unchangeable nature is responsible. For instance, Sigmund Freud (1968) and Konrad Lorenz (1963) have argued that aggression is innate, stemming from humans' genetic programming and psychological makeup. Noting that Homo sapiens is the most deadly species, ethologists (those who study animal behavior in order to understand human behavior) have similarly argued that humankind is one of the few species practicing "intraspecific" aggression (routine killing of its own kind). Most other species practice "interspecific" aggression (they kill only other species, except in the most unusual circumstances—cannibalism in certain tropical fishes is one exception).

These theories have been challenged on empirical and logical grounds. If warfare is an inevitable impulse deriving from human nature, critics have asked, then how can the relative infrequency of war be explained? If aggression is inherent in human nature, presumably all humans should express this genetically determined form of behavior. But some people are consistently nonaggressive, and genetics does not explain why the same individuals are often belligerent and nonbelligerent at different times.

Many social scientists have concluded that war is a learned trait, that it is a part of humankind's cultural and environmental heritage, not its biological nature.[6] Aggression is a propensity acquired early in life as a result of socialization and learning and, therefore, is a conditioned response to conflict for which substitutes can be found and learned. The fact that many societies have managed conflict without recourse to war suggests that human nature can express itself in a variety of ways; it also suggests that violence is not an inborn drive or trait that makes war inevitable. Violence is more accurately understood as a response to stimuli arising from particular environments under particular types of conditions. Hence, changes in environmental circumstances can alter its frequency.

Because foreign policies are typically made by individuals operating within groups rather than by themselves (and hence under conditions that circumscribe individual discretion), social-psychological factors are especially important as factors that constrain the impact of human nature and individual choice. Both the setting for decision making and the global environments may exert "an influence independent of the actions and beliefs of individual policymakers. . . . War seems less like something decision makers choose than something that somehow happens to them," even as it happens "through them," through the choices they make (Beer, 1981).

For these reasons most observers have rejected the once prevalent belief that violence derives from an innate aggressiveness in human nature. Violence may derive from conditions, but not from human nature. As Ted Robert Gurr (1970) puts it, "The capacity, but not the need, for violence appears to be biologically entrenched in men." Thus human nature allows war to occur but does not make it occur. Together, these theoretical orientations point out that war is best seen as a phenomenon rooted in a plethora of underlying conditions.

Even if we acknowledge that war results if, and only if, policymakers choose to initiate it, it is clear that human nature and the process by which foreign policy decisions are made greatly constrain the freedom of choice by which human nature and volition are given expression (recall Chapter 3). It is thus important, in considering the causes of war, to assume that the decision for war also stems in part from the domestic political pressures that diplomats experience. Therefore, it is relevant to ask, What are the prevalent domestic factors believed to encourage policymakers to elect war as a means of conflict resolution? Let us next examine some theories addressing the internal conditions that may cause nations to become involved in war (as either the attacker or the attacked).

---

6. The debate over the nature–nurture question will probably never be resolved. For reviews as it pertains to political conflict, see Nelson (1974) and Lewontin, Rose, and Kamin (1984).

Which Nations Are Prone to War?

Conventional wisdom holds that some states are more warlike than others. Among the national attributes believed most likely to influence the probability that a country will become involved in war are its size, ideology, geographical location, population dynamics, ethnic composition and homogeneity, wealth, economic performance, type of economic system and political institutions, military capabilities, level of educational attainment, industrialization, and historical traditions.[7] Which among these attributes makes nations most prone to participate in war?

NEW NATIONS　In his inspection of war in previous historical periods, Quincy Wright (1942) concluded in his seminal study that new nations are more likely to initiate wars than are mature states. Part of the reason for this is that newly independent nations tend to go through a period of intense nationalistic feelings, and nationalism has often served as a catalyst to war.[8] The drives to acquire independence or to settle territorial disputes have been prominent motives for the initiation of wars. It is thus not coincidental that since World War II, nearly all wars have occurred in the Third World.

TYPE OF POLITICAL SYSTEM　It is noteworthy that the nature of states' political systems appear to have little bearing on the likelihood that they will participate in war. Some, such as the philosopher Immanuel Kant, have assumed that liberal democratic governments are inherently peaceful. But historically democracies have been involved in war as frequently as have autocracies (Wright, 1942). The character of the participants in wars since 1945 suggests that this pattern continues today, as democratic and autocratic regimes appear to be equally likely to initiate or otherwise to become involved in wars (Small and Singer, 1976). This casts considerable doubt on the proposition that "making the world safe for democracy" will produce peace; indeed, history has not been kind to the theory that democratic states are necessarily peaceful. They have entered war much too frequently to place much confidence in their ability to extinguish the penchant for violence. Instead, as the French sociolo-

---

7. Implicit in this view is the assumption that the differences in the types or classes of nations will determine whether they will engage in war. A (perhaps dubious) corollary is that the leaders' personalities and perceptual idiosyncrasies are relatively immaterial—that the prospects for war will be conditioned more by the effects of national attributes than by the impact of leaders on the countries they lead. The decision for war, in other words, will be affected more by the circumstances that leaders encounter than by their preferences.

8. Nationalism entails a sense of loyalty and devotion to a nation, an attitude of national consciousness exalting one nation above all others and emphasizing the promotion of its culture and interests, as opposed to those of other nations or supranational groups. Kenneth Boulding has commented on the violence-provoking consequences of this disposition by noting that nationalism is "the only religion that still demands human sacrifice" (cited in Nelson, 1974).

gist Alexis de Tocqueville suggested in the last century, not only is democracy not a safeguard against war, but also, once engaged in war, democracies tend to be the most unrestrained. The arousal of mass involvements and hatreds in democratic societies is presumably responsible.

LEVEL OF ECONOMIC DEVELOPMENT   Closely associated with length of independence is another national attribute related to the probability of war involvement: the level of economic development. Advanced industrialized societies with relatively high standards of living tend to be satisfied states and therefore less apt to initiate a war that might risk that valued status. (There are exceptions, of course, such as Germany in 1939.) On the other hand, historically the most warlike states have been relatively poor states. At least in regard to the geographic locus of war, this pattern continues to prevail. Since 1945 most wars have been fought on the territories of the developing countries (although many of these have involved the great powers either directly or covertly).

Several hypotheses have been proposed to explain this tendency. Some have argued, for example, that poor societies are internally unstable and that instability breeds war. In this context Robert S. McNamara, then the U.S. secretary of defense, argued in 1966 that "there is no question but that there is evidence of a relationship between violence and economic backwardness." A variant of this idea contends that aggression is primarily a response to frustration and that relatively deprived and impoverished societies, being frustrated in their ability to satisfy their needs, are more prone toward war. This notion helps explain war in the Third World as an attack on problems of self-esteem through attack on foreign enemies: These countries attack what is feared or envied.

Alternatively, war in the developing world may be seen as an effort to rectify perceived status discrepancies, wherein the nation initiating the war seeks to reduce the difference between its achieved status (what it believes its status deserves to be) and its ascribed status (the status that others confer on it as a result of their image of its attainments). Other explanations of war in preindustrial societies include the hypothesis that such wars are stimulated by the desire to sever dependency relationships with advanced nations, and especially with their exploitative former colonial masters. The Algerian and Indochinese wars are often cited as cases in point.

But before we conclude that poverty breeds war, it is important to note that generally the most impoverished nations have been the least prone to initiate wars against others. The most plausible explanation of the relative infrequency of conventional war in the poorest countries is that although they share all the frustrations and deprivations that might be expected to be expressed through war, they are inhibited from venting their frustrations aggressively because they lack the military or economic resources to sustain its costs. Thus the poorest nations share one attribute with the wealthiest: the infrequency with which they engage in war. Neither can afford to wage war, but for quite different reasons: for the former, because they lack the means of war; for the latter, because their abundant weapons are too destructive to use.

This pattern certainly does not mean that the poorest nations will always remain peaceful. Indeed, if the past is a guide to the future, then the impoverished nations that attain a degree of development will be those most likely to participate in future wars, as economic growth and the rising expectations and the arms that growth permits lead to outbursts of aggressiveness (Chouchri and North, 1975).

An extension of this view argues that changes in nations' relative growth rates affect the chance that they will go to war. War is most likely when competitive states' power ratios undergo rapid transition as a result of industrialization and economic growth, with the result that power differentials between states become confused. Dubbed the *power transition* theory, this view assumes that

> an even distribution of political, economic, and military capabilities between contending groups of states is likely to increase the probability of war; peace is preserved best when there is an imbalance of national capabilities between disadvantaged and advantaged nations; the aggressor will come from a small group of dissatisfied strong countries; and it is the weaker, rather than the stronger, power that is most likely to be the aggressor. (Organski and Kugler, 1980: 19)

During the transition from developing to developed status, incentives are created for emergent challengers to achieve through force the power and recognition to which they believe their new-formed muscles entitle them. Conversely, established powers often are willing to employ force to arrest their relative decline and to avert or postpone the loss of their dominant position. Thus during periods of social unrest, wealthy, urbanized countries seem especially prone to war (Haas, 1965). When change is rapid and the international hierarchy is undergoing restructuring, war becomes especially likely as advancing and retreating states simultaneously seek to accommodate themselves to these changes in relative power. National circumstances thus influence which nations are most likely to respond by resort to arms to the threats posed by rapid global transformation.

ARMS PROLIFERATION   The dispersion of weapons to the developing nations may also increase the probability of war (see also Chapter 11). As Third World countries accumulate the economic resources to equip their military establishments, the future may well witness the specter of a peaceful, developed world surrounded by a violent, less-developed world. Evidence is found in the historical development of Europe. During its transition from relative poverty to the apex of development, Europe was the location of the world's most frequent and deadly wars. The major European states are estimated to have been at war about 65 percent of the time in the sixteenth and seventeenth centuries (Wright, 1942). Violence decreased only as the European nations moved up the ladder of development in later centuries.[9] Significantly, interstate war has not occurred in Europe since 1945.

If the Third World nations follow the European pattern, the world promises to be an even less peaceful place for the foreseeable future. As these states develop, the imbalance of national capabilities between disadvantaged and advantaged nations will be reduced, and these new centers of power will challenge the privileged position of the advanced industrial societies. According to the power transition theory, therefore, the transition to a system of diffused power will create conditions conducive to a new wave of war in the twenty-first century.

This discussion of nations' characteristics that relate to their war proneness hardly exhausts the subject. Other potential causes internal to the state include the aggressive search for new markets, attributed by Marxist-Leninists to capitalist states, or the misperceptions that result from bureaucratic decision-making procedures (see Levy, 1983a, 1986). But however important domestic influences might be as a source of war, many believe that the nature of the international system is even more important.

The Systemic Sources of Interstate War

At the level of the entire global system, virtually every global trend identified in this book may be seen as a factor either promoting or inhibiting the probability of war. Some of these factors relate more directly and powerfully to the prospects for peace than do others, and there are many theories that trace the linkages between structural or systemic properties and war (see Levy, 1988). Usually included are such global conditions as the number of alliances and international organizations, the rules of international law, the extent to which power is dispersed or concentrated in polarity configurations, and the degree of inequalities in the distribution of wealth worldwide. At issue is how systemic factors influence war's frequency. Historical trends convey the impression that war may be likened to a contagious disease, whose causes are located in the way that the international system is structured. From this premise, it is assumed that war is best understood as an epidemic caused by many viruses resulting from the environmental conditions in which states interact. That view, in turn, prompts two inquiries.

DOES VIOLENCE BREED VIOLENCE?   The adage "violence breeds violence" reflects the view that the seeds of future wars are found in past wars. World War

---

9. Francis Beer (1974: 28) similarly notes that over a third of the major wars occurring in the world since 3600 B.C. took place in Europe. The majority of these were initiated when the European states were adjusting to economic growth; the preceding prolonged period of economic stagnation was also a period of relative peace.

II—often viewed as an outgrowth of World War I—and the recurrent wars in the Middle East—seemingly the same battle fought over and over—are consistent with this interpretation. The conclusion that past wars have caused subsequent wars cannot be made on the basis of available evidence. But the data do support the proposition that the frequency of past wars tends to be correlated with the incidence of wars in later periods.[10] This finding conforms to the well-known view that "other things being equal, the more frequently things have happened in the past, the more sure you can be they will happen in the future" (Horst, 1963). War may be contagious; to some its future outbreak is therefore inevitable.[11] If so, then something within the dynamics of world politics—its anarchical nature, its weak legal system, its uneven distribution of power, or some combination of structural attributes—makes the system a war system.

ARE THERE CYCLES OF WAR AND PEACE?   If war is recurrent but not necessarily inevitable, how might temporal variations in the amount of war be explained? The absence of a clear trend in the frequency of war does not discount the possibility that individual nations or groups of nations engage in war periodically and that therefore the overall incidence of war might rise and fall over long stretches of time as latent enmities erupt into violence. Another theoretical interpretation is thus suggested: that processes are at work in the anarchic world system that create cycles. According to this perspective, world history oscillates rhythmically between periods of war and periods of peace. The peaks and valleys are guided by an all-powerful invisible hand built into the system's dynamics that causes the pattern to continue. Or, more real-

---

10. Care should be exercised in drawing conclusions from correlational analysis. No association or correlation between two variables, no matter how strong, constitutes proof that one is the cause of the other.

11. Those subscribing to the belief in war's inevitability have often taken their ammunition from the historical fact just noted that war has been so repetitive. Could war's recurrence be a kind of self-fulfilling prophecy? Expecting war and violence, do people prepare for it in order to deter it, and only then discover that their actions have promoted the very conditions that make war more likely?

Despite the possibility of war's inevitability, the available evidence fails to support the thesis. That history has been replete with war does not necessarily mean that we will always have it in the future. Preoccupation with violence may blind us to the fact that war as a mode of international intercourse is the exception, not the rule. Historically, most nations have been at peace much longer than they have been at war.

Indeed, social scientists have demonstrated that war is not a universal institution (Etzioni, 1968; Kluckhohn, 1944; Mead, 1968; Sumner, 1968). There are societies that have never known war, and some nations have been immune to it for prolonged periods (Switzerland and Sweden, for example). This indicates that war is not necessarily inevitable and that peace may be possible; historical forces do not deterministically control people's freedom of choice or experiences. Moreover, as described, the outbreak of war (but not the number of wars under way) since 1945 has stabilized and may even be declining somewhat. Because this decline has occurred despite the substantial increase in the number of nations extant since 1945, it would appear that the possibility that a nation will escape war is improving. This temporal variation, making war for most nations in fact less likely, undermines confidence in theories of war's inevitability.

istically perhaps, if war occurs cyclically, it may be caused by some combination of systemic phenomena that produce the regularity, such as the changes and repetitions cyclically occurring within the stable structure of the capitalist system, as described by the well-known theories of Nikolai Kondratieff (see Goldstein, 1988).

There may be deterministic overtones in such theories, but they have intuitive appeal. It seems plausible, for example, that just as long-term downswings and recoveries in business cycles profoundly affect subsequent behaviors and conditions, so a war experience produces aftereffects that may last for generations. Presumably, therefore, a nation at war will become exhausted and lose its enthusiasm for another war, but only for a time. This idea has been labeled the *war weariness* hypothesis (Blainey, 1973). Italian historian Luigi da Porto expresses one version: "Peace brings riches; riches brings pride; pride brings anger; anger brings war; war brings poverty; poverty brings humanity; humanity brings peace; peace, as I have said, brings riches, and so the world's affairs go round." The implication is that it takes time to move through these stages, which explains why there may be alternations between periods of enthusiasm for war and weariness of war which are influenced by learning, forgetting, and aging.

Arnold J. Toynbee's *A Study of History* (1947) is a classic illustration of the view that history alternates between periods of war and periods of peace, with the cycle taking over a century. The *long-cycle theory* seeks to explore historical cycles (Goldstein, 1988; Modelski, 1987; Rosecrance, 1987; Thompson, 1989). In particular, proponents of the theory have explored the regularity of cycles of world leadership and global war over the past five centuries to determine whether a "general war" repeats itself once every century, as many of these theorists maintain.

Tests of cyclical theories have led to conflicting results. Quincy Wright (1942) suggested that if periods of peace and war do exist, they can best be described as comprising intervals of peace lasting about fifty years between major outbreaks of war. Lewis F. Richardson (1960a) and Pitirim Sorokin (1937) collected data that indicated the possibility of cycles of over 200 years from peak to peak (although both were somewhat skeptical and cautioned against attaching too much causal importance to their existence), and Edward Dewey (1964) estimated a 177-year cycle. And looking at the proposition that "periods of high violence in the system will be followed by a decrease in the level of violence" (and, conversely, that "periods of low systemic violence will be followed by an increase in violence"), Frank Denton and Warren Phillips (1971) measured the amount of war under way rather than the number of wars begun and concluded that peaks in international violence occur every 20 to 30 years.

More recent research lends support to the thesis that processes are embedded in global political and economic dynamics that propel a great power to a hegemonic (preponderant) position about every hundred years (such as Portugal and the Netherlands at the beginning of the sixteenth and seventeenth centuries, respectively, Britain at the beginning of both the eighteenth and nineteenth centuries, and the United States at the end of World War II). During their reign, hegemonic powers monopolize military power and trade and determine the system's rules. However, no hegemonic power has been able to retain its position for more than three to four decades. In each cycle, overcommitments, the costs of empire, and ultimately the appearance of rivals lead to the delegitimation of the hegemon's authority and to the deconcentration of power globally. The recurrent result has been the outbreak of a "general war" every century (1494–1517, 1579–1609, 1688–1713, 1792–1815, and 1914–1945) which established, at its conclusion, a new world leader (Modelski, 1978, 1987). The cyclical process thus begins anew.

The validity of these interpretations depends in part on the measures of war's frequency and magnitude to which one refers (see Goldstein, 1988, for a review of long-cycle theory). For example, the evidence accumulated by the Correlates of War project does not point to the existence of a cycle since 1815 in the frequency with which war has begun. There is a pattern in the rate at which new wars are initiated, but that pattern does not conform to a regular, periodic propensity. The onset of war occurs at irregular intervals, suggesting the need to reject theses about cycles in international war (Singer, 1981; Small and Singer, 1982).[12]

When we consider the amount of war under way since 1815 instead of the number of wars begun, a slightly different picture emerges. Here the evidence does suggest that the amount of war occurring worldwide has peaked every fifteen or twenty years since the Congress of Vienna. But although peaks and troughs in the amount of war under way can be observed, this periodicity is not sufficiently regular to demonstrate that cycles of war are an inherent property of world politics. Rather, the evidence "suggests not so much that discrete wars come and go with some regularity, but that, with *some* level of such violence almost always present, there may be certain periodic fluctuations in the amount of that violence" (Small and Singer, 1982). That cautious conclusion seems reasonable and applies to the post–World War II era especially well (Figure 12.1).

From several theoretical standpoints, therefore, statements regarding the extent to which warfare in the global system is undergoing a transformation might be questioned. Newspaper headlines notwithstanding, the available evidence does not support the notion that the number of wars is increasing. Wars appear, instead, to be stable in number and may even be declining. War has been nonexistent among the great powers since 1945, for example. Furthermore, there is little evidence to support the proposition that war is necessarily an inexorable feature of world politics. But likewise there is little to support the utopian dream that a warless world is just around the corner.

---

12. Melvin Small and J. David Singer (1972) also conclude that "no cyclical patterns are apparent when we examine the military experiences of the individual nations which participated in several wars."

If a radical transformation in the incidence and extent of war is unlikely, the character of war may nevertheless be undergoing a fundamental change in terms of the other ways in which armed conflict is practiced on the world's stage. We now turn from this exploration of the multiple causes of war to inspect these alternative forms of violence.

OTHER MODES OF ARMED CONFLICT AND VIOLENCE IN WORLD POLITICS

The adage that ours is an age of violence finds expression not only in the wars between states that have already occurred or in the destruction that will undoubtedly result from future wars, but also because the threat of violence is always present in still other ways. Four additional modes of armed conflict— or the threat thereof—must be considered: crises, "low-intensity conflict," civil war, and terrorism.

Between War and Peace: Crisis and Crisis Management

It is a cliché that we live in an age of crisis. President Dwight D. Eisenhower, for instance, reflected in his memoirs that he could not "remember a day that had not brought its major or minor crisis."

The relationship between international crisis and international violence is close but ambiguous. *Crises* are situations of intense conflict between parties, usually accompanied by dramatic increases in hostile messages that threaten to escalate to war (Zinnes et al., 1972). They result when one actor confronts another with words and deeds in an effort to force the adversary to alter its posture toward certain issues and outcomes, but without the initiation of warfare. Crises therefore are something less than international war, even though they encompass extremely hostile acts to bend an enemy to one's will. They lie somewhere "between peace and war" (Lebow, 1981). How decision makers manage these tense relationships that typically threaten to escalate to war determines whether war will in fact result.[13]

Because of the extraordinary risks and costs of contemporary war, crises may best be seen as a hostile form of competitive bargaining that serves as a substitute for the use of force. The threat of warfare is designed to influence the perceptions and decisions of others in order to induce their compliance. A crisis thus performs the function that war often traditionally played, namely, forcing an enemy to submit to another's wishes. "Their . . . function is to

---

13. Crises threaten to escalate to war because of the time pressures that decision makers face, inadequate information, fear and anxiety, and personal stress that normally accompany decision-making procedures during crisis situations (see Herek et al., 1987; Rhodes, 1988).

resolve without violence, or with only minimal violence, those conflicts that are too severe to be settled by ordinary diplomacy and that in earlier times would have been settled by war" (Snyder and Diesing, 1977). Because the use of war as an instrument of policy has been severely restricted in the post–World War II period, "the threat of force has become more important than its actual use" (Williams, 1976). *Confrontations*—the military challenges of an enemy without the use of force—have therefore become common.

Crises are fraught with peril because they are provocative situations that take hostilities to the brink of war. Indeed, such threatening conditions in the past have often triggered war itself. Nevertheless the risky game of crisis politics and brinkmanship has been played repeatedly. Implicit in diplomats' willingness to practice it has been their belief that crises can be effectively managed because, as rational actors, nations will ultimately keep their hostility within controllable bounds in order to avoid the final step to war.[14] This belief is a premise on which much of American strategic thinking has been based (Schelling, 1960, 1966).

To contend that crises may be substitutes for war (and precursors to them) begs the question of what a crisis is. Unfortunately, few observers seem able to agree on its meaning, despite the frequency with which the term is used. Charles F. Hermann's (1972) definition is widely accepted as authoritative: "A crisis is a situation that (1) threatens the high-priority goals of the decision-making unit, (2) restricts the amount of time available for response before the decision is transformed, and (3) surprises the members of the decision-making unit by its occurrence." These attributes have been featured in some of the most conspicuous crises of our age, such as the Cuban missile crisis, the Berlin blockade, the Sino-Soviet border clash, and the Formosan Straits crisis. Each contained the elements of surprise, threat, and time pressure, as well as the risk of war. In each, a sense of urgency precipitated by unanticipated maneuvers by others was involved. But all were managed successfully in the sense that none crossed the line into overt military hostilities.[15]

The frequency of international crises provides a crude measure of global tension. In practice, tensions often translate into situations in which one state confronts another with a military threat, thereby creating a *militarized dispute*.

---

14. Ole R. Holsti (1972) questions the validity of this assumption: "There is scant evidence that along with more lethal weapons we have evolved leaders more capable of coping with stress."

15. According to this conception, crises that culminate in violence cease to be crises and become wars. Examples of violence that were preceded by crisis include World War I (1914), Kashmir (1948), Suez (1956), Tibet (1959), the Cuban Bay of Pigs (1961), and Goa (1961), among others. Conversely, some situations popularly termed crises in fact do not meet these criteria. The global energy crisis during the 1970s is an example. Surely the situation involved "threat," but neither "surprise" nor, but somewhat less so, "time pressure" describes it appropriately. Crises are pervasive nonetheless. One inventory has determined that an average of 7.7 crises erupted every year between 1945 and 1979 (Brecher et al., 1988).

Militarized disputes have been recurrent throughout history, but their number has risen in the twentieth century (compared with that of the nineteenth), and especially in the nuclear era. Over 40 percent of all militarized disputes occurring between 1816 and 1976 arose in the last three decades of that period (Gochman and Maoz, 1984: 592). The fact that the more recent periods had greater numbers of militarized disputes demonstrates why contemporary world politics seems to be in perpetual crisis.

Another picture of the chronic nature of international crises and their temporal variation is provided in Figure 12.3. It displays the distribution of 325 interstate crises initiated between 1928 and 1985. An international crisis is defined for purposes of this chronological profile as a "situational change characterized by an increase in the intensity of disruptive interactions between two or more adversaries, with a high probability of military hostilities in time

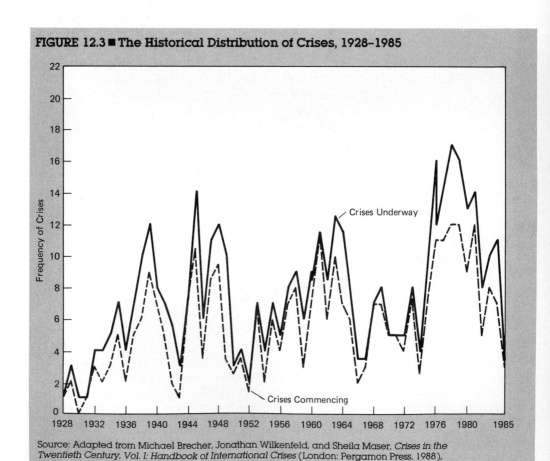

FIGURE 12.3 ■ The Historical Distribution of Crises, 1928–1985

Source: Adapted from Michael Brecher, Jonathan Wilkenfeld, and Sheila Maser, *Crises in the Twentieth Century, Vol. I: Handbook of International Crises* (London: Pergamon Press, 1988), with data for 1979-1985 provided by Professor Wilkenfeld.

of peace and, during a war, an adverse change in the military balance'' (Brecher et al., 1988). The continuing presence of ''higher-than-normal conflictual interactions'' that ''destabilize existing relationships and pose a challenge to the existing structure of an international system'' is made evident. So too is the constant stream of newly initiated system-threatening crises.

The data suggest several patterns. One is the way that crisis is concentrated around the major war in the system during this time frame (World War II), with the years 1936 to 1941 and 1945 to 1950 periods of particular instability. Second, the global atmosphere has been charged with the threat of war, especially during the transition from a bipolar to a bipolycentric power distribution between roughly 1960 and 1963—a ''turning point'' in international affairs that witnessed important shifts in the strategic balance toward parity and an accompanying shift in strategic thinking about the role of nuclear weapons away from compellence toward deterrence (see Chapter 11). And third, these data suggest a general increase over time in the incidence with which threats to global peace under conditions of crisis have arisen. The large number of interstate crises in the 1980s suggests that the onset of crises has not receded.

Given their frequency, an important question is the extent to which crises actually do escalate to war. The evidence indicates that once they erupt, many crises do end in war (Holsti, 1972). In fact, the proportion of crises that eventually resulted in the use of force has risen steadily in the twentieth century. Between 1946 and 1976 three-quarters of militarized disputes culminated in the use of force (Gochman and Maoz, 1984: 600).

It is important to remember, however, that the proportion of crises escalating to the use of force *among the major powers* has actually fallen since World War II. For disputes between the strongest states, the correlation between the onset of crisis and war has declined. As previously suggested, many crises involving the great powers have arisen, but all have been managed successfully without recourse to war. The great powers seem to have learned skills in crisis management as a result of their many prior experiences and to have developed tacit rules for this purpose that both respect (George, 1986). Fear of the dire consequences should their management efforts fail doubtlessly has contributed to the learning process (see Gaddis, 1986).

> The widespread recognition that military force has become dangerously volatile and potentially uncontrollable ensures that many states resort to it only in the face of serious provocation and after the most careful consideration. Faith in victory at an acceptable cost is far less well entrenched than in the past. Consequently, in some circumstances that previously might have led to hostilities, force has been replaced by a more amicable—or at least, less violent—means of settling disputes. (Williams, 1976: 46)

If threats to the peace posed by great power crises have been averted since World War II (in contrast with earlier periods, when they frequently crossed the threshold to full-scale warfare), that has not been the case with respect to war-threatening disputes between unequals—those between powerful and weak states (Brecher and Wilkenfeld, 1989). These have been relatively frequent. Indeed, overt foreign military intervention, such as the U.S. military intervention in the Dominican Republic (1965) and the Soviet intervention in Afghanistan (which began in 1979), has been repetitive in the Third World, which has been the target for these interventions. To interventionist activity the characteristics of an international crisis can appropriately be ascribed because every act of great power intervention has threatened to escalate to a war. A crisis atmosphere has prevailed because

> foreign overt military intervention [has been] a constant feature of contemporary international politics. Not a single day since World War II has failed to see it somewhere. It erupts regularly. The worldwide frequency of intervention has remained about the same throughout the post-war era, averaging nearly fifteen interventions initiated per year. (Tillema, 1987: 13)

Overt militarized interventions in Third World countries have been recurrent and prolonged and have involved relatively modest levels of military operations (Tillema, 1987). Their occurrence nonetheless has heightened the global tension level and has heated up the climate of world politics, with the threat of major warfare through great power involvement a continual fear. The boundary between peace and war remains narrow.

Low-Intensity Conflict

If the destructiveness of modern weapons has reduced the incentives for great and small powers alike to resort to armed force and to substitute the threat of force for its actual use, other modes of conflict have arisen that still allow states to resolve their disputes through violence or the threat of violence. Filling the void has been the development of *low-intensity conflict* (LIC) and an elaborate set of strategies and methods by which armed conflict short of warfare might be waged. Low-intensity conflict has become a part of the vocabulary of world politics as a way of describing the most prevalent form of armed conflict practiced today.

> [Low-intensity conflict] is warfare that falls below the threshold of full-scale military combat between modern armies (of the sort that occurred in the Korean War and at the onset of the Iran–Iraq War). Under U.S. doctrine, low-intensity conflict encompasses four particular types of operations: (1) *counterinsurgency*, [such as] combat against revolutionary guerrillas, as . . . waged in El Salvador and the Philippines; (2) *proinsurgency*, [meaning] U.S. support for anticommunist insurgents, such as the contras in Nicaragua and UNITA in Angola; (3) *peacetime contingency operations*, [including] police-type actions like the U.S. invasion of Grenada and the April 1986 bombing of Tripoli; and (4) *military "shows of force,"* [which are]

threatening military maneuvers of the sort the U.S. conducted in 1987 and 1988 in the Persian Gulf. (Klare, 1988: 12)

Many of the foregoing operations have a long history. For example, much of the early involvement of the United States in the Vietnam War was, for it, essentially an experiment in counterinsurgency warfare. Similarly, the United States has used "shows of force" as a kind of postwar variant on "gunboat diplomacy." In fact, systematic evidence indicates that the United States engaged in shows of force designed to alter the behavior of other actors on 286 different occasions between 1946 and 1984 (Blechman and Kaplan, 1978: 547–553; Zelikow, 1987: 34–36), or an average of 7.3 times per year since World War II (but with a marked increase between 1981 and 1984, when the average climbed to more than 11 incidents per year). The Soviet Union has likewise used shows of force to pursue its foreign policy objectives, engaging in such behavior over 150 times between the mid-1940s and late 1970s (Kaplan, 1981: 689–693).

What distinguishes low-intensity conflict as the concept is now used, then, is that it has become a symbol of warfare between the haves and have-nots, a method for combating terrorism, insurgency, and guerrilla activities in the Third World in order to protect the interests of the powerful. Proxy wars, wars fought with mercenaries, counterinsurgency, psychological operations to terrorize the populace, death squads—these are part and parcel of the modern face of warfare below the level of overt military operations by the soldiers of a state's regular army. American military and economic support for the *contras* in Nicaragua exemplifies the ways in which low-intensity means of fighting are conducted. "What is crucial to recognize," notes Michael T. Klare (1988), "is that low-intensity conflict is a form of warfare in which *your* side suffers very little death or destruction, while the other side suffers as much damage as possible without producing undue hardship for your own society. . . . [Low-intensity conflict] doctrine . . . states that the privileged nations of the industrialized 'North' are vitally threatened by the starving, nonwhite masses of the underdeveloped 'South'" and that this threat to the industrial West must be met by force short of war. Low-intensity conflict is thus a growing method by which great powers have sought to influence political developments in the Third World. Three other characteristics are notable: "It is almost certain to be pervasive, is likely to be prolonged, and is often sufficiently unconventional as to defy being labeled as conflict in any traditional sense. It may be indistinguishable from police work; it can always be labeled police action" (Yarmolinsky, 1988). Despite its name, however, low-intensity conflict does not necessarily mean low levels of death or destruction. "The low-intensity conflict in Guatemala, for instance, [had by 1988] already claimed well over 100,000 lives" (Klare, 1988: 12).

Because low-intensity conflict occurs largely in and against societies in which poverty and desperation breed domestic turmoil, it is related to internal wars—another dimension of the changing character of conflict and violence in contemporary world politics to which our attention now turns.

Armed Conflict Within States: Civil Wars

Wars within nations—civil wars—comprise still another form of violence in today's world that has an impact on world politics. Evan Luard (1968) speculates that civil wars "have become perhaps the most common of all types of international military activity" and estimates that they have been almost twice as common in the post–World War II period as in the period between the world wars—impressions that are supported by empirical evidence (Sivard, 1987: 28–31; Tillema, 1987). It is thus internal wars and insurgencies, more than international wars, that tend to capture the headlines.[16]

In an examination of civil wars resulting in at least one thousand civilian and military deaths per year, Small and Singer (1982) identified 106 civil wars in the 165 years between 1816 and 1980. The outbreak of these has been somewhat irregular. At least 1 civil war began in "only" 75, or less than half, of these years. Some periods, such as that between 1816 and 1840, were relatively more immune from the onset of civil strife than were others. And clearly, civil war is not an exclusively modern phenomenon. But civil war has been more frequent recently, as shown in Table 12.2. Each decade, on the average, has experienced 7 civil wars, but that figure has risen through time. Thirty-eight percent of the 106 civil wars in the last century and a half began between 1948 and 1980. However, this apparent trend is at least in part a consequence of the increase in the number of independent states in the international system, which makes the incidence of civil war more probable statistically (Small and Singer, 1982).

Perhaps the amount of civil war under way provides a better picture of the extent to which civil war has become a characteristic of world politics. This indicator monitors how extensive civil war as a worldwide phenomenon has become: Civil wars have been under way internationally 80 percent of the time, or 134 years, between 1816 and 1980 (Small and Singer, 1982: 251–267). Thus civil wars start more frequently, and once begun, they last longer.

Indicators of the severity of civil wars are also noteworthy. The number of lives lost in civil violence has remained high throughout the span of 165 years (see Table 12.2), and casualty rates show an alarming growth, especially since World War II. One symptom is that "of the 15 most [destructive civil] wars, 10 are from the twentieth century; 7 of those 10 are from the post–World War II era, perhaps another tribute to the greater lethality of weapons in our time" (Small and Singer, 1982: 241). Another accounting of war fatalities between

---

16. Ted Robert Gurr (1970: 3) found that "ten of the world's thirteen most deadly conflicts in the past 160 years have been civil wars and rebellions; since 1945 violent attempts to overthrow governments have been more common than national elections."

TABLE 12.2 ■ The Frequency and Severity of Civil Wars, 1816–1980

Period	Number of Civil Wars Begun	Total Months of Nations' Involvement in Civil War	Battle Deaths	Number/Percentage of Civil Wars Internationalized Through Large-Scale Military Intervention
1816–1848	12	333.1	93,200	3 (25%)
1849–1881	20	625.4	2,891,600	1 (5%)
1882–1914	18	286.0	388,000	3 (17%)
1915–1947	15	343.3	2,622,300	4 (27%)
1948–1980	41	1191.4	3,022,300	10 (25%)
Totals	106	2778.8	9,017,400	21

Source: Calculations derived from data published in Melvin Small and J. David Singer, *Resort to Arms: International and Civil Wars, 1816–1980* (Beverly Hills, Calif.: Sage, 1982).

1960 and 1982 estimated that three-quarters of some 10.7 million war deaths occurred in civil wars (Sivard, 1982: 15).

Civil war and revolution have been simultaneously defended as instruments of justice and condemned as the immoral acceptance of violent change. They contain ingredients of both. The American, Russian, and Chinese revolutions all used violence but have been rationalized as necessary to realize social change, political freedom, and independence.

Civil wars stem from a wide range of ideological, demographic, religious, ethnic, economic, social-structural, and political conditions (see Eckstein, 1972). Internal violence also can be seen as a reaction to frustration and deprivation, especially when the distribution of wealth and opportunities are highly unequal (see Gurr, 1970); these conditions partially account for the pervasiveness of civil war today in the developing countries.

The destabilization caused by rapid growth accounts for much of the ubiquity of internal war (see Olson, 1971). Civil violence seems to occur in countries in which conditions are improving because modernization generates expectations that often cannot be satisfied. Governments, in other words, are often unable to keep pace with rising expectations (Gurr, 1970). "Economic modernization leads to political instability rather than political stability," former U.S. Secretary of State Henry A. Kissinger has postulated.

It is tempting to think of civil war as only an internal problem, stemming exclusively from conditions within countries. But revolutions and rebellions also are often influenced by external factors. How other states react to civil disturbance is also a part of the civil war syndrome. According to George Modelski (1964), "Every war has two faces. It is a conflict both between and within political systems; a conflict that is both external and internal. [It is undeniable that] internal wars affect the international system [and that] the international system affects internal wars."

Global trends have been associated with changes in the incidence of civil war. For example, the relatively high levels of civil war between 1848 and 1870 were related to the effects of imperialism, industrialization, nationalism, mass communication, and ideology, whereas the frequent incidence with which civil war erupted between the end of World War II and the 1960s can be traced to the disruptions associated with the breakup of the European colonial empires.

The possible causal relationship between internal wars and systemic conditions is suggested by the close connections between wars within and those between nations. Indeed, it is often difficult to determine where an internal war ends and an international one begins. The possibility that civil wars will lead to interstate wars is always present. Because the great powers, in particular, have global interests and are concerned with fostering the growth of friendly governments and preventing hostile ones from coming to power elsewhere, they are apt to intervene militarily in civil wars in order to protect their perceived political interests. Thus they intervene to help maintain existing governments, to overthrow them, or to prevent unstable foreign situations from challenging their national interests.

Participants in civil wars are also often tempted to invite external support for their cause. Foreign assistance may be the margin between defeat and victory in a civil struggle, hence the search for external assistance. Intervention then often breeds further intervention: "Where one outside power or alliance becomes involved in a dispute of this kind, another almost invariably becomes so in due course" (Luard, 1968).

As Table 12.2 reveals, a consistently high percentage of civil wars became internationalized through large-scale military intervention by an external power. More than half of all large-scale military interventions have occurred since 1944, and nearly half of the internationalized civil wars have appeared since that date.[17] Typically, one in five civil wars becomes an interstate war.

From the point of view of the interveners, periods of high civil violence may generate pressures for involvement in international wars. Some of America's more recent foreign entanglements, for example, were responses to internal instability (Lebanon, the Dominican Republic, Korea, Vietnam, and El Salvador), and Soviet interventions have also occurred in countries undergoing violent internal disruptions (Hungary, Ethiopia, and Afghanistan). In 1987, foreign combat troops were present in sixty-eight Third World countries, the

---

17. A military intervention by one state into the civil war in another is said to occur if that participation is direct: One thousand troops or more must be committed to a battle zone, or one hundred casualties sustained. According to this measure, thirty-three cases of intervention were recorded between 1816 and 1980, resulting in the internationalization of twenty-one civil wars (see Small and Singer, 1982; see also Kegley and Raymond, 1983, for an analysis of the factors that lead internal wars to become internationalized).

majority of which were experiencing civil strife at the time (Sivard, 1987: 13). On the basis of the historical record, the possibility that these foreign adventures might lead to international war is ever present. As *The Defense Monitor* (vol. 12, no. 1, 1983) warned, "World War III could grow out of a 'local' war. Numerous conventional and guerrilla conflicts have the potential for regional expansion and superpower confrontation. Foreign weapons . . . have in many cases prolonged conflicts and encouraged their escalation."

A consideration of the international consequences of civil wars would not be complete without examining the related proposition that civil unrest promotes external aggression, not by provoking great power intervention but, rather, because under conditions of civil disturbance political leaders may try to mitigate internal disorder by diverting their citizens' attention toward foreign adversaries. The assumption is that national cohesion will rise in the face of external threat and that the leaders facing domestic unrest will seek to control it by initiating foreign adventures. From this perspective, then, civil strife breeds foreign conflict and war.

This hypothesis has a rich folklore as well as an intuitive appeal. At least since Thucydides, it has been part of the conventional wisdom that conflict at home is related to conflict abroad and that leaders wage the latter in order to manage the former. Machiavelli, for instance, advised the Prince to undertake foreign wars whenever turmoil within the state became too great. Hermann Goering advocated the same idea in Nazi Germany by contending: "Voice or no voice, the people can always be brought to do the bidding of the leaders. That is easy. All you have to do is tell them they are being attacked and denounce the pacifists for lack of patriotism." Similarly, before he became the secretary of state, John Foster Dulles (1939) reflected: "The easiest and quickest cure of internal dissension is to portray danger from abroad. Thus group authorities find it convenient always to keep alive among the group members a feeling that their nation is in danger from one or another of the nation-villains with which it is surrounded."

Implicit in this view is the expectation that external war will result in increased domestic support for political leaders. "To put it cynically, one could say that nothing helps a leader like a good war. It gives him his only chance of being a tyrant and being loved for it at the same time. He can introduce the most ruthless forms of control and send thousands of his followers to their deaths and still be hailed as a great protector. Nothing ties tighter the in-group bonds than an out-group threat" (Morris, 1969).

Whether war in fact reduces internal problems and political leaders actually initiate wars in order to deal with domestic conflict are empirical questions. Studies by Cattell (1949), Rummel (1963), and Tanter (1966), among others (see Scolnick, 1974; Stein, 1976), have sought to test the proposition that domestic conflict is a prelude to foreign conflict. These empirical examinations fail to confirm the thesis that a close connection exists between a country's level of domestic instability and external aggression. Thus, an otherwise plausible theory must be rejected. Civil unrest does not lead to foreign aggressiveness.

Perhaps the most compelling reason for the absence of a direct linkage is that "when domestic conflict becomes extremely intense it would seem more reasonable to argue that there is a greater likelihood that a state will retreat from its foreign engagements in order to handle the situation at home" (Zinnes and Wilkenfeld, 1971).

Terrorism

Television and newspaper reports repeatedly portray the growing incidence of yet another alarming kind of violence that is transforming the global system: transnational terrorism. Almost daily, the media tell of kidnappings and, at times, the murder of diplomats and other government and corporation leaders, bombings, sabotage, and the taking of hostages. The instruments of terror are varied and the motivations of terrorists diverse. But all terrorist activity employs violence designed to achieve political objectives. "Experts agree that terrorism is the use or threat of violence, a method of combat or a strategy to achieve certain goals, that its aim is to induce a state of fear in the victim, that it is ruthless and does not conform to humanitarian norms, and that publicity is an essential factor in terrorist strategy" (Laqueur, 1988).

Although some terrorist activities begin and end in a single country, many transcend national borders. Thus terrorism today has a uniquely transnational character. Global in scope, terrorism's prevalence in today's world is depicted in Figure 12.4: The general trend is one of an increasing level of transnational terrorist activity.

Terrorism did not originate in the contemporary era, but it does seem to be a disorder distinctive to the modern world. "Terrorism has grown from an esoteric aspect of aggression and violence to a predominant means for international and intranational conflict resolution" (Blair and Brewer, 1977). It arises so frequently perhaps because it is a strategy that even the weak can employ. Modern technology may also have contributed inadvertently to its incidence, for a crucial part of the terrorists' strength derives from the instant access that television provides as a medium of communication through which to publicize their grievances. Indeed, international communication has made any terrorist act against prominent figures an instant media event. The ability to bring the terrorist act into the global spotlight by securing publicity is a catalyst to the fear that the act is intended to generate (which is why international terrorism has so often been likened to theater). And part of what makes terrorism so terrifying is the message that anyone can become its victim.

Terrorist activities also have grown more lethal. Terrorism has always threatened human life, but terrorist acts are now targeted more frequently at people instead of property. And terrorists have shown a growing willingness to kill, not just to threaten their victims, as indicated by the increasing number of terrorist incidents resulting in fatalities since the 1970s. (Jenkins, 1986). In fact, many acts are calculated to produce casualties in large numbers. The trend toward large-scale indiscriminate violence becomes even more alarming be-

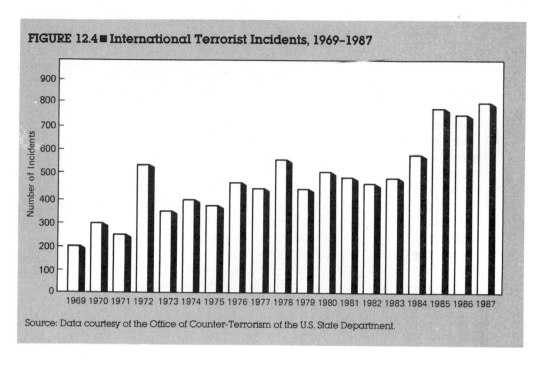

FIGURE 12.4 ■ International Terrorist Incidents, 1969–1987

Number of Incidents

Source: Data courtesy of the Office of Counter-Terrorism of the U.S. State Department.

cause the "terrorists' growing lack of regard for human life heightens fears that they could escalate their activities to threats of mass slaughter—biological, chemical, or nuclear" (Kempe, 1983).

International terrorists use a variety of methods to pursue their goals. Included are some traditional techniques for inflicting terror, such as kidnappings, assassinations, hijackings, hostage takings, and sabotage. But governments have strengthened their capabilities to deter these methods, by providing greater security at airports, guarding likely kidnap targets, securing embassies, deploying specially trained commandos to deal with hostage situations, collecting and sharing intelligence data, announcing "no concession" policies, and the like. In response, terrorists have adjusted their modes of operation, moving to hit-and-run tactics, especially through the increased use of bombings and tactics that inflict more violence. Sniping and direct armed attacks are examples. One aspect of this trend, beside its deadliness, is that although now, as before, "terrorists want a lot of people watching, not a lot of people dead," the more violent tactics have found greater prominence as a way of gaining attention. For, as one expert on terrorism has observed, "if terrorism stops terrorizing—if it ceases to have an explosive impact on public opinion—then terrorists have an innate tendency to escalate [the violence] in order to recapture the headlines" (cited in Kempe, 1983). Thus the international terrorist can be expected to use a greater variety of even more lethal methods directed at an expanded spectrum of targets in the future. "Because terrorists can attack anything, anywhere, any time, and governments cannot protect everything, everywhere, all the time, terrorists always retain a certain advantage'' (Jenkins, 1986).

Other trends reveal that transnational terrorism has spread throughout the world, becoming a global epidemic. In 1970, terrorist acts occurred in only forty-eight countries, but in 1981 terrorist incidents occurred in ninety-one countries (U.S. Department of State, 1982: 10). Terrorism nevertheless afflicts some countries more than others. The United States, France, Israel, the United Kingdom, and Turkey have been the targets of half of all international terrorist attacks, whereas only ten countries bear the brunt of three-quarters of all terrorist incidents (Jenkins, 1986: 779). When the geographical distribution of terrorist incidents over time is examined, regional trends suggest that transnational terrorism, like a virus, is spreading, but at varying rates. In 1979 nearly half of all incidents occurred in Western Europe. By 1985 that region was the site of little more than a quarter of the terrorist incidents, and the Middle East had come to be the site of some 45 percent (Bremer, 1987: 3).

When considering where transnational terrorism occurs, one must also examine the terrorists' intended victims. One pattern is revealed in the tendency for "officials and businessmen—and especially individuals who are symbols of Western power and wealth—[to be] the primary targets" (U.S. Central Intelligence Agency, 1980). This suggests that transnational terrorism is often an attack by the disadvantaged on the advantaged and that it takes place where the representatives of the wealthy and powerful live.

A corollary to this idea is the tendency for long-standing terrorist movements to be motivated by the political causes of the ethnic groups to which they belong. Minorities seeking sovereign independence, such as Palestinians in the Middle East, the Basques in Spain, and Puerto Rican nationalists, typify the kinds of aspirations of transnational terrorists, whose major complaint is that they lack a country. And terrorism in the industrialized world often occurs where discrepancies in income are severe and where minority groups are sometimes deprived of the political rights and freedoms enjoyed by the majority. In these locations and circumstances, rural guerrilla warfare is not a route to self-assertion, but terrorist tactics are.

Examination of the likely causes of terrorist activity suggests that terrorism is not perceived by all to be a disease. One person's terrorist may, to another, be a liberator. In fact, both governments and countergovernment movements claim to seek liberty, and both are labeled terrorists by those they oppose. The difference between a freedom fighter and a protector of freedom often lies in the eye of the beholder, a problem that makes the identity of a terrorist group not altogether obvious (see O'Brien, 1977).

Indeed, when terrorism is put into a broad historical context, it can be seen as something more than the effort of relatively powerless movements to upset by means of the threat of violence the established hierarchy within and among nations. Although most terrorist groups in the contemporary era are undeniably organizations without sovereignty or power, a broader definition would acknowledge that some terrorist groups are state sponsored and that, accordingly, it is important to recognize "the state as terrorist" (see Stohl and Lopez, 1984). States finance, train, equip, and provide sanctuaries for terrorists whose activities serve their foreign policy objectives. They support the terrorist activities of movements espousing philosophies that they embrace (or challenge the security of states that they see as enemies). The United States has accused the Soviet Union, Cuba, Libya, North Korea, and Syria, among others, of practicing state terrorism.[18] In much the same way, the United States has been accused of sponsoring terrorist activities in Vietnam, Chile, and Nicaragua.

From another angle, terrorism may be seen as an instrument of foreign policy, a method directly pursued by states themselves to achieve their objectives abroad. Terrorism by ideologically motivated fanatics, extremists, and minorities at the periphery of society may not be that different from the kinds of terrorism conducted by the state governments that they oppose. This is especially true given the way in which modern (conventional) warfare is often conducted.

> Those who are described as terrorists, and who reject that title for themselves, make the uncomfortable point that national armed forces, fully supported by democratic opinion, have in fact employed violence and terror on a far vaster scale than what liberation movements have as yet been able to attain. The "freedom fighters" see themselves as fighting a just war. Why should they not be entitled to kill, burn and destroy as national armies, navies and air forces do, and why should the label "terrorist" be applied to them and not to the national militaries? (O'Brien, 1977: 56–57)

The growth of international terrorism represents a trend in world politics that appears likely to continue. Andrew J. Pierre speculates:

> It is unlikely that international terrorism is a passing and transitory phenomenon. The trend toward the weakening of central authority in governments, the rise in ethnic and subnational sentiments, and the increasing fractionalization of the global political process point toward its growth as a form of political protest and persuasion. Classic balance of power diplomacy is of little utility in dealing with it, for violent acts of small groups of people, or individuals, are difficult for governments to control. International terrorism is likely to continue and to expand because in the minds of many of its perpetrators it has proven to be "successful." (Pierre, 1984: 85)

---

18. The attack by Libyan embassy personnel on anti-Qaddafi demonstrators in London in April 1984 is an example of terrorist actions conducted by representatives of a state government. Those who retaliate against terrorist attacks become, in the eyes of the target, terrorist attackers. Thus the U.S. air strike against Libya in April 1986 provoked the charge that the United States itself practiced terrorism.

International terrorism is also likely to grow because it offers an alternative mode of armed conflict to state and nonstate actors alike. Given the costs and impracticality of conventional war, terrorism provides an available instrument of force that the weak can use, whereas "open, interstate armed conflict" is not a viable option. The face of violence has been transformed by contemporary technology, making for an international system in which the use of force has changed in character:

> We may be on the threshold of an era of armed conflict in which limited conventional warfare, guerrilla warfare, and international terrorism will coexist, with governments and subnational entities employing them individually, interchangeably, sequentially, or simultaneously—and having to defend against them. Warfare in the future may be less destructive than that in the first half of the twentieth century, but it may also be less coherent. Warfare will cease to be finite. The distinction between war and peace will dissolve. Armed conflict will not be confined to national frontiers. No contest will be local. Local belligerents will mobilize foreign patrons. Terrorists will attack foreign targets both at home and abroad. (Jenkins, 1986: 778)

In sum, terrorism, like warfare, has been both condemned as a repugnant form of violence and defended as a necessary instrument of justice in the war against oppression and persecution. As long as pronounced inequalities of wealth and opportunity are perceived to exist, the attempt to justify violence to remove them can be expected. Because the sources from which international terrorism springs are deeply rooted and embedded in the structure of the international system (Kegley et al., 1988), international terrorism is likely to persist.

THE HUMAN TRAGEDY OF VIOLENT CONFLICT

The preceding review of trends in the incidence and severity of various forms of armed conflict suggests that violence within and among nations remains an entrenched characteristic of world politics.

The raw statistics documenting this condition do not reveal the terrible toll on human lives that wars extract or the costs to human welfare that the wages of war involve. Preparations for war reduce the standard of living of the globe's inhabitants, and violent conflict reduces their numbers and threatens their habitat. War leaves an indelible mark, commemorated publicly by black flags of mourning that flutter from the homes of the war dead and memorials at grave sites worldwide. Monuments are built to honor the courage displayed by the soldiers who gave their lives in their nations' wars, even though innocent civilians are contemporary war's most frequent victims. In 1987, four-fifths of the world's war victims were civilians (Sivard, 1987: 5). Fear, vulnerability, dependence, and desperation are the primary emotions from which acts of violence originate; death, destruction, and depression are the primary products of the violent responses to these emotions.

The tragic human consequences of violence are also revealed every day by the efforts of individuals and families seeking to escape its scourge. They can be observed fleeing from one country in hopes of finding refuge, and perhaps a better life, in another country. The refugee asylum problem has assumed global dimensions, and it bears a direct relationship to the prospects for world peace (see Kegley, 1984).

The global dimensions of the refugee problem are suggested by the fact that in 1982 alone over ten million people were estimated to have crossed national borders in the hope of escaping the dangers they faced in their home countries (U.S. Committee for Refugees, 1982). The number of refugees has more than doubled in less than a decade (*New York Times*, February 16, 1986, p. E3; see also Chapter 9). They escape by air, they march by foot, and they travel the oceans by boat; but whatever the means and the destination, their goal is the same: to find a place where survival is a possibility. But today's world seems unable to provide either personal or national security. Religious preference, the color of one's skin, and the expression of political dissent are some of the factors that motivate refugees. But along with poverty, persecution, and the pain of hunger and starvation, war—whether intranational or international—remains a paramount cause. Could it be that a world so ingenious in perpetrating violence will also learn that war and violence are too costly, too destructive to continue? If so, can it discover viable paths to peace? Some solutions that have been proposed are considered in the subsequent chapters.

SUGGESTED READINGS

Ashley, Richard K. *The Political Economy of War and Peace.* New York: Nichols, 1980.

Beer, Francis A. *Peace Against War: The Ecology of International Violence.* San Francisco: Freeman, 1981.

Brecher, Michael, Jonathan Wilkenfeld, and Sheila Moser. *Crises in the Twentieth Century: Vol. 1·1 Handbook of International Crises.* Oxford, England: Pergamon Press, 1988.

Gilpin, Robert. *War and Change in World Politics.* Cambridge, England: Cambridge University Press, 1981.

Howard, Michael. *The Causes of Wars,* 2nd ed. Cambridge, Mass.: Harvard University Press, 1984.

Laqueur, Walter. "Reflections on Terrorism," *Foreign Affairs* 65 (Fall 1986): 86–100.

Lebow, Richard Ned. *Between Peace and War: The Nature of International Crisis.* Baltimore: Johns Hopkins University Press, 1981.

Siverson, Randolph M. "War and Change in the International System," pp. 211–232 in Ole R. Holsti, Randolph M. Siverson, and Alexander L. George, eds., *Change in the International System.* Boulder, Colo.: Westview Press, 1980.

Small, Melvin, and J. David Singer. *Resort to Arms: International and Civil War, 1816–1980.* Beverly Hills, Calif.: Sage, 1982.

Stohl, Michael, ed. *The Politics of Terrorism,* 3rd ed. New York: Dekker, 1988.

THIRTEEN

Military Paths to Peace: Power Balances and Arms Control

It is an unfortunate fact that we can only secure peace by preparing for war.
JOHN F. KENNEDY, 1960

I went into the British Army believing that if you want peace you must prepare for war. I now believe that if you prepare thoroughly for war you will get it.
SIR JOHN FREDERICK MAURICE, 1883

Many nations now have the capacity to inflict enormous destruction on their enemies. As a consequence, national security is often their preeminent problem. But security remains, as ever, elusive. Many paths to deter aggression and avoid war have been proposed, but most states' sense of security has diminished, not increased, during this century, and a workable solution to the security dilemma does not exist.

This chapter explores the paths to peace that emphasize arms. They differ in concept and in prescription, but all converge on the belief that the incidence of war is directly related to the distribution of arms in the world. Who has how much of different kinds of military capabilities is assumed to determine whether war will occur and which countries will experience and possibly be vanquished by it.

Three strategies are available to states who seek security through arms: (1) to aggregate military power by forming alliances with others in such a way that a balance of power will keep the peace, (2) to reduce or redistribute the level of weapons through disarmament or arms control, and (3) to develop military might of sufficient deterrent capability that no adversary will risk launching a war against them. Most countries approach national security and war avoidance through some combination of all three strategies. Because deterrence was discussed in Chapter 11, our attention in this chapter is on balance of power and arms control as approaches to national security.

THE BALANCE OF POWER

The global system is presently structured in such a way that it encourages states to compete with one another for power, wealth, and resources. The anarchical system places responsibility for the preservation of peace on each individual state, which must rely on self-help to preserve its own security. Accordingly, the international political system resembles a Hobbesian "war of all against all," a dynamic of perpetual conflict and struggle. To political realists (recall Chapter 2) this condition is a permanent condition, and states must therefore attempt ceaselessly to maximize their own power. Peace cannot come by reforming the system.

How might such a disorderly and war-prone system be effectively managed? A traditional prescription has been to tie the survival of the states and the maintenance of peace to the functioning of a system of military balances. What is meant by this approach, broadly captured in the phrase "balance of power"?

Balance of power is an ambiguous concept that has been used in a variety of ways (see Claude, 1962; Haas, 1953a, 1953b). At the core of its many meanings is the idea that peace will result when the power of states (defined in this instance primarily in military terms) is distributed in such a way that no one state is strong enough to pose a meaningful threat to the others. Should one state, or a combination of states, acquire enough power to constitute a threat, others would unite out of self-interest and form a defensive alliance to restore the balance and maintain the status quo. The equilibrium or balancing of power that would result from such collusion would be sufficient to deter the would-be attacker from pursuing its expansionist goals. Peace would thus be produced from the equilibrium resulting from the balance of contending factions.

There are many corollaries to the balance-of-power approach to world peace. Foremost is the conviction that faith in the goodwill and peaceful intentions of others is unwarranted. Political realists see all nations as driven by self-interest; all are perceived to define those interests in terms of power and its relentless quest. All therefore are expected to expand their power until checked by a countervailing power. Thus all are locked into a perpetual struggle for power as each competitively attempts to enhance its position relative to others.

Classic balance-of-power theory is predicated on the notion that weakness leads to war, that vulnerability invites attack from power-seeking aggressors, and that potential aggressors can be deterred from attacking only by intimidating them with countervailing power. Hence we encounter again the realist idea that the best way to preserve peace is to prepare for war. When all nations are seen as driven by expansionist power drives, the conclusion easily follows that one's own military capability should be strengthened as a means of protecting against the hegemonical aspirations of potential adversaries. Invariably, this reasoning rationalizes the quest for military superiority which, because it is pursued by others as well, inevitably results in arms races. Indeed, balance-of-power theory is predicated on an acceptance of arms and war as necessary tools of foreign policy. In addition, armaments and warfare are seen as vehicles for maintaining states' sovereign independence. A state is entitled to resort to force whenever its preservation is threatened (see Gulick, 1955).

On the surface, these assumptions of balance-of-power theory appear dubious, premises that in a self-fulfilling way breed the very outcome most feared—war. But the proponents of balance-of-power theory as it was practiced in seventeenth-, eighteenth-, and nineteenth-century Europe were not irrational. They thought that a system founded on suspicion, antagonism, fear, and competition could produce peace. The mechanism believed to translate these presumably violence-promoting features into international stability was alliance, a time-honored means of enhancing the prospects for security and national survival by affecting the distribution of power.

Alliance Politics

European policymakers believed during the heyday of the balance-of-power system that coalitions were formed out of self-interest in an almost mechanistic fashion so as to protect any state threatened or under attack by a more powerful adversary. But the process was seldom automatic. In practice, one among the powers favoring the status quo typically had to take the lead in building a coalition with the other powers by convincing them of the threats they faced. Nevertheless, counteralliances were expected to be formed; states sitting on the sidelines could not afford the risk that a potential aggressor with greater capabilities might ultimately turn against them. Thus, rational calculations would compel states to align with others threatened by more powerful ones, not because of concern for the plight of weaker states, but because their own vulnerability would leave the uncommitted states exposed to the threat of an aggressive state with hegemonic ambitions. The result of these individual calculations would be the formation of coalitions approximately equal in power.[1]

In the classic European balance-of-power system, permanent alliances were eschewed. To facilitate maintenance of an even distribution of power, the system embraced rules promoting fluid, flexible, rapidly shifting alliances. Alliances were not to be based on friendships or loyalties but on interests and capabilities. The principle "no permanent ties, only permanent interests" lubricated the dynamics of alliance politics and thereby made a balance, an

---

1. According to the so-called size principle, rational actors will tend to form coalitions sufficient in size to ensure victory and no larger; hence political coalitions tend to be roughly equal in size. See Riker (1962) for a discussion with applications to international coalitions in the context of balance-of-power theory. Morgenthau (1973) and Gulick (1955) also discuss the rationality of policies aimed at equalizing the power of competing coalitions.

equilibrium, more probable. Why? Ironically, through such competitive jock-eying for power, nations seeking advantages by attempting to increase their power created strong incentives for others to form coalitions designed to prevent any one nation from achieving dominance. In principle, then, coali-tion politics would produce a stalemate, with no state sufficiently powerful to impose its will on others. The system would be policed by competition. Critical in policing the system was "the balancer"—a role often played by Great Britain in the eighteenth and nineteenth centuries, when it gave its support to one or another coalition to ensure that no one achieved prepon-derance. Winston Churchill (1948) once described Britain's policy thus: "For 400 years the foreign policy of England has been to oppose the strongest, most aggressive, most dominating power on the continent, in joining the weaker states." The search for preponderance by one state or coalition of states would thus produce a peace founded on parity rather than war.

However, alliance competition could not achieve equilibrium automat-ically, but only if certain rules of behavior were followed. The classical bal-ance-of-power system seemed to produce a balance preserving peace if, and only if, nations behaved according to the following "essential rules":

(1) increase capabilities but negotiate rather than fight; (2) fight rather than fail to increase capabilities; (3) stop fighting rather than eliminate an essen-tial actor; (4) oppose any coalition or single actor which tends to assume a position of predominance within the system; (5) constrain actors who subscribe to supranational organizational principles; and (6) permit de-feated or constrained essential national actors to reenter the system as acceptable role partners. (Kaplan, 1975: 259)

According to these rules, competition is appropriate. Power is to be sought, not disdained. Force and war are approved as means to obtain power. The independence of each national unit is cherished; to preserve one's own auton-omy, the autonomy of others must be supported out of self-interest. Efforts to subvert national independence through international organization or world government are to be restrained. Competition leads to the equalization of weapons capabilities among the major competitors. Defensive alliances emerge to counter nations with preponderant capabilities. Alliances dissolve when the threat of aggression diminishes; they are never permanent. And because today's adversary may be tomorrow's friend, those defeated in war must be treated with moderation and neither annihilated nor otherwise re-moved from the system.

These postulates of the balance-of-power approach assume that peace is produced by distributing power through the dynamics of alliance politics. As such, the approach deals with the problem of war in a way that preserves the problem, for warfare is not abolished. Instead, it is a way of measuring national power and becomes a means of changing the distribution of power and the position of various countries within the system's hierarchy. The balance of power is thus a set of rules for managing war's frequency but not for preventing its occurrence; it seeks not to end war but to prevent the acquisition of overwhelming power by any one state or group of states.

It has often been noted that the successful operation of a balance-of-power system presupposes not only that nations act according to the rules of the system but also that the essential prerequisites for its successful operation be present.[2] For example, states must seek to maintain a balance through the rational pursuit of their self-interest guided by the possession of sufficient and accurate information. But in addition the theory argues that there must also be (1) a sufficiently large number of independent states to make alliance formation and dissolution readily possible;[3] (2) a limited geographic area; (3) freedom of action for the central decision makers of the states comprising the system; (4) relative equality in their capabilities; (5) a common political culture in which the rules of the system are recognized and respected; (6) a modicum of homogeneity within the system's political culture; (7) a weapons technology that inhibits quick mobilization for war, prevents prolonged wars, and reduces the prospects of wars of annihilation; and (8) the absence of international or supranational institutions capable of determining states' policies.

The Eurocentric system that existed from the mid-seventeenth century until World War I is generally regarded as the heyday of balance-of-power politics. But even during that time, the proposition that peace would result from the "invisible hand" of balance-of-power dynamics was not without its critics. War may have been relatively limited in scope, duration, and severity during the alleged "golden age of diplomacy" (especially during the century between the Congress of Vienna in 1815 and the outbreak of World War I in 1914), but the restraints on the incidence of interstate violence may have been the result more of technological, cultural, and geographical conditions than of the constraints exerted by an equilibrium of forces. As Ludwig Dehio (1962) observes, the classic European balance of power was always precarious at best.

Indeed, the regularity with which wars broke out in Europe between the mid-1600s and the early twentieth century (when the fundamental prerequisites of the balance of power presumably existed) attests to the repeated failure of its mechanisms to preserve peace. Although the balance of power may at times have prolonged the length of peacetime between wars and

---

2. The conditions necessary for the successful operation of the balance-of-power mechanisms remain unclear. Waltz (1979) provides a useful review and critique of the conventional reasoning associated with this topic and advances the realist thesis that "balance-of-power politics prevail whenever two, and only two, requirements are met: that the order be anarchic and that it be populated by units wishing to survive."

3. Kaplan (1957) postulates that a stable balance-of-power system requires at least five powerful states or blocs of states.

possibly limited their duration and damage when they occurred, it is question-able that a balancing of power has ever been able to keep the peace for long.[4]

Equally questionable is the assumption that relative strength leads to peace. It has been shown that the preparation for war and the acquisition of relative superiority over an adversary may actually invite attack: In five of the nine wars involving the great powers in the 150 years following the Congress of Vienna, for example, the nations that were attacked were appreciably stronger militarily than those initiating the war (Singer and Small, 1975: 233). This empirical regularity does not speak well for the hypothesis that seeking mili-tary advantages over others deters aggression. Instead, the growth of a state's military power may so terrify its adversaries that they are motivated to initiate a preemptive strike in order to prevent their subjugation. In fact, surprisingly, and contrary to the logic of balance-of-power theorizing, research shows that ''major power wars are often initiated by nations which are relatively inferior, but gaining vis-à-vis the leaders'' (Singer and Small, 1975).

The outbreak of World War I, perhaps more than any other event, dis-credited balance-of-power politics and promoted the search for alternatives to it. The catastrophic proportions of that general war led many to view the balance-of-power mechanism as a *cause* of war instead of an instrument for its prevention. Indeed, the arms races, the secret treaties, and the entangling alliances that were connected with balance-of-power politics before the out-break of the war were frequently cited as its causes.

Opposition to balance-of-power politics was articulated most vehemently by President Woodrow Wilson. He and other political idealists in particular hoped to supersede the balance of power by replacing it with the principle of *collective security*.

The League of Nations embodied that principle. It was built on the assump-tion that peace-loving nations could collectively deter—and, if necessary, counteract—aggression. Instead of accepting war as a legitimate instrument of national policy, collective security sought to prohibit any war and fashioned a set of rules to prevent it through collective action. In contrast with the rules of balance of power, the theory of collective security proposed: (1) to retaliate against any aggressive act or attempt to establish hegemony—not just those acts that threatened hegemony within the system; (2) to involve the participa-tion of all member states—not just a sufficient number to stop the aggressor; and (3) to create an international organization to identify acts of aggression and to organize a military response to such acts—not just to let individual states decide for themselves whether to undertake self-help measures.

---

4. It could be argued that the relative peace of nineteenth-century Europe was *not* the product of an equilibrium resulting from balance-of-power politics but, instead, was a result of the extraordi-nary preponderance of power possessed and used by Great Britain to keep peace among its European rivals (see Organski, 1968).

To the great disappointment of its proponents, collective security also failed. Japan's aggression against Manchuria in 1931 and China proper in 1937 and Italy's invasion of Ethiopia in 1935 were widely condemned, but collective resistance was not forthcoming. Furthermore, there was no collective response to Germany's aggression against Czechoslovakia and other European nations in the 1930s. Collective security failed to prevent World War II and, like the balance of power, became a discredited theory because it failed to ensure the security of individual states in an anarchical international environment.

But the balance of power gained renewed support following World War II. A number of theorists and political leaders sought to restore the balance concept, perceiving it as the only "realistic" approach to security under prevailing conditions. The effort reaffirmed the beliefs that national self-reliance is the only trustworthy safeguard of security, that peace will come through strength, and that a potential aggressor must be confronted with a preponderance of power if it is to be successfully deterred. President Richard Nixon echoed an approach to peace that has many historical precedents, when he stated, "We must remember the only time in the history of the world that we have had any extended period of peace is when there has been a balance of power. . . . It will be a safer world . . . if we have a strong, healthy United States, Europe, Soviet Union, China, Japan, each balancing the other."

The reasons for the persistence of balance-of-power theorizing rest on a number of assumptions about the nature of contemporary world politics. Two deserve special attention: (1) that alliances deter war and (2) that systemic polarization leads to war.

Do Alliances Deter War?

As observed in both classical balance-of-power theory and in the precepts underlying post–World War II efforts to achieve global equilibrium, alliances are thought to be fundamental. They are assumed to be the trigger that makes the balance work, by pitting antagonistic coalitions against one another in such a way that neither is able to obtain superiority over its opponent. They are believed to create balances precisely because they aggregate power.

Presumably what makes two nations join in an alliance is their mutual fear of a third party; the alignment can help each offset the power of an adversary, both by adding an ally's power to its own and by denying the addition of that power to the enemy. The assumption is that by combining power, the probability of war is decreased.[5]

---

5. Classic balance-of-power theory presumed that alliances also would form *after* war erupts to redress the new threat to the balance and to restore the *status quo ante bellum* (the condition that existed before the outbreak of war).

Is this assumption valid? Is international order a product of alliance formation, as some contend (Liska, 1968; Osgood, 1968)? Or do alliances diminish rather than enhance states' security?

If the assumptions of the balance-of-power theory are correct, then historical periods in which there are many alliances should also be periods in which its members become involved in war less frequently. Studies have shown that during the nineteenth century, alliance formation was indeed associated with the absence of war. Throughout the first half of the twentieth century, however, this hypothesis no longer holds: As many nations became members of alliances, the international system was relatively more war-prone (Singer and Small, 1968).

The greater war-proneness of the first half of the twentieth century underwent a significant change, however, with the advent of the nuclear era. The incidence of war involving advanced industrialized societies that belong to alliances such as NATO and the Warsaw Pact has been virtually nonexistent since World War II. The contemporary period is aptly characterized as a remarkably "long peace" among the great powers (Gaddis, 1986). But the source of this stability cannot be attributed to alliance formation. More accurately, the relationship between alliance and the maintenance of peace was transformed by the moderating influence of nuclear weapons on great power belligerence. In the process, alliance systems themselves were transformed. The growing proportion of states entangled in security organizations, the declining flexibility of today's alliance systems, the development of rigid enmities between certain states, and the ideological colorations and bureaucratization of most alliance systems may have undermined the stabilizing function that balance-of-power theory envisions and may have reduced the capacity of power balances to shelter many Third World states from military intervention and armed attack (recall Chapter 12). So, too, the destructiveness of today's weapons systems may have eliminated the deterrent function that alliance formation traditionally performed. The fact is that neither the United States nor the Soviet Union depends on its allies to protect its own security.

Regardless of the reasons, and recognizing the special circumstances relating to the NATO and Warsaw Pact alliances, historical evidence demonstrates that during this century at least, nations that join alliances tend to be the ones most likely to go to war (Singer and Small, 1969, 1975). The marked preference of many Third World nations for nonalignment may represent a policy reflecting awareness of today's realities and astute self-interest. But then again, quite obviously many governments, notably those making up the Eastern and Western blocs as well as other industrialized countries living under the Soviet or American nuclear umbrella, still see in alliance a form of protection and a means of avoiding war. Whether their security has been increased or reduced by that choice is uncertain, as is expressed by the division of opinion on this issue exhibited in Europe in recent years (see Domke et al., 1987).

Post–World War II Models of the Global Distribution of Power

Power can be distributed in different ways. Some power configurations (such as world government) are largely hypothetical, having few historical manifestations. The configurations that have existed historically range from those highly concentrated, on one end of the continuum, to those highly dispersed, on the other. The former embraces regional empire, as with the Roman Empire, and an example of the latter is the approximate equality of power possessed by the European nations that acquired sovereignty at the conclusion of the Thirty Years War in 1648.

The structure of the global distribution of power has undergone a fundamental transformation since World War II. Most nations were devastated by the war that ended in 1945, a situation that left the United States in a clearly superordinate position, with its economy accounting for half the combined GNP of the world's nations. And of course the United States was the only nation that possessed the awesome new weapon, the atomic bomb. The fact that the United States had already demonstrated that it was willing to use the weapon merely underscored for others that it had acquired military capabilities without historical precedent.[6] However ephemeral, the immediate postwar environment can be regarded as a *unipolar* power configuration. Power was concentrated in the hands of a single dominant actor.

This period was short-lived, however. The recovery of the Soviet economy, the growth of its military capabilities, and the maintenance of a large Soviet army helped transform the system. The Soviets broke the American monopoly of atomic weapons in 1949 and exploded a thermonuclear device in 1953, less than a year after the United States. These developments thus contributed to the emergence of a *bipolar* distribution of power. Power came to be concentrated in the hands of the two superpowers, and their competition with each other for global influence became the most salient factor shaping politics worldwide.

The concept of two poles is especially apt in this context because a pole is a fit metaphor for a magnet—it both repels and attracts (Nogee, 1975). The formation of the North Atlantic Treaty Organization (NATO), linking the United States to the defense of Western Europe, and the Warsaw Pact, linking the Soviet Union in a formal alliance with its Eastern European clients, were manifestations of the emerging bipolar power structure. The opposing alliance systems were formed partly because of the pressure that the superpowers exerted to attract allies and partly because of the tendency of less-powerful nations to look to one or the other of the superpowers for protection in a highly insecure international environment. Correspondingly, each super-

---

6. In contrast, consider the position of America's closest rival, the Soviet Union, at that time. Its industrial, agricultural, and transportation systems had either been destroyed or severely damaged. An estimated twenty million Soviets had lost their lives; the ratio of Soviet to American war deaths was about seventy to one. The USSR was left exhausted, with its greatest asset being its large but underequipped army.

power's allies gave it forward bases from which to carry on the competition. The competition was punctuated by recurrent confrontations and crises that marked the superpowers' quest for power and position in an atmosphere pervaded by mutual suspicion.

The bipolar distribution of power itself contributed to the crisis-ridden postwar atmosphere. By grouping the system's nation-states into two blocs, each led by a superpower, the bipolar structure bred insecurity among all (Spanier, 1975). The balance was constantly at stake. Each bloc leader feared that its adversary would attain hegemony In such a system, every move, however defensive, was interpreted as an attempt to achieve superior status; what one side gained was seen as a loss for the other. Great importance was therefore attached to recruiting new friends and allies, and fear that an old ally might desert the fold was ever present. Little room was left for compromise or maneuver. Each superpower initiative was viewed as the first step toward the anticipated goal of world conquest; hence every hostile challenge was to be met by a retaliatory challenge. Endemic to the struggle was the notion that peace was impossible, that the most that could be hoped for was a momentary pause in overt hostilities based on a mutual respect for the territorial status quo.

To a significant extent, according to this line of reasoning, the cause of the competition between the United States and the Soviet Union in the postwar period was simply the concentration of power in the hands of the two super-powers. Each posed the only meaningful military threat to the other. To be sure, ideological differences and political incompatibilities reinforced the per-ception of threat each felt from the other, but the concentration of power in two poles (two states) was its principal source (see also Chapter 4). Conse-quently, the alliance configurations (NATO and the Warsaw Pact), which so often came to be seen as synonymous with bipolarity, were in fact little more than reflections of (rather than causes of) Soviet-American military dominance.

The major Cold War coalitions associated with bipolarity began to disinte-grate in the 1960s and early 1970s under the pressure of changing conditions. As their internal cohesion eroded and bipolarity deteriorated, what has been described as a bipolycentric system (Spanier, 1975) began to emerge. *Bipoly-centrism* describes the continued military superiority of the United States and the Soviet Union, and the continued reliance, at least ultimately, of the alliance partners on their respective superpower patrons for security. At the same time, the concept draws attention to the considerable room for maneuver created for weaker alliance partners. Hence the term *polycentrism*, indicating the existence at this second tier of multiple centers of power and diverse relation-ships among the nations subordinate to the superpowers (such as those friendly relations that were nurtured between the United States and Romania, on the one hand, and those between France and the Soviet Union, on the other). At the same time, the secondary powers are assumed to use these ties, as well as others established across alliance boundaries by the secondary powers themselves (such as between Poland and West Germany), to enhance their bargaining position within their own alliance. Although the superpowers remain dominant militarily, there is much greater fluidity in the actual foreign policy behavior of the alliance partners than is true in a strictly bipolar system. And new foreign policy roles (other than simply aligned or nonaligned) are created for actors in this less rigid system.

Rapid technological innovation in the superpowers' major weapons systems was one of the principal catalysts of change at the level of military capabilities in the polarity structure of the international system. In particular, the advent of technologically sophisticated intercontinental ballistic missiles (ICBMs) eroded the necessity of forward-base areas for striking at the heart of the adversary, thereby diminishing the drive to create and maintain tight, cohesive alliance systems composed of reliable partners.

In addition, the loosening of the ties that had bound allies to one another was accelerated by the narrowing of the difference between Soviet and American military capabilities. The European members of NATO in particular began to question whether the United States would indeed, as it had pledged, trade New York City for Paris or Bonn. Under what conditions might Washington or Moscow be willing to risk a nuclear holocaust? The uncertainty aroused by such questioning has not abated. "It's not conceivable," former CIA director Stansfield Turner wrote in 1986, "that any president would risk the very existence of [the United States] in order to defend our European allies from a conventional assault" (cited in Ignatius, 1987). In partial response to the dilemma posed, others, particularly France, decided to protect themselves by developing their own nuclear capabilities. Thus power became increasingly diffused. At the same time, fears of aggression and territorial expansion lessened, which contributed further to the erosion of the once-cohesive Cold War alliances.

As changes have occurred in the attributes and policies of many communist and capitalist countries, Cold War categories used to classify these states' political systems and foreign policy alignments have lost some of their relevance, as the concept of bipolycentrism implies. This is illustrated especially well with respect to the communist countries, where a strong capitalistic revival in the late 1980s transpired in countries as diverse as China, Cambodia, Laos, Vietnam, Poland, and Hungary (Diehl, 1987; Hoagland, 1987; Richburg, 1987). These changes promise to challenge further the adhesive bonds that ideology formerly helped tie states to one another, as well as their ability to confront their security problems from a common posture. Orthodox ways of thinking about alliances may in the process become obsolete as new orientations and alignments become more visible. Similarly, disputes in the Western alliance over strategic doctrine, arms control, American military bases on allies' territory, "out-of-area conflicts" (those beyond the traditional geographical boundaries of NATO), and a multitude of other issues speak to an era of decomposing bloc structures and declining support generally for the sanctity of commitments among parties to treaties of alliance (Kegley and Raymond, 1989).

Against the background of these important domestic and external developments, how can the present world distribution of power be most accurately described?[7] The decline of East–West tension in Europe (Goldmann, 1973; Goldmann and Lagerkranz, 1977), the emergence of Japan and the European Community as significant and powerful new actors, and the rise of China and its open competition with the Soviet Union are forces for the continuing transformation of the international political system. They also make a multipolar system (approximating the structural characteristics of the classic European balance of power) a potential model for accurately describing emerging political realities.

Yet, although one might envision a multipolar system in which the United States, the Soviet Union, Japan, China, and a united Europe are the major actors, the equilibrating mechanisms of the classical balance of power are of doubtful relevance to the contemporary world. The classical system was maintained by the major actors' willingness to enter into alliances with anyone (ideology did not matter) and to use war as an instrument of policy. The applicability of these conditions to present-day international politics is doubtful—despite the dispersion of power to multiple centers, the failure of some postwar security pacts, such as the ANZUS (Australia, New Zealand, United States) alliance, and, most significantly, the broad decline of American and Soviet power relative to others (Kennedy, 1988; Mead, 1987; Thompson, 1989). (In the parlance of long-cycle theory, the "world leadership" phase of American domination between 1945 and 1973 has ended, and a new phase in which its power has become challenged and its authority "delegitimatized" has begun [Modelski, 1987].) Because of technological requirements, among other things, alliances (such as NATO and the Warsaw Pact) are today relatively binding, with quasi-permanent bureaucracies and infrastructures that preclude adjustments of the power distribution through shifts in their membership. The global system is now universalized, comprising not a handful of states but more than 160. The freedom of the decision makers responsible for making foreign policies has become more constrained by domestic factors and global interdependence than was the case in earlier periods. The system is fragmented politically and culturally, and states' capabilities are not evenly matched. Furthermore, the destructiveness of contemporary weapons systems precludes the aggregation of power through coalitions, because the possession of nuclear weapons by any one state gives it the ability to destroy an adversary without the assistance of allies. Thus, even if one could plausibly envision a relative equilibrium of military capabilities among the United States, the Soviet

---

7. The fluid nature of the present system makes its characterization difficult. The difficulty is multiplied because analyses are based on different assumptions. Nogee (1975) illustrates this difficulty by noting the many terms employed to designate the postwar distribution of power: "bimodal, bipolar, loose bipolar, very loose bipolar, tight bipolar, bimultipolar, bipolycentric, complex conglomerate, detente system, diffuse bloc, discontinuity model, heterosymmetrical bipolarity, multipolar, multihierarchical, multibloc, pentapolar, policentric, oligopolistic, tripolar, and three-tiered multidimensional system within a bipolar setting."

Union, China, Japan, and a united Europe by, say, the beginning of the new millennium in 2001, the destructiveness of modern weapons, which seems more likely to increase than decrease by that time, makes it difficult to imagine a reemergent balance-of-power system analogous to the classical European state system.

The erosion of the diplomatic relationships of both the United States and the Soviet Union with their principal allies (Ball, 1985; Volgyes, 1988) and the growing independence of China from either's influence make it necessary to contemplate China's role in the world power equation.[8] For that purpose, a focus on the nature of triangular politics may be the most relevant.

Tripolarity[9] entails a system comprising three nations with relatively equal power potential vis-à-vis one another as defined by their economic and military capabilities, especially in the area of nuclear weapons capability. The description does not apply to present-day strategic realities. Objectively, China cannot be defined as the military rival of either the United States or the Soviet Union, although diplomatically China's role has taken on increasing importance. Nor is it likely to achieve such a capability quickly. But as the Chinese continue to develop nuclear weapons and a capacity to deliver them, at least in Asia, they may transform the power distributions that have heretofore dominated world politics. Deterrence under such conditions would have to be directed at two actors, and in particular toward preventing a military attack by two against one.

Preventing two against one would appear to be the key element defining foreign policy behavior in a (nuclear) tripolar system. Foreign policy behavior in a tripolar world would thus be based on a rational calculation of interest and power in which ideology is a peripheral consideration. "As a broad generalization, it can probably be hypothesized that, whereas in a bipolar system the great fear of each power is becoming militarily inferior lest the opponent achieve military superiority and a dominance that may not be reversible, in a tripolar system the fear of each pole is diplomatic isolation" (Spanier, 1975, emphasis deleted). Restraints on behavior in such a system derive from the fear that if there were a nuclear exchange involving only two of the actors, the combatants would probably be so severely devastated that the uninvolved actor would emerge as "the victor"—even if the noncombatant were initially the weakest of the three, such as China.

Restraints also derive from the fear of becoming permanently isolated. A tripolar system would encourage two actors to coalesce against one, particularly if the third appears unduly aggressive or interferes in the sphere of influence of another (such as China's sphere in Asia, the Soviet Union's sphere

---

8. Related to the ability of the People's Republic of China to steer an assertively independent foreign policy course is its rapid desertion from strict adherence to Marxist principles and its embrace of "capitalistic communism" to propel economic growth (Schlesinger, 1987).

9. Our discussion of tripolarity draws on Yalem (1972) and especially Spanier (1975).

in Eastern Europe, or the American sphere in the North Atlantic and the Western Hemisphere). Nonaggressiveness and noninterference therefore appear compatible with the interests of all and become more rather than less probable under the conditions of nuclear tripolarity.

In the current international system, the possession of a second-strike nuclear capacity and the means to deliver it are preconditions for a power to be considered a "pole." China does not possess such a capacity and is unlikely to for some time. It is therefore best to use the triangular concept to describe the diplomatic behavior exhibited by the Americans, Soviets, and Chinese toward one another rather than to use it to describe the international polarity system as a whole (see Starr, 1982, for an analysis of triangular relationships). Thus the concept helps explain China's apprehensiveness of Soviet-American détente; it provides insight into Soviet concerns about Sino-American rapproachement; and it makes understandable the American support of polycentric tendencies in the communist camp generally (and fear of Sino-Soviet attempts at fence mending particularly). It also explains the manifest caution of all three central actors.

The possibility that Japan, the world's second largest industrial democracy, might seek to play a more assertive diplomatic role and perhaps even a military role commensurate with its economic prowess makes the globe's future power equation even more uncertain. Several alternative polar configurations can be imagined that may apply to new combinations of conflict and accommodation. For instance, one view foresees the crystallization of a Washington–Tokyo–Peking axis balancing another composed of Bonn–Paris–Moscow (Brucan, 1984). Another predicts that both China and Japan will have the economic capacity to act as major world powers early in the twenty-first century, with a number of lesser powers, notably South Korea and India, assuming more commanding roles as their economies grow substantially relative to those of a number of industrialized nations. This view also sees the Soviet Union's share of the world economy shrinking "unless [Gorbachev's] 'restructuring' produces startling new gains" (Commission on Integrated Long-Term Strategy, 1988).

Regardless of which geopolitical or economic configuration develops, it is clear that the prospects for peace and the probability of war will be influenced by the degree to which the global power configuration concentrates or disperses power. Thus it is important to consider a theoretical question: Which is the more probable product of a concentration of power, war or peace?

Do Power Concentrations Promote or Inhibit War?

Whether an excessive concentration of military power is a condition inviting war, especially among the great powers, remains an unresolved question. The conventional view maintains that peace is preserved when power is evenly distributed. But others, noting the *pax Romana, pax Britannica,* and *pax Americana* of previous historical periods, contend that peace may depend, instead, on the existence of a preponderance or an imbalance of power. A. F. K. Organski observes, for example, that periods of equal power between states are periods of war "while the periods of known preponderance are periods of peace":

> . . . it is often claimed that a balance of power brings peace. . . . [There] were periods when an equal distribution of power between contenders actually existed . . . but these were the exception rather than the rule. . . . [Closer] examination reveals that they were periods of war, not peace. (Organski, 1968: 293)

If this view is accurate, then peace will occur when the most powerful state, but one *without hegemonic ambitions*, can deter others' expansionist ambitions. The proposition springs from the arguments that "an unequal power distribution (or preponderance) promotes peace because the more powerful opponent has no need to go to war, while the weaker side would be foolish to do so" but that "an equal power distribution between opponents increases the likelihood of war because each opponent thinks it can win" (Simowitz, 1982). If we think of the United States as the hegemonic power in the post–World War II system, these seemingly plausible conclusions do not bode well for the future. For if present trends are not arrested, the 1990s are likely to witness the continuing deconcentration of power as the United States' capabilities and influence relative to those of others recede further. According to this argument, as the dispersion of power proceeds, the likelihood of war increases.

Whether it is appropriate to think of the United States as the hegemon since World War II in the way that the foregoing implies is questionable. As noted earlier, the United States was clearly the dominant power immediately after World War II—and hence the configuration of the system can be described as unipolar—but this was a brief period that quickly gave way to a bipolar configuration. Thus the question that is usually asked is whether a bipolar power configuration is more peaceful than a multipolar system (like the classic balance-of-power system). Put somewhat differently, which of these arrangements improves the prospects for a viable system of power balancing power?

Many have argued that by its very nature a polarized system concentrating power in two competing blocs will lead to war. The hardening of alliances, it is reasoned, invariably will lead to a struggle for dominance. This situation promotes a crisis-prone environment of pure competition, because by definition, a bipolar configuration generates the fear that tempts each bloc to attain superior military capability. There are no constraints on the recourse to violence (especially the possible intervention of third parties to restore the balance), because the balancer role is absent. Similarly, a bipolar world may be violence prone because national decision makers will identify the enemy and estimate its capabilities more readily than when there are multiple adversaries (Deutsch and Singer, 1975).

Multipolar systems, on the other hand, are regarded as more stable in part because the existence of a larger number of autonomous actors gives rise to more potential alliance partners to counterbalance a would-be aggressor. Shifting alliances can occur only when there are several independent actors or power centers; a relatively large number of actors is essential to the operation of a balance. Moreover, because multipolar systems permit more contact among its members, the relative amount of information-processing time that the decision makers can allocate to any one of them will decrease, thus generating a kind of uncertainty that breeds caution (Deutsch and Singer, 1975) In such a system, national policy should seek to accommodate different national needs, with the result that alliance formation to counterbalance a threatening coalition becomes more probable.[10] As a consequence, war is believed to be less likely.

Arguments defending bipolarity as a means of maintaining peace also exist. For instance, Kenneth Waltz (1971) has asserted that a bipolar world like the one that emerged after World War II is stable because the heightened tension accompanying it encourages states to exercise caution, to assume greater responsibility for their actions, and to restrain the crisis-provoking, aggressive actions of their subordinate allies. Ironically, stability may result from threats that often reach the brink of war. Under such conditions, the major actors will, if rational, seek to manage crises peacefully and to prevent minor conflicts from escalating to a larger war that could engulf the world. It is also thought that uncertainty keeps nations' leaders alert and stimulates the pursuit of information that, in turn, reduces misperceptions and miscalculations regarding rivals' intentions during crises. This interpretation is reinforced by the argument that "the division of all nations into two camps raises the costs of war to such a high level that all but the most fundamental conflicts are resolved without resort to violence" (Bueno de Mesquita, 1975).

Thus, different assumptions lead to contradictory but equally plausible conclusions about the relationship between polarities and global stability. Which theory, when confronted with evidence, has the most to recommend it?

As is often the case with complex questions, the evidence is mixed. The argument that a bipolar world is more stable than a multipolar one is supported by the fact that in the bipolar environment of the 1950s, when the threat of war was endemic, major war did not occur. The superpowers repeatedly went to the brink of war as a seemingly unending series of crises marked their relations. But they never went over the brink. Hence, the perpetual competition that marked the bipolar world might, paradoxically, have produced caution and restraint rather than recklessness and violence. Clearly, the fear of large-scale destruction that might be caused by the use of nuclear weapons,

---

10. The concept of *interaction opportunities* refers to the fact that as the number of autonomous actors increases, the probability that more actors will develop relationships with an expanding number of other actors also grows, thereby increasing the number of possible coalitions.

which by themselves were the single most important manifestation of the superpowers' military capabilities, was an important constraint on the willingness of the United States and the Soviet Union to breach the brink. Thus the "long peace" between the superpowers that has persisted since 1945 has rested on very precarious foundations, but stability has resulted nonetheless (see Gaddis, 1986).

Quantitative historical studies also have examined the relationship between the number of poles in the system and the amount of war. They show that in the twentieth century, increased polarization led to more wars (Singer and Small, 1975) of greater duration (Bueno de Mesquita, 1975).[11] But empirical research also indicates that the overall relationship between polarity and war is not a direct one. One probe of the linkage found that the global system has been least stable under either very high or very low polarization (Rosecrance, 1966), whereas another concluded similarly: "By and large, when the system has been either very diffuse or highly polarized, interstate war has increased" (Singer and Small, 1975).

Thus, in general, increases in the extent to which power is concentrated in the hands of a few make for a more war-prone system (although the concentration of power in the hands of only one actor appears to be a means of avoiding war). Likewise, extensive dispersions of power throughout the system (which imply a lack of effective supervision by two or three giants) increase the probability of war.

In addition, war historically has often followed changes in the dispersion and concentration of power. That is, periods in which global power distributions have rapidly undergone substantial modification have been the periods most susceptible to war. This, again, does not inspire confidence about future stability, as it implies that swift change in the present structure of the global system will likely increase the probability of war (see Gilpin, 1981). Yet, as described earlier, a long-term change in the distribution of global power is clearly unfolding:

> While hegemony and balance of power models represent the tendency to centralize a system that remains organically decentralized, the emergence of more than 160 sovereign political units scattered over the continents has produced a new international setting in which it is no longer possible to run the world from one or two centers. We are witnessing a crucial conflict in world politics: the old thrust toward centralization of power is now clashing with the drive to decentralize power. (Brucan, 1984: 103)

Nonetheless, a measure of assurance can be taken in the fact that historically, polarity structures have seldom undergone rapid alterations, and that

---

11. What these findings do not mention is that war among the major powers has not occurred since World War II, or roughly the second half of the twentieth century, which reinforces the proposition articulated in earlier chapters as well as here, namely, that nuclear weapons have radically altered the role of force in contemporary world politics.

the present period does not appear to be an exception. The shift from a bipolar structure to the gradual emergence of a bipolycentric system and possibly a tripolar world indicates that the rapid reemergence of either an extremely polarized (unipolar) or extremely diffused (multibloc) structure is unlikely in the near future. This relative lack of polarity fluctuation should have a stabilizing effect, even though changes currently unfolding in the distribution of power operate as a source of tension and conflict, particularly as the ability of the United States to exercise disproportionate influence wanes.

By way of conclusion, the use made by states of the balance of power as a method of aggregating capabilities to preserve peace has had a rather checkered history. Often, the alliances formed and the distributions of power produced have failed to avert a breakdown of world order. But history also suggests that certain distributions of power may be more conducive to the preservation of peace than others are. When these and the conditions defining them stabilize, the prospects for the prevention of war improve.

DISARMAMENT AND ARMS CONTROL

To threaten the use of force to prevent the use of force by others, and to balance power with power to preserve peace are timeworn approaches to war avoidance. But the repeated failure of states to make those ideas work has stimulated the search for other solutions to the problem of war. One such proposal is to do away with the instruments of violence themselves. This approach constitutes a frontal attack on the theory that power can be balanced with power, in that it proposes to eliminate the instruments of destruction themselves. The idea can be traced to the biblical prescription that nations should beat their swords into plowshares. The destructiveness of today's weapons gives added urgency to the advice.

Do the weapons of war contribute to its frequency? A number of reasons suggest that they do.[12] Arms are designed for use in conflict. A nation that arms signals to others its potentially aggressive designs. If others fear that the arms are directed toward them, they often will feel compelled to arm themselves. Furthermore, the possession of arms may tempt the threatened party to use them, as, for example, in a preemptive strike.

On the other hand, if war is defined as the use of force to settle interstate differences, then it cannot occur if the instruments of force are not available. Nations without weapons cannot initiate wars; nor are they always the most likely targets of aggression by their armed neighbors (although they are not freed from that fear). Instead, could it be, as the Bible suggests and as evidence supports, that those who live by the sword usually die by the sword (Midlarsky, 1975; Richardson, 1960a; Small and Singer, 1982)? The acquisition of arms may invite attack because weapons elicit fear and aggression in others

---

12. Recall the discussion in Chapter 11, which advances an opposing proposition, namely, that because weapons deter, those nations who possess them are not likely to experience war.

(Berkowitz and LePage, 1970). If enemies are most dangerous when they are provoked—and nothing is more provocative than a sophisticated system of delivering destruction—then the creation of intimidating weapons systems with which to threaten enemies may be counterproductive. In the contemporary period, this principle translates into the observation that each new increment of military power may give states that much less security.

The incentives for controlling arms have increased greatly since the horrors of Hiroshima and Nagasaki. The threat that nuclear weapons pose to stability and survival was expressed by President Kennedy in a 1961 address to the United Nations that still retains its relevance:

> Today, every inhabitant of this planet must contemplate the day when this planet may no longer be habitable. Every man, woman and child lives under a nuclear sword of Damocles, hanging by the slenderest of threads, capable of being cut at any moment by accident or miscalculation or by madness. The weapons of war must be abolished before they abolish us.
>
> Men no longer debate whether armaments are a symptom or a cause of tension. The mere existence of modern weapons—ten million times more powerful than any that the world has ever seen, and only minutes away from any target on earth—is a source of horror, and discord and distrust. Men no longer maintain that disarmament must await the settlement of all disputes—for disarmament must be a part of any permanent settlement. And men may no longer pretend that the quest for disarmament is a sign of weakness—for in a spiraling arms race, a nation's security may well be shrinking even as its arms increase.

These words conjure up Nikita Khrushchev's prediction in 1962 that in the event of a nuclear exchange "the survivors would envy the dead." The conventional wisdom that arms produce security is called into question. Indeed, the right to arm is itself questioned. When the destructiveness of weapons threatens the very fate of the earth (see Sagan, 1983–1984; Schell, 1982, 1984), abolishing the source of that threat ceases to appear to be a radical, utopian aspiration.

Although the idea that war can be controlled by eliminating the world's military arsenals is not new—even if it has taken on a new urgency—one of the few constants in the changing international system has been the repetition with which disarmament proposals have been voiced but simultaneously ignored in practice.[13] To be sure, some nations occasionally have decreased their armaments levels.[14] But these instances have often been temporary and invol-

---

13. Disarmament proposals figured prominently in the Hague peace conferences of 1899 and 1907, the League of Nations' World Disarmament Conference of 1933, and rather continuously in the United Nations since 1946 but especially in its Special Sessions on Disarmament.

14. The Chinese states in 600 B.C. formed a disarmament league that produced a peaceful century for the league's members, and Canada and the United States agreed in 1818 that the Great Lakes area should be disarmed.

untary—disarmament imposed by coercion on the vanquished by the victors in the immediate aftermath of a war, as when the Allied powers attempted (unsuccessfully) to disarm permanently a defeated Germany after World War I. Even less frequent have been the instances of unilateral disarmament in the absence of coercion, wherein individual nations have voluntarily reduced their arms levels, or of policies of explicit arms restraint such as that carried out by the Japanese after their defeat in World War II.[15] In short, governments have rarely disarmed. To speak of disarmament, then, is to speak of a phenomenon with few historical examples. The one that stands out, precisely because it is so rare, is the intermediate-range nuclear forces (INF) agreement reached between the United States and the Soviet Union in 1987, that established the basis for the elimination of an entire class of nuclear delivery systems.[16]

Disarmament (the reduction of armaments, if not their abolition) may be usefully distinguished from a related concept, *arms control*. The latter term generally refers to agreements designed to regulate arms levels either by limiting their growth or by restricting how they might be used. Arms control is less ambitious than is disarmament because it seeks not to reduce or eliminate weapons but to moderate the pace at which they are developed and to limit the ways in which they can be employed. These more modest objectives perhaps explain why efforts to control arms have been more successful than have efforts to disarm and why the control of arms is a foreign policy goal of many nations. Arms control, in fact, is widely perceived as an essential component of national security policy. To seek to control the development of some kinds of arms while expanding others is a strategy consistent with the policies of many nations, including the superpowers. The tendency to couple arms limitations and defense preparations helps explain one of the major paradoxes of world politics—the simultaneous pursuit of an arms race and arms control.

Historical examples of arms control efforts can be found as early as 1139, when the Second Lateran Council prohibited the use of crossbows in fighting. Early twentieth-century examples include the 1899 and 1907 International Peace Conferences at the Hague which restricted the use of some weapons and prohibited others, and the agreement among the United States, Britain, Japan, France, and Italy at the Washington Naval Conferences (1921–1922) adjusting the relative tonnage of their fleets (followed and extended by the London Treaties of 1930 and 1936). An unsuccessful example is found in the 1921

---

15. Note that Japan's insistence on not rearming has often been cited as an example that disarmed states are not necessarily insecure ones. (This may have been because the Japanese felt that they could count on the United States to ensure Japan's security.) By choosing not to compete militarily, Japan may have been able to compete more successfully economically. Indeed, the Japanese experience suggests that political power can derive from economic power and that military power can be a liability of sorts (see Rosecrance, 1986).

16. As discussed later, the 1987 intermediate-range nuclear force (INF) treaty between the United States and the Soviet Union, which is designed to eliminate short-range (SRINF) and long-range (LRINF) intermediate-range missiles from Europe, is an agreement that for the first time since World War II opens the way for a meaningful reduction of armaments.

League of Nations effort to realize an arms production moratorium, a proposal that culminated in 1933 in the League of Nations' abortive World Disarmament Conference. Other examples include the 1919 St. Germain Convention on the export of arms, the 1925 Geneva Convention on arms trade, and the 1929 Geneva draft convention on arms manufacture.

The post–World War II period has witnessed a variety of arms control proposals. The Baruch Plan (1946) called for the creation of a United Nations Atomic Development Authority that would have placed atomic energy under an international authority to ensure its use for only peaceful purposes, but the proposal was never implemented. (However, American and Soviet scientists also have met informally since 1957 at the so-called Pugwash Conference to discuss problems regarding the control of nuclear weapons.) At the Geneva summit conference of 1955, President Eisenhower made an "open skies" proposal for aerial reconnaissance to monitor military maneuvers in the United States and the Soviet Union, but it failed to result in an agreement. So, too, did the Rapacki Plan of 1957, which would have prevented the deployment of nuclear weapons in Central Europe.

Nonetheless, efforts to resolve differences so that formal arms control agreements might be realized have been recurrent. For instance, arms control was the dominant topic in no less than fifteen summit conferences between American and Soviet leaders between July 1955, when President Eisenhower and Nikita Khrushchev, then first secretary of the Soviet Communist party, met in Geneva, and May 1988, when President Reagan and General Secretary Gorbachev met in Moscow and ratified the INF treaty. Among other things, the summits sought, and often resulted in, an improved atmosphere for serious arms control negotiations.

In addition to summitry, negotiations on particular issues have sometimes taken on the character of institutionalized efforts to resolve differences among nations so as to realize arms control agreements. Examples include the United Nations Committee on Disarmament (created in 1979), the Comprehensive Test Ban Negotiations (initiated in 1978 but suspended by the Reagan administration), the Conference on Security and Cooperation in Europe (CSCE) (1975), designed to establish confidence-building measures in Europe (such as the requirement for prior modification of military maneuvers), and the Mutual and Balanced Force Reduction (MBFR) talks (1973) aimed at reducing the conventional military forces of the NATO and Warsaw Pact alliances in the European theater.

Other issues that have been the subject of still incomplete negotiations include efforts to impose a verifiable ban on the production and stockpiling of chemical weapons, to strengthen the verification provisions of the (unratified) Comprehensive Threshold Test Ban and the Peaceful Nuclear Explosions Treaty, and to improve the international safeguards on technology relating to the production of nuclear material.

Although the list of unresolved negotiating topics is long, some of the efforts have produced concrete achievements. As shown in Table 13.1, ten

TABLE 13.1 ■ Major Multilateral Arms Control Treaties and Agreements

Date	Agreement	Principal Objectives
1959	Antarctic Treaty	■ prevents the military use of the Antarctic, including the testing of nuclear weapons
1963	Limited Test Ban Treaty	■ prohibits nuclear weapons in the atmosphere, outer space, and underwater
1967	Outer Space Treaty	■ outlaws the use of outer space for testing or stationing any weapons, as well as for military maneuvers
1967	Treaty of Tlatelolco	■ creates the Latin America Nuclear Free Zone by prohibiting the testing and possession of nuclear facilities for military purposes
1968	Nuclear Nonproliferation Treaty	■ prevents the transfer of nuclear weapons and nuclear weapons production technologies to non-nuclear weapon states
1971	Seabed Treaty	■ prohibits the deployment of weapons of mass destruction and nuclear weapons on the seabed beyond a 12-mile coastal limit
1972	Biological Weapons Convention	■ prohibits the production and storage of biological and toxins; calls for the destruction of biological weapons stocks
1977	Environmental Modification Convention	■ bans the use of technologies that could alter the earth's weather patterns, ocean currents, ozone layer, or ecology
1981	Inhumane Weapons Convention	■ prohibits the use of such weapons as fragmentation bombs, incendiary weapons, booby traps, and mines to which civilians could be exposed
1985	South Pacific Nuclear Free Zone Treaty	■ prohibits the testing, acquisition, or deployment of nuclear weapons

major multilateral arms control agreements have been reached since 1959. These agreements may help alter the environment in which states compete, by reducing suspicions, the risk of war, and the potential for destruction in the event that armed conflict erupts. Thus they may make for a more predictable and orderly global environment by fostering international communication and understanding. And because some limit the range of permissible actions and weapons systems available to states, they may have helped slow the global arms race.

Controlling Nuclear Arms

Particularly conspicuous in any chronicle of arms control achievements are those agreements reached between the United States and the Soviet Union, and between them and other nations as a result of the superpowers' efforts.

Soviet and American arms control efforts have understandably focused on ways to minimize the threat of nuclear war. The results of these endeavors are summarized in Table 13.2, which lists the bilateral arms control agreements reached between the United States and the Soviet Union since 1960. To these might be added an indeterminate number of tacit understandings about the level and use of weapons to which the two powers seem to have agreed, understandings that have not achieved the status of formal agreements but that the two superpowers have nonetheless observed. In this category, for example, might be included the superpowers' commitment to refrain from the nondefensive use of their nuclear arsenals, as indicated by President Carter's pledge that the United States would not be the first country to use nuclear weapons in war and Soviet Foreign Minister Andrei Gromyko's promise that the Soviet Union would never be the first to use nuclear weapons in any conflict. Such commitments are not legally binding, but they take both superpowers in the direction of a no-first-use doctrine that could demarcate the line between conventional and nuclear weapons and thus reduce the risk of nuclear war.

Of the explicit, formal arms control agreements reached by the superpowers, the two so-called SALT (Strategic Arms Limitation Talks) agreements were precedent setting. SALT I, signed in 1972, consisted of (1) a treaty that restricted the deployment of antiballistic missile defense systems by the United States and the Soviet Union to equal and very low levels and (2) a five-year interim accord on strategic offensive arms, which restricted the number of ICBM (intercontinental ballistic missile) and SLBM (submarine-launched ballistic missile) launchers that each side was permitted to have. The SALT I agreement was essentially a confidence-building, "stopgap" step toward a longer-term, more comprehensive treaty. The SALT II agreement of 1979 sought to realize that objective in that it substantially increased the quantitative restrictions of SALT I and began as well to place certain qualitative constraints on the superpowers' strategic arsenals.

The essentials of SALT II, although until then perhaps the most extensive and complicated arms control agreement ever negotiated, were nevertheless quite simple. First, the agreement called for placing an eventual overall ceiling of 2,250 on the number of ICBM launchers, SLBM launchers, heavy bombers, and ASBMs (air-to-surface ballistic missiles with ranges over six hundred kilometers) that each side was permitted to maintain. Within this overall ceiling, several subceilings specified additional restrictions on particular types of nuclear systems. Taken together, these limitations were estimated at the time that SALT II was signed to have reduced by as many as 8,500 the total number of strategic nuclear weapons that the United States and the Soviet Union would have possessed by 1985 without the agreement. The number of strategic nuclear delivery vehicles that SALT II permitted the Soviet Union to deploy was also substantially less than the number that American defense planners believed it would otherwise have deployed.

But the difficulty of agreeing to control arms is illustrated by the problems that SALT II encountered. The United States Senate deferred ratification of the SALT II treaty "indefinitely" following the Soviet invasion of Afghanistan. Although both superpowers continued to abide by the basic terms of SALT II during the confrontation in the early 1980s, the "final result as embodied in SALT II was a clear disappointment to the hopes generated in the early 1970s. In essence, SALT II failed to achieve actual arms reductions. Its basic fault was that it would have permitted substantial growth in the strategic forces of both sides" (U.S. Department of State, 1983).

Against this background of what the United States labeled "the failed promise of SALT," the agenda was set for new approaches to strategic arms control. In June 1982 the Reagan administration initiated a new round of arms talks aimed at significant reductions in the strategic arsenals of both superpowers. Termed START (Strategic Arms Reduction Talks), the initiative resumed the SALT process but expanded its agenda by seeking to remove asymmetries that had developed in the superpowers' weapons systems.

In addition to negotiations involving strategic weapons, the United States and the Soviet Union have pursued arms control on other fronts. Most dramatic among these efforts are the negotiations begun in 1981 aimed at limiting intermediate-range nuclear forces in Europe, an initiative that culminated in the historic agreement ratified in the 1988 Moscow summit to ban an entire category of weapons—the first such disarmament agreement in modern history not implemented by the victors in war. Although the agreement requires that less than 5 percent of the world's nuclear arsenals be dismantled over a period of three years (the United States would destroy 859 missiles, the Soviets an estimated 1,752), it set important precedents. The Soviet Union, for example, agreed to a treaty that would require it to make greater quantitative reductions than the United States did. The Soviets also accepted the American "zero-option position," that is, the complete elimination of LRINF (long-range intermediate-range nuclear force) weapons, and came closer to the American

TABLE 13.2 ■ Major Bilateral Arms Control Agreements Between the United States and the Soviet Union

Date	Agreement	Principal Objectives
1963	Hot Line Agreement	■ establishes a direct radio and telegraph communication system between the governments to be used in times of crisis
1971	Hot Line Modernization Agreement	■ puts a hot line satellite communication system into operation
1971	Nuclear Accidents Agreement	■ creates a process for notification of accidental or unauthorized detonation of a nuclear weapon; creates safeguards to prevent accidents
1972	ABM Treaty (SALT I)	■ restricts the deployment of antiballistic missile defense systems to one area, and prohibits the development of space-based ABM system
1972	SALT I Interim Agreement on Offensive Strategic Arms	■ freezes the superpowers' total number of ballistic missile launchers for a 5-year period
1972	Protocol to the Interim Agreement	■ clarifies and strengthens prior limits on strategic arms
1973	Agreement on the Prevention of Nuclear War	■ commits the superpowers to the goal of preventing the onset of nuclear war; requires consultation if a threat of nuclear war emerges
1974	Threshold Test Ban Treaty with Protocol	■ restricts the underground testing of nuclear weapons above a yield of 150 kilotons
1974	Protocol to the ABM Treaty	■ strengthens the limits imposed by the ABM Treaty
1976	Treaty on the Limitation of Underground Explosions for Peaceful Purposes	■ broadens the ban on underground nuclear testing stipulated in the 1974 Threshold Test Ban Treaty; requires on-site observers of tests with yields exceeding 150 kilotons

TABLE 13.2 ■ Continued

Date	Agreement	Principal Objectives
1977	Convention on the Prohibition of Military or Any Other Hostile Use of Environmental Modification Techniques	■ bans weapons that threaten to modify the planetary ecology
1979	SALT II Treaty (never ratified)	■ places ceilings on the number of strategic delivery vehicles, MIRVed missiles, long-range bombers, cruise missiles, ICBMs, and other weapons; restrains testing
1987	INF Treaty	■ calls for the elimination of U.S. and USSR intermediate- and shorter-range nuclear weapons in Europe within 3 years and enables extensive verification measures

position in the START talks. These concessions stemmed from their desire to see the U.S. Pershing IIs removed from West Germany, to reduce the U.S. commitment to SDI (the Strategic Defense Initiative, popularly known as the "Star Wars" defense against intercontinental ballistic missile forces). Most importantly, perhaps, both sides agreed to a system of reciprocal on-site inspections which addressed in a concrete and positive fashion the touchy issue of verification that had long plagued efforts to reach mutual understandings.

The INF agreement inspired hope for what British Foreign Secretary Sir Geoffrey Howe called "the beginning of the beginning of the whole arms control process."[17] That view reflected the hope of many that its importance was primarily as a prelude to the more comprehensive and far-reaching goal of reaching an agreement on strategic weapons. Reagan and Gorbachev did agree at the 1987 Washington summit to the principle that each superpower halve its arsenal of strategic nuclear warheads (to approximately 6,000). In addition, the

---

17. The spirit and hopes for the treaty were expressed by Ronald Reagan's comment: "The arms race is not pre-ordained and not part of some inevitable course of history. We can make history"; and Mikhail Gorbachev's declaration: "May December 8, 1987, become a date that will be inscribed in the history books, a date that will mark a watershed separating the era of mounting risk of nuclear war from the era of a demilitarization of human life."

United States sought a sublimit of 3,300 on land-based missiles as well as a ban on mobile missiles. But many obstacles stand in the way of further agreements on strategic weapons, including the issue of verification and the insistence of the United States on pursuing a Star Wars ballistic missile defense system. Thus Senate Majority Leader Robert Byrd aptly warned in 1988 that the INF accord "could very well be either the beginning or the end of arms control—the first step or the last step."

How Meaningful Are Arms Control Agreements?

As promising as the superpowers' initiatives might appear, the troubled history of their past efforts, as illustrated in the long list of ongoing but unresolved negotiations, is testimony to how difficult it is for adversaries to reach arms control agreements. That history raises the question of whether most of the arms control agreements reached thus far have in fact restrained the arms race or reduced the military potential of states. In many respects, it could be argued that "the weapons prohibited have had little, if any, military importance, and the outlawed activities have never been seriously contemplated as methods of war. Negotiations on measures which could make a significant impact on the arms situation in the world have stagnated for years" (Goldblat, 1982). Indeed, critics have cynically noted that arms control agreements may instill a false sense of security by encouraging people to think that the arms race is being controlled when it actually is not.

They have also wondered whether the international agreements designed to control arms are unimportant because they deal with comparatively trivial issues. Because the notion persists that security derives from arms accumulation, do nations seek to control only those armaments that they have little intention of or incentive for developing in the first place or that have become obsolete? Are the most threatening problems left beyond control? These are troublesome questions, for they do not speak well of the history of contemporary efforts to bring arms under control.

The potential impotence of some of the agreements listed in Table 13.1, for example, is illustrated by the disregard that some signatories have demonstrated toward them. For example, there have been twelve alleged instances of the use of chemical and biological warfare between 1975 and 1981 that violate the 1972 Biological Weapons Convention (Goldblat, 1982: 100). Included among the allegations are the Vietnamese forces' use of poison gas against China (1979), the United States' use of chemical weapons in covert action in Cuba (1978–1981), the Iraqis' use of "chemical bombs" in occupied Iranian territory (1980), and the Soviet Union's use of lethal chemical weapons in Laos and Afghanistan over prolonged periods in such quantities as to produce a toxic "yellow rain."

Consider also the record of the continued development and testing of nuclear weapons. The six known nuclear states have conducted more than thirteen hundred nuclear explosions since 1945. Nor has the pace slowed since the partial test ban treaty of 1963, which proscribed atmospheric and under-water testing but not underground explosions.[18] In fact, more explosions have taken place since 1963 than before. Nor is the "threat" system of armaments seriously challenged by the abolition of nuclear weapons from such areas as Antarctica or Latin America, where the temptations for their deployment were not great to begin with.[19]

Nagging questions about the nature and utility of arms control efforts apply especially to the United States and the Soviet Union. Both, for example, but especially the United States, have lodged many complaints about violations of existing agreements by their adversary. More importantly, when the super-powers have perceived their vital interests to be at stake, their penchant to accumulate ever more deadly weapons systems has not been moderated. The skeptic might argue that arms control has been largely a fraud devised to disguise the continuation of the arms race or even a conspiracy conducted by the superpowers' military establishments to spread complacency in the public mind. The continued use of arms talks as propaganda forums and the propen-sity for new weapons to be created (for "bargaining" purposes) but seldom traded away lend credence to this cynical view.

A related charge is that arms control accomplishments have not imposed meaningful restrictions on arms races; they merely stabilize, legitimize, and provide orderly rules for the continuation of the races. The SALT agreements, for example, were widely perceived as significant pauses in the extraordinarily expensive Soviet-American arms race, and they were presented to the Ameri-can and Soviet publics as important steps toward that end. Yet it is noteworthy that during the five years covered by the SALT I agreement (1972–1977), the superpowers' combined military spending exceeded $1 trillion. This was a rate of spending greater than that of the quarter-century between the end of World War II and the signing of the SALT I agreements, when total military spending was $2.3 trillion. Since 1977 the military spending of both super-powers has accelerated in an upward spiral. The SALT agreements, in short, failed to produce reductions in the military spending of either superpower.

Also revealing is what the SALT agreements failed to restrict. SALT I, for example, froze the number of strategic launchers in operation or in the process of construction at the time of the agreement, but it failed to cover strategic bombers or to prevent the kinds of qualitative improvements that can make quantitative thresholds meaningless. One such improvement was in the num-

---

18. Neither France nor China is a party to the partial test-ban treaty. China has conducted atmospheric testing of nuclear weapons, but since 1974 France has conducted all of its nuclear explosions underground.

19. Latin America was made a nuclear weapon–free zone in the 1967 Treaty of Tlatelolco. How-ever, neither Brazil nor Argentina, the only two countries in the area with nuclear potential and aspirations, had still by the mid-1980s refused to agree fully to the provisions of the treaty. "Nuclear weapon–free zones" (NWFZs) have been proposed for a number of other regions as well (see Karem, 1988).

ber of strategic warheads that a single missile could launch against an enemy. And in fact the number of multiple independently targetable warheads (MIRVs) deployed on missiles by the superpowers in 1977 was four times greater than when the SALT talks began, even though SALT I froze the number of delivery vehicles at the superpowers' disposal. Perhaps this is the kind of situation that Herbert Scoville, Jr., a former deputy director of the U.S. Central Intelligence Agency, had in mind when he noted at the time of the signing of SALT I: "Arms control negotiations are rapidly becoming the best excuse for escalating rather than toning down the arms race" (cited in Barnet, 1977). The pattern revealed in this and other developments led one former American policymaker to conclude that "three decades of U.S.-Soviet negotiations to limit arms competition have done little more than to codify the arms race" (Gelb, 1979).

Perhaps because of fear of the relentless arms race and the futility of the arms control process, the idea of a "nuclear freeze" gained momentum on both sides of the Atlantic in the early 1980s. The United States Congress debated the issue, and the Catholic church became involved when the American Catholic bishops composed a pastoral letter that called for an immediate end to the arms race and asserted that the deliberate initiation of nuclear warfare, on however restricted a scale, could not be morally justified.

Freeze advocates were motivated by the view that more weapons will not produce more security; indeed, they believed that continuation of the arms race threatens rather than strengthens national security. According to this view, it is a "delusion" to see "nuclear weapons as just one more weapon, like any other weapon, only more destructive" (Kennan, 1982).

As a policy proposal, a total freeze on the testing, production, and deployment of nuclear weapons envisions a path to disarmament that first stops new weapons systems before starting to reduce the existing ones. To do that, the present strategic balance would first be frozen (for both sides' deterrent capabilities currently are invulnerable, freeze advocates assert, and a freeze would keep them that way). Once the arms race was curtailed, arms reductions could be considered. But whether that can be accomplished remains doubtful.

Impediments to Effective Arms Control

Why have agreements to control the size and dispersion of weapons been so modest? Why have states taken decisions to arm that have apparently imprisoned them in the grip of perpetual insecurity? The incentives for meaningful arms control would seem to be many and mutually beneficial. Significant controls on the weapons of war would save money, reduce tension and hence the dangers of war, symbolize the desire for peace, lessen health hazards, reduce the potential destructiveness of war, dampen the incentive for one state to seek a power advantage over others, diminish the possibility of being the target of a preemptive attack, and achieve a propaganda advantage for those advocating peace (Van Dyke, 1966). To these might be added moral satisfaction and the opportunity to live in a global environment free of fear.

But arms are not being controlled in today's international system, and the reasons for the continued reliance on military preparedness as a path to peace are many. They stem from the fear that is endemic to the international system as it is now structured. Most nations are reluctant to engage in arms limitations in an atmosphere in which trust of their adversaries is lacking, and such trust is unlikely to be cultivated in an anarchical environment that encourages adversaries to arm. Hence nations find themselves caught in a vicious circle of fear that creates the security dilemma: Others' arms provoke fear; fear stimulates the desire to arm for defense; arms encourage the enemy to increase its arms; and so it goes in a never-ending spiral. Conversely, when states talk of beating swords into plowshares, each wants the last sword.

The fear of others helps explain nations' seemingly self-defeating posture in arms control negotiations. "The military establishments on both sides subscribe to the same two basic principles: (1) 'Don't negotiate when you are behind. Why accept a permanent position of number two?' and (2) 'Don't negotiate when you are ahead. Why accept a freeze in an area of military competition when the other side has not kept up with you?'" (Barnet, 1977). The result of this syndrome is clear: When fearful nations abide by the axiom that they should never negotiate from a position of weakness, then they are left with no option but to refuse to negotiate. It is little wonder that meaningful agreements have been so hard to achieve (and why states develop weapons systems as bargaining chips for future negotiations). Arms bargaining is a game of give and take, but all participants typically want to take much and give little. As described by a former United States arms negotiator, "U.S. negotiators are almost invariably given instructions, in effect, to close all of the other side's loopholes but to keep their own open. Not surprisingly, Soviet instructions seem similar" (Gelb, 1979).

The problems of arriving at meaningful arms control agreements are compounded by other obstacles. A precondition to agreement is the perception of the achievement of secure *mutual* deterrence (Smoke, 1975), but strategic parity is seldom perceived. Arms ratios are also particularly unstable in the face of rapid technological innovations (such as those that have led to the miniaturization of weapons and improvements in the precision of delivery systems). Technology can make weapons systems obsolete and at the same time enable qualitative refinements of existing weapons systems. The possibilities of such innovations and the asymmetries they create exacerbate the difficulties of comparing the relative military strengths of parties to an agreement. "What are equivalent weapons?" is a question on which few observers (even within a given country) are able to agree, because no single measure of military strength is adequate to determine which country is ahead and which is behind. The two superpowers' weapons systems are qualitatively different and therefore not easily compared, which is one reason that some measures invariably point to an American advantage and others show a Soviet lead. And of course achieving agreement on ratios of strength and verifying compliance with such agreements are political as well as technical problems of considerable magnitude.

Orchestrating arms negotiations to keep them in balance with political negotiations in other areas and convincing various publics and pressure groups that the benefits of an agreement outweigh the costs require considerable energy and skill.[20]

Equally troublesome is the difficulty of separating the control of weapons from other issues.[21] Nowhere is this more evident than in the Soviet-American rivalry, in which arms talks often have been linked to the vicissitudes of the Soviet-American competition in other areas. Arms control and détente have proved in fact to be symbiotic—the former has assisted the development of the latter, and the latter has fostered the former. The deterioration of East–West relations in nonmilitary areas can therefore jeopardize the prospects for arms control, just as an escalating arms race can reduce considerably the probability of improved Soviet-American political relationships. The linkage between arms control and the superpowers' conduct overall means that their inability to reach accommodation in areas not directly related to arms control will likely deter progress on arms control. Conversely, arms agreements, if reached, could contribute to a climate conducive to constructive economic and political relationships.

IN SEARCH OF PEACE

The obstacles to the control of arms are formidable. The idea that a disarmed world would be a more secure one does not have the force of history behind it, whereas the idea that military preparedness produces security does. It may be that peace via disarmament and arms control is, as critics have charged, a utopian dream. Arms control efforts may also be doomed to failure, not because the control of arms is idealistic, but because it does not go far enough. "Arms control does not solve the basic problem of armaments. States still have them, and if they have them, they can use them" (Ziegler, 1977).

---

20. Many people benefit financially from the perpetuation of arms races and become lobbyists against arms agreements because they can lose their jobs by an abatement of military spending. Groups exist in all societies whose influence is tied to the continuation of the arms race. For assessments of military-industrial complexes, see Rosen (1973) and the series of articles "The Military Industrial Complex: USSR/USA" in the *Journal of International Affairs* (1972).

21. In fact, policymakers have often sought to link these issues, particularly, as noted in Chapter 4, during the period of détente. At least one major study questioned the wisdom of this strategy, concluding that

to the extent that arms control is to serve the security, economic and other interests of all parties, participating in negotiations for arms control agreements should not be treated as a favor done to another state or as a reward for "good international behaviour." Therefore, linking arms control talks with the global policies of the negotiators is bound to be futile: it impedes progress in arms control without promoting the solution of other international problems. If anything, it is a prescription for an uncontrolled arms race. (Goldblat, 1982: 354)

U.S. Secretary of State George Shultz echoed dissatisfaction with the linkage strategy in an early 1988 (and hence post–Washington summit) speech in which he said, "It yields the initiative to the Soviets to set the pace and scope of relations with us and with our allies."

Alternatively, it may be that the control of arms is a practical necessity, even though the international milieu is not conducive to a far-reaching realization of that goal.[22] Problems that cannot be solved are seldom raised. States have failed to control their proclivity to arm because the race for armaments is only a symptom of larger problems. Managing political conflicts without violence may be the key to arms control. For arms, after all, are less causes of war than they are symptoms of political tension: "Men do not fight because they have arms. They have arms because [they are afraid and] they deem it necessary to fight" (Morgenthau, 1967). From this perspective, controlling arms is contingent on removing the fears that underlie nations' political conflicts.

Because the quest for national security in an anarchical world springs from states' fear of one another, the realization of security by one nation may provoke insecurity in others. This explains why nations continue to emphasize preparations for war.

States, of course, pursue many paths to the realization of their national objectives, of which security is the preeminent one. Thus they seek through deterrence to balance power with power while seeking simultaneously through arms control to remove the incentives for war that arms provide, because the weapons themselves may aggravate political tensions. In this sense the military paths to peace discussed in this chapter are intimately related to the quest for national security discussed in Chapter 11. Whether global security is served by nations' search for their own national security remains at issue, however. Perhaps the seeds of the world's destruction have been sown by the forces that propel the pursuit of peace and security through military might. Nothing makes the search for peace through political means more compelling. Hope may be inspired by the observations of a former U.S. Secretary of Defense, Robert McNamara: "We have reached the present dangerous and absurd confrontation by a long series of steps, many of which seemed rational in their time. Step-by-step we can undo much of the damage."

SUGGESTED READINGS

Bueno de Mesquita, Bruce. *The War Trap*. New Haven, Conn.: Yale University Press, 1981.

Claude, Inis L., Jr. *Power and International Relations*. New York: Random House, 1962.

---

22. See Sibley (1963) for a statement that argues for both the necessity and the possibility of unilateral disarmament. The idea that the world might have to choose between an arms race and the human race was expressed by President Eisenhower in 1956, who felt that "in any general hostilities . . . destruction will be both reciprocal and complete" and "because we are rapidly getting to the point that no war can be won, we had better begin to plan for restraint." To this might be added the proposition that the invigorated efforts to inhibit the arms race through arms control in the late 1980s was stimulated by financial necessities. Neither superpower, whose economic circumstances have deteriorated in part because of its enormous expenditures for arms, can afford to continue that level of expenditure without fear of destroying the economic foundation on which national strength ultimately rests (see Kennedy, 1988).

Gasteyger, Curt. *Searching for World Security: Understanding Global Armament and Disarmament*. New York: St. Martin's Press, 1987.

Goldblat, Jozef. *Agreements for Arms Control: A Critical Survey*. London, England: Taylor Francis, 1982.

Gulick, Edward Vose. *Europe's Classical Balance of Power*. Ithaca, N.Y.: Cornell University Press, 1955.

Haas, Ernst B. "The Balance of Power: Prescription, Concept, or Propaganda?" *World Politics* 5 (July 1953): 442–477.

Jensen, Lloyd. *Bargaining for National Security: The Postwar Disarmament Negotiations*. Columbia: University of South Carolina Press, 1988.

Kaplan, Morton. *System and Process in International Politics*. New York: Wiley, 1957.

Mayers, Teena Karsa. *Understanding Nuclear Weapons and Arms Control*, 3rd rev. ed. Washington, D.C.: Pergamon-Brassey's, 1986.

Sabrosky, Alan Ned, ed. *Polarity and War: The Changing Structure of International Conflict*. Boulder, Colo.: Westview Press, 1985.

FOURTEEN

Political Paths to Peace: International Law and Organization

In the conflict of arms, laws must be silent.

HUGO GROTIUS, 1625

Everything that is done in international affairs must be done from the viewpoint of whether it will advance or hinder the establishment of world government.

ALBERT EINSTEIN, 1946

Since antiquity, two primary paths to peace have been pursued. One emphasizes the use of *military* power to deter war. The other seeks avoidance of war through *political* solutions. Advocates of the latter approach maintain that the outbreak of war is symptomatic of the failure of politics and, in the words of Emil Brunner, regard the widely accepted claim of the theoretician Karl von Clausewitz that "war is the *ultima ratio* of politics" as "simply a superstition."

In this chapter, we consider a series of ideas associated with the political pursuit of world peace. Although they differ in important ways, they converge on the conviction that the prospects for world order can be enhanced through appropriate political and institutional strategies.

INTERNATIONAL LAW AND WORLD ORDER

Legal procedures are a potential source for the peaceful control of interstate conflict, but their contribution has often been questioned. Because legal orders are created to deter violence and are evaluated according to their ability to perform this function (Falk, 1968), the recurrence of war has led some critics to conclude that international law is irrelevant, inapplicable, and impotent. International law appears to skeptics as "weak and defenseless," hopelessly "vague," "in its infancy," and debilitated by "the virtual absence of a reliable, powerful, impartial enforcement machinery" (see Fried, 1971). Noting the frequency with which states ignore international law when their

455

national interests appear to require it, many have asked, Is international law really law?

For many reasons, the answer to this question is clearly in the affirmative. Although international law performs imperfectly, like all systems of law, it is relied on daily by governments, international organizations, multinational corporations, and individuals to redress grievances (see Joyner, 1988; Kim, 1985). The vast majority of this regulatory activity is focused on routinized transnational intercourse in such areas as commerce, communications, and travel, in which the record of performance and compliance compares favorably with that achieved in domestic legal systems (Brownlie, 1981). Sometimes referred to as *private* international law, this legal domain is largely invisible to the public because its accomplishments only infrequently command public attention. Yet private international law is the locus for all but a small fraction of international legal activities, and it is here that the majority of transnational disputes are regularly and successfully settled.

In contrast, *public* international law, which addresses government-to-government relations, captures the headlines; it also captures most of the criticism, for it is here that failures, when they occur, are so conspicuous. This is especially true with respect to the high politics of peace and security and particularly issues involving the use of force. It is here that cynical views tend to be directed, like that expressed by Israeli Ambassador Abba Eban (1983), who claimed, "International law is that law which the wicked do not obey and the righteous do not enforce." It is here, then, where it is appropriate to ask, Is international law really law?

Because we are concerned in this chapter with the capacity of public international law to control global conflict, it is important to examine its attributes. Our discussion emphasizes only the body of international law and the institutional machinery designed to manage it that pertains to the maintenance of world order—that is, it emphasizes precisely that segment of international law popularly regarded as most deficient.[1]

The Nature of Law at the International Level

International law is generally defined as the body of rules that governs the conduct of states in their relations with one another.[2] It derives from prece-

---

1. The dichotomy between private and public law conforms in some respects to the separation that international law itself sometimes makes between the law of peace and the law of war.

2. This definition avoids the controversy created by interpretations of law as "commands" from a sovereign authority that restrain its subjects from behaving in a particular manner, for as we shall see, the international system lacks a central, law-giving authority. The absence of central authorities and institutions, which has characterized the state system since its inception with the Peace of Westphalia in 1648, contributes to the notion that international law is, say, "positive morality," but not really law as it is known in domestic (municipal) systems. The view reflects the "command theory of law" associated with the legal philosopher John Austin, which suggests that law works because it is a command backed by superior force.

In fact, however, the command theory of law is as inappropriate to an understanding of why governments obey the law in domestic systems as it is at the international level. As Roger Fisher

dents found in the historical development of the international political system itself, on which it continues to rest (Kaplan and Katzenbach, 1961). The *corpus juris gentium* (the body of the law of nations) has grown considerably over the past three centuries, changing according to custom and state practice. A (selective) inventory of some of the legal principles relevant to the control of war illuminates the nature of this general body of rules.[3]

PRINCIPLES OF INTERNATIONAL LAW   No principle of international law is more important than the doctrine of state *sovereignty*. Sovereignty means that no authority in the global hierarchy is legally above the state, except the authority that the state voluntarily confers on the organizations that it creates. Indeed, in foreign policy, international law "permits a complete freedom of action" (Parry, 1968) and maintains that the preservation of sovereignty is the primary foreign policy objective of states.

Nearly every tenet of international law supports and elaborates the cardinal principle that the subjects of international law are independent, sovereign nation-states. For instance, state sovereignty justifies the principle of the equality of states. *Equality* stipulates that each state is entitled to full respect by other states and full protection of the legal rules that the system acknowledges (but it does not assume that all are equal in military power, resources, or size). As a corollary, the right of independence guarantees states autonomy in their internal affairs and external relations, under the logic that the independence of each presumes that of all others.

Furthermore, international law stipulates that states must not interfere in the internal affairs of other states. The *noninterference* principle forms the basis for the states' duty of *nonintervention*, that is, the duty to refrain from uninvited involvement in activities within another's borders. States have routinely violated this classic norm in recent decades as their capabilities to penetrate other countries through new channels (telecommunications and clandestine operations, for example) have become more varied and sophisticated. They also have intervened through classic military means. Nonetheless,

---

(1969) observes, in dealing with national governments, domestic law "is backed up by less force than is international law." Yet governments routinely comply with domestic (municipal) law because the political costs of failing to do so outweigh the gains realized from breaking the law. Thus the president of the United States routinely complies with the decisions of the Supreme Court even if they run counter to what the president wants—and even though the president (executive branch) is in charge of the force presumed to make law work. The best example, perhaps, is when President Richard Nixon complied with the U.S. Supreme Court's edict in 1974 that he surrender tape recordings that were sought as evidence by the House Judiciary Committee in its impeachment proceedings against him in the Watergate scandal. No superior force compelled Nixon to abide by the Court's rulings, but failing to do so would have profoundly, and adversely, affected the political consequences that Nixon faced.

Similarly, at the international level, states routinely abide by international law, not because a superior force backs up authoritative commands, but because law affects the political climate in which they must make choices (see Fisher, 1969, for elaboration).

3. Reviews of the rules of international law are lengthy and often complicated. Von Glahn (1986); Akehurst (1987); Brownlie (1973); and Sørensen (1968) are representative. The discussion here follows Sørensen.

the rule of noninterference is consistent with the right of states to exercise jurisdiction over only their own territory; each is granted control over practically all things on, under, or above its bounded territory. (There are exceptions to which states have agreed and that have been codified in international law, such as immunity for other nations' diplomatic envoys while they represent their country abroad, but the premise of territorial integrity remains sacrosanct.)[4]

In practice, domestic jurisdiction permits a state to establish and interpret whatever laws it wishes for its own citizens, including the rules for determining the conditions under which individuals can acquire citizenship.[5] It can create whatever type of political system or form of government it desires without regard to its acceptability to other states. It also has freedom to regulate economic transactions within its boundaries, and it is empowered to compel those living on its soil to fight—and die, if necessary—for the state's survival.[6]

To enjoy the many legal prerogatives that *statehood* confers, those aspiring to become members of the international legal system must first acquire that privileged status. The Montevideo Convention of 1933 on the Rights and Duties of States summarizes the major components of statehood. A political entity aspiring to it must possess a permanent population, a well-defined territory, and a government capable of ruling its citizens (claiming legitimacy) and of entering into formal diplomatic relations with other states. Other rules specify how and when these conditions are satisfied. Essentially, the acquisition of statehood is dependent on a political entity's recognition as such by other states. Whether or not a state exists thus rests in the hands of other states;

---

4. It was the violation of this principle by Iran when American diplomats were incarcerated in 1979 that distinguished that situation from other hostage takings or acts of terrorism. As the World Court explained in its 1980 ruling in favor of the United States, "This case is unique and of very particular gravity because here it is not only private individuals or groups that have disregarded and set at naught the inviolability of a foreign embassy, but the Government of the receiving state itself." The principle of diplomatic immunity—which rules out the prosecution of diplomatic personnel for almost any offense, from routine parking violations to murder—also played a part in Britain's decision in 1984 to break diplomatic relations with Libya but not to prosecute its embassy staff after members of it machine-gunned a British policewoman and fourteen anti-Qaddafi demonstrators in London.

5. There are different conventions regarding the acquisition of nationality. Two principles generally have been selected to confer nationality—*jus soli* (citizenship is determined by the state on whose territory the birth took place) or *jus sanguinis* (nationality is acquired by birth from descent from a parent of a national). In some states a combination of these two principles governs.

6. Because the state is under the legal influence of no superior power, sovereignty is absolute—states are the only legitimate subjects of international law. Individuals and transnational institutions, although of increasing concern to international law, do not have sovereign rights; they have gained standing only because states see benefits in making them for limited purposes the subjects of international law. It has been said in this context that "laws are made to protect the state from the individual and not the individual from the state" (noted in Gottlieb, 1982). It should be remembered, however, that with the dramatic expansion of transnational activities undertaken by individuals, multinational corporations, and other transnational entities have come new rules to protect the rights of these actors, even when that protection has meant a reduction of the state's control over them.

that is, preexisting states are entitled to extend *diplomatic recognition* to another entity. *De facto* recognition is provisional and capable of being withdrawn in the event that the recognized government is superseded by another; it does not carry with it the exchange of diplomatic representatives or other legal benefits and responsibilities. The government that is recognized *de jure*, on the other hand, obtains full legal and diplomatic privileges from the granting state. The distinction emphasizes that recognition is a political tool of international law, implying approval or disapproval of a government.

Today, with the exception of Antarctica, no significant land mass remains *terra nullius* (territory belonging legally to no one).[7] Because, with the exception of a few trust territories under the control of the United Nations, nearly all of the earth's land surfaces are now within some state's sovereign control, none remains for colonization, and the birth of a new state must necessarily be at the expense of an existing one. Hence, the recognition of a new state almost always means the recognition of a new government's control over a particular piece of territory. Because recognition is a voluntary political act, *nonrecognition* is a legally institutionalized form of public insult to a government aspiring to be accepted as legitimate by other governments, a form of sanction against an unwanted political regime.

The doctrine of *neutrality* flows from the concept of sovereignty and enables states to avoid taking sides in disputes between other contending parties, thereby enhancing their ability to avoid involvement in others' fights while simultaneously confining their scope. On the other hand, international law prescribes that states seek to negotiate their disputes, and it spells out rules for the conduct of negotiations (but it does not obligate nations to reach agreement or to resolve their disputes peacefully).

States are free to enter into treaty arrangements with other states. Again, a large body of rules specifies how treaties are to be activated and interpreted. International law holds that treaties voluntarily entered into are binding (*pacta sunt servanda*), but it also reserves for states the right to unilaterally abrogate treaties previously agreed to by reference to the escape clause known as *rebus sic stantibus*—the principle that a treaty is binding only as long as there is no vital change in the circumstances that existed when the treaty was concluded.

The right of self-defense reinforces a state's ability to do whatever it deems necessary to safeguard its independence. The doctrine of *military necessity* justifies taking "protective" military measures to guard national interests.

---

7. The Antarctic Treaty, put into force with the support of the superpowers in 1961, places this territory outside the jurisdiction of any state. Antarctica is administered jointly by a number of states, including the United States and the Soviet Union. Recently, the Antarctic regime has been challenged by some Third World nations, who wish access to its considerable resources. These conflicting claims to sovereignty may jeopardize the regime's stability—and ultimately peace in a world region that has thus far avoided violent conflict. Nonetheless, the treaty, which by 1988 had been ratified by thirty-five states, serves as a paragon of the potential for international law to make an important contribution to the peaceful management of a portion of the global habitat.

From this it is a short step to the traditional *jus ad bellum* (the right to resort to war) and to the claim that states have an unlimited right both to threaten and to make war. Indeed, the legal justification for belligerency "in defense of the system's rules" (Kelsen, 1945) or for "humanitarian" purposes enjoys a long history in international law. When national interests were perceived to demand it, states were legally free to engage in a variety of forceful self-help measures, including war.

Laws also specify conditions under which coercive procedures short of war are legitimate. Acts such as military occupations, blockades, embargoes, and boycotts are acceptable means to redress grievances, as are reprisals, retortions, invasions, shows of strength, and mobilizations as forms of retaliation.

Jus belli (the law of war) comprises a significant proportion of the body of law among nations, including rules for declaring, conducting, and terminating war as well as prohibiting certain weapons and nonhumanitarian practices during war itself. States have the right to judge the propriety of their conduct with respect to many of these activities. As the eminent publicist J. L. Brierly (1944) concluded, international law thus creates a seemingly curious system wherein states are "legally bound to respect each other's independence and other rights, and yet free to attack each other at will."

STRUCTURAL ATTRIBUTES OF INTERNATIONAL LAW   Sovereignty and the legal principles derived from it shape the international political system and reinforce the anarchical, state-centric nature of contemporary world politics. The global condition is thus legally dependent on what governments elect to do with one another and to their own populations, as well as the kinds of rules they voluntarily support. It is a legal system by and for them.

Because the international legal system depends so much on the attitudes and behaviors of those it governs, many theorists regard it as structurally defective. Formal legal institutions (resembling those within states) capable of performing its essential functions do not exist at the international level. Because of this, critics make the following points.

First, every legal system must make rules through recognized procedures, but in world politics a legislative body capable of creating the law does not exist. Rules are made only when states willingly observe them or embrace them in the treaties to which they voluntarily subscribe. There is no systematic method of amending or revoking them. Noteworthy in this respect are the provisions of Article 38 of the Statute of the International Court of Justice (or World Court), generally accepted as the authoritative statement on the sources of international law. It states that international law derives from (1) custom, (2) international treaties and agreements, (3) national and international court decisions, (4) the writings of legal authorities and specialists, and (5) the "general principles" of law recognized since the Roman Empire as part of "natural law" and "right reason" and perceived as inherent in the legal systems of all states.[8] The absence of any reference to a world parliament or congress reflects the lack of global legislative mechanisms.

Second, every legal system must interpret the rules enacted, but in world politics no authoritative judicial body is empowered to identify the rules accepted by states, record the substantive precepts reached, specify when and how the rules apply, and identify instances of violation. Instead, states are responsible for performing these tasks themselves according to their own definition and concept of justice. The World Court does not have the power to perform these functions without states' consent. Furthermore, the use of the court is not required, and compliance with its verdicts is not mandatory.

Finally, every legal system must execute the law, but in world politics there is no executive body capable of enforcing the rules. The United Nations Security Council may try to enforce a World Court ruling, but usually it is enforced (if at all) through the self-help procedures of individual states. Compliance is thus voluntary, and retaliatory sanctions are exercised by one state against another if and when it chooses to punish it for its perceived violation of the states' rights or the system's rules. The whole system rests, therefore, on states' willingness to abide by the rules to which they consent and on the ability of each to enforce through reprisals or other measures the norms of behavior it values. No centralized enforcement procedures exist.

In sum, international law rests on a consensual foundation: States are accountable to no one and abide by only those regulations to which they freely subscribe. This reinforces the self-help nature of the international system generally: The rules governing interactions among states are made by the states themselves (not by a higher authority). Each state can determine what the rules are, when they apply, and when and how they should be enforced. Given the consensual nature of international law, nearly anything becomes permissible as long as it is justified as contributing to the state's self-preservation, which is the highest value in the system. But when everyone is above the law, can anyone be ruled by it?

Other attributes of the international legal order also make its character suspect. Five of the more conspicuous of its supposed structural defects warrant comment.

❏ *International law lacks universality*. An effective legal system must represent the norms shared by those it governs. According to the precept of Roman law *ubi societas, ibi jus* (where there is society, there is law), the existence of community values is the minimal requirement for the formation of a legal system. The contemporary international order is

---

8. The law of treaties comprises by far the largest proportion of the law of nations. Treaties have a lawmaking function, and the precedents they establish contribute to the creation of rules for the signatory parties. The number and diversity of treaties have grown rapidly as states have negotiated agreements covering an increasing array of new problems.

culturally and ideologically heterogeneous and lacks a common value consensus (Bozeman, 1971). Instead of an integrated community of nations, diverse systems of public order exist throughout the global system (McDougal and Lasswell, 1959). The claim that the Western-based international legal order approximates universality is contradicted by state practice and by the simultaneous operation of often incompatible legal traditions throughout the world.

❑ *International law perpetuates competition among states and justifies the pursuit of national advantage without regard to morality or justice.* Indeed, international law is said to legitimize the drive for superiority rather than to restrain it. Hence, international law contributes to conflict, not just cooperation (Lissitzyn, 1963). Self-help does not control power; it is a concession to power. By worshiping the unbridled autonomy of sovereign independence, international law follows the "iron law of politics"—that legal obligations must yield to the national interest (Morgenthau, 1973).

As in any legal system, in international politics the legal thing to do is not necessarily the moral thing to do (see Nardin, 1983). Is it moral to allow some to starve while others live in comparative opulence?

❑ *International law is an instrument of the powerful to oppress the weak.* In a voluntary consent system, the rules to which the powerful willingly agree are usually those that serve their interests. In the contemporary international political system, these tend to preserve the existing hierarchy, to perpetuate the privileges of the powerful, and to further the discrepancy between the dominant and the subordinate. International law protects the prerogatives of the haves and discounts the aspirations of the have-nots (see Friedheim, 1965). Thus it is sometimes claimed that international law supports the so-called structural violence that afflicts world politics, which improves the welfare of the powerful at the expense of the weak (see Galtung, 1969).

International law reflects the legal preferences of the Western European actors who established its basic rules. Many Third World states do not share the world view expressed in Western culture and resent their dependence on rules outside their own traditions perceived to be biased and inimical to their own needs.

Even the process of law enforcement favors the strong over the weak. Because states alone monopolize the legitimate means whereby international law is enforced, enforcement is left "to the vicissitudes of the distribution of power between the violator of the law and the victim of the violation. It makes it easy for the strong both to violate the law and to enforce it, and consequently puts the rights of the weak in jeopardy. A great power can violate the rights of a small nation without having to fear effective sanctions on the latter's part" (Morgenthau, 1973).

❑ *International law is little more than a justification of existing practices.* The process of lawmaking at the international level says that when a particular behavior pattern becomes widespread, it becomes legally obligatory. Rules *of* behavior come to be rules *for* behavior (Hoffmann, 1971). Like laws in primitive societies that are created in the absence of formal government, this tendency explains why custom is an important source of international law. Kelsen's contention that states ought to behave as they have customarily behaved (see Onuf, 1982) and Hoebel's (1961) dictum that "what the most do, others should do," reflect this perspective in positivist international legal theory.[9] Most (positivist) theorists assert that if a type of behavior, such as war, occurs frequently, then it ought to be legally approved. The dependence of rules on custom means that international law is shaped by the policies of states, not vice versa.

In fact, relatively little international law has been codified, in part because it is difficult to identify what principles have sufficient consensual support to be classified as legal.[10] Often what has been codified deals with the relatively trivial or with agreed-upon norms so hopelessly vague (such as "treaties ought to be fulfilled in good faith") that their impact on behavior is minimal, and in many areas international law remains silent. Law thus modifies state practice less than it is modified by it.

❑ *Ambiguity and the lack of central institutions encourage the use of international law for propaganda purposes.* When states alone define the rules and interpret them, almost any action is legitimate. "The problem here," observes Samuel Kim (1985), "is that every declaratory statement of principles . . . embodies mutually contradictory principles: for example, the [UN] Charter principle of non-threat and non-use of force (Article 2) versus the principle of the inherent right of individual or collective self-defense (Article 51)." This makes international law a foreign policy tool, a symbol of rectitude, instead of a guide to conduct. The malleability of international law for policy purposes led Quincy Wright (1953) to note that most states characteristically use international law to get what they can and to justify what they have obtained.

Other deficiencies in contemporary international law could be added to this list. But these are sufficient to demonstrate the inadequacies generally perceived to afflict the international legal order. International law does not police states' actions. They retain the right to define for themselves what the

---

9. Positivists stress states' practices and customs as the most important sources from which laws derive. In the absence of formal machinery for creating rules at the international level, positivist theories turn to customary rules for evidence of what the law is. Positivists seek evidence of customary practice by observing leaders' foreign policy pronouncements, repeated usage in conventions voluntarily accepted by states, general practice (by an overwhelmingly large number of states), judicial decisions of national and international tribunals, and legal principles stated in United Nations resolutions.

10. For instance, international law does not clearly define the conditions that make armed violence illegal. Can a state engage in covert activity, supporting and arming rebels within another country? Is "anticolonialist" intervention in the name of self-determination permissible? What are the differences among involvement, interference, and intervention? Are acts of terrorism illegal when committed by individuals but legal when practiced by states? The United Nations' Definition of Aggression (Resolution 3314, 1974) does not define aggression precisely (Kim, 1985). The ambiguity inherent in these questions is illustrated by the United States' invasion of Grenada in 1983, an overt military action regarded by some as a violation of international law but by others as supported by it.

law is. International law is most developed and consistently followed in the domain of low politics remote from states' security interests, according to this viewpoint. It is relatively primitive when states' security is at issue. It is here that nations are least inclined to agree. When national survival is perceived to be at stake, legal restraints no longer control behavior.

The Relevance of International Law

International law is clearly fraught with deficiencies, but the proposition that it is irrelevant to contemporary international politics can be challenged on both theoretical and empirical grounds.

Empirically, it is clear that states themselves do not deem international law irrelevant. In fact, they attach much importance to it and expend considerable resources to affect its evolution. All are decidedly interested in revising it in ways that serve their purposes and in maintaining those rules already in operation that advance their own interests. "If international law were meaningless as some of the more extreme 'realistic' theorists suggest," George Quester (1971) observes, "reasonable men would not spend so much time haggling and fighting over its interpretation."

An important reason why nations value international law is because their long-term political interests are served by a legal system that promotes a common understanding of the "rules of the game." Law helps shape expectations, and common rules enhance predictability in international affairs. This reduces uncertainty and facilitates planning:

> In the most primitive sense international law posits boundaries upon conflict. These boundaries function as limits upon the means available to states in contention with one another. . . . Among the most essential boundary rules the following may be mentioned: 1. No concerted use of military force across international boundaries for unspecified objectives; 2. No use of nuclear weapons to influence outcomes . . . ; 3. No overt military intervention . . . within a state belonging to a rival superpower's bloc or sphere of influence; 4. No extension of the scope of overt violence associated with an internal war . . . across an international frontier; 5. No insistence upon victory in a violent encounter. . . . (Falk, 1970: 52–53)

International law also provides a mechanism for communication between states. It is an "institutional device for communicating to the policy makers of various states a consensus on the nature of the international system," that is, for offering a definition of international reality (Coplin, 1975). Such communication helps contribute to the formation of a shared global political culture. But the consensus that international norms express is imperfect (what Coplin, 1966, calls an "immature political culture") because the system's members usually agree on certain general values at the same time that they fail to recognize the implications of these values for their own behavior.

These functions of international law serve every member of the international system, and the benefits they confer explain why international law receives states' support and why states usually accommodate voluntarily their actions and policies to it. World politics would undoubtedly be worse off in the absence of this system, however inchoate and primitive it might be.

It is nonetheless tempting to agree with the critics that the lack of an authority possessing supranational sanctioning powers makes international law useless for one of its most important functions, the control of violence. The view is strengthened by comparisons of the international legal order with nation-states' highly centralized systems, but the comparison is questionable. The differences between domestic (municipal) and international law hide similarities and obscure the really important comparative question: Which type of legal order is more effective? Comparison invites the specious conclusion that the presence of a formal legal structure (a centralized, vertical system of law) is automatically superior to the decentralized, self-help, horizontal system that characterizes the international legal system.

The absence of a reliable procedure of identifying a violation of international law and of an authority monopolizing the instruments to enforce international rules does not mean that states exercise their sovereign freedoms without restraint or routinely disobey existing customs and rules. A voluntary compliance system need not be normless, with a high incidence of disrespect for rules. In fact, disobedience is rare. States *do* police themselves, and they *do* comply with existing laws, even though they do not have to and the means to compel compliance are haphazard and imperfect. "The reality as demonstrated through their behavior," Christopher Joyner (1988) observes, "is that states do accept international law as law and, even more significant, in the vast majority of instances they usually obey it."

Why is this so? Self-restraint often works because even the most powerful states appreciate its benefits. International reputations are important. Those who play the game of international politics by recognized rules are rewarded. An enlightened view of one's long-term self-interests recommends voluntary compliance with agreements and deference to legal obligations. A preference for order over disorder is also rooted in self-interest. Those who ignore international law or who break customary norms may pay costs for doing as they please; other nations thereafter may be reluctant to cooperate with them. Reprisals and retaliation by those victimized by a transgression are also to be feared, which inhibits the temptation to break a rule. Rule breakers also face criticism from abroad and perhaps at home, and a diplomatically costly loss of international prestige. Because law provides sanctions for the breach of treaties and norms, only the most ambitious or reckless state is apt to disregard it.

Evidence that unorganized or primitive legal systems succeed in containing violence and ensuring compliance with rules is revealing (Masters, 1969). Even in systems in which reliable coercive sanctions are absent, other self-help measures may operate effectively. As Michael Barkun (1968) notes, "law without sanctions" is possible in the absence of the kinds of institutionalized procedures for punishing rule violation typically found in municipal legal systems.

Conversely, the mere presence of formal institutions for rule enforcement is no guarantee of rule compliance. Indeed, no legal system is capable of deterring all of its members from breaking existing laws. Thus it is a mistake to expect any legal system, including the international legal system, to prevent all criminal behavior or to insist that any violation of the law proves the inadequacy of the legal structure. That asks too much of law. Correspondingly, every breakdown of international law should not be interpreted as confirming general international lawlessness any more than a single murder or burglary in a domestic system should be regarded as indicating the absence of law. Law is designed to deter crime, but it is unreasonable to expect it to prevent it.

Similarly, the illegal use of force to settle a dispute does not indicate that international law generally has failed, however unwelcome that violation. All legal systems are strained under conditions of crisis, and few, when tested severely, are able to contain all violence. As many people have died from civil wars as have perished from wars between sovereign states (see Small and Singer, 1982). By this bloody criterion, the allegedly "deficient" international legal system would appear to be performing its central job—the prevention of interstate violence—more effectively than do the supposedly more sophisticated systems found in domestic societies. Perhaps the usual criteria by which legal systems are evaluated are dubious. Perhaps we should be less concerned with structures and institutions and more with performance. If so, the proposition that international law is irrelevant to the containment of violence hardly seems warranted (Brownlie, 1981).

As we noted, international law also contributes to the regulation of the routinized transactions constantly carried out across national borders on a daily basis worldwide. As transnational contacts among nations have become more frequent, the need for rules to manage them has grown. International law has responded to that need. States routinely abide by the rules regulating international trade, foreign travel, mail flows, currency exchange, debt obligations, and similar types of transactions. Although the development and application of international rules governing these transactions remain somewhat primitive, their content is often sophisticated. The growth of international litigation, for example, has been most dramatic in the area of routine, non-political transactions; yet compliance with regulations in these areas has been consistently high. Thus, mutually beneficial collaborative experiences seem to generate expectations for their continuation. The ascendance of new kinds of nonstate actors has also created a need for new laws to regulate their internal administration as well as their intercourse with one another and with the nations with which they come into contact.[11] Here again international law has responded.

---

11. The expansion of the number and competencies of international organizations has stimulated the growth of international law. Resolutions by the United Nations General Assembly perform a lawmaking function, for instance, and these rules strengthen further the legal ties that bind states together. Noteworthy is the legislation that has emerged through this mechanism in the areas of decolonization, the New International Economic Order, and *apartheid*.

Equally important is the long-term contribution of the growth of international law in these areas to the avoidance of international conflict. To use regime parlance (recall Chapter 2), the principles, rules, and decision-making procedures that give order and regularity to numerous issue-areas on the global agenda reduce states' incentives to resort to force to resolve them to their own satisfaction. Consider the agreements that have been struck to deal with the world economy, the high seas, human rights, and environmental protection, and the impressive degree to which regime participants regard them as binding and abide by their provisions (see Kim, 1985; Soroos, 1986). By removing these issues from possible resolution by armed force, the potential sources for discord, disagreement, and violence may have been reduced.

Regrettably, however, the growth of international norms in these areas has not been matched by similar growth in areas proximate to states' vital security interests. As Alberto R. Coll (1986) warns, "The international legal norms on the use of force are in a state of crisis that threatens to engulf international law itself." There remains, therefore, great need to strengthen the rules inhibiting the use of force if peace is to be preserved.

Efforts to bring interstate disputes under the control of an international legal order stem from states' need in a decentralized, anarchical world to coordinate their decision making so as to avoid unnecessary injury to themselves. Because self-interests are served by states' willingness to collaborate and voluntarily restrain their freedom of choice, they increasingly have participated together in decision making according to agreed-upon rules compatible with their needs. This helps make an anarchical world nonetheless an orderly world.

Legal Procedures for Conflict Management

As useful as international law is and as promising as the prospects for its further development might be, the skeptic might counter by noting that these contributions clearly fail to address the most destructive of all behavior—war. Does not international law encourage war by making rules for it? Does it therefore fail to perform the most vital function of law, the deterrence of violence?

There are several responses to these important questions. First, international law as presently conceived is not intended to prevent all warfare. Aggressive war is illegal, but defensive war is not. Therefore, it would be a mistake to claim that international law has broken down whenever war has broken out.

Second, instead of doing away with war, international law preserves it as a sanction against the breaking of rules. Thus war is a device of last resort to punish aggressors and thereby maintain the system's legal framework.

Third, international law is an institutional substitute for war. That is, there are legal mechanisms that enable states to resolve their conflicts before they erupt into open hostilities. In this sense, legal procedures can be an alternative to war, if not a deterrent to it, because in theory they may make recourse to violence unnecessary and thereby preserve peace.

Included among the legal means of conflict resolution (that is, the methods of dispute resolution short of force) are procedures for registering protests, expressing denials, making accusations, withdrawing ambassadors, and articulating threats, all in the context of the laws of negotiation. Similarly, international law has clear rules regarding the use of mediation (when a third party proposes a nonbinding solution to a controversy between two other states, as illustrated by President Carter's historic mediation at the 1978 Camp David meeting between the leaders of Egypt and Israel); good offices (when a third party offers a location for discussions among disputants but does not participate in the actual negotiations, as Switzerland often does); and conciliation (when a third party assists both sides but does not offer any solution). Two more powerful techniques for settling interstate disputes are arbitration (when a third party gives a binding decision through an *ad hoc* forum) and adjudication (when a third party offers a binding decision through an institutionalized tribunal, such as a court). All of these mechanisms are based on the expectation that pacific (that is, non-warlike) means can resolve controversies.

The historical record provides support for the view that states are able to resolve their differences short of war. Of ninety-seven interstate conflicts between 1919 and 1986, for instance, K. J. Holsti (1988: 420) found 168 attempts by the contending parties to negotiate, mediate, adjudicate, or otherwise settle their disputes through formal procedures of conflict resolution (note that one conflict may entail several types of settlement attempts). Sixty-eight of these attempts were successful. In other words, since World War I, states have been able to resolve their differences 70 percent of the time through use of one or more pacific settlement procedures. This proportion is not overwhelming, but it also seems likely that if legal procedures had not been available, at least some of these sixty-eight cases would have resulted in settlement by force. In this sense, at least, law has made a positive contribution to peace.

This is not to suggest, however, that international adjudicative machinery is well developed or functionally effective. Nowhere is this more evident than with the International Court of Justice (ICJ), presumably created as the highest court on earth for the judicial settlement of interstate disputes, but in practice a very inactive legal institution. Between 1946 and 1986, it heard only fifty-three contentious cases and handed down only seventeen advisory opinions; worse still, only twenty-three of the contentious cases resulted in judgments (Riggs and Plano, 1988: 194–195).

Part of the reason for this is that the court's jurisdiction is not compulsory. Although all members of the United Nations are members of the court, only a fraction have affirmed their willingness to accept automatically the court's jurisdiction in conflicts involving them. The United States, for example, defines its position in the so-called Connally amendment (a reservation attached to the statute of the World Court by the Senate in 1946), which defends U.S. sovereignty by reserving for the United States the right to determine the cases in which it will allow the court jurisdiction.

The World Court's weakness against powerful states was dramatized in 1984, when the Reagan administration announced that it would unilaterally withdraw from the World Court's jurisdiction disputes between the United States and Central American countries. What provoked the move was Nicaragua's charge that the United States Central Intelligence Agency was illegally trying to "overthrow and destabilize" the Sandinista government by assisting in the mining of Nicaraguan ports and otherwise supplying money, military assistance, and training to the rebel *contra* forces. In denying the tribunal's authority, the United States was certainly not acting without precedent; others had done so previously. But by thumbing its nose at the court and the rule of law it represents, some felt that the United States had become the "international outlaw."[12] Others, however, felt that the United States was acting within its rights and appropriately in defense of its interests. The World Court supported the former view. In a preliminary judgment handed down in 1984, the Court (by a vote of fifteen to one), without addressing the jurisdictional issue, ruled as follows:

> The right to sovereignty and to political independence possessed by the Republic of Nicaragua, like any other state of the region or of the world, should be fully respected and should not in any way be jeopardized by any military and paramilitary activities which are prohibited by the principles of international law, in particular the principle that states should refrain in their international relations from the threat or the use of force against the territorial integrity or the political independence of any state, and the principle concerning the duty not to intervene in matters within the domestic jurisdiction of a state, principles embodied in the United Nations Charter and the Charter of the Organization of American States. (*New York Times*, May 11, 1984, p. 8)

Most judicial settlements of conflicts in fact take place in the domestic courts of one of the contestants, rather than in international or supranational tribunals. Here there is strong evidence of compliance with decisions that are reached—although, not surprisingly, there is also evidence of ethnocentricism and partiality in the judicial process (Falk, 1964, Lillich, 1972; Nagel, 1969).

Apart from mechanisms for dispute settlement, international law has shown a capacity to change in response to changing global conditions, and some of these changes have affected the world climate of opinion regarding

---

12. The American Society of International Law voted overwhelmingly (April 12, 1984) to urge the United States to reverse its decision. Harvard Law Professor Abram Chayes, who earlier in his career laid the legal foundations for the Kennedy administration's naval quarantine of Cuba during the 1962 missile crisis with the Soviet Union, elected to represent Nicaragua in its suit against the United States. Believing that the Nicaraguan leaders were acting "to uphold the rule of law in international affairs," Chayes stated that he thought it appropriate for the United States, which "purports to be bound by the rule of law," to be judged under "appropriate international procedures." He stated that "there is nothing wrong with holding the United States to its own best standards and best principles" (*New York Times*, April 11, 1983).

international politics and war. For example, there has been a gradual but steady decline in the international community's tolerance of war and a growing disaffection with the absolute right of states to employ force to achieve their foreign policy objectives, particularly in the twentieth century. Even the classic concept of the so-called just war (the circumstances in which use of force in self-defense is justified) has become the target of criticism and increasingly restrictive definitions of the just war precept have gained acceptance (see Johnson, 1984).

The Hague conferences of 1899 and 1907, which devised rules for limiting the violence of war, were early developments in shaping new attitudes toward war. However, World War I revealed that the rules of warfare could neither contain destruction nor reduce its scope. In fact, the rules of warfare may have inadvertently contributed to the level of destruction by helping maintain and support the rule of force.

However, in the aftermath of World War I and in response to it, a decisive step was taken with the signing of the Covenant of the League of Nations. Articles 11 to 17 of the covenant stipulated that in no case could a state resort to war until three months after a judicial determination by the League had elapsed. Another important signal that international values were changing occurred in 1928 with the signing of the Treaty Providing for the Renunciation of War As an Instrument of National Policy. Known as the Kellogg–Briand Pact (officially the Pact of Paris), this treaty (signed by sixty-two states by 1939) for the first time prohibited recourse to force as an instrument of national policy. The prohibition was reaffirmed in the 1933 Anti-War Treaty of Rio de Janeiro and in the Nuremberg war crimes trials at the end of World War II, both of which spoke of war as "the supreme international crime." The United Nations Charter (Article 2) reflected the emergent view of warfare by unequivocally outlawing war and the threat of war in pursuit of national political objectives.

One survey (Kegley, 1982; Raymond, 1980) of the contents of major international legal texts from 1810 to the present demonstrates the transformation of international values regarding warfare (see Figure 14.1). Clearly, attitudes in the international environment have changed demonstrably. "The willingness of nations to subscribe, even in principle, to the renunciation of their rights to use force (except in self-defense) is a significant step, an expression of willingness to move in one direction rather than the other, and a disclosure of consensus on the most important aspect of political order in world affairs" (Falk, 1965).[13]

---

13. There are many reasons for this historic transformation in the international community's values. It is tempting to speculate that the most important is the growing awareness of the horrors of modern warfare, that the perceived legitimacy of war has declined in association with each incremental increase in the magnitude, brutality, and destructiveness of war. But this does not suggest that the rejection of war necessarily has been related to changes in the incidence of war. Instead, its rejection has declined more in proportion to increases in the violence of modern warfare than in the frequency of its occurrence.

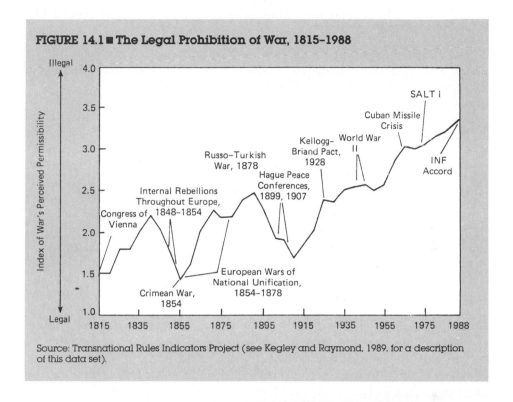

FIGURE 14.1 ■ The Legal Prohibition of War, 1815–1988

Source: Transnational Rules Indicators Project (see Kegley and Raymond, 1989, for a description of this data set).

Even though attitudes toward war have changed, it is difficult to demonstrate that state behavior has also changed. True, since World War II the major powers have avoided direct combat with one another. But they have also frequently used force against other states, and their behavior has not been restrained by legal rules; between 1946 and 1980, France, Great Britain, the United States, and the Soviet Union intervened militarily on seventy-one occasions in ways arguably prohibited by international law. Despite their professed respect for the nonintervention principle, the record indicates that major states exhibit more respect for power than they do for international law (Tillema and Van Wingen, 1982: 220). Still, the rejection of war's permissibility signals a departure from previous standards of conduct and may reduce its incidence. When war is no longer licensed and when the global system itself has abrogated *jus ad bellum* (the right to make war), then *animus belligerandi* (the intention to make war) becomes a crime. Those who initiate war thus become criminals. That may be an important psychological restraint on policymakers' choices. (Political realists, however, would undoubtedly disagree, arguing that aggressive leaders will not be restrained by the mere delegitimization of violence.)

Along with this emerging consensus on the prohibition of war, there has been a growth of law regulating the methods that may be used in war—*jus in bello* (war's means).[14] Although the cynic may conclude that this component of the law of nations comprises little more than instructions for killing, the greater restrictions placed on the weapons that can be used and the conditions under which fighting is permissible may reduce the extent to which conventional wars produce death (see Weston et al., 1980). The objections voiced in international law to the use of poison gas as a military weapon or prohibitions against biological and chemical warfare move world politics toward civility and away from barbarism. So, too, do rules for the treatment of prisoners and the wounded. The rule of noncombatant immunity, prohibiting direct attacks on civilians; the rule of proportionality, requiring that the damage inflicted not be more than that necessary for victory; and the rules of combat limiting the amount and kind of damage that soldiers and their commanders may impose on targets all seek to limit the suffering caused by modern warfare.

Most significant is the emerging consensus proscribing the first use of nuclear weapons. Although this tacit rule is not enforceable, it is instructive that not one of the states capable of breaking it has done so since the United States used two atomic bombs against Japan in 1945. Admittedly, there is tragic irony in the fact that this rule, if ever broken, could destroy the very foundations of civilization as they are presently known. But this should not blind us to the significance of normative restraints on states' behaviors, even though those restraints cannot free humankind from the threat of nuclear annihilation.

Finally, international law helps preserve world peace by improving the prospect for crisis management. At the onset of interstate crises, international law "serves as a sort of signal to tell states which of these clashes are acceptable and which are deserving of retaliation" (D'Amato, 1982). Once under way, norms of conduct contribute to crisis management and negotiation by eliminating the need to decide on a procedure for deciding—and this is no small service.

As norms such as those described become widely accepted, they strengthen the role that legal understandings can play in moderating future conduct. Even the most skeptical of theorists must acknowledge that the existence of international legal norms contributes to a more orderly world. Indeed, it would be difficult to imagine a peaceful world without them.

But whether prevailing global trends will lead to the creation of a more effective legal system remains to be seen. There is evidence that the most

---

14. The most dramatic evidence of this development was the conclusion in 1977 of the four-year Geneva Conference on Humanitarian Law attended by more than one hundred nations. Two protocols were adopted; one added twenty-eight rules to the one principle governing internal wars since the 1949 Geneva Conventions; the other provided new instruments for "Red Cross law" stipulating regulations for the treatment of noncombatants and prisoners of war. Characteristically, North–South issues dominated much of the conference, crosscutting East–West differences about the rules of warfare. Subsequently, in 1980 at Geneva, the United Nations Conference on Prohibition or Restrictions of the Use of Certain Conventional Weapons Which May Be Deemed to Be Excessively Injurious or to Have Indiscriminate Effects adopted a convention and three protocol statements.

complex societies usually possess the most developed legal systems (see Onuf, 1982). Applied to the international level, we can speculate that a transnational society characterized by complex interdependence may develop institutions that are authoritative and capable of effectively enforcing transnational norms. International society may yet impose legal controls on the exercise of military might so as to rely on law instead of the balance of power to keep peace.

The future will nevertheless depend to a considerable extent, as it has in the past, on the purposes to which states choose to put international law. International law's alleged shortcomings lie not with the laws but their creators— nation-states. The intentions of nations acting individually or in concert, and not the slow processes by which legal developments tend to unfold, will be decisive. From this perspective, the prospects are dim that international law will develop into world law, because the international political system has yet to make the transition from an unorganized collectivity of independent units to an organized community or, as John F. Kennedy expressed it, to one in which "a beachhead of cooperation may push back the jungle of suspicion," and the world joins "in creating . . . not a new balance of power, but a new world of law, where the strong are just and the weak secure and the peace preserved."[15] That conclusion leads naturally to a consideration of the role that international organizations have played in maintaining world peace.

INTERNATIONAL ORGANIZATION AND WORLD ORDER

The creation of international institutions designed to preserve world order is a second major political path toward peace. The growth of international organizations designed to protect their members from the threat of war has been persistent, particularly in the twentieth century. To understand this political approach, its theoretical underpinnings must also be understood. Those foundations are exemplified by the expectations about and performance of the United Nations.

The United Nations and the Preservation of Peace

As in the case of its predecessor, the League of Nations, the primary mission of the United Nations, as its charter states, is the "maintenance of international

---

15. There are various reform movements designed to strengthen legal approaches to peace. The World Peace Through World Law movement, for instance, predicates its approach on the belief that the present legal order is inadequately structured to prevent war. Its proponents see substantial reform of existing international legal institutions as a necessary precondition to the establishment of world peace, consistent with the view that to reduce the incidence of interstate violence, legal change must occur. The peace-through-law movement has created a voluminous literature that continues to grow. Clark and Sohn (1966) remains the definitive statement.

peace and security." The stipulation that membership is open to all "peace-loving" countries reaffirms this purpose, as does the charter's requirement that members "settle their international disputes by peaceful means in such a manner that international peace and security, and justice, are not endangered." Moreover, members are pledged to "refrain in their international relations from the threat or use of force against the territorial integrity or political independence of any state."

Collective security is generally regarded as the cornerstone of the United Nations' role in keeping international peace. In principle, collective security stands as an alternative to competitive alliances and the balance of power as mechanisms for maintaining peace among nations. Whereas the balance-of-power concept assumes that each nation, acting in its own self-interest for its individual protection, will form coalitions offsetting others and that the resulting equilibrium will ensure international peace and stability, collective security is a shared approach to peace. It asks that each state take responsibility for every other state's security. Joint action against any transgressor is to be undertaken; and all are to act in concert to check the expansionist drives of any one state or group of states. The superior power of the entire community is presumed sufficient to deter any aggression from occurring in the first place or, failing that, to defeat any violator of the peace.

Although the principle of collective security was considered one of the main tenets of the League of Nations, the history of the interwar years makes clear that it was not successful in preserving peace. The League's inability to muster a collective response to the Italian invasion of Ethiopia and the Japanese invasion of Manchuria signaled the collapse of collective security. Under the leadership of Adolf Hitler, Nazi Germany was the most potent threat to the existing order. It repudiated one element after another of the Versailles peace treaty that formally concluded World War I, and undertook territorial aggrandizement in Europe. As it did so, the League of Nations and the Western democracies proved incapable of stopping the Nazi onslaught. Then—in 1938 at Munich—Germany, Great Britain, and France agreed to the German annexation of a large part of Czechoslovakia in return for what then British Prime Minister Neville Chamberlain called "peace in our time." The appeasement at Munich was nothing more than that. On September 1, 1939, Germany attacked Poland. Shortly thereafter Britain and France declared war on Germany, and World War II commenced.

There are many reasons for the failure of the League of Nations to put collective security into practice. In the aftermath of its failure, some critics noted sadly the perhaps illusory expectations on which the design was built, for many of the preconditions necessary for an effective system of collective security were lacking. Among them was the absence of the United States, which refused to join the organization that President Woodrow Wilson had so vigorously championed. A sense of membership in a common international society was missing, and the idea of collective measures was resisted by the great powers who feared that the collectivity might use its strength against them. Other factors contributed to the undermining of the collective security system, including the tendency to give lip service to the value of general peace but to organize resistance only against those violations deemed threatening to one's own security; the fear of inequities in sharing the risks and costs of an organized response; and the problem of objectively defining an instance of aggression in which all concurred. In the final analysis, states rejected collective security because they feared it would unnecessarily involve them in war and thereby, paradoxically, broaden rather than restrain war.

Furthermore, as a principle, collective security is designed essentially to preserve existing interstate power hierarchies. The perpetuation of the status quo runs counter to the interests and aspirations of the majority at the bottom of the global system's pyramid. The theory's central fallacy was that it expected a state's desire to see other states protected to be as strong as its desire to protect itself. The assumption was not upheld in the interwar period, with the result that collective security was stillborn. The League of Nations never managed to put it into practice.

The architects of the United Nations were painfully aware of this experience and the lessons it suggested. As a consequence, the United Nations rejected resurrecting the principles of collective security and basing the organization on them (see Claude, 1962, 1971). Instead, the United Nations was structured in a manner that partially restored the balance of power as a mechanism for maintaining peace. Through the voting procedures of the Security Council in particular, the principle of individual self-defense was supported, and the United Nations' capacity to ensure collective self-defense was undermined.

The United Nations Charter is replete with evidence that its designers sought to sanctify nation-states as the fundamental units of world politics and to leave their sovereign rights unimpaired. The principle of collective security was given token support in the (unrealistic) assumptions that the Security Council's permanent members would find themselves in agreement on security issues and act in concert to protect the peace. This consensus never materialized and was breached almost from the United Nations' inception. As a result, collective security was not embraced, for at the very least that concept leaves to an international organization the determination of when states are to use force for the collective good. Noteworthy is that collective response to external aggression is contingent on the willingness of the individual member states of the United Nations to agree on a response. This is most evident in the Security Council, in which a veto by any of the five permanent members can block a resolution or enforcement action designed to cope with threats to international peace. Similarly, the General Assembly is severely restricted in its capacity to mount collective action in response to international crises, for it can only initiate studies of conflict situations, call perceived threats to peace and security to the attention of the Security Council, and make recommendations for peacekeeping initiatives. The secretary general and the working staff of the Secretariat are confined by the charter to alerting the Security Council to any situation considered a threat to world peace and providing administrative support for peacekeeping operations that the Security Council initiates. In practice, these restrictions have meant that collective efforts to maintain international peace and security tend to occur only with the consent of the disputing states or when the members of the Security Council are in agreement—a rare event in a postwar world dominated by Cold War issues.

In short, sovereignty reigns supreme. The United Nations is a concession to the independence and nationalistic motives of states; it was not designed to supersede them by placing supranational controls on national initiatives. Inis Claude summarizes the manner in which the principle of collective security was largely bypassed in the United Nations Charter:

> In the final analysis, the San Francisco Conference must be described as having repudiated the doctrine of collective security as the foundation for a general, universally applicable system for the management of power in international relations. The doctrine was given ideological lip service, and a scheme was contrived for making it effective in cases of relatively minor importance. But the new organization reflected the conviction that the concept of collective security has no realistic relevance to the problems posed by conflict among the major powers. (Claude, 1962: 164–165)

Does this realization seriously flaw the United Nations as an instrument for realizing its primary purpose—preserving world peace? To be sure, yes, but only to a degree. The structural deficiencies built into the United Nations resemble and replicate those evident in world politics, rather than providing a meaningful substitute for them. But the United Nations is more than a mere debating society, a forum for discussing world problems, and a theater for nations to dramatize their positions in staged pronouncements. It is also more than an institutionalized arena for the conduct of power politics by its members. Although the United Nations has fallen short of the ideals envisioned by its founders (principally because of the absence of cooperation between at least two of the five permanent members of the Security Council), it has nevertheless made important contributions to the management of global conflicts. Like any adaptive institution, it has responded to changing international circumstances and the advent of new kinds of threats to the peace, thus mirroring transformations in world politics generally.

The conflict between the United States and the Soviet Union that erupted almost simultaneously with the United Nations' founding prevented the organization from pursuing an institutional approach to world peace according to the precepts of collective security. The Korean police action provided a glimmer of hope, but that brief interlude in global responsibility for world peace was so colored by unusual circumstances that it was never a harbinger of things to come. Nor, indeed, was it a true collective security operation; instead, it was largely perceived as an intervention sponsored for and fought by the United States under United Nations auspices. The disillusioning Korean experience proved to be the last "enforcement" mission in which United Nations troops sought to defeat an enemy.

Other, less ambitious military operations to preserve peace were under-taken in the uncertain formative period of the United Nations (including, for example, the United Nations Truce Supervision Organization for the countries contiguous to Israel and the United Nations Military Observer Group in India and Pakistan concerned with the Kashmir cease-fire zone; see Figure 14.2). But for the most part, these experiences revealed the weaknesses of the United Nations' system in dealing with threats to international peace and security or, for that matter, in orchestrating military sanctions generally.

The real innovation in the United Nations' approach to collective conflict management occurred in 1956 when the General Assembly, acting under the Uniting for Peace resolution, created the first United Nations Emergency Force (UNEF) and charged the secretary general with primary responsibility for its operation. The principles of UNEF were quite different from the principle of collective security. The latter emphasized checking aggression through collec-tive enforcement. UNEF, by contrast, emphasized noncoercive activities aimed at reestablishing and maintaining peaceful international intercourse. In particu-lar, UNEF was designed to forestall the superpowers' competitive intrusion into a potentially explosive situation. Similar principles guided the creation of the United Nations Operation in the Congo (ONUC, 1960) and the United Nations Force in Cyprus (UNFICYP, 1964).[16]

Secretary General Dag Hammarskjöld articulated the principles of *preven-tive diplomacy*—a term that has since become virtually synonymous with United Nations peacekeeping—in his annual report to the General Assembly in 1960:

> Preventive diplomacy . . . is of special significance in cases where the original conflict may be said either to be the result of, or to imply risks for, the creation of a power vacuum between the main blocs. Preventive action in such cases must in the first place aim at filling the vacuum so that it will not provoke action from any of the major parties, the initiative for which might be taken for preventive purposes but might in turn lead to counter-action from the other side. The ways in which a vacuum can be filled by the United Nations so as to forestall such initiatives differ from case to case, but they all have this in common: temporarily . . . the United Nations enters the picture on the basis of its noncommitment to any power bloc . . . so as to provide to the extent possible a guarantee in relation to all parties against initiatives from others. (Hammarskjöld, 1965: 402)

---

16. The decisions to conduct those operations were facilitated by the agreement to restrict Soviet and American military participation in them. UNEF-II, created after the 1973 Yom Kippur War, included a military contingent from Poland, the first time a Warsaw Pact member had been included in a United Nations peacekeeping operation. For accounts of United Nations peacekeep-ing operations during the organization's first four decades, see Wiseman (1983), Haas (1986), and Riggs and Plano (1988).

Figure 14.2 ■ UN Peacekeeping Operations

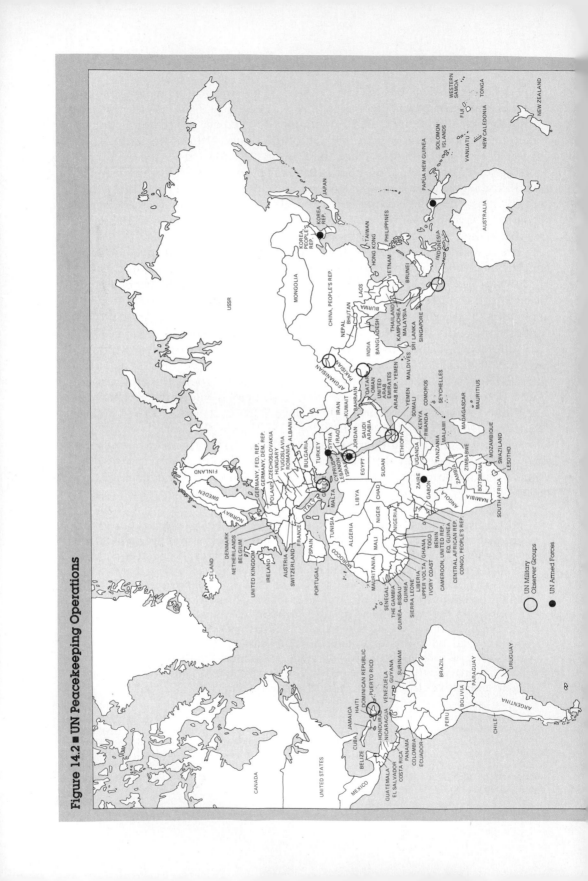

As the universal organ of collective security, the United Nations promotes disarmament and encourages peaceful solutions to international disputes. Through the voluntary cooperation of its members, the United Nations also has taken steps to suppress aggression, prevent or end armed hostilities, and maintain peace and order in territories where local authority is not fully established. These "peacekeeping" operations take the form of military observer groups supervising truces or cease-fires or of armed forces prepared for more direct intervention. The oldest UN military observer group is UNTSO, created during the Arab-Israeli hostilities in 1948. In size, observer: groups range from fewer than 10 to more than 130 persons, while armed forces' strength has varied from UNSF's 1,500 Pakistanis to ONUC's peak of 16,000 drawn from many nations. In the Korean war, where the object was to repel large-scale aggression, peak UN strength was about 400,000, the bulk accounted for by the United States. (The maximum strength of Republic of Korea forces under the UN Command was somewhat more than 400,000.)

Latin America

IAPF. Inter-American Peace Force, 1965-66: Moderate civil strife in the Dominican Republic (dispatched by the Organization of American States; UN representative and military observer present concurrently with IAPF).

Africa

ONUC. French initials for the UN Operation in the Congo, 1960-64: Keep peace and order, preserve unity.

Europe

UNMOG. UN Military Observers in Greece, 1952-54: Investigate incidents along borders with Albania, Yugoslavia, and Bulgaria.

UNFICYP. UN Force in Cyprus, 1974-present: Keep law and order and peace between Greek and Turkish communities.

Middle East

UNTSO. UN Truce Supervision Organization in Palestine, 1948-present: Supervise armistice among Israel, Jordan, Lebanon, and Syria.

UNEF. UN Emergency Force. 1956-67, 1973-79: Prevent Israeli-Egyptian hostilities, keep peace and order in Sinai and Gaza Strip.

UNOGIL. UN Observer Group in Lebanon, June-December 1958: Police Lebanon-Syria border.

UNDOF. UN Disengagement Observer Force, 1974-present: Maintain cease-fire between Syria and Israel.

UNIFIL. UN Interim Force in Lebanon, 1978-present: Police Lebanon-Israel border.

UNYOM. UN Yemen Observation Mission, 1963-64: Report on withdrawal of Saudi Arabian and Egyptian forces.

Asia/Pacific

UNMOGIP. UN Military Observer Group in India and Pakistan, 1948-present: Supervise cease-fire in Jammu-Kashmir.

UNCFI. UN Commission for Indonesia, 1949-51: Settle dispute with Netherlands.

United Nations Command in Korea, 1950-present: Established to repel armed attack by forces from North Korea and restore international peace in Korea.

UNSF. UN Security Force, 1962-63: Facilitate transfer of West Irian to Indonesia.

UNIPOM. UN India-Pakistan Observation Mission, 1965-66: Supervise cease-fire in Rann of Kutch.

Source: Harry F. Young, *Atlas of United States Foreign Relations* (Washington, D.C.: U.S. Government Printing Office, 1985), p. 20.

Preventive diplomacy thus maintains that one of the ways that diplomacy might prevent wars is by isolating Third World crises from great power involvement. It is an approach to control conflict that employs relatively small troop contingents (typically troops from Scandinavia or from nonaligned nations), whose perilous assignment is to stand in the cross fire between opposing armies and attempt to mediate and cool the situation.

Figure 14.2 summarizes the fifteen most important UN military and peacekeeping operations (other than Korea) undertaken since 1946, each of which has enjoyed some success in pursuit of modest objectives. Observer missions, for instance, have succeeded in creating buffers between the warring disputants, negotiating cease-fires, and ensuring compliance with the provisions of agreements. More impressively, the peacekeeping missions have successfully intervened between combatants and facilitated withdrawal from territory by the advancing party. These UN operations thus have helped contain conflicts that seriously threatened to escalate, and it is reasonable to classify only two of these (UNYOM, in Yemen, and UNTAG, in Namibia) as outright failures and only one (UNIFIL, in Lebanon) as limited in success (Haas, 1986: 36, 38–39).

Preventive diplomacy came about because of the changing international political environment, particularly the Cold War competition between the United States and the Soviet Union, the threat that competition posed for the entire world because of the destructiveness of modern weapons, and the increase in the number of Third World nations whose interests and objectives have often diverged from those of the superpowers.

What to one state is impartial intervention in a conflict is not, however, necessarily impartiality to another. The Soviet Union turned against the United Nations' Congo operation because it saw the organization pursuing policies that were inimical to Soviet interests. The Soviets pressed their opposition in various ways, most visibly in their refusal to support the principle of collective financial responsibility for the peacekeeping operation. The Congo experience proved in the long run to have a debilitating impact on the United Nations' ability to deal with other conflicts. Significantly, it was almost a full decade before the world organization launched another major peacekeeping operation, when it sent a force to Cyprus. The force assigned to the Sinai peninsula in 1973 (UNEF-II) was agreed upon only after the policy of détente, to which the United States and the Soviet Union were committed, had been severely threatened by the eruption of war in the Middle East. Furthermore, control of the force was placed firmly in the hands of the Security Council, thus reaffirming the primacy of the great powers in matters of international peace and security.

The assertion of Security Council authority undermined the ability of the secretary general to pursue an independent role in world politics. Preventive diplomacy as defined by Hammarskjöld reflected his frustration with the United Nations' legal structure, particularly the Security Council's inability to perform adequately its central purpose, maintaining peace. Given the charter's constraints, Hammarskjöld sought to redefine and expand the constitutional authority granted his office to undertake actions on behalf of the world community. More than his predecessor, Trygve Lie of Norway, Hammarskjöld saw his role as an active participant in the management of crises. Consequently, Hammarskjöld enlarged the responsibilities of the executive organ of the United Nations by using his "good offices" to moderate international disputes before they escalated into war, by mediating conflicts between the contending parties, and by strengthening the United Nations' administrative support for peacekeeping operations. The 1956 UNEF-I operation and later the Congo force were only the most visible and ambitious manifestations of Hammarskjöld's preventive diplomacy efforts.

Hammarskjöld's successor, U Thant of Burma, pursued a much less activist role. Responding to increasing pressure from both the United States and the Soviet Union, U Thant's efforts concentrated on the management of crises identified by the Security Council or the General Assembly rather than by the secretary general. This approach to the use of the United Nations was more akin to the emphasis in the 1950s, which stressed crisis response rather than crisis prevention. The shift reflected the reality on which the United Nations is built—that its effectiveness depends ultimately on the willingness of the great powers to take concerted actions to deter violence. Accordingly, U Thant adopted a low profile on security issues and instead tried to act as a world spokesman on issues relating to the emerging North–South confrontation and, in particular, as an advocate for the principles of justice, stability, and equality.

Kurt Waldheim, who took over the post of secretary general in 1972, continued U Thant's policy. He sought to resolve interstate disputes (as exemplified by his efforts to obtain release of the American hostages seized in Iran in 1979). But he exhibited appreciation of the constraints imposed by the charter on his office (and on the United Nations generally), as well as by the political realities that the United Nations more often mirrors than influences.

Waldheim's successor, Javier Pérez de Cúellar, likewise appreciated the United Nations' deficiencies as an instrument for global conflict management. Although he expressed pride in the organization's record of peacekeeping over the years, he was more vocally critical of its failures and less accepting of the constraints imposed on it by its members. In his first annual report, he spoke of an "alarming succession of international crises" in which "the United Nations . . . has been unable to play as effective and decisive a role as the Charter certainly envisaged for it." To correct its impotence, he called for renewed use of the Security Council which "too often finds itself on the sidelines" because of alleged "partisanship, indecisiveness or incapacity arising from divisions among Member States." The council's collective security function could be performed with respect to critical problems and not merely noncontroversial issues, de Cúellar contended, if it were willing "to keep an active watch on dangerous situations and, if necessary, initiate discussions with the parties before they reach the point of crisis" so that they might be defused "at an early stage before they degenerate into violence." In issuing this challenge, the secretary general alleged the council's abrogation of responsibility as one of the main reasons that the United Nations is perceived to be powerless and that "our divided international community" is "so perilously near to a new international anarchy" (de Cúellar, 1984).

This candid assessment draws attention to the fact that the United Nations cannot preserve world peace through efforts organized by the secretary general alone. But whether the political obstacles to great power collaboration designed to prevent and resolve international disputes can be transcended is problematic. As a result, the mission of the United Nations has increasingly been directed toward "rear door" approaches to creating a warless world—to alleviate the conditions of poverty, inequality, frustration, and despair that plague the daily lives of so many millions in the world—unacceptable conditions to which people are inclined to respond violently. In other words, the United Nations has stressed not the high politics of peace and security but, rather, the low politics of economic, social, and cultural development.[17] In this sense, the United Nations has shown a preference to address some of the deepseated, structural causes of war rather than the immediate causes—such as the motives that underpin a state's decision to attack an adversary—that bring about a threat to the peace. But whether in this domain the United Nations is any better equipped for the enormous task is questionable indeed, especially with a meager annual budget and a modest number of civil servants scattered around the world. But its search for solutions constitutes a step along the path toward a more secure world, inasmuch as the United Nations' nonsecurity functions may ultimately make important positive differences in the kind of global environment in which nations operate.

In some respects this cautious conclusion also applies to any evaluation of the United Nations' future role in coping with security issues. The record of its efforts to mitigate, abate, and settle conflicts is not without its successes; yet it is amenable to differing interpretations, depending on one's criteria. Holsti (1988: 423) estimates that "only about two out of five" of the United Nations' attempts to mediate conflicts succeed. Similarly, Haas (1986: 9) records a total of 319 international disputes in which some fighting occurred between 1945 and 1984, and notes that only 137, or 43 percent, of these were referred to the United Nations for management. Moreover, distressingly, the United Nations failed to abate 47 percent of these disputes and failed to settle fully 75 percent of them; its capacity to stop ongoing hostilities, moreover, has declined since the 1960s (Haas, 1986: 17).[18]

A reading of the United Nations' historical record suggests a number of propositions about the factors that most contribute to its efficacy. It appears

---

17. For evidence that officials in the United Nations' Secretariat place economic welfare and social justice above peace in their priorities, see Sylvester (1980).

18. A different, more reassuring picture is produced when attention is restricted to the subset of major disputes that involved, not just skirmishes, but "serious" fighting. Forty-nine percent of 122 of these were referred to the United Nations, a proportion that has increased since 1980 (Haas, 1986: 20).

that its effectiveness as an instrument of conflict management is greatest when a conflict (1) does not involve the superpowers, (2) is outside the context of the East–West rivalry, (3) is opposed by both superpowers and other members of the Security Council, (4) is intense and in danger of spreading geographically, (5) entails fighting (albeit at a limited level), (6) centers on a decolonization dispute, (7) involves "middle" and "small" states possessing relatively modest military capabilities, and (8) is identified as a threat to peace by the secretary general, who leads efforts to organize the organization's resistance to its continuation.

It should be noted here that the United Nations' *peacekeeping* record has been substantially more distinguished than have its *peacemaking* achievements. In most cases of UN involvement, the principal causes of conflict have either remained or been removed by forces external to the organization itself. By no means does this denigrate the organization's violence-preventing achievements. Despite its weaknesses, the United Nations may be what John F. Kennedy labeled "our last hope in an age where the instruments of war have far outpaced the instruments of peace." But it does raise the question of whether, in succeeding more in peacekeeping than in peacemaking, a United Nations presence will postpone political solutions by muting the urgency of political compromise among the parties directly involved in a conflict.

Our assessment of the United Nations will be colored by what we expect of it, and this should be tempered by an appreciation of the constraints under which it must operate. The United Nations, after all, is a creation of sovereign nations, and it can accomplish no more than what its members permit it to accomplish. As Trygve Lie noted in 1946, "The United Nations is no stronger than the collective will of the nations that support it. Of itself it can do nothing. It is a machinery through which nations can cooperate. It can be used and developed . . . or it can be discarded and broken." To expect the United Nations to replace international conflict with cooperation asks it to accomplish something that its members have yet to empower it to achieve and that no other institution has heretofore accomplished.

Regional Security Organizations and Conflict Management

If the United Nations reflects the lack of shared values and a common purpose characteristic of a global community, perhaps regional organizations of states that already share some interests and cultural traditions offer better prospects for dealing politically with the problems of conflict and war.

One piece of evidence consistent with the view that regionalism may be the path to peace is found in the fact that although both universal and regional IGOs (international intergovernmental organizations) have increased in number in response to rising international interdependence and the perceived need to confront mutual problems through collective problem-solving mechanisms, the proportionate growth of regional IGOs has substantially exceeded that of the universal IGOs.

The North Atlantic Treaty Organization (NATO) and the Warsaw Pact (WTO) are the best-known examples of regional security organizations. Others include the ANZUS pact (which disintegrated in 1986 when New Zealand withdrew from its defense arrangement with the United States and Australia over the issue of nuclear-armed submarines in its harbors), and the now-defunct Southeast Asia Treaty Organization (SEATO). Regional organizations with somewhat broader political mandates include the Organization of American States (OAS), the League of Arab States, the Organization of African Unity (OAU), the Nordic Council, and the Association of Southeast Asian Nations (ASEAN).

The possibility of regional organizations was anticipated in Article 51 of the United Nations Charter, which provides that "nothing in the present Charter shall impair the inherent right of individual or collective self-defense if an armed attack occurs against a Member of the United Nations, until the Security Council has taken the measures necessary to maintain international peace and security."

The contribution of regional organizations to world peace has, nevertheless, been open to dispute. NATO and the other mutual security arrangements that the United States established in the 1950s were a direct consequence of the American government's disappointment with the United Nations. These organizations were created under the rubric of Article 51 and are frequently described as instruments of "collective security." But they are not. They are regional alliance systems designed to promote "collective self-defense" in the face of a common external enemy. According to Ernst B. Haas, "Collective security properly refers to a global or regional system in which *all* member countries insure each other against *every* member; no state is singled out in advance as the enemy, and each might be an aggressor in the future. Alliances, however, usually come into existence when the members are agreed on the identity of the enemy and wish to insure each other against him" (Haas, 1969).

For the United States, the external enemy was, of course, the Soviet Union. Although this was historically true for the other members of NATO as well, in other American-sponsored mutual security systems, particularly the OAS and SEATO, differences of opinion about the enemy became a source of political controversy among the coalition partners. The growing polycentrism in NATO during the 1960s and 1970s can likewise be partially attributed to a decline in the members' perception of a common external threat.

If the Soviet Union was the common threat stimulating the creation of NATO, the United States (and, to a lesser but more immediate extent, an independent West Germany) was the perceived enemy of the Warsaw Pact. Thus the two principal Cold War alliance systems were created to enhance mutual security because each faced an enemy that fostered insecurity. The alliances may have contributed to global security by ensuring the effective operation of a deterrence system based on a delicately tuned balance of terror. But neither alliance is appropriately interpreted as an institutional approach to the problem of war that has effectively inhibited the incidence of interstate violence generally.

Have other regional organizations fared better as conflict-resolving mechanisms? The management of disputes between 1945 and 1984 by the Organization of American States (OAS), the Arab League, the Organization for African Unity (OAU), and the Council of Europe shows a general decline in effectiveness that parallels (but is less steep) than that of the United Nations (Haas, 1986: 14).[19] Of 319 disputes existing in this period, 86, or 27 percent, were referred to these regional organizations for management (in comparison with 43 percent considered by the United Nations). The regional organizations failed to abate 44 percent and failed to settle 74 percent of these referrals (for the United Nations, the rates are 47 percent and 75 percent, respectively) (Haas, 1986: 17). The conclusion that follows is that like the United Nations, regional organizations have often been unable to terminate ongoing hostilities, and even their limited success has eroded over time. Moreover, the disputes referred to regional organizations tend to be less intense than those referred to the United Nations, to be localized (confined to the geographic region in which the organization has special interest), and to involve minimal fighting. Whereas nearly half the serious interstate disputes involving military operations are referred to the United Nations, only one in five serious disputes are referred to the regional organizations (Haas, 1986: 20). These facts indicate that although regional organizations in some ways perhaps compete with the United Nations for responsibility in the management of conflict, in the sense that regional organizations may "now seek to compensate for the deficiencies of global arrangements" (Haas, 1983), they appear to complement the mission of the United Nations more than to substitute for it. But in bringing even some of the regional conflicts under control, these organizations reduce the burden of security management faced by the United Nations and contribute thereby to the maintenance of international peace and security.

In the long run, international organizations, particularly at the regional level, may help build security communities in which the expectation of peaceful modes of conflict resolution ultimately becomes more widespread than the expectation of violence. The processes through which such metamorphoses might occur are addressed by the functional and neofunctional approaches to peace.

Political Integration and the Functional and Neofunctional Approaches to Peace

Political integration refers either to the process or the product of efforts to build new political communities. Usually these are assumed to be suprana-

---

19. The comparative rates at which four regional organizations have successfully managed conflicts between 1945 and 1984, based on a scale ranging from 0 to 100, vary, and are as follows: OAS, 32; Arab League, 19; OAU, 18; and the Council of Europe, 18 (Haas, 1986: 13–14).

tional institutional structures that transcend the nation-state.[20] Integration theorists therefore frequently focus on the question of how international organizations might be transformed from instruments *of* states to structures *over* them. Functionalism and neofunctionalism are bodies of theory directed toward the following question: "Within what environment, under what conditions, and by what processes does a new transnational political unit emerge peacefully from two or more initially separate and different ones?" (Puchala, 1988; emphasis deleted).

Functionalism in its various manifestations is not an argument for a frontal attack on the nation-state, proposing that it be replaced by some form of world government. The *world federalists*, however, do advocate this approach. They recommend a world government in which political and military power would be transferred from competitive nation-states to a central authority that would monopolize the use of force and hence suppress war-threatening conflict throughout the world. Federalists (such as Barr, 1953) believe that this transformation will occur because people will see (presumably before it is too late) that the benefits of transferring power and loyalty to a world government outweigh the costs. The transfer would thus be a rational act; survival would be valued more highly than relative national advantage, and people would act according to the calculation that destruction can be averted by dismantling the multistate system that produces war.

Critics of the federalist plan contend that it is based on rather naive assumptions (see Claude, 1971, for an elaboration), including the proposition that governments are bad but people are good, wise, and enlightened. "People" are therefore assumed to be eager "to take the federalist plunge," even though their governments may resist it. But in an age of intense nationalism that buttresses the concept of state sovereignty, such an assumption is clearly unwarranted. That necessity will lead to global institutional innovation is also questionable—the need for something will not automatically bring it into existence. Aversion to war and raised consciousness of its dangers do not guarantee replacement of the system presumed to cause it. Even if they did, the expectation that world government could be created quickly is unrealistic.

Functionalism differs from federalism by focusing on immediate self-interest and by not requiring that authority be transferred immediately to supranational institutions. *Classical functionalism* (Mitrany, 1966, 1975) is based not on creating a world federal structure with all its constitutional paraphernalia but, rather, on building "peace by pieces" through transnational organizations that emphasize the "sharing of sovereignty" rather than its surrender.

Rather than addressing the immediate sources of national insecurity, the functionalists' peace plan calls for transnational cooperation in technical areas,

---

20. Compare Deutsch and colleagues (1957), in which "integrated" communities are characterized by the absence of intracommunity warfare and the expectation of a peaceful resolution of conflict rather than by the presence of supranational structures. See Puchala (1988) for a survey of integration theory and its relationship to the larger corpus of international relations theory.

primarily social and economic, as a means to promote prosperity and peace. Technical experts and the knowledge they generate and disseminate, rather than professional diplomats, are seen as the agents bridging national borders. Functionalists assume that habits of cooperation learned in one technical area will eventually spill over into another, especially if the experience proves to be mutually beneficial. To enhance the probability that cooperative endeavors will prove rewarding rather than frustrating, functionalists recommend that less difficult tasks be tackled first. The successful mastering of one problem will then encourage attacking another collaboratively. If the process continues unabated, the tics among nations will multiply, and collaboration will culminate in the transfer of sovereignty to supranational, welfare-oriented institutions. "Hence, the mission of functionalism is to make peace possible by organizing particular layers of human social life in accordance with their particular requirements, breaking down the artificialities of the zoning arrangements associated with the principle of sovereignty" (Claude, 1971). Sovereignty divides people; functional cooperation unites them into a peaceful community of interests.

Functionalism assumes that war originates in poverty, misery, and despair. If these conditions can be eliminated, the incentive for military rivalry will recede—a view that follows Sigmund Freud's contention that "all that produces ties of sentiment between man and man must serve as war's antidote." Technical experts are preferable to professional diplomats for achieving the transformation, because the latter are overly protective of selfish national interests at the expense of collective human interests. In this sense functionalism rests on a kind of international version of the assumption that "politics is dirty."

The intellectual father of functionalism, David Mitrany (1966; originally published in 1943), argues that functionalism is *A Working Peace System* because it is based on self-interest.

> Functionalism proposes not to squelch but to utilize national selfishness; it asks governments not to give up sovereignty which belongs to their peoples but to acquire benefits for their peoples which were hitherto unavailable, not to reduce their power to defend their citizens but to expand their competence to serve them. It intimates that the basic requirement for peace is that states have the wit to cooperate in pursuit of national interests that coincide with those of other states rather than the will to compromise national interests that conflict with those of others. (Claude, 1971: 386)

Functionalism draws its historical insights from the formation of the universal problem-solving organizations in the 1800s (such as the Universal Postal Union) and from the growth of international organizations in the twentieth century. It helps explain some of the early organizational ideology of the activities of the United Nations' specialized agencies. And it provides insight into the reasons behind the growth of IGOs and INGOs alike, seeing the latter as supporting the former's efforts to promote transnational collaboration in solving technical problems.

Although in its original formulation, functionalism did not pertain to multinational corporations (MNCs), it is tempting to speculate that MNCs may facilitate the transformation of world politics in a manner consistent with functionalist logic. Individuals who manage global corporations often think and talk of themselves as a "revolutionary class" possessing a holistic, cosmopolitan vision of the earth that challenges traditional nationalism (Barnet and Müller, 1974). This ideology and the corresponding slogan "down with borders" are based on the assumptions that the world can be managed as an integrated unit, that global corporations can serve as agents of social change, that governments interfere unnecessarily with the free flow of capital and technology, and that the MNCs can mediate disputes and encourage compromise between contending states. It is also assumed that MNCs will act in this manner because their interests (and corporate profits) will be served by so doing, in part because free trade and the reduction of sovereign states' tendencies to interfere with it through protective tariffs are powerful incentives.

As a theory of peace and world order, however, functionalism does not take into account some important political realities. First, its assumption about the causes of war is questionable. Do poverty and despair cause war, or does war cause poverty and despair? Indeed, may not material deprivation sometimes breed—instead of aggression—apathy, anomie, and hostility without recourse to violence (see Gurr, 1970)? Why should we assume that the functionalist theory of war is more accurate than the many other explanations of global violence?

Second, functionalism supposes that political differences among nations will be dissolved by the habits of cooperation learned by experts organized transnationally to cope with technical problems. The reality is that technical cooperation is often more strongly influenced by politics than the other way around. For example, the United States' withdrawal from and subsequent reentry into the International Labor Organization (ILO) because of the organization's politicized nature dramatized the primacy of politics. Indeed, functionalists naively believe that technical (functional) undertakings and political affairs can be separated. They cannot. If technical cooperation becomes as important to state welfare as the functionalists argue it will be, states will not step aside. Welfare and power cannot be separated, because the solution of economic and social problems cannot be divorced from political considerations. Whether the authority and competency of transnational institutions can readily be expanded at the expense of national governments is, therefore, unlikely. Functionalism, in short, is an idea whose time has passed.

Neofunctionalists share the intellectual traditions of functionalism, but they differ from the classical functionalists on the question of politics. Classical functionalism is sometimes regarded as essentially a nonpolitical approach to solving political problems, in that the latter would be resolved by focusing on technical activities (health, agriculture, and so forth).

In contrast, *neofunctionalism* explicitly emphasizes the political factors in the process of merging formerly independent states.

> *Neofunctionalism* holds that political institutions and policies should be crafted so that they lead to further integration through the process of . . . "the expansive logic of sector integration." For example, as [first] president of the ECSC [European Coal and Steel Community], [Jean] Monnet sought to use the integration of the coal and steel markets of the six member countries as a lever to promote the integration of their social security and transport policies, arguing that such action was essential to eliminate distortions in coal and steel prices. Finally, the neofunctionalism of Monnet and others has as its ultimate goal . . . the creation of a federal state. (Jacobson, 1984: 66)

Neofunctionalism thus proposes to reach its goal of a supranational community by stressing cooperation in areas that are politically controversial, rather than by avoiding them. It proposes to hurdle political obstacles standing in the way of cooperation by demonstrating the benefits common to all members of a potential political union. Furthermore, this demonstration requires the proponents of integration to bring political pressure to bear at crucial decision points in order to win against their opponents.

Western Europe is the preeminent example of the application of neofunctionalist principles to the development of an integrated political community. As described in Chapter 6, within a single generation, cooperation across European boundaries has led to economic union and the creation of common institutions that may lead to political unity among the member countries of the European Community. Whether political union is realized depends on both continued economic integration and the integration of social and economic sectors. But politics may intrude on the process of realizing ultimate political union. The historical record of Europe's efforts to build the community now in place demonstrates the many points at which politics can impede—or accelerate—the integrative process. Nevertheless, Western Europe has already constructed the ingredients for a pluralistic security community, in which the expectation of war has receded in one of the historically most violence-prone regions of the world. Symbolic of the changing climate in Europe over the past four decades is the reflection of Chancellor Helmut Kohl of West Germany: "We have learned history's lesson, that violence is not a means of politics. European national states have no future. We need a European roof, and my goal . . . is the political unification of Europe."

In contrast with this vision remains the reality of a collection of often quarrelsome polities that currently make up the European Community. Given the chronic suspicion, selfishness, and tenacious national memories of the dark side of Europe's twentieth-century history, it is unclear whether the dream of true European unity will some day become a reality. The dream persists nonetheless, even as the obstacles remain.

European integration has served as a model for neofunctionalist logic in other regions of the world. Parts of Latin America, Africa, Asia, and Eastern Europe also have engaged in similar institution-building efforts. However, because integration is a multidimensional phenomenon involving the political and social as well as the economic systems, there is no guarantee that the "logic of sector integration" will proceed automatically. Spillover, involving either the deepening of ties in one sector or their expansion to another so as to ensure the members' satisfaction with the integrative process, may lead to further integration. But there is no inherent expansive momentum in integration schemes. "Spillback" (when a regional integration scheme fails, as in the case of the East African Community) and "spill-around" (when a regional integration scheme stagnates or its activities become encapsulated) are also possibilities.

The substantial difficulty that other world regions have experienced in achieving the same level of institution building as has Western Europe suggests something about the barriers extant to the creation of new political communities out of previously divided ones. Furthermore, the paradox that political integration in some portions of the globe is proceeding at the same time that disintegration characterizes others is noteworthy. A United States of Europe may be in its nascent stages, but Northern Ireland, Great Britain, South Africa, and Canada are being pressured by centrifugal political forces that threaten to fragment them. Thus societies may either amalgamate or decay; there is no reason to expect integrative processes, once under way, to progress through the pull of their own momentum.

The factors associated with successful integration efforts are many and their mixture complex. It is not enough that two countries choose to interact cooperatively for the process to commence. Research indicates that the probability that such cooperative behavior will culminate in integration is remote in the absence of geographical proximity, similar political systems, favorable public opinion, cultural homogeneity, similar experiences in historical and internal social development, stability of regime, similar levels of military preparedness and economic capabilities, bureaucratic compatibilities, and previous collaborative endeavors (Cobb and Elder, 1970; Deutsch, 1975). Although not all of these conditions must be present for integration to occur, history suggests that the absence of more than a few will considerably diminish the chances of success. The integration of two or more societies, let alone the entire world, is, in short, not easily accomplished. The evidence to date in fact suggests that the integration of nation-states into larger political communities may be peculiarly relevant to advanced industrial societies but has doubtful applicability to the Third World.

LAW, ORGANIZATION, AND WORLD ORDER

It is revealing that the theories of the contribution of international law and organization to conflict regulation (especially those advanced by idealists) tend to perceive war as deriving from the deficiencies built into the state system itself. That system is a Hobbesian anarchical arena of competitive states driven to pursue national advantage at the expense of others. Security is dear because global welfare is subservient to national welfare. The schemes devised to avert bloodshed and to produce a more peaceful world seek to address the inadequacies of the state system and the inability of governments to meet the challenges posed by an interdependent world. Seeing the international system as underdeveloped, underinstitutionalized, and in a latent state of anarchy, proponents of international law and organization believe that approaches that address the inadequacies of the state system can extirpate the roots from which war has so often grown. Although the contributions of law and organization to this grand purpose have, to date, been marginal, as long-term historical processes their importance should not be minimized. Inis L. Claude makes a cogent argument regarding the process of organization internationally:

> Particular *organizations* may be nothing more than playthings of power politics and handmaidens of national ambitions. But international *organization*, considered as an historical process, represents a secular trend toward the systematic development of an enterprising quest for political means of making the world safe for human habitation. It may fail, and peter out ignominiously. But if it maintains the momentum that it has built up in the twentieth century, it may yet effect a transformation of human relationships on this planet which will at some indeterminate point justify the assertion that the world has come to be governed—that mankind has become a community capable of sustaining order, promoting justice, and establishing the conditions of that good life which Aristotle took to be the supreme aim of politics. (Claude, 1971: 447–448, emphasis added)

Somewhat ironically, the complex interdependence that now characterizes the relations among key world political actors suggests that a quiet if revolutionary transformation in global politics may be unfolding, one that makes political probes for peace through multilateral approaches more compelling in the face of the dangers posed by modern warfare. All those who think about war wish to avoid it. The incentives for preventing war in an age of collective vulnerability may make the ancient dream of global community more likely. But until human effort and power are organized more effectively for the security of all, and legal and political institutions are developed to protect it, it is doubtful that peace will become widespread in our transforming world.

SUGGESTED READINGS

Bennett, A. Leroy. *International Organizations: Principles and Issues*, 4th ed. Englewood Cliffs, N.J.: Prentice Hall, 1988.

de Cúellar, Javier Pérez. "The United Nations and World Politics," pp. 178–185 in Charles W. Kegley, Jr., and Eugene R. Wittkopf, eds., *The Global Agenda: Issues and Perspectives*, 2nd ed. New York: Random House, 1988.

Haas, Ernst B. *Why We Still Need the United Nations: The Collective Management of International Conflict, 1945–1984*. Berkeley, Calif.: Institute of International Studies, University of California-Berkeley, 1986.

Joyner, Christopher C. "The Reality and Relevance of International Law," pp. 186–197 in Charles W. Kegley, Jr., and Eugene R. Wittkopf, eds., *The Global Agenda: Issues and Perspectives*, 2nd ed. New York: Random House, 1988.

Kim, Samuel S. "The United Nations, Lawmaking, and World Order," *Alternatives* 10 (no. 4, 1985): 643–675.

Luck, Edward C. "The U.N. at 40: A Supporter's Lament," *Foreign Policy* 57 (Winter 1984–1985): 143–159.

Onuf, Nicholas Greenwood, ed. *Law-Making in the Global Community*. Durham, N.C.: Carolina Academic Press, 1982.

Puchala, Donald J. "The Integration Theorists and the Study of International Relations," pp. 198–265 in Charles W. Kegley, Jr., and Eugene R. Wittkopf, eds., *The Global Agenda: Issues and Perspectives*, 2nd ed. New York: Random House, 1988.

Weston, Burns, Richard A. Falk, and Anthony A. D'Amato. *International Law and World Order*. St. Paul: West Publishing, 1980.

PART V

Global Change and the Future of World Politics

FIFTEEN

Understanding Global Transformation: From Evidence to Inference

Trend is not destiny.

RENE DUBOS, 1975

We must plan our civilization or we must perish.

HAROLD LASKI, 1945

The forces propelling change in world politics are multifaceted and deeply rooted. Among them are unprecedented numbers of national political units with internal characteristics significantly different from those in the past; new kinds of subnational and transnational actors; and more people. Because many of these actors seek unconventional political objectives, new cleavages and controversies have been produced. The capabilities of nation-states have changed drastically, making economic modes of exercising influence increasingly practicable and the specter of human extinction possible. Technological innovations have altered the means by which foreign policy goals are pursued. And long-standing patterns of relationships among states—from coalition configurations and power distributions to status hierarchies and income rankings—have been disrupted.

These changes are recorded on a global agenda crowded with new issues and problems and articulated in a new vocabulary of policy rhetoric. Moreover, the global system has been knit into a complex web of interdependence, which has made the political interconnections among transnational actors qualitatively different from those exhibited previously. An accelerated pace of change can be added to this list of conditions characterizing contemporary world politics. And the unparalleled dangers and challenges of the present add an element of urgency to world affairs. As UN Secretary General U Thant warned, if current trends continue, the future of life on earth could be endangered. Perhaps this explains why, given the present state of global politics, contemplations of the future so often seem to be punctuated by the language of desperation (Falk, 1979, 1983).

The preceding chapters have treated these trends as major elements in the transformation of world politics. The convergence of so many of them in the twilight of the twentieth century suggests that a transformation is well under way—that, indeed, it may already have been accomplished.

Compelling as this impression is, it assumes a common understanding of the elements that distinguish change or evolution from transformation. It assumes, in other words, a consensus on the distinctions among changes that inevitably occur with the passage of time (including long-term changes as well as temporary fluctuations) from the kinds of changes that culminate to produce a fundamental shift from one global pattern to another. Furthermore, it assumes that the influences propelling change are more powerful than the forces promoting continuity. This chapter will examine the interaction among global trends and explore the elements that make for global transformation. We first identify various types of global change (and ways of conceptualizing it), then consider its sources, and finally, evaluate some perspectives on the future global condition.

TYPES OF GLOBAL CHANGE

What does it mean to assert that world politics is changing? What is transformation? How can it be detected? It may seem facile to describe today's international system as one marked by change, because every historical period is marked to some extent by change.[1] It is useful, therefore, to think of transformation as the culmination of piecemeal developments that produce a qualitative difference in the overall texture of world politics. The direction and force of transnational changes, however, are rarely uniform. Only infrequently do trends unfold at the same rate and in the same direction so as to signal the disappearance of the prevailing international system and the emergence of another. The multiple developments monitored in this book exhibit different characteristics, which suggests the need to discriminate among several categories of change at work simultaneously, namely, discontinuity, continuity, and the interaction between them.

---

1. Nonetheless, a case can be made that the change occurring today is unprecedented. As Richard Barnet has observed:

Every generation is by definition an era of transition, but our own time portends bigger changes in the organization of the planet than we have had for at least five hundred years. A crisis of values has swept across both the capitalist and socialist worlds. The rapid process of decolonization following four hundred years of imperial conquest in Asia, Africa, and Latin America is far from completed. Profound struggles are taking place or are in the offing—between rich and poor nations over their share of the world product, within the industrial world over sharing resources and markets, and between cities and regions within nations over access to food, fuel, minerals, and water. The world is already in the midst of a transition to a postpetroleum civilization. (Barnet, 1980a: 19)

Discontinuity

Numerous signs portend a potentially revolutionary restructuring of world politics—recurrent crises, resource scarcities, monetary disorder, trade dependence, debt accumulation, environmental deterioration, weapons proliferation, overpopulation, terrorism, fragmentation of the bipolar world, diffusion of global power, and intranational and international conflict and war. These momentous developments, many of which represent sharp discontinuities from the past, suggest that world politics is perhaps more conducive to a reshaping—a transformation—than at any time since the end of World War II.

Further, these trends are changing at different rates. Some are changing so fast that they can be labeled revolutionary in both rapidity and scope. Others fluctuate widely in the short run, but within confined limits. Still others move so slowly that they appear not to be trends at all. Thus it is easy to confuse a temporary interruption with an enduring alteration. Change may be either ephemeral or continuous, with the former signaling discontinuity and the latter a potential transformation. To differentiate ephemeral change from continuing change requires tracing change against the backdrop of long historical periods. Thus, detecting real transformations or historical watersheds in world politics is hazardous (Aron, 1958). The so-called breakpoints of international systems do not fall neatly into easily defined periods, signaling that one system has truly ended and a new one has commenced.[2]

Nevertheless, the most important turning points in world history usually have been demarcated by major wars, in part because their far-reaching effects have often disrupted or perhaps destroyed preexisting international arrangements. World Wars I and II have often been interpreted as fundamental breaks with the past because each set in motion major transformations in world politics.

Other watersheds are marked by the advent of major technological developments, such as the splitting of the atom, which gave states an unprecedented capacity to cause massive destruction. More subtle but equally seminal transformations in world politics may be triggered by the cumulative impact of incremental developments, such as the disintegration of colonial empires and the consequent creation of new states, the effects of resource scarcities, or the rise of new but powerful transnational actors such as multinational corporations. Likewise, the very foundations and structure of the world economy have changed gradually but irreversibly to the point that it is now appropriate to

---

2. This distinction assumes, of course, that we are speaking only of major global changes, touching many other features of world politics. The distinction is important because a "small" but "permanent" change is hardly equivalent to a "transformation." The disagreement among analysts about the dates of previous transformations in world politics testifies to the problems posed. See Hoffmann (1961), Kaplan (1957), Oren (1984), and Rosecrance (1963) for examples and discussions of alternative periodizations of world politics.

ask, "Have we come to the end of the 300-year-old attempt to regulate and stabilize money, on which, after all, both the modern nation-state and the international system are largely based?" (Drucker, 1986).

Regardless of the criteria used to delineate chronological transformations in world politics and distinguish momentary disruptions of prevailing tendencies from actual metamorphoses, it is important that the differentiation be made. Otherwise, any random fluctuation, unexpected accident, or short-term perturbation might be mistaken for a transformation. And because foreign policy decision makers base their judgments in part on their assessments of probable changes and projections of long-term developments, any misinterpretation could be costly and even dangerous.

Continuity

Although change is an intrinsic facet of world politics, some political features central to the functioning of the international system have endured for centuries.[3] The obvious illustrations of relatively stable properties of world politics are the perpetuation of the territorial nation-state and the corresponding support of the principle of sovereignty that have lasted for over three centuries. Whether the modern nation-state, born in 1648 to cope with the then-emergent political conditions in Europe, is equipped to deal adequately with the problems posed by contemporary global circumstances is questionable, but it has survived nonetheless.

Paralleling the continuation of the nation-state has been continued support in the global political culture for many of the system's central norms. People have remained reluctant to construct political institutions that would transcend nation-states and to give them supranational authority. The continued reliance on self-help measures to achieve national political objectives (including the use of violence without international mandate), the continuing derivation of international legal norms and obligations from both custom and formal consent, and the continuing acceptance of the pursuit of power through preparation for war all reflect and reinforce continuities within the existing international system. It is these persistent attitudes that lead to the maintenance of an international society that remains anarchical if not also archaic (Bull, 1977).

The persistence of various hierarchies in world politics provides another illustration of the enduring structural properties of the global political order. The economic hierarchy that divides the rich from the poor, the political hierarchy that separates the rulers from subordinates, the resource hierarchy

---

3. Dina A. Zinnes (1980) summarizes a wide body of literature on the factors believed most important to the system's operation that identifies the following variables: (1) the number of nations, (2) the distribution of power, (3) nations' goals, (4) countries' types of governments and decision-making processes, (5) international rules and customs, (6) the patterns of relations among states, and (7) perceptual patterns among the system's nations.

that makes some suppliers and others dependents, and the military asymmetries that pit the strong against the weak all still shape the relations among nations, as they have in the past. The particular nations populating the various strata in these pecking orders have changed during the twentieth century, but the underlying structural inequalities remain.

The Interplay of Continuity and Discontinuity

Because global conditions exhibit both change and constancy and because global trends often move in divergent directions, the impression is conveyed that in world politics "the more things change the more they stay the same." It is in the vortex of stable properties and changing characteristics that the ultimate direction of world politics is determined. Interaction between the continuous and the discontinuous may thus produce different kinds of systemic changes.[4] What are some of these possibilities?

First, the international system may exhibit *equilibrium*, with the forces of change and continuity balancing each other to produce a kind of kinetic movement (like a motor running but going nowhere). The result is a dynamic system filled with movement but maintaining its essential parameters. Stated differently, countervailing trends may combine to preserve the central properties of the system within confined limits of variation, producing fluidity at the same time that the patterns of relations in world politics are prevented from deviating substantially from their equilibrium or steady state (see Liska, 1957).[5] As one observer of system dynamics framed it,

> Because the complexity and dynamism of political turbulence involves swift-moving flows of activity, flows that often gather in strength and surge irregularly in diverse directions, [the perception of] constant flux conveys the impression of endless change, of individuals, officials, collectivities, and institutions being caught up in the course of events and adjusting to them by altering their ways. Yet, as in the case of whirlpools and hurricanes, all the commotion and activities of turbulent social systems need not always result in change. They can form repetitive patterns that are marked by constancy: both people and societies can be on the move, only to converge back on their starting points as their changes encounter constraints that redirect them back to where they began, a circular process that is distinguished by both short-term changes and long-term continuities. (Rosenau, 1988: chap. 4, p. 3)

---

4. In the terminology of future studies, investigation of the various effects that trends have on one another is called *cross-impact analysis*. This mode of analysis is often popular because some of the hardest issues are *polycentric policy problems*—problems for which solutions have often unwelcome implications for other problems.

5. These concepts are derived from the analytic approach of *general systems theory*, which might be regarded as the intellectual forerunner of the *interdependence* perspective as it applies to the study of world politics (see Chapter 2).

Social systems maintain their steady states through what are called self-regulatory or *homeostatic* mechanisms.[6] These "system-maintenance" mechanisms make global transformations infrequent (McClelland, 1966), reduce the impact of transforming agents, and thus promote only incremental adaptations of the status quo. System-maintenance mechanisms monitor the environment and regulate it, much like a thermostat maintains within certain limits the temperature in a room.

Various regulatory devices built into the framework of world politics slow transformations and preserve systemic stability. Examples of processes and procedures that inhibit global transformation include international legal norms, past treaty agreements and other commitments, ties within and among international organizations, and strategic balances of power. The homeostatic propensities of complex systems thus encourage recurrent patterns of world politics, steering world political developments along a relatively even path and preventing extreme deviations from the general course. The obstacles to transformation imposed by these self-adjusting mechanisms should not be underestimated. Through their force, the basic properties of world politics tend to remain durable and resilient.

Despite these obstacles, a second pattern is one in which some trends may interact cumulatively to propel world politics into a new and transformed steady state. Using the vocabulary of futures studies, global trends and constants may cohere synergistically to produce an *envelope curve*—one that combines several subsidiary developments—capable of producing a new pattern of world political relationships. Thus "threshold effects" may transform international politics; the slow accumulation of small changes that by themselves have no apparent impact may, when they interact with and reinforce one another, open the way for a substantial transformation in the world's political processes.

The resistance of global politics to transformation notwithstanding, cumulative transforming forces can be potent in the long run. The growth of interstate interdependence through transnational exchanges is one example. Although the high politics of military posturing continues to command the world's headlines, the compound effects of transnational travel, communication, investment, trade, and the like have been quietly reshaping the global environment. Whether the additive effects of these changes have reached a threshold point, capable of spilling over to transform world politics, is uncertain. The potential for such transformation is evident, nonetheless, and in many important respects these developments have already considerably altered the global environment.

Incremental transformation through cumulative and compound changes should not be seen as somehow inevitable, however. Trends in world politics rarely unfold in a constant, linear direction. Indeed, persistence forecasting

---

6. In domestic political systems, for example, educational institutions often promote system maintenance through the socialization process that transmits the system's supportive values (the political culture) from one generation to the next.

(pointing to automatic eventual transformation) usually fails because the conditions that coalesce to produce a given trend almost never continue indefinitely. As conditions change, they produce effects different from those observable at any given moment and breed obstacles to their continuation. Historical trends sometimes exhaust themselves; others stabilize or even reverse themselves as natural or manufactured obstacles interrupt their evolutionary progression. The radical change in the global energy picture forecast for the 1990s compared with projections made only a few years ago is a striking case in point. Thus, a third mode of change in world politics is possible: the capacity for international systems to exhibit, over time, *reversibility*.

Reversibility suggests that world politics may in the future emulate its distant past. Indeed, the historically minded observer of world affairs may encounter a sense of *déjà vu*, because, over a long time, cycles make today's changes look only like a reversion to the politics dominant in earlier periods. One example is in the changes in the rankings of nations in the international hierarchy over long stretches of time. Those once at the top—the hegemons, such as Spain, France, the Netherlands, and Great Britain—all were subsequently replaced by other world leaders. A long cycle of world leadership is observable, in that no preeminent state has managed to retain a position at the pinnacle of wealth and power (see Modelski, 1987; Thompson, 1988). Yet, every hundred years a single power has risen to dominate the international political system, thereby indicating one significant way in which global conditions at any point in time often resemble those that existed before. To the extent that long cycles are operative in world politics, the historical interaction between forces of continuity and change "holds within itself the seeds of its own dissolution" (Modelski, 1978).

The potential for recurrent cyclical alterations in world politics has important implications for world politics in the 1990s and beyond. Some observers, for instance, claim that the world of the 1990s is much like that of the 1890s or 1930s and that changes presently unfolding may soon give way to the reassertion of long-standing patterns, perhaps replicating the kind of atmosphere that will eventually precipitate another worldwide depression or even a third (and final?) world war.

What cyclical alterations in world politics portend for the world's political future remains uncertain, however. Some analysts see the fragmentation of political authority into smaller parcels, whereas others see its consolidation into large competitive power blocs. Some see science and technology as propelling the world into abundance and affluence, whereas others see them turning the world back toward poverty and hopelessness.

To recapitulate, world politics consists of interacting continuities and discontinuities. Clearly, it is difficult to predict which of these forces will dominate the future. But in seeking to do so it is also clear that we must think in multicausal terms. No trend or trouble stands alone; all interact simultaneously. The path toward the future is influenced by multiple determinants. Each is connected to the rest in a complex set of linkages that promises to grow even tighter in the future. The expanding complexity of relationships among causal forces may produce stability by inhibiting the impact of any single force or trend. On the other hand, if interacting forces converge, their combined effects may accelerate the pace at which a transformation in world politics occurs and move it in directions not possible in the absence of this symbiosis.

THE SOURCES OF TRANSFORMATION IN WORLD POLITICS

Every chapter in this book implies that the trend or issue on which it focuses constitutes *the* key to understanding the many problems that confront world politics. The East–West conflict, the gap between rich and poor nations, the mounting sense of mutual vulnerability created by growing economic interdependence, the unprecedented pressures on the global habitat, the militarization of the entire globe, and the rise of new forms of international conflict and violence all compete with one another for attention as the principal force shaping conduct in the world and the chief cause of its afflictions.

The admonition that the future of world politics will flow from many causes suggests, however, that transformation in world politics depends on how many discordant global trends simultaneously affect one another. Future global conditions thus depend on how changes and continuities eventually coalesce. But in a sense this conclusion begs another question, as it does not consider the sources from which transformation in world politics may derive.

The Global Past As Prologue?

Some have assumed that global trends are propelled by their own, almost irreversible momentum. The past, in other words, molds the future. Is this an appropriate way to describe the forces that transform world politics? Or is the inference wrong that history somehow moves irresistibly by the force of its own momentum?

Especially when the status quo appears obsolete and change inevitable, it is tempting to regard change as a real, material phenomenon that occurs as a result of its own volition. The future may appear to be predetermined by the pull of history—a philosophical tradition known as *historical determinism*. Among other claims, historical determinism contends that history dictates its own pace and sets the course of subsequent developments.[7] From this per-

---

7. The ideas associated with historical determinism are more complicated and varied than suggested here. Generally, historical determinism maintains that there are certain types of factors—reason, class struggle, or whatever—that guide historical change in certain patterns or preordained ways. The view is not incompatible with the belief that a divine entity is responsible for the fate of humankind, as long as that belief holds that such a god permits humankind to choose its own destiny by exhibiting either virtuous or sinful behaviors. Thus historical determinism need not deny free choice. It can also mean that choices are constrained by the factors that determine history. This was the position of Karl Marx, for instance, whose economic determinism maintained that the mode of production determines the kinds of political choices that people make. More broadly, individuals' choices are strongly influenced by the social milieu in which they live.

spective, the transformation of world politics may be interpreted as moving toward a preordained destiny in (fatalistic?) response to a collection of predetermined trends.

A corollary of this conviction is the proposition that human destiny has an overall purpose. This view is based on *teleological* reasoning, which presumes that a purpose can be attributed to nature, that a master design is in operation, and that therefore any development can be interpreted as a consequence of the overall scheme of things foreordained by nature. Consistent with this logic, it was once popular to explain the expansion of the borders of the United States on and beyond the North American continent by reference to a preprogrammed plan, namely, *manifest destiny*. Even today it is not uncommon to see explanations of Soviet foreign policy behavior that claim that the Soviets, like their czarist predecessors, are driven by "nature's design" to seek a warm-water port.

Neither historical determinism nor teleological reasoning is compatible with scientific thinking. They both fail to inform us adequately about the origins of the trends and transformations in world politics, as both deny the ability of humankind to shape its own destiny. They thus run counter to an indisputable fact—that change is conditioned by human choice. What people have elected to do has molded the world we currently inhabit. Accordingly, the fate of nations and the world is not predetermined according to some master plan; if it were, the study of human life and society would be a wasted activity, because no one would have any incentive to try to make things different.

It is more fruitful to recognize that the transformation of world politics has and will continue to be determined by the collective impact of individual and group behaviors, bounded as they are by ecological and structural opportunities and constraints. Nature does not act, humans do. Human choice alone can modify prevailing tendencies (see Childe, 1962). Thus, because it is easier to describe a trend than it is to explain it, it is tempting—but fallacious—to assume that trends are self-propelling and therefore caused by the force of their own inertia. Global trends are in fact governed by a variety of causal factors, and their direction and pace of change must be explained by reference to these human and nonhuman determinants. This principle is perhaps what Ronald Reagan had in mind when in 1987 he argued that "the arms race is not pre-ordained and not part of some inevitable course of history. We can make history." Similarly, John F. Kennedy noted, "Our problems are manmade. Therefore they can be solved by man."

Change in world politics therefore is neither autonomous nor automatic. Because trend is not destiny, historical transformations are not a necessity. Historical developments may impose circumstantial limits that constrain the free exercise of choice, but history itself cannot move a trend along a designated trajectory. Trends are not "natural" laws (Popper, 1957). What makes political behavior central to future worlds is that such behavior places world politics in a human context, emphasizing that humankind's fate is conditioned by the way that people allocate values through political conduct. Perhaps this axiom is the reason why the ancient Greek philosopher Aristotle called politics the master science.

Individual Behaviors and Collective Consequences

If the transformation of world politics is a function of human choice, then, clearly, individuals matter. Parenting a child, purchasing a foreign-produced car, writing an overseas pen pal, saluting a flag, traveling abroad, voting for a jingoistic politician—each of these individual actions affects, however imperceptibly, the quality of life on earth. Vast impersonal forces may appear to rule the world, but Walt Whitman was helpful in reminding us that even in politics and metaphysics, sooner or later we come down to one single, solitary soul.

Although the role of the individual in world politics cannot be denied, the causal linkage between individual actions and the overall state of the world is extraordinarily difficult to unravel. The structure of the global system may be conditioned by the cumulative, interactive effects of individuals' choices, but macroprocesses are not tied directly to microbehaviors (see Schelling, 1978, 1984). How these microparts fit together to make the whole is therefore very complicated. Why world political trends assume a shape that no one fully expected may be due to the inability to trace how individual acts interrelate to affect collective outcomes. "The trouble with change in human affairs," Ralf Dahrendorf (1986) observes, "is that it is so hard to pin down. It happens all the time. But while it happens it eludes our grasp, and once we feel able to come to grips with it, it has become past history."

This analytic obstacle complicates the task of understanding trends and transformations in world politics. A microperspective yields a worm's-eye view of the world, and a macroperspective provides a bird's-eye view. But how to get from the former to the latter has eluded scholarship. The tragedy of the commons metaphor introduced in Chapter 9 is useful in understanding the causes of ecological overshoot precisely because it links micro (individual) choices to macro (global) consequences. In a similar manner, the security dilemma described in Chapter 11 is a valuable analytic tool because it illuminates how preparations for war by one actor to enhance its defense unintentionally provoke the same kinds of efforts by others. The unsought result is that weapons decisions made independently by individual states create conditions that reduce the security of all. But because the commons metaphor and the security dilemma are not relevant or applicable to all micro-macro processes, we must search elsewhere to understand the connection between individual behavior and macropolitics. This requires consideration of another analytic distinction relevant to studying the multiple sources of global transformation which was introduced in Chapter 2, namely, the distinction among various levels of analysis.

Levels of Analysis

All people may contribute individually to the macro trends under way in the world arena, but they do not contribute equally, and their impacts are not all uniform. Thus we cannot use reductionist logic, which seeks to locate all world developments in individual choices. Instead, we must discriminate among the relative contributions of different actors at different levels according to their ability to influence global circumstances.

Two facts make this necessary. First, political power in the global system is distributed unevenly. Hence, the best place to look for the major forces of systemic transformation is in those sectors in which power is concentrated. Second, individual choice is typically exercised in a group context. The decisions reached are therefore affected strongly by the collective needs, values, and preferences of the groups to which individuals belong. These empirical facts of social life make it important to study world politics by reference to both individuals and the various groups and collectivities they form and the significant reference groups to which humans habitually defer. We must, in other words, approach world politics by studying the variety of collectivities to which people extend their loyalty, from small special-interest groupings to larger entities like nation-states.

In international politics, this analytic prescription is conventionally referred to as the levels-of-analysis problem. It underscores the necessity of tracing changes in world politics to different groups of actors, their attributes, and their activities. By scholarly convention, the actors can be categorized according to the relative size and scope of their composition.

At the smallest (narrowest) level is the so-called idiosyncratic or individual level of analysis—the personal characteristics of each human being, from the average citizen to the head of a state. At a second level are the authoritative decision-making units that govern nation-states as well as various subnational groupings of individuals (for example, pressure groups and political parties) that shape the choices of those who govern. At the systemic level are the conditions that result from the interactions of all transnational actors with one another around the globe. These sometimes combine on a regional scale to form transnational associations (such as the European Community, NATO, and the Warsaw Pact). At this level also are those transnational actors purporting universality, such as the United Nations. The "system" or international level of analysis is also used to refer to those macro properties that influence the actors within the global environment, such as its international legal rules, distribution of power, or the amount of alliance aggregation and war occurring in a given historical period.

This differentiation of levels draws attention to the need to attribute transformations in world politics not to any one of these levels but to the influence of all of them. The existence of interconnections across levels means that any global development is likely to be linked simultaneously to forces operating at each level. The behavior of any one nation, for instance, will likely be affected by the dispositions of its leaders, its domestic political and social conditions, and its external environment and the stimuli it receives from abroad. Similarly, any future increase or relaxation of worldwide international tension will be governed in part by how actors at each level choose to act internationally today.

One conclusion derived from the levels-of-analysis distinction is that exclusive attention to the nation-state in world affairs is unwarranted. As this book has tried to make clear, there are other kinds of actors, and their actions and interaction make substantial contributions to the global political condition.

Nonetheless, the traditional state-centric focus of the theory of political realism is understandable. Political power remains embedded primarily in the central decision-making institutions of the national actors that make up the international system. This underscores the continuing importance of analyzing comparatively the foreign policies of nation-states. Until global or regional collective problem-solving institutions amass greater power over nation-states, human destiny will continue to be shaped principally by government-to-government relationships. Thus the transformation of world politics will continue to be mediated mainly through the decisions of those governing national political units.

EVALUATING THE GLOBAL CONDITION

The trends and transformations in world politics already under way invite still another kind of analytic question—the normative one of how the transformations occurring and the continuities persisting should be judged. Are they for better or worse? Should global conditions evoke optimism or pessimism? Do the structures and institutions underlying world politics promote good or ill?

The contemporary facts defining the global condition provide no consistent message. Selective human perception and value discrepancies point to alternative scenarios and disparate evaluations. Assessments differ because they focus on different dimensions of world politics, each of which is judged according to personal values. This is why, perhaps, so many analytic perspectives in the study of international relations exist (recall Chapter 2), each seeking to address and explain the diverse questions posed by rapidly changing global circumstances.

Two categories of value assessment warrant special consideration because of the important questions they raise about continuity and change as they relate to the future of world politics. The first is the image of global *progress*. For some (for example, Kahn, 1976; Simon and Kahn, 1984), the future inspires confidence and hope, not despair. Optimists contend that degradation and decay in future global conditions are unlikely. On the contrary, many trends are favorable. For instance, the standard of living enjoyed by a considerable proportion of humanity far surpasses that enjoyed by even the most advantaged in even the recent past. Dismal worldwide trends such as monetary disorder, food shortages, and violence are partially offset by the presence of regional and national countertrends. Despite the friction between contending nations and the dangers posed by the destructiveness of their weapons, for instance, the superpowers have avoided war between them for nearly five decades, and their crisis-management capabilities seem to have improved considerably over time. Such assessments thus take comfort in recalling the world's impressive track record in coping successfully with previous challenges; indeed, all previous predictions of apocalyptic doom have proved unfounded in subsequent periods. Equipped with a raised social consciousness about global problems and new tools of science and technology, humankind's prospects for improvement appear better than ever before.

According to the interpretation that today's problems do not necessarily mean greater problems tomorrow, the twilight of the twentieth century is full of possibilities, not just problems. Futurists subscribing to this perspective appreciate the extent to which material progress is contingent on the current implementation of political solutions to today's challenges. The real problem is that the progress under way in some quarters of the globe is not exhibited throughout the world. It is dispersed unevenly. Political analysts have long believed that the maintenance of wide welfare differentials within and among countries breeds instability and violence. Reducing these differences in order to provide the greatest number with the greatest good is not only the greatest challenge; it is also a necessity, for the absence of stability and peace will surely impair humanity's ability to control change for the better by reversing those trends toward deteriorating conditions. Optimists also argue, however, that among these inequalities will be found the building blocks for creating institutions capable of ensuring a more just and peaceful international environment.

A second perspective is that of global *regress*, the belief that the global condition is experiencing a regressive decline. Whereas optimists view the future with hope, pessimists see the global condition and its prospects quite differently. To them, we live in a system dominated by scarcity and fear. Harsh realities must be faced. Paranoia is a heightened state of awareness. If people today are not at least somewhat paranoid about the trends emanating from prevailing circumstances and the dangers they pose, then surely the threatening direction in which the world is headed will be misunderstood.

From the perspective of global regress, the signs point toward a period of deteriorating conditions, diminishing expectations, and generally dismal prospects. Already we live with unimaginable brutality. For the majority of humankind, poverty, hunger, and degradation are everyday experiences. Violence is an ever-present danger, and the expectation of a better life is an unknown or forgotten hope. Even personal survival is precarious. As the influential *Global 2000 Report* of the United States government warned,

> If present trends continue, the world in 2000 will be more crowded, more polluted, less stable ecologically, and more vulnerable to disruption than the world we live in now. Serious stresses involving population, resources, and environment are clearly visible ahead. Despite greater material output, the world's people will be poorer in many ways than they are today. (*The Global 2000 Report to the President*, 1980a)

Because the world shows no sign of mounting a meaningful response to these dangers, the human prospect is dim (Asimov, 1979; Heilbroner, 1975).

The despondency of the pessimists is rooted in a cluster of assumptions. Apocalypse is around the corner, if not already here, because the unaddressed trends threatening the world have reached the point that they may be impossible to reverse. The dispersion of weapons, the proliferation of nuclear know-how, the depletion of the world's finite resources, the destruction of its ecosystem, and the continuous growth of the world's population all point to real, perhaps insurmountable, hazards. The dangers reinforce one another, making efforts to control any one an obstacle to controlling the others. Each decision not only opens alternatives; it also forecloses others. In short, global trends constitute a time bomb, and the time required to make adaptive adjustments is rapidly ticking away.

Although the scenarios of the pessimists differ, all the outcomes are grim. Options have narrowed, and the pace of change itself inhibits the implementation of solutions. The earth imposes real limits that no technology can escape without encroaching on the natural limits imposed by nature. Indeed, technology itself may contribute to problems, not solutions—"what man makes unmakes man," Norman Cousins has contended. In sum, it may be too late: The existing problems dwarf the remedies; the adequacy of existing institutional structures is a delusion; the probability that humankind will collaborate peacefully to reorder the planet's political system is remote.

IS GLOBAL CHANGE BEYOND CONTROL?

The future has few political advocates. To be sure, there are those in academic circles who can persuasively argue that the future ought to be considered. But for most politicians the future is near term and its requirements clear-cut— winning the next election or averting an impending coup. In neither process do future generations figure prominently.

Even if politicians and policymakers were able to look beyond their immediate problems, efforts to cope with the complexities of contemporary problems often produce unintended consequences as policymakers and others create conditions that were not part of their intent. Andrew Scott provides one compelling illustration of the unintended consequences of foreign policy choice:

> The Bretton Woods system was designed to foster increased trade, the improvement of payments procedures, and economic development. It succeeded in accomplishing these objectives. It also "accomplished" a number of other things that were not intended—it furthered inequality between developed and less-developed nations, it contributed to the build-up of international debt, it provided the institutional framework within which an extraordinary growth of multinational enterprises took place, it tied global economic conditions to domestic and foreign policy decisions of the United States, [and] by contributing to the increase of trade it also contributed to the growth of interdependence and to the vulnerability of the global economic system to disruption. (Scott, 1979: 2–3)

Under circumstances that connect the choices made in one society to consequences in others, determining what is in the interest of humanity is not simple. Even conditions once believed to be altogether desirable, such as growth, are now questioned (see Schumacher, 1973). The first step in doing good things, the ancient Greek philosophers believed, was to know what is good. The overlap of actors, issues, interests, and values obscures the identification of what is good. Every good has its costs, and every policy option risks unintended consequences.

The paradox of world politics under conditions of complex interdependence is that these circumstances have simultaneously enlarged the responsibilities and expanded the issues to be confronted while narrowing the available options and spreading thin the attention of leaders. This means that it is more difficult, not less, to implement needed global reforms. The barriers are evident everywhere. National actors seem to muddle through problems as crises arise, rather than to mold the world to preferred plans. A Band-Aid approach that deals with symptoms, as opposed to causes, is usually taken. Policies proposing comprehensive or radical solutions are avoided because they are the most controversial politically. Instead, trial-and-error and incremental approaches to new realities tend to be pursued. The world seems to be surprised on a regular basis as problems appear for which no one seems prepared.

Is the transformation of world politics beyond the capacity of any actor or set of actors to control? If what can still be done is less than what could once be done, is the efficient management of world politics impossible? Under contemporary world conditions, must foreign policy at its best involve a choice only between the lesser of evils? Or will humankind join together to address global problems and enhance transcendent common interests? Can it, in Jean Monnet's phrase, "put [its] problems on one side of the table and all of us on the other?"

These are challenging, even apocalyptic questions. They ask that we think some uncomfortable thoughts—whether humankind can control its fate and whether it can steer the direction of the global transformation that may well determine the course of human destiny.

SUGGESTED READINGS

Bertsch, Gary K., ed. *Global Policy Futures*. Beverly Hills, Calif.: Sage, 1982.

Brecher, Michael, and Patrick James. *Crisis and Change in World Politics*. Boulder, Colo.: Westview Press, 1986.

Ferguson, Yale H., and Richard W. Mansbach. *The Elusive Quest: Theory and International Politics*. Columbia: University of South Carolina Press, 1988.

Gilpin, Robert. *War and Change in World Politics*. New York: Cambridge University Press, 1981.

Holsti, Ole R., Randolph M. Siverson, and Alexander L. George, eds. *Change in the International System*. Boulder, Colo.: Westview Press, 1980.

Morse, Edward L. *Modernization and the Transformation of International Relations*. New York: Free Press, 1976.

Oren, Nissan, ed. *When Patterns Change: Turning Points in International Politics.* New York: St. Martin's Press, 1984.

Schelling, Thomas C. *Choice and Consequence.* Cambridge, Mass.: Harvard University Press, 1984.

Scott, Andrew M. *The Dynamics of Interdependence.* Chapel Hill: University of North Carolina Press, 1982.

Vasquez, John A., and Richard W. Mansbach. "The Issue Cycle: Conceptualizing Long-Term Global Change," *International Organization* 37 (Spring 1983): 257–280.

SIXTEEN

The Global Predicament:
Ten Questions for a Tense Era

We are at risk. . . . We have all by ourselves generated . . . dangers. . . .
Joining forces against these new [common] enemies requires us to make
courageous efforts at self-knowledge, because we ourselves—all nations of the
Earth—bear responsibility for the perils we now face. . . . History has placed
a burden on our shoulders. It is up to us to build a future worthy of our
children and grandchildren.

CARL SAGAN, 1988

Human history becomes more and more a race between education and
catastrophe.

H. G. WELLS, 1921

The trends and transformations described in this book provoke many questions about the meaning of change for world politics. Answers to them are likely to be elusive and to be colored by the vantage point of the observer. What the eminent scientist Johannes Kepler noted about the age in which he lived applies to ours as well:

> These are strange and marvelous times in which we live, that such transformations are wrought in our view of the nature of things. Yet . . . it is only our vision which is being expanded and altered. . . . Curious, how easy it is for us little creatures to confuse the opening of our eyes with the coming into being of a new creation: like children conceiving the world remade each morning when they awake.

Whether the changes sweeping the contemporary world portend the advent of a new creation is uncertain. But what is certain is that the pace of change challenges the wisdom of old beliefs and orthodox visions of the world. These picture the world as stable and static, when in fact present-day political reality is a world of borders permeated and transcended by the flow of goods and capital, the passage of people, communication through airwaves, airborne traffic, and space satellites. Because change, mobility, and turmoil are characteristic of contemporary life, they require that unconventional ques-

511

tions be asked about conventional ideas and that we realize that complicated and interrelated problems cannot be solved by simple formulas.

In this final chapter we ask ten questions that are linked to the preceding description of trends and transforming forces in contemporary world politics. How they are answered may influence significantly the kind of world that will unfold.

1. Are Nation-States Obsolete?

Changes in the world since the dawn of the twentieth century have been profound. Collectively, they have brought into existence an environment in which the role of the primary actor in world politics, the territorial nation-state, has been altered:

> One of the hallmarks of human history in the late twentieth century is the increasing internationalization of the world: in production, trade, finance, technology, threats to security, communications, research, education, and culture. One major consequence of this is that the mutual penetration of economic, political, and social forces among the nations of the world is increasingly salient; and it may be the case that the governments of nation-states are progressively losing degrees of direct control over the global forces that affect them. (Smelser, 1986: 1)

"A myth" is what John F. Kennedy called "the untouchability of national sovereignty." Henry Kissinger labeled the nation-state "inadequate" and the emergence of a global community an "imperative." Zbigniew Brzezinski asserted that "we are witnessing the end of the supremacy of the nation-state on the international scene" and noted that although "this process is far from consummated . . . the trend seems irreversible." Implicit in these views is an attack on the utility of the nation-state as a political entity capable of adequately handling global challenges.

The sociologist Auguste Comte argued that societal institutions are created to address problems and meet human needs and that they disappear when they can no longer perform these functions. Throughout the world, the legitimacy of governments is being disputed by minorities seeking separation and sovereignty. And nation-states everywhere find their economies influenced by others because "technology has created a world no longer effectively composed of individual national economic entities. . . . There is now one world capital market." As a consequence, "national policies [are] bound to prove frustrating, and often counterproductive as well" (Blumenthal, 1988). Nation-states' viability is also critically undermined by their inability to protect their citizens from foreign aggression. In an age of weapons of mass extinction, no nation can make credible its claim to guarantee the common defense. The nation-state's primary *raison d'être* may no longer exist (Herz, 1976).

Indeed, the nation-state's managerial capabilities everywhere, irrespective of form of government, fail to inspire confidence. Lack of faith in governmental efficiency has reached epidemic proportions. No government is immune from attacks by its own citizens for its inability to protect its population or improve its life. Making war, preserving peace, maintaining domestic stability, providing for the general welfare, ensuring a just distribution of income, engineering economic growth, promoting civil liberties—in few countries can citizens be found expressing satisfaction with their government's performance in meeting these goals.

But at the same time, other forces infuse the nation-state with vigor and encourage its persistence. "Obviously in some respects the nation-state is flourishing and in others it is dying," observes Pierre Hassner (1968), adding, "it can no longer fulfill some of the most important traditional functions, yet it constantly assumes new ones which it alone seems able to fulfill." Thus, at the core of contemporary international politics lies a paradox: "At a time when the nation-state has appeared to be functionally obsolete, it has been reaffirmed by the same process which would call for its transcendence" (Morse, 1976). Will the current phase in which global problems are addressed through national solutions be replaced by a transformed system in which global problems will be confronted by transnational institutions?

2. Is Interdependence a Cure or a Curse?

Global interdependence poses perhaps the greatest threat to the nation-state. It has expanded the range of global issues while making their management more difficult, and mutual vulnerabilities have reduced states' autonomy and curtailed their sovereign control over their national destinies. Whether in the long run interdependence will prove to be a cure or a curse is, therefore, a question of pressing concern to the next generation.

From one perspective, global interdependence may eventually prove to be a cure by drawing the world's diverse components together in pursuit of mutual survival and welfare. Awareness of the common destiny of all may necessitate cooperation among states. In this sense, the mutual challenges facing the world may serve a constructive purpose, energizing efforts to put aside national competition in order to address shared problems collaboratively. Ignoring these challenges—for example, pollution, debt, and protection of the oceans and atmosphere—is no longer a realistic policy alternative. Similarly, under conditions of tightening global interdependence, violent conflict will recede, for people's willingness to fight those on whom their continued welfare rests can be expected to decline. At a minimum, so this reasoning goes, conflict among interdependent states will be limited because few nations will be able to disentangle themselves from the transnational ties that bind them together. From this perspective, then, the continued tightening of interstate linkages is to be welcomed, for it strengthens the seams that bind together the fragile tapestry of international relations.

But from another, more pessimistic perspective, global interdependence may prove to be a force that prevents the world from effectively addressing the many problems confronting it. Adherents to this view warn, for example, that global interdependence does not necessarily mean global organization, regardless of how compelling the need for coordination may be. Contact and mutual dependence may instead breed conflict. The absence of a community of nations remains, and there is ample evidence of a nostalgia for the relative autonomy that nation-states once possessed. Under conditions of scarcity, the temptation to use force to acquire perceived national necessities may be overwhelming. Indeed, frustration over the inability to sever dependency relationships may lead to war instead of peace. Similarly, the temptation to seek isolation from foreign economic competition by creating barriers to free trade may be irresistible. That a new wave of protectionism could result once again in global economic collapse seems possible.

Thus, the tightening web of global interdependence foretells both opportunity and danger. It has mixed consequences (see Gasiorowski, 1983, 1986). If, on balance, the advantages of interdependence outweigh the disadvantages, then the means for accelerating its development should be used to benefit the greatest number. Conversely, if global interdependence undermines national and international welfare and security, then the means for containing and perhaps reversing its effects need to be found. But is the capacity to realize either goal within the power of a politically disorganized and fragmented world community?

3. What Is the "National Interest"?

What policy goals should nation-states pursue? What is the national interest? This question has preoccupied policymakers for centuries. In earlier times, the answer could be comfortably put: It was perceived appropriate for the state to do whatever was necessary to promote its internal welfare, protect itself from external attack, and preserve its values and way of life.

Similar goals are sought today. But the options available for their realization are increasingly limited, and the choices are not nearly so viable as they seemingly once were. We live in an age of trade-offs; as Ronald Reagan observed in 1983, "as some problems are resolved, others are sure to pop up." Many problems can be resolved only at the price of exacerbating others. Under these conditions, the quest for narrow self-advantage often can carry prohibitively high costs, and the drive for power can result in destruction. Thus, when every nation is dependent on others for its welfare, a search for independence can be self-defeating. Moreover, the historic tendency to define the national interest chauvinistically (my country, right or wrong) is counterproductive domestically as well as internationally. No country can afford to assume a self-righteous posture, to quest for power in a way that reduces the security of its enemies, or to take comfort in the tribulations of others.

In the past, those questioning orthodox definitions of the national interest seldom were applauded for their criticisms. But increasingly the call is heard for more sophisticated definitions of it. As Margaret Mead mused, "Substantially we all share the same atmosphere today, and we can only save ourselves by saving other people also. There is no longer a contradiction between patriotism and concern for the world." This idea was also voiced by the former secretary of state Cyrus Vance in a speech before the United Nations General Assembly, when he stated that "more than ever cooperative endeavors among nations are a matter not only of idealism but of direct self-interest."

Years ago, the eminent political realist E. H. Carr (1939) articulated his convictions about the realism of idealism, maintaining that self-interest is not served by opposing the general interests of humankind. Nor is it served by failing to recognize that the plight of others can ultimately threaten oneself—a view underlined by Martin Luther King's reminder that "injustice anywhere is a threat to justice everywhere."

4. Technological Innovation: Blessing or Burden?

Underlying the uncertainty accompanying change is the irresistible growth of technology:

> There is one circumstance which overshadows all else and has set the current period apart: unprecedented, deep and continual technological change. In the 1970s and 1980s extraordinarily rapid technological change has thrust upon us new and as yet unresolved problems of governance in the national and international spheres. There appears to be a fundamental lag between the current rate of technological change and the rate of adjustment to these changes among decision-makers. (Blumenthal, 1988: 531–532)

Technology in all its forms profoundly affects our lives and shapes our future. Discoveries in microelectronics, information processing, transportation, energy, agriculture, communications, medicine, and biotechnology have transformed life within and between societies. As a result, "the world is not what it was only a few short years ago. World industry and commerce are being reshaped by technological change in many . . . ways, as are the national and international problems to which new technologies give rise" (Blumenthal, 1988).

These changes propel growth and alter behavior patterns. They can, accordingly, either be a blessing or impose a burden. They may provide solutions to some problems but cause others. They may lead to the discovery of new ways to prevent disease or foreign attack but may also make possible new ways to transmit disease across borders or to make war.

Technological advance is, therefore, two-sided in its effects. It can improve life as well as improve the capacity of humankind to destroy life. Ultimately, its consequences will depend on human values—on the choices the powerful make about the purposes to which new technologies will be put. As Wassily

Leontief warned in 1987, "Technology is now, for better or worse, the principal driving force behind the ongoing rapid economic, social, and political change. Like any irrepressible force, the new technology can bestow on us undreamed of benefits but also inflict irreparable damage." The technological catalyst of change can promote progress only if properly and constructively managed and if the interconnectedness of technological change and economic, political, and military conditions is recognized.

5. Of What Value Is Military Power?

The changing role of military force in world politics has raised questions about the uses to which it can be put. In the past, force enabled a state to project its power, exercise influence, and dominate others. Today, the destructiveness of both sophisticated conventional and nuclear weapons makes them dangerous to employ, and the threat of their use is less convincing than ever before. But their existence poses new questions and reinforces old ones. Is proper control possible? Is accidental holocaust avoidable? Do arms deter attack by others? Or, instead, because of the threats they elicit, might weapons instead invite preemptive attacks by the fearful adversaries on whom they are targeted? Security is a psychological phenomenon, but is it augmented by the acquisition of more weapons of war? Or are preparations for war for purposes of defense responsible for the security dilemma that all nations face?

Policy debate has not often centered on the issue of whether arms should be acquired. To be sure, most national political leaders agree with Aristotle that "a people without walls is a people without choice" and hence continue to assume that preparation for war is the best route to the maintenance of peace. But much debate does center on questions concerning the costs of weapons. What priorities should be attached to military expenditures compared with other needs? How much military strength is necessary to ensure peace without destroying industrial productivity and economic growth?

That military power may no longer confer influence on its possessor is another challenge. "The paradox of contemporary military strength," Henry Kissinger explained, is that "the capacity to destroy is difficult to translate into a plausible threat even against countries with no capacity for retaliation." The threat of force is often not very credible. Military power is rendered impotent by its very strength. Whether it can be used as a mode of leverage in bargaining is therefore questionable.

Weapons do perform a deterrent function. But if military strength can no longer be used to extract compliance from others, then weapons will have lost their capacity to function as a basis—or a substitute—for diplomacy, and the militarily powerful will no longer be able to command influence. And if military power is impotent, why pay the price of vigilance? Inasmuch as no amount of military might can make a nation invulnerable, escalating military buildups can be assessed only in terms of other consequences, so that it becomes relevant to ask if there are thresholds beyond which the addition of greater destructive power is meaningless. That further increases in weapons may be counterproductive was reflected in U Thant's observation that "the massive sums devoted to armaments do not increase international or human security or happiness. On the contrary, they serve to feed the escalating arms race, to increase insecurity, and to multiply the risks to human survival."

6. Is War Obsolete?

John F. Kennedy described the superpowers as "both racing to alter that uncertain balance of terror that stays the hand of mankind's final war." The fear that this race engenders has led to critical reassessments of the role of force in international politics. Empirically, however, it is obvious that war is not obsolete. War—traditionally regarded as a foreign policy option of last resort—remains a recurrent means to the forceful pursuit of political objectives.

This is not to say that war as an institution is necessarily permanent or to assert that it will always be a dominant element in world politics (see Levi, 1981). Eventually, institutions wither away when they cease to serve their intended purpose. Could this trend already be under way with regard to war? Since World War II, war has been confined to battles among and within the nonindustrialized nations. Peace has endured among the major powers, making the postwar period the longest span of great power peace since the seventeenth century. And as the number of nations has steadily climbed, the total number of wars between them worldwide has not increased. This runs counter to the laws of probability: More wars should be expected, other things being equal. But they have not become more frequent.

Of course, whether the proverbial unthinkable use of today's most destructive weapons will someday make war itself unthinkable is uncertain. It may be, instead, that the eventual disappearance of war will occur in another, far more frightening way—that war will disappear because the use of weapons will obliterate humankind. The only puzzle is when and by what means war will become obsolete. "The choice is either nonviolence or nonexistence," Martin Luther King, Jr., declared.

7. Is Empire Dead?

Since humans first began to roam the planet, the possibility that some would attain hegemony over others has been feared. Much of world history has been written in terms of dreams of world conquest, the quest of peoples for world domination, and the efforts of others to prevent it (Doyle, 1986).

Whether territorial conquest remains a possibility or even a desire in the contemporary world is questionable (even if domination through economic imperialism remains an active force worldwide). Occasionally borders do change and territory does shift hands through legitimate means. But the pursuit of territorial expansionism and of empire has waned noticeably. If anything, borders are changed more often as a result of national disintegration than of territorial expansion.

Many continue to think and act as if nations are actively planning to conquer others. But the past forty-five years of international politics have witnessed a trend on the part of the great powers to relinquish their possessions and dismantle their empires. Since World War II, the great powers' forceful acquisition of territory beyond the confines of their historic boundaries has been rare. And among the lesser powers—to whom threats to the integrity of their borders remain a pressing concern—the goal of expanding one's sovereign reach at the expense of others is not as pervasive as it once was.

Why has the quest for empire apparently largely passed from the scene? A plausible explanation is that empire did not benefit the imperial powers materially (Boulding, 1978). William Langer, writing in the early 1960s when the decolonization process was at its peak, argued similarly:

> It is highly unlikely that the modern world will revert to the imperialism of the past. History has shown that the nameless fears which in the late nineteenth century led to the most violent outburst of expansionism were largely unwarranted. The Scandinavian states and Germany since Versailles have demonstrated that economic prosperity and social well-being are not dependent on the exploitation of other peoples, while better distribution of wealth in the advanced countries has reduced if not obviated whatever need there may have been to seek abroad a safety-value for the pressures building up at home. Even in the field of defense, the old need for overseas bases or for the control of adjacent territories is rapidly being outrun. (Langer, 1962: 129)

If imperialism, empire building, and territorial acquisition are no longer in a nation's self-interest, why should nations continue to prepare for military defense against the imagined expansionist aims of others?

8. *What Price Preeminence?*

Although the presumed desire for world conquest may be little more than an echo from a previous period of international politics, national competition for status in the international pecking order remains a central feature of world politics. Prestige, respect, and wealth remain the core values of many societies and the central goals for which they strive internationally. To remain or become first in the international political system means competing for the political and economic means to bend others to one's will.

The potential long-term consequences of this competition are not entirely favorable, for gross differentials of power and wealth are a constant source of strain. Inequality and military contests among nations have been the price associated with the pursuit of prominence. The perpetuation of poverty in some nations, often exacerbated by their exploitation by other nations, has been another. The instability produced by the divisiveness of rising expectations and diminishing prospects is a third. In struggles among unequals, some nations are victimized. Alienation, resentment, and oppression are among the by-products of inequality. And the ethics of a global arrangement that perpetuates unequal divisions is certainly questionable.

However deplorable the overall situation may be (especially to the disadvantaged), the pursuit of preeminence remains, and its appropriateness has seldom been disputed. Yet the problems of primacy are numerous, the disadvantages of advantage many. With leadership comes the burden of responsibility and the necessity of setting the pace. Moreover, the dominant nations are often the targets of other nations' resentment, envy, hostility, fear, and blame.

It seems likely that the quest for preeminence will be more seriously questioned in national capitals as its costs are acknowledged (see Howell, 1981; Iklé, 1979). Military superiority reduces a great power's industrial growth, weakens its ability to compete economically, and, ultimately, undermines its ability to preserve its dominant position:

> It has been a common dilemma facing previous "number-one" countries that even as their relative economic strength is ebbing, the growing foreign challenges to their position have compelled them to allocate more and more of their resources into the military sector, which in turn squeezes out productive investment and, over time, leads to the downward spiral of slower growth, heavier taxes, deepening domestic splits over spending priorities and a weakening capacity to bear the burdens of defense. (Kennedy, 1988: 533)

Many will not take this message seriously, however, for the one predicament that nearly every nation finds worse than being preeminent is being subject to another's dictates. The pursuit of preeminence is thus likely to continue.

9. Is the World Preparing for the Wrong War?

The destructive power of modern weapons understandably creates tremors in national capitals, and a sense of the apocalyptic haunts the world. The universal formula for national security is that in order to preserve peace, one must prepare for war. But we should ask whether nations would not be wiser to prepare to conquer the conditions that undermine prosperity, freedom, and welfare. As Martin J. Siegel (1983) pointed out, "war for survival is the destiny of all species. In our case, we are courting suicide [by waging war against one another]. The world powers should declare war against their common enemy—the catastrophic and survival-of-the-fittest forces that destroyed most of the species of life that came before us."

Not all world leaders can be accused of single-mindedly preparing to wage the wrong war. Voices that challenge the prevailing penchant are occasionally heard. President Miguel de la Madrid of Mexico in 1983 noted that "scarce resources are being used to sustain the arms race, thereby hindering the economic development of nations and international cooperation." Similarly, President François Mitterrand of France in the same year warned that "together we must urgently find the solutions to the real problems at hand—especially unemployment and underdevelopment. This is the battlefield where the outlines of the year 2000 will be drawn." And India's Prime Minister Indira Gandhi predicted that "either nuclear war will annihilate the human race and destroy the earth, thus disposing of any future, or men and women all over must raise their voices for peace and for an urgent attempt to combine the insights of different civilizations with contemporary knowledge. We can survive in peace and goodwill only by viewing the human race as one, and by looking at global problems in their totality." Each of these rhetorical positions doubtlessly reflects the problems and self-interests of these leaders' countries, but they nonetheless disclose what often seems to be a minority viewpoint. The war of people against people goes on. Humankind may consequently plummet, not because of the absence of opportunities, but because of its collective inability to see and to seize them. "Perhaps we will destroy ourselves. Perhaps the common enemy within us will be too strong for us to recognize and overcome," Carl Sagan (1988) lamented. "But," he continued, "I have hope. Lately there have been signs of change. . . . Is it possible that we humans are at last coming to our senses and beginning to work together on behalf of the species and the planet?"

10. Is Growth Progress?

This rarely examined question promises to command attention as policymakers deal with a world of rapid change. At issue is not just whether there may be limits to growth (see Meadows et al., 1974) but also whether, in a world of finite resources and expanding populations, progress can any longer be equated with economic growth. The possibility that science and the technology it produces can create more problems than they solve is already evident in advanced industrial countries.

"A rise in the GNP," Kenneth Boulding (1978) found, "does not necessarily mean things are better; it may only mean that some things are bigger." But a rise in a state's gross national product can have different consequences for people currently living in poor societies compared with those in rich societies. For the inhabitants of most Third World countries, growth in GNP may mean more food, better housing, better education, and an increased standard of living. Because most people living in the First World already have these basic amenities, additional increments of income usually lead to the satisfaction of relatively trivial needs.

The impact on the global commons of the continued striving for growth is nevertheless substantial. "The incremental person in poor countries contributes negligibly to production, but makes few demands on world resources," explains Herman Daly (1973). By contrast, "the incremental person in the rich country contributes to his country's GNP, and to feed his high standard of living contributes greatly to depletion of the world's resources and pollution of its spaces." In both cases, then, continued population growth is detrimental—for poor societies, because it inhibits increases in per-capita income and welfare, and for rich societies, because it further burdens the earth's delicate ecological system.

An alternative to perpetual growth for the world's rich nations is a steady-state economy, which seeks a constant stock of capital and population combined with as modest a rate of production and consumption of goods as possible. Because most advanced industrial nations have already approached zero-population growth, or a steady state, realizing zero economic growth will require profoundly altered attitudes toward production and consumption. It will also require an alteration in attitudes toward cultural norms regarding leisure and satisfaction. The durability of goods will have to be maximized, and junk will have to be recycled. The profit motive that sustains the perceived need for growth in order to satisfy the craving for items that are not really necessary (for which demand is often created through advertising) will have to be disciplined. Domestic political systems will have to devise means of managing conflict other than by doling out increments of an ever-expanding pie—for in a steady-state economy the pie will no longer be growing.

These prescriptions shake the very foundations on which much of Western civilization has been built. But is there an alternative? Can growth in a finite world proceed infinitely? How many fish can be taken from a fishery before the offtake exceeds the fishery's maximum sustainable yield? How long can a finite energy source sustain consumption before automobiles sputter to a stop, industries grind to a halt, and lights go out? How many pollutants can be dumped into the atmosphere before irreparable environmental damage is done? And how many people can a delicately balanced ecosystem support?

THE CONTINUING TRANSFORMATION OF WORLD POLITICS

In framing the foregoing list of questions we have purposely focused on the puzzles and seeming dilemmas that lie at the core of international politics as it has traditionally been conceptualized and practiced. The potential for present trends to accelerate, move in different directions, or reverse themselves makes conventional wisdom suspect. Indeed, the failure to acknowledge the existence of important global trends and transformations may risk making humanity a victim of its own prevailing orthodoxies.

From the vantage point of the twilight of the twentieth century, the inescapable impression is that the world is undergoing a fundamental restructuring. Previously established patterns and relationships seem to have been interrupted, perhaps irreversibly. Something revolutionary, not simply novel, seems to be happening.

Juxtaposed against the revolutionary is the persistent—the durability of accepted rituals, existing rules, established institutions, and entrenched customs. These resist the pull of some of the revolutionary transformations under way. Change and persistence coexist uneasily in world politics, and it is this intertwined mixture that makes so uncertain the future direction of the international system.

If a new world politics is in the process of unfolding, that process cannot be regarded as complete. A new structure has not emerged to replace the preexisting one. Hence the global system as it currently exists defies easy characterization. It is clearly moving, but discordantly and in seemingly divergent directions. Because the path to the future has not yet assumed recognizable definition, the description of the present as an age *in transformation* is most compelling.

Two races govern the path between the world that is and the world that will be. The first is the race between knowledge and oblivion. Ignorance is the greatest obstacle to global progress and justice. Advances in science and technology have far outpaced resolution of the social and political problems they have generated. Building the knowledge to confront these problems, revolutionary transformations in world politics may therefore present the ultimate challenge. "The splitting of the atom," Albert Einstein warned, "has changed everything save our modes of thinking, and thus we drift toward unparalleled catastrophe. Unless there is a fundamental change in [our] attitudes toward one another as well as [our] concept of the future, the world will face unprecedented disaster."

"Knowledge is our destiny," the philosopher Jacob Bronowski declared. If the world is to forge a future of promise for itself, it must acquire more sophisticated knowledge, and sophistication requires seeing the world as a whole as well as in terms of its individual parts. The temptation to picture others according to our images of ourselves and to project onto them our own aims and values must be overcome. The belief that there is a simple formula for a better tomorrow must be discarded. The limits of rational choice and the political obstacles to reform must be acknowledged. Toleration of ambiguity, even its pursuit, is essential.

The future of world politics—and of humankind—also rests on a race between the ability of nations to act in concert to protect their communal destiny and the forces militating against transnational collaboration. What is being tested is the world's capacity to summon the political will to implement those reforms necessary to meet global challenges.

"Since there is now a risk of mankind destroying itself," former West German chancellor Willy Brandt warned, "this risk must be met by new methods." Can new methods be found? Can a comprehensive reordering of international priorities be effected in time to avert global disaster? Humankind raises only those questions it can solve, argued Karl Marx. Are the world's political problems beyond solution? Whether humankind will be victim or victor may well depend on the answer.

In facing an uncertain global future, it is important to recall that the future is in our hands. The moving words of President Kennedy thus describe a posture we might well assume: "However close we sometimes seem to that dark and final abyss, let no man of peace and freedom despair. For he does not stand alone. . . . Together we shall save our planet or together we shall perish in its flames. Save it we can, and save it we must, and then shall we earn the eternal thanks of mankind."

SUGGESTED READINGS

Brucan, Silviu. "The Global Crisis," *International Studies Quarterly* 28 (March 1984): 97–109.

Cornish, Edward, ed. *Global Solutions*. Bethesda, Md.: World Future Society, 1984.

Falk, Richard. *The End of World Order*. New York: Holmes & Meier, 1983.

Heilbroner, Robert L. *An Inquiry into the Human Prospect: Updated and Reconsidered for the 1980s*. New York: Norton, 1980.

Johansen, Robert C. *The National Interest and the Human Interest*. Princeton, N.J.: Princeton University Press, 1980.

Kim, Samuel S. *The Quest for a Just World Order*. Boulder, Colo.: Westview Press, 1984.

Kothari, Rajni. "Peace in an Age of Transformation," pp. 323–361 in R. B. J. Walker, ed., *Culture, Ideology, and World Order*. Boulder, Colo.: Westview Press, 1984.

Mathisen, Trygve. *Sharing Destiny: A Study of Global Integration*. Oslo: Norwegian University Press, 1985.

McKinley, R. D., and R. Little. *Global Problems and World Order*. Madison: University of Wisconsin Press, 1986.

Miller, Lynn H. *Global Order: Values and Power in International Politics*. Boulder, Colo.: Westview Press, 1985.

REFERENCES

ABRAHAMSSON, BERNHARD J. (1975) "The International Oil Industry," pp. 73–88 in Joseph S. Szyliowicz and Bard E. O'Neill (eds.), *The Energy Crisis and U.S. Foreign Policy*. New York: Praeger.

"THE AGE OF AGING." (1982) *UN Chronicle* 19 (July): 82–84.

AGGARWAL, VINOD K. (1987) *International Debt Threat: Bargaining Among Creditors and Debtors in the 1980s*. Berkeley: Institute of International Studies, University of California.

AKEHURST, MICHAEL. (1987) *A Modern Introduction to International Law*, 5th ed. London: Allen & Unwin.

ALGER, CHADWICK F. (1965) "Personal Contact in Intergovernmental Organizations," pp. 523–547 in Herbert C. Kelman (ed.), *International Behavior*. New York: Holt, Rinehart & Winston.

ALLISON, GRAHAM T. (1971) *Essence of Decision: Explaining the Cuban Missile Crisis*. Boston: Little, Brown.

ALPEROVITZ, GAR. (1985) *Atomic Diplomacy: Hiroshima and Potsdam*. New York: Penguin.

———. (1970) *Cold War Essays*. Garden City, N.Y.: Doubleday-Anchor.

ALSOP, JOSEPH, AND DAVID JORAVSKY. (1980) "Was the Hiroshima Bomb Necessary? An Exchange," *New York Review of Books*, October 23, pp. 37–42.

AMBROSE, STEPHEN E. (1985) *Rise to Globalism*, 4th rev. ed. New York: Penguin.

AMIN, SAMIR. (1987) "Democracy and National Strategy in the Periphery," *Third World Quarterly* 9 (October): 1129–1156.

———. (1974) *Accumulation on a World Scale. A Critique of the Theory of Underdevelopment*. New York: Monthly Review Press.

AMUZEGAR, JAHANGIR. (1987) "Dealing with Debt," *Foreign Policy* 68 (Fall): 140–158.

APTER, DAVID E., AND LOUIS W. GOODMAN (ed.) (1976) *The Multinational Corporation and Social Change*. New York: Praeger.

ARAD, RUTH W., AND UZI B. ARAD. (1979) "Scarce Natural Resources and Potential Conflict," pp. 23–85 in Ruth W. Arad, Uzi B. Arad, Rachel McCulloch, José Piñera, and Ann L. Hollick, *Sharing Global Resources*. New York: McGraw-Hill.

ARCHER, CLIVE. (1983) *International Organizations*. London: Allen & Unwin.

ARMS CONTROL ASSOCIATION. (1988) "Strategic Nuclear Forces of the United States and the Soviet Union," Press Release, May. Washington, D.C.: Arms Control Association.

ARON, RAYMOND. (1958) "Evidence and Inference in History," *Daedalus* 87 (Fall): 11–39.

ASHLEY, RICHARD K. (1984) "The Poverty of Neorealism," *International Organization* 38 (Spring): 255–286.

———. (1980) *The Political Economy of War and Peace*. New York: Nichols.

ASIMOV, ISAAC. (1979) *A Choice of Catastrophes*. New York: Simon & Schuster.

AVERY, DENNIS. (1985) "U.S. Farm Dilemma: The Global Bad News Is Wrong," *Science*, October 25, pp. 408–412.

AYITTEY, GEORGE B. N. (1986) "The Real Foreign Debt Problem," *Wall Street Journal*, April 8, p. 30.

BALDWIN, DAVID A. (1985) *Economic Statecraft*. Princeton, N.J.: Princeton University Press.

BALL, DESMOND. (1983) *Targeting for Strategic Deterrence*. Adelphi Papers No. 185. London: International Institute for Strategic Studies.

BALL, GEORGE W. (1985) "Erosion of U.S. Foreign Relations," *Bulletin of the Atomic Scientists* 41 (August): 110–113.

———. (1971) "Cosmocorp: The Importance of Being Stateless," *Columbia Journal of World Business* 6 (November–December): 25–30.

BARAN, PAUL. (1968) *The Political Economy of Growth*. New York: Monthly Review Press.

BARKUN, MICHAEL. (1968) *Law Without Sanctions: Order in Primitive Societies and the World Community.* New Haven, Conn.: Yale University Press.

BARNET, RICHARD J. (1988) "An Absence of Trust: Roots of Discord in the Soviet-American Relationship," pp. 127–137 in Charles W. Kegley, Jr., and Eugene R. Wittkopf (eds.), *The Global Agenda,* 2nd ed. New York: Random House.

———. (1980a) *The Lean Years.* New York: Simon & Schuster.

———. (1980b) "The Profits of Hunger," *The Nation,* February 9, pp. 1, 145–148.

———. (1979) "Challenging the Myths of National Security," *New York Times Magazine,* April 1, pp. 25, 56 passim.

———. (1977) *The Giants: Russia and America.* New York: Simon & Schuster.

BARNET, RICHARD J., AND RONALD E. MÜLLER. (1974) *Global Reach: The Power of the Multinational Corporations.* New York: Simon & Schuster.

BARON, SAMUEL H., AND CARL PLETSCH. (eds.) (1985) *Introspection in Biography: The Biographer's Quest for Self Awareness.* Hillsdale, N.J.: Analytic Press.

BARR, STRINGFELLOW. (1953) *Citizens of the World.* Garden City, N.Y.: Doubleday.

BEER, FRANCIS A. (1981) *Peace Against War: The Ecology of International Violence.* San Francisco: Freeman.

———. (1974) *How Much War in History: Definitions, Estimates, Extrapolations and Trends.* Sage Professional Papers in International Studies, vol. 3, series no. 02–030. Beverly Hills, Calif.: Sage.

BENNETT, A. LEROY. (1988) *International Organizations,* 4th ed. Englewood Cliffs, N.J.: Prentice-Hall.

BERGESEN, ALBERT. (1980) "From Utilitarianism to Globology: The Shift from the Individual to the World As a Whole As the Primordial Unit of Analysis," pp. 1–12 in Albert Bergesen (ed.), *Studies of the Modern World-System.* New York: Academic Press.

BERGESEN, ALBERT, AND RONALD SCHOENBERG. (1980) "Long Waves of Colonial Expansion and Contraction, 1415–1969," pp. 231–277 in Albert Bergesen (ed.), *Studies of the Modern World-System.* New York: Academic Press.

BERGSTEN, C. FRED. (1973) "The Threat from the Third World," *Foreign Policy* 11 (Summer): 102–124.

BERKOWITZ, LEONARD, AND ANTHONY LEPAGE. (1970) "Weapons As Aggression-Eliciting Stimuli," pp. 132–144 in Edwin I. Megaree and Jack E. Kokanson (eds.), *The Dynamics of Aggression.* New York: Harper & Row.

BERKOWITZ, MORTON, P. G. BOCK, AND VINCENT J. FUCCILLO. (1977) *The Politics of American Foreign Policy.* Englewood Cliffs, N.J.: Prentice-Hall.

BERLIN, MICHAEL J. (1987–1988) "Moscow Takes the High Road," *The Inter Dependent* 13 (December–January): 5.

BERTELSEN, JUDY S. (ed.) (1977) *Nonstate Nations in International Politics.* New York: Praeger.

BIERSTECKER, T. J. (1978) *Distortion or Development: Contending Perspectives on the Multinational Corporation.* Cambridge, Mass.: MIT Press.

BLAINEY, GEOFFREY. (1973) *The Causes of War.* New York: Free Press.

BLAIR, BRUCE G., AND GARRY D. BREWER. (1977) "The Terrorist Threat to World Nuclear Programs," *Journal of Conflict Resolution* 21 (September): 379–403.

BLAKE, DAVID H., AND ROBERT S. WALTERS. (1987) *The Politics of Global Economic Relations,* 3rd ed. Englewood Cliffs, N.J.: Prentice-Hall.

BLECHMAN, BARRY M., AND STEPHEN S. KAPLAN, WITH DAVID K. HALL, WILLIAM B. QUANDT, JEROME N. SLATER, ROBERT M. SLUSSER, AND PHILIP WINDSOR. (1978) *Force Without War.* Washington, D.C.: Brookings Institution.

BLOCK, FRED L. (1977) *The Origins of International Economic Disorder.* Berkeley and Los Angeles: University of California Press.

BLUMENTHAL, W. MICHAEL. (1988) "The World Economy and Technological Change," *Foreign Affairs* 66 (No. 3): 529–550.

BOGDANOWICZ-BINDERT, CHRISTINE A. (1985–1986) "World Debt: The United States Reconsiders," *Foreign Affairs* 64 (Winter): 259–273.

BOHI, DOUGLAS R., AND WILLIAM B. QUANDT. (1984) *Economic Security in the 1980s: Economic and Political Perspectives.* Washington, D.C.: Brookings Institution.

BOONEKAMP, CLEMENS F. J. (1987) "Voluntary Export Restraints," *Finance and Development* 24 (December): 2–5.

BORNSCHIER, VOLKER. (1984) "The Role of MNCs in Economic Growth," *Journal of Conflict Resolution* 28 (March): 157–164.

BOULDING, KENNETH E. (1978) *Stable Peace*. Austin: University of Texas Press.

_____. (1975) "National Images and International Systems," pp. 347–360 in William D. Coplin and Charles W. Kegley, Jr. (eds.), *Analyzing International Relations*. New York: Praeger.

_____. (1962) *Conflict and Defense: A General Theory*. New York: Harper & Row.

BOULDING, KENNETH E., AND TAPAN MUKERJEE (eds.) (1972) *Economic Imperialism*. Ann Arbor: University of Michigan Press.

BOUVIER, LEON F., AND ROBERT W. GARDNER. (1986) "Immigration to the U.S.: The Unfinished Story," *Population Bulletin*, vol. 41, no. 4. Washington, D.C.: Population Reference Bureau.

BOZEMAN, ADDA B. (1971) *The Future of Law in a Multicultural World*. Princeton, N.J.: Princeton University Press.

BP Statistical Review of World Energy. (1987) London: British Petroleum Company. *BP Statistical Review of World Energy*. (1984) London: British Petroleum Company.

BRADY, LAWRENCE J. (1987) "The Utility of Economic Sanctions As a Policy Instrument," pp. 297–302 in David Leyton-Brown (ed.), *The Utility of Economic Sanctions*. New York: St. Martin's Press.

BRECHER, MICHAEL, AND JONATHAN WILKENFELD. (1989) *Crises in the Twentieth Century: Vol. III: The Analysis of International and Foreign Policy Crises*. Oxford, England: Pergamon Press.

BRECHER, MICHAEL, JONATHAN WILKENFELD, AND SHEILA MOSER. (1988) *Crises in the Twentieth Century: Vol. I: Handbook of International Crises*. Oxford, England: Pergamon Press.

BREMER, L. PAUL, III. (1987) "Practical Measures for Dealing with Terrorism," Address before the Discover Conference on Terrorism in a Technological World, January 22. U.S. Department of State, Bureau of Public Affairs, Current Policy no. 913.

BRESLAUER, GEORGE W. (1983) "Why Détente Failed: An Interpretation," pp. 319–340 in Alexander L. George (ed.), *Managing U.S.-Soviet Rivalry: Problems of Crisis Prevention*. Boulder, Colo.: Westview Press.

BRIERLY, JAMES L. (1944) *The Outlook for International Law*. Oxford, England: Clarendon Press.

BROCK, WILLIAM E. (1984) "Trade and Debt: The Vital Linkage," *Foreign Affairs* 62 (Summer): 1037–1057.

BRONFENBRENNER, URIE. (1975) "The Mirror Image in Soviet-American Relations," pp. 161–166 in William D. Coplin and Charles W. Kegley, Jr. (eds.), *Analyzing International Relations*. New York: Praeger.

BROWN, HAROLD. (1983) *Thinking About National Security: Defense and Foreign Policy in a Dangerous World*. Boulder, Colo.: Westview Press.

BROWN, LESTER R. (1986) "New Dimensions of National Security," pp. 209–299 in Joseph Kruzel (ed.), *American Defense Annual 1986–1987*. Lexington, Mass.: Lexington Books.

_____. (1982) *U.S. and Soviet Agriculture: The Shifting Balance*. Worldwatch Paper No. 51. Washington, D.C.: Worldwatch Institute.

_____. (1979) *Resource Trends and Population Policy: A Time for Reassessment*. Worldwatch Paper No. 29. Washington, D.C.: Worldwatch Institute.

_____. (1978) *The Twenty-Ninth Day*. New York: Norton.

_____. (1972) *World Without Borders*. New York: Vintage Books.

BROWN, LESTER R., EDWARD C. WOLF, LINDA STARKE, WILLIAM U. CHANDLER, CHRISTOPHER FLAVIN, CYNTHIA POLLOCK, SANDRA POSTEL, AND JODI JACOBSON. (1987) *State of the World 1987*. New York: Norton.

BROWN, SEYOM. (1977) "A Cooling-off Period for U.S. Soviet Relations," *Foreign Policy* 28 (Fall): 3–21.

BROWNLIE, IAN. (1981) "The Reality and Efficacy of International Law," *British Yearbook of International Law 1981* 52: 1–8.

_____. (1973) *Principles of Public International Law*. London: Clarendon Press.

BRUCAN, SILVIU. (1984) "The Global Crisis," *International Studies Quarterly* 28 (March): 97–109.

BRZEZINSKI, ZBIGNIEW. (1970) *Between Two Ages: America's Role in the Technetronic Era*. New York: Viking.

BRZEZINSKI, ZBIGNIEW, AND SAMUEL P. HUNTINGTON. (1964) *Political Power: USA/USSR*. New York: Viking.

BUENO DE MESQUITA, BRUCE. (1981) *The War Trap*. New Haven, Conn.: Yale University Press.

_____. (1975) "The Effect of Systemic Polarization on the Probability and Duration of War." Paper presented at the Annual Meeting of the International Studies Association, Washington, D.C., February 19–22.

BULL, HEDLEY. (1984) "Rethinking Non-Proliferation," pp. 65–70 in Charles W. Kegley, Jr., and Eugene R. Wittkopf (eds.), *The Global Agenda*. New York: Random House.

_____. (1977) *The Anarchical Society: A Study of Order in World Politics*. New York: Columbia University Press.

BUNCE, VALERIE. (1981) *Do New Leaders Make a Difference?* Princeton, N.J.: Princeton University Press.

BUNDY, WILLIAM P. (1977) "Elements of National Power," *Foreign Affairs* 56 (October): 1–26.

BURKI, SHAHID JAVED. (1983) "UNCTAD VI: For Better or for Worse?" *Finance and Development* 20 (December): 16–19.

BURNEY, MAHMUD A. (1979) "A Recognition of Interdependence: UNCTAD V," *Finance and Development* 16 (September): 15–18.

BYWATER, MARION. (1975) "The Lomé Convention," *European Community* 184 (March): 5–9.

CALDWELL, DAN. (1977) "Bureaucratic Foreign Policy Making," *American Behavioral Scientist* 21 (September–October): 87–110.

CALVERT, PETER. (1986) *The Foreign Policy of New States.* New York: St. Martin's Press.

CAMERON, DAVID R. (1978) "The Expansion of the Public Economy: A Comparative Analysis," *American Political Science Review* 72 (December): 1243–1261.

CAPORASO, JAMES A. (1987) "International Political Economy: Fad or Field?" *International Studies Notes* 13 (Winter): 1–8.

———. (1980) "Dependency Theory: Continuities and Discontinuities in Development Studies," *International Organization* 34 (Autumn): 605–628.

———. (ed.) (1978) "Dependence and Dependency in the Global System." Special issue, *International Organization* 32 (Winter): 1–300.

CARNESALE, ALBERT, PAUL DOTY, STANLEY HOFFMANN, SAMUEL P. HUNTINGTON, JOSEPH S. NYE, JR., AND SCOTT D. SAGAN. (1985) "How Might Nuclear War Begin?" pp. 242–257 in Charles W. Kegley, Jr., and Eugene R. Wittkopf (eds.), *The Nuclear Reader.* New York: St. Martin's Press.

CARPENTER, TED GALEN. (1986) "The U.S. and the ANZUS Alliance: Pursuing a Strategic Divorce," *USA Today* 115 (July): 41–45.

CARR, E. H. (1939) *The Twenty-Years' Crisis, 1919–1939: An Introduction to the Study of International Relations.* London: Macmillan.

CATTELL, RAYMOND B. (1949) "The Dimensions of Culture Patterns by Factorization of National Characteristics," *Journal of Abnormal and Social Psychology* 44 (October): 443–469.

CENTRE ON TRANSNATIONAL CORPORATIONS. (1987) *Foreign Direct Investment, the Service Sector, and International Banking.* New York: United Nations.

———. (1985a) *Transnational Corporations and International Trade.* New York: United Nations.

———. (1985b) "Trends and Issues in Foreign Direct Investment and Related Flows: A Technical Paper," U.N. Doc. ST/CTC/59, United Nations Centre on Transnational Corporations.

CHAN, STEVE. (1987) "Military Expenditures and Economic Performance," pp. 29–37 in U.S. Arms Control and Disarmament Agency, *World Military Expenditures and Arms Transfers 1986.* Washington, D.C.: U.S. Government Printing Office.

CHASE-DUNN, CHRISTOPHER. (1981) "Interstate System and Capitalist World-Economy: One Logic or Two?" *International Studies Quarterly* 25 (March): 19–42.

CHERNUS, IRA. (1987) *Dr. Strangegod: On the Symbolic Meaning of Nuclear Weapons.* Columbia: University of South Carolina Press.

CHILDE, V. GORDON. (1962) *Man Makes Himself.* New York: Mentor Books.

CHIROT, DANIEL. (1986) *Social Change in the Modern Era.* San Diego: Harcourt Brace Jovanovich.

CHIROT, DANIEL, AND THOMAS D. HALL. (1982) "World-System Theory," *Annual Review of Sociology* 8: 81–106.

CHOUCHRI, NAZLI. (1972) "Population, Resources, and Technology: Political Implications of the Environmental Crisis," *International Organization* 26 (Spring): 175–212.

CHOUCHRI, NAZLI, AND ROBERT C. NORTH. (1975) *Nations in Conflict.* San Francisco: Freeman.

———. (1972) "Dynamics of International Conflict: Some Policy Implications of Population, Resources, and Technology," pp. 80–122 in Raymond Tanter and Richard H. Ullman (eds.), *Theory and Policy in International Relations.* Princeton, N.J.: Princeton University Press.

CHRISTENSEN, CHERYL. (1978) "World Hunger: A Structural Approach," *International Organization* 32 (Summer): 745–774.

CHURCHILL, WINSTON. (1948) *The Second World War: The Gathering Storm.* Boston: Houghton Mifflin.

CLAIRMONTE, FREDERICK, AND JOHN CAVANAGH. (1982) "Transnational Corporations and Global Markets: Changing Power Relations," *Trade and Development: An UNCTAD Review* 4 (Winter): 149–182.

CLARK, GRENVILLE, AND LOUIS B. SOHN. (1966) *World Peace Through World Law.* Cambridge, Mass.: Harvard University Press.

CLAUDE, INIS L., JR. (1971) *Swords into Plowshares,* 4th ed. New York: Random House.

_____. (1967) *The Changing United Nations*. New York: Random House.

_____. (1962) *Power and International Relations*. New York: Random House.

COATE, ROGER A. (1988) *Unilateralism, Ideology, and U.S. Foreign Policy: The United States In and Out of UNESCO*. Boulder, Colo.: Lynne Rienner.

COBB, ROGER, AND CHARLES ELDER. (1970) *International Community*. New York: Harcourt, Brace & World.

CODY, EDWARD. (1987) "A Farewell to Arms Sales," *Washington Post National Weekly Edition*, May 4, p. 22.

COHEN, BENJAMIN J. (1983) "Trade and Unemployment: Global Bread-and-Butter Issues," *Worldview* 26 (January): 9–11.

_____. (1979) "Europe's Money, America's Problem," *Foreign Policy* 35 (Summer): 31–47.

_____. (1973) *The Question of Imperialism*. New York: Basic Books.

COHEN, RAYMOND. (1980) "Rules of the Game in International Politics," *International Studies Quarterly* 24 (March): 129–150.

COHEN, STEPHEN D., AND RONALD I. MELTZER. (1982) *United States International Economic Policy in Action*. New York: Praeger.

COLL, ALBERTO R. (1986) "The Limits of Global Consciousness and Legal Absolutism: Protecting International Law from Some of Its Best Friends," *Harvard International Law Journal* 27 (Spring): 599–620.

COMMAGER, HENRY STEELE. (1983) "Misconceptions Governing American Foreign Policy," pp. 510–517 in Charles W. Kegley, Jr., and Eugene R. Wittkopf (eds.), *Perspectives on American Foreign Policy*. New York: St. Martin's Press.

COMMISSION ON INTEGRATED LONG-TERM STRATEGY. (1988) *Discriminate Deterrence*. Washington, D.C.: U.S. Government Printing Office.

COMMISSION ON TRANSNATIONAL CORPORATIONS. (1986) "Recent Developments Related to Transnational Corporations and International Economic Relations," U.N. Doc. E/C.10/1986/2, United Nations Economic and Social Council.

COMMONER, BARRY. (1976) *The Poverty of Power*. London: Jonathan Cape.

CONNELLY, PHILIP, AND ROBERT PERLMAN. (1975) *The Politics of Scarcity*. London: Oxford University Press.

COPELAND, MILES. (1969) *The Game of Nations*. New York: Simon & Schuster.

COPLIN, WILLIAM D. (1975) "International Law and Assumptions About the State System," pp. 270–279 in William D. Coplin and Charles W. Kegley, Jr. (eds.), *Analyzing International Relations*. New York: Praeger.

_____. (1971) *Introduction to International Politics*. Chicago: Markham.

_____. (1966) *The Functions of International Law*. Chicago: Rand McNally.

COSER, LEWIS. (1956) *The Functions of Social Conflict*. London: Routledge & Kegan Paul.

CUTLER, LLOYD N. (1978) *Global Interdependence and the Multinational Firm*. Headline Series no. 239 (April). New York: Foreign Policy Association.

CUTLER, ROBERT M. (1983) "East–South Relations at UNCTAD: Global Political Economy and the CMEA," *International Organization* 37 (Winter): 121–142.

DAHRENDORF, RALF. (1986) "The Europeanization of Europe," pp. 5–56 in Andrew J. Pierre (ed.), *A Widening Atlantic? Domestic Change and Foreign Policy*. New York: Council on Foreign Relations.

DALY, HERMAN E. (1973) "Introduction," pp. 1–29 in Herman E. Daly (ed.), *Toward a Steady-State Economy*. San Francisco: Freeman.

D'AMATO, ANTHONY. (1982) "What 'Counts' As Law?" pp. 83–107 in Nicholas Greenwood Onuf (ed.), *Law-Making in the Global Community*. Durham, N.C.: Carolina Academic Press.

DARMSTADTER, JOEL, AND HANS H. LANDSBERG. (1976) "The Economic Background," pp. 15–37 in Raymond Vernon (ed.), *The Oil Crisis*. New York: Norton.

DARMSTADTER, JOEL, HANS H. LANDSBERG, AND HERBERT C. MORTON, WITH MICHAEL J. CODA. (1983) *Energy Today and Tomorrow: Living with Uncertainty*. Englewood Cliffs, N.J.: Prentice-Hall.

DE CUÉLLAR, JAVIER PÉREZ. (1984) "The United Nations and World Politics," pp. 167–175 in Charles W. Kegley, Jr., and Eugene R. Wittkopf (eds.), *The Global Agenda*. New York: Random House.

DEGER, SAADET, AND RON SMITH. (1983) "Military Expansion and Growth in Less Developed Countries," *Journal of Conflict Resolution* 27 (June): 335–353.

DEHIO, LUDWIG. (1962) *The Precarious Balance*. Translated by Charles Fullman. New York: Knopf.

DENTON, FRANK, AND WARREN PHILLIPS. (1971) "Some Patterns in the History of Violence," pp. 327–338 in Claggett G. Smith (ed.), *Conflict Resolution*. Notre Dame, Ind.: University of Notre Dame Press.

DeRivera, Joseph H. (1968) *The Psychological Dimension of Foreign Policy*. Columbus, Ohio: Merrill.

Deutsch, Karl W. (1975) "The Growth of Nations: Some Recurrent Patterns of Political and Social Integration," pp. 306–319 in William D. Coplin and Charles W. Kegley, Jr. (eds.), *Analyzing International Relations*. New York: Praeger.

Deutsch, Karl W., Sidney A. Burrell, Robert A. Kann, Maurice Lee, Jr., Martin Lichterman, Raymond E. Lindgren, Francis L. Loewenheim, and Richard W. Van Wagenen. (1957) *Political Community and the North Atlantic Area*. Princeton, N.J.: Princeton University Press.

Deutsch, Karl W., and Richard L. Merritt. (1965) "Effects of Events on National and International Images," pp. 132–187 in Herbert C. Kelman (ed.), *International Behavior*. New York: Holt, Rinehart & Winston.

Deutsch, Karl W., and J. David Singer. (1975) "Multipolar Power Systems and International Stability," pp. 320–337 in William D. Coplin and Charles W. Kegley, Jr. (eds.), *Analyzing International Relations*. New York: Praeger.

Dewey, Edward R. (1964) *The 177 Year Cycle in War, 600 B.C.–A.D. 1957*. Pittsburgh: Foundation for the Study of Cycles.

DeYoung, Karen. (1987) "Need a Weapon? Call Portugal," *Washington Post National Weekly Edition*, February 9, p. 17.

Diaz-Briquets, Sergio. (1986) *Conflict in Central America: The Demographic Dimension*. Washington, D.C.: Population Reference Bureau.

Diehl, Jackson. (1987) "In Hungary, the Horn of Plenty Plays a Free-Market Tune," *Washington Post National Weekly Edition*, April 20, pp. 7–8.

DiRenzo, Gordon J. (ed.) (1974) *Personality and Politics*. Garden City, N.Y.: Doubleday-Anchor.

Domke, William K., Richard C. Eichenberg, and Catherine M. Kelleher. (1987) "Consensus Lost? Domestic Politics and the 'Crisis' in NATO," *World Politics* 39 (April): 382–407.

Doyle, Michael W. (1986) *Empires*. Ithaca, N.Y.: Cornell University Press.

Drucker, Peter F. (1986) "The Changed World Economy," *Foreign Affairs* 64 (Spring): 768–791.

———. (1974) "Multinationals and Developing Countries: Myths and Realities," *Foreign Affairs* 53 (October): 121–134.

Dulles, John Foster. (1939) *War, Peace, and Change*. New York: Harper.

Dyson, Freeman. (1984) *Weapons and Hope*. New York: Harper & Row.

East, Maurice A., Stephen Salmore, and Charles F. Hermann (eds.) (1978) *Why Nations Act*. Beverly Hills, Calif.: Sage.

Easton, David. (1969) "The New Revolution in Political Science," *American Political Science Review* 63 (December): 1051–1061.

Easton, Stewart C. (1964) *The Rise and Fall of Western Colonialism*. New York: Praeger.

Eban, Abba. (1983) *The New Diplomacy: International Affairs in the Modern Age*. New York: Random House.

Ebinger, Charles. (1985) "A 'Complacent' U.S. Courts New Oil Crisis," *U.S. News and World Report*, May 27, pp. 37–38.

———. (1982) *The Critical Link: Energy and National Security in the 1980s*. Cambridge, Mass.: Ballinger.

Eckaus, Richard S. (1977) *Appropriate Technologies for Developing Countries*. Washington, D.C.: National Academy of Science.

Eckstein, Harry. (1972) "On the Etiology of Internal Wars," pp. 9–30 in Ivo K. Feierabend, Rosalind L. Feierabend, and Ted Robert Gurr (eds.), *Anger, Violence, and Politics*. Englewood Cliffs, N.J.: Prentice-Hall.

Ehrlich, Paul R., Anne H. Ehrlich, and John P. Holdren. (1977) *Ecoscience*. San Francisco: Freeman.

Ehrlich, Paul R., John Harte, Mark A. Harwell, Peter H. Raven, Carl Sagan, George M. Woodwell, Joseph Berry, Edward S. Ayensu, Anne H. Ehrlich, Thomas Eisner, Stephen J. Gould, Herbert D. Grover, Rafael Herrera, Robert M. May, Ernst Mayr, Christopher P. McKay, Harold A. Mooney, Norman Myers, David Pimentel, and John M. Teal. (1983) "Long-Term Biological Consequences of Nuclear War," *Science*, December 23, pp. 1293–1300.

Ekirch, Arthur A., Jr. (1966) *Ideas, Ideals, and American Diplomacy*. New York: Appleton-Century-Crofts.

Emmanuel, Arghiri. (1972) *Unequal Exchange: An Essay on the Imperialism of Trade*. New York: Monthly Review Press.

Etzioni, Amitai. (1968) "Toward a Sociological Theory of Peace," pp. 403–428 in Leon Bramson and George W. Goethals (eds.), *War*. New York: Basic Books.

Ewing, David W. (1974) "The Corporation As Peacemonger," pp. 150–157 in Peter A. Toma,

Andrew Gyorgy, and Robert S. Jordan (eds.), *Basic Issues in International Relations*. Boston: Allyn & Bacon.

FALK, RICHARD A. (1983) *The End of World Order*. New York: Holmes & Meier.

———. (1979) "The Clear and Present Danger of World War III," *Transition* 4 (November): 1–2.

———. (1976) *Future Worlds*. Headline Series no. 229 (February). New York: Foreign Policy Association.

———. (1975) *A Study of Future Worlds*. New York: Free Press.

———. (1970) *The Status of Law in International Society*. Princeton, N.J.: Princeton University Press.

———. (1968) *Legal Order in a Violent World*. Princeton, N.J.: Princeton University Press.

———. (1965) "World Law and Human Conflict," pp. 227–249 in Elton B. McNeil (ed.), *The Nature of Human Conflict*. Englewood Cliffs, N.J.: Prentice-Hall.

———. (1964) *The Role of Domestic Courts in the International Legal Order*. Syracuse, N.Y.: Syracuse University Press.

FALKENHEIM, PEGGY L. (1987) "Post-Afghanistan Sanctions," pp. 105–130 in David Leyton-Brown (ed.), *The Utility of International Economic Sanctions*. New York: St. Martin's Press.

FALLOWS, JAMES. (1983) "Immigration: How It's Affecting Us," *The Atlantic* 252 (November): 45–52.

———. (1982) "Reagan: The Fruits of Success," *New York Review of Books*, October 27, pp. 68–73.

FELD, WERNER J. (1972) *Nongovernmental Forces and World Politics*. New York: Praeger.

FELD, WERNER J., AND ROBERT S. JORDAN, WITH LEON HURWITZ. (1983) *International Organizations: A Comparative Approach*. New York: Praeger.

FESHARAKI, FEREIDUN. (1981) "World Oil Availability: The Role of OPEC Policies," pp. 267–308 in Jack M. Hollander, Melvin K. Simmons, and David O. Wood (eds.), *Annual Review of Energy*. Palo Alto, Calif.: Annual Review.

FIELDHOUSE, D. K. (1973) *Economics and Empire, 1830–1914*. Ithaca, N.Y.: Cornell University Press.

"FINANCING THE UNITED NATIONS." (n.d.) *UNA–USA Fact Sheet*. United Nations Association of the United States of America.

FINKELSTEIN, LAWRENCE S. (1980) "The IR of IGOs." Paper presented at the Annual Meeting of the International Studies Association, Los Angeles, March 19–22.

FISCHER, DIETRICH. (1987) "Reagan's Military Buildup Puts World on Perilous Path Toward Nuclear Holocaust," *Atlanta Constitution*, December 28, p. 11.

FISHER, ROGER. (1969) *International Conflict for Beginners*. New York: Harper & Row.

FLAVIN, CHRISTOPHER. (1987) *Reassessing Nuclear Power: The Fallout from Chernobyl*. Worldwatch Paper no. 75. Washington, D.C.: Worldwatch Institute.

FOOD AND AGRICULTURE ORGANIZATION OF THE UNITED NATIONS. (1982) *FAO Trade Yearbook, 1981*. Rome: Food and Agriculture Organization of the United Nations.

———. (n.d.) *Billions More to Feed*. Rome: Food and Agriculture Organization of the United Nations.

"FOOD 1983." (1983) *UN Chronicle* 20 (January): 65–72.

FRANK, ANDRE GUNDER. (1969) *Latin America: Underdevelopment or Revolution*. New York: Monthly Review Press.

FRANKEL, GLENN. (1987) "Weapons: The Global Commodity," *Washington Post National Weekly Edition*, January 12, pp. 6–7.

FREUD, SIGMUND. (1968) "Why War," pp. 71–80 in Leon Bramson and George W. Goethals (eds.), *War*. New York: Basic Books.

FRIED, JOHN H. E. (1971) "International Law—Neither Orphan nor Harlot, Neither Jailer nor Never-Never Land," pp. 124–176 in Karl W. Deutsch and Stanley Hoffmann (eds.), *The Relevance of International Law*. Garden City, N.Y.: Doubleday-Anchor.

FRIEDEN, JEFF. (1981) "Third World Indebted Industrialization: International Finance and State Capitalism in Mexico, Brazil, Algeria, and South Korea," *International Organization* 35 (Summer): 407–431.

FRIEDHEIM, ROBERT L. (1965) "The 'Satisfied' and 'Dissatisfied' States Negotiate International Law," *World Politics* 18 (October): 20–41.

GADDIS, JOHN LEWIS. (1986) "The Long Peace: Elements of Stability in the Postwar International System," *International Security* 10 (Spring): 99–142.

———. (1983) "Containment: Its Past and Future," pp. 16–31 in Charles W. Kegley, Jr., and Eugene R. Wittkopf (eds.), *Perspectives on American Foreign Policy*. New York: St. Martin's Press.

_____. (1972) *The United States and the Origins of the Cold War*. New York: Columbia University Press.

GALBRAITH, JOHN KENNETH. (1983) *The Anatomy of Power*. Boston: Houghton Mifflin.

_____. (1982–1983) "The Second Imperial Requiem," *International Security* 7 (Winter): 84–93.

GALTUNG, JOHAN. (1969) "Violence, Peace, and Peace Research," *Journal of Peace Research* 6 (no. 3): 167–191.

GARDNER, LLOYD C. (1970) *Architects of Illusion*. Chicago: Quadrangle.

GARTHOFF, RAYMOND L. (1985) *Détente and Confrontation: American-Soviet Relations from Nixon to Reagan*. Washington, D.C.: Brookings Institution.

GASIOROWSKI, MARK J. (1986) "Economic Interdependence and International Conflict: Some Cross-National Evidence," *International Studies Quarterly* 30 (March): 23–38.

_____. (1985) "The Structure of Third World Economic Interdependence," *International Organization* 39 (Spring): 331–342.

GASTIL, RAYMOND D. (1978) "The Comparative Survey of Freedom—VIII," *Freedom at Issue* 44 (January–February): 3–19.

GATI, TOBY TRISTER (ed.) (1983) *The US, The UN, and the Management of Global Change*. New York: New York University Press.

GAUHAR, ALTAF F. (1985) "Who Wants the Bomb?" *South* 59 (September): 14–18.

GAWAD, ATEF. (1986) "Moscow's Arms-for-Oil Diplomacy," *Foreign Policy* 63 (Summer): 147–168.

GELB, LESLIE H. (1983) "Oil = X in a Strategic Equation," *New York Times*, October 7, pp. 33, 36.

_____. (1979) "The Future of Arms Control: A Glass Half Full," *Foreign Policy* 36 (Fall): 21–32.

_____. (1976) "What Exactly Is Kissinger's Legacy?" *New York Times Magazine*, October 31, pp. 13–15 passim.

GELB, LESLIE H., AND MORTON H. HALPERIN. (1973) "The Ten Commandments of the Foreign Affairs Bureaucracy," pp. 250–259 in Steven L. Spiegel (ed.), *At Issue: Politics in the World Arena*. New York: St. Martin's Press.

GEORGE, ALEXANDER L. (1986) "U.S.-Soviet Global Rivalry: Norms of Competition," *Journal of Peace Research* 23 (September): 247–262.

_____. (1972) "The Case for Multiple Advocacy in Making Foreign Policy," *American Political Science Review* 66 (September): 751–785.

GILPIN, ROBERT. (1985) "The Politics of Transnational Economic Relations," pp. 171–194 in Ray Maghroori and Bennett Ramberg (eds.), *Globalism Versus Realism: International Relations' Third Debate*. Boulder, Colo.: Westview Press.

_____. (1984) "The Richness of the Tradition of Political Realism," *International Organization* 38 (Spring): 287–304.

_____. (1981) *War and Change in World Politics*. Cambridge, England: Cambridge University Press.

_____. (1975) *U.S. Power and the Multinational Corporation*. New York: Basic Books.

"GLOBAL POPULATION TRENDS: CHALLENGES FACING WORLD LEADERS." (n.d.) Washington, D.C.: Population Reference Bureau.

The Global 2000 Report to the President. (1980a) Vol. I: Entering the Twenty-First Century. Washington, D.C.: U.S. Government Printing Office.

The Global 2000 Report to the President. (1980b) Vol. II: The Technical Report. Washington, D.C.: U.S. Government Printing Office.

GOCHMAN, CHARLES S., AND ZEEV MAOZ. (1984) "Militarized Interstate Disputes, 1816–1976: Procedures, Patterns, and Insights," *Journal of Conflict Resolution* 28 (December): 585–616.

GOLDBLAT, JOZEF. (1982) *Agreements for Arms Control: A Critical Survey*. London: Taylor & Francis.

GOLDMANN, KJELL. (1973) "East–West Tension in Europe, 1946–1970: A Conceptual Analysis and a Quantitative Description," *World Politics* 26 (October): 106–125.

GOLDMANN, KJELL, AND JOHAN LAGERKRANZ. (1977) "Neither Tension nor Détente: East–West Relations in Europe, 1971–1975," *Cooperation and Conflict* 12 (no. 4): 251–264.

GOLDSTEIN, JOSHUA. (1988) *Long Cycles: Prosperity and War in the Modern Age*. New Haven: Yale University Press.

GORDON, LINCOLN. (1979) *Growth Policies and the International Order*. New York: McGraw-Hill.

GOTTLIEB, GIDON. (1982) "Global Bargaining: The Legal and Diplomatic Framework," pp. 109–130 in Nicholas Greenwood Onuf (ed.), *Law-Making in the Global Community*. Durham, N.C.: Carolina Academic Press.

GRAHAM, THOMAS R. (1979) "Revolution in Trade Politics," *Foreign Policy* 26 (Fall): 49–63.

GRAY, COLIN S., AND KEITH PAYNE. (1980) "Victory Is Possible," *Foreign Policy* 39 (Summer): 14–27.

GREENSTEIN, FRED I. (1987) *Personality and Politics*. Princeton, N.J.: Princeton University Press.

GREGG, ROBERT W. (1977) "The Apportioning of Political Power," pp. 69–80 in David A. Kay (ed.), *The Changing United Nations*. New York: Academy of Political Science.

GREY, EDWARD. (1925) *Twenty-five Years, 1892–1916*. New York: Frederick Stokes.

GRIEVES, FOREST L. (1977) *Conflict and Order*. Boston: Houghton Mifflin.

GRUHN, ISEBILL V. (1976) "The Lomé Convention: Inching Toward Interdependence," *International Organization* 30 (Spring): 241–262.

GULICK, EDWARD VOSE. (1955) *Europe's Classical Balance of Power*. Ithaca, N.Y.: Cornell University Press.

GURR, TED ROBERT. (1970) *Why Men Rebel*. Princeton, N.J.: Princeton University Press.

HAAS, ERNST B. (1986) *Why We Still Need the United Nations: The Collective Management of International Conflict, 1945–1984*. Berkeley, Calif.: Institute of International Studies, University of California.

_____. (1983) "Regime Decay: Conflict Management and International Organizations, 1945–1981," *International Organization* 37 (Spring): 189–256.

_____. (1969) *Tangle of Hopes*. Englewood Cliffs, N.J.: Prentice-Hall.

_____. (1953a) "The Balance of Power As a Guide to Policy Making," *Journal of Politics* 15 (August): 370–398.

_____. (1953b) "The Balance of Power: Prescription, Concept, or Propaganda?" *World Politics* 5 (July): 442–477.

HAAS, MICHAEL. (1965) "Societal Approaches to the Study of War," *Journal of Peace Research* 2 (no. 4): 307–323.

HAGGARD, STEPHAN, AND BETH A. SIMMONS. (1987) "Theories of International Regimes," *International Organization* 41 (Summer): 491–517.

HALEY, P. EDWARD, AND JACK MERRITT (eds.) (1986) *Strategic Defense Initiative: Folly or Future?* Boulder, Colo.: Westview Press.

HALLIDAY, FRED. (1987) "Gorbachev and the 'Arab Syndrome': Soviet Policy in the Middle East," *World Policy Journal* 4 (Summer): 415–442.

HAMED, MAZHER A. (1987) "Mecca Showed That Saudi Arabia Is More Stable Than It Used to Be," *Washington Post National Weekly Edition*, August 24, p. 24.

HAMMARSKJÖLD, DAG. (1965) "Introduction to the Annual Report of the Secretary-General on the Work of the Organization, 16 June 1959–15 June 1960," pp. 399–409 in Joel Larus (ed.), *From Collective Security to Preventive Diplomacy*. New York: Wiley.

HANRIEDER, WOLFRAM F. (1978) "Dissolving International Politics: Reflections on the Nation-State," *American Political Science Review* 72 (December): 1276–1287.

HANSEN, ROGER D. (1980) "North–South Policy—What's the Problem?" *Foreign Affairs* 58 (Summer): 1104–1128.

_____. (1979) *The North–South Stalemate*. New York: McGraw-Hill.

HARDEN, BLAINE. (1988) "Fighting with Guns and Butter," *Washington Post National Weekly Edition*, January 18–24, pp. 6–7.

_____. (1987) "AIDS May Replace Famine As the Continent's Worst Blight," *Washington Post National Weekly Edition*, June 15, pp. 16–17.

HARDIN, GARRETT. (1977) "The Tragedy of the Commons," pp. 16–30 in Garrett Hardin and John Baden (eds.), *Managing the Commons*. San Francisco: Freeman.

_____. (1968) "The Tragedy of the Commons," *Science*, December 13, pp. 1243–1248.

HARDIN, GARRETT, AND JOHN BADEN (eds.) (1977) *Managing the Commons*. San Francisco: Freeman.

HART, JEFFREY A. (1978) "The New International Economic Order Negotiations: From the Sixth Special Session to the End of the North–South Dialogue." Paper presented at the Meeting of the Peace Science Society, Boca Raton, Fla., April 6–7.

HARWOOD, RICHARD. (1979) "Will SALT Impede World's Race Toward Nuclear Death?" Reprinted in *The State* (Columbia, S.C.), June 10, p. 1 passim.

HASSNER, PIERRE. (1968) "The Nation-State in the Nuclear Age," *Survey* 67 (April): 3–27.

HATHAWAY, DALE E. (1983) "The Internationalization of U.S. Agriculture," pp. 81–111 in Emery N. Castle and Kent A. Price (eds.), *U.S. Interests and Global Natural Resources*. Washington, D.C.: Resources for the Future.

HAYES, DENIS. (1977) *Rays of Hope: The Transition to a Post-Petroleum World*. New York: Norton.

HAYTER, TERESA. (1971) *Aid As Imperialism*. Baltimore: Penguin.

HEENAN, DAVID A., AND WARREN J. KEEGAN. (1979) "The Rise of Third World Multinationals," *Harvard Business Review* 57 (January–February): 101–109.

HEILBRONER, ROBERT L. (1977) "The Multinational Corporation and the Nation-State," pp. 338–352 in Steven L. Spiegel (ed.), *At Issue: Politics in the World Arena*. New York: St. Martin's Press.

_____. (1975) *An Inquiry into the Human Prospect*. New York: Norton.

HENRY, JAMES S. (1987) "Brazil Says: Nuts," *New Republic*, October 12, pp. 25, 28–29.

_____. (1986) "Where the Money Went," *New Republic*, November 14, pp. 20–23.

HEREK, GREGORY M., IRVING L. JANIS, AND PAUL HUTH. (1987) "Decision Making During International Crises: Is Quality of Process Related to Outcome?" *Journal of Conflict Resolution* 31 (June): 203–226.

HERMANN, CHARLES F. (1988) "New Foreign Policy Problems and Old Bureaucratic Organizations," pp. 248–265 in Charles W. Kegley, Jr., and Eugene R. Wittkopf (eds.), *The Domestic Sources of American Foreign Policy*. New York: St. Martin's Press.

_____. (1972) "Some Issues in the Study of International Crisis," pp. 3–17 in Charles F. Hermann (ed.), *International Crises*. New York: Free Press.

HERMANN, CHARLES F., CHARLES W. KEGLEY, JR., AND JAMES N. ROSENAU (eds.) (1987) *New Directions in the Study of Foreign Policy*. Boston: Allen & Unwin.

HERMANN, MARGARET G. (1988) "The Role of Leaders and Leadership in the Making of American Foreign Policy," pp. 266–284 in Charles W. Kegley, Jr., and Eugene R. Wittkopf (eds.), *The Domestic Sources of American Foreign Policy*. New York: St. Martin's Press.

_____. (1987) "Role Theory and Foreign Policy Dynamics: The African Arena," pp. 161–198 in Stephen G. Walker (ed.), *Role Theory and Foreign Policy Analysis*. Durham, N.C.: Duke University Press.

_____. (1976) "When Leader Personality Will Affect Foreign Policy: Some Propositions," pp. 326–333 in James N. Rosenau (ed.), *In Search of Global Patterns*. New York: Free Press.

HERZ, JOHN H. (1976) *The Nation-State and the Crisis of World Politics*. New York: McKay.

_____. (1951) *Political Realism and Political Idealism*. Chicago: University of Chicago Press.

HEWETT, ED A. (1984) *Energy, Economics, and Foreign Policy in the Soviet Union*. Washington, D.C.: Brookings Institution.

HIGGINS, BENJAMIN, AND JEAN DOWNING HIGGINS. (1979) *Economic Development of a Small Planet*. New York: Norton.

HILSMAN, ROGER. (1971) *The Politics of Policy Making in Defense and Foreign Affairs*. New York: Harper & Row.

_____. (1967) *To Move a Nation*. New York: Doubleday.

HOAGLAND, JIM. (1987) "Communist Leaders Administer a Dose of Capitalism," *Washington Post National Weekly Edition*, April 20, pp. 6–7.

HOEBEL, E. ADAMSON. (1961) *The Law of Primitive Man*. Cambridge, Mass.: Harvard University Press.

HOFFMANN, STANLEY. (1971) "International Law and the Control of Force," pp. 34–66 in Karl W. Deutsch and Stanley Hoffmann (eds.), *The Relevance of International Law*. Garden City, N.Y.: Doubleday-Anchor.

_____. (1961) "International Systems and International Law," pp. 205–237 in Klaus Knorr and Sidney Verba (eds.), *The International System*. Princeton, N.J.: Princeton University Press.

_____. (1960) *Contemporary Theory in International Politics*. Englewood Cliffs, N.J.: Prentice-Hall.

HOLLOWAY, DAVID. (1983) *The Soviet Union and the Arms Race*. New Haven, Conn.: Yale University Press.

HOLMES, JOHN W. (1977) "A Non-American Perspective," pp. 30–43 in David A. Kay (ed.), *The Changing United Nations*. New York: Academy of Political Science.

HOLMES, LESLIE. (1981) *The Policy Process in Communist States*. Beverly Hills, Calif.: Sage.

HOLSTI, K. J. (1988) *International Politics: A Framework for Analysis*, 5th ed. Englewood Cliffs, N.J.: Prentice-Hall.

_____. (1980) "Détente and Peaceful Co-existence: Assessing the Possibilities," *Coexistence* 17 (April): 1–19.

_____. (1970) "National Role Conceptions in the Study of Foreign Policy," *International Studies Quarterly* 14 (September): 233–309.

HOLSTI, OLE R. (1975) "The Belief System and National Images: A Case Study," pp. 22–33 in William D. Coplin and Charles W. Kegley, Jr. (eds.), *Analyzing International Relations*. New York: Praeger.

_____. (1972) *Crisis Escalation War*. Montreal: McGill–Queen's University Press.

HOLSTI, OLE R., AND JAMES N. ROSENAU. (1984) *American Leadership in World Affairs*. Boston: Allen & Unwin.

HOPKINS, RAYMOND F., ROBERT L. PAARLBERG, AND MITCHEL B. WALLERSTEIN. (1982) *Food in the Global Arena*. New York: Holt, Rinehart & Winston.

HOPKINS, TERENCE K., IMMANUEL WALLERSTEIN & ASSOCIATES. (1982) *World-Systems Analysis*. Beverly Hills, Calif.: Sage.

HOROWITZ, DAVID. (1971) "The Cold War Continues, 1945–1948," pp. 42–74 in Michael Parenti (ed.), *Trends and Tragedies in American Foreign Policy*. Boston: Little, Brown.

HORST, PAUL. (1963) *Matrix Algebra for Social Scientists*. New York: Holt, Rinehart & Winston.

HOWARD, MICHAEL E. (1983) *The Causes of War*. Cambridge, Mass.: Harvard University Press.

———. (1981) "On Fighting a Nuclear War," *International Security* 35 (Spring): 3–17.

HOWELL, LLEWELLYN D. (1981) "America's Role in the International Arena: Why Not Number Two?" *USA Today* 109 (January): 15–18.

HUFBAUER, GARY CLYDE, AND JEFFREY J. SCHOTT. (1985a) *Economic Sanctions Reconsidered: History and Current Policy*. Washington, D.C.: Institute for International Economics.

———. (1985b) "Economic Sanctions and U.S. Foreign Policy," *PS* 18 (Fall): 727–735.

———. (1983) *Economic Sanctions in Support of Foreign Policy Goals*. Washington, D.C.: Institute for International Economics.

HUNTER, ROBERT E. (1988) "Changing Roles for Military Power," *Los Angeles Times*, January 5, p. 7.

HUNTINGTON, SAMUEL P. (1987) "Patterns of Intervention: America and Soviets in the Third World," *The National Interest* 7 (Spring): 39–47.

———. (1978) "Trade, Technology, and Leverage: Economic Diplomacy," *Foreign Policy* 32 (Fall): 63–80.

———. (1973) "Transnational Organizations in World Politics," *World Politics* 25 (April): 333–368.

HYLAND, WILLIAM G. (1987) "Reagan–Gorbachev III," *Foreign Affairs* 66 (Fall): 7–21.

IGNATIUS, DAVID. (1987) "We've Learned to Stop Worrying and Love Arms Control—And in the Process, the U.S. and the Soviets Reversed Roles," *Washington Post National Weekly Edition*, September 14, p. 25.

IKLÉ, FRED CHARLES. (1979) *What It Means to Be Number Two*. Washington, D.C.: Ethics and Public Policy Center.

INSEL, BARBARA. (1985) "A World Awash in Grain," *Foreign Affairs* 63 (Spring): 892–911.

INTERNATIONAL ENERGY AGENCY. (1982) *World Energy Outlook*. Paris: Organization for Economic Cooperation and Development.

INTERNATIONAL MONETARY FUND. (1987) *World Economic Outlook*. Washington, D.C.: International Monetary Fund.

ISAAK, ROBERT A. (1975) *Individuals and World Politics*. North Scituate, Mass.: Duxbury Press.

ISLAM, SHADA. (1982) "Stabex Sour Note As Brussels Rings Changes," *South* 24 (October): 71–72.

JACOBS, JANE. (1984) "The Dynamic of Decline," *Atlantic Monthly* 253 (April): 98–114.

JACOBSEN, KURT. (1978) *The General Assembly of the United Nations*. New York: Columbia University Press.

———. (1969) "Sponsorships in the United Nations: A System Analysis," *Journal of Peace Research* 6 (3): 235–256.

JACOBSON, HAROLD K. (1984) *Networks of Interdependence: International Organizations and the Global Political System*. New York: Knopf.

JANIS, IRVING. (1982) *Groupthink: Psychological Studies of Policy Decisions and Fiascoes*, 2nd ed. Boston: Houghton Mifflin.

JENKINS, BRIAN M. (1986) "Defense Against Terrorism," *Political Science Quarterly* 101 (no. 5): 773–786.

JENSEN, LLOYD. (1982) *Explaining Foreign Policy*. Englewood Cliffs, N.J.: Prentice-Hall.

JERVIS, ROBERT. (1986) "The Nuclear Revolution and the Common Defense," *Political Science Quarterly* 101 (no. 5): 689–703.

———. (1982) "Security Regimes," *International Organization* 36 (Spring): 357–378.

———. (1976) *Perception and Misperception in World Politics*. Princeton, N.J.: Princeton University Press.

———. (1969) "Hypotheses on Misperception," pp. 239–254 in James N. Rosenau (ed.), *International Politics and Foreign Policy*. New York: Free Press.

JESSUP, ALPHEUS W. (1988) "Oil Prices: The Sobering Security Dilemma," pp. 326–332 in Charles W. Kegley, Jr., and Eugene R. Wittkopf (eds.), *The Global Agenda*, 2nd ed. New York: Random House.

JOFFE, JOSEF. (1985) "The Foreign Policy of the Federal Republic of Germany," pp. 72–113 in Roy C. Macridis (ed.), *Foreign Policy in World Politics*, 6th ed. Englewood Cliffs, N.J.: Prentice-Hall.

JOHNSON, JAMES TURNER. (1984) *Can Modern War Be Just?* New Haven, Conn.: Yale University Press.

JÖNSSON, CHRISTER. (1982) "The Ideology of Foreign Policy," pp. 91–110 in Charles W. Kegley, Jr., and Pat McGowan (eds.), *Foreign Policy: USA/USSR*. Beverly Hills, Calif.: Sage.

JOYNER, CHRISTOPHER C. (1988) "The Reality and Relevance of International Law," pp. 186–197 in Charles W. Kegley, Jr., and Eugene R. Wittkopf (eds.), *The Global Agenda*, 2nd ed. New York: Random House.

KAHN, HERMAN. (1976) *The Next 200 Years*. New York: Morrow.

KAPLAN, MORTON A. (1975) "Models of International Systems," pp. 257–269 in William D. Coplin and Charles W. Kegley, Jr. (eds.), *Analyzing International Relations*. New York: Praeger.

_____. (ed.) (1968) *New Approaches to International Relations*. New York: St. Martin's Press.

_____. (1957) *System and Process in International Politics*. New York: Wiley.

KAPLAN, MORTON A., AND NICHOLAS DEB. KATZENBACH. (1961) *The Political Foundation of International Law*. New York: Wiley.

KAREM, MAHMOUD. (1988) *A Nuclear-Weapon-Free Zone in the Middle East*. New York: Greenwood.

KAPLAN, STEPHEN S. (1981) *Diplomacy of Power*. Washington, D.C.: Brookings Institution.

KATZ, ARTHUR M. (1982) *Life After Nuclear War*. Cambridge, Mass.: Ballinger.

KATZENSTEIN, PETER J. (1975) "International Interdependence: Some Long-term Trends and Recent Changes," *International Organization* 29 (Autumn): 1021–1034.

KEENY, SPURGEON M., JR., AND WOLFGANG K. H. PANOFSKY. (1981) "MAD vs. NUTS: Can Doctrine or Weaponry Remedy the Mutual Hostage Relationship of the Superpowers?" *Foreign Affairs* 60 (Winter): 287–304.

KEGLEY, CHARLES W. (1984) "The Refugee Asylum Problem and World Peace Efforts," *International Journal on World Peace* 1 (Autumn): 45–52.

KEGLEY, CHARLES W., JR. (1988) "Neoidealism: A Practical Matter," *Ethics and International Affairs* 2: 173–197.

_____. (1982) "Measuring Transformation in the Global Legal System," pp. 173–209 in Nicholas Greenwood Onuf (ed.), *Law-making in the Global Community*. Durham, N.C.: Carolina Academic Press.

KEGLEY, CHARLES W., JR., AND GREGORY A. RAYMOND. (1989) *When Trust Breaks Down: Alliance Norms and World Politics*. Columbia: University of South Carolina Press, forthcoming.

_____. (1983) "Civil War and Great Power Intervention: A Statistical Re-examination," *Korea & World Affairs* 7 (Fall): 445–459.

KEGLEY, CHARLES W., JR., GREGORY A. RAYMOND, AND RICHARD A. SKINNER. (1980) "A Comparative Analysis of Nuclear Armament," pp. 231–255 in Patrick J. McGowan and Charles W. Kegley, Jr. (eds.), *Threats, Weapons, and Foreign Policy*. Beverly Hills, Calif.: Sage.

KEGLEY, CHARLES W., JR., T. VANCE STURGEON, AND EUGENE R. WITTKOPF. (1988) "Structural Terrorism: The Systemic Sources of State-Sponsored Terrorism," pp. 13–31 in Michael Stohl and George Lopez (eds.), *Terrible Beyond Endurance: The Foreign Policy of State Terrorism*. Westport, Conn.: Greenwood Press.

KEGLEY, CHARLES W., JR., AND EUGENE R. WITTKOPF. (eds.) (1989) *The Nuclear Reader: Strategy, Weapons, War*, 2nd ed. New York: St. Martin's Press, forthcoming.

_____. (1987) *American Foreign Policy: Pattern and Process*, 3rd ed. New York: St. Martin's Press.

KELMAN, HERBERT C. (1970) "The Role of the Individual in International Relations," *Journal of International Affairs* 24 (no. 1): 1–17.

_____. (ed.) (1965) *International Behavior: A Social-Psychological Analysis*. New York: Holt, Rinehart & Winston.

KELSEN, HANS. (1945) *General Theory of Law and State*. Translated by A. Weldberg. Cambridge, Mass.: Harvard University Press.

KEMPE, FREDERICK. (1983) "Terrorist Attacks Grow But Groups Are Smaller and Narrower Focus," *Wall Street Journal*, April 19, pp. 1, 20.

KENNAN, GEORGE F. (1984) "Soviet-American Relations: The Politics of Discord and Collaboration," pp. 107–120 in Charles W. Kegley, Jr., and Eugene R. Wittkopf (eds.), *The Global Agenda*. New York: Random House.

_____. (1982) *The Nuclear Delusion*. New York: Pantheon.

_____. (1976) "The United States and the Soviet Union, 1917–1976," *Foreign Affairs* 54 (July): 670–690.

_____. (1967) *Memoirs*. Boston: Little, Brown.

_____. (1954) *Realities of American Foreign Policy*. Princeton, N.J.: Princeton University Press.

_____. (1951) *American Diplomacy, 1900–1950*. New York: New American Library.

_____. (''X'') (1947) ''The Sources of Soviet Conduct,'' *Foreign Affairs* 25 (July): 566–582.

KENNEDY, PAUL. (1988) *The Rise and Fall of the Great Powers*. New York: Random House.

_____. (1987a) ''The (Relative) Decline of America,'' *Atlantic Monthly* 260 (August): 29–38.

_____. (1987b) ''What Gorbachev Is Up Against,'' *Atlantic Monthly* 259 (June): 29–43.

KEOHANE, ROBERT O. (ed.) (1986a) *Neorealism and Its Critics*. New York: Columbia University Press.

_____. (1986b) ''Realism, Neorealism and the Study of World Politics,'' pp. 1–26 in Robert O. Keohane (ed.), *Neorealism and Its Critics*. New York: Columbia University Press.

_____. (1984) *After Hegemony: Cooperation and Discord in the World Political Economy*. Princeton, N.J.: Princeton University Press.

_____. (1983) ''Theory of World Politics: Structural Realism and Beyond,'' pp. 503–540 in Ada Finifter (ed.), *Political Science: The State of the Discipline*. Washington, D.C.: American Political Science Association.

_____. (1982) ''Hegemonic Leadership and U.S. Foreign Economic Policy in the 'Long Decade' of the 1950s,'' pp. 49–76 in William P. Avery and David P. Rapkin (eds.), *America in a Changing World Political Economy*. New York: Longman.

_____. (1980) ''The Theory of Hegemonic Stability and Changes in International Economic Regimes, 1967–1977,'' pp. 131–162 in Ole R. Holsti, Randolph M. Siverson, and Alexander L. George (eds.), *Change in the International System*. Boulder, Colo.: Westview Press.

KEOHANE, ROBERT O., AND JOSEPH S. NYE, JR. (1984) ''Complex Interdependence, Transnational Relations, and Realism: Alternative Perspectives on World Politics,'' pp. 245–260 in Charles W. Kegley, Jr., and Eugene R. Wittkopf (eds.), *The Global Agenda*. New York: Random House.

_____. (1977) *Power and Interdependence*. Boston: Little, Brown.

_____. (1975) ''International Interdependence and Integration,'' pp. 363–414 in Fred I. Greenstein and Nelson W. Polsby (eds.), *International Politics: Handbook of Political Science*, vol. 8. Reading, Mass.: Addison-Wesley.

KIDRON, MICHAEL, AND DAN SMITH. (1983) *The War Atlas: Armed Conflict—Armed Peace*. New York: Pluto Press/Simon & Schuster.

KIM, SAMUEL S. (1985) ''The United Nations, Lawmaking, and World Order,'' *Alternatives* 10 (no. 4): 643–675.

_____. (1979) *China, the United Nations, and World Order*. Princeton, N.J.: Princeton University Press.

KINDLEBERGER, CHARLES P. (1977a) *America in the World Economy*. Headline Series no. 237 (October). New York: Foreign Policy Association.

_____. (1977b) ''U.S. Foreign Economic Policy, 1976–1977,'' *Foreign Affairs* 55 (January): 395–417.

_____. (1969) *American Business Abroad*. New Haven, Conn.: Yale University Press.

KING, MARTIN LUTHER, JR. (1967) *Where Do We Go from Here? Chaos or Community*. New York: Harper & Row.

KISSINGER, HENRY A. (1982) *Years of Upheaval*. Boston: Little, Brown.

_____. (1979) *White House Years*. Boston: Little, Brown.

_____. (1973) ''Secretary Kissinger at *Pacim in Terris*,'' news release of the Bureau of Public Affairs, U.S. Department of State (October 10).

_____. (1969) ''Domestic Structure and Foreign Policy,'' pp. 261–275 in James N. Rosenau (ed.), *International Politics and Foreign Policy*. New York: Free Press.

_____. (1964) *A World Restored*. New York: Grosset & Dunlap.

KLAPP, MERRIE G. (1982) ''The State—Landlord or Entrepreneur?'' *International Organization* 36 (Summer): 575–607.

KLARE, MICHAEL T. (1988) ''Low-Intensity Conflict,'' *Christianity and Crisis*, February 1, pp. 11–14.

_____. (1987) ''The Arms Trade: Changing Patterns in the 1980s,'' *Third World Quarterly* 9 (October): 1257–1281.

_____. (1986) ''The State of the Trade: Global Arms Transfer Patterns in the 1980s,'' *Journal of International Affairs* 40 (Summer): 1–21.

KLUCKHOHN, CLYDE. (1944) ''Anthropological Research and World Peace,'' pp. 143–152 in L. Bryson, Laurence Finkelstein, and Robert M. MacIver (eds.), *Approaches to World Peace*. New York: Conference on Science, Philosophy, and Religion.

KNORR, KLAUS. (1977) ''International Economic Leverage and Its Uses,'' pp. 99–126 in Klaus Knorr and Frank N. Trager (eds.), *Economic Issues and National Security*. Lawrence: Regents Press of Kansas.

_____. (1975) *The Power of Nations*. New York: Basic Books.

KNORR, KLAUS, AND JAMES N. ROSENAU (eds.) (1969) *Contending Approaches to International Politics*. Princeton, N.J.: Princeton University Press.

KNORR, KLAUS, AND FRANK TRAGER (eds.) (1977) *Economic Issues and National Security*. Lawrence: Regents Press of Kansas.

KNORR, KLAUS, AND SIDNEY VERBA (eds.) (1961) *The International System*. Princeton, N.J.: Princeton University Press.

KNUDSEN, BAARD BREDRUP. (1984) *Europe Versus America: Foreign Policy in the 1980s*. Paris: Atlantic Institute for International Affairs.

KORANY, BAHGAT. (1986) *How Foreign Policy Decisions Are Made in the Third World*. Boulder, Colo.: Westview Press.

KORBONSKI, ANDRZEJ. (1973) "Theory and Practice of Regional Integration: The Case of Comecon," pp. 152–175 in Richard A. Falk and Saul H. Mendlovitz (eds.), *Regional Politics and World Order*. San Francisco: Freeman.

KRASNER, STEPHEN D. (1985) *Structural Conflict: The Third World Against Global Liberalism*. Berkeley, Calif.: University of California Press.

_____. (1983) *International Regimes*. Ithaca, N.Y.: Cornell University Press.

_____. (1982) "Structural Causes and Regime Consequences," *International Organization* 36 (Spring): 185–206.

_____. (1981) "Transforming International Regimes: What the Third World Wants and Why," *International Studies Quarterly* 25 (March): 119–148.

_____. (1979) "The Tokyo Round: Particularistic Interests and Prospects for Stability in the Global Trading System," *International Studies Quarterly* 23 (December): 491–531.

_____. (1978) *Defending the National Interest*. Princeton, N.J.: Princeton University Press.

_____. (1976) "State Power and the Structure of International Trade," *World Politics* 28 (April): 317–347.

_____. (1974) "Oil Is the Exception," *Foreign Policy* 14 (Spring): 68–84.

_____. (1972) "Are Bureaucracies Important? (Or Allison Wonderland)," *Foreign Policy* 7 (Summer): 159–179.

KRATOCHWIL, FRIEDRICH, AND JOHN GERARD RUGGIE. (1986) "International Organization: A State of the Art on the Art of the State," *International Organization* 40 (Autumn): 753–775.

KRAUTHAMMER, CHARLES. (1983) "From OPEC to ODEC," *New Republic*, November 28, pp. 19–21.

KREPON, MICHAEL. (1984) *Strategic Stalemate*. New York: St. Martin's Press.

KUCZYNSKI, PEDRO-PABLO. (1987) "The Outlook for Latin American Debt," *Foreign Affairs* 66 (Fall): 129–149.

KUDRLE, ROBERT T. (1987) "The Several Faces of the Multinational Corporation: Political Reaction and Policy Response," pp. 230–241 in Jeffry A. Frieden and David A. Lake (eds.), *International Political Economy*. New York: St. Martin's Press.

KUHLMAN, JAMES A. (1976) "Eastern Europe," pp. 444–465 in James N. Rosenau, Kenneth W. Thompson, and Gavin Boyd (eds.), *World Politics*. New York: Free Press.

KUHN, THOMAS S. (1970) *The Structure of Scientific Revolutions*. Chicago: University of Chicago Press.

KURIAN, GEORGE THOMAS. (1979) *The Book of World Rankings*. New York: Facts on File.

LANGER, WILLIAM L. (1962) "Farewell to Empire," *Foreign Affairs* 41 (October): 115–130.

LAQUEUR, WALTER. (1988) "Reflections on Terrorism," pp. 102–112 in Charles W. Kegley, Jr., and Eugene R. Wittkopf (eds.), *The Global Agenda*, 2nd ed. New York: Random House.

LASZLO, ERVIN, JORGE LOZOYA, A. K. BHATTACHARYA, JAIME ESTEVEZ, ROSARIO GREEN, AND VENKATA RAMAN. (1980) *The Obstacles to the New International Economic Order*. Elmsford, N.Y.: Pergamon Press.

LEBOW, RICHARD NED. (1981) *Between Peace and War: The Nature of International Crisis*. Baltimore: Johns Hopkins University Press.

LEVI, WERNER. (1981) *The Coming End of War*. Beverly Hills, Calif.: Sage.

LEVY, JACK. (1988) "Contending Theories of War," pp. 54–62 in Charles W. Kegley, Jr., and Eugene R. Wittkopf (eds.), *The Global Agenda*, 2nd ed. New York: Random House.

_____. (1986) "Organizational Routines and the Causes of War," *International Studies Quarterly* 30 (June): 193–222.

_____. (1983a) "Misperception and the Causes of War," *World Politics* 35 (October): 76–99.

_____. (1983b) *War in the Modern Great Power System, 1495–1975*. Lexington: University of Kentucky Press.

LEVY, WALTER J. (1978–1979) "The Years That the Locust Hath Eaten: Oil Policy and OPEC Development Prospects," *Foreign Affairs* 57 (Winter): 287–305.

LEWIS, JOHN P., AND VALERIANA KALLAB (eds.) (1983) *U.S. Foreign Policy and the Third World: Agenda 1983.* New York: Praeger.

LEWIS, KEVIN N. (1979) "The Prompt and Delayed Effects of Nuclear War," *Scientific American* 241 (July): 35–47.

LEWIS, W. ARTHUR. (1978) *The Evolution of the International Economic Order.* Princeton, N.J.: Princeton University Press.

LEWONTIN, R. C., STEVEN ROSE, AND LEON J. KAMIN. (1984) *Not in Our Genes: Biology, Ideology, and Human Nature.* New York: Pantheon.

LEYTON-BROWN, DAVID. (1987) "Introduction," pp. 1–4 in David Leyton-Brown (ed.), *The Utility of Economic Sanctions.* New York: St. Martin's Press.

LIEBER, ROBERT J. (1982) "Cohesion and Disruption in the Western Alliance," pp. 320–348 in Daniel Yergin and Martin Hillenbrand (eds.), *Global Insecurity.* New York: Penguin.

LIFTON, ROBERT JAY, AND RICHARD FALK. (1982) *Indefensible Weapons: The Political and Psychological Case Against Nuclearism.* New York: Basic Books.

LIGHTHIZER, ROBERT E. (1983) "The Summit: What Is Likely to Happen and How It Will Affect U.S. Policy." Remarks before the University of South Carolina Seminar on International Economic and Political Issues, Columbia, S.C., May 15.

LIJPHART, AREND. (1974) "The Structure of the Theoretical Revolution in International Relations," *International Studies Quarterly* 18 (March): 42–49.

LILLICH, RICHARD B. (1972) "Domestic Institutions," pp. 384–424 in Cyril E. Black and Richard A. Falk (eds.), *The Future of the International Legal Order.* Princeton, N.J.: Princeton University Press.

LINDBLOM, CHARLES E. (1977) *Politics and Markets.* New York: Basic Books.

LINDSAY, JAMES M. (1986) "Trade Sanctions As Policy Instruments: A Re-examination," *International Studies Quarterly* 30 (June): 153–173.

LIPSON, CHARLES. (1984) "International Cooperation in Economic and Security Affairs," *World Politics* 37 (October): 1–23.

LISKA, GEORGE. (1968) *Alliances and the Third World.* Baltimore: Johns Hopkins University Press.

———. (1957) *International Equilibrium.* Cambridge, Mass.: Harvard University Press.

LISSITZYN, OLIVER J. (1963) "International Law in a Divided World," *International Conciliation* 542 (March): 3–69.

LISTER, FREDERICK K. (1986) "Fairness and Accountability in U.N. Financial Decision-Making." United Nations Management and Decision-making Project, United Nations Association of the United States of America.

LITTLE, RICHARD. (1975) *Intervention: External Involvement in Civil Wars.* Totowa, N.J.: Rowman and Littlefield.

LORENZ, KONRAD. (1963) *On Aggression.* New York: Harcourt, Brace & World.

LOVELL, JOHN P. (1970) *Foreign Policy in Perspective.* New York: Holt, Rinehart & Winston.

LUARD, EVAN. (1968) *Conflict and Peace in the Modern International System.* Boston: Little, Brown.

LUCKHAM, ROBIN. (1984) "Militarisation and the New International Anarchy," *Third World Quarterly* 6 (April): 351–373.

LUKE, TIMOTHY W. (1983) "Dependent Development and the Arab OPEC States," *Journal of Politics* 45 (November): 979–1003.

MACRIDIS, ROY C. (ed.) (1985a) *Foreign Policy in World Politics*, 6th ed. Englewood Cliffs, N.J.: Prentice-Hall.

———. (1985b) "French Foreign Policy: The Quest for Rank," pp. 22–71 in Roy C. Macridis (ed.), *Foreign Policy in World Politics*, 6th ed. Englewood Cliffs, N.J.: Prentice-Hall.

MANSBACH, RICHARD W., YALE H. FERGUSON, AND DONALD E. LAMPERT. (1976) *The Web of World Politics.* Englewood Cliffs, N.J.: Prentice-Hall.

MARANTZ, PAUL. (1987) "Economic Sanctions in the Polish Crisis," pp. 131–146 in David Leyton-Brown (ed.), *The Utility of International Economic Sanctions.* New York: St. Martin's Press.

MARRIS, STEPHEN. (1987) *Deficits and the Dollar Revisited.* Washington, D.C.: Institute for International Economics.

MASTERS, ROGER D. (1969) "World Politics As a Primitive Political System," pp. 104–118 in James N. Rosenau (ed.), *International Politics and Foreign Policy.* New York: Free Press.

MAYUR, RASHMI. (1984) "The Third World and Tomorrow," *The Futurist* 18 (April): 21–23.

McCartney, James. (1987) "Chinese Feel Justified in Continued Arms Sales to Iran," *The State* (Columbia, S.C.), November 15, p. 3B.

McCartney, Robert J. (1987) "A Silent Killer Heard 'Round the World," *Washington Post National Weekly Edition*, March 30, p. 9.

McClelland, Charles A. (1966) *Theory and the International System*. New York: Macmillan.

McDougal, Myres S., and Harold D. Lasswell. (1959) "The Identification and Appraisal of Diverse Systems of Public Order," *American Journal of International Law* 53 (January): 1–29.

McGowan, Patrick J., and Charles W. Kegley, Jr. (eds.) (1983) *Foreign Policy and the Modern World System*. Beverly Hills, Calif.: Sage.

——. (eds.) (1980) *Threats, Weapons and Foreign Policy*. Beverly Hills, Calif.: Sage.

McGowan, Patrick J., with the Assistance of Bohdan Kordan. (1981) "Imperialism in World-System Perspective," *International Studies Quarterly* 25 (March): 43–68.

McLaughlin, Martin M. (1979) *The United States and World Development: Agenda 1979*. New York: Praeger.

McNamara, Robert S. (1984) "Time Bomb or Myth: The Population Problem," *Foreign Affairs* 62 (Summer): 1107–1131.

——. (1983) "The Military Role of Nuclear Weapons," *Foreign Affairs* 62 (Fall): 59–80.

——. (1977) "Population and International Security," *International Security* 2 (Fall): 25–55.

Mead, Margaret. (1968) "Warfare Is Only an Invention—Not a Biological Necessity," pp. 270–274 in Leon Bramson and George W. Goethals (eds.), *War*. New York: Basic Books.

Mead, Walter Russell. (1987) *Mortal Splendor: The American Empire in Transition*. Boston: Houghton Mifflin.

Meadows, Donella H., Dennis L. Meadows, Jørgen Randers, and William W. Behrens III. (1974) *The Limits to Growth*. New York: New American Library.

Merrick, Thomas W. (1986) "World Population in Transition," *Population Bulletin*, vol. 41, no. 2. Washington, D.C.: Population Reference Bureau.

Midlarsky, Manus I. (1975) *On War*. New York: Free Press.

Mills, C. Wright. (1956) *The Power Elite*. New York: Oxford University Press.

Minter, William. (1986–1987) "South Africa: Straight Talk on Sanctions," *Foreign Policy* 65 (Winter): 43–63.

Mitrany, David. (1975) *The Functional Theory of Politics*. New York: St. Martin's Press.

——. (1966) *A Working Peace System*. Chicago: Quadrangle.

Modelski, George (ed.) (1987) *Exploring Long Cycles*. Boulder, Colo.: Lynne Rienner.

——. (1978) "The Long Cycle of Global Politics and the Nation-State," *Comparative Studies in Society and History* 20 (April): 214–235.

——. (1964) "The International Relations of Internal War," pp. 14–44 in James N. Rosenau (ed.), *International Aspects of Civil Strife*. Princeton, N.J.: Princeton University Press.

Moon, Bruce E., and William J. Dixon. (1985) "Politics, the State, and Basic Human Needs: A Cross-National Study," *American Journal of Political Science* 29 (November): 661–694.

Morawetz, David. (1977) *Twenty-five Years of Economic Development, 1950 to 1975*. Washington, D.C.: World Bank.

Morgenthau, Hans J. (1983) "Defining the National Interest—Again," pp. 32–39 in Charles W. Kegley, Jr., and Eugene R. Wittkopf (eds.), *Perspectives on American Foreign Policy*. New York: St. Martin's Press.

——. (1973) *Politics Among Nations*, 5th ed. New York: Knopf.

——. (1969) "Historical Justice and the Cold War," *New York Review of Books*, July 10, pp. 10–17.

——. (1967) *Politics Among Nations*, 4th ed. New York: Knopf.

——. (1948) *Politics Among Nations*. New York: Knopf.

Morris, David. (1979) *Measuring the Condition of the World's Poor: The Physical Quality of Life Index*. New York: Pergamon Press.

Morris, Desmond. (1969) *The Human Zoo*. New York: Dell.

Morse, Edward L. (1986) "After the Fall: The Politics of Oil," *Foreign Affairs* 64 (Spring): 792–811.

——. (1976) *Modernization and the Transformation of International Relations*. New York: Free Press.

Mossavar-Rahmani, Bijan. (1983) "The OPEC Multiplier," *Foreign Policy* 52 (Fall): 136–148.

Mowlana, Hamid. (1983) "Needed: A New World Information Order," *USA Today* 112 (September): 42–44.

MOYNIHAN, DANIEL P. (1975) "The United States in Opposition," *Commentary* 59 (March): 31–44.

MOYNIHAN, DANIEL P., WITH SUZANNE WEAVER. (1978) *A Dangerous Place*. Boston: Little, Brown.

MÜLLER, RONALD. (1973–1974) "Poverty Is the Product," *Foreign Policy* 13 (Winter): 71–103.

MULLINS, A. F., JR. (1987) *Born Arming: Development and Military Power in New States*. Stanford, Calif.: Stanford University Press.

MURPHY, CRAIG N. (1983) "What the Third World Wants: An Interpretation of the Development and Meaning of the New International Economic Order Ideology," *International Studies Quarterly* 27 (March): 55–76.

MURRAY, ANNE FIRTH. (1985) "Population: A Global Accounting," *Environment* 27 (July–August): 7–11, 33–34.

NAGEL, STUART S. (1969) *The Legal Process from a Behavioral Perspective*. Homewood, Ill.: Dorsey Press.

NARDIN, TERRY. (1983) *Law, Morality, and the Relations of States*. Princeton, N.J.: Princeton University Press.

NAU, HENRY R. (1987) "Trade and Deterrence," *The National Interest* 7 (Summer): 48–60.

NEF, JOHN U. (1968) *War and Human Progress*. New York: Norton.

NELSON, STEPHAN D. (1974) "Nature/Nurture Revisited: A Review of the Biological Bases of Conflict," *Journal of Conflict Resolution* 18 (June): 285–335.

The New Population Debate: Two Views on Population Growth and Economic Development. (1985) Washington, D.C.: Population Reference Bureau.

NIEBUHR, REINHOLD. (1947) *Moral Man and Immoral Society*. New York: Scribner's.

NINCIC, MIROSLAV. (1982) *The Arms Race: The Political Economy of Military Growth*. New York: Praeger.

NOGEE, JOSEPH L. (1975) "Polarity: An Ambiguous Concept," *Orbis* 28 (Winter): 1193–1224.

NOGEE, JOSEPH L., AND ROBERT L. DONALDSON. (1981) *Soviet Foreign Policy Since World War II*. Elmsford, N.Y.: Pergamon Press.

NORMAN, COLIN. (1979) *Knowledge and Power: The Global Research and Development Budget*. Worldwatch Paper no. 31. Washington, D.C.: Worldwatch Institute.

NOVE, ALEC. (1978) *East–West Trade: Problems, Prospects, Issues*. The Washington Papers, vol. 6, no. 53. Beverly Hills, Calif.: Sage.

NYE, JOSEPH S., JR. (1987) "Nuclear Learning and U.S.-Soviet Security Regimes," *International Organization* 41 (Summer): 371–402.

————. (1979) "We Tried Harder (and Did More)," *Foreign Policy* 36 (Fall): 101–104.

————. (1971) *Peace in Parts*. Boston: Little, Brown.

NYE, JOSEPH S., JR., AND ROBERT O. KEOHANE. (1971) "Transnational Relations and World Politics: An Introduction," *International Organization* 25 (Summer): 329–349.

O'BRIEN, CONOR CRUISE. (1977) "Liberty and Terrorism," *International Security* 2 (Fall): 56–67.

O'BRIEN, PATRICK M. (1988) "Agricultural Productivity and the Global Food Market," pp. 394–408 in Charles W. Kegley, Jr., and Eugene R. Wittkopf (eds.), *The Global Agenda*, 2nd ed. New York: Random House.

The Oil Rollercoaster. (1987) Washington, D.C.: Fund for Renewable Energy and the Environment.

O'KEEFE, BERNARD J. (1983) *Nuclear Hostages*. Boston: Houghton Mifflin.

OLSON, MANCUR. (1982) *The Rise and Decline of Nations*. New Haven, Conn.: Yale University Press.

————. (1971) "Rapid Growth As a Destabilizing Force," pp. 215–227 in James C. Davies (ed.), *When Men Revolt and Why*. New York: Free Press.

ONUF, NICHOLAS GREENWOOD. (1982) "Global Law-Making and Legal Thought," pp. 1–82 in Nicholas Greenwood Onuf (ed.), *Law-Making in the Global Community*. Durham, N.C.: Carolina Academic Press.

OREN, NISSAN (ed.) (1984) *When Patterns Change: Turning Points in International Politics*. New York: St. Martin's Press.

ORGANSKI, A. F. K. (1968) *World Politics*. New York: Knopf.

ORGANSKI, A. F. K., AND JACEK KUGLER. (1980) *The War Ledger*. Chicago: University of Chicago Press.

OSGOOD, ROBERT E. (1968) *Alliances and American Foreign Policy*. Baltimore: Johns Hopkins University Press.

OTTAWAY, DAVID B. (1987) "It Looks Like Pakistan Can Have Its Bomb and Eat It, Too," *Washington Post National Weekly Edition*, March 23, p. 15.

PAARLBERG, ROBERT L. (1984) "Coercive Resource Power," pp. 20–29 in Charles W. Kegley, Jr., and Eugene R. Wittkopf (eds.), *The Global Agenda*. New York: Random House.

———. (1982) "A Food Security Approach for the 1980s: Righting the Balance," pp. 69–95 in Roger D. Hansen, *U.S. Foreign Policy and the Third World: Agenda 1982*. New York: Praeger.

———. (1980) "Lessons of the Grain Embargo," *Foreign Affairs* 59 (Fall): 144–162.

PAPP, DANIEL S. (1986) *Soviet Policies Toward the Developing World During the 1980s*. Maxwell Air Force Base, Ala.: Air University Press.

PARENTI, MICHAEL. (1969) *The Anti-Communist Impulse*. New York: Random House.

PARRY, CLIVE. (1968) "The Function of Law in the International Community," pp. 1–54 in Max Sorensen (ed.), *Manual of Public International Law*. New York: St. Martin's Press.

PATERSON, THOMAS G. (1979) *On Every Front: The Making of the Cold War*. New York: Norton.

PEASE, DON J., AND J. WILLIAM GOOLD. (1985) "The New GSP: Fair Trade with the Third World," *World Policy Journal* 2 (Spring): 351–366.

PFISTER, ULRICH, AND CHRISTIAN SUTER. (1987) "International Financial Relations As Part of the World-System," *International Studies Quarterly* 31 (September): 239–272.

PIERRE, ANDREW J. (1984) "The Politics of International Terrorism," pp. 84–92 in Charles W. Kegley, Jr., and Eugene R. Wittkopf (eds.), *The Global Agenda*. New York: Random House.

———. (1982) *The Global Politics of Arms Sales*. Princeton, N.J.: Princeton University Press.

PIPES, RICHARD. (1977) "Why the Soviet Union Thinks It Could Fight and Win a Nuclear War," *Commentary* 26 (July): 21–34.

PIRAGES, DENNIS. (1986) "World Energy Crisis 1995," *Futures Research Quarterly* 2 (Fall): 31–47.

———. (1983) "The Ecological Perspective and the Social Sciences," *International Studies Quarterly* 27 (September): 243–255.

———. (1978) *The New Context for International Relations: Global Ecopolitics*. North Scituate, Mass.: Duxbury Press.

PLATT, JOHN. (1987) "The Future of AIDS," *The Futurist* 21 (November–December): 10–17.

POATS, RUTHERFORD M. (1982) *Development Co-operation: 1982 Review*. Paris: Organization for Economic Cooperation and Development.

POPPER, KARL R. (1957) *The Poverty of Historicism*. Boston: Beacon Press.

Population in Perspective. (1986) Washington, D.C.: Population Reference Bureau.

POPULATION REFERENCE BUREAU. (1981) *World Population: Toward the Next Century*. Washington, D.C.: Population Reference Bureau.

POSTEL, SANDRA. (1986) *Altering the World's Chemistry: Assessing the Risks*. Worldwatch Paper no. 71. Washington, D.C.: Worldwatch Institute.

"PROGRESS REPORT ON EUROPE'S SINGLE INTERNAL MARKET." (1987) *Europe* (265) (April): 22–23.

PRUITT, DEAN G. (1965) "Definition of the Situation As a Determinant of International Action," pp. 393–432 in Herbert C. Kelman (ed.), *International Behavior*. New York: Holt, Rinehart & Winston.

PRUITT, DEAN G., AND RICHARD C. SNYDER (eds.) (1969) *Theory and Research on the Causes of War*. Englewood Cliffs, N.J.: Prentice-Hall.

PUCHALA, DONALD J. (1988) "The Integration Theorists and the Study of International Relations," pp. 198–265 in Charles W. Kegley, Jr., and Eugene R. Wittkopf (eds.), *The Global Agenda*, 2nd ed. New York: Random House.

———. (ed.) (1983) *Issues Before the 38th General Assembly of the United Nations, 1983–1984*. New York: United Nations Association of the United States of America.

———. (1982–1983) "American Interests and the United Nations," *Political Science Quarterly* 97 (Winter): 571–588,

QUESTER, GEORGE H. (ed.) (1971) *Power, Action, and Interaction*. Boston: Little, Brown.

RAPKIN, DAVID P., AND WILLIAM P. AVERY. (1982) "U.S. International Economic Policy in a Period of Hegemonic Decline," pp. 3–26 in William P. Avery and David P. Rapkin (eds.), *America in a Changing World Political Economy*. New York: Longman.

RAVENHILL, JOHN. (1984) "What Is to Be Done for Third World Commodity Exporters? An Evaluation of the STABEX Scheme," *International Organization* 38 (Summer): 537–574.

RAWLS, LUCIA. (1986) "Saudi Arabia, Aramco, and the American Political Process: Cause for Concern?" *American-Arab Affairs* 18 (Fall): 92–105.

RAYMOND, GREGORY A. (1980) *Conflict Resolution and the Structure of the State System: An Analysis of Arbitrative Settlements*. Montclair, N.J.: Allanheld, Osmun.

"THE REALITIES OF ECONOMIC INTERDEPENDENCE." (1984) *Finance and Development* 21 (March): 28–32.

REICH, ROBERT B. (1983) "Why Democracy Makes Economic Sense," *New Republic*, December 19, pp. 25–32.

RENNER, MICHAEL G. (1987) "Shaping America's Energy Future," *World Policy Journal* 4 (Summer): 383–414.

REPETTO, ROBERT. (1987) "Population, Resources, Environment: An Uncertain Future," *Population Bulletin*, vol. 42, no. 2. Washington, D.C.: Population Reference Bureau.

REUTLINGER, SHLOMO. (1985) "Food Security and Poverty in LDCs," *Finance and Development* 22 (December): 7–11.

RHODES, EDWARD. (1988) "Nuclear Weapons and Credibility: Deterrence Theory Beyond Rationality," *Review of International Studies* 14 (January): 45–62.

RICHARDSON, LEWIS F. (1960a) *Arms and Insecurity*. Pittsburgh: Boxwood Press.

———. (1960b) *Statistics of Deadly Quarrels*. Chicago: Quadrangle.

RICHBURG, KEITH B. (1987) "As Marxist Economies Wither Away," *Washington Post National Weekly Edition*, April 27, pp. 10–11.

RIENOW, ROBERT, AND LEANA RIENOW. (1967) *Moment in the Sun*. New York: Dial Press.

RIGGS, ROBERT E. (1978) "The United States and the Diffusion of Power in the Security Council," *International Studies Quarterly* 22 (December): 513–544.

———. (1977) "One Small Step for Functionalism: UN Participation and Congressional Attitude Change," *International Organization* 31 (Summer): 515–539.

RIGGS, ROBERT E., AND JACK C. PLANO. (1988) *The United Nations: International Organization and World Politics*. Chicago: Dorsey Press.

RIKER, WILLIAM H. (1962) *The Theory of Political Coalitions*. New Haven, Conn.: Yale University Press.

ROCA, SERGIO. (1987) "Economic Sanctions Against Cuba," pp. 87–104 in David Leyton-Brown (ed.), *The Utility of International Economic Sanctions*. New York: St. Martin's Press.

ROKEACH, MILTON. (1960) *The Open and Closed Mind*. New York: Basic Books.

ROSECRANCE, RICHARD. (1988) "Force or Trade: The Costs and Benefits of Two Paths to Global Influence," pp. 21–30 in Charles W. Kegley, Jr., and Eugene R. Wittkopf (eds.), *The Global Agenda*, 2nd ed. New York: Random House.

———. (1987) "Long Cycle Theory and International Relations," *International Organization* 42 (Spring): 283–301.

———. (1986) *The Rise of the Trading State: Commerce and Conquest in the Modern World*. New York: Basic Books.

———. (1966) "Bipolarity, Multipolarity, and the Future," *Journal of Conflict Resolution* 10 (September): 314–327.

———. (1963) *Action and Reaction in World Politics*. Boston: Little, Brown.

ROSECRANCE, RICHARD N., A. ALEXANDROFF, W. KOEHLER, J. KROLL, S. LAQUE STOCKER. (1977) "Whither Interdependence?" *International Organization* 31 (Summer): 425–471.

ROSECRANCE, RICHARD N., AND ARTHUR STEIN. (1973) "Interdependence: Myth or Reality?" *World Politics* 24 (October): 1–27.

ROSEN, STEVEN J. (ed.) (1973) *Testing the Theory of the Military-Industrial Complex*. Lexington, Mass.: Heath.

ROSENAU, JAMES N. (1988) "Turbulence in World Politics." Unpublished manuscript.

———. (1980) *The Scientific Study of Foreign Policy*. New York: Nichols.

ROSTOW, W. W. (1960) *The Stages of Economic Growth*. Cambridge, England: Cambridge University Press.

ROTHSCHILD, EMMA. (1980) "Boom and Bust," *New York Review of Books*, April 3, pp. 31–34.

ROTHSTEIN, RICHARD. (1988) "Give Them a Break: Third World Debtors and a Cure for Reaganomics," *New Republic*, February 1, pp. 20–24.

ROTHSTEIN, ROBERT L. (1979) *Global Bargaining: UNCTAD and the Quest for a New International Economic Order*. Princeton, N.J.: Princeton University Press.

———. (1972) "On the Costs of Realism," *Political Science Quarterly* 83 (September): 347–362.

ROWE, EDWARD T. (1969) "Changing Patterns in the Voting Success of Member States in the United Nations General Assembly: 1945–1966," *International Organization* 23 (Spring): 231–253.

RUGGIE, JOHN GERARD. (1985) "The United States and the United Nations: Toward a New Realism," *International Organization* 39 (Spring): 343–356.

RUMMEL, R. J. (1963) "Dimensions of Conflict Behavior Within and Between Nations," *General Systems Yearbook* 8: 1–50.

RUSSETT, BRUCE. (1985) "The Mysterious Case of Vanishing Hegemony: Or, Is Mark Twain Really Dead?" *International Organization* 39 (Spring): 207–231.

———. (1984) "Dimensions of Resource Dependence: Some Elements of Rigor in Concept and Policy Analysis," *International Organization* 38 (Summer): 481–499.

————. (1982) "Defense Expenditures and National Well-Being," *American Political Science Review* 76 (December): 767–777.

————. (1978) "The Marginal Utility of Income Transfers to the Third World," *International Organization* 32 (Autumn): 913–928.

————. (1965) *Trends in World Politics.* New York: Macmillan.

SAGAN, CARL. (1988) "The Common Enemy," *Parade*, February 7, pp. 4–7.

————. (1983–1984) "Nuclear War and Climatic Catastrophe: Some Policy Implications," *Foreign Affairs* 62 (Winter): 257–292.

SAMPSON, ANTHONY. (1978) "Want to Start a War?" *Esquire*, March 1, pp. 58–69.

————. (1975) *The Seven Sisters.* New York: Bantam Books.

SANDERSON, STEVEN E. (ed.) (1984) *The Americas in the New International Division of Labor.* New York: Holmes & Meier.

SANDLER, TODD (ed.) (1980) *The Theory and Structures of International Political Economy.* Boulder, Colo · Westview Press.

SCHECHTER, MICHAEL G. (1979) "The Common Fund: A Test Case for the New International Economic Order." Paper presented at the Annual Meeting of the International Studies Association/South, Athens, Ga., October 4–6.

SCHELL, JONATHAN. (1984) *The Abolition.* New York: Knopf.

————. (1982) *The Fate of the Earth.* New York: Avon Books.

SCHELLING, THOMAS C. (1984) *Choice and Consequence.* Cambridge, Mass.: Harvard University Press.

————. (1978) *Micromotives and Macrobehavior.* New York: Norton.

————. (1966) *Arms and Influence.* New Haven, Conn.: Yale University Press.

————. (1960) *The Strategy of Conflict.* Cambridge, Mass.: Harvard University Press.

SCHLESINGER, ARTHUR, JR. (1987) "At Last: Capitalistic Communism," *Wall Street Journal*, August 4, p. 34.

————. (1983) "Pretension in the Presidential Pulpit," *Wall Street Journal*, March 17, p. 26.

————. (1967) "Origins of the Cold War," *Foreign Affairs* 46 (October): 22–52.

SCHNEIDER, WILLIAM. (1976) *Food, Foreign Policy, and Raw Materials Cartels.* New York: Crane, Russak.

SCHREIBER, ANNA P. (1973) "Economic Coercion As an Instrument of Foreign Policy: U.S. Economic Measures Against Cuba and the Dominican Republic," *World Politics* 25 (April): 387–413.

SCHUMACHER, E. F. (1973) *Small Is Beautiful.* New York: Harper & Row.

SCOLNICK, JOSEPH M., JR. (1974) "An Appraisal of Studies of the Linkage Between Domestic and International Conflict," *Comparative Political Studies* 6 (January): 485–509.

SCOTT, ANDREW M. (1979) "Science and Surprise: The Role of the Inadvertent in International Affairs." Paper presented at the Annual Meeting of the International Studies Association/South, Athens, Ga., October 4–6.

SEGAL, DAVID. (1987) "Could Iran Become the Next Member of the Nuclear Bomb Club?" *Washington Post National Weekly Edition*, May 11, p. 25.

SEWELL, JOHN W., AND CHRISTINE E. CONTEE. (1987) "Foreign Aid and Gramm–Rudman," *Foreign Affairs* 65 (Summer): 1015–1036.

SEWELL, JOHN W., AND STUART K. TUCKER. (1988) *Growth, Jobs, and Exports in a Changing World Economy.* New Brunswick, N.J.: Transaction Books.

SEWELL, JOHN W., AND THE STAFF OF THE OVERSEAS DEVELOPMENT COUNCIL. (1980) *The United States and World Development: Agenda 1980.* New York: Praeger.

————— (1979) "Can the North Prosper Without Growth and Progress in the South?" pp. 45–76 in Martin M. McLaughlin, *The United States and World Development: Agenda 1979.* New York: Praeger.

SHAPLEN, ROBERT. (1983) "Reporter at Large: The Paradox of Nonalignment," *New Yorker*, May 23, pp. 83–84 passim.

SHERRY, MICHAEL. (1977) *Preparing for the Next War.* New Haven, Conn.: Yale University Press.

SHONFIELD, ANDREW. (1980) "The World Economy 1979," *Foreign Affairs.* Special issue, *America and the World 1979*, 58 (no. 3): 596–621.

SHULMAN, MARSHALL D. (ed.) (1986) *East–West Tensions in the Third World.* New York: Norton.

SHULTZ, GEORGE P. (1983) "Security and Economic Assistance for FY 1984." Statement before the House Foreign Affairs Committee, February 19. U.S. Department of State, Bureau of Public Affairs, Current Policy no. 454 (February 16).

SIBLEY, MULFORD Q. (1963) "Unilateral Disarmament," pp. 112–140 in Robert A. Goldwin (ed.), *America Armed.* Chicago: Rand McNally.

SIEGEL, MARTIN J. (1983) "Survival," *USA Today* 112 (August): 1–2.

Simon, Herbert A. (1957) *Models of Man*. New York: Wiley.

Simon, Julian L. (1981) *The Ultimate Resource*. Princeton, N.J.: Princeton University Press.

Simon, Julian L., and Herman Kahn (eds.) (1984) *The Resourceful Earth: A Response to Global 2000*. Oxford, England: Blackwell Publisher.

Simowitz, Roslyn. (1982) *The Logical Consistency and Soundness of the Balance of Power Theory*. Denver: Graduate School of International Studies, University of Denver.

Simpson, Smith. (1967) *Anatomy of the State Department*. Boston: Houghton Mifflin.

Singer, Hans W., and Javed A. Ansari. (1988) *Rich and Poor Countries*, 4th ed. London: Unwin Hyman.

Singer, J. David. (1981) "Accounting for International War: The State of the Discipline," *Journal of Peace Research* 18 (no. 1): 1–18.

———. (ed.) (1968) *Quantitative International Politics*. New York: Free Press.

———. (ed.) (1965) *Human Behavior and International Politics*. Chicago: Rand McNally.

———. (1961) "The Level-of-Analysis Problem in International Relations," pp. 77–92 in Klaus Knorr and Sidney Verba (eds.), *The International System*. Princeton, N.J.: Princeton University Press.

———. (1960) "Theorizing About Theory in International Politics," *Journal of Conflict Resolution* 4 (December): 431–442.

Singer, J. David, and Melvin Small. (1975) "War in History and in the State of the World Message," pp. 220–248 in William D. Coplin and Charles W. Kegley, Jr. (eds.), *Analyzing International Relations*. New York: Praeger.

———. (1969) "National Alliance Commitments and War Involvement, 1815–1945," pp. 513–542 in James N. Rosenau (ed.), *International Politics and Foreign Policy*. New York: Free Press.

———. (1968) "Alliance Aggregation and the Onset of War, 1815–1945," pp. 247–285 in J. David Singer (ed.), *Quantitative International Politics*. New York: Free Press.

Singer, J. David, and Michael Wallace. (1970) "Intergovernmental Organization and the Preservation of Peace, 1816–1964: Some Bivariate Relationships," *International Organization* 24 (Summer): 520–547.

Sivard, Ruth Leger. (1987) *World Military and Social Expenditures 1987–88*. Washington, D.C.: World Priorities.

———. (1986) *World Military and Social Expenditures 1986*. Washington, D.C.: World Priorities.

———. (1982) *World Military and Social Expenditures 1982*. Leesburg, Va.: World Priorities.

———. (1981) *World Energy Survey*. Leesburg, Va.: World Priorities.

———. (1979a) *World Energy Survey*. Leesburg, Va.: World Priorities.

———. (1979b) *World Military and Social Expenditures 1979*. Leesburg, Va.: World Priorities.

Slater, Jerome, and David Goldfischer. (1988) "Can SDI Provide a Defense?" pp. 74–86 in Charles W. Kegley, Jr., and Eugene R. Wittkopf (eds.), *The Global Agenda*, 2nd ed. New York: Random House.

Small, Melvin, and J. David Singer. (1982) *Resort to Arms: International and Civil Wars, 1816–1980*. Beverly Hills, Calif.: Sage.

———. (1979) "Conflict in the International System, 1816–1977: Historical Trends and Policy Futures," pp. 89–115 in Charles W. Kegley, Jr., and Patrick J. McGowan (eds.), *Challenges to America*. Beverly Hills, Calif.: Sage.

———. (1976) "The War Proneness of Democratic Regimes," *Jerusalem Journal of International Relations* 1 (Summer): 50–59.

———. (1972) "Patterns in International Warfare, 1816–1965," pp. 121–131 in James F. Short, Jr., and Marvin E. Wolfgang (eds.), *Collective Violence*. Chicago: Aldine-Atherton.

Smart, Ian. (1976) "Uniqueness and Generality," pp. 259–281 in Raymond Vernon (ed.), *The Oil Crisis*. New York: Norton.

Smelser, Neil J. (1986) "External and Internal Factors in Theories of Social Change." Paper presented to the German-American Conference on Social Change and Modernization, Berkeley, Calif., August 26–28.

Smith, Ron P., and George Georgiou. (1983) "Assessing the Effect of Military Expenditures on OECD Economies: A Survey," *Arms Control* 4 (May): 3–15.

Smith, Roger K. (1987) "Explaining the Non-Proliferation Regime: Anomalies for Contemporary International Relations Theory," *International Organization* 41 (Spring): 251–281.

Smith, Steve, and Michael Clarke. (1985) *Foreign Policy Implementation*. London: Allen & Unwin.

Smith, Tony. (1981) "The Logic of Dependency Theory Revisited," *International Organization* 35 (Autumn): 755–776.

_____. (1979) "The Underdevelopment of Development Literature: The Case of Dependency Theory," *World Politics* 31 (January): 247–288.

SMOKE, RICHARD. (1975) "National Security Affairs," pp. 247–362 in Fred I. Greenstein and Nelson W. Polsby (eds.), *International Politics: Handbook of Political Science*, vol. 8. Reading, Mass.: Addison-Wesley.

SNIDAL, DUNCAN. (1985) "The Limits of Hegemonic Stability Theory," *International Organization* 49 (Autumn): 579–614.

SNYDER, GLENN H. (1984) "The Security Dilemma in Alliance Politics," *World Politics* 36 (July): 461–495.

SNYDER, GLENN H., AND PAUL DIESING. (1977) *Conflict Among Nations: Bargaining, Decision-Making, and System Structure in International Crisis*. Princeton, N.J.: Princeton University Press.

SNYDER, RICHARD C. (1955) "Toward Greater Order in the Study of International Politics," *World Politics* 7 (April): 461–468.

SONDERMANN, FRED A. (1957) "The Study of International Relations, 1956 Version," *World Politics* 9 (October): 102–111.

SØRENSEN, MAX. (1968) *Manual of Public International Law*. New York: St. Martin's Press.

SORENSEN, THEODORE C. (1963) *Decision Making in the White House*. New York: Columbia University Press.

SOROKIN, PITIRIM A. (1937) *Social and Cultural Dynamics*. New York: American Book.

SOROOS, MARVIN S. (1988) "The Tragedy of the Commons in Global Perspective," pp. 345–357 in Charles W. Kegley, Jr., and Eugene R. Wittkopf (eds.), *The Global Agenda*, 2nd ed. New York: Random House.

_____. (1986) *Beyond Sovereignty: The Challenge of Global Policy*. Columbia: University of South Carolina Press.

_____. (1984) "Coping with Resource Scarcity: A Critique of Lifeboat Ethics," pp. 350–366 in Charles W. Kegley, Jr., and Eugene R. Wittkopf (eds.), *The Global Agenda*. New York: Random House.

_____. (1977) "The Commons and Lifeboat As Guides for International Ecological Policy," *International Studies Quarterly* 21 (December): 647–674.

SPANIER, JOHN. (1987) *Games Nations Play*, 6th ed. Washington, D.C.: CQ Press.

_____. (1975) *Games Nations Play*, 2nd ed. New York: Praeger.

SPECTOR, LEONARD. (1986) "Nuclear Proliferation: The Silent Spread," *National Forum* 66 (Fall): 5–7.

_____. (1985) "Silent Spread," *Foreign Policy* 58 (Spring): 53–78.

SPERO, JOAN EDELMAN. (1985) *The Politics of International Economic Relations*, 3rd ed. New York: St. Martin's Press.

_____. (1983) "Trade in Services: Removing Barriers," *PS* 16 (Winter): 17–24.

SPIEGEL, STEVEN L. (1985) *The Other Arab-Israeli Conflict*. Chicago: University of Chicago Press.

SPIVACK, NEAL, AND ANN FLORINI. (1986) *Food on the Table: Seeking Global Solutions to Chronic Hunger*. New York: United Nations Association of the United States of America.

SPROUT, HAROLD, AND MARGARET SPROUT. (1984) "The Ecological Perspective on International Politics," pp. 322–326 in Charles W. Kegley, Jr., and Eugene R. Wittkopf (eds.), *The Global Agenda*. New York: Random House.

_____. (1971) *Toward a Politics of the Planet Earth*. New York: Van Nostrand.

_____. (1968) *An Ecological Paradigm for the Study of International Politics*. Research Monograph no. 30, Center of International Studies. Princeton, N.J.: Princeton University.

STARR, HARVEY. (1982) " 'Détente' or 'Two Against One'? The China Factor," pp. 185–212 in Charles W. Kegley, Jr., and Pat McGowan (eds.), *Foreign Policy: USA/USSR*. Beverly Hills, Calif.: Sage.

"STATE OF WORLD POPULATION '82." (1982) *UN Chronicle* 19 (July): 77–82.

State of World Population 1985. (1984) New York: United Nations Fund for Population Activities

STEIN, ARTHUR. (1984) "The Hegemon's Dilemma: Great Britain, the United States, and the International Economic Order," *International Organization* 38 (Spring): 355–386.

_____. (1976) "Conflict and Cohesion: A Review of the Literature," *Journal of Conflict Resolution* 20 (March): 143–172.

STERN, ERNEST, AND WOUTER TIMS. (1976) "The Relative Bargaining Strength of the Developing Countries," pp. 6–50 in Ronald G. Ridker (ed.), *Changing Resource Problems of the Fourth World*. Washington, D.C.: Resources for the Future.

STEWART, MICHAEL. (1984) *The Age of Interdependence: Economic Policy in a Shrinking World*. Cambridge, Mass.: MIT Press.

STOBAUGH, ROBERT. (1982) "World Energy to the Year 2000," pp. 29–57 in Daniel Yergin and Martin Hillenbrand (eds.), *Global Insecurity*. New York: Penguin.

STOBAUGH, ROBERT, AND DANIEL YERGIN. (1980) "Energy: An Emergency Telescoped," *Foreign Affairs*. Special issue, *America and the World 1979*, 58 (no. 3): 563–595.

——. (1979) "After the Second Shock: Pragmatic Energy Strategies," *Foreign Affairs* 57 (Spring): 836–871.

STOESSINGER, JOHN G. (1977) *The United Nations and the Superpowers: China, Russia, and America*. New York: Random House.

STOHL, MICHAEL, AND GEORGE A. LOPEZ (eds.) (1984) *The State As Terrorist*. Westport, Conn.: Greenwood Press.

STRANGE, SUSAN (ed.) (1984) *Paths to International Political Economy*. London: Allen & Unwin.

——. (1982) "*Cave! Hic Dragones*: A Critique of Regime Analysis," *International Organization* 36 (Spring): 479–496.

——. (1971) "The Politics of International Currencies," *World Politics* 23 (January): 215–231.

STREETEN, PAUL. (1974) "World Trade in Agricultural Commodities and the Terms of Trade with Industrial Goods," pp. 207–223 in Nurul Islam (ed.), *Agricultural Policy in Developing Countries*. London: Macmillan.

SULZBERGER, C. C. (1987) "How Brezhnev Offered to 'Split the World' with Nixon," *International Herald Tribune*, July 27, p. 7.

SUMNER, WILLIAM GRAHAM. (1968) "War," pp. 205–228 in Leon Bramson and George W. Goethals (eds.), *War*. New York: Basic Books.

SYLVESTER, CHRISTINE. (1980) "UN Elites: Perspective on Peace," *Journal of Peace Research* 17 (no. 4): 305–324.

TANTER, RAYMOND. (1966) "Dimensions of Conflict Behavior Within and Between Nations, 1958–1960," *Journal of Conflict Resolution* 10 (March): 143–164.

TANTER, RAYMOND, AND RICHARD ULLMAN (eds.) (1972) *Theory and Policy in International Relations*. Princeton, N.J.: Princeton University Press.

TAYLOR, PHILLIP. (1984) *Nonstate Actors in International Politics*. Boulder, Colo.: Westview Press.

THOMPSON, KENNETH W. (1960) *Political Realism and the Crisis of World Politics*. Princeton, N.J.: Princeton University Press.

——. (1958) "The Limits of Principle in International Politics," *Journal of Politics* 20 (August): 437–467.

THOMPSON, WILLIAM R. (1988) *On Global War: Historical-Structural Approaches to World Politics*. Columbia: University of South Carolina Press.

——. (1983) "The World-Economy, the Long Cycle, and the Question of World-System Time," pp. 35–62 in Pat McGowan and Charles W. Kegley, Jr. (eds.), *Foreign Policy and the Modern World System*. Beverly Hills, Calif.: Sage.

THUROW, LESTER. (1988) "America, Europe, and Japan: A Time to Dismantle the World Economy," pp. 308–316 in Charles W. Kegley, Jr., and Eugene R. Wittkopf (eds.), *The Global Agenda*, 2nd ed. New York: Random House.

TILLEMA, HERBERT K. (1987) "Foreign Overt Military Intervention, International Armed Conflict and Contemporary International War." Unpublished manuscript.

TILLEMA, HERBERT K., AND JOHN R. VAN WINGEN. (1982) "Law and Power in Military Intervention: Major States After World War II," *International Studies Quarterly* 26 (June): 220–250.

TODARO, MICHAEL P. (1981) *Economic Development in the Third World*. New York: Longman.

TOFFLER, ALVIN. (1980) *The Third Wave*. New York: Morrow.

——. (1970) *Future Shock*. New York: Random House.

TOWNSEND, JOYCE CAROL. (1982) *Bureaucratic Politics in American Decision Making*. Washington, D.C.: University Press of America.

TOYNBEE, ARNOLD J. (1947) *A Study of History*. New York: Oxford University Press.

TRIFFIN, ROBERT. (1978–1979) "The International Role and Fate of the Dollar," *Foreign Affairs* 57 (Winter): 269–286.

TUCKER, ROBERT W. (1980) "America in Decline: The Foreign Policy of 'Maturity'," *Foreign Affairs*. Special issue, *America and the World 1979*, 58 (no. 3): 449–484.

TUGWELL, REXFORD GUY. (1971) *Off Course: From Truman to Nixon*. New York: Praeger.

ULAM, ADAM B. (1983) *Dangerous Relations: The Soviet Union in World Politics, 1970–82*. New York: Oxford University Press.

——. (1971) *The Rivals: America and Russia Since World War II*. New York: Viking.

UNGERER, HORST. (1983) "Main Developments in the European Monetary System," *Finance and Development* 20 (June): 16–19.

U.S. Arms Control and Disarmament Agency. (1988) *World Military Expenditures and Arms Transfers 1987*. Washington, D.C.: U.S. Government Printing Office.

———. (1984) *World Military Expenditures and Arms Transfers 1972–1982*. ACDA Publication no. 117 (April). Washington, D.C.: U.S. Government Printing Office.

———. (1979) *Arms Control 1978*. Washington, D.C.: U S. Government Printing Office.

U.S. Central Intelligence Agency. (1980) "International Terrorism in 1979." Report Prepared by the National Foreign Assessment Center. Washington, D.C.: Director of Public Affairs, U.S. Central Intelligence Agency (April).

———. (1977) *The International Energy Situation: Outlook to 1985*. Washington, D.C.: U.S. Central Intelligence Agency.

U.S. Committee for Refugees. (1982) *World Refugee Survey 1982*. New York: U.S. Committee for Refugees.

U.S. Department of Commerce. (1978) *Selected Trade and Economic Data of the Centrally Planned Economies*, December 1977. Washington, D.C.: U.S. Government Printing Office.

U.S. Department of Energy. (1987a) Energy Information Administration. *Monthly Energy Review* (October).

———. (1987b) *Energy Security*. Washington, D.C.: U.S. Department of Energy.

U.S. Department of State. (1983) *Security and Arms Control: The Search for a More Stable Peace*. Washington, D.C.: U.S. Government Printing Office.

———. (1982) *Combatting Terrorism*. Washington, D.C.: U.S. Department of State.

———. (1978a) "World Population: The Silent Explosion—Part 2," *Department of State Bulletin* 78 (November): 1–8.

———. (1978b) "World Population: The Silent Explosion—Part 1," *Department of State Bulletin* 78 (October): 45–54.

U.S. Environmental Protection Agency. (1983) *Can We Delay Greenhouse Warming?* Washington, D.C.: U.S. Government Printing Office.

U.S. Office of Technology Assessment. (1981) *Technology and Soviet Energy Availability*. Washington, D.C.: U.S. Government Printing Office.

Valenta, Jiri, and William Potter (eds.) (1984) *Soviet Decisionmaking for National Security*. London: Allen & Unwin.

van de Kaa, Dirk J. (1987) "Europe's Second Demographic Transition," *Population Bulletin*, vol. 42, no. 1. Washington, D.C.: Population Reference Bureau.

Van Dyke, Vernon. (1966) *International Politics*. New York: Appleton-Century-Crofts.

Vanous, Jan. (1986) "The Soviets' Dilemma: Will It Be Tanks or Tractors?" *Washington Post National Weekly Edition*, September 1, p. 23.

Varon, Bension, and Kenji Takeuchi. (1974) "Developing Countries and Non-Fuel Minerals," *Foreign Affairs* 52 (April): 497–510.

Verba, Sidney. (1969) "Assumptions of Rationality and Non-Rationality in Models of the International System," pp. 217–231 in James N. Rosenau (ed.), *International Politics and Foreign Policy*. New York: Free Press.

Vernon, Raymond. (1982) "International Trade Policy in the 1980s: Prospects and Problems," *International Studies Quarterly* 26 (December): 483–510.

———. (1979) "The Fragile Foundations of East–West Trade," *Foreign Affairs* 57 (Summer): 1045–1051.

———. (1976) "An Introduction," pp. 1–14 in Raymond Vernon (ed.), *The Oil Crisis*. New York: Norton.

———. (1975) "Foreign Operations," pp. 275–298 in James W. McKie (ed.), *Social Responsibility and the Business Predicament*. Washington, D.C.: Brookings Institution.

———. (1971) *Sovereignty at Bay*. New York: Basic Books.

Volgy, Thomas J., and Jon E. Quistgard. (1974) "Correlates of Organizational Rewards in the United Nations: An Analysis of Environmental and Legislative Variables," *International Organization* 28 (Spring): 179–205.

Volgyes, Ivan. (1988) "Troubled Friendship or Mutual Dependence? Eastern Europe and the USSR in the Gorbachev Era," pp. 159–162 in Charles W. Kegley, Jr., and Eugene R. Wittkopf (eds.), *The Global Agenda*, 2nd ed. New York: Random House.

von Glahn, Gerhard. (1986) *Law Among Nations*, 5th ed. New York: Macmillan.

Waldheim, Kurt. (1984) "The United Nations: The Tarnished Image," *Foreign Affairs* 63 (Fall): 93–107.

Wallace, Michael, and J. David Singer. (1970) "Intergovernmental Organization in the Global System, 1815–1964: A Quantitative Description," *International Organization* 24 (Spring): 239–287.

WALLERSTEIN, IMMANUEL. (1980) *The Modern World-System II*. New York: Academic Press.
_____. (1974) "The Rise and Future Demise of the World Capitalist System: Concepts for Comparative Analysis," *Comparative Studies in Society and History* 16 (September): 387–415.
WALLIS, ALLEN. (1986)"U.S.-EC Relations and the International Trading System." Address before the Luxembourg Society for International Affairs, October 8. U.S. Department of State, Bureau of Public Affairs, Current Policy no. 889.
_____. (1983) "A Collective Approach to East–West Economic Relations." Address before the American Society of Business Press Editors, Chicago, June 20. U.S. Department of State, Bureau of Public Affairs, Current Policy no. 495.
WALTERS, ROBERT S. (1983) "America's Declining Industrial Competitiveness: Protectionism, the Marketplace and the State," *PS* 16 (Winter): 25–33.
WALTZ, KENNETH N. (1979) *Theory of International Politics*. Reading, Mass.: Addison-Wesley.
_____. (1975) "Theory of International Relations," pp. 1–85 in Fred I. Greenstein and Nelson W. Polsby (eds.), *International Politics: Handbook of Political Science*, vol. 8. Reading, Mass.: Addison-Wesley.
_____. (1971) "The Stability of the Bipolar World," pp. 333–342 in William D. Coplin and Charles W. Kegley, Jr. (eds.), *A Multi-Method Introduction to International Politics*. Chicago: Markham.
_____. (1970) "The Myth of National Interdependence," pp. 205–223 in Charles P. Kindleberger (ed.), *The International Corporation*. Cambridge: MIT Press.
_____. (1954) *Man, the State, and War*. New York: Columbia University Press.
WATTENBERG, BEN J. (1987) *The Birth Dearth*. New York: Pharos Books.
WELCH, WILLIAM A. (1970) *American Images of Soviet Foreign Policy*. New Haven, Conn.: Yale University Press.
WELLER, ROBERT H., AND LEON F. BOUVIER. (1981) *Population: Demography and Policy*. New York: St. Martin's Press.
WELLS, LOUIS T. (1983) *Third World Multinationals*. Cambridge, Mass.: MIT Press.
WELTMAN, JOHN J. (1974) "On the Obsolescence of War," *International Studies Quarterly* 18 (December): 395–416.
WENDZEL, ROBERT L. (1980) *International Relations: A Policymaker Focus*. New York: Wiley.
WESTON, BURNS, RICHARD A. FALK, AND ANTHONY A. D'AMATO. (1980) *International Law and World Order*. St. Paul: West Publishing.
WHELAN, JOSEPH G., AND MICHAEL J. DIXON. (1986) *The Soviet Union in the Third World: Threat to World Peace?* Washington, D.C.: Pergamon-Brassey's.
WHITE, RALPH K. (1984) *Fearful Warriors: A Psychological Profile of U.S.-Soviet Relations*. New York: Free Press.
WHITING, ALLEN S. (1985) "Foreign Policy of China," pp. 246–290 in Roy C. Macridis (ed.), *Foreign Policy in World Politics*, 6th ed. Englewood Cliffs, N.J.: Prentice-Hall.
WICKER, TOM. (1982) "War by Accident," *New York Times*, November 21, p. E19.
WILLIAMS, PHIL. (1976) *Crisis Management: Confrontation and Diplomacy in the Nuclear Age*. New York: Wiley.
WILLRICH, MASON. (1975) *Energy and World Politics*. New York: Free Press.
WINBERG, ALAN R. (1979) "Resource Politics: The Future of International Markets for Raw Materials," pp. 178–194 in David W. Orr and Marvin S. Soroos (eds.), *The Global Predicament: Ecological Perspectives on World Order*. Chapel Hill: University of North Carolina Press.
WISEMAN, HENRY. (1983) "United Nations Peacekeeping: An Historical Overview," pp. 19–58 in Henry Wiseman (ed.), *Peacekeeping: Appraisals and Proposals*. Elmsford, N.Y.: Pergamon Press.
WITTKOPF, EUGENE R. (1975) "Soviet and American Political Success in the United Nations General Assembly, 1946–70," pp. 179–204 in Charles W. Kegley, Jr., Gregory A. Raymond, Robert M. Roud, and Richard A. Skinner (eds.), *International Events and the Comparative Analysis of Foreign Policy*. Columbia: University of South Carolina Press.
WOHLSTETTER, ALBERT. (1976–1977) "Spreading the Bomb Without Quite Breaking the Rules," *Foreign Policy* 25 (Winter): 88–96, 145–179.
WOLF, EDWARD C. (1986) *Beyond the Green Revolution: New Approaches for Third World Agriculture*. Worldwatch Paper no. 73. Washington, D.C.: Worldwatch Institute.
WOLFERS, ARNOLD. (1952) "National Security As an Ambiguous Symbol," *Political Science Quarterly* 67 (December): 481–502.
WOLF-PHILLIPS, LESLIE. (1987) "Why 'Third World'?: Origin, Definitions and Usage," *Third World Quarterly* 9 (October): 1311–1327.

WOLPIN, MILES. (1983) "Comparative Perspectives on Militarization, Repression, and Social Welfare," *Journal of Peace Research* 20 (no. 2): 129–156.

World Bank Atlas 1987. (1987) Washington, D.C.: The World Bank.

World Development Report 1987. (1987) New York: Oxford University Press.

World Development Report 1986. (1986) New York: Oxford University Press.

World Development Report 1985. (1985) New York: Oxford University Press.

World Development Report 1984. (1984) New York: Oxford University Press.

World Development Report 1983. (1983) New York: Oxford University Press.

World Resources 1986: A Report by the World Resources Institute and the International Institute for Environment and Development. (1986) New York: Basic Books.

WRIGGINS, W. HOWARD. (1978) "Third World Strategies for Change: The Political Context of North–South Interdependence," pp. 19–117 in W. Howard Wriggins and Gunnar Adler-Karlsson, *Reducing Global Inequities.* New York: McGraw-Hill.

WRIGHT, QUINCY. (1955) *The Study of International Relations.* New York: Appleton-Century-Crofts.

———. (1953) "The Outlawry of War and the Law of War," *American Journal of International Law* 47 (July): 365–376.

———. (1942) *A Study of War.* Chicago: University of Chicago Press.

WU, YUAN LI. (1973) *Raw Material Supply in a Multipolar World.* New York: Crane, Russak.

YALEM, RONALD J. (1972) "Tripolarity and the International System," *Orbis* 15 (Winter): 1051–1063.

YARMOLINSKY, ADAM. (1988) "Low-Intensity Conflict: Causes, Consequences, and Questionable Cures," pp. 96–101 in Charles W. Kegley, Jr., and Eugene R. Wittkopf (eds.), *The Global Agenda,* 2nd ed. New York: Random House.

Yearbook of International Organizations, 1987/88. (1987) *Vol. 1: Organization Descriptions and Index.* Munich: K. G. Saur.

Yearbook of International Organizations, 1987/88. (1987) *Vol. 2: Geographic Volume.* Munich: K. G. Saur.

Yearbook of International Organizations, 1986/87. (1986) *Vol. 3: Subject Volume.* Munich: K. G. Saur.

Yearbook of of International Organizations, 1983. (1983) *Vol. 1: Organization Descriptions and Index.* Munich: K. G. Sauer.

YERGIN, DANIEL. (1977) "Politics and Soviet-American Trade: The Three Questions," *Foreign Affairs* 55 (April): 517–538.

YOUNG, ORAN. (1986) "International Regimes: Toward a New Theory of Institutions," *World Politics* 39 (October): 104–122.

———. (1980) "International Regimes: Problems of Concept Formation," *World Politics* 32 (April): 331–356.

YOUNG, PETER. (1987) "Privatization Around the World," pp. 190–206 in Steve H. Hanke (ed.), *Prospects for Privatization.* New York: Academy of Political Science.

ZACHER, MARK W. (1987) "Trade Gaps, Analytical Gaps: Regime Analysis and International Commodity Trade Regulation," *International Organization* 41 (Spring): 173–202.

ZELIKOW, PHILIP. (1987) "The United States and the Use of Force: A Historical Summary," pp. 31–81 in George K. Osborn, Asa A. Clark IV, Daniel J. Kaufman, and Douglas E. Lute (eds.), *Democracy, Strategy, and Vietnam.* Lexington, Mass.: Lexington Books.

ZIEGLER, DAVID W. (1977) *War, Peace, and International Politics.* Boston: Little, Brown.

ZIMMERMAN, WILLIAM, AND HAROLD K. JACOBSON. (1987) "Whither Détente? Conflict and Cooperation in U.S.-Soviet Relations." Paper presented at the Annual Meeting of the International Studies Association, Washington, D.C., April 16–18.

ZINNES, DINA A. (1980) "Prerequisites for the Study of System Transformation," pp. 3–21 in Ole R. Holsti, Randolph M. Siverson, and Alexander L. George (eds.), *Change in the International System.* Boulder, Colo.: Westview Press.

ZINNES, DINA A., AND JONATHAN WILKENFELD. (1971) "An Analysis of Foreign Conflict Behavior of Nations," pp. 167–213 in Wolfram F. Hanrieder (ed.), *Comparative Foreign Policy.* New York: McKay.

ZINNES, DINA A., JOSEPH L. ZINNES, AND ROBERT D. McCLURE. (1972) "Hostility in Diplomatic Communication," pp. 139–161 in Charles F. Hermann (ed.), *International Crises.* New York: Free Press.

INDEX

Note: Page numbers in italics refer to material in figures, tables, or boxes.